NEW AVENUES IN BIBLICAL EXEGESIS
IN LIGHT OF THE SEPTUAGINT

THE SEPTUAGINT IN ITS ANCIENT CONTEXT
PHILOLOGICAL, HISTORICAL AND THEOLOGICAL APPROACHES

VOLUME 1

series edited by
Eberhard Bons

in collaboration with
Françoise Vinel and
Christoph Kugelmeier

New Avenues in Biblical Exegesis in Light of the Septuagint

Edited by

LEONARDO PESSOA DA SILVA PINTO

DANIELA SCIALABBA

BREPOLS

D/2022/0095/137
ISBN 978-2-503-59806-2
eISBN 978-2-503-59807-9
DOI 10.1484/M.SEPT-EB.5.127220

Printed in the EU on acid-free paper.

Table of Contents

Preface

The present volume originates from the international conference 'New Avenues in the Exegesis of the Bible in the Light of the LXX' held at the Pontifical Biblical Institute in Rome on 23 and 24 October 2019 in honor of Professor R. P. Stephen Pisano, S. J. († 7 October 2019). The book brings together the papers of this conference and is complemented by articles from other experts in Septuagint studies who were invited to contribute to this publication.

The scope of this volume is to highlight the importance of the Septuagint within the broad field of biblical studies and to foster the dialogue between different perspectives and approaches. Our aim, therefore, has been to assemble contributions that offer a glimpse into the variety of recent research on the Septuagint. We are convinced that a multifaceted approach to the Septuagint sheds new light not only on the Greek Bible as such but allows for a better understanding of its importance for biblical studies in general.

Without excluding exegetical approaches considered traditional, the authors of this volume leave trodden paths in order to develop new questions and hypotheses and to offer new perspectives. On the one hand, these studies have an impact on the understanding of issues like the textual history of specific passages or biblical books. On the other, the papers place the Septuagint on a much broader horizon: rather than focusing on its character as a translation from Hebrew to Greek and the problems resulting from translating from a Semitic source language to an Indo-European target language, the authors emphasize the specific features of the Septuagint as a collection of texts whose literary value is undoubtedly unique due to its stylistic, compositional, literary and historical heterogeneity. However, it is necessary to go even further. In fact, a difficult but rewarding task is to explain the Septuagint and its linguistic features against the background of classical and Hellenistic Greek literature. The Septuagint, moreover, has left its traces in the so-called intertestamental literature, in the New Testament and in early Christian texts. Consequently, these proceedings gathers contributions that range from general methodological issues to the broad spectrum of possible innovations on the level of theology whenever the Septuagint departs from the Hebrew texts available today. In this sense, the authors of the various contributions investigate different areas including philology, lexicography, exegesis and, as for the latter, the fields of textual criticism, narratology, rhetoric, pragmatics of discourse, intertextuality and reception criticism.

Such a multifaceted approach offers new insights into the various aspects of the Septuagint texts and the numerous uses to which they lend themselves. It opens new horizons in the understanding of the biblical texts and provides biblical studies with fresh impetus, namely by shifting the frontiers towards a broader vision that includes literary, historical and theological aspects hitherto neglected. Needless to say, this approach is able to shed some new light on the complex framework of the history of translation, reception and interpretation of the biblical texts. In conclusion, the present volume is intended as a plea that the Septuagint be taken seriously in all areas of the exegetical work and as a demonstration that attention to the Greek version can only enrich the discipline.

Our thanks are due to all the authors who have contributed with their articles. We are thankful to our colleagues Prof. Peter Dubovsky and Prof. Benedetta Rossi who worked with us in the organization of the conference and to the Pontifical Biblical Institute of Rome for taking the opportunity of publishing the conference proceedings and for supporting our scientific activity as editors of this collection. Special thanks go to the international committee of the series 'The Septuagint in its Ancient Context' (Brepols) in the persons of Prof. Eberhard Bons (University of Strasbourg, director of the series), Prof. Françoise Vinel (University of Strasbourg) and Prof. Christoph Kugelmeier (University of Saarbrücken) for having accepted this volume into the series. Finally, we would like to thank the Brepols publishing house and, in particular, Dr Tim Denecker, who made possible the publication of this volume.

Rome, 29 June 2021, Feast of Saints Peter and Paul
Leonardo Pessoa and Daniela Scialabba

SIEGFRIED KREUZER

'Bringing forth from the Treasure New and Old'

Septuagint Studies and Exegetical Methods

The title of this volume poses an interesting but also challenging question. The question about new avenues may be understood in the sense of adding new approaches, yet it also seems to imply some devaluation or at least some relativization of the old avenues. Therefore, the challenge is to reflect on the traditional methods and on possible new approaches and how they relate to Septuagint studies.

As a first step for these deliberations, it seems worthwhile to look at what we consider as our exegetical methods; not the least because so far, scholarly exegesis would claim that the exegetical methods in principle do not differ from scholarly approaches to any text, at least as long as one takes into account its specifics. For example, establishing the text by text critical methods or taking into account the specific form and the traditions that have influenced it are procedures that would apply to any text, independent also from the question of whether these steps should be called textual criticism, form criticism and tradition history or whether they should be given a different name.

Considering the history of research, one may observe that exegetical methods have developed and changed over the time. New perspectives and questions have been added, and new material has been discovered. Both aspects may have altered the balance of specific questions. Does the new awareness of the Septuagint result in new methods or does it lead to new applications and adaptations?

In order to answer this question, we first take a look at what can be considered to constitute our exegetical methods, and then move on to relating them to Septuagint research and new approaches.

1. The Inventory of Exegetical Methods

The inventory of exegetical methods has developed over about three centuries. It started with the basic idea that a text has to be interpreted within the horizon of the time of its origin, which also implies that the text is studied in its original language. This intention was not entirely new, but it received fresh interest and new emphasis during the period of Renaissance humanism and the Reformation because of the idea that the true meaning of a text can only be discovered if it is interpreted literally and in its original setting. This approach reinstated the text in its own right (not only, for example, being a proof text for something known before) and also set free its creative potential.

New Avenues in Biblical Exegesis in Light of the Septuagint
ed. by Leonardo Pessoa da Silva Pinto and Daniela Scialabba, Turnhout, 2022 (SEPT, 1), pp. 9–26
© BREPOLS ❧ PUBLISHERS   DOI 10.1484/M.SEPT-EB.5.127708

Historically, this started with the editions of the biblical texts in the sixteenth century and the development of hermeneutical rules and continued with the development of rules for textual criticism towards the end of the seventeenth and in the early eighteenth century. One may recall the large Polyglot Bibles (e.g. the Complutensian (1514–17) and later on the Antwerp (1569–72) and the London Polyglot (1654–57) and the text critical rules established by Johann Albrecht Bengel (1687–1752).[1]

At the same time, critical questions about the age and the unity of the biblical texts were asked. One may think of Baruch Spinoza's *Tractatus theologico-politicus* from 1670, and especially of the investigations that started with Johann Bernhard Witter in 1711 and Jean Astruc in 1753, with their questions about the sources of the book of Genesis,[2] which by the time under the name of literary criticism developed into a method applicable to any biblical text (or any other text).

While the nineteenth century saw the climax of literary criticism, other questions arose as well, especially: What was before the written texts? Are there features specific to the Hebrew language and its poetics?[3] In other words, the question of oral history and oral traditions began to be asked. Deliberations about these matters can already be found in Heinrich Ewald's History of Israel 1843–55, e.g. a discussion about the characteristics of the sagas and how they may relate to history.[4] Important aspects of the poetic texts were considered as well, e.g. by Johann Gottfried Herder in his *Vom Geist der ebräischen Poesie* (1782–83). However, the second half of the nineteenth century was dominated by literary criticism. Not only the Pentateuch but also the prophetic books and even the wisdom books were split up into many sources.

In the twentieth century, the question of form criticism and of tradition history came up. Together with the discoveries of ancient Mesopotamian and Egyptian texts, it became important to ask how ancient oriental traditions influenced the religion of Israel and its literature. This was supported by a new awareness of the form of the texts, especially of forms that were suited for oral transmission and that would, therefore, indicate an oral prehistory. For both aspects, one may mention Herrmann Gunkel (1862–1932) and his commentaries on Genesis and Psalms, yet he was not the only scholar working on these questions.

---

1   Johann Albrecht Bengel, *Prodromus Novi Testamenti Graeci recte cauteque adornandi* (Stuttgart: Mezler and Erhard, 1725) established the rule of the *lectio difficilior* (originally: *Proclivi scriptioni praestat ardua*).

2   Henning Bernhard Witter, *Jura Israelitarum in Palestinam terram Chananaeam* (Hildesheim: Schröderus, 1711), who discerned two sources in Genesis 1–11, and Jean Astruc with his *Conjectures sur les mémoires originaux dont il paroit que Moyse s'est servi pour composer le livre de la Genèse* (Brussels: Chez Fricx, 1753), who discerned four different authors of the book of Genesis. Not surprisingly, they started with the book of Genesis, not only because there the phenomena were most clear, but also because — as Astruc's title nicely indicates — even under the assumption of Mosaic authorship one could inquire about the sources for that earlier time.

3   Especially Johann Gottfried Herder, *Vom Geist der ebräischen Poesie: Eine Anleitung für die Liebhaber derselben und der ältesten Geschichte des menschlichen Geistes*, 2 vols (Dessau: auf Kosten der Verlags-Kasse, und zu finden in der Buchhandlung der Gelehrten, 1782–83).

4   The much-used example of the three texts Genesis 12; 20; 26 is already used in his prolegomena and for the problem of possible historical relevance of oral traditions.

Together with the generally traditional tendencies in society and also in the churches after World War II, many scholars were certainly over-confident concerning the feasibility of discovering the pre-literary conditions and traditions of early Israel, i.e. in pre-monarchic times and in the early monarchy. It is not surprising that around 1970 the pendulum began to swing back. For a number of reasons, at this point the later history of the texts also came into focus.

It became of interest how a text was received, re-read and re-interpreted. In other words, redaction criticism became the dominant method and perspective. This again had practical consequences: While literary criticism searched for the sources from which a text was compiled, not only in the Pentateuch but also in e.g. the prophetic books, redaction criticism looks for additions, corrections and reinterpretation. This naturally changes the perspective. While, for example, in the book of Jeremiah, former exegetes found the sources A, B, C, and D, Winfried Thiel asked about the deuteronomistic redaction and post-deuteronomistic additions,[5] and for Robert P. Carroll the book of Jeremiah became a 'rolling corpus' altogether.[6]

In other words, literary criticism and tradition history looked upstream, whereas redaction criticism looks downstream. As other methods also have their own tendencies, redaction criticism tends to see texts as younger and younger.

This tendency meets with another perspective that was also initiated around 1970: The canonical approach and the search for the meaning of the text's final form. This approach originated partly out of frustration with the different and often contradictory results of critical analysis and, on the other hand, from the insight that it is the so-called final form or the canonical text that became normative and relevant for the religious communities. As pioneer and influential author of this approach, Brevard S. Childs is well known. The title of his book *Biblical Theology in Crisis* indicates the problem he wanted to solve.[7]

A similar development can also be observed concerning the Pentateuch. One argument put forward against the classical source model was about the different answers and unsolved questions which would speak against the classical model and call for new solutions. However, as the new redaction critical models show at least as much discrepancy, this argument quite soon disappeared.[8] While the canonical

5 Winfried Thiel, *Die deuteronomistische Redaktion des Jeremiabuches 1–25*, WMANT, 41 (Neukirchen-Vluyn: Neukirchener, 1973); *Die deuteronomistische Redaktion von Jeremia 26–45*, WMANT, 52 (Neukirchen-Vluyn: Neukirchener, 1981).

6 Robert P. Carroll, *Jeremiah*, OTL (London: SMC, 1986).

7 Brevard S. Childs, *Biblical Theology in Crisis* (Philadelphia: The Westminster Press, 1970); later complemented especially by Brevard S. Childs, *Introduction to the Old Testament as Scripture* (Philadelphia: Fortress, 1979). It is almost unknown that Childs was a doctoral student with Walther Eichrodt in Basel, whose *Theologie des Alten Testaments* appeared in eight editions until 1968, and who integrated theological perspectives with historical-critical exegesis and also with religio-historical discoveries. Childs's dissertation had been: *A Study of Myth in Genesis I–XI* (1955).

8 In the first edition of Erich Zenger and others, *Einleitung in das Alte Testament* (Stuttgart: Kohlhammer, 1995), p. 70, he wrote: 'Wenn die Divergenzen bei den Vertretern des gleichen Modells so gravierend waren bzw. sind, muss man dann nicht folgern, dass das Problem im "Modell" selbst liegt?' In the later editions, this sentence is not repeated.

interpretation certainly has its own strengths, it became also clear that this approach as well has its ambiguities and does not produce simple solutions.[9]

Presently, synchronic and diachronic approaches appear well established and accepted. Especially in commentaries, there are attempts to combine both;[10] yet it often does not yet go beyond an addition. The relationship between the two approaches still needs to be worked on.

It is interesting that not only has the exegetical pendulum swung back to the so-called final form,[11] but that, especially because of the Qumran biblical texts, fresh interest has arisen in textual history and textual criticism. The new interest in the Septuagint dovetails nicely with this development, not the least as one may say that the Septuagint translators read their Holy Scriptures synchronically.

There is another interesting convergence: The historical development of the exegetical methods as just presented is more or less analogous to the way of analyzing a given text, at least in the sense of historical-critical exegesis: The first step is to lay a clear textual foundation by doing the text critical work (textual criticism). The next step is to analyze the sequence of the text, i.e. its narrative sequence or the sequence of the argumentation or of the presentation (linguistic description).[12] The observations would allow checking the integrity of the text, i.e. whether it is a coherent literary unit or whether it consists of different parts, and demonstrating some development (literary criticism). From there, one may go on to the formal aspects: if the form of the text or its elements relates to specific usage, and if it is likely that the text had a prehistory e.g. in everyday life or in cultic procedures or in court annals, etc. (form criticism, *Sitz im Leben*).[13] The question about underlying traditions, their influence and their reshaping (tradition history) is also situated at this point.[14]

---

9   Zenger already in the first edition of his *Einleitung* (see n. 8) stated in view of the synchronic models: 'Ob freilich angesichts der oben angedeuteten literarischen Komplexität des Endtextes eine *naive* synchrone Interpretation des Endtextes überhaupt möglich ist, ist fraglich'. (p. 116).

10   See e.g. the new *International Exegetical Commentary of the Old Testament* series (Stuttgart: Kohlhammer, 2012).

11   But what is the final form? Is it the text that was used by the Septuagint translators? Is it the proto-masoretic text that needs to be identified among other forms of the biblical texts, e.g. in Qumran? Is it the text of *Codex Leningradensis* with its vocalization from the tenth century, which is partly old but partly also a late tradition?

12   In older research, this is not mentioned separately, but the observations were collected and used in the argumentation.

13   Oral tradition and literary tradition usually are in historical sequence, but often also interrelated: Literary traditions may influence oral traditions and literary traditions may be accompanied by oral tradition. On these interactions, see David Carr, *Writing on the Tablet of the Heart: Origins of Scripture and Literature* (Oxford: Oxford University Press, 2005).

14   While in German *Überlieferungsgeschichte* and *Traditionsgeschichte* are basically interchangeable, Odil Hannes Steck, *Exegese des Alten Testaments: Leitfaden der Methodik*, 14th edn (Neukirchen-Vluyn: Neukirchener, 1990), strictly differentiated between *Traditionskritik/Tradititonsgeschichte* for the content (in the sense of Latin *traditum*) and *Überlieferungskritik/Überlieferungsgeschichte* as referring to the process of transmission (Latin *traditio*) and he limited *Überlieferungsgeschichte* to the oral transmission (as different from *Redaktionskritik* for the literary transmission). This distinction and limitation has become widely followed in German scholarship, while e.g. Martin Noth had used

From literary criticism, form criticism, and tradition-historical inquiries, which looked mainly upstream, so to speak, exegesis would now turn to looking downstream at the development of the text, from the first literary recording through additions, new emphasis and other redactional interventions (redaction criticism), down to the text we find in the oldest manuscripts.

The following figure gives a general overview of the development of a text and the related exegetical steps.[15] The Septuagint is added at two places, which will be explained below.

Development of a text and related exegetical methods

Influence	↓		Event or theme			↑	Influence
			⇩ ⇩ ⇩				
			Oral transmission				
by ⇨	TrH		⇩ ⇩ ⇩			FC	⇦ by the
	↓		*(First) written text*			TrC	historical
traditional actions,			⇩ ⇩ ⇩			↑	situation(s)
ideas, ⇨	↓		Literary transmission			↑	and by the
			and redaction(s)				
forms of expression	RC		⇩ ⇩ ⇩			LC	⇦ intention of
performance ⇨	↓		*Canonical Text*			↑	the authors
			"End-text"				
			Oldest reachable text			TxC	⇦ the redactors
(LXX)			⇩ ⇩ ⇩ ⇩				(LXX)
(Historical)			Transmission of the text				
Interpretation			*Textual history*				
of the text			*Reception History*				

Abbreviations: TxC = Textual Criticism / LC = Literary Criticism / FC = Form Criticism / TrC = Tradition Criticism / TrH = Transmission History / RC = Redaction Criticism

Basically, there are three levels or three transits through a text. The first level is the basic approach to the text, this means reading and, in most cases, translating the text. In most cases one will need a lexicon for less well-known words or also for specific meanings of well-known words. Often also a grammar will be useful for specific questions. A first translation of the text forces one to give a clear expression of this first understanding and shows problems and uncertainties in the understanding.

Überlieferungsgeschichte for the whole process from oral transmission to the final redaction, cf. his *Überlieferungsgeschichte des Pentateuch* (Stuttgart: Kohlhammer, 1948); English trans.: *A History of Pentateuchal Traditions*, Translated with an Introduction by Bernhard W. Anderson (Englewood Cliffs, NJ: Prentice-Hall, 1972). In English, there is 'tradition' only, therefore one has to distinguish between tradition criticism (analyzing the content) and tradition history (the passing on of the tradition).

15   Cf. Siegfried Kreuzer, 'Aufgabe und Geschichte der Exegese', in *Proseminar I. Altes Testament*, ed. by Siegfried Kreuzer and others, 3rd edn (Stuttgart: Kohlhammer, 2019), pp. 13–25 (p. 17).

This first translation will certainly need to be improved by the ongoing work. This understanding may be refined by a linguistic analysis and/or by a narratological analysis. This basically synchronic approach may also give some first impressions about the historical situation, but it will also give some indications of tensions in the text or, to express it in a different way, about the coherence of the text. If there are disturbances in the coherence of the text, they indicate that the text had some prehistory, whether through the development of the text, or whether through influences on the writer, e.g. by fixed formulas or by specific ideas or traditions.

This leads to the next level or transit through a text, basically the questions and methods outlined above and today called diachronic interpretation. As shown above, these methods lead to different insights about the growth and development of a text and the different aspects that influenced it. The questions of form and content accompany the development of a text through its different phases (therefore Form*geschichte* and Traditions*geschichte*, history of form and history of tradition).

From this diachronic tour the exegete will return to the given text and interpret it with all the insights gained before. This third level and transit also deals with the whole text, enriched by the insights from the previous steps. If this interpretation proceeds verse by verse or in more condensed form, or in a combination of both, as most commentaries do, is a matter of space and of the purpose of the exercise.

The important point is that all three levels or transits go through the whole text and that they have their specific questions and answers, that are different and should be distinguished, but they also have some overlap and connections.

At this point, I would like to add that beyond the basic steps that I mentioned, there are several additional approaches like sociological and psychological interpretation or literary approaches like narratology, intertextuality, and reception history.

These additional approaches may be heuristic tools that bring out specific aspects of a text, but primarily I would place them in the realm of hermeneutics. However, they may put forward new questions and bring out aspects that were not seen before.

From this overview, we now turn to the Septuagint.

2. The Relation of the Exegetical Methods to Septuagint Studies

2.1. The Place of Septuagint Studies

From an Old Testament perspective, the Septuagint comes, *grosso modo*, after the Old Testament, as (most of) it is the translation of the Hebrew Bible/Old Testament writings. This is different from the New Testament perspective. For the New Testament, the Septuagint is older, so to say its precursor and an important reference text.[16] For

---

16 Cf. the theological lexica of the New Testament, e.g. the *Theologisches Wörterbuch zum Neuen Testament* (ThWNT) or its younger counterparts, that usually have passages on the one hand on the prehistory of the terms in Greek, and on the other hand on the prehistory in the Old Testament,

the New Testament, the Septuagint is similar to what the Ancient Near Eastern texts, e.g. the texts from Ugarit or from Mari, are for the Old Testament, at least from a chronological perspective. The relationship is not the same, because the New Testament throughout relates to, and many times explicitly quotes, the Septuagint, while the traces of the Ancient Near Eastern texts — or, more properly, traditions — in the Old Testament are in most cases more beneath the surface.

In any case, the Septuagint is later than the Old Testament. It is the translation of the Hebrew Bible, and probably the oldest, and for its time the most comprehensive, interpretation of it. Therefore, as shown above, for the exegesis of the Old Testament/ Hebrew Bible, the Septuagint has its place in the textual criticism but also in the exegesis of the text, as it presents its oldest or one of the oldest understandings of the Hebrew (and Aramaic) Old Testament.

However, there is a hermeneutical approach that goes beyond these two aspects. This is intertextuality. Intertextuality — as I understand it — is different from tradition history and reception history: Tradition history asks about older traditions and how they influenced a given text; reception history shows how a text was received and interpreted later on. Different from the, so to say, downstream perspective on the historical development, intertextuality asks about interaction in any direction: Intertextuality not only interprets texts in historical sequence, but also looks, so to say, backwards, as it were, by inviting later texts to question earlier ones.[17]

However, this is not entirely different from reception history, because reception history also has the effect that one goes back to the original text in order to ask if the text really wanted to say this, or if it at least allows a specific interpretation. Let me give two examples: The הָעַלְמָה in Isaiah 7. 14 and also the Greek rendering as παρθένος certainly would have received much less exegetical attention if there was no Christian usage of this verse to justify the idea of virgin birth. Another interesting example is Exodus 22. 27, אֱלֹהִים לֹא תְקַלֵּל 'You shall not revile God'. In the Septuagint this has become: θεοὺς οὐ κακολογήσεις, 'You shall not revile Gods'. This is most probably not what the Hebrew text intended, but it is certainly not a mistake. The Greek translation says: If we, as a Jewish minority in Egypt or in other places of the diaspora, want to be respected with our religion, we should not be disrespectful to others. This translation can even be justified by the parallelism in the verse ('nor curse a ruler of your people') and by later rabbinical exegetical rules.[18] That is not the issue now. My point is that having realized this translation and its meaning, one would probably also see the Hebrew text with different eyes. The Greek rendering is different from the original meaning of the text, but the rendering in the Septuagint also works backward and influences our perception of the Hebrew text (at least in the sense of asking if the translation is possible and why). This working backward

---

especially in the Septuagint. See now also the Historical and Theological Lexikon of the Septuagint (HTLS).

17 To my mind, this is the specific difference between intertextuality and the tradition-historical approach.

18 Interestingly, the King James Version in this case follows the Greek translation, as did Jerome in the Vulgate.

is what I see as the basic difference between classical tradition-history or reception history and intertextuality.

At this point, I would also like to mention an influence of modern Septuagint studies, not on exegetical methods but on the primary genre of exegetical literature, that is, on commentaries: Many commentaries have begun to add a passage on the Septuagint, not just regarding textual criticism as was also done in the past, but as a separate chapter on the text's reception. In these passages, the Septuagint is not only considered interesting in itself, but also because of the expectation that the Greek translation may shed light on the original Hebrew text. One may compare Hans-Joachim Kraus's commentary on the Psalms with its quotations from Calvin[19] and, fifty years later, Erich Zenger's commentary with a passage on the Septuagint of each Psalm.[20]

Let us now turn to the Septuagint and some of the traditional exegetical methods.

2.2. *Septuagint and Textual Criticism*

In all textbooks on exegetical methods, and especially those on textual criticism, the Septuagint and its history are, at least briefly, presented. This is necessary in order to understand the apparatus in the text critical editions and in order to be able to reconstruct the oldest text of the Hebrew Bible. This modest role of the Septuagint is mirrored in the apparatus where the Septuagint is present only in bits and pieces. We all know about this and lament it.

However, in the second half of the twentieth century, the influence of the Septuagint has even decreased. This can be demonstrated by the Bible translations. All recent Bible translations that I am familiar with, only use the Hebrew Masoretic text (except in cases where the text makes no sense at all). Contrary to this, earlier editions, e.g. the *Zürcher Bibel* (published in 1931), relied on text critical work and often followed the Septuagint. As mentioned above in view of Exodus 22. 27(28), also the King James Version sometimes followed the Septuagint (and the Vulgate).

What is the reason for this recent exclusive reliance on the Masoretic text? There are two main causes. The first one is that from 1937 onward, with the third edition of the *Biblia Hebraica*, the so-called Kittel Bible, an excellent Masoretic text had become available. The other reason is the discovery of the Qumran biblical texts. Suddenly, there was a Hebrew text that was one thousand years older than the oldest manuscripts that had been available before, and this text showed a very reliable transmission of the biblical text for a whole millennium. The resulting enthusiasm led to a new estimation of the Hebrew Masoretic text and, one may say, to an overestimation. Unfortunately,

---

19 Hans Joachim Kraus, *Psalmen*, Biblischer Kommentar, 2 vols (Neukirchen-Vluyn: Neukirchener, 1960; 5th edn 1978). In defense of Kraus one has to remember the devaluation of the Hebrew Bible in the preceding years, and that one of the aims of the *Biblischer Kommentar* series was to regain the Old Testament for the Christian church.

20 Erich Zenger and Frank-Lothar Hossfeld, *Die Psalmen*, HThKAT (Freiburg: Herder, 2000; 3rd edn 2007), II. Psalm 51–100 (English trans. 2005); *Die Psalmen*, HThKAT (Freiburg: Herder, 2008), III. Psalm 101–50.

the other side of the Qumran biblical texts, the fact that there were different Hebrew textual traditions, the so-called textual plurality in early Judaism, disappeared from both, the general and the scholarly perception. Only recently, and slowly, has the overestimation of the Hebrew Masoretic text begun to change.

2.3.   *Textual Criticism or Literary Criticism?*

The Qumran discoveries have not only changed the perception of the Hebrew biblical texts, but also that of the Septuagint. This is primarily because some of the Qumran biblical texts confirmed the Septuagint as they showed that many of the specifics of the Greek text are not inventions of the translators but go back to a Hebrew *Vorlage*. However, this is not entirely new. For a long time, it was known that many readings of the Septuagint agree with readings in the Samaritan Pentateuch, e.g. in Exodus 12. 40 it says that Israel had been in Egypt for 430 years. The Septuagint and also the Samaritan Pentateuch include the time of the Patriarchs and count the 430 years from Abraham and the covenant in Genesis 15.[21] The Qumran texts have confirmed the Septuagint text for many books beyond the Pentateuch.

There is also a methodological side to such observations: Is a textual difference, like the one I just mentioned, a purely text critical problem or does it belong to literary criticism (or rather: redaction criticism) because it is evidently an intentional change? Normally, textual criticism is defined and limited by what can be reached on the basis of manuscripts, while literary criticism starts from there.[22] Emanuel Tov in his textbook has collected most of the texts relevant to this question.[23] The question was already discussed by Rainer Stahl in the 1970s. In the 1990s, Hermann-Josef Stipp and Ludger Schwienhorst-Schönberger intensively debated the question. Heinz-Josef Fabry made some wise suggestions.[24]

I think that one has to give up the idea that there must be a strict border between textual and literary criticism, rather there is an overlap between both methods.

---

21   Siegfried Kreuzer, 'Zur Priorität von Exodus 12,40 MT — Die chronologische Interpretation des Ägyptenaufenthalts in der judäischen, samaritanischen und alexandrinischen Exegese', *ZAW*, 103 (1991), 252–58.

22   See e.g. Siegfried Kreuzer, 'Textkritik', in *Proseminar I. Altes Testament*, ed. by Siegfried Kreuzer and others, 3rd edn (Stuttgart: Kohlhammer, 2019) pp. 26–48 (p. 26); Alexander A. Fischer, *Der Text des Alten Testaments* (Stuttgart: Deutsche Bibelgesellschaft, 2009), devotes a chapter to the definitions of textual criticism: '7.3 Definitionen der Textkritik', pp. 197–201.

23   Emanuel Tov, *Textual Criticism of the Hebrew Bible*, 3rd edn (Minneapolis: Fortress 2011), pp. 283–326.

24   Rainer Stahl, 'Die Überlieferungsgeschichte des hebräischen Bibeltextes als Problem der Textkritik: Ein Beitrag zu gegenwärtig vorliegenden textgeschichtlichen Hypothesen und zur Frage nach dem Verhältnis von Textkritik und Literarkritik' (unpublished doctoral thesis, Jena, 1978); cf. *ThLZ*, 105 (1980), 475–78; Ludger Schwienhorst-Schönberger, *Die Eroberung Jerichos: Exegetische Untersuchungen zu Josua 6*, SBS, 122 (Stuttgart: Katholisches Bibelwerk, 1986), pp. 20–21; Hermann-Josef Stipp, 'Das Verhältnis von Textkritik und Literarkritik in neueren alttestamentlichen Veröffentlichungen', *BZ*, 34 (1990), 16–37; Heinz-Josef Fabry, 'Der Altarbau der Samaritaner — ein Problem der Text- und Literargeschichte?', in *Die Texte vom Toten Meer und der Text der Hebräischen Bibel*, ed. by Ulrich Dahmen and others (Neukirchen-Vluyn: Neukirchener 2000), pp. 35–52 (pp. 46–49).

The Qumran biblical texts have confirmed what could already be seen from the Septuagint, that the Septuagint, and now also the Qumran texts, allow a glimpse at the intentional growing and changes. Adrian Schenker would talk about literary variants, i.e. intentional differences that change the literary character of the text.[25]

This leads to the fact that what we can do based on manuscripts is not only textual criticism but, to some extent, also literary criticism. Or to say it differently: The method of literary criticism has, for its later phases, gained some evidence in the manuscripts.[26] Yet, on the other hand, there are not only unintentional changes but also intentional changes that belong to the realm of textual criticism and not to literary or redactional criticism of the original text.

These observations and discoveries have not changed the business of literary or redactional criticism (i.e. determining the development of a text in its literary stage) and of textual criticism (reconstructing the oldest text that can be reached according to the manuscripts and explaining the variants). These methods have merely gained some new perspectives and areas of application.

2.4. *Form Criticism and Tradition Criticism*

Form criticism[27] or genre criticism intends to describe the literary form of a specific text and, by comparing it with the genre to which the text belongs, to discern particular deviations from expected conventions. One may use such observations, insofar as it is possible, to draw conclusions about the intention and message of a specific text, perhaps even to give some idea about the life situation (*Sitz im Leben*) and usage of the text. In a similar way, tradition criticism intends to discover the traditions that a particular text draws on or is influenced by, and thereby call attention to new aspects of a text and establish its specific message.[28]

These methods of form criticism and tradition criticism are, in my view, not changed by the Septuagint; I would rather say that they can also be fruitfully applied to the Septuagint. There is merely a change in perspective. Form criticism in the Septuagint is now clearly related to the literary text, with a twofold comparative perspective: Identity with, or differences from, the Hebrew form, and possible influences from

---

25   The phenomenon is now also taken up in the new *Biblia Hebraica Quinta*. Literary differences that are not relevant for the textual criticism of a specific form of the textual tradition are tagged as 'lit'.

26   However, one has to admit, that hardly anyone would be able to identify the additions in the MT without knowing e.g. the shorter version of Jeremiah as preserved in the Septuagint.

27   It may be mentioned that in the English realm, form criticism sometimes has been criticized as being too formalistic. This seems to be influenced by a misunderstanding of the word 'form', because in English the word 'form' not only means the form of a text, but also a form that just needs to be filled in. But this in German would be a *Formular*.

28   In present day's research, the question of earlier transmission or even oral tradition is usually set aside. While it may be that much more is fictitious than assumed by earlier scholarship, there still remains the question on how, e.g. information from monarchic or even pre-monarchic times may have been transmitted down to the times of the oldest written texts, composed, for example, in the seventh century or later. While today these questions often are neglected, they still exist.

other literature. Accordingly, one has to consider what it means if the old form is maintained or if it is changed in a new cultural context.

The same holds true for tradition criticism. There are the traditions of the Hebrew *Vorlage* and the Jewish community for whom the text is translated, there are the literary and cultural traditions of the environment, and there are the intentions of the translators.

2.5. Interpretation of the Text

The different exegetical steps are interesting in themselves and they may suffice for specific questions.

However, basically they should contribute to the understanding of a given text. This may be a narrative from the book of Genesis or from the books of Samuel, or a psalm or a wisdom passage. The different exegetical methods may answer a specific question, but in the end, they should help towards a better understanding of a given text and its meaning.[29]

2.6. The Septuagint as Part of the Reception History
of the Old Testament Text

As mentioned above, the Septuagint represents the oldest and most comprehensive exegesis of the (Hebrew and Aramaic) Old Testament. This holds true in different ways: The Septuagint represents how the Old Testament was understood in its time. But the Septuagint also reflects the hermeneutics of the biblical texts. This is reflected in the original translation which, *grosso modo*, tries to be faithful to its *Vorlage*, but also comprehensible to the readers (and listeners), while later translations and especially the revisions lay more emphasis on the (holy and perfect) source text that should shine through the translation.[30] Because of this contribution of the Septuagint to the interpretation of a given Old Testament text, I have placed the Septuagint also on the left side of the above scheme showing the exegetical methods.

---

29 Basically, this meaning will be the intention of the text. 'Meaning' and 'intention' touch on a much-debated problem. Especially in the 1990s, several authors wanted to avoid the question of intention and asked (in the sense of Wolfgang Iser's *Rezeptionsästhetik*) only about the (possible) receptions of a text. However, most of these studies ended up close to the question about the intention (if not of the author, but at least) of the text. This, to my mind, is necessary, at least if one does not allow any use of a text, but if one also asks about the limits of interpretation; see Umberto Eco, *The Limits of Interpretation* (Indiana: Indiana University Press, 1990); Tom Kindt and Tilmann Köppe (ed.), *Moderne Interpretationstheorien: Ein Reader* (Göttingen: Vandenhoeck & Ruprecht, 2008).

30 This is especially the intention of the kaige- and the semi-kaige-recension, that, in the first century BCE, isomorphically reworked the Old Greek text towards the original and holy Hebrew text. Because it is a holy and perfect text, also formal details that (at least for us) make no difference in the meaning are important and become reflected in the kaige-recension, e.g. the difference between the long and the short form of the personal pronoun 1st sg; or word order or the presence of a visible article (even contrary to the rules of determination).

3. Exegetical Methods for the Septuagint

3.1. Textual Criticism and Septuagint Studies

The Septuagint is not only a very important factor for textual criticism of the Hebrew Bible, but textual criticism is also an aspect within Septuagint research. The saying that 'textual criticism is the door to exegesis, there is no back door'[31] holds true for the Septuagint as well. It is necessary to keep this in mind even in view of the eclectic editions. Working just with an edition bears the danger of not analyzing e.g. the translation technique of a specific book, but (at least to some part) rather the editorial principles of its editor.

Basically, there were text critical reflections early on. Origen in his Hexapla decided for the text closest to the Hebrew text of his time. Was it because he assumed that this was the oldest text or because it was closest to the Hebrew text and in this way the most original one (at least according to his assumptions)? We also do not know for sure if the text he reconstructed in the Hexapla was intended for use in the church or for scholarly discussion, including discussion with the Jews.

For Jerome, we know more. In his letter to Sunnia and Fretela he writes about two text forms: the generally used Greek text, and the text taken from what he called the Hexaplaric manuscripts, which he preferred. For Jerome, the best text was not the oldest text but the text closest to the Hebrew, in other words: closest to the *veritas hebraica* (as it was available in his time and known to him).

Today, we think differently. Beginning with humanism, the best text is the oldest text, the text closest to the original. For the Septuagint this is the oldest Greek text. This evidently was already the goal of the first printed editions, i.e. the Complutensian Polyglot and the Aldine edition.[32] Unfortunately, we do not know about the criteria for the best manuscripts for which the editors had searched as basis for their printed editions. Later on, the goal of textual criticism was explicitly to present the oldest text, at least the oldest text that could be reached.

This was clearly the goal for Johann Ernestus Grabe around 1700,[33] for Paul Anton de Lagarde and many others in the nineteenth century, or for Alfred Rahlfs and others in the twentieth century, and especially of the Göttingen edition.

However, the rules that were used for establishing the text have undergone some changes. In 1863, de Lagarde published his famous axioms:[34] The first proposition

---

31 'Die Textkritik ist das Tor zur Exegese, eine Hintertür gibt es nicht'. (Fischer, *Text des Alten Testaments*, p. 187).

32 These earliest editions are based on manuscripts, but they are not simply diplomatic editions, because the editors emphasize that they looked for the best manuscripts available; they evidently followed not just one manuscript, and they also included variant readings.

33 See his *Epistola ad Clarissimum Virum, Dn. Joannem Millium ... Qua ostenditur, Libri Iudicum Genuinam LXX. Interpretum Versionem eam esse, quam MS Codex Alexandrinus exhibit* (London: E Theatro Sheldoniano, 1705), demonstrating that *Codex Alexandrinus* had the oldest text of Judges (reachable at his time), which also prompted his edition of the *Codex Alexandrinus* of 1709–20.

34 Paul Anton de Lagarde, *Anmerkungen zur griechischen Übersetzung der Proverbien* (Leipzig: Brockhaus, 1863), p. 3. Similar rules were already put forward by Heinrich W. J. Thiersch, *Ad Pentateuchi versionem Alexandrinam critice pertractandam prolegomena* (Erlangen: Junge, 1837), p. 17.

claims that one must work eclectically: 'I. die manuscripte der griechischen übersetzung des alten testaments sind alle, entweder unmittelbar oder mittelbar das resultat eines eklektischen verfahrens: darum muss, wer den echten text wiederfinden will, ebenfalls eklektiker sein'.

Propositions II and III elaborate these rules:

II. wenn ein vers oder verstheil in einer freien und in einer sklavisch treuen übertragung vorliegt, gilt die erstere als die echte. III. wenn sich zwei lesarten nebeneinander finden, von denen die eine den masoretischen text ausdrückt, die andre nur aus einer von ihm abweichenden urschrift erklärt werden kann, so ist die letztere für ursprünglich zu halten.[35]

These axioms simply apply the rules of textual criticism. In fact, they contain only one real axiom, which is the assumption that the Greek text has been reworked towards the later authoritative Hebrew text, what today is called the proto-Masoretic text. Yet this assumption has also been proven, both in antiquity by Origen's work in the Hexapla and today by the kaige-recension discovered by Barthélemy in the Naḥal Ḥever scroll and in manuscripts of several books of the Septuagint.

One may even say that de Lagarde's third axiom has also been confirmed by the Qumran texts, as they show the plurality of the Hebrew texts that is presupposed by de Lagarde.

Interestingly, de Lagarde later changed his view. Although still in 1881,[36] he had been quite critical of Jerome's statements, under the influence of Frederick Field's *Hexaplorum fragmenta quae supersunt* of 1875 he took over the idea of the *trifaria varietas*. In 1891 he declared that his goal was to identify those three recensions and from there to proceed to the oldest text. Interestingly, even Field did not really write about three text forms; rather in the introduction to his book he only discussed the Hexaplaric and the Lucianic text but not the Hesychian text. Basically, the same happened in the case of de Lagarde and later on also with Alfred Rahlfs.

However, the idea of the three Christian recensions of the Septuagint gained an unexpected relevance because de Lagarde's new idea was taken up into the guidelines for the Göttingen edition when they were established around 1907.

With this idea of the three Christian recensions a new framework was introduced, not only a framework for the manuscripts and their readings but also a time frame: Readings from a specific group of manuscripts belong to a specific text type and therefore

---

35   'II. If a verse or part of a verse is present in a free translation and in a slavishly faithful translation, the first is the true one. III. If two readings are present next to each other, one of which expresses the Masoretic text and the other of which can be explained only by a source text that deviates from [the Masoretic], the latter is to be considered original'.

36   Still in 19 November 1881 de Lagarde wrote about his sceptical view of Jerome's statements: 'Für die Septuaginta öffentlich an Hesych, Lucian und die palaestinische κοινή zu denken, verbot mir mein in den Clementina [de Lagarde refers to his edition of the Clementina from 1865] xxvii unverholen ausgesprochenes mistrauen gegen den eigentlich einzigen gewärsmann jener drei recensionen, Hieronymus'; Paul Anton de Lagarde, *Ankündigung einer neuen Ausgabe der griechischen Übersetzung* (Göttingen: Dieterich, 1882), p. 22.

cannot be old. Contradictory evidence such as agreement with Josephus or with the Old Latin or with the New Testament was explained away as later cross-influence. The basic idea of three rather late Christian recensions is maintained, although there are other statements by Jerome as well, and despite the fact that Alfred Rahlfs already in 1926 declared that he had given up this idea,[37] not to mention the discoveries from Qumran and the Judaean Desert and their consequences.[38]

This is not the place to go into details. The main point concerning methods is that in this case some specific assumptions were allowed to override the basic text critical rules.

Sometimes there is the claim that one would have to look at single cases separately. However, deciding a single case implies knowledge about the weight of the manuscripts or ideas about the textual history. This cannot be avoided; therefore, it is necessary to lay open the implied assumptions and to reflect on them. Regarding the question of methodology, I would say that text critical deliberations at least in some areas of Septuagint research should regain priority over mere assumptions.

3.2. Specific Approaches in Septuagint Studies?

Because most books of the Septuagint are translated texts, there arise some questions that are different from the exegesis of the original texts: In general, there is no question about the prehistory or about oral traditions of the text.

On the other hand, there is the question of translation technique and also of the linguistic realms the translators could draw on. Translation technique may be investigated under many different aspects, from the choice of words to the rendering of specific grammatical forms of the Hebrew in Greek and to the rendering of specific expressions. Even the transcription of names or expressions may be a characteristic of the translation, not least because transcription was not only used because of ignorance but also out of reverence for the original.

While translation is a specific act, the factors that play a role in it are not too different from what is usually considered under the heading of tradition history:

---

37 Alfred Rahlfs, *Genesis*, Septuaginta: Vetus Testamentum Graecum, I (Stuttgart: Privilegierte Württembergische Bibelanstalt, 1926), Introduction: 'Daß das, was ich hier biete, noch viel weniger als das im Buch Ruth Gebotene dem Lagardeschen Ideal eines Aufbaues nach den berühmten Rezensionen des Origenes, Lukian und Hesych entspricht, verkenne ich keineswegs. Aber wenn wir vorwärtskommen wollen, müssen wir uns nicht von vorgefaßten Theorien, sondern lediglich von dem gegebenen Material leiten lassen'. ('I certainly do not ignore that what I offer here follows even less than in the book of Ruth the ideal of Lagarde to order according to the famous recensions of Origen, Lucian and Hesych. But if we want to advance, we do not have to follow preconceived ideas but the material given to us').

38 Especially the discovery of the kaige-recension by Dominique Barthélemy and the consequences this had for the picture of the transmission of the Septuagint: Dominique Barthélemy, *Les Devanciers d'Aquila*, V.T.S, 10 (Leiden: Brill, 1963); see e.g. Siegfried Kreuzer, '"Lukian redivivus" or Barthélemy and beyond?', in *Congress Volume Helsinki 2010*, ed. by Melvin K. Peters, SBLSCS, 59 (Atlanta: SBL 2013), pp. 243–61; 'The Origin and Transmission of the Septuagint', in *Introduction to the Septuagint*, ed. by Siegfried Kreuzer (Waco, TX: Baylor University Press 2019), pp. 3–56 (pp. 37–43).

The words used by the translator are loaded with meaning; that is exactly why they are chosen. This meaning certainly is connected with the use of the words in the Greek, but often also influenced by the usage in books of the Septuagint that were translated earlier. Basically, the questions of lexicography and translation technique are variations of tradition criticism and tradition-history.

Besides translation, the phenomenon of revision, and revision technique, and the implied hermeneutics may also be considered. There is the phenomenon of the largely isomorphic kaige-recension with its goal of bringing the Greek text close to the Hebrew text which implies a specific understanding of Scripture. Basically, this means shaping and reshaping a given content, i.e. a given (textual) tradition.

As the translators of the Septuagint usually kept close to their *Vorlage*, the form of the text was about the same in Greek. However, even minor changes and especially larger transpositions or additions of passages influence the form of a text and such changes modify the meaning.[39] Sometimes, the other way around, a new understanding of a tradition may have influenced the form or the place of a text.[40] Observing such modifications and asking for their cause and intention is also the goal of form criticism and tradition criticism. As these are changes on the literary level, they are also a matter of redaction criticism.

Also for the writings without (or without known) Hebrew *Vorlagen*, e.g. the four (very different) books of the Maccabees, Psalms of Solomon, or Tobit, all the traditional exegetical methods are of relevance, although, as is always the case, they have to be adapted to the specific texts.

Altogether, I would maintain that the exegetical methods that were developed and that are used for the Old Testament (and basically also for the New Testament), are of relevance and need to be applied to the Septuagint as well. This always also includes the necessary adaptation to the specific texts (which is necessary for their application to the Old or the New Testament as well).

3.3. *Additional and Alternative Approaches*

As mentioned above, there are several additional or also alternative approaches in exegesis: linguistic approaches, sociological studies, gender studies, reception history, or iconography and archaeology.[41]

---

39 For example, the differences in Exodus 35–40; cf. Martha L. Wade, *Consistency of Translation Techniques in the Tabernacle accounts of Exodus in the Old Greek*, SBLSCS, 49 (Leiden: Brill, 2003); or the differences in I Kings 11–14, cf. Frank Ueberschaer, *Vom Gründungsmythos zur Untergangssymphonie: Eine text- und literaturgeschichtliche Untersuchung zu 1Kön 11–14*, BZAW, 481 (Berlin: de Gruyter, 2015); or the additions in the book of Esther, cf. Kristin de Troyer, 'Esther', in *Introduction to the Septuagint*, ed. by Siegfried Kreuzer (Waco, TX: Baylor, 2019), pp. 235–43.

40 E.g.: As resurrection in Ezekiel 37 became understood not as resurrection of the people but as individual resurrection, this chapter consequently was placed after the final wars with Gog in Ezekiel 38f. (see p. 967).

41 For a presentation of some of these methods and approaches, see e.g. the second part in the study book *Proseminar I. Altes Testament*, ed. by Siegfried Kreuzer and others, 3rd edn (Stuttgart: Kohlhammer, 2019).

Iconography may elucidate a given text, and archaeological insights may help to understand the historical, the cultural, and also the religious background. These approaches have their specific materials and their specific methods that should be applied before the results are used for comparison. However, using them for the Septuagint is not too different from their use for Old Testament or New Testament studies.

Linguistic approaches and sociological studies often have very specific systems of working and also of terminology that are not always easily accessible. Yet they certainly may be useful for specific insights, be it into the literary features of the text or the sociological situation that is behind the text and reflected in it.

Gender studies are a modern approach to biblical and other texts. They apply specific questions and by doing so they certainly help to discover aspects of the text that so far had not been observed. However, as with other forms of so-called *engagierte Exegese* there is the danger of not only gaining new insights in the text but also of imposing one's own expectations on the text.

Reception history to my mind is not an exegetical method as such, however, looking at reception history may raise awareness to aspects in the text that are (presently) overlooked. At the same time, one may also ask, whether a specific reception of a given text was really justified by the text, or if it was a misuse or a misunderstanding, and why it came about.

3.4. *Dangers and Pitfalls in Septuagint Exegesis*

1) As also in other areas there are some specific problems and dangers in Septuagint studies. One problem is the dependence on traditional assumptions. Certainly, no one can start from scratch. One is always dependent on prior work, beginning with lexica to specific approaches of interpretation or evaluation. One such problem is mentioned above, some traditional assumptions about the history of the text that influenced even the decisions in the eclectic editions. Therefore, it is important to consider underlying assumptions and consider the alternatives. — This also concerns a so called single case approach. Also a single case is never approached without underlying assumptions like the value of manuscripts or the lexical meaning of specific expressions.

2) Another problem is overinterpretation of small details (and sometimes their generalization to a whole biblical book). Certainly, there are differences between the Hebrew and the Greek text or in the transmission of the Greek text that are intended. And also a mistake or an unintentional variant may be prompted by the expectation of the translator or of a scribe. However, a difference may still be the result of a simple misreading or of a misunderstanding, and it is not always part of a far-reaching theological of philosophical reinterpretation.

3) A third problem is overdependence on modern translations, especially for understanding the Hebrew text. For comparison between the Hebrew and the Greek text, often modern translations are adduced, and the Hebrew text is often understood in the sense of a modern translation. However, one has to keep in

mind, that a translation has to decide between different possibilities,[42] and that even very reliable translations have the intention of conveying the sense of the text to a modern reader. Therefore, they often explicate the text in a certain sense, or they (necessarily) pick one specific meaning, while the Septuagint translator may have chosen another, equally possible, understanding. To give an example: Job 28 describes the amazing work of mining. For this, the Hebrew text uses 3rd sg ('he does') in the general sense ('one does'), e.g. in v. 3: 'He (one) puts an end to darkness'. The *NRSV* makes the subject explicit and additionally uses the plural: 'Miners put an end to darkness'.[43] However, the Septuagint translator relates the verse to God because he is the one able to put an end to darkness. This is an important difference, but there is no grammatical change from plural to singular. The translator only identified the subject of the verb differently.

Conclusions: Exegetical Methods and Septuagint Studies

1) The exegetical methods as they have developed and as they are available today are basically relevant and applicable to the Septuagint as well as to the Hebrew Bible or any other given text.

2) The exegetical methods have their specific questions and their specific rules. However, they must be adapted to the given text. Regarding the Septuagint, this means: The Septuagint does not change the exegetical methods, that is, their basic question and intention, but the Septuagint changes the application of the methods. This is not different from other areas of research as there must always be an interaction between the specific object and the methods applied.

3) The exegetical methods have developed over a long time. Often one specific method dominated, yet it is important to combine different aspects and approaches. Comparing and confronting different methods and their results shows the specific possibilities as well as the limitations.

4) Exegetical methods, as also other methods, always imply specific assumptions and perspectives. These assumptions are the result of prior research. Yet it is important to be aware of these assumptions and to be open to modifying them because of new insights.

5) Exegetical methods have developed over time and they may and will develop. New approaches may help to bring forward new insights, also about the Septuagint. The criterion is, whether their use and their results are adequate for the given text. The answer to this question is not provided at once nor by a single person, not even by a once adopted position, but it grows out of continued scholarly debate.

---

42 This is what the philosopher Hans-Georg Gadamer, *Wahrheit und Methode: Grundzüge einer philosophischen Hermeneutik*, 4th edn (Tübingen: J. C. B. Mohr, 1975), p. 362, meant saying 'die Übersetzung ist die Vollendung der Auslegung' ('translation is the completion of interpretation'). For the translation, the translator must decide for one of the possibilities of understanding a given text.

43 The *NRSV* often uses the plural for the singular in order to avoid a male form of the subject.

▼ ABSTRACT The paper takes up the question of if and how the new awareness of the Septuagint or the Septuagint per se changes the exegetical methods, not the least in view of the claim that the usual exegetical methods basically are applicable to any text. In a first step, the classical exegetical methods in their development and their interrelation are presented, and the relation of the Septuagint to Old and New Testament is reflected upon. In a second part, the mutual relations and influences between specific exegetical methods (textual criticism, literary criticism, tradition history etc.) and Septuagint studies are discussed, including the aspects of intertextuality and reception history. In the third part, the question about specific approaches in Septuagint research is taken up again, including the problem of some specific pitfalls in Septuagint research. The conclusion sums up the result in five points.

DANIELA SCIALABBA

Non-Israelites and the God of Israel

The Vocabulary of 'Conversion' in the Septuagint and Greek
Jewish Literature against its Greek-Hellenistic Background

In recent years, I have researched the relationship between non-Israelites and the God of Israel in the Hebrew Bible, paying special attention to the role of non-Israelites in some texts (such as, for example, the book of Jonah).[1] This frequently brought me to 'conversion' and the Hebrew and Greek presumed to denote this concept.[2]

'Conversion' is key theological term in the New Testament, used in present day translations. It refers to Gentiles who decide to become members of the Christian community.[3] In the context of the so-called Council of Jerusalem, Acts 15. 3 reads: 'So they [Paul and Barnabas] were sent on their waẏ by the church, and as they passed through both Phoenicia and Samaria, they reported the conversion of the Gentiles [ἐκδιηγούμενοι τὴν ἐπιστροφὴν τῶν ἐθνῶν] and brought great joy to all the believers' (*NRSV*). Likewise, in Acts 26. 20 Paul sums up the aim of his missionary activities as follows: The Gentiles 'should repent and turn to God and do deeds consistent with repentance', μετανοεῖν καὶ ἐπιστρέφειν ἐπὶ τὸν θεόν, ἄξια τῆς μετανοίας ἔργα πράσσοντας. From the above quotations, the author of the Acts of the Apostles uses two terms, μετανοέω and ἐπιστρέφω/ἐπιστροφή to refer to Gentiles prompted to believe in God. Finally, the apostle Paul uses the same terminology to praise the Thessalonians for having 'turned to God from idols, to serve a living and true God'

---

1   In this regard, see e.g. Daniela Scialabba, *Creation and Salvation: Models of Relationship between the God of Israel and the Nations in the Book of Jonah, Psalm 33 (MT and LXX) and the Novel Joseph and Aseneth*, FAT, II 106 (Tübingen: Mohr Siebeck, 2019); see also Daniela Scialabba, 'The LXX translation of Jonah 1:6b — Text-critical and exegetical considerations', in *Die Septuaginta — Orte und Intentionen: 5. Internationale Fachtagung veranstaltet von Septuaginta Deutsch (LXX.D), Wuppertal 24.-27. Juli 2014*, ed. by Siegfried Kreuzer and others, WUNT, I 361 (Tübingen: Mohr Siebeck, 2016), pp. 645–54.
2   On this topic, see e.g. Daniela Scialabba, 'La conversione dei pagani in Giuseppe e Aseneth e Atti degli Apostoli', *Ho Theológos*, 30 (2012), 369–96; 'The Vocabulary of Conversion in Joseph and Aseneth and in the Acts of the Apostles', in *Die Septuaginta — Text, Wirkung, Rezeption: 4. Internationale Fachtagung veranstaltet von Septuaginta Deutsch (LXX.D), Wuppertal 19.-22. Juli 2012*, ed. by Wolfgang Kraus and Siegfried Kreuzer, WUNT, I 325 (Tübingen: Mohr Siebeck, 2014), pp. 501–14.
3   This specific aspect has not been highlighted by David A. Lambert, *How Repentance became Biblical: Judaism, Christianity and the Interpretation of Scripture* (Oxford: Oxford University Press, 2016), p. 184.

New Avenues in Biblical Exegesis in Light of the Septuagint
ed. by Leonardo Pessoa da Silva Pinto and Daniela Scialabba, Turnhout, 2022 (*SEPT*, 1), pp. 27–39
© BREPOLS 🐝 PUBLISHERS   DOI 10.1484/M.SEPT-EB.5.127709

(I Thessalonians 1. 9: πῶς ἐπεστρέψατε πρὸς τὸν θεὸν ἀπὸ τῶν εἰδώλων δουλεύειν θεῷ ζῶντι καὶ ἀληθινῷ).

In the Hebrew Bible and the Septuagint, however, the situation is quite different, for two reasons:

- In a small number of texts in the Hebrew Bible, their translation in the Septuagint as well as in so-called intertestamental literature, there is mention of Gentiles showing some interest in entering into closer contact with Israel and its God. However, the textual evidence is very limited. Accordingly, the vocabulary is not very rich.
- As for 'conversion', the question arises whether this is still an appropriate general term for the wide range of ways in which Gentiles express their positive relationship with the God of Israel and his people, extending from mere admiration to full membership of the Jewish community.[4] That is why recent research uses the term 'conversion' only *cum grano salis*.

The aim of this paper is to consider the Septuagint terminology denoting the metaphorical 'crossing of boundaries' by Gentiles when they are interested in establishing a positive relationship with the God of Israel and the Jewish community.[5] In particular, I shall focus on the following questions:

- Which verbs and nouns in the Septuagint and in so-called intertestamental literature are used to express this phenomenon?
- Which verbs and nouns are introduced in intertestamental literature or even in the New Testament and which others disappear gradually?
- To what degree is the choice of this vocabulary in line with non-Jewish or non-Christian usage of the terms in question? And how does intertestamental literature give certain words a new connotation?
- Which terms become *termini technici* as Jewish-Hellenistic literature and later Christian writings evolve over time?

The first step is to make an inventory of the texts and terms to be analyzed. The second is to review the most important terms, especially against their non-biblical background, in order to illustrate the specific nuance in their meaning.

---

4 For more details, see Shaye J. D. Cohen, 'Crossing the Boundary and Becoming a Jew', *HTR*, 82 (1989), 13–33 (p. 14), who distinguishes between 'seven forms of behavior by which a gentile demonstrates respect or affection for Judaism'.
5 In this article, which focuses on terminological issues, different other problems concerning conversion are not dealt with, namely historical and social-historical questions. For example, the question arises of whether the knowledge of the Greek Bible really prompted a non-Jew to convert to Judaism. For this question, see e.g. Louis H. Feldman, *Jew and Gentile in the Ancient World: Attitudes and Interactions from Alexander to Justinian* (Princeton, NJ: Princeton University Press, 1993), especially pp. 311–14, who wonders whether the Septuagint had missionary tracts in order to attract proselytes in the Greek world. For the social and historical problem of conversion in a society highly influenced by the system of patronage, see Zeba A. Crook, *Reconceptualising Conversion Patronage, Loyalty, and Conversion in the Religions of the Ancient Mediterranean*, BZNW, 130 (Berlin: de Gruyter, 2004).

1. The Gentiles and the God of Israel: A Brief Overview of Some Key Texts in the Hebrew Bible, the Septuagint and Intertestamental Literature

In the Hebrew Bible and in translations of texts of the Septuagint only very few passages deal with Gentiles, either individuals or groups of individuals, interested in establishing some sort of relationship with the people of Israel and with their God. Three of these texts mention different groups of people:

—   In the law on joining the assembly of the Lord in Deuteronomy 23. 2–9, the verb used of those permitted to 'join' the community and those excluded from it, is in each case εἰσέρχομαι, 'come (in, into), enter', a literal rendering of the underlying Hebrew verb בא, literally 'to enter'. In this context, the refusal to allow the Ammonites and the Moabites into the community is of particular interest because this idea is simply expressed by the verb εἰσέρχομαι.

—   With reference to the nations, the verb ἐπιστρέφω/ἐπιστρέφομαι is used twice in the Septuagint. In fact, two texts announce that in the future (at the end of time?),[6] the nations will 'turn' to the Lord, though the exact circumstances are unexplained. Thus, LXX-Psalm 21. 28 reads: μνησθήσονται καὶ ἐπιστραφήσονται πρὸς κύριον πάντα τὰ πέρατα τῆς γῆς καὶ προσκυνήσουσιν ἐνώπιόν σου πᾶσαι αἱ πατριαὶ τῶν ἐθνῶν, 'All the ends of the earth shall remember and turn to the Lord and all the paternal families of nations shall do obeisance before him'. Here, the verb ἐπιστρέφομαι corresponds to the Hebrew verb שוב.[7] Likewise, the book of Tobit mentions a similar *scenario* in which turning towards God means the abandonment of idols: LXX[B,A]-Tobit 14. 6–7: καὶ πάντα τὰ ἔθνη ἐπιστρέψουσιν ἀληθινῶς φοβεῖσθαι κύριον τὸν θεὸν καὶ κατορύξουσιν τὰ εἴδωλα αὐτῶν καὶ εὐλογήσουσιν πάντα τὰ ἔθνη τὸν κύριον [...], 'Then all the nations will turn back truly to fear the Lord God and they will bury their idols. And all the nations will bless the Lord [...]' (*NETS*). In this case there is no extant Hebrew source text.

—   A key text in the MT and in the LXX is Isaiah 56, a passage that announces the salvation of all those who 'keep judgment and do justice' (Isaiah 53. 1). Two categories, in particular, are mentioned: the stranger who is 'attached to the Lord' (Isaiah 56. 3: ὁ ἀλλογενής ὁ προσκείμενος πρὸς κύριον, MT: בֶּן־הַנֵּכָר הַנִּלְוָה אֶל־יְהֹוָה; see also v. 6) as well as the eunuch. God will bring the strangers 'to His holy mountain and make them joyful in His house of prayer' (Isaiah 56. 7), and the eunuchs who observe the Sabbaths and 'hold fast his covenant' (Isaiah 56. 4) will receive 'an honorable place, better than sons and daughters' in God's house and will be granted 'an everlasting name' (Isaiah 56. 5). In this text, the verb describing how these two categories — strangers and eunuchs, probably Persian

---

6   For this idea, see e.g. Tiziano Lorenzin, *I Salmi: Nuova versione, Introduzione e Commento* (Milano: Paoline, 2001), p. 117.

7   Luis Alonso Schökel and Cecilia Carniti, *Salmi*, 2nd edn (Rome: Borla, 2007), I, p. 445, understand here the verb שוב as a conversion or radical change of religion but advocates a more nuanced interpretation: the people mentioned would acknowledge YHWH as their God, without worshipping him exclusively.

officials — hold fast to the God of Israel[8] is πρόσκειμαι, 'to reside alongside the native population' or 'to act with dedication and devotion',[9] a translation of the Hebrew *niphal* participle הַנִּלְוָה of the verb לוה, 'one who joins himself to somebody'.

- In Ruth 1. 16 the well-known declaration 'your God is my God', that Ruth addresses to Noemi, does not contain any verb indicating that she will share her mother-in-law's faith.[10] Only in Ruth 2. 12 does her future husband Boaz note that she has placed her trust in the Lord: πρὸς ὃν ἦλθες πεποιθέναι ὑπὸ τὰς πτέρυγας αὐτοῦ, 'to whom you came, to put your trust under his wings'. The LXX faithfully translates a Hebrew text analogous to that preserved in the MT: אֲשֶׁר־בָּאת לַחֲסוֹת תַּחַת־כְּנָפָיו.

- Finally, a text dealing with the topic of Gentiles seeking to worship the God of the Patriarchs *par excellence* is the novel *Joseph and Aseneth*, an intertestamental text of Jewish origin and written in a Greek style strongly influenced by the language of the Septuagint. In this novel, the verb μετανοέω plays a very important role insofar as it becomes a key word designating the radical change in a formerly idolatrous person — Aseneth, daughter of an Egyptian priest — when she decides to believe in God. The verb μετανοέω is found in Aseneth's prayer in *Jos. Asen.*, 9. 2 where it is connected to her resolute and definitive decision to abandon idols: Καὶ ἔκλαυσε κλαυθμῷ μεγάλῳ καὶ πικρῷ καὶ μετενόει ἀπὸ τῶν θεῶν αὐτῆς, ὧν ἐσέβετο, καὶ προσώχθισε τοῖς εἰδώλοις πᾶσι, 'And she wept with great and bitter weeping and repented of her [infatuation with the] gods whom she used to worship, and spurned all the idols'[11] (see also 15. 7–8). Furthermore, the cognate noun μετάνοια occurs in connection with the verb πρόσκειμαι (*Jos. Asen.*, 16. 14): καὶ μακάριοι πάντες οἱ προσκείμενοι κυρίῳ τῷ θεῷ ἐν μετανοίᾳ,[12] 'and happy [are] all who attach themselves to the Lord God in repentance'.

As an *interim* conclusion, we can state that there is undoubtedly considerable divergence in the aforementioned texts. However, even if they appear to share the idea of Gentiles establishing a more or less close relationship with the God of the Patriarchs and/or his people, there is no *terminus technicus* in either the

---

8 For the interpretation of this text, namely in the MT, see e.g. Hubert Irsigler, 'Ein Gottesvolk aus allen Völkern? Zur Spannung zwischen universalen und partikularen Heilsvorstellungen in der Zeit des zweiten Tempels', *BZ*, 56 (2012), 210–46 (pp. 227–31).

9 See Takamitsu Muraoka, *A Greek-English Lexicon of the Septuagint* (Leuven: Peeters, 2009), p. 595, s.v. πρόσκειμαι.

10 Feldman, *Jew and Gentile in the Ancient World*, p. 289: 'There is no mention of a formal conversion for Ruth, although the rabbis (*Yavamoth* 47b) understand her statement "The people shall be my people" (Ruth 1:16) to indicate that she embraced Judaism'.

11 The English translations of *Joseph and Aseneth* are taken from Christoph Burchard, 'Joseph and Aseneth', in *The Old Testament Pseudepigrapha*, ed. by James H. Charlesworth, 2 vols (New York: Doubleday, 1985), II, pp. 202–47.

12 In *Joseph and Aseneth* the same expression, οἱ προσκείμενοι, associated with the noun μετάνοια occurs again in 15. 17: καὶ ἐν τῷ τείχει σου φυλαχθήσονται οἱ προσκείμενοι τῷ θεῷ τῷ ὑψίστῳ ἐν τῆς ὀνόματι μετανοίας, 'and behind your walls will be guarded those who attach themselves to the Most High God in the name of Repentance'.

Septuagint or the intertestamental literature for this. Thus, it seems that the LXX and intertestamental literature do not have any specific vocabulary to denote the desire of Gentiles to abandon their former religious practices in order to worship the God of Israel.[13] On the contrary, the texts cited above use various verbs and nouns: εἰσέρχομαι, πεποιθέναι, πρόσκειμαι, μετανοέω/μετάνοια and ἐπιστρέφω/ἐπιστροφή, each of which has its own nuance.

2. Remarks on the Specific Use of πρόσκειμαι, μετανοέω/ μετάνοια and ἐπιστρέφω/ἐπιστρέφομαι/ἐπιστροφή in the Context of the So-Called 'conversion' of Gentiles

In the next paragraph, I will focus on πρόσκειμαι, μετανοέω/μετάνοια and ἐπιστρέφω/ ἐπιστρέφομαι/ἐπιστροφή. I will leave aside εἰσέρχομαι and πεποιθέναι because their wide semantic range means that these verbs appear to be too unspecific to denote the process traditionally called 'conversion'.

2.1. Use of πρόσκειμαι in Religious Contexts

In the biblical and non-biblical Greek texts of Jewish origin, the verb πρόσκειμαι does not have an exclusively religious meaning. The verb, which means literally 'to lie beside, cling on' (LSJ) occurs in the LXX around twenty-four times, mostly referring to the προσήλυτοι (MT: גֵרִים), who are 'abiding among Israel' (e.g. Leviticus 16. 29). Moreover, πρόσκειμαι expresses Israel's attachment to its Lord in Deuteronomy 4. 4 and Joshua 22. 5 (MT: דָּבֵק) and to His commandments in Deuteronomy 1. 36 (MT: מלא piel, 'to fulfill').[14] Finally, in Job 26. 2, Job asks his friend Baldad: 'To whom are you devoted?' The prophetic passage Isaiah 56. 3, 6 and, *mutatis mutandis*, the macarism in *Jos. Asen.*, 16. 14 are the only passages that use πρόσκειμαι with reference to non-Israelites who hold fast to the God of the patriarchs (in the case of Aseneth) or of Israel (in the case of the strangers in Isaiah 56). However, it is important to note that the verb does not describe a process but a state: somebody who has already found his or her way to God, regardless of the practices or worship left behind, e.g. idolatry. In this context, the verb was not a likely candidate when it came to finding a term to denote so-called 'conversion', whether in a Jewish or Christian context. It is interesting to note that neither Philo nor Josephus use the verb with this particular

13 Probably the same holds true for the authors of the New Testament writings. In fact, according to Jean Bouffartigue, in the New Testament era, authors did not have at their disposal Greek terminology denoting the act of conversion by Gentiles; see Jean Bouffartigue, 'Par quels mots le grec ancien pouvait-il désigner le passage d'une religion à une autre?', in *Le problème de la christianisation du monde antique*, ed. by Hervé Inglebert, Sylvain Destephen and Bruno Dumézil (Paris: Éditions A. et J. Picard, 2010), pp. 19–31 (p. 25).

14 Concerning the usage of the verb πρόσκειμαι in the book of Deuteronomy, see Cécile Dogniez and Marguerite Harl, *Le Deutéronome*, La Bible d'Alexandrie, 5 (Paris: Cerf, 1992), pp. 120, 134.

meaning,[15] and in Greek literature the specific religious connotation of the verb is only rarely attested, namely in texts of the Roman era. On Crassus's military campaigns in Northern Greece, Cassius Dio, *Historiae Romanae*, 51. 25, remarks: ὅτι τῷ τε Διονύσῳ πρόσκεινται […] ἐφείσατο, 'these [= the Odrysians, a Thracian tribe] he [= Crassus] spared because they are attached to the service of Dionysus'. In a philosophical and ethical context, without reference to a particular cult, the stoic philosopher Epictetus, *Dissertationes ab Arriano digestae*, 4. 7. 20, pleads for the following option: κρεῖττον γὰρ ἡγοῦμαι ὃ ὁ θεὸς θέλει ἢ ὃ ἐγώ. προσκείσομαι διάκονος καὶ ἀκόλουθος ἐκείνῳ, 'for I think that what God chooses is better than what I choose. I will be attached as a minister and follower to him'.

In conclusion, if the verb πρόσκειμαι did not become a *terminus technicus* for 'conversion', this was probably due to the fact that it does not focus on the process that involves a radical change in religious practice and conviction but rather on a state: the person is already attached to a specific god, and this attachment is no longer up for debate.

2.2. The Use of μετανοέω and μετάνοια: Regret, Repentance and Change of Conduct

The verb μετανοέω and cognate noun μετάνοια could possibly be appropriate terms for the so-called conversion of Gentiles because in texts that are not influenced by Jewish or Christian ideas the words sometimes denote a more or less radical decision or a fundamental change of purpose motivated by regret, something going far beyond a mere change of opinion. In these cases, there is a clear before and after, with past choices totally abandoned in favor of the new orientation. A good example is Xenophon's, *Hellenica*, 1. 7. 19, where Euryptolemus exhorts his audience to follow his advice in order that they might not find out later, to their sorrow, that they have sinned against the gods and against themselves: καὶ ὅθεν μάλιστ' ἀληθῆ πεύσεσθε καὶ οὐ μετανοήσαντες ὕστερον εὑρήσετε σφᾶς αὐτοὺς ἡμαρτηκότας τὰ μέγιστα ἐς θεούς τε καὶ ὑμᾶς αὐτούς, 'which will best enable you to learn the truth and to avoid finding out hereafter, to your sorrow, that it is you yourselves who have sinned most grievously, not only against the gods, but against yourselves'. Admittedly, in this example, the regret that is evoked in a solemn warning is only potential. Nevertheless, there is no doubt that the verb μετανοέω refers to the conviction that past choices turn out to be wrong and that a new path, diametrically opposed to past ways, has to be taken.

In another probably more recent text, the romance *Chaereas and Callirhoe* written by a certain Chariton, a young newly married woman, Callirhoe, has been kidnapped by pirates. Her husband, Chaereas, fearing that she has been married against her will to someone else, in his despair writes her a letter imploring her to come back (4. 4. 8): θάνατον μὲν γὰρ ἄνθρωπος ὢν προσεδόκων, τὸν δὲ σὸν γάμον οὐκ ἤλπισα. Ἀλλ' ἱκετεύω,

---

15   Philo quotes Deuteronomy 4. 4 in *De fuga et inventione*, 56 as well as in *De Specialibus legibus*, 1. 31, 345, but in the respective commentaries on the quotation the verb πρόσκειμαι is lacking.

μετανόησον. Κατασπένδω τούτων μου τῶν γραμμάτων δάκρυα καὶ φιλήματα, 'as a man I expected death, but I did not fear you marriage. But I beg you, repent, I pour out tears and kisses over my letters'. As the text describes, the situation of the couple, separated against their will, is really dramatic. For the husband, there is only one solution: for his wife to declare that she is married to him, thereby refusing any other marriage. Here, the verb μετανοέω denotes not only a change of mind but first and foremost a decision that implies the refusal of another marriage and the young wife's return to her legitimate husband. The two options in the romance are mutually exclusive: Callirhoe has to decide either to stay with her new partner or to return to Chaereas.

Of course, it is possible to illustrate uses of μετανοέω by quoting several other examples in Greek literature of the Hellenistic or Roman epochs.[16] Nevertheless, the two examples quoted above are sufficient to show that the verb μετανοέω has two connotations, which may be more or less present: regret and the decision to change one's behavior completely.

Returning to the biblical writings, as we have already seen, use of μετανοέω with reference to the Gentiles seeking to enter into closer contact with Israel and its God is not found in the LXX. On the contrary the LXX occurrences of μετανοέω often refer to God who changes his mind (e.g. Joel 2. 14; Jonah 3. 9; 4. 2; Amos 7. 3)[17] or to Israel (or an individual in Israel) who is invited to repent and to turn to the Lord on account of its sins (Jeremiah 8. 6; 38(31). 19; Sirach 48. 15). Against this background, it is interesting to observe that the novel *Joseph and Aseneth* is an exception insofar Aseneth's 'conversion', which is accompanied by rites of repentance, self-abasement and the resolute abandonment of idolatry, is described as follows: μετενόει ἀπὸ τῶν θεῶν αὐτῆς, a phrase that expresses *in nuce* both her contrition and her abandonment of the gods she had previously worshipped. This specific use of μετανοέω is unparalleled in the LXX and Jewish-Hellenistic literature, but as we have seen, it appears *mutatis mutandis* in the New Testament referring to the 'conversion' of the Gentiles who wish to worship the only God (Acts 17. 30; 26. 20).[18]

2.3. The Verb ἐπιστρέφω/ἐπιστρέφομαι – Metaphorical Use of a Verb of Movement

Beginning with the two texts already quoted above, Psalm 21. 28 and LXX[B,A]-Tobit 4. 6–7, we should note that in the first case the verb is passive while in the second example, the

---

16 See already the examples quoted by E. F. Thompson, *ΜΕΤΑΝΟΕΩ and ΜΕΤΑΜΕΛΕΙ in Greek Literature until 100 A.D., Including Discussion of their Cognates and of their Hebrew Equivalents* (Chicago: University of Chicago Press, 1908), Chapter III.

17 Muraoka, *A Greek-English Lexicon of the Septuagint*, p. 454, s.v. μετανοέω.

18 For this idea, see also Czeslaw Lukasz, *Evangelizzazione e conflitto: Indagine sulla coerenza letteraria e tematica della pericope di Cornelio (At 10, 1–11,18)*, Europäische Hochschulschriften, XXIII 484 (Frankfurt: Peter Lang, 1993), p. 214: '*Metanoia* usata nei contesti pagani ha come oggetto l'abbandono dell'idolatria. Questo è evidente in 17,30 e implicito nei "sommari" 20,21 e 26,20, nei quali Paolo riassume tutta la sua missione sia ai pagani timorati di Dio (13,16.26; 17,4; 18,7) che ai pagani idolatri (14,8–18; 17,16–34; 19,9)'.

active form is used. Nevertheless, both are intransitive in meaning,[19] i.e. 'to turn (oneself)' towards'. In both texts the verb refers to the non-Israelites turning to the God of Israel.

Mutatis mutandis we find the same intransitive use of the verb in its active and middle-passive forms in the New Testament, sometimes with and sometimes without any complement (e.g. Acts 3. 19: μετανοήσατε οὖν καὶ ἐπιστρέψατε; 9. 35: πάντες οἱ κατοικοῦντες Λύδδα καὶ τὸν Σαρῶνα, οἵτινες ἐπέστρεψαν ἐπὶ τὸν κύριον; 11. 21: πολύς τε ἀριθμὸς πιστεύσας ἐπέστρεψεν ἐπὶ τὸν κύριον; 14. 15: ἐπιστρέφειν ἐπὶ θεὸν ζῶντα; 15. 19: τοῖς ἀπὸ τῶν ἐθνῶν ἐπιστρέφουσιν ἐπὶ τὸν θεόν; 26. 20: καὶ τοῖς ἔθνεσιν ἀπήγγελλον μετανοεῖν καὶ ἐπιστρέφειν ἐπὶ τὸν θεόν; I Thessalonians 1. 9: καὶ πῶς ἐπεστρέψατε πρὸς τὸν θεὸν ἀπὸ τῶν εἰδώλων). As for the other Jewish literature in Greek, ἐπιστρέφω only occurs with this meaning in *Jos. Asen.*, 11. 11: ὅθεν τολμήσω κἀγὼ καὶ ἐπιστρέψω πρὸς αὐτὸν καὶ ἐπ᾽ αὐτὸν καταφεύξομαι καὶ ἐξομολογήσομαι αὐτῷ πάσας τὰς ἁμαρτίας μου καὶ ἐκχέω τὴν δέησίν μου ἐνώπιόν αὐτοῦ, 'Therefore I will take courage too and turn to him, and take refuge with him, and confess all my sins to him, and pour out my supplication before him'.[20]

On first sight, this terminology is not surprising at all and does not seem sufficiently important to arouse the interest of scholars. On closer inspection, however, several issues arise. The first question is: how to explain this specific use by the LXX of the verb ἐπιστρέφω/ἐπιστρέφομαι in contexts dealing with the relationship of non-Israelites with the only God? Is this use of the metaphor restricted to the Septuagint and Jewish and Christian literature influenced by it? To what degree does the phrase ἐπιστρέφω/ἐπιστρέφομαι πρὸς or ἐπὶ τὸν θεόν/τὸν κύριον express the idea of a more or less profound change of religious belief and practise?

In order to answer these questions, I will present two ways in which the verb is used in different corpora of Greek literature, papyri and Jewish and Christian texts. As a second step, I will seek to draw conclusions by comparing this evidence with the biblical occurrences of the verb.

2.3.1. The Most Common Meanings of the Verb ἐπιστρέφω/ἐπιστρέφομαι

To begin with, we should keep in mind that the verb ἐπιστρέφω/ἐπιστρέφομαι is first of all a verb of movement whose basic meaning is 'to turn round', 'to turn towards'. This meaning is widely attested in ancient Greek literature, in the Septuagint, in the NT and in more recent texts.[21] Normally, in this case, the subjects of the verb are humans, sometimes gods, spirits or animals.

---

19 See e.g. Cyril Aslanoff, 'Les notions de retour à Dieu et de repentir dans la Septante', in *Retour, repentir et constitution de soi*, ed. by Annick Charles-Saget (Paris: Vrin, 1998), pp. 50–63 (p. 54).

20 According to Matthew Thiessen, 'Aseneth's Eight-Day Transformation as Scriptural Justification for Conversion', *JSJ*, 45 (2014), 229–49 (p. 237), Aseneth's decision could be understood as a conversion because 'the author of *Joseph and Aseneth* describes Aseneth's conversion as an eight-day process in order to parallel circumcision, another eight-day process, thereby legitimizing her conversion'.

21 For the different usages of the verb ἐπιστρέφω/ἐπιστρέφομαι in the Septuagint, as well as the prepositions governed by the verb, see Robert Helbing, *Die Kasussyntax der Verba bei den Septuaginta: Ein Beitrag zur Hebraismenfrage und zur Syntax der Κοινή* (Göttingen: Vandenhoeck & Ruprecht, 1928), pp. 284–85.

For humans, a striking example can be found in Euripides' tragedy *Alcestis*, 185–89 where the female protagonist bewails her fate and turns to her chamber after weeping: ἐπεὶ δὲ πολλῶν δακρύων εἶχεν κόρον, στείχει προνωπὴς ἐκπεσοῦσα δεμνίων, καὶ πολλὰ θαλάμων ἐξιοῦσ' ἐπεστράφη κἄρριψεν αὑτὴν αὖθις ἐς κοίτην πάλιν, 'When she had had enough of weeping, [...] after going out of the chamber, she turned back and threw herself upon the bed once more'. Likewise, in the Septuagint, the verb is used in the sense of turning to the place of origin in Exodus 4. 20: ἀναλαβὼν δὲ Μωυσῆς τὴν γυναῖκα καὶ τὰ παιδία ἀνεβίβασεν αὐτὰ ἐπὶ τὰ ὑποζύγια καὶ ἐπέστρεψεν εἰς Αἴγυπτον, 'Then Moyses took his wife and children and put them on draft animals, and he went back to Egypt'. In the NT, in Mark 13. 16, Jesus gives instructions on how to behave on the day when the kingdom comes, exhorting those who are in the field, not to turn back to take their clothes: καὶ ὁ εἰς τὸν ἀγρὸν ὢν μὴ ἐπιστρεψάτω εἰς τὰ ὀπίσω, ἆραι τὸ ἱμάτιον αὐτοῦ, 'and let him who is in the field not turn back to get his cloak' (see also Matthew 24. 18; Luke 17. 31).

Sometimes the verb ἐπιστρέφω/ἐπιστρέφομαι occurs with reference to divine movements. Plato, talking about life in heaven, affirms in *Phaedrus*, 247a5: πολλαὶ μὲν οὖν καὶ μακάριαι θέαι τε καὶ διέξοδοι ἐντὸς οὐρανοῦ, ἃς θεῶν γένος εὐδαιμόνων ἐπιστρέφεται πράττων ἕκαστος αὐτῶν τὸ αὑτοῦ, 'There are many blessed sights and many ways hither and thither within the heaven, along which the blessed gods go to and fro attending each to his own duties'.

As for spirits, the verb ἐπιστρέφω/ἐπιστρέφομαι appears in the New Testament, for example in Matthew 12. 44 where Jesus speaks of possession by unclean spirits: as soon as it has left one person, the unclean spirit seeks a resting place in the desert. Not finding any such place, it decides to return with other seven spirits to the house, e.g. the person, whence it came:[22] Τότε λέγει, Ἐπιστρέψω εἰς τὸν οἶκόν μου ὅθεν ἐξῆλθον, 'Then it says, "I will return to my house from which I came"'.

The verb is used of an animal e.g. in Aristotle, *Historia Animalium*, 629b15, which describes the behaviour of the lion confronted by hunters: Ἐν δὲ ταῖς θήραις ὁρώμενος μὲν οὐδέποτε φεύγει οὐδὲ πτήσσει, ἀλλ' ἐὰν καὶ διὰ πλῆθος ἀναγκασθῇ τῶν θηρευόντων ὑπαγαγεῖν βάδην ὑποχωρεῖ καὶ κατὰ σκέλος, κατὰ βραχὺ ἐπιστρεφόμενος, 'In the chase, as long as he is in view, he makes no attempt to run and shows no fear, but even if he be compelled by the multitude of the hunters to retreat, he withdraws step by step, little by little'.

In the Septuagint, the verb is also used with reference to animals. A well-known example is Genesis 8. 12, where Noah is waiting for the end of the flood, confirmation depending on whether or not the dove returns to the ark: πάλιν ἐξαπέστειλεν τὴν περιστερὰν καὶ οὐ προσέθετο τοῦ ἐπιστρέψαι πρὸς αὐτὸν ἔτι, 'again he sent forth the dove, and it did not continue to turn back to him any more'.

In the papyri from the Ptolemaic period, the verb ἐπιστρέφω/ἐπιστρέφομαι is not very frequent and is attested in only very fragmentary documents. Where used,

---

22 For other texts sharing the same idea, see also William D. Davies and Dale C. Allison, *A Critical and Exegetical Commentary on the Gospel according to Saint Matthew*, ICC (London: T&T Clark, 2004), II. Matthew VIII–XVIII, p. 361.

it has the same meaning as in the texts already quoted, i.e. the movement or act of returning. Suffice to quote one example dating from the second century BCE. *Papyrus Tebtunis*, 3. 1. 729, in a letter about the seizure of livestock, writes: αὐτὸς δ' εἰς τὰς περιοίκους κώμας ἐπέδραμεν ὑπολιπόμενος Διονύσιον τὸν διαδεχόμενον αὐτόν. καὶ μετὰ ταῦτα ἐπέστ[ρ]εψεν, […] μέχρι δὲ τοῦ γράφειν ἔτι ἐστὶν ἐν τῆι κώ(μηι), 'He hastened himself to the neighboring villages, leaving Dionysios as his deputy. After this he returned, […] and up to the time of writing is still in the village'.

We could quote many other examples from Greek literature and biblical writings. However, other examples would only confirm the impression that usually the verb ἐπιστρέφω/ἐπιστρέφομαι is used in contexts of real or imagined movements by gods, spirits, humans or animals in real or imagined places.

The second meaning of ἐπιστρέφω/ἐπιστρέφομαι, is rarer and more abstract, the idea of movement being absent. Here, the verb can govern an infinitive or an object in the genitive. In some contexts the verb means 'to pay attention', 'to think of ', 'to reflect'.[23] That is, it refers to a mental activity which is sometimes followed, or accompanied, by a decision. The verb ἐπιστρέφω/ἐπιστρέφομαι is used in this sense in Demosthenes, *In Aristocratem*, 11. 319 (23. 136) where Cotys intends to rob Iphicrates of everything that makes life worth living (including honours, statues and countries). It is said that he is unconcerned by the deprivation he is causing Iphicrates (νομίζων ἀποστερήσειν οὐκ ἐπεστράφη).

The verb is used in this negative sense (of being unconcerned) several times in writings of Jewish origin. The first example that deserves attention is in Philo, *Quod deus sit immutabilis*, 17. In this treaty the philosopher speaks of selfish people who do not bother about their duty to family, society or even God: […] μὴ γονέων τιμῆς, μὴ παίδων εὐκοσμίας, μὴ σωτηρίας πατρίδος, μὴ νόμων φυλακῆς, μὴ ἐθῶν βεβαιότητος, μὴ ἰδίων μὴ κοινῶν ἐπανορθώσεως, μὴ ἱερῶν ἁγιστείας, μὴ τῆς πρὸς θεὸν εὐσεβείας ἐπιστρεφόμενοι, 'not with a view to the honor of their parents, or the proper regulation of their children, or the salvation of their country, or the guardianship of the laws, or the preservation of good morals, or with a view to the due performance of any public or private duty, or of a proper celebration of sacred rites, or the pious worship due to the gods, they will be deservedly miserable'.

Likewise, Josephus, *Antiquitates Iudaicae*, 6. 43, describes the Israelites who do not listen to Samuel, but insist on having a king: Ἦν δ' ἄρα καὶ πρὸς τὰς προρρήσεις τῶν συμβησομένων ἀνόητον τὸ πλῆθος καὶ δύσκολον […] οὐδὲ γὰρ ἐπεστράφησαν οὐδ' ἐμέλησεν αὐτοῖς τῶν Σαμουήλου λόγων ἀλλ' ἐνέκειντο λιπαρῶς καὶ χειροτονεῖν ἠξίουν ἤδη τὸν βασιλέα καὶ μὴ φροντίζειν τῶν ἐσομένων, 'But the multitude was still so foolish as to be deaf to these predictions of what would befall them; […] they did not reflect and they did not regard the words of Samuel, but peremptorily insisted on their resolution, and desired him to ordain them a king immediately, and not trouble himself with fears of what would happen hereafter'.

---

23   For the specific meaning of the noun ἐπιστροφή 'consideration, attention', see e.g. Georg Bertram, 'ἐπιστρέφω, ἐπιστροφή', in *Theologisches Wörterbuch zum Neuen Testament*, ed. by Gerhard Kittel and Gerhard Friedrich, 12 vols (Stuttgart: Kohlhammer, 1933–78), VII (1935), pp. 722–29 (p. 722).

This negative sense is attested also in a papyrus of the Roman period where the writer complains about people slow in paying their debts: *BGU* 2. 436 dupl:

Στοτοῆτις ὁ καὶ Φανῆσις Στοτοήτιος καὶ οἱ ἀδελφοὶ Ἁρπαγάθης καὶ Ὧρος ὀφείλοντές μοι κατ᾽ οὐδὲν ἐπιστρέφονται ἀποδοῦναί μοι διαπλανῶντες καὶ ὑπερτιθέμενοι, ἀλλ᾽ ἔτι καὶ ἐπήλθοσάν μοι καὶ ὕβριν οὐ τὴν τυχοῦσαν συνετελέσαντο καὶ πληγὰς ἐπή[νε] γκαν καταρήξ[α]ντες καὶ ὃν εἶχον κιτῶνα.[24]

Even if these texts stem from different authors and origins, they have in common that they disapprove the lack of reflection or thoughtlessness that leads to reprehensible behaviour. On the other hand, thought, implied by ἐπιστρέφω/ἐπιστρέφομαι leads to the application of reason whereby the person in question is convinced of something. This idea appears for example in two texts by Josephus:

- Thus, in *Antiquitates Iudaicae*, 17. 62, Herodes is convinced by Pheroras's freedmen to inquire into the mysterious death of their master. Herodes 'was convinced by [their] words' (τοῦ δ᾽ ἐπιστραφέντος τοῖς λόγοις).
- Likewise, Josephus in *Bellum Iudaicum*, 5. 416, encourages his Jerusalem compatriots not to fight the Romans but to have regard for the beauty of the city, its temple and treasures (ὦ σιδήρειοι ῥίψατε τὰς πανοπλίας, λάβετε ἤδη κατερειπομένης αἰδῶ πατρίδος ἐπιστράφητε καὶ θεάσασθε τὸ κάλλος ἧς προδίδοτε, οἷον ἄστυ, οἷον ἱερόν, ὅσων ἐθνῶν δῶρα, 'O hard hearted wretches as you are! cast away all your arms, and take pity on your country already going to ruin; pay attention to have regard to the excellency of that city which you are going to betray, to that excellent temple with the donations of so many countries in it').

All these occurrences of the verb have in common that they allude to the thought processes that lead to a change of mind or behaviour. At least once in Greek literature, the verb ἐπιστρέφω/ἐπιστρέφομαι has this meaning, namely in Sophocles, *Antigone*, 1111, the focus being less on the act of reflection than on its result. In this case, the subject δόξα governs the verb ἐπιστρέφομαι: ἐπειδὴ δόξα τῇδ᾽ ἐπεστράφη, αὐτός τ᾽ ἔδησα καὶ παρὼν ἐκλύσομαι, 'But since my judgment has taken this turn, I will be there to set her free, as I myself confined her'.

2.3.2. Remarks on the Use of ἐπιστρέφω/ἐπιστρέφομαι in Jewish and Christian Writings

This specific use of ἐπιστρέφω/ἐπιστρέφομαι as found in the LXX, in the NT and in *Joseph and Aseneth*, 11. 11, i.e. with a complement like ἐπὶ τὸν θεόν/κύριον, is attested neither in Greek literature nor in the extant papyri. As for the first occurrence, Psalm 21. 28, this Greek translation can easily be explained against the background of the

---

24 'Although Stotoetis alias Phanesis, son of Stotoetis, and his brothers Harpagathes and Horos, are in debt to me, they are making no effort to repay me, but making excuses and delaying, and on top of that they came up to me, acted violently in a quite unfitting manner, belaboured me with blows and even ripped the chiton which I was wearing […]'.

Hebrew text that uses the verb שוב, ἐπιστρέφω/ἐπιστρέφομαι being the standard LXX translation of this word. From the point of view of a Greek speaking reader, the expression ἐπιστρέφω/ἐπιστρέφομαι πρὸς or ἐπὶ τὸν θεόν/τὸν κύριον would sound like a metaphor composed of a verb of movement, on the one hand, and a non-spatial destination on the other, the God of Israel. If the other more recent Jewish and Christian writings — namely *Joseph and Aseneth*, the Acts of the Apostles, and Paul — used the same metaphor, their authors obviously took for granted that it was understood by their respective readers. In other words, probably it was a frequent and crystallised image already present in the language of the Greek speaking Jewish and Christian communities.

On the assumption that the process expressed by the phrase ἐπιστρέφω/ἐπιστρέφομαι πρὸς or ἐπὶ τὸν θεόν/τὸν κύριον requires a more or less profound change of mind and behaviour, notably the abandonment of idolatry, it should be pointed out that the focus of the phrase is not primarily on this aspect. The phrase alludes more to a movement of individuals or groups/communities willing to approach the only God, and less to the idea of regret and repentance. Nevertheless, as the examples from Demosthenes, Philo and Josephus have shown, the idea of a more or less radical change is not foreign to the verb ἐπιστρέφω/ἐπιστρέφομαι whose basic meaning is 'to turn around'.

The fact that the verb ἐπιστρέφω/ἐπιστρέφομαι with this specific meaning is not attested in non-Jewish or non-Christian literature is, at best, explained by the social and religious circumstances: faith in the gods, in the plural, was commonly accepted and to worship one god did not generally exclude worship of others.[25]

Conclusions

As we have seen, specific use of the verbs μετανοέω and ἐπιστρέφω/ἐπιστρέφομαι and their cognate nouns as *termini technici* of so-called 'conversion' of the Gentiles has its origin either in the Septuagint or in Jewish-Hellenistic literature, namely in the novel *Joseph and Aseneth*. Although both terms sometimes appear in parallel, it should be kept in mind that each of them has a specific nuance.[26] In *Joseph and Aseneth* the verb μετανοέω appears in the context of abandonment of the sin of idolatry. Therefore, repentance, i.e. μετάνοια, is required. The verb ἐπιστρέφω/ἐπιστρέφομαι, however, does not convey these connotations. The underlying idea is rather one of movement. In LXX-Psalm 21. 28, the nations will turn to the Lord and worship before him (ἐπιστραφήσονται πρὸς κύριον [...] καὶ προσκυνήσουσιν). In this case, the

---

25 Paul Aubin, *Le problème de la 'Conversion': Étude sur un terme commun à l'Hellénisme et au Christianisme des trois premiers siècles* (Paris: Beauchesne, 1963), p. 47, observes concerning the Septuagint use of ἐπιστρέφω/ἐπιστρέφομαι that two ideas have been associated: 'Attention' and 'retour physique'.

26 Johannes Behm, 'μετανοέω/μετάνοια', in *Theologisches Worterbuch zum Neuen Testament*, ed. by Gerhard Kittel and Gerhard Friedrich, 12 vols (Stuttgart: Kohlhammer, 1933–78), IV (1942), pp. 986–98, however, claimed that in the LXX the verbs μετανοέω and ἐπιστρέφω, when used in religious contexts, are nearly synonyms (e.g. Jeremiah 38. 18–19; Isaiah 46. 8).

idea of repentance is not mentioned but only the 'movement' of nations turning to the Lord. A text like LXX^{B,A}-Tobit 14. 5–6 is certainly more explicit, speaking even of burying idols. Nevertheless, the idea of repentance is absent from this text. The situation is different in *Jos. Asen.*, 11. 11: here, 'turning to God' is certainly spatial, albeit in a metaphorical sense: Once she has abandoned the idols, Aseneth turns to the Lord and takes refuge in him. The idea of repentance, however, is of paramount importance in the novel and plays a decisive role in the abandonment of idols and the rites of repentance of the protagonist.

To conclude, traces of two different meanings of the terms ἐπιστρέφω/ἐπιστρέφομαι and μετανοέω are to be found in the New Testament texts as well. In some cases, e.g. Acts 15. 3, the idea of repentance might be presupposed but is not explicitly mentioned. In Acts 26. 20, however, both ideas are present: the 'movement' of the Gentiles to God and their concomitant repentance, manifest in particular by deeds worthy of repentance. Finally, Paul no longer mentions repentance in I Thessalonians 1. 9, but only the idea of movement that is two-fold: the Thessalonians have turned to God which at the same time means turning away from the idols.

▼ ABSTRACT 'Conversion' is key theological term in the New Testament, used in present day translations of the Bible. However, the New Testament terminology cannot be understood without the Septuagint background. The aim of this paper is to consider the Septuagint terminology denoting the metaphorical 'crossing of boundaries' by Gentiles when they are interested in establishing a positive relationship with the God of Israel and the Jewish community. In particular, this article will address the following questions: a) which verbs and nouns in the Septuagint and in so-called intertestamental literature are used to express this phenomenon? b) Which verbs and nouns are introduced in intertestamental literature or even in the New Testament and which others disappear gradually? c) To what degree is the choice of this vocabulary in line with non-Jewish or non-Christian usage of the terms in question? And how does intertestamental literature give certain words a new connotation? d) Which terms become *termini technici* as Jewish-Hellenistic literature and later Christian writings evolve over time?

In a first stage it is necessary to make an inventory of the texts and terms to be analyzed. In the second I shall review the most important terms, especially against their non-biblical background, in order to illustrate the specific nuance in their meaning.

EMANUEL TOV

The Use of the Septuagint in Critical Commentaries

While critical commentaries on Old Testament books such as ICC, *Biblischer Kommentar*, and Anchor Bible focus on the Masoretic text (MT), they also turn to additional textual sources, often in a special apparatus. It is well known that some of these sources are very relevant for the writing of commentaries because they are as significant as MT itself, and often more so. Consulting Hebrew sources such as the Dead Sea Scrolls for commentaries is rather straightforward, but the use of the ancient versions is not. In these cases, additional sets of criteria need to be employed. Now, among these ancient versions, the LXX is especially important because of the wealth of data embedded in that version. The data are in Greek, and we need special skills in order to integrate them in a text critical analysis. In this study, my main interest is the text critical sources in general, and especially the LXX.

It appears to be an almost impossible task for the average commentator to use the LXX due to the immensity of this assignment. Yet scholars do so all the time. They mainly interact with MT, while occasionally referring to the LXX. In my view, a good perusal of the LXX requires that the scholar be an expert in all aspects of that translation. The scholar would have to be at home in all the features of a specific Greek unit and that would require extensive *Vorarbeiten*. One can only understand a detail in the translation if one has a good understanding of the translation character of the complete book. Thus, if a detail in MT is lacking in the LXX one would have to decide whether that detail was not found in the translator's parent text and that can only be done if we have a thorough understanding of the translator's faithfulness to his *Vorlage*. This would allow us a judgment on the question whether the lacking detail was found in the translator's *Vorlage* or was omitted by him.

Obviously, a commentator cannot make a thorough investigation of the features of the LXX, and therefore one uses the Septuagint and other textual tools to the best of one's ability. Ideally, the writing of a commentary should be a team effort, in which an expert in textual criticism is involved but I do not know whether such a collaborative effort has ever taken place. Occasionally, a commentator is himself/ herself an expert in either the Septuagint or other areas of textual criticism.

It has been established by many scholars since the time of Cappellus (1650) that the ancient versions need to be employed in the exegesis of the Hebrew Bible and

New Avenues in Biblical Exegesis in Light of the Septuagint
ed. by Leonardo Pessoa da Silva Pinto and Daniela Scialabba, Turnhout, 2022 (*SEPT*, 1), pp. 41–58
© BREPOLS ❧ PUBLISHERS   DOI 10.1484/M.SEPT-EB.5.127710

indeed this has been done all the time.[1] But how well is it done, and can we expect that a commentator with an expertise in literary criticism also have a mastery in textual criticism? When I consult the commentaries known to me in the European languages and Hebrew, this is not the case.

Should the commentator use a shortcut such as listings of variants in scholarly editions or consult all the ancient sources himself/herself? The latter seems to be required. After all, if the commentator's textual preference is based on the selection of the variants and guidance provided by *BHS*, much material will be missed. The selection of variants in the earlier *BH* was wider than that in *BHS*.[2] The commentator is much better off with the selection of variants and guidance in *BHQ*. At the same time, the textual guidance in *BHQ* is often problematic; for example, in Genesis and Judges virtually no readings in the textual sources are preferred to those of MT.[3] In the case of the *HUB*, the selection of variants is optimal, but no guidance is offered regarding the choice of textual readings. On the other hand, in the only extant modern eclectic edition, that by Michael Fox of Proverbs,[4] guidance is provided as the editor preferred a few readings to MT, but the preferred text is very close to MT. Furthermore, in the text of that edition, the evidence of the LXX is not fully taken into consideration and therefore a future commentator on Proverbs cannot use this edition as a suitable base for a textual-literary analysis of the Hebrew book. The many volumes of Barthélemy are gems of textual analysis, but they discuss far too few cases; further, in these studies, MT is usually preferred and therefore these studies are not a good basis for writing a commentary.[5]

In short, in my view there are no suitable tools that a commentator can use as adequate guidance in textual judgment, and one needs to turn to the ancient versions themselves, and this is how it should be. A commentator should have first-hand contact with the ancient sources, although the selection of the textual variants of the *HUB* and *BHQ* is of great help.

---

1   Ludovicus Cappellus, *Critica Sacra sive de variis quae in sacris Veteris Testamenti libris occurrunt lectionibus libri sex* (Paris: Cramoisy, 1650; Halle: Hendel, 1775–[86]).

2   See the data I provided in my review article 'Biblia Hebraica Stuttgartensia', *Shnaton*, 4 (1980), 172–80 (Hebrew with English summary).

3   For Genesis, see my review article, 'A New Volume in the *Biblia Hebraica Quinta* Series: *Genesis*', in *Festschrift Peter Gentry 2019*, by Abraham Tal, forthcoming. For Judges, see my article '*Biblia Hebraica Quinta*, Vol. 7, Judges (ed. Natalio Fernández Marcos)', in *Textual Criticism of the Hebrew Bible, Qumran, Septuagint: Collected Essays*, ed. by Emanuel Tov, V.T.S, 167 (Leiden: Brill, 2015) III, pp. 258–64.

4   Michael V. Fox, *Proverbs: An Eclectic Edition with Introduction and Textual Commentary*, HBCE, 1 (Atlanta: SBL, 2015).

5   Dominique Barthélemy and others, *Preliminary and Interim Report on the Hebrew Old Testament Text Project — Compte rendu préliminaire et provisoire sur le travail d'analyse textuelle de l'Ancien Testament hébreu*, 5 vols (New York: United Bible Societies, 1973–80); Dominique Barthélemy and others, *Critique textuelle de l'Ancien Testament*, OBO, 50/1 (Fribourg: Éditions Universitaires; Göttingen: Vandenhoeck & Ruprecht, 1982), I. Josué–Esther, and all the subsequent volumes on the other books (1986, 1992, 2005, 2015).

In my necessarily subjective review, I now turn to the series of commentaries, first to four series of commentaries on the LXX itself. Their usefulness for this purpose is very limited since they involve the Hebrew text only infrequently. The volumes of the *Bible d'Alexandrie* provide an excellent inner-Septuagintal commentary, focusing on how that text was regarded in Hellenistic times. The earlier volumes disregard the Hebrew text and therefore sometimes misrepresent the intentions of the translators,[6] while the more recent ones are often engaged with the possible *Vorlage* of the LXX.[7]

The *Septuagint Commentary Series* by Brill (Leiden: Brill: 2005–) is likewise an inner-Septuagintal enterprise that focuses on *Codex Vaticanus*, the most important LXX manuscript. Some volumes are more inner-Septuagintal than others. The Joshua volume, by a biblical exegete, interacts occasionally with the Hebrew text.[8] Most volumes, however, view the LXX as a Hellenistic document.[9] Thus, in her Genesis commentary,[10] Brayford recognizes a philological problem in the relation between the MT and LXX in Genesis 18. 12,[11] where Sarah is depicted in completely different

---

6   For example, in Genesis 3. 17, אֲרוּרָה הָאֲדָמָה בַּעֲבוּרֶךָ ('Cursed be the ground because of you') was misread or misinterpreted as אֲרוּרָה הָאֲדָמָה בַּעֲבֹד(ת)ךָ ('Cursed is the earth in your labors'). Likewise, 8. 21 לֹא אֹסִף לְקַלֵּל עוֹד אֶת הָאֲדָמָה בַּעֲבוּר הָאָדָם ('Never again will I doom the earth because of man'), was rendered as οὐ προσθήσω ἔτι τοῦ καταράσασθαι τὴν γῆν διὰ τὰ ἔργα τῶν ἀνθρώπων ('I will not proceed hereafter to curse the earth because of the deeds of men'). In both cases, בַּעֲבוּר was not recognized at the beginning of the translation enterprise and was read with a *dalet*. These textual problems were not mentioned in the commentary by Marguerite Harl, *La Genèse*, La Bible d'Alexandrie, 1 (Paris: Cerf, 1986), p. 139 who, instead, read a theological intention into the LXX of Genesis 8. 21: 'God does not take the nature of human beings into consideration, but the actions of everyone'.
7   In the case of the Minor Prophets, the following volumes have appeared to date: Jan Joosten and others, *Les Douze Prophètes, Osée*, La Bible d'Alexandrie, 23.1 (Paris: Cerf, 2002); Marguerite Harl and others, *Les Douze Prophètes, Joël, Abdiou, Jonas, Naoum, Ambakoum, Sophonie*, La Bible d'Alexandrie, 23.4–9 (Paris: Cerf, 1999); Marguerite Harl and others, *Les Douze Prophètes, Aggée, Zacharie*, La Bible d'Alexandrie, 23.10–11 (Paris: Cerf, 2011); Laurence Vianès, *Les Douze Prophètes, Malachie*, La Bible d'Alexandrie, 23.12 (Paris: Cerf, 2011). The remarks in these volumes list the pluses and minuses of the LXX as well as the qualitative differences without taking a position regarding their textual status.
8   Alan Graeme Auld, *Joshua, Jesus Son of Naüe in Codex Vaticanus*, Septuagint Commentary Series (Leiden: Brill, 2005), provides occasional remarks on Hebrew-Greek equivalents. Further, the lacking MT segments at the beginning of Chapter 20 (cities of refuge) are mentioned briefly on p. 202, but not analyzed. By the same token, the importance of the long plus of the LXX at the end of Joshua 24. 33 is mentioned but not discussed (p. 229).
9   Susan Brayford, *Genesis*, Septuagint Commentary Series (Leiden: Brill, 2007); Daniel Gurtner, *Exodus*, Septuagint Commentary Series (Leiden: Brill, 2013); Mark Awabdy, *Leviticus*, Septuagint Commentary Series (Leiden: Brill, 2019); Georg Walzer, *Jeremiah*, Septuagint Commentary Series (Leiden: Brill, 2012); John Olley, *Ezekiel*, Septuagint Commentary Series (Leiden: Brill, 2013); William Edward Glenny, *Amos*, Septuagint Commentary Series (Leiden: Brill, 2013); William Edward Glenny, *Hosea*, Septuagint Commentary Series (Leiden: Brill, 2013); William Edward Glenny, *Micah*, Septuagint Commentary Series (Leiden: Brill, 2015).
10 Brayford, *Genesis*, p. 313.
11 Genesis 18. 12 MT וַתִּצְחַק שָׂרָה בְּקִרְבָּהּ לֵאמֹר אַחֲרֵי בְלֹתִי הָיְתָה־לִּי עֶדְנָה וַאדֹנִי זָקֵן, 'And Sarah laughed to herself, saying, "Now that I am withered, am I to have enjoyment — with my husband so old?"' (*NJPS*). LXX ἐγέλασεν δὲ Σαρρα ἐν ἑαυτῇ λέγουσα Οὔπω μέν μοι γέγονεν ἕως τοῦ νῦν, ὁ δὲ κύριός μου πρεσβύτερος, 'And Sarah laughed within herself, saying: "it has not yet happened to me up to the present, and my lord is rather old"'.

ways in these sources due to a textual difference.[12] However, she prefers to explain this difference at the philosophical level, which in my view is irrelevant.[13]

Most references to the parent text of the LXX are found in the important commentaries of John William Wevers on the five books of the Torah.[14] Wevers was in the first place interested in the internal problems of the LXX, but he also remarked on the relation of the LXX to the MT. His approach was conservative: Hardly, if ever, did Wevers assume a different Hebrew reading at the base of the LXX, as was already visible in his early study on Kings.[15]

The German *Septuaginta Deutsch* provides a valuable commentary, referring to the Hebrew text more than other LXX commentaries. It is brief and the quality differs in the various books.[16]

The Genesis commentary in Modern Hebrew by Moshe A. Zipor is probably the single best critical commentary on the LXX in existence in that or any other language.[17] It provides a translation of the LXX in Modern Hebrew as well as a very extensive commentary.

Except for the Genesis commentary of Zipor and *Septuaginta Deutsch*, the LXX commentaries do not pay attention to the full range of textual problems. I now turn to general commentaries of the Hebrew Bible, while examining the range of their interest in textual issues. It is often difficult to single out the LXX from the plethora of textual witnesses. Usually, the commentary provides an eclectic translation of the biblical text, selecting elements from MT, the LXX, other versions, and the author's own conjectures.[18] At other times, it contains a central Bible translation. Thus the

---

12 For these insights, Brayford, *Genesis*, p. 313, quotes the commentary of John William Wevers, *Notes on the Greek Text of Genesis*, SBLSCS, 35 (Atlanta: Scholars Press, 1993), p. 252.

13 Brayford, *Genesis*, p. 313: 'They [the differences between the MT and LXX] also reflect differences in the social and gender attitudes characteristic in the translator's Hellenistic environment. Instead of pondering the possibility of sexual pleasure in her old age and withered state, the LXX-G Sarah merely comments on her lifetime problem. Furthermore, by replacing Sarah's thoughts of pleasure with an allusion to her continued barrenness, the LXX-G Sarah accepts the blame for the couple's lack of progeny. Doing so downplays the significance of Abraham's age. His virility is less threatened, especially since he had earlier fathered a son through Hagar. Like a proper Hellenistic matron, Sarah thinks not of her own sexual pleasure'.

14 Wevers, *Genesis*; John William Wevers, *Notes on the Greek Text of Exodus*, SBLSCS, 30 (Atlanta: Scholars Press, 1990); *Notes on the Greek Text of Leviticus*, SBLSCS, 44 (Atlanta: Scholars Press, 1997); *Notes on the Greek Text of Numbers*, SBLSCS, 46 (Atlanta: Scholars Press, 1998); *Notes on the Greek Text of Deuteronomy*, SBLSCS, 39 (Atlanta: Scholars Press, 1995).

15 John William Wevers, 'A Study in the Hebrew Variants in the Books of Kings', *ZAW*, 61 (1945–48), 43–76.

16 *Septuaginta Deutsch, Erläuterungen und Kommentare zum griechischen Alten Testament*, ed. by Martin Karrer and Wolfgang Kraus, 2 vols (Stuttgart: Deutsche Bibelgesellschaft, 2011).

17 Moshe A. Zipor, *The Septuagint Version of the Book of Genesis* (Ramat-Gan: Bar-Ilan University Press, 2005; Hebrew).

18 See Emanuel Tov, *Textual Criticism of the Hebrew Bible*, 3rd edn, Revised and Expanded (Minneapolis: Fortress Press, 2012), pp. 369–76; Stephen C. Daley, *The Textual Basis of English Translations of the Hebrew Bible*, Supplements to the Textual History of the Hebrew Bible, 2 (Leiden: Brill, 2019).

volumes of *The JPS Torah Commentary* comment on the translation of the *NJPS*,[19] the volumes of the *Old Testament Library* comment on the translation of the *RSV*, and the volumes of *Die Neue Echter Bibel* comment on the *Einheitsübersetzung*. Many commentaries present the text in the supposed sequence of its sources,[20] and Noth (OTL) and others indicate the Pentateuchal sources in detail in the translation.

Commentaries incorporate details from the non-Masoretic sources in order to present the various witnesses of 'the Bible' in an egalitarian way. These elements are included in the eclectic translations mentioned in the preceding paragraph, in special textual notes, and in the course of the running commentary. However, time and again, the commentaries mainly comment on MT; under the assumption that this text includes mistakes and/or does not reflect the original literary shape of the Hebrew Bible, the textual data are used to 'correct' MT. Furthermore, often MT is corrected without any textual basis. These are the so-called emendations.

While commenting mainly on MT, commentators often correct MT based on other sources. For example, in his ICC commentary on Ezekiel,[21] George A. Cooke considers the LXX a 'weapon' in the attempt to correct MT. Sometimes scholars will say: 'The text has been preserved well in MT',[22] but such formulations are irrelevant since the full scope of the textual material will never be known. Therefore, no claim can be made that the text has been well preserved in MT as possibly better texts may have perished. It should be understood that the survival of the texts is to some extent coincidental (note the discovery of the Dead Sea Scrolls).

We are faced with tens of series and hundreds of individual volumes. I limit myself to the series and commentaries in English, German, and Hebrew, and even the works written in these languages cannot be exhausted. I realize that it is difficult

---

19 For example, Jeffrey H. Tigay, *The JPS Torah Commentary, Deuteronomy* דברים (Philadelphia: Jewish Publication Society, 1996).

20 See below with reference to Gunkel on Genesis (HAT), Procksch on Genesis (KAT), and Bright on Jeremiah (AB).

21 George Albert Cooke, *Ezekiel*, ICC (Edinburgh: T&T Clark, 1936), p. xli.

22 I attach an anthology of such remarks: George Buchanan Gray, *Numbers*, ICC (Edinburgh: T&T Clark, 1903), p. xxxix: 'Like the remaining books of the Pentateuch, and unlike such books as Samuel and the Minor Prophets, the text of Numbers appears to have suffered comparatively little from simple errors of transcription. The most corrupt passages are to be found in some of the poems, and in these the most serious corruption is a more ancient than G, and, consequently, only to be amended, if amended at all, by conjecture'; William Rainy Harper, *Amos and Hosea*, ICC (Edinburgh: T&T Clark, 1905), p. clxxiii: 'The text of Amos is as well preserved as perhaps any text in the Hebrew Bible, the number of unintelligible passages being remarkably small (cf. 3^{10}, 4^9, 5^6, $6^{1,2}$, 7^2)'; Edward Lewis Curtis and Albert Alonzo Madsen, *Chronicles*, ICC (Edinburgh: T&T Clark, 1910), p. 36: 'The text of Chronicles is in fair condition, though by no means up to the standard of many of the older Old Testament books'; Julius A. Bewer, *Micah, Zephaniah, Nahum, Habakkuk, Obadiah and Joel*, ICC (Edinburgh: T&T Clark, 1911), p. 68: 'The text of Joel is well preserved and no special discussion of it is needed here'; Wilhelm Rudolph, *Esra und Nehemia* (Tübingen: Mohr Siebeck, 1949), p. xix: 'Der Text ist im algemeinen nicht schlecht erhalten [...]'; Roland E. Murphy, *The Song of Songs, A Commentary*, Hermeneia (Minneapolis: Fortress Press, 1990), p. 7: 'The Hebrew text of the Song in M appears to be in good repair, relative especially to the condition of the traditional Hebrew text of Job or even Proverbs'.

to characterize commentaries without a more comprehensive study. I refer solely to their approach to textual criticism, which is but a limited part of the task of a commentator.

I pay attention especially to those passages and books in which the LXX makes a difference. The evidence of the LXX is very important for commentaries, especially when it offers material that is relevant not only for the textual but also for the literary history.[23] This is the case especially in Joshua, Samuel, Kings, Jeremiah, Ezekiel, and Proverbs, but also in key chapters in Genesis, Isaiah, and Esther. In the cases of Ezekiel and Jeremiah, the Greek texts are respectively 5% and 16% shorter than their Hebrew counterparts, in words, phrases, sentences, and small and large sections. The Greek text of Proverbs has pluses, minuses, and displays differences in sequence. I do not express an opinion on the type of solution suggested by the commentator, but I investigate whether the commentator is aware that there is a textual problem or that we are dealing at times with a global textual issue in a section or book.

I examine whether the commentaries dwelled on key textual issues, such as the chronological differences between MT, SP, and the LXX in Genesis 5 and 11, the major differences between MT and the LXX in Exodus 30–35, the differences between the LXX and the MT at the end of Genesis 31, many details in the blessing of Jacob in Genesis 49, the short text of the LXX of Ezekiel, etc. In almost every book there are key textual issues on which a commentator is expected to remark, although there are several books that do not offer many such challenges, when the non-Masoretic sources do not differ significantly from MT, such as Judges, Ruth, Qohelet, and Lamentations. However, also those books offer textual challenges. Among other things, I wanted to see whether the commentaries display an awareness of the major differences between MT and the LXX, but very often they do not. They are not all of the same caliber as that of Julius Wellhausen, who understood already in 1871 that the LXX sometimes relates to the literary criticism of Samuel.[24] My general feeling is that as a rule attention to textual details is underdeveloped in commentaries and that is why I embarked on this investigation. On the other hand, some text critical monographs focusing on certain books fill a vacuum.

Focusing on textual criticism only, I distinguish between several types of commentaries. In my view, an ideal commentary characterizes the textual sources and the commentator summarizes his/her approach to these sources. When these elements are included in an introduction, the commentator can refer to those paragraphs when a variation between MT and an ancient source is discussed.

I distinguish between: (1) semicritical and (2) critical commentaries. Within each series, the volumes are of a variable character with regard to their attention

---

23 On the other hand, Moshe Greenberg, *Ezekiel 1–20*, AB (Garden City, NY: Doubleday, 1983), p. 20, and *Ezekiel 21–37*, AB (Garden City, NY: Doubleday, 1997), p. 396, downplayed the evidence of the LXX after he had indicated in a separate study that the MT and LXX display two different worlds: 'The Use of the Ancient Versions for Interpreting the Hebrew Text: A Sampling from Ezekiel ii 1 – iii 11', in *Congress Volume Göttingen 1977*, VT.S, 29 (Leiden: Brill, 1978), pp. 131–48.

24 Julius Wellhausen, *Der Text der Bücher Samuelis* (Göttingen: Vandenhoeck & Ruprecht, 1871), p. xi.

to textual criticism. Among the critical commentaries, I distinguish between: (2.1) those that devote little or no attention to textual criticism, mainly the LXX; (2.2) those that devote variable attention to textual criticism; and (2.3) those that devote constant attention. In my sample, the largest group is group 2.2, series that devote variable attention to textual criticism. In other words, in those series, some pay attention to textual criticism, while others or most do not. It remains remarkable that many volumes of semicritical and critical character pay little or no attention to textual criticism, while they are very developed in other areas, especially in their source-critical analysis. In other words, these commentaries apply their criticism to the printed text of MT.

I present the various series in approximate chronological sequence, although they often overlap to some extent.

1. Semicritical Commentaries

Semicritical commentaries pay little or no attention to textual criticism, for example:
-   *Cambridge Bible for Schools and Churches* (CB) (1882–). The discussion is very brief, also by well-known scholars such as Samuel R. Driver on Exodus.[25] On the other hand, George A. Cooke pays attention to the LXX in Joshua;[26]
-   *The Cambridge Bible Commentary on the New English Bible*, e.g. Ernst W. Nicholson on Jeremiah;[27]
-   *Die Neue Echter Bibel*,[28] providing the text of the *Einheitsübersetzung*, without introduction to the textual sources and with a minimum of textual notes.

2. Critical Commentaries

2.1.   Critical Commentaries with Little or No Attention to Textual Criticism

Critical commentaries with little or no attention to textual criticism:
-   *Die Heilige Schrift des Alten Testaments* makes use of the textual data and provides an eclectic translation, e.g. in I–II Kings.[29] The remarks are very brief and impressionistic and there is no introduction to the textual sources;

---

25   Samuel Rolles Driver, *Exodus*, CB (Cambridge: Cambridge University Press, 1911).
26   George Albert Cooke, *The Book of Joshua in the Revised Version with Introduction and Notes*, CB (Cambridge: Cambridge University Press, 1918).
27   Ernst W. Nicholson, *Jeremiah 1–25, Jeremiah 26–52*, CBC (Cambridge: Cambridge University Press, 1973, 1975).
28   For example, Georg Hentschel, *Eins Könige, Zwei Könige*, NEchtB (Würzburg: Echter, 1984, 1985).
29   Otto Eissfeldt, *Das erste Buch der Könige, Das zweite Buch der Könige*, Die Heilige Schrift des Alten Testaments, II.5–6 (Tübingen: Mohr Siebeck, 1922).

- *Das Alte Testament Deutsch* (ATD), *Old and New Series*, the German counterpart to the OTL series. Most volumes provide no introduction to textual criticism, contain no special segment on textual criticism, and have very few textual notes;[30]
- *Old Testament Library* (OTL), *Old Series*. The Old Testament Library is a critical scholarly series, based on source criticism, including volumes by Martin Noth on Exodus, Leviticus, Joshua, and Kings, among others.[31] Typically for the series, Noth pays little attention to textual variants and, as Noth's main interest is source criticism, he marks the various sources in the *RSV* translation with different typefaces. Without any reference to textual sources other than MT, he reconstructs the 'original' text by bracketing words, parts of verses, verses, and complete sections that do not belong to that text. None of Noth's commentaries contains a section devoted to textual criticism, except for a brief statement in Joshua.[32] By stating that the MT of Joshua is 'good', Noth implies that there is no need to consult any other text; this assertion, however, does not take the LXX adequately into account. It is rather symptomatic of this system that the Leviticus volume has a joint section named 'Literary Criticism and Textual History' (pp. 10–15) that does not refer at all to textual criticism. Also the other volumes have very few textual notes.[33] The volume by John Gray on Kings has an introduction to the text (pp. 43–54), including some attention to the LXX (pp. 44–46), mainly on the chronological discrepancies between the texts.[34]

2.2. Critical Commentaries with Variable Attention to Textual Criticism

The following are critical commentaries with variable attention to textual criticism:
- *Handkommentar zum Alten Testament* (HAT), *Old and New Series*. Hermann Gunkel's famous commentary on Genesis is innovative, but it seldom refers to the versions, since 'we can really improve the transmitted text of Genesis only in relatively few places'.[35] Gunkel rearranged the text in accord with the source-critical analysis based on the printed text of MT. Thus, the commentary starts with the

---

30 For example, Ernst Würthwein, *Das Erste Buch der Könige, Kapitel 1–16* (Göttingen: Vandenhoeck & Ruprecht, 1977). For newer volumes, see Karl-Friedrich Pohlmann, *Das Buch des Propheten Hesekiel (Ezechiel) Kapitel 1–19*, ATD, 22/1 (Göttingen: Vandenhoeck & Ruprecht, 1996); Werner H. Schmidt, *Das Buch Jeremia, Kapitel 1–20*, ATD, 20 (Göttingen: Vandenhoeck & Ruprecht, 2008); Werner H. Schmidt, *Das Buch Jeremia, Kapitel 21–52*, ATD, 21 (Göttingen: Vandenhoeck & Ruprecht, 2013); Magne Saebo, *Sprüche*, ATD (Göttingen: Vandenhoeck & Ruprecht, 2012).
31 Martin Noth, *Exodus*, OTL (London: SCM Press, 1966); *Leviticus*, OTL (London: SCM Press, 1965); *Deuteronomy*, OTL (London: SCM Press, 1966); *Joshua*, OTL (London: SCM Press, 1972). These volumes were translated from the *Das Alte Testament Deutsch* series.
32 Noth, *Joshua*, p. 18: 'The Hebrew text of Joshua is generally good, although it has preserved, as Baldi has observed, a number of traditional errors [...]'.
33 For example, Arthur Weiser, *The Psalms: A Commentary*, OTL (London: SCM Press, 1962); Norman W. Porteous, *Daniel: A Commentary*, OTL (London: SCM Press, 1965).
34 John Gray, *I & II Kings: A Commentary*, OTL (Philadelphia: Westminster, 1963).
35 Hermann Gunkel, *Genesis*, HAT (Göttingen: Vandenhoeck & Ruprecht, 1902), p. vii: 'der überlieferte Text von Genesis kann von uns nur an verhältnissmässig wenigen Stellen wirklich verbessert werden'.

story of the Paradise of J in 2. 4b–3. 24, while the preceding creation history of P in 1. 1–2. 4a appears only on p. 89. Some of the other volumes in HAT likewise pay little attention to textual criticism,[36] while yet other volumes like that by Wilhelm Frankenberg pay appropriate attention to that discipline.[37] This volume appropriately consults the LXX in Chapters 16, 17, 31, and 36. On the other hand, in the textually significant Jeremiah, Wilhelm Rudolph's commentary lacks background information: The introduction is too short and there is no analysis of the translation technique of the LXX.[38] In the new HAT series, Hermann-Josef Stipp places full weight on text critical analysis combined with literary analysis.[39] This is the only commentary known to me that systematically translates the text of the LXX alongside or within the translation from MT, and also exegetes both texts.

- *Kurzer Hand-Commentar zum Alten Testament* (KHC). Together with a brief introduction to textual criticism, the Kings volume provides a good guide to text critical matters.[40] Likewise, the Genesis and Samuel volumes provide brief but appropriate textual notes.[41] The introductions are very brief.
- *Kurzgefasster Kommentar zu den Heiligen Schriften Alten und Neuen Testamentes sowie zu den Apokryphen.* This series provides very brief commentaries, such as in Genesis[42] and the remainder of the Torah, without textual introductions, and sometimes the notes are a little more extensive as in the case of Samuel–Kings[43] and Jeremiah.[44]
- *Biblischer Kommentar* (BKAT), *Old Series.* Except for the commentary by Walther Zimmerli on Ezekiel (see the analysis below of the English translation in the Hermeneia series),[45] none of the prefaces to the volumes in this series include an introduction to textual criticism. The Kings commentary by Noth includes only a few references to the LXX.[46]
- *International Critical Commentary* (ICC), *Old Series.* ICC provides separate notes of textual and philological content, and occasionally includes these remarks in

---

36 Bernhard Duhm, *Jesaja*, HAT, 2nd edn (Göttingen: Vandenhoeck & Ruprecht, 1902); Ernst Würthwein, Kurt Galling and Otto Plöger, *Die Fünf Megilloth*, 2nd edn (Tübingen: Mohr Siebeck, 1969); Wilhelm Rudolph, *Chronikbücher*, HAT (Tübingen: Mohr Siebeck, 1955).

37 Wilhelm Frankenberg, *Die Sprüche, Prediger, und Hoheslied*, HAT (Göttingen: Vandenhoeck & Ruprecht, 1898).

38 Wilhelm Rudolph, *Jeremia*, 2nd edn, HAT (Tübingen: Mohr Siebeck, 1958), pp. xx–xxi.

39 Hermann-Josef Stipp, *Jeremia 25–52*, HAT, I 12,2 (Tübingen: Mohr Siebeck, 2019).

40 Immanuel Benzinger, *Die Bücher der Könige*, KHC, IX (Tübingen: Mohr Siebeck, 1899).

41 Heinrich Holzinger, *Genesis*, KHC, I (Tübingen: Mohr Siebeck, 1898); Karl Budde, *Die Bucher Samuel*, KHC, VIII (Tübingen: Mohr Siebeck, 1902).

42 Hermann L. Strack, *Die Genesis*, KHC, A 1 (Munich: Beck, 1905).

43 August Klostermann, *Die Bücher Samuelis und der Könige*, Kurzgefasster Kommentar zu den Heiligen Schriften Alten und Neuen Testamentes sowie zu den Apokryphen (Nordlingen: Beck, 1887).

44 Conrad von Orelli, *Der Prophet Jeremia*, KHC, A 4,2 (Munich: Beck, 1905).

45 Walther Zimmerli, *Ezechiel*, BKAT (Neukirchen-Vluyn: Neukirchener Verlag des Erziehungsvereins, 1969).

46 Martin Noth, *Könige*, BKAT (Neukirchen-Vluyn: Neukirchener Verlag des Erziehungsvereins, 1968).

the text when they pertain to exegesis. The quality of the textual remarks varies much from volume to volume. The volumes of Kings, Isaiah, Ezekiel, Psalms, Ecclesiastes, and Daniel[47] engage seriously in textual criticism in introductory remarks on the ancient versions and in the commentary while all other volumes treat these issues briefly or not at all.[48] The lack of a serious analysis of the nature of the LXX is felt in Hosea where William R. Harper notes that '[t]he text of Hosea, however, is one of the most corrupt in the O.T., the number of passages which almost defy interpretation being extremely large' (p. clxxiii). Harper notes that the LXX is 'most helpful' in the correction of MT and the Targum (p. clxxiv), but he does not analyze that translation. Ezekiel is a good example of a positive use of the LXX in the correction of the Hebrew text, which, according to George A. Cooke, is very corrupt.[49] The description of the LXX, more extensive than in most ICC volumes (pp. xli–xlvii), includes a list of the verses in which the LXX is used in order to correct the text of MT and provides a selection of the features of the LXX. Cooke does not offer a full-blown analysis of the translation technique, but he has a well-based view on the LXX. Cooke considers the LXX a 'weapon' in the correction of the Hebrew text (p. xli), and he does not consider the possibility that MT and the LXX once represented different literary traditions of the Hebrew text.[50] The volume on Kings by James A. Montgomery probably devotes the most attention to matters of textual criticism in the old ICC series. Its author, Montgomery, and reviser, Henry S. Gehman, are well at home in textual criticism.[51]

---

47 James A. Montgomery, *Kings*, ed. by Henry Snyder Gehman (Edinburgh: T&T Clark, 1951); George Buchanan Gray, *Isaiah I–XXVII* (Edinburgh: T&T Clark, 1912); George Albert Cooke, *Ezekiel* (Edinburgh: T&T Clark, 1936); Charles Augustus Briggs, *Psalms*, ICC (Edinburgh: T&T Clark, 1906); George Aaron Barton, *Ecclesiastes*, ICC (Edinburgh: T&T Clark, 1908); James A. Montgomery, *Daniel*, ICC (Edinburgh: T&T Clark, 1927).

48 John Skinner, *Genesis*, 2nd edn, ICC (Edinburgh: T&T Clark, 1930); George Buchanan Gray, *Numbers*, ICC (Edinburgh: T&T Clark, 1903); Samuel Rolles Driver, *Deuteronomy* (Edinburgh: T&T Clark, 1908); George Foot Moore, *Judges*, ICC (Edinburgh: T&T Clark, 1895); Henry Preserved Smith, *Samuel*, ICC (Edinburgh: T&T Clark, 1899); William Rainy Harper, *Amos and Hosea*, ICC (Edinburgh: T&T Clark, 1905); John Merlin Powis Smith and others, *Micah, Zephaniah, Nahum, Habakkuk, Obadiah and Joel* (Edinburgh: T&T Clark, 1911); Crawford H. Toy, *Proverbs*, ICC (Edinburgh: T&T Clark, 1899); Samuel Rolles Driver and George Buchanan Gray, *Job*, ICC (Edinburgh: T&T Clark, 1921); Lewis Bayles Paton, *Esther*, ICC (Edinburgh: T&T Clark, 1908) — although this commentary introduces the various texts in a long analysis of forty-seven pages, the exegesis itself is based on MT; Loring W. Batten, *Ezra and Nehemiah*, ICC (Edinburgh: T&T Clark, 1913); Edward Lewis Curtis and Albert Alonzo Madsen, *Chronicles*, ICC (Edinburgh: T&T Clark, 1910).

49 Cooke, *Ezekiel*, p. xxvii.

50 MT may well represent an expansion of the shorter Greek text. This MT layer of some five percent was added to the earlier layer now represented by the Greek text. See my study: 'Recensional Differences between the MT and LXX of Ezekiel', *ETL*, 62 (1986), 89–101. Revised version: Emanuel Tov, *The Greek and Hebrew Bible: Collected Essays on the Septuagint*, VT.S, 72 (Leiden: Brill, 1999), pp. 397–410.

51 Montgomery, *Kings*. Among the important remarks in the introduction, the author says: '[…] but this process of comparison does not become scientific until statistics of the right and wrong in a given version have been gathered. It will actually be found that a small percentage of the variations of

–   *Anchor Bible* (AB). In the Anchor Bible series, the volume with the greatest openness to textual criticism is probably that of Samuel by P. Kyle McCarter with ample attention to the scrolls and the LXX.[52] It provides a brief history of the research and some words on the textual sources but does not characterize these sources. Neither does this volume offer a general approach on each of these sources, from which it would have benefitted. Some AB volumes provide insufficient attention to the intricacies of textual criticism. For example, the Jeremiah volume by the historian John Bright did not investigate the LXX thoroughly, although that version has not been neglected. He reconstructed his own *Urtext* in English translation based on MT, the LXX, and his intuition, by rearranging and omitting sections.[53] Some volumes in the AB pay little attention to textual criticism because their authors believed that the textual witnesses reflect few relevant textual details.[54] The translation and commentary in Mitchell Dahood's volume on Psalms, based on the consonantal framework of MT, disregard the ancient versions 'because they have relatively little to offer toward a better understanding of the difficult texts'.[55] At the same time, Dahood does not follow MT closely, as he frequently changes the MT vocalization in accordance with what he considers valid parallels from Ugaritic. Likewise, Francis I. Andersen and David N. Freedman base their thorough commentary of Amos on MT.[56]

–   *Kommentar zum Alten Testament* (KAT), *Old Series*. This series pays some attention to textual criticism and has very brief introductions to the texts. The book of Samuel, which has drawn much textual attention in other series, has no

---

the Old Greek translations, for example, have any value for text-correction. The bulk of the notable ones will be found to be in the way of interpretation, following the endeavor to obtain sense out of a passage difficult rhetorically or grammatically, or to improve it, especially when theology is involved' (p. 23).

52   Peter Kyle McCarter, *I Samuel*, AB, 8 (Garden City, NY: Doubleday, 1980); *II Samuel*, AB, 9 (Garden City, NY: Doubleday, 1984).

53   John Bright, *Jeremiah*, AB (Garden City, NY: Doubleday, 1965). For example, Bright created the following sequence in translation: 24. 1–19, 24, 20–23; 21. 1–10 followed by 34. 1–7; 34. 8–22; 37. 1–10, etc. In order to find a certain section in the commentary, one needs to consult the table of contents.

54   The terminology used by Baruch A. Levine, *Numbers 1–20*, AB (New York: Doubleday, 1993), p. 86 on Numbers 1–20 shows his approach to MT: 'Taken as a whole, the variants exhibited by the Qumran scrolls cannot be said to undermine the Masoretic text of Numbers, and they seldom indicate that the Qumran scribes had before them, to start with, texts different from those underlying the Masoretic version'. The use of the term 'undermine' indicates the central place ascribed to MT. The thorough commentary on Leviticus by Jacob Milgrom, *Leviticus 1–16*, AB (New York: Doubleday, 1991); *Leviticus 17–22*, AB (New York: Doubleday, 2000); *Leviticus 23–27*, AB (New York: Doubleday, 2001), is based on MT, with occasional notes on the versions, and the introduction to this commentary of 2714 pages devotes a mere six lines to the textual condition of the book.

55   Mitchell Dahood, *Psalms*, AB (Garden City, NY: Doubleday, 1965), I. 1–50, p. xxiv.

56   Francis I. Andersen and David N. Freedman, *Amos: A New Translation with Notes and Commentary*, AB (New York: Doubleday, 1989), pp. 140–41: 'The study of MT as it stands is a straightforward and intrinsically legitimate activity. If more justification is needed, then MT is self-vindicating to the extent that it can be shown to make sense. Sometimes it is not possible to do so […] We keep the MT in the first place of interest and with first claim to be Amos' text'.

introduction to the text in KAT and contains only few textual notes.[57] The Genesis volume by Otto Procksch pays more attention to textual criticism, including a brief introduction.[58] This approach goes together with a complete rearrangement of the book of Genesis according to its sources, and in order to find the chapter one is interested in, one needs to use the table in the introduction.

- *Kommentar zum Alten Testament* (KAT), *New Series.* The new series provides only slightly more attention to textual criticism than the old series; see the volumes of Samuel and Job.[59] On the other hand, textual notes abound in the KAT volume of Ezra.[60]
- *Biblischer Kommentar* (BKAT), *New Series.* Genesis by Claus Westermann, containing more than 1800 pages,[61] does not include an introduction to textual criticism and its exegesis does not give the full weight to textual sources. The Samuel volume by Walter Dietrich contains too short an introduction to textual criticism (pp. 39*–41*),[62] but the textual observations are extensive.
- *Old Testament Library* (OTL), *New Series.* Several volumes in this series pay full attention to textual criticism, some without[63] and some with an introduction to that field, e.g. Alan Graeme Auld on Samuel,[64] Jon D. Levenson on Esther,[65] and Sara Japhet on Chronicles.[66] On the other hand, the volumes by Marvin A. Sweeney (Kings) and Leslie C. Allen (Jeremiah) are based more or less on MT.[67]
- *Hermeneia.* The volume with the greatest openness to textual criticism is probably the one of Daniel by John Collins.[68] Not only does this commentary have a judicious introduction to all the textual materials, it also takes that material into serious consideration in the philological commentary. In Chapters 4–6, the MT and OG texts differ so much from each other that scholars find it difficult to determine the relation between them. Collins therefore translated

---

57 Wilhelm Caspari, *Die Samuelbücher*, KAT (Leipzig: Deichert, 1926).

58 Otto Procksch, *Die Genesis*, KAT (Leipzig: Deichert, 1913).

59 Hans Joachim Stoebe, *Das erste Buch Samuelis*, KAT (Gütersloh: Mohn, 1973); the introduction to the textual witnesses is bibliographical and does not analyze these witnesses like the monograph of Driver (see n. 89). Georg Fohrer, *Das Buch Hiob*, KAT (Gütersloh: Mohn, 1963). The introduction to the textual sources on pp. 55–56 barely scratches the surface.

60 Antonius H. J. Gunneweg, *Esra*, KAT (Gütersloh: Mohn, 1985).

61 Claus Westermann, *Genesis 11*, BKAT (Neukirchen-Vluyn: Neukirchener Verlag des Erziehungsvereins, 1974); *Genesis 12–36* (Neukirchen-Vluyn: Neukirchener Verlag des Erziehungsvereins, 1981); *Genesis 37–50* (Neukirchen-Vluyn: Neukirchener Verlag des Erziehungsvereins, 1982).

62 Walter Dietrich, *Samuel (1 Sam 1–12)* (Göttingen: Neukirchener Theologie, 2010); *Samuel (1 Sam 13–26)* (Göttingen: Neukirchener Theologie, 2015).

63 Richard D. Nelson, *Deuteronomy: A Commentary*, OTL (Louisville: Westminster John Knox, 2002).

64 Alan Graeme Auld, *I & II Samuel*, OTL (Louisville: Westminster John Knox, 2011).

65 Jon D. Levenson, *Esther: A Commentary* (London: SCM Press, 1997).

66 Sara Japhet, *I & II Chronicles: A Commentary*, OTL (Louisville: Westminster John Knox, 1993), pp. 28–31.

67 Marvin A. Sweeney, *I & II Kings: A Commentary* (Louisville: Westminster John Knox, 2007); Leslie C. Allen, *Jeremiah: A Commentary* (Louisville: Westminster John Knox, 2008).

68 John J. Collins, *Daniel: A Commentary on the Book of Daniel*, Hermeneia (Minneapolis: Fortress Press, 1993).

and explained both texts, something I remember only from Stipp's commentary on Jeremiah (see n. 39). Likewise, William L. Holladay's commentary on Jeremiah does full justice to the LXX.[69] The commentary does not suggest a literary solution for the LXX, but it recognizes the possibility that the LXX may reflect an earlier layer of the book, lacking inter alia, Jeremiah 33. 14–26. On the other hand, the Hermeneia commentary by Zimmerli (translated from his BKAT commentary)[70] did not present an overall view of the literary character of the LXX, but this author devotes very little attention to the LXX in the introduction.[71] This volume comments mainly on MT.[72] Some volumes in this series do not present any introduction to textual criticism,[73] while others have a very extensive introduction.[74]

- *Mikra Leyisrael, A Bible Commentary for Israel,* in Modern Hebrew, provides brief introductions to the text and versions and textual notes on the most important textual variations. Thus, in the most recent volume in that series, by Sara Japhet, the parallel lists in Ezra 2 // Nehemiah 7 and Nehemiah 11 // 1 Chronicles 9 receive detailed text critical attention.[75]

---

69 William L. Holladay, *Jeremiah 1: A Commentary on the Book of the Prophet Jeremiah Chapters 1–25,* Hermeneia (Philadelphia: Fortress Press, 1986); William A. Holladay, *Jeremiah 2: A Commentary on the Book of the Prophet Jeremiah Chapters 26–52,* Hermeneia (Minneapolis: Fortress Press, 1989), pp. 2–9, gives a good introduction to the textual situation in Jeremiah and to the nature of the LXX.

70 Walther Zimmerli, *Ezekiel 1,* trans. by Ronald E. Clements, Hermeneia (Philadelphia: Fortress Press, 1979); Walther Zimmerli, *Ezekiel 2,* trans. by James D. Martin, Hermeneia (Philadelphia: Fortress Press, 1983).

71 That Zimmerli does not attach much importance to the evidence of the LXX is clear from the structure of the commentary. The paragraphs in the introduction relate to such matters as 'The contents of the book of Ezekiel', 'The personality of Ezekiel', 'The language and form of the prophecies of the book of Ezekiel', 'Notes on the vocabulary and language of the book of Ezekiel' etc. Now, the language of the book of Ezekiel cannot be analyzed before its textual character has been settled, for possibly some of the words of MT were added only in a late layer of that version, as many scholars believe. Therefore, it is imperative that any analysis should start with the textual evidence, which should not be left to paragraph 9 on p. 74 as part of the so-called 'Later history of the book and its text'.

72 In the words of Zimmerli, *Ezekiel 1,* p. 75: 'The text tradition of the book of Ezekiel offers particular problems. Critical scholarship was first aroused by them. It is once noticeable in M how different things are in the separate complexes'. Zimmerli then spells out what help we should expect from the versions: 'The versions offer some help towards a recognition of corruptions that have entered later, among which the Septuagint (G) naturally stands first. Even if we do not emphasize their value for the reconstruction of the text as strongly as Cornill, or so enthusiastically as Jahn, they yet remain at many points a help that is not to be undervalued for the recovery of a better text'. (p. 75).

73 Hans Walter Wolff, *A Commentary on the Book of the Prophet Hosea,* Hermeneia (Philadelphia: Fortress Press, 1974); Shalom M. Paul, *A Commentary on the Book of Amos,* Hermeneia (Minneapolis: Fortress Press, 1991), p. 75.

74 Holladay, *Jeremiah,* 2003; Marvin A. Sweeney, *Zephaniah: A Commentary,* Hermeneia (Minneapolis: Fortress Press, 2003), pp. 1–41.

75 Sara Japhet, *Ezra–Nehemiah,* Mikra Leyisrael, A Bible Commentary for Israel (Tel-Aviv: Am Oved, 2019; Hebrew).

2.3. Critical Commentaries with Constant Attention to Textual Criticism

Critical commentaries with constant attention to textual criticism are:

- *Kurzgefasstes exegetisches Handbuch zum Alten Testament* (KeHAT). This old series has paid ample attention to textual criticism, especially in the Samuel volume by Otto Thenius.[76] Together with Thenius's commentary on Kings[77] in the same series and Julius Wellhausen's monographic textual commentary on the same book (see below), this is probably the most remarkable gem of the German text critical literature.[78]

- *International Critical Commentary* (ICC), *New Series.* The revived ICC series of the twentieth century offers more involvement in textual matters as seen in the volumes by Hugh G. M. Williamson of Isaiah, Andrew A. Macintosh of Hosea, and Robert B. Salters of Lamentations.[79] Combining literary and textual remarks, the Jeremiah volume by McKane[80] provides the best that ICC or any commentary has to offer in textual criticism.[81]

---

76   Otto Thenius, *Die Bücher Samuels*, rev. by Max Löhr, KeHAT, 3rd edn (Leipzig: Hirzel, 1898). The first edition by Thenius himself (Leipzig: Weidmann, 1842) already had a remarkable introduction to textual criticism (pp. xxiv–xxxii), but the third edition was the most extensive (pp. lxix–xcv).

77   Otto Thenius, *Die Bücher der Könige*, 2nd edn, KeHAT (Leipzig: Hirzel, 1873), pp. xxv–xxxiii.

78   For example, on pp. xxviii–xxix, Thenius mentioned long minuses in MT that have been preserved in the LXX (in other words, pluses of the LXX) in I Samuel 1. 18, 25; 3. 15, 21; 6. 1; 10. 1; 12. 6, 8; 13. 8, 15; 14. 41, 42; 15. 12; 21. 7; 23. 6; 25. 34; 30. 11, 24, 28; II Samuel 2. 22; 11. 22; 13. 21, 27, 34; 14. 30; 15. 20; 20. 22; 24. 25. According to Thenius, these pluses show that MT was 'corrupt' (p. xxviii) and that the *Vorlage* of the LXX was 'better' and 'more complete' than MT (p. xxix). Thenius's trust in the LXX may have been exaggerated in favor of that version since only some examples showed possible cases of textual corruption of MT (haplography or homoioteleuton). Most examples pertain to possible literary differences between the two texts that could have been multiplied several times and countered by reverse examples of minuses of the LXX vis à vis MT. Often the LXX indeed offered a better text, although further examples would have been called for, while in other cases the LXX and MT offered an equally good text.

79   Andrew A. Macintosh, *A Critical and Exegetical Commentary on Hosea*, ICC (London: T&T Clark, 1997); Hugh G. M. Williamson, *A Critical and Exegetical Commentary on Isaiah 1–27*, ICC (London: T&T Clark, 2006); Robert B. Salters, *A Critical and Exegetical Commentary on Lamentations*, ICC (London: T&T Clark, 2011).

80   William McKane, *A Critical and Exegetical Commentary on Jeremiah*, ICC (London: T&T Clark, 1986, 1996).

81   The introduction (pp. xv–xli) describes the problems of the short text of the LXX as well as other features of that and the other versions in great detail. In another segment of the introduction (pp. l–lxxxiii), McKane describes the relation between the long MT text and the short LXX text as a 'rolling corpus'. McKane thus has an overall approach that he applies to individual instances, and in this regard his approach is preferable to that of most other commentators, whether one agrees with him or not. Furthermore, the analysis of Chapter 27 (vol. II, pp. 684–708) is a good example of the interaction between textual and literary criticism. In the system of this volume, a first set of notes refers to 'Text, Grammar, Translation', a second analysis analyzes 'The Degree of Literary Coherence in Chapter 27', and a third analysis deals with 'The Composition of Chapter 27'. In all three analyses, textual data are employed. This system is employed in an improved manner in the second volume and is invoked also in other instances (Chapter 35, pp. 885–98).

- *Anchor Bible, New Series.* The Jeremiah volume by Jack R. Lundbom gives all the attention to the LXX. His view may be unusual, as he prefers the MT,[82] but he analyzed the LXX in much detail. According to Lundbom, the translator freely shortened the text and changed the sequence of its chapters, while MT remains preferable.[83] Lundbom believes that the translator erroneously omitted various elements in sixty-four percent of the cases of a shorter text.[84] Undoubtedly some of the minuses were due to textual mishaps, but not so many.
- *Herders Theologischer Kommentar zum Alten Testament* (HThKAT). These volumes devote much attention to textual criticism and have good introductions; see e.g. the volumes of Genesis and Jeremiah by Georg Fischer and Jürgen Ebach and Nahum by Heinz-Josef Fabry.[85]

2.4. Textual Monographs

The very best commentaries that give the most attention to the Septuagint are not necessarily those that are written as part of a series. Some are written as stand-alone textual monographs:
- *Wellhausen on Samuel.* In this exemplary study,[86] Julius Wellhausen was preceded by another great scholar, namely Otto Thenius, *Die Bücher Samuels* (1842). Wellhausen's textual intuition and his integration of textual and literary analysis made this commentary into a classic of the exegetical literature.
- *Cornill on Ezekiel.*[87] In the nineteenth century, Carl H. Cornill used the LXX extensively in his commentary on Ezekiel, in which he reconstructed the original text of that book. Can one use the LXX too much? Yes, I think Cornill did, but he did it in a masterly way.[88]

---

82 Jack R. Lundbom, *Jeremiah 1–20: A New Translation with Introduction and Commentary*, AB, 21A (New York: Doubleday, 1999), pp. 57–71, 885–87.
83 A similar view had been expressed earlier by Georg Fischer, 'Jer 25 und die Fremdvölkersprüche: Unterschiede zwischen hebräischem und griechischem Text', *Bib*, 72 (1991), 474–99; 'Zum Text des Jeremiabuches', *Bib*, 78 (1997), 305–28; Georg Fischer and Andreas Vonach, 'Tendencies in the LXX Version of Jeremiah', in *Der Prophet wie Mose: Studien zum Jeremiabuch*, BZABR, 15 (Wiesbaden: Harrassowitz, 2011), pp. 64–72.
84 Jack R. Lundbom, 'Haplography in the Hebrew Vorlage of LXX Jeremiah', *HS*, 46 (2005), 301–20.
85 Georg Fischer, *Genesis 1–11*, HThKAT (Freiburg: Herder, 2018); Jürgen Ebach, *Genesis 37–50*, HThKAT (Freiburg: Herder, 2018); Georg Fischer, *Jeremia 1–25*, HThKAT (Freiburg: Herder, 2005); Heinz-Josef Fabry, *Nahum*, HThKAT (Freiburg: Herder, 2006).
86 Wellhausen, *Bücher Samuelis*, pp. 3, 14. He started his introduction with the words: 'The enterprise, to improve the badly transmitted text of Samuel, as is commonly recognized [...]' (p. 1). Wellhausen referred in very general terms to instances of homoioteleuton and vertical dittography as well as to other scribal mistakes in MT with very few examples (pp. 14–21). For a summary of Wellhausen's views, see Arie van der Kooij, 'De tekst van Samuel en het tekstkritisch onderzoek', *NedTT*, 36 (1982), 177–204.
87 Carl Heinrich Cornill, *Das Buch des Propheten Ezechiel* (Leipzig: Hinrichs, 1886), pp. 99–109.
88 This edition is based on sound, mature scholarship and therefore it is hard to imagine that it was not preceded by earlier editions; however, I do not know of any such editions. However, Cornill's masterly product was preceded by several eclectic translations included in scholarly commentaries

– *Driver on Samuel.*[89] In his textual notes on Samuel, Driver provided a very insightful commentary focusing on the contribution of the LXX, preceded by a long introduction on the features of the various textual witnesses. This is the first concise introduction to textual criticism in modern times.

– *Burney on Kings.*[90] As Charles F. Burney remarked in his preface, this monograph is based on the first edition of Driver's introduction. It has a long description of the textual witnesses, though not as long as that of Driver, and the notes turn to questions of text.

– *Holmes on Joshua.* The small Joshua volume by Samuel Holmes pays careful attention to the LXX.[91]

– *Burney on Judges* is of the same caliber as his commentary on Kings.[92]

– *Dominique Barthélemy, Interim Report* (see n. 5).

– *Dominique Barthélemy, Critique textuelle,* 1982, 1986, 1992, 2005, 2015 (see n. 5). Barthélemy is the master of detailed textual analysis of key problems on the verse, especially those of interest for translators.

Less known are several additional textual monographs.[93]

---

that must have influenced the production of such editions in Hebrew. In his preface (p. v), Cornill noted that he decided to edit the biblical text in the same way a classical philologist would have treated any ancient Greek or Latin composition. In an introduction of no less than 175 pages, Cornill described the versions in detail.

89 Samuel Rolles Driver, *Notes on the Hebrew Text and the Topography of the Books of Samuel, with an Introduction on Hebrew Palaeography and the Ancient Versions,* 2nd edn (Oxford: Clarendon Press, 1913), pp. xxxiv–xxxvii. No examples were given, but some rules were formulated for the removal of corruptions from MT. The LXX is said to contain a 'purer' text (p. xxxvii). Driver also provided long lists of scribal processes from MT to the LXX (pp. lix–lxix), but he too readily ascribed the deviations to the LXX.

90 Charles Fox Burney, *Notes on the Hebrew Text of the Book of Kings* (Oxford: Clarendon Press, 1903).

91 Samuel Holmes, *Joshua: The Hebrew and Greek Texts* (Cambridge: Cambridge University Press, 1914).

92 Charles Fox Burney, *The Book of Judges, with Introduction and Notes* (London: Rivington, 1918).

93 According to the sequence of the biblical books: George James Spurrell, *Notes on the Text of the Book of Genesis* (Oxford: Clarendon Press, 1896); Andrés Fernández Truyols, *I Sam. 1–15: crítica textual* (Rome: Pontifical Biblical Institute, 1917); Pieter Arie Hendrik de Boer, *Research into the Text of 1 Samuel I–XVI: A Contribution to the Study of the Books of Samuel* (Amsterdam: H. J. Paris, 1938); Paul Volz, *Studien zum Text des Jeremia,* BWANT, 25 (Leipzig: Hinrichs, 1920); John Taylor, *The Massoretic Text and the Ancient Versions of the Book of Micah* (London: Williams & Norgate, 1891); Mayer I. Gruber, *Hosea: A Textual Commentary,* LHBOTS, 653 (London: T&T Clark, 2017); Johann Lachmann, *Das Buch Habbakuk: Eine textkritische Studie* (Aussig: Selbstverlag des Verfassers, 1932); Sidney Zandstra, *The Witness of the Vulgate, Peshitta and Septuagint to the Text of Zephaniah,* Contributions to Oriental History and Philology, IV (New York: Columbia University Press, 1909); Melville Scott, *Textual Discoveries in Proverbs, Psalms, and Isaiah* (London: Society for Promoting Christian Knowledge, 1927); Georg Beer, *Der Text des Buches Hiob* (Marburg: Elwert, 1897); Martijn Theodoor Houtsma, *Textkritische Studien zum Alten Testament, I: Das Buch Hiob* (Leiden: Brill, 1925); Georg Richter, *Textstudien zum Buche Hiob,* BWANT, 3.7 (Stuttgart: Kohlhammer, 1927); Eduard Dhorme, *Job,* EBib (Paris: Gabalda, 1926; repr. Nashville: T. Nelson, 1984); Bertil Albrektson, *Studies in the Text and Theology of the Book of Lamentations* (Lund: Gleerup, 1963); Julius August Bewer, *Der Text des Buches Ezra,* FRLANT (Göttingen: Vandenhoeck & Ruprecht, 1922); Herbert Gotthard, *Der Text des Buches Nehemia* (Wiesbaden: Harrassowitz, 1958).

Summary

Maybe it is unreasonable to expect from a commentator to be at home in exegesis, literary criticism, and the intricacies of textual criticism. Indeed, most commentators are not up to the task of absorbing and accessing the non-Masoretic evidence. These commentators comment upon the printed text of MT, with occasional or frequent remarks on the LXX and sometimes also on the other versions. Among commentators, the view that all ancient sources have equal rights has yet to develop. To give one example, although it is difficult, it would make sense to write a commentary on some chapters in the LXX of Ezekiel alongside those in MT if one believes that both texts may reflect different literary layers. I have done this myself in a commentary on Jeremiah 27.[94] In his commentary on Daniel, John Collins made a bold decision to translate and comment upon both MT and the OG of Daniel 4–6, and the same system was followed consistently by Stipp in Jeremiah (see n. 39). Exceptional are also the commentaries of McKane, Holladay, and Lundbom, which give much attention to the LXX-Jeremiah. I further note the commentaries of Otto Thenius on Samuel and Kings and those of Cooke on Joshua and Ezekiel, as well as several textual monographs, such as those of Cornill on Ezekiel, Wellhausen and Driver on Samuel, and the many studies by Barthélemy. Long ago, Thenius (Samuel, 1842), Driver (Samuel, 1913), and Montgomery (Daniel, 1927 and Kings, 1951) set good precedents by providing thorough introductions to the versions. This tradition should be continued in order to prevent improvised and impressionistic textual remarks as we find too often in the commentaries. I know, this is difficult, and possibly the writing of a commentary requires a joint undertaking with the involvement of a textual scholar. But possibly this is an endless process since others may say that a commentator should also be an established linguist or historian. If I am not mistaken, there is a certain trend to involve more textual evidence in the most recent commentaries, probably due to the discovery of the Dead Sea Scrolls. This trend should be continued, together with the understanding that all textual sources are equal, and that commentaries should not be written on the basis of the printed editions of MT.

▼ ABSTRACT   The average commentator mainly interacts with MT, while occasionally referring to the LXX, and less so to the other textual sources. It is indeed an almost impossible task to be an expert in both literary and textual criticism. As a result, text critical sources are usually underused in commentaries, while they are well represented in

---

94 'Exegetical Notes on the Hebrew Vorlage of the LXX of Jeremiah 27 (34)', ZAW, 91 (1979), 73–93. Revised version: Emanuel Tov, *The Greek and Hebrew Bible: Collected Essays on the Septuagint*, VT.S, 72 (Leiden: Brill, 1999), pp. 315–31.

a number of such tools. This study reviews the approach of different groups of commentaries to textual criticism, especially the LXX. Since textual data are crucial for the understanding of several Scripture books, the hope is expressed that more attention be given to the textual sources in commentaries.

ADRIAN SCHENKER

Elisha's Posthumous Miracle in Textual History (II Kings 13. 20–21)

What does This Story Teach Us
*about the Textual History of the Books of Kings?**

1. The Issue

The story of the dead man brought back to life by contact with the prophet Elisha's bones serves as the final crowning of the whole Elisha story. This latter has been transmitted principally in two different literary forms: in the Masoretic Text (MT) and in the witnesses to the Old Greek Bible, namely, the Septuagint (LXX) and the Old Latin Bible, the *Vetus Latina* (OL). The OL reflects that LXX from which it was translated. The OL originated in North Africa and was first produced around 200 CE.[1]

The textual tradition, therefore, is complex. To understand it, one must examine the three oldest witnesses, MT, LXX and OL, each in its own right and in comparison to the others. Matthieu Richelle has carried out this task in an exemplary manner.[2] His result was that OL represents the oldest form of LXX, a form that has not been preserved in any textual witness to LXX in Greek, but only in OL, in Latin translation.[3] Richelle refrains from choosing between MT and OL,[4] which, in his view, corresponds to the original LXX.

Here one must attempt to make and justify a decision. Of course, the Syriac and Aramaic versions and the Vulgate must have their say in this investigation, if applicable.

---

* Our gratitude goes to Kevin Zilverberg for the English translation of this paper.
1 Pierre-Maurice Bogaert, 'The Latin Bible', in *The New Cambridge History of the Bible*, ed. by James Carleton Paget and Joachim Schaper (Cambridge: University Press, 2013), I. From the Beginnings to 600, pp. 505–26.
2 Matthieu Richelle, *Le testament d'Elisée: Texte massorétique et Septante en 2 Rois 13,10–14,16*, CRB, 76 (Paris: Gabalda, 2010), pp. 73–87.
3 Richelle, *Le testament*, p. 83.
4 Richelle, *Le testament*, pp. 85–86. For Richelle it is just slightly more likely that OL rather than MT corresponds to the original narrative.

New Avenues in Biblical Exegesis in Light of the Septuagint
ed. by Leonardo Pessoa da Silva Pinto and Daniela Scialabba, Turnhout, 2022 (*SEPT*, 1), pp. 59–69
© BREPOLS ❦ PUBLISHERS   DOI 10.1484/M.SEPT-EB.5.127711

2. The Story in MT

The extreme concision with which the author recounts the story raises various questions, which must be clarified so that no misinterpretations taint the judgment about the textual history.

Four points need clarification:

(1) A phrase in v. 20a is difficult: בא שנה. How does it fit within the context in which it appears? The syntactical structure is complex but linguistically meaningful, as Rudolf Meyer has shown.[5] A main storyline, 'they threw the man into Elisha's grave', follows three preparatory adverbial phrases: 'bands of robbers from Moab came into the land' (circumstance 1), 'a year had passed' (circumstance 2), 'a man was about to be buried' (circumstance 3). The first two adverbial phrases are of a general nature; the third mentions a specific circumstance of the main action. The second temporal adverbial phrase follows the first asyndetically, as in the syntactically parallel passage Genesis 24. 1. The narrative requires the second circumstance, 'a year had passed' (since the death of Elisha), for it clarifies that the incident of v. 21 took place not at the prophet's burial but only a year later. Without this indication of time, listeners and readers must assume that, at the same time Elisha was laid in the grave, a funeral procession with a dead man passed by and Moabite robbers appeared. With the adverbial phrase 'a year had come/passed', this meeting is avoided.[6]

(2) The personal pronoun in the third person, masculine, plural, has an impersonal meaning here: 'they' in the sense of 'someone', since there is no antecedent to which this pronoun refers. The impersonal use of personal pronouns in the third person, masculine, plural, without a previous antecedent is rare, but there are examples of this use: Isaiah 24. 15; 25. 2.

(3) The word גדוד, here in the plural of the construct state, usually denotes a band of robbers. Nevertheless, in II Samuel 22. 30 it is employed for an individual, the psalmist David, where it has a positive sense: 'in you I run quickly and jump over walls'. The context is war. The psalmist performs superbly in foot races and the high jump. The word גדוד, therefore, can have both plural or collective and singular meanings, and its sense mostly has a negative connotation: 'robber band'. Yet it also possesses a positive meaning: 'extremely strong'. In Genesis 49. 19 גדוד characterizes the tribe of Gad or the tribe's eponymous patriarch, either in the sense of a fearsome gang of looters or in the sense of an extremely strong warrior.

(4) The verb הלך, which is applied to the dead man who flies in a high arc into Elisha's grave, often means 'to go, to reach'. Here it means 'to reach' in the sense of 'to arrive at': he reached the prophet's bones, so that he touched them. The purpose of the phrase is to indicate that the corpse thrown into the grave came unintentionally

---

5 Rudolf Meyer, *Hebräische Grammatik*, Sammlung Göschen, 3rd edn (Berlin: de Gruyter, 1972), III, § 121, pp. 107–08 = Rudolf Meyer, *Hebräische Grammatik* (Berlin: de Gruyter, 1992), § 121, pp. 449–50.

6 This is the simplest and most obvious interpretation of the phrase in its context. The narrative in OL, which does not provide this temporal circumstance, shows that Elisha's burial temporally coincides with the event of the dead man thrown into his grave (see here sections 5 and 6).

into contact with Elisha's bones. The undertakers did not throw him directly and dishonorably onto the bones, but the corpse slid upon them by itself.

In summary, the narrative in MT can be stylistically and narratively characterized thus: its style is extremely concise, and some phrases are rare, yet it is linguistically possible and understandable.

Four protagonists appear in the story: Elisha (at the beginning and end), robbers from Moab, anonymous undertakers and an anonymous deceased man, whom they carry to the grave.

3. The Story in the Textual Witnesses to LXX

The story in LXX is essentially the same as in MT. There are the same four protagonists, and the same narrative concision prevails. Nevertheless, the textual witnesses to LXX differ so greatly from one another, that it is necessary to establish the oldest obtainable form in the Greek textual tradition.[7] There are nine principal variants (in just two verses!):

(1) In v. 20, the Lucianic translation (LXX[L]) presents the sequence subject ('and Elisha') — predicate ('died'); all the other witnesses, like MT, place the predicate at the beginning ('and he died') and the subject ('Elisha') after it. The same syntax appears in II Kings 13. 4 in LXX[L], against all the other textual witnesses. However, the placement of the subject ('Joash') first, followed by the subsequent predicate ('fell ill'), occurs in MT and LXX in II Kings 13. 13. At this point, it marks a particularly decisive, fresh start in the narrative flow of II Kings 13. LXX obviously had the same Hebrew *Vorlage* as MT, in 13. 4, 13. 13 and 13. 20. It is probable that LXX[L], according to the pattern of 13. 13, introduced two further breaks (vv. 4 and 20) as text division indicators. LXX[L] often makes stylistic corrections. That is probably also here the cause for the altered syntactic order in which the subject precedes and the predicate follows. There is likewise a caesura in MT, the *Setumah*, but it is not of a syntactical nature.

(2) LXX[L] renders the Hebrew narrative tense ויקברהו with the Greek present. The historical present occurs predominantly in the original LXX.[8] LXX[L] may have preserved here the original form of LXX.

(3) The rendering of גדוד with μονόζωνοι is indicative of the kaige recension.[9] The OL attests *piratae* (see below, section 4). This is the original rendering. Nevertheless, all the textual witnesses attest the rendering μονόζωνοι, 'lightly armed'. This means that all the witnesses to LXX present a secondary reading, which was probably taken from the Hexapla.

(4) Most of the Greek witnesses interpret בארץ with the article as a preposition with the dative, but the Syrohexapla (Syh) and OL interpret it as a preposition with

---

7 Richelle, *Le testament*, assumes that the Antiochene or Lucianic (LXX[L]) is the oldest form of LXX. This is partly true but also partly not. Here, as elsewhere, it contains secondary material in I–II Kings.

8 Dominique Barthélemy, *Les Devanciers d'Aquila*, V.T.S, 10 (Leiden: Brill, 1963), pp. 63–65.

9 Barthélemy, *Les Devanciers*, pp. 81–82.

the accusative. Syh offers this phrase with the accusative, 'they came into the land', without any Aristarchian symbol (asterisk). Hence, this reading represents that which Origen found in his LXX text, on which he based the Hexapla. It is, therefore, a pre-hexaplaric reading, which corresponds to the reading in the original version of LXX. The fact that OL attests an accusative reading also supports this (see further on, section 4).

The interpretation of the expression as a preposition with the dative is difficult, at first glance. The reading cannot mean 'they came into the land'. However, it makes good sense within the narrative unit, since it clarifies why the looters had come to Elisha's grave precisely as the funeral procession also arrived there. One can obviously understand 'they had reached the land <there>', that is, Elisha's grave. In this way the passage prepares for understanding the indispensable event of the convergence of the funeral procession and the looters at Elisha's grave.

This also leads to understanding גדודי מאב. Here it cannot mean 'bands of robbers', for the Israelites with their corpse did not see multiple bands but a Moabite looter (LXX singular) or 'a' band of robbers (In LXX^L the one band is plural). In MT there are perhaps not 'bands' but, in the sense of II Samuel 22. 30, the 'lightly armed' (who only wear one weapon belt), therefore 'lightly armed (robbers from Moab)'.

V. 21

(5) Instead of ἄνθρωπον ἕνα in LXX^L, the other witnesses to LXX read τὸν ἄνδρα. This latter rendering surprises in its context, since the article here is not anaphoric; 'the man' was not mentioned before. If one assumes a Hebrew *Vorlage* for it, the article here probably corresponds to a possessive pronoun.[10] In fact, איש is never used with a plural suffix. There is a close relationship between the funeral procession and the dead man being carried to the grave: he is their (dead) man. LXX^L has probably introduced a stylistic alteration. The reading with the article is the more difficult variant.

(6) Instead of the phrase 'and behold, they saw the robber', LXX^L reads καὶ ἤγγισεν τὸ πειρατήριον αὐτοῖς. This reading corresponds neither to the other witnesses to LXX nor to OL, except the predicate 'it approached'. In LXX^L the band of robbers, πειρατήριον, approaches the funeral procession. In OL the looters approach the grave. The funeral procession does not occur in OL. The witnesses to LXX do not report the robbers' approach but the undertakers' taking notice. LXX^L, conversely, recounts only the robber band's approach. Since OL also recounts the latter, it is probably an element of the original LXX.

(7) καὶ ἔφυγον of LXX^L lacks in LXX. It is translated in OL, but with a different subject: in LXX^L these are the grieving Israelites, in OL the robbers.

(8) The verb וילך forms a phrase in MT, whose subject is the dead man. The majority of the witnesses to LXX translate the verb with ἐπορεύθη, and LXX^L with

---

10 Paul Joüon, *Grammaire de l'hébreu biblique* (Rome: Institut biblique pontifical, 1947), § 137f, p. 422 = Paul Joüon and Takamitsu. Muraoka, *Grammar of Biblical Hebrew*, Subsidia biblica, 14-II (Rome: Pontificio Istituto Biblico, 1991), § 137f, p. 507.

ἦλθε. This is a stylistic Greek variant, which is probably secondary. The Hexaplaric LXX (LXX^O), according to Syh, here reads the plural 'and they went', with the grieving Israelites as the subject. This is the reading of Origen's pre-hexaplaric LXX. This is all the more likely since Syh offers a reading corresponding to that of Symmachus, in which Symmachus translates וילך in the singular. Therefore, the verb in the plural does not correspond to LXX^O, which in all likelihood employed the singular, like Symmachus.[11] The verb in the plural here plays the same role as the reading ἔφυγον in LXX^L (and OL). It explicitly reports that the mourners fled in terror.

The difference between the plural and singular can be explained on a text-critical or literary basis. It could be a matter of dittography: after וילך the ו from ויגע was written twice, or the event was told differently. Barthélemy proposes yet another possible explanation.[12] It is based on a rule of many Hebrew copyists, which Samuel David Luzzato has recognized: if a word ending with ו is followed by one beginning with ו, the copyist writes just one ו. This letter does double duty as the last of one word and the first of the next. Hence, Barthélemy considers the word וילך to be the *Vorlage* of καὶ ἐπορεύθησαν. The plural was intended.[13]

However, given the extremely concise narrative style, which here reaches a climax, the question arises whether the singular-plural variation might be an attempt to let the logic of the narrative emerge more clearly. In that case, a literary or redactional alteration would be the more likely explanation. A reviser saw that no one was present when the dead man in Elisha's grave rose, since the mourners (and the robbers) had departed. A miracle without witnesses is difficult to accept. This explanation of the variant may be more likely, since the story as a whole has had such a thorough redactional reworking.

An observation of the narrative and stylistic order supports this content-based justification. In MT and all the witnesses, except OL, the narrator recounts this moment of the event in four very short sentences consisting of four verbs in the narrative tense with the preformative ו. Of these four, sentences 2 and 4 each have a noun as the complement to the verb: 1) 'and he arrived', 2) 'and he touched Elisha's bones', 3) 'and he lived (again)', 4) 'and he stood on his feet'. It is quite possible that a redactor and editor perceived the plural 'and they went (away)' to be flat, in comparison with the singular 'and he went/arrived (there)'. The plural disrupts the story. Someone throws the dead man into Elisha's grave. From a narrative standpoint, this immediately

---

11 The Symmachus reading is only preserved in Syriac. The Greek verb can no longer be determined with certainty. Frederick Field, *Origenis Hexaplorum quae supersunt* (Oxford: Clarendon Press, 1875), I, p. 678, suspected the participial *Vorlage* ἐνεχθεῖς δε. In any case, this rendering could be a less-than-literal reproduction of 'and he went' in this altogether singular context, as would be fitting for Symmachus. Another possibility, however, is that the Symmachus reading derives from ויגע.

12 Dominique Barthélemy, *Critique textuelle de l'Ancien Testament*, OBO, 50/1 (Fribourg: Éditions Universitaires; Göttingen: Vandenhoeck & Ruprecht, 1982), I. Josué–Esther, pp. 401–02, with reference to Luzzato.

13 Explanations based on scribal practices not directly attested should probably be employed only when a reading would otherwise make no sense or be extremely difficult to understand. Is that the case here? The ancient textual witnesses MT, LXX, Symmachus, Targum, Peshitta and Vulgate saw no particular difficulty with this verb being in the singular.

raises the question 'and what happens now to him?' Here, the undertakers and the robbers are no longer a concern. Considering all aspects of these four sentences in terms of content and style, it is perhaps more likely that sequence of the four parallel concluding sentences is secondary, since the plural in sentence 1 disrupts the logically unfolding event and is narratively less effective. The argument would be: the better narrative proceeds from the poorer one, and not vice versa.

(9) In MT, after יגע comes האיש. For this, LXX^L reads ὁ ἀνὴρ ὁ θαπτόμενος, while Syh offers 'this man', with an asterisk. Origen took over the demonstrative pronoun from Symmachus. Since the asterisked reading in Symmachus encompasses the whole rendering 'this man', the conclusion follows that Origen, in his LXX, read neither the demonstrative pronoun nor the noun 'man'. A reading with an implicit subject fits well within the extremely concise style of this narrative. However, it was obvious for a writer or editor (recensor) to make the subject explicit. Only LXX preserved what is probably the original reading.

As a result of this review of the narrative form in LXX, one can see that LXX^B, with the majority of the witnesses, corresponds almost exactly to MT. LXX^L contains all the LXX readings and at the same time numerous stylistic changes which are found only in it. LXX^O, true to its nature, contains Hexaplaric elements and at the same time shows elements of the text of the original LXX. Hence, no surviving textual witness to LXX corresponds to the form which the narrative had in the original LXX.

4. The Old Latin Version of II Kings 13. 20–21

The Old Latin narrative is completely preserved in a palimpsest manuscript of the fifth century, from Africa.[14] It was edited by Bonifatius Fischer.[15] In addition, there is a OL citation in the margin of Vulgate manuscripts in Spain.[16]

Here follows the text and translation of II Kings 13. 20–21:

> V. 20 et mortus est helisseus / et sepelierunt eum / et piratae moab venerunt in terram illam. /
> V. 21 et factum est / cum sepellirent piratae hominem unum / accesserunt at monumentum / et proiecerunt hominem in monumentum helissei / et fugerunt / et adplicitus est homo ossibus helissei / et vixit homo / et surrexit super pedes suos.

---

14 OL^{115}: Roger Gryson, *Altlateinische Handschriften. Manuscrits vieux latins: Répertoire descriptif*, Vetus Latina, 1/2A (Freiburg: Herder, 1999), p. 181.

15 Bonifatius Fischer, 'Palimpsestus Vindobonensis', in *Beiträge zur Geschichte der lateinischen Bibeltexte*, Vetus Latina, 12 (Freiburg: Herder, 1986), pp. 308–438 (p. 379).

16 Antonio Moreno Hernández, *Las glosas marginales de Vetus Latina en las Biblias Vulgatas españolas*, 1–2 Reyes, TECC, 49 (Madrid: CSIC, 1992). The citation is at p. 136. In Gryson, *Altlateinische Handschriften*, pp. 147–55, these manuscripts bear numbers 91–94. The main witness is *Codex Gothicus Legionensis* (León), a copy of an older *Vorlage* presumably from the tenth century.

Translation:

> V. 20 and Elisha died / and they buried him / and robbers from Moab came into that land /
> V. 21 and it happened / when the robbers were burying a man / they came to the grave (or: to a grave) / and threw the man into Elisha's grave / and fled / and the man contacted Elisha's bones / and the man lived / and rose up upon his feet.

The text of the story in OL can easily be retroverted into Greek and Hebrew. It is very probable that it indirectly reflects a Hebrew *Vorlage*.

The passage in OL[91–94] differs from OL[115] in the expression *praedones* instead of *piratae* and in the prepositional phrase *in Moab*. OL[115], with *piratae*, corresponds to the Old Greek translation of גדוד (cf. Genesis 49. 19). *Praedo* seeks to translate μονόζωνος, a rendering of the kaige recension.

The prepositional phrase *in Moab* eliminates the determination 'the' from 'the robbers of Moab' by the indeterminate expression 'robbers in Moab'; or it makes clear that Moab is a toponym and designates a place or territory. Such a clarification is typical for a scholion, but it is less suitable for a translation. OL[91–94] contains not only OL citations but also scholia.[17] It follows that OL[115] has preserved the good reading here.

5. OL[115] in Comparison with MT and LXX

It is worthwhile to first compare the narrative of II Kings 13. 20–21 as a whole, in OL[115], MT and LXX. It immediately becomes clear that MT and LXX recount the same story with four protagonists: Elisha, robbers, a dead man, and grave diggers. OL, however, recounts a different one, for it presents only three protagonists. In MT and LXX anonymous mourners bury a likewise anonymous dead man. Then robbers from Moab suddenly appear and frighten them so greatly that they throw the dead man into Elisha's grave. Therefore, the event plays out in the land of Israel, and, accordingly, the mourners and the dead man are Israelites. In OL one does not know whether the deceased is an Israelite or perhaps a Moabite robber. There is only mention of a 'person' (ἄνθρωπος), and the context gives no indication of his ethnicity. From this fact it follows that for the narrator in OL[115] the only important thing was the miracle of the resurrection of a dead man, by touching the bones of the prophet. The provenance of the deceased has no pertinence for him.

This is a different matter for the narrator in MT and LXX, for he makes clear precisely this fact. A criterion is thereby established for comparing the two versions

---

17 Adrian Schenker, 'Der Platz der altlateinischen Randlesarten des Kodex von León und der Valvanera-Bibel in der griechischen Textgeschichte (1–4 Kgt)', in *Der antiochenische Text der Septuaginta in seiner Bezeugung und in seiner Bedeutung*, ed. by Siegfried Kreuzer and Marcus Sigismund, DSI, 4 (Göttingen: Vandenhoeck & Ruprecht, 2013), pp. 199–210.

of II Kings 13. 20–21. Nevertheless, there is no doubt that this is one and the same narrative, extant in two recensions, of which the recension of MT and LXX itself falls into two subgroups. Even so, in the narrative's main point presently under consideration, on the one hand there are Israelites who want to bury their dead man, and on the other hand there are Moabite robbers who want to bury a dead man in all haste. These are two recensions of the same material.

So, the question is: is it likely that the narrative of MT and LXX is more original than that in OL? The converse ordering is more plausible.

Indeed, it is easily understood that Elisha's miracle happened for an Israelite dead man, who was carried by Israelites to the grave, while Moabite looters threatened and disturbed the Israelite funeral procession. It would be difficult, however, to understand a recensor or editor who had completely erased the Israelites from the narrative. It is therefore probable that OL has preserved the narrative's oldest form.

An additional argument for this likelihood is the fact that Flavius Josephus presupposes the narrative's form as in OL.[18]

6. Comparison of Some Differences between MT, LXX and OL

V. 20 (1) OL[115] reads *piratae* instead of μονόζωνοι, against all the Greek witnesses. In this, OL is more original (cf. above, section 3,3).

(2) OL[115] and OL[91–94] read *in terram illam*. The demonstrative *ille* in OL usually stands for οὗτος.[19] Syh and the Armenian translation read εἰς, like OL. Syh lacks the asterisk, which means that it likely reflects the reading of Origen's Bible. Thus, the preposition with the accusative corresponds more likely to the original LXX. The demonstrative also seems original (see above, section 3,4), since it fits well with the preposition with the accusative but not with *in* followed by the ablative.

(3) MT and LXX conclude v. 20 with the adverbial phrase 'one year had come'. It does not occur in OL[115]. The purpose of this temporal precision is to create a difference between Elisha's death and burial (v. 20) and the event recounted in vv. 20–21: the emergency burial of v. 21 took place one year after Elisha's burial. Narratively, however, it is clear that Elisha's burial coincides with the emergency burial of the anonymous dead man by robbers in v. 21 — just as the narrative in OL implies, since the emergency burial of the unnamed deceased presumes an open grave.[20] It all must have happened, according to both recensions, in great haste. There was no question of keeping once-closed graves open again for a long time. The most likely scenario is that, at Elisha's funeral his grave was not yet closed. Thus, either the overtaken funeral procession of MT and LXX, or the robbers of

---

18 Josephus, *Ant.*, 9. 183, Greek text and French translation: Étienne Nodet, *Les antiquités juives* (Paris: Cerf, 2005), IV. Livres VIII et IX, pp. 179 and 179*.

19 Moreno Hernández, *Glosas marginales*, p. 371.

20 Nodet, *Les antiquités*, p. 179, correctly points out that Josephus implies that the grave must have been easily accessible. He deduced this from the oldest LXX = OL.

OL, were able to throw their dead man into Elisha's grave in an instant, for it was still open.

It is more conceivable that a narrator wanted to separate the incident of the dead man thrown into Elisha's grave from Elisha's funeral, than the converse. The latter would be a reworking in which the phrase 'one year had passed' was eventually removed, despite all the reasons for the plausibility of the temporal coincidence of the two burials of vv. 20 and 21. One could also interpret the separation of the two burials as an expansion of the prophet's posthumous miracle.

V. 21 (1) MT presents the word איש three times. OL reads *homo* in the three instances. The Greek witnesses to LXX render ἀνήρ in the first two instances in the verse. In the third, 'and he touched Elisha's bones', the LXX witnesses do not repeat ἀνήρ. Only Syr adds 'this man' with an asterisk (cf. above, section 3,9). Thus, Origen had the Greek reading without an explicit subject. The explicit subject 'person/man' in MT, LXX^L, and OL is probably secondary, since there are frequently explanatory additions in LXX, which facilitate understanding. Supplementary elements of this sort, later added to the narrative, also occur in MT. LXX^L adds yet another explicit characterization of the man: 'the buried man'.

As for the difference between 'man', ἀνήρ, and 'person', the translators vary: OL reads *homo* three times, never *vir*. LXX^L once presents 'person' and twice 'man'. Variations of a stylistic nature are a hallmark of the Antiochene-Lucianic edition (recension): LXX reads 'man' twice. LXX is original here, with regard to the lack of an explicit subject at the third place of the verse, where MT has איש. The rendering with 'man' in LXX and LXX^L (twice) is possibly secondary to the transmission of 'person'. An indirect observation points in the direction of this presumption. The kaige recension replaces the pronoun 'each' with 'man', in those places where איש means 'each', even though this rendering greatly impedes understanding.[21] This shows that in the kaige group the correspondence איש – ἀνήρ was prominent. In light of this preference of the kaige group, one might assume that they more thoroughly and intentionally rendered איש with ἀνήρ than the early LXX translators had done. The latter fluctuated between ἀνήρ and ἄνθρωπος.

(2) At the beginning of the verse, LXX reads 'the man' with the definite article (cf. section 3,5). The determination lacks in LXX^L and OL, where the indetermination is emphasized with the word ἕνα, *unum*. MT also lacks the article. The determined reading is surprising and difficult. It explains itself linguistically, if it is based on a Hebrew *Vorlage* with the article (cf. section 3,6). It likewise explains itself satisfactorily on narrative grounds: 'the dead man' belongs to the funeral procession, which consists of Israelites (cf. section 5). MT, LXX^L and OL agree. Perhaps this fact gives witness to the undetermined form's originality. But this is not certain.

(3) LXX^L and OL read 'it was approaching'. The expression lacks in MT and the other witnesses to LXX. This has a narrative ground: in MT and LXX the funeral procession is terrified, since they see the robbers, and in terror they throw the dead

---

21 Barthélemy, *Les Devanciers*, pp. 48–54.

man into Elisha's grave. In OL the robbers themselves throw the dead man into the grave.[22] Here LXX^L probably preserved the original form of the verb, together with OL.

(4) OL alone reads '(the robbers approached) the grave', *monumentum*. This comes from the original narrative, in which there is no funeral procession for the looters to approach.

(5) OL and LXX^L recount that 'they fled', in OL the robbers, in LXX^L the mourners. This rendering lacks in MT and in the other witnesses to LXX. However, Syh without an asterisk and the Coptic version read the plural ἐπορεύθησαν instead of the singular ἐπορεύθη. Origen has read this plural in the version of LXX available to him. This corresponds to an old form of LXX. It is obvious that καὶ ἐπορεύθησαν in the plural renders וילכו. LXX^L and OL have understood and translated this departure of the robbers or mourners specifically as flight. This rendering seems to correspond to the original LXX and the original Hebrew narrative. The singular, וילך, καὶ ἐπορεύθη is probably secondary. The narrator's three short concluding sentences in the singular have led a redactor to put the preceding sentence in the singular as well (cf. above, section 2,4; 3,8). LXX^L, accordingly, has a doublet: one verb in the plural and one in the singular.

(6) Concerning the subject 'the person' in the predicate 'touched' in OL, cf. section 6 at v. 21, point 1.

Overall, it follows from this comparison of readings from LXX and OL, that OL usually, but not always, reflects the oldest form of LXX.

7. Result

7.1. Among the versions of the narrative II Kings 13. 20–21, OL comes closest to the narrative's most original form. Nevertheless, even it is not an image of the oldest narrative in every detail.

7.2. MT, LXX and LXX^L, for the most part, agree with one another. Above all, the funeral procession is common to them all, which the robbers from Moab disrupt. This lacks in OL. Besides this, there is the space of one year between Elisha's burial and the incident narrated. In OL the two events coincide, which is narratively plausible.

7.3. The Greek witnesses essentially reflect MT. LXX^L is the most deviant textual witness. It possesses elements of the original LXX version alongside many stylistic changes. This mixture of preservation of an earlier text and freedom for textual intervention is characteristic of LXX^L.

7.4. The narrative recasting of the story of the prophet Elisha's last, posthumous miracle is clear in its purpose. It would like to present the miracle as a sign performed

---

22   Richelle, *Le testament*, p. 81, explains the event in LXX^L in such a way that it was the robbers who threw the dead man into Elisha's grave (as is recounted in OL), for 'a band of robbers approached **them**'. This implies the group of undertakers. The pronoun 'them' precedes the phrase: 'and they threw him into Elisha's grave', they, the undertakers. LXX^L differs from MT and the other LXX witnesses insofar as it recounts the robbers' approach instead of the undertakers' notice of it.

for the benefit of the Israelites.[23] The older narrative specifically concerned the unexpected miraculous power of Elisha's bones. This power simply works, regardless of the recipient of its working. The posthumous miracle thereby resembles Naaman's cleansing from leprosy in II Kings 5. He was a foreigner with nothing to give him precedence ahead of all the Israelite lepers for such a great miracle, as Jesus declares in Luke 4. 27.

7.5. The other ancient versions, the Targum, Peshitta and Vulgate, have translated MT. At the end of v. 21 the Peshitta reads 'in the same year' instead of 'one year had come/passed'. It or its Hebrew *Vorlage* has interpreted the Aramaizing בא as a preposition with a pronoun in the demonstrative sense. The Targum avoids the touching of Elisha's bones; the man thrown into the grave only came near them. But that sufficed to raise him back to life! Peshitta translates it 'he came', which corresponds to MT verbatim. Both are variants implying no other Hebrew *Vorlage*. They are merely interpretations.

7.6. Besides the actual textual variants, one finds editorial modifications both in the versions and also in LXX, including OL. The narrative of Elisha's posthumous miracle proves the **literary** transformation of a more original narrative.

7.7. MT is likewise the result of literary recasting, which is secondary in comparison with the oldest form of LXX attested principally in OL. Association with Israel was more important for the reviser than for the original narrator. The latter focused on the prophetic power to work miracles.

▼ ABSTRACT The conclusion of the prophetical narrative of Elisha is a posthumous miracle. A dead man comes back to life after a contact with the prophet's bones, II Kings 13. 20–21. It is an outstanding example of classical Hebrew narrative style aiming at utmost concision. Moreover, the three earliest textual witnesses, MT, LXX and Old Latin, differ widely between themselves on the textual and on the literary level. An analysis of their literary forms, relationship, causes and origins, in one specific pericope, may reveal their stylistic and literary interests, as well as their qualities and weaknesses in textual transmission. Despite the shortness of II Kings 13. 20–21, its textual history is likely to be representative for the whole book of I-II Kings, and to shed light on the textual witnesses and the text history of Kings, and even of all Former and Latter Prophets for most of them were transmitted in the same circles in the last three centuries BCE.

---

23 In my opinion, it is not a matter of profaning Elisha's grave by defilement and impious treatment. Every corpse defiles, whether Israelite or Moabite, and the throwing of a dead man into a grave out of fear or haste is not blameworthy. It is only a matter of the miracle of reviving the dead.

JULIO TREBOLLE, PABLO TORIJANO
AND ANDRÉS PIQUER*

The Septuagint's Faculty of Putting Things in Their Right Place

Challenges of a Critical Edition
of IV Kingdoms / II Kings 10. 30–31; 13. 14–21

The title of this paper is suggested by the statement of James Montgomery 'Lucian is a weak authority, even with his faculty of putting things in their right place'.[1] Montgomery acknowledges that the Lucianic text (MSS 19 82 93 108 127) places the conclusive formula of the reign of Joash of Israel in 'its right place', after II Kings 13. 24–25. However, in Montgomery's opinion Lucian or the 'Lucianic' recension remains 'a weak authority'.[2] In his commentary to the books of Kings Montgomery manifests 'strong sympathy' to the movement that shortly before the middle of the last century promoted a 'return to the Masoretic text' (*zurück zum masoretischen Texte*).[3] This movement then led by Henrik S. Nyberg and Joseph Reider reacted to the prevailing trend to resort to conjectures based on the LXX as practiced by Duhm, Ehrlich or Cheyne.[4] The discredit of the Lucianic text manifested by Montgomery survives still today to a large extent due to the influence of Rahlfs's work *Lucians Rezension der Königsbücher*.[5] Rahlfs's manual edition of the Septuagint does not take into account the Antiochene text (*L*) if it is not a testimony of the Hexaplaric text.

---

* This is a joint paper by Julio Trebolle and Pablo Torijano, editors of III–IV Kingdoms in the LXX Göttingen Series, and Andrés Piquer, editor of II Kings in *The Hebrew Bible. A Critical Edition*.
1 James Alan Montgomery, *The Books of Kings*, ed. by Henry Snyder Gehman, ICC (Edinburgh: T&T Clark, 1951), p. 434. The Antiochene text is quoted according to the edition of Natalio Fernández Marcos and José Ramón Busto Saiz, *El texto antioqueno de la Biblia griega* (Madrid: CSIC, 1992), II. 1–2 Reyes.
2 Also according to Jan Joosten, '*The Antiochene text is a narrow basis, however, for constructing the correct Hebrew text*'; Sidnie White Crawford, Jan Joosten and Eugene Ulrich, 'Sample Editions of the Oxford Hebrew Bible: Deuteronomy 32:1–9, 1 Kings 11:1–8, and Jeremiah 27:1–10', *VT*, 58 (2008), 352–66 (p. 359).
3 Montgomery, *The Books Kings*, p. 24 n. 9.
4 Henrik S. Nyberg, *Studien zum Hoseabuche: Zugleich ein Beitrag zur Klärung des Problems der Alttestamentlichen Textkritik* (Uppsala: A.-B. Lundequistska, 1935); 'Das textkritische Problem des Alten Testaments am Hoseabuch demonstriert', *ZAW*, 53 (1934), 241–54; Joseph Reider, 'The Present State of Textual Criticism of the Old Testament', *HUCA*, 7 (1930), 185–315.
5 Alfred Rahlfs, *Septuaginta-Studien*, 3 vols (Göttingen: Vandenhoeck & Ruprecht, 1904–11), III: Lucians Rezension der Königsbücher (1911).

New Avenues in Biblical Exegesis in Light of the Septuagint
ed. by Leonardo Pessoa da Silva Pinto and Daniela Scialabba, Turnhout, 2022 (*SEPT*, 1), pp. 71–91
© BREPOLS ❧ PUBLISHERS   DOI 10.1484/M.SEPT-EB.5.127712

But research on the Qumran manuscripts, particularly on 4QSam[a] and the Twelve Prophets scroll of Naḥal Ḥever, has made it clear that the Lucianic MSS 19 82 93 108 127 transmit a pre-Lucianic text very close to the Old Greek text (OG). Therefore 'Lucian's faculty of putting things in their right place' is not an ability of the Lucianic recensor of the fourth century but a distinctive feature of the Old Greek, that translates a Hebrew edition different from the one transmitted by the proto-MT. After Qumran, textual criticism does not attempt to correct the MT, but to recognize the Hebrew original of the Septuagint and to value both Hebrew editions on their own merits. As stated by Barthélemy, 'the Books of the Kingdoms are perhaps of all the books of the Bible those for which one can expect from a recovery of the ancient Septuagint the most valuable insights for the restoration of the original Hebrew text'.[6]

The textual history of the Septuagint in the Pentateuch and many other books is that of the original version carried out in the third or second century BCE and revised centuries later by Aquila, Symmachus and Theodotion and finally in the Hexaplaric and Lucianic recensions.[7] But the textual history of LXX-Kings is considerably more complex due to two intermediate textual levels: the kaige-Theodotionic recension and the pre-Lucianic level underlying the late Lucianic text. The kaige-Theodotionic recension was the first attempt to bring the OG in line with an early form of the Hebrew Masoretic text. This recension, accomplished around the turn of the era, affected the text of two sections of III–IV Kingdoms as established by Thackeray: III Kingdoms 1. 1–2. 11 (βγ) and III Kingdoms 22. 1–IV Kingdoms 25. 30 (γδ). In these kaige sections the B-text represented by *Codex Vaticanus* and MSS 121 509 transmits the text of the kaige revision.[8]

The pre-Lucianic level of the Antiochene text is very close or substantially identical with the OG.[9] It is attested by the Old Latin (OL), Coptic and Aethiopic versions, the pre-Hexaplaric stratum of the Armenian version, Josephus, readings of the parallel passages of Chronicles and *Paralipomena*.[10] In the kaige sections it is often the only way of attaining the oldest preserved Greek text. Accordingly, the text critical problem of I–II Kings lies mostly in identifying the kaige and the pre-Lucianic readings in order to establish the pre-recensional text closest to the OG. Precisely the OL fulfills this function. The antiquity of the version, prior to the Hexaplaric and Lucianic recensions, and a literalism that reveals the underlying pre-Hexaplaric and pre-Lucianic Antiochene text make it possible to discriminate between pre-Lucianic/

---

6 Dominique Barthélemy, *Les Devanciers d'Aquila* (Leiden: Brill, 1963), p. 140.
7 Christian Schäfer, *Benutzerhandbuch zur Göttinger Septuaginta* (Göttingen: Vandenhoeck & Ruprecht, 2012), I. Die Edition des Pentateuch von John William Wevers, pp. 93–112.
8 Barthélemy, *Les Devanciers d'Aquila*, p. 47.
9 See the information offered by Siegfried Kreuzer, '5.4 Septuagint (Samuel)', *Textual History of the Bible: The Hebrew Bible*, ed. by Armin Lange and Emanuel Tov (Leiden: Brill, 2017), I.B. Pentateuch, Former and Latter Prophets, pp. 349–61; '5.5. Septuagint (Kings)', pp. 362–66.
10 The New Testament contains previous 'Theodotionic' readings, but also 'pre-Lucianic' readings like Romans 11. 3 ὑπελείφθην in a quotation of III Kingdoms 19. 14 according to the Antiochene text ὑπελείφθην (ὑπολέλειμμαι B); Folker Siegert, *Zwischen Hebräischer Bibel und Altem Testament: Eine Einführung in die Septuaginta* (Münster: LIT, 2001), p. 90.

OG readings and secondary kaige readings and to reconstruct readings of a Hebrew edition different from that of MT. The OL translates an OG passage located 'in the right place' (II Kings / IV Kingdoms 10. 31–32) that was relocated by the kaige text in 13. 14–21 according to the rearrangement accomplished by the new edition represented by the MT.

1. The Different Arrangement of the Literary Units in the Old Greek/Old Latin Versions and the Masoretic Text

The textual history of LXX-Kings differs considerably in the non-kaige γγ section and in the kaige βγ and γδ sections. In the non-kaige γγ section the B and L texts preserve the OG without major variations between them, both attesting the numerous transpositions between MT and LXX in Chapters 2–14. The γδ kaige section also contains numerous transpositions between MT and LXX, but they are mainly attested only by the 'Lucianic' text: III Kingdoms 22. 41–51 // III Kingdoms 16. 28a–h; IV Kingdoms 1. 17–18a // 3. 1; 8. 27 // L 10. 36+, and L 10. 23–24; 12. 1; 13. 23; 13. 24–25. The 'weak authority' attributed to the 'Lucianic' text explains that the different arrangement of the Hebrew and Greek texts in this kaige section has hardly received any attention. An example of this is the reading of II Kings 13. 23 'and [the Lord] would not cast them from his presence up to now' (עַד־עָתָּה). *Codex Vaticanus* and the majority text followed by Rahlfs omit the MT expression 'up to now'. According to Barthélemy this omission betrays a purpose of modernization by the Greek translator.[11] But the OG does not omit ἕως τοῦ νῦν, since this reading is preserved by the pre-Lucianic text that witnesses the original location of v. 23 after v. 7.

The text of MT 13. 23 breaks the flow of the notice about the Aramean war developed in vv. 22, 24–25: 'And the Lord was gracious unto them, and had compassion on them, and had respect unto them, because of his covenant with Abraham, Isaac, and Jacob, and would not destroy them, neither cast he them from his presence as yet'. In the Antiochene text v. 23 is placed after v. 7, as part of the Deuteronomistic comment of 13. 2–7, 23. This movable verse is an addition that, as in similar cases, appears in a different location in MT and LXX. The transposition of a verse or of a literary unit from one place to another often carries with it textual variants at the beginning and end of the transposed text. At the beginning of the addition the kaige B-text has the reading 'The Lord was gracious to them', καὶ ἠλέησεν κύριος αὐτούς, while the Antiochene text (placed after v. 7) preserves the reading 'The Lord repented', καὶ μετεμελήθη (נחם) κύριος.

B (*kaige*) καὶ ἠλέησεν (MT וַיָּחָן) κύριος αὐτοὺς καὶ οἰκτίρησεν αὐτοὺς καὶ ἐπέβλεψεν πρὸς αὐτούς

L (OG) καὶ μετεμελήθη (נחם) κύριος καὶ οἰκτίρησεν αὐτούς

---

11 Dominique Barthélemy, *Critique textuelle de l'Ancien Testament* (Fribourg: Éditions universitaires; Göttingen: Vandenhoeck & Ruprecht, 1982), I, p. 402.

A similar change is found in II Samuel 24. 16 (also in a kaige section): καὶ μετεμελήθη Κύριος ἐπὶ τῇ κακίᾳ, μετεμελήθη L] παρεκλινεν 245; παρεκληθη rell (Rahlfs). The OL *et poenitentiam habuit Dominus in malitiam* confirms the pre-Lucianic and OG character of μετεμελήθη.[12] In II Kings 13. 23 the Antiochene text further omitts καὶ ἐπέβλεψεν πρὸς αὐτούς, 'and he turned toward them', a kaige reading that reflects MT וַיִּפֶן אֲלֵיהֶם. MT presents a double reading 'was gracious to them' and 'he turned toward them', that seems originated from the pair of terms חנן / פנה אל, found also in Psalms 25. 16; 69. 17; 86. 16; 119. 132. The Antiochene text attests here the short OG reading.

At the end of this addition the verb ἀπέρριψεν translating (הִשְׁלִיכָם מֵעַל־פָּנָיו), '[the Lord] cast them out of his presence', appears only here and in 17. 20 (הִשְׁלִיכָם מִפָּנָיו) and 24. 20 (הִשְׁלִכוֹ אֹתָם מֵעַל פָּנָיו). But this expression is usually constructed with the verb סור in *hiphil* הסיר מעל פני and translated with the verb ἀφίστημι (ἀπὸ τοῦ προσώπου) as in II Samuel 7. 15 and in II Kings in kaige section in IV Kingdoms 17. 18, 23; 23. 27; 24. 3. In this way the use of השליך instead of הסיר is an additional indication of the secondary character of 13. 23 and also of 17. 20 which for other reasons is also considered an addition.[13] The translation characteristics OG ἀφίστημι = סור and kaige ἀπορρίπτω = שלך reveal that at a late stage of the Hebrew the expression 'the Lord cast them out [...]' began to be constructed with the השליך instead of הסיר.

The passages selected are II Kings / IV Kingdoms 10. 30–36; 13. 1–25 and particularly 10. 30–31; 13. 14–21.[14] The main literary units that make up these passages are the initial and conclusive formulae of the reigns of Israel and Judah, the story on the death and burial of Elisha, several notices on the Aramean kings Hazael and Ben-Hadad and a comment in deuteronomistic style. The units located in different contexts in MT and LXX appear marked in bold in the chart below. The arrows indicate the transpositions that differentiate the two texts: the conclusive formulae of the reign of

---

12   'The verb נחם *nip'al* occurs *in the Books of Samuel* in the meaning "to regret" and with God as the subject in 1 Sam 15:11, 29*bis*, 35 and 2 Sam 24:16... "God does not regret" is a significant theological statement shared by the Torah (second Balaam oracle) and 1 Sam 15. This statement must have provided the motivation for the *kaige*-type corrections we have been discussing: if God does not change his mind, then נחם *nip'al* should not be understood in the mening "to regret" and not translated with μεταμέλομαι or μετανοέω, but rather παρακαλέομαι "to be comforted"'; Anneli Aejmelaeus, 'Does God Regret? A Theological Problem that Concerned the *Kaige* Revisers', in *Legacy of Barthélemy: 50 Years after 'Les Devanciers d'Aquila'*, ed. by Anneli Aejmealeus and Tuukka Kauhanen (Göttingen: Vandenhoeck & Ruprecht, 2017), pp. 41–53 (pp. 46, 53).

13   'verses 19–20 form a gloss-like addition, made to interpret further the mention of "only Judah remaining" in 18b'; Timo Tekoniemi, 'A Game of Thrones: Textual History of 2 Kings 17 in Light of Old Latin' (unpublished doctoral dissertation, University of Helsinki, Faculty of Theology, 2019), p. 184.

14   Matthieu Richelle, *Le testament d'Élisée: texte massorétique et septante en 2 Rois 13.10–14.16* (Pandé: J. Gabalda, 2010); 'Revisiting 2 Kings 13,14–21 (MT and LXX): The Transposition of a Pericope and Multiple Literary Editions in 2 Kings', in *Making the Biblical Text: Textual Studies in the Hebrew and the Greek Bible*, ed. by Innocent Himbaza (Fribourg: Academic Press; Göttingen: Vandenhoeck & Ruprecht, 2015), pp. 62–81; Adrian Schenker, *Älteste Textgeschichte der Königsbücher: Die hebräische Vorlage der ursprünglichen Septuaginta als älteste Textform der Königsbücher*, OBO, 199 (Fribourg: Academic Press; Göttingen: Vandenhoeck & Ruprecht, 2004), pp. 134–45.

Joash, the deuteronomistic comment and the story of the death and burial of Elisha, as well as the unit about Ahazaiah of Judah transmitted by *L* and OL.

The location of a passage in two different places raises the question of which of the two locations is the original. I Kings contains numerous transpositions between MT and LXX in Chapters 2–14. Critics argue that the order of LXX was modified by the MT or, conversely, that the Masoretic text was rearranged by the Greek translator or by the editor of the Septuagint's *Vorlage*. The second book of Kings also contains numerous transpositions between MT and LXX, but they have barely been studied for the simple reason that they are attested only by the supposedly late 'Lucianic' text: III Kingdoms 22. 41–51 // III Kingdoms 16. 28a–h; IV Kingdoms 1. 17–18a // 3. 1; 8. 27 // *L* 10. 36+; *L* 10. 23–24; 12. 1; 13. 23; 13. 24–25.[15] The OL also presents other transpositions, among them vv. 9–14 and 15–19 of II Kings 17.[16]

Old Greek (LXX^L)		MT = LXX^B (kaige)	
	JEHU		JEHU
10. 30	"The Lord said to Jehu…"	10. 30	"The Lord said to Jehu…"
	OL: Elisha's death and burial		
10. 31	Judgement on the reign o Jehu	10. 31	Judgement on the reign o Jehu
10. 32–33	Notice on Hazael	10. 32–33	Notice on Hazael
10. 34–36	Conclusive formulae of Jehu	10. 34–36	Conclusive formulae of Jehu
11. 1–12.			
22			
	JOAHAZ		JOAHAZ
13. 1	Initial formulae	13. 1	Initial formulae
13. 2–7	Deuteronomistic comment	13 2–7	Deuteronomistic comment
	13. 23		
13. 8–9	Conclusive formulae of Joahaz	13. 8–9	Conclusive formulae of Joahaz
	JOASH		JOASH
13. 10–11	Initial formulae	13. 10–11	Initial formulae
		13. 12–13	**Conclusive formulae of Joash**
		13. 14–21	**Elisha's death and burial**
13. 22	Notice on Ben-Hadad	13. 22	Notice on Ben-Hadad
		13. 23	**Addition**
13. 24–25	Notice on Ben-Hadad	13. 24–25	Notice on Ben-Hadad
13. 12–13	**Conclusive formulae of Joash**		
	AMAZIAH		AMAZIAH
14. 1–4	Initial formulae of Amaziah	14. 1–4	Initial formulae of Amaziah
14. 5–7	Notice	14. 5–7	Notice
14. 8–14	Narrative	14. 8–14	Narrative
		14. 15	**Conclusive formulae of Joash**
14. 16–17	Joash and Amaziah	14. 16–17	Joash and Amaziah

---

15 Julio Trebolle, 'Textual Criticism ant the Literary Structure and Composition of 1–2 Kings / 3–4 Reigns. The Different Sequence of Literary Units in MT and LXX', *Die Septuaginta: Entstehung, Sprache, Geschichte*, ed. by Siegfried Kreuzer, Martin Meiser and Marcus Sigismund (Tübingen: Mohr Siebeck, 2010), pp. 55–78.

16 Andrés Piquer Otero, 'What Text to Edit? The Oxford Hebrew Bible Editon of 2 Kings 17.1–23', *After Qumran: Old and Modern Editions of the Biblical Texts — The Historical Books*, ed. by Hans Ausloos, Benedicte Lemmelijn, Julio Trebolle Barrera (Leuven: Peeters, 2012), pp. 227–43; Tekoniemi, 'A Game of Thrones'.

1.1.   The Conclusive Formulae of the Reign of Joash: MT-II Kings 13. 12–13; 14. 15, Located in L (OG) after 13. 25

In the Masoretic text the initial formula of the reign of Joash (II Kings 13. 10–11) and the conclusive one (13. 12–13) follow each other, leaving the narrative about Elisha's death and burial (vv. 14–21) and the notice on the Aramean war (vv. 22, 24–25) outside the frame of the reign of Joash. In this way the textual layout of MT breaks a composition rule of Kings according to which every literary unit (a story, a notice or a deuteron-omistic comment) must be included between the initial and final formulas of the corresponding reign. Furthermore, MT repeats the conclusive formula of 13. 12–13 later on in 14. 15–16 (LXX ignores v. 15 as attested by the Antiochene text). On the other hand, the Antiochene text (and Josephus) attests the OG text which presents the conclusive formulae of Joash after 13. 25, in the 'right place' as recognized by Montgomery. In this way the OG integrates between the initial and final formulae of the reign of Joash the story and notice which synchronize with it, in accordance with the aforementioned composition rule of the books of Kings. Gray and Würthwein among other authors recognize that the 'right' arrangement of the Antiochene text is also 'original'.[17]

1.2.   The Story of Elisha's Death: II Kings 13. 14–19

The narrative of Elisha's death appears in MT and in the kaige, B-text in II Kings 13. 14–19, • 20–21, outside the frame of Joash reign to which it is related. This location breaks the aforementioned composition rule of the book. MT also requires the assuming that Elisha lived around eighty years since he appears as Elijah's disciple already in Ahab's days (I Kings 19. 19–21; 20).[18] The OL text, preserved in the *Vindobonensis* palimpsest, places this narrative in Chapter 10, between vv. 30 and 31, after the initial formulae of Jehu's reign. The king of Israel who takes part in this narrative is not Joash, but Jehu, who reigned from 841 to 815/14 (Gershon Galil) or from 839 to 822 (James M. Miller and John H. Hayes), quite a bit before Joash (806/5–791/90 or 804–789).[19]

The actual location of this narrative in MT is to be connected with the topic of Israel's salvation alluded three times in Chapter 13. The deuteronomistic comment mentions 'a saviour' (מושיע) in v. 5; the prophetic narrative talks of 'salvation' or 'victory' (תשועה) in v. 17; and the notice about the Aramean war confirms the victory or salvation from the Aramean oppression: 'Three times did Joash beat him [Benhadad the son of Hazael] and recovered the cities of Israel' (13. 24–25).

The Cambridge edition of the Septuagint collects the OL variants in the context of 13. 14–21 (LXX/MT). This location is wrong or at least misleading. The OL variants

---

17   John Gray, *I & II Kings*, 2nd edn (London: SCM Press, 1970), p. 597; Ernst Würthwein, *Die Bücher der Könige 1. Kön. 17–2. Kön. 25* (Göttingen: Vandenhoeck & Ruprecht, 1984), p. 363.

18   The historians are quite divided about dating the wars against the Arameans (II Kings 6. 24–7. 20; 13) in the period of Jehu's dynasty, during the reigns of Jehoahaz or Joash, or even in the period of Omri's dynasty.

19   Gershon Galil, *The Chronology of the Kings of Israel & Judah* (Leiden: Brill, 1996), pp. 71–73; James Maxwell Miller and John Haralson Hayes, *A History of Ancient Israel and Judah* (London: SCM Press, 1985), p. 337.

selected in the apparatus of Brooke-McLean point to the 'omission' of Ιωας at 13. 14 and the 'addition' of *Ieu* in 13. 16:

τῷ βασιλεῖ] *at Ieu regem israel*
Ιωας τὴν χεῖρα αὐτοῦ] *manum suam Ieu*
τοῦ] pr *Ieu*

Also in 13. 18:

Ελισαιε] *helisseus Ieu regi*

Also the edition of *Palimpsestus Vindobonensis* by B. Fischer points in the wrong direction when it notes that the name *ieu* 'must stand instead of *ioas* because of the transposition in the text'.[20] The OL did not add or omit nor substitute *Ioas* for *Jehu*. It simply represents the OG text that differs from LXX[B,L] in 13. 14–21. It preserves the oldest recognizable account of Elisha's death and burial.

The reading 'Arrow of victory for Yahveh and arrow of victory for Israel' (*sagitta salutis Domini et sagitta salutis Israel*) translates an OG that reads Ισραηλ (a genitive that parallels the previous genitive *Domini*) instead of the kaige reading ἐν Συρίᾳ (LXX[B,L], MT בַּאְרָם).[21] The OL reading *in aseroth quae est contra faciem samariae* places the battle against the Arameans in Ḥatseroth while MT locates it in Aphek (LXX[B,L] ἐν Αφεκ).[22] A place known as חצרות (LXX Ασηρωθ, Vulgate *Aseroth*, Numbers 11. 35 (2x); 12. 16; 33. 17, 18 and Deuteronomy 1. 1) is located in the Sinai.[23] A place called Ḥatseroth, located *c*. 8 km southeast of Samaria is mentioned several times in the Samaria Ostraka, dated in the eighth century, *c*. two decades after the battle against the Arameans happened.[24] The expression *quae est contra faciem samariae* suggests a situation toward the East of Samaria, as if one was facing the sunrise. There are two places called Aphek, one in the Golan Heights in the road from Damascus to Samaria,[25] and another one southwest of Samaria, quoted several times in the biblical texts and well known in extra biblical sources. A little known place, חצרות, seems to have been replaced with a better known place, Aphek. However, the two

---

20 Bonifatius Fischer with the collaboration of Eugene Ulrich and Judith E. Sanderson, 'Palimpsestus Vindobonensis', in Bonifatius Fischer, *Beiträge zur Geschichte der lateinischen Bibeltexts* (Freiburg: Herder, 1986), pp. 308–86 (p. 379).
21 According to Steven L. McKenzie, *1 Kings 16–2 Kings 16* (Stuttgart: Kohlhammer, 2019), p. 466: 'Since it is the same arrow of victory, the reading in Israel makes more sense, especially in view of the geographical setting'. However, as the note of the editor of *Palimpsestus Vindobonensis* indicates, the correct OL reading is *sagitta salutis Israel* as further in the same verse.
22 According to Adrian Schenker, *Älteste Textgeschichte der Königsbücher*, p. 140, 'Als Ergebnis zeichnet sich die Testgestalt der VL als die ursprünglichste ab'.
23 Yohanan Aharoni, *The Land of the Bible: A Historical Geography* (London: Burns & Oates, 1968), p. 378.
24 Aharoni, *The Land of the Bible*, p. 325.
25 Miller and Hayes place the battle against the Arameans in the same location where Saul fought his last battle against the Philistines, that is, in the Gilboa mountains, identifying there a place called Aphek as well; see James Maxwell Miller and John Haralson Hayes, *A History of Ancient Israel and Judah*, 2nd edn (Louisville: Westminster John Knox Press, 2006), p. 346.

places seem to correspond to two different battles in two different periods. The text represented by the OL refers to a battle against Hazael that took place near Samaria in Hatserot in the time of Jehu's reign, while MT and the Greek kaige text (LXX[B,L]) make reference to a battle against Ben-Hadad in Aphek in the time of Joash's reign. This battle is also referred to in the notice of 13. 22, 24–25 according to the Antiochene text: 'And Hazael took the Philistine from the hand of Jehoahaz from the sea of the West to Aphek (καὶ ἔλαβεν Αζαηλ τὸν ἀλλόφυλον ἐκ χειρὸς αὐτοῦ ἀπὸ θαλάσσης τῆς καθ' ἑσπέραν ἕως Αφεκ) [...] And Joash struck Ben-Hadad, son of Hazael, three times in the war, in Aphek (καὶ ἐπάταξεν Ιωας τὸν υἱὸν Αδερ υἱὸν Αζαηλ τρὶς ἐν τῷ πολέμῳ ἐν Αφεκ)'. Wellhausen and Stade accepted the Antiochene text as original material. Rahlfs classified this reading among the pre-Lucianic material ('vorlucianisches Gut'), but saying at the same time that 'Luc. misunderstood "the sea of the Arabah", 14[25], as "the sea of the West", i.e., the Mediterranean, and so similarly at 25[4, 5] with "the Arabah" = "the West".[26] Montgomery attributes this misunderstanding to Lucian himself and qualifies as midrash the Antiochene text of this vv. 22, 25.

The location of the story about Elisha's death and of the notice about the battle against the Arameans during Jehu's reign poses a challenge to the historical study of this period, but also to exegetes that try to trace the 'deuteronomistic' redaction history of Kings. The historians are quite divided about dating the wars against the Arameans (I Kings 20–22; II Kings 6. 24–7. 20; 13) in the period of Omri's dynasty or in the period of Jehu's dynasty, during the reigns of Jehu, Jehoahaz or Joash.[27] The studies about the composition and redaction of Kings do not take into account the LXX and especially the Antiochene text and the OL when they diverge from MT.[28] According to Walter Dietrich, the narrative about Jehu was the final piece of a 'Prophetic Narrative on Yhwh's battle against Baal in Israel'. This large-scale narrative contained most of the material found in I Kings 17 to II Kings 10 and only later was inserted in the work of the Deuteronomistic historian (DtrH).[29] In our opinion the collection of stories about Elisha concludes in Chapter 10 but including the prophetic stories of Chapter 13. In this way the story about the revolt of Jehu begins and ends with an intervention by the prophet Elisha. A comparative analysis of how the Elijah-Elisha narratives (and the stories about the Aramean wars) appear introduced in each Hebrew edition (MT and LXX) is a previous step for the study of how these narratives were integrated into the deuteronomistic history.

---

26 According to Montgomery, 'L replaces the foll. Hebrew with invented midrash: "And Ioas smote the son of Ader, son of Azael thrice in the battle at Aphek according to the word of the Lord, and recovered the cities of Israel and what he took"', The Books Kings, p. 438.

27 Lester L. Grabbe, Ancient Israel: What Do We Know and How Do We Know It? (London: T&T Clark, 2017), p. 147.

28 See the studies reviewed by G. N. Knoppers, R. L. Cohen, B. Halpern and A. Lemaire in The Books of Kings: Sources, Composition, Historiography and Reception, ed. by André Lemaire and Baruch Halpern, VT.S, 129 (Leiden: Brill, 2010): Gary N. Knoppers, 'Theories of the Redaction(s) of Kings', pp. 69–88; Robert L. Cohen, 'The Literary Structure of Kings', pp. 107–22; Baruch Halpern and André Lemaire, 'The Composition of Kings', pp. 123–53.

29 Walter Dietrich, 'Jehus Kampf gegen den Baal von Samaria', TZ, 57 (2001), pp. 115–34.

1.3. The Story of Elisha's Burial: II Kings 13. 20–21

The OL transmits a version of the story very different from that of MT and LXX^{B,L}. According to the MT/LXX^{B,L} version of the story (II Kings 13. 20–21) a man was carried to his last abode by the same people who had formerly buried Elisha. When coming into contact with Elisha, the man (obviously an Israelite) revives. Following the OL version of the story, in one of their inroads into the land of Israel, some Moab's bandits rashly cast the corpse of one fellow bandit into Elisha's grave. When coming into contact with Elisha, the Moabite man revives:[30]

> [20] et mortus est helisseus et sepelierunt eum et piratae moab uenerunt in terram illam. [21] Et factum est cum sepeliirent pirate hominem unum accesserunt ad monumentum et proiecerunt hominem in monumentum helissei et fugerunt et adplicitus est homo ossibus helissei et uixit homo et surrexit super pedes suos [10.31 et Ieu non obseruauit ire in uiam Domini Dei Israel ex toto corde suo].[31]

The extreme literalism of the OL text located after 10. 30 allows an easy inverse translation into Greek and Hebrew. Doubts can be raised about the repeated subject and object of the action. The term *iterum* in 10. 30f can be an addition from the OL or the LXX (πάλιν) or even the Hebrew (עוֹד), related to the previous interpolation of 10. 30e that causes the repetition of *usq·at finem* […] *totam* — ἕως συντελείας […] ἕως συντελείας — עַד־כַּלֵּה[…] עַד־כַּלֵּה (*Wiederaufnahme*) (cf. below).[32] The OG readings underlying the OL are underlined, as opposed to the kaige B/L readings in 13. 14–19:

10. 30h καὶ ἀπέθανεν Ελισαιε καὶ <u>θάπτουσιν</u> (B ἔθαψαν) αὐτόν καὶ <u>πειραταὶ</u> (B μονόζωνοι) Μωαβ ἦλθον ἐν τῇ γῇ ἐλθόντος τοῦ ἐνιαυτοῦ 10. 30i καὶ ἐγένετο αὐτῶν θαπτόντων <u>ἄνθρωπον ἕνα</u> (B τὸν ἄνδρα) καὶ ἤγγισε τὸ πειρατήριον αὐτοῖς (B καὶ ἰδοὺ <u>εἶδον</u> τὸν μονόζωνον) καὶ ἔρριψαν τὸν ἄνδρα ἐν τῷ τάφῳ Ελισαιε <u>καὶ ἔφυγον</u> (καὶ ἦλθε L / καὶ ἐπορεύθη B) καὶ ἤψατο τῶν ὀστέων Ελισαιε καὶ ἔζησε καὶ ἀνέστη ἐπὶ τοὺς πόδας αὐτοῦ.

The historical present θάπτουσιν is a well-known OG translation feature, in opposition to the aorist ἔθαψαν. The OG ἄνθρωπον ἕνα is attested by the OL *hominem unum*; πειραται and πειρατήριον are also OG readings preserved by the Antiochene text and

---

30 Julio Trebolle, 'Dos textos para un relato de resurrección: 2 Re 13,20-21 TM LXX-B / LXX–L VL', *Sefarad*, 43 (1983), pp. 3–16, translated in Julio Trebolle, 'Two Texts for a Story of a Resurrection: 2 Kings 13:20–21', in *Textual and Literary Criticism of the Books of Kings: Collected Essays*, ed. by Andrés Piquer and Pablo A. Torijano (Leiden: Brill, 2020), pp. 152–62.

31 10. 30h/13. 20 And Elisha died, and they buried him, and pirates from Moab came to that land. 10. 30i/13. 21 And it came to pass, as the pirates were burying a man, they approached the grave and they cast the man into the grave of Elisha and fled, and when the man touched the bones of Elisha, he revived, and stood up on his feet [10. 31 But Jehu was not careful to walk in the law of the Lord the God of Israel with all his heart].

32 In Exodus 3. 15 the word 'yet' (עוֹד) may conceal the addition of a second speech by repeating 'and said to': '14 Elohim said to Moses: "I am he that I am" […] 15 And Elohim also (עוֹד) said to Moses […]'. The second speech alludes to the promise of long lineage that appears later in 17. 20 and 21. 13, 18.

OL (*piratae*), while μονόζωνοι and μονόζωνον are kaige readings;[33] καὶ ἔφυγον is the pre-Lucianic and OG reading attested by the OL *et fugerunt*. The reading καὶ ἦλθε (*L*) or καὶ ἐπορεύθη (B) translating MT וַיֵּלֶךְ offers special difficulty.

The resurrection of a Moabite, just like the resurrection of the Sareptas's widow's son by Elijah and the healing of the Syrian Naaman performed by Elisha, affects a foreign character. The figures of Elijah and Elisha and the period in which they lived are mostly characterized by anti-Canaanite fanaticism and anti-Baalist polemics, but these accounts of healings and resurrections of foreign individuals, as well as the political activity of the prophets *vis a vis* the neighbor countries, complement and enrich the image of the prophet Elisha.

A comparative study of the edition represented by the MT and the edition translated in the OG (and OL) is very productive both for the historical study of the period of the Israelite monarchy[34] and for the studies on the redaction history and the editorial process of the books of Kings. The exegesis of these books is to be based both on the text order reached in the MT edition and on the previous arrangement of the literary units that characterized the edition known by the *Vorlage* of LXX.

2. The Challenge of Integrating OL's Testimony in a Critical Edition of the Septuagint (IV Kingdoms 10. 30–31a–i)

The critical edition of LXX-Kings is to replace numerous kaige readings of the Rahlfs's edition with the corresponding OG reading. The frequent 'Lucianic' duplicates of the Antiochene text are composed of a pre-Lucianic/OG reading and the corresponding kaige variant. The kaige-Theodotionic recension is responsible for having introduced into the OG new readings that replaced the originals with variants more in line with the MT. The critical edition follows the pre-Lucianic/OG reading reflected in the OL while assigning the B-text, kaige reading to the critical apparatus, as in the following cases:

> 3 *Reg* 22. 10 ἐν ὁδῷ πύλης OG (*ad viam portae* OL 91–95) / ἐν ταῖς πύλαις B (פתח שער MT, בשערי)
>
> 4 *Reg* 1. 4.6 διὰ τοῦτο OG (*ideo* OL) (לכן) / οὐχ οὕτως B (לא כן)
>
> 4 *Reg* 2. 23 καὶ ἐλίθαζον αὐτόν OG (*et lapidabant illum* OL) (ויסקלו) / καὶ κατέπαιζον αὐτοῦ B (ויתקלסו)
>
> 4 *Reg* 3. 4 ἦν φέρων OG (*ferebat* OL) / ἐπιστρέφων B (השיב)

---

33   4 Reg 5. 2 μονόζωνοι] + πειρατηριον V 52 106–06 92–314–489 134 119 55 372 554; 6. 23 μονόζωνοι] πειραται L SyrH^mg(uid); 13. 20 μονόζωνοι] praedones 91–95; 13. 21 μονόζωνον] πειρατηριον L; 24. 2 μονόζωνοι 4x] om. μονοζωνους 4° L. Cf. Barthélemy, *Les Devanciers d'Aquila*, p. 81.

34   Matthieu Richelle, 'The Relevance of the Septuagint for Reconstructing the History of Ancient Israel', in *Die Septuaginta — Geschichte, Wirkung, Relevanz: 6. Internationale Fachtagung veranstaltet von Septuaginta Deutsch (LXX.D), Wuppertal 21.–24. Juli 2016*, ed. by Martin Meiser and others, WUNT, 405 (Tübingen: Mohr Siebeck, 2018), pp. 573–87.

4 Reg 3. 21 καὶ παρήγγειλαν παντὶ περιζωννυμένῳ παραζώνην (*et denuntiaverunt omni praecincto gladium* OL) καὶ παρατείνοντι OG / καὶ ἐβόησαν ἐκ παντὸς παραζωννυμένου παραζώνην B

4 Reg 4. 16 εἰς τὸ μαρτύριον τοῦτο OG (*in testimonio erit sermo hic* OL) / εἰς τὸν καιρὸν τοῦτον B

4 Reg 7. 5 ἤδη διαυγάζοντος OG (*lucent* OL) / ἐν τῷ σκότει B

4 Reg 8. 1 καὶ παρέσται ἐπὶ τὴν γῆν ἑπτὰ ἔτη (*et erit in terra tribus annis* OL) / καί γε ἦλθεν ἐπὶ τὴν γῆν ἑπτὰ ἔτη B

4 Reg 9. 37 καὶ οὐκ ἔσται ὁ λέγων Οἴμμοι (*et non est qui dicat: Vae mihi!* OL) / ὥστε μὴ εἰπεῖν αὕτη Ιεζαβελ *kaige* (μὴ εἰπεῖν αὐτούς Rahlfs = לֹא־יֹאמְרוּ)

4 Reg 18. 34 καὶ ποῦ εἰσὶν οἱ θεοὶ τῆς χώρας Σαμαρείας (*ubi sunt dii terrae Samariae* OL) / μὴ ἐξείλαντο τὴν Σαμάρειαν ἐκ χειρός μου *kaige* (καὶ ὅτι ἐξείλαντο Rahlfs)

Similarly, the critical edition should restore the text of II Kings 13. 23 to its original location after 13. 7 with the corresponding pre-Lucianic / OG text, while relegating the kaige text of 13. 23 to the critical apparatus. It would not make sense to produce a duplicate of OG + kaige readings. However, in view of a better understanding of the text and its history, it will surely be more appropriate to reproduce the kaige text in the lemma, enclosed in square brackets to signify that it is not an OG text.

Robert Hanhart has edited *Paralipomenon II* before *Paralipomenon I* in the Göttingen series because the full OL text of *Paralipomenon II* has been preserved in manuscript La¹⁰⁹ (Madrid, Biblioteca de la Universidad Complutense 31). This OL text allows him to connect the text of *Paralipomenon II* with III–IV Kingdoms, and with the Antiochene text in particular. Hanhart points out an editorial rule that is mandatory in the Göttingen series: not to pick up text forms transmitted by secondary versions if they are not attested in the Greek tradition.[35] The purpose of textual criticism is to reach the oldest text attested or the oldest which can be recovered. But this text may not be among those attested in the Greek textual tradition and can only be retrieved through a version as in the case of OL 10. 30a–i. If strictly following the norm referred to, this OL text should appear in the critical apparatus, but in this way it would be implied that it is a late text, when in fact it represents the oldest recoverable text, although not preserved in the Greek manuscript tradition.

A critical edition cannot contain duplicates that were not part of the OG text. However, Rahlfs's LXX edition contains the OG text of III Kingdoms 16. 28a–h and also the parallel kaige text of III Kingdoms 22. 41–51, omitted by the Antiochene text which represents the OG here. A critical edition of III Kingdoms should assign the kaige, B-text of III Kingdoms 22. 41–51 to the critical apparatus. However, given the transmission conditions of the LXX text — OG in some sections and kaige in others — it is surely advisable to also include the text of III Kingdoms 22. 41–51 in the lemma but indicating with some graphic sign that it is in fact a kaige text. Otherwise, the reader finds that

35 '[...] eines Gesetzes, das in der Göttinger Edition grundsätzlich eingehalten werden muss: für den Verzicht auf die Aufnahme in den Sekundärübersetzungen überlieferter Textformen, die griechisch nicht mitbezeugt sind'; *Paralipomenon liber II*, ed. by Robert Hanhart, Septuaginta Vetus Testamentum Graecum, VII 2 (Göttingen: Vandenhoeck & Ruprecht, 2014), p. 4.

on some occasions the edition reproduces kaige readings as the oldest recoverable text and on others they are relegated to the critical apparatus. For this same reason we have chosen to include in the lemma of the edition the OL text of 10. 30a–i in its own location, enclosed in square brackets, and also include in the lemma the *L* and B-text of 13. 14–21, giving preference to pre-Lucianic readings of *L* over the kaige variants of B:

> 10. 30 …υἱοὶ τέταρτοι καθήσονταί σοι ἐπὶ θρόνου Ισραηλ. [[OL cf. 13. 14–21: … *sedebunt tibi fili quarti in throno Israel* 10:30a/13:14 *et helisseus infirmatus est infirmitatem suam qua mortus est et descendit at eum rex israel et plorauit super faciem eius dicens pater pater rector israel et eques eius* 10. 30b/13. 15 *et dixit at eum helisseus accipe arcum et sagittas accepit arcum et sagittas* 10. 30c/13. 16 *et dixit at ieu regem israel inpone manum tuam super arcum et inposuit manum suam ieu et superinposuit manus suas helisseus super manus ieu regis* 10. 30d/13. 17 *et dixit aperi fenestram quae ab oriente est et aperuit et dixit helisseus sagittare et sagittauit et dixit helisseus sagitta salutis domini et sagitta salutis <in> israel et percuties syriam in aseroth quae est contra faciem samariae usq at finem.* 10. 30e *Et aperuit fenestram secundam et dixit sagittare et sagittauit sagittam salutis domini et sagittam salutis israel et dixit helisseus percuties syriam totam* 10. 30f/13. 18 *Et iterum dixit helisseus ieu regi percute in terram et percussit ter et stetit* 10. 30g/13. 19 *et contristatus est homo dei pro eo et dixit si percussisses quinques aut sexies tunc percutiebas syriam totam usq·at finem et nunc percuties syriam ter* 10. 30h/13. 20 *et mortus est helisseus et sepelierunt eum et piratae moab uenerunt in terram illam* 10. 30i/13. 21 *Et factum est cum sepeliirent pirate hominem unum accesserunt (ad monumentum) et proiecerunt hominem in monumentum helissei et fugerunt et adplicitus est homo ossibus helissei et uixit homo et surrexit super pedes suos et Ieu non obseruauit ire in uiam Domini Dei Israel ex toto corde suo.*]] 10:31 καὶ Ιου οὐκ ἐφύλαξεν πορεύεσθαι ἐν νόμῳ κυρίου θεοῦ Ισραηλ ἐν ὅλῃ καρδίᾳ αὐτοῦ.

4 Kgdms 13. 14–21

¹⁴Καὶ Ελισαιε ἠρρώστησεν τὴν ἀρρωστίαν αὐτοῦ, δι᾽ ἣν ἀπέθανεν. Καὶ κατέβη πρὸς αὐτὸν βασιλεὺς Ισραηλ καὶ ἔκλαυσεν ἐπὶ πρόσωπον αὐτοῦ καὶ εἶπεν Πάτερ πάτερ, ἅρμα Ισραηλ καὶ ἱππεὺς αὐτοῦ. ¹⁵Καὶ εἶπεν αὐτῷ Ελισαιε Λαβὲ τόξον καὶ βέλη· καὶ ἔλαβεν πρὸς αὐτὸν τόξον καὶ βέλη.
¹⁶Καὶ εἶπεν τῷ βασιλεῖ Ισραηλ Ἐπιβίβασον τὴν χεῖρά σου ἐπὶ τὸ τόξον· καὶ ἐπεβίβασεν τὴν χεῖρα αὐτοῦ ὁ βασιλεὺς ἐπὶ τὸ τόξον, καὶ ἐπέθηκεν Ελισαιε τὰς χεῖρας αὐτοῦ ἐπὶ τὰς χεῖρας τοῦ βασιλέως. ¹⁷Καὶ εἶπεν Ἄνοιξον τὴν θυρίδα κατ᾽ ἀνατολάς· καὶ ἤνοιξεν. Καὶ εἶπεν Ελισαιε Τόξευσον· καὶ ἐτόξευσεν. καὶ εἶπεν Βέλος σωτηρίας τῷ κυρίῳ καὶ βέλος σωτηρίας ἐν Ισραηλ, καὶ πατάξεις τὴν Συρίαν ἐν Αφεκ ἕως συντελείας. ¹⁸Καὶ εἶπεν αὐτῷ Ελισαιε Λαβὲ πέντε βέλη· καὶ ἔλαβεν. Καὶ εἶπεν τῷ βασιλεῖ Ισραηλ Πάταξον εἰς τὴν γῆν· καὶ ἐπάταξεν τρὶς καὶ ἔστη. ¹⁹Καὶ ἐλυπήθη ὁ ἄνθρωπος τοῦ θεοῦ ἐπ᾽ αὐτῷ καὶ εἶπεν Εἰ ἐπάταξας πεντάκις ἢ ἑξάκις, τότε ἂν ἐπάταξας τὴν Συρίαν ἕως συντελείας· καὶ νῦν τρὶς πατάξεις τὴν Συρίαν. ²⁰Καὶ ἀπέθανεν Ελισαιε καὶ θάπτουσιν αὐτόν καὶ πειρᾶται Μωαβ ἦλθον ἐν τῇ γῇ ἐλθόντος τοῦ ἐνιαυτοῦ. ²¹Καὶ ἐγένετο αὐτῶν θαπτόντων ἄνθρωπον ἕνα καὶ ἤγγισε τὸ πειρατήριον αὐτοῖς καὶ ἔρριψαν τὸν ἄνδρα ἐν τῷ τάφῳ Ελισαιε καὶ ἔφυγον καὶ ἥψατο τῶν ὀστέων Ελισαιε καὶ ἔζησε καὶ ἔστη ἐπὶ τοὺς πόδας αὐτοῦ

B M V *O L CI CII b d f o s t. x z al* [>] Aeth Arm Sa Lat¹¹⁵ SyrH

14 Ελισαιε Bᶜ V 64 55 158 372] ελισεαι 108; ελισσεαι 82-93; ελισσαιος 372 460 700; *Helisseus* (apud 4 Reg 10. 30–31); ελεισαιε B*; ελισσαιε rel | αὐτοῦ] εαυτου B; > 246 Arm | ἤν] ης 247 121 488 460 | ἀπέθανεν B A*f* 71 245 Lat¹¹⁵ (apud 4 Reg 10. 30–31)] pr και rel Arm SyrH; *moriebatur* Aeth; + αυτος 246 | om πρὸς – βασιλεύς 530ᵗˣᵗ | πρὸς αὐτόν] post Ισραηλ¹ tr *L* 460 700; om αὐτόν 120 *z* | βασιλεὺς scripsi cf. Lat¹¹⁵ (apud 4 Reg 10. 30–31)] pr ιωαβ 313; pr ιωραμ 236-242-530; pr Ιωας (pr ο 158) rel | om Ισραηλ¹ 68 | πρόσωπον] προσωπου B *CI* 56 158 244 | καὶ εἶπεν] *dicens* Lat¹¹⁵ (apud 4 Reg 10. 30–31);> 93 | ἅρμα] *rector* Lat¹¹⁵ (apud 4 Reg 10. 30–31) | ἱππεὺς] ιππεις Arm Aeth.

15 om αὐτῷ 82 44 | Ελισαιε Bᶜ V 127 64 55 158 372] ελισεαι 108; ελισσεαι 82-93; ελισσαιος 700 342 460; *Helisseus* La¹¹⁵ (apud 4 Reg 10. 30–31); ελεισαιε B*; ελισσαιε rel | τόξον¹] pr το 93| βέλη¹] βολιδας *L* 460 700; βολιδα 71 | καὶ³ – βέλη²] bis scr 55; > 247 245 554 Aeth; om πρὸς – βέλη *d*⁻¹⁰⁶ 381 | ἔλαβεν] + ιωας *L* 460; + ιας 700 | πρὸς αὐτόν] > 93 700 Lat¹¹⁵ (apud 4 Reg 10. 30–31) Arm; post τόξον tr 460 | αὐτόν] εαυτον Bᶜ 82-127 460 | τόξον²] pr το 93; τοξα 71.

16 εἶπεν] + ελισεαι 108; + ελισσεαι 82-93; + ελισαιε 127; + ελισσαιε 19; + ελισσαιος 460; + ιωας 700; + *elissaeus* Sa | τῷ βασιλεῖ Ισραηλ A *L* 460 700 Arm Syh] *at Ieu regem israel* Lat¹¹⁵ (apud 4 Reg 10:30-31); αυτω 381; τω βασιλει rel; > 44 | om ἐπὶ¹ – αὐτοῦ¹ 313 245 | τὸ τόξον¹] τω τοξω 328; om V* A | καὶ² – τόξον²] και εποιησεν ουτως 44; > 19 *CII*⁻⁵²ᶜ ³¹³ 527 | τὴν χεῖρα αὐτοῦ (>460) ὁ βασιλεὺς 82 460] *manum suam Ieu* Lat¹¹⁵ (apud 4 Reg 10. 30–31); ο βασιλευς την χειρα αυτου *L*⁻⁸² 700; την χειρα αυτου ιωας ο 372; ιωας την χειρα αυτου (> 246) rel | ἐπὶ τό τόξον²] > B; ε. τω τωξω 799 | Ελισαιε Bᶜ V 127 64 55 158 372] ελισαιε 108; ελισσεαι 82-93; ελισσαιος 460 700; ελεισαιε B*; > 342; ελισσαιε rel | τὰς χεῖρας¹] την χειρα A Aeth Arm Cop | om αὐτοῦ² 19′ | τοῦ βασιλέως] pr *ieu* Lat¹¹⁵ (apud 4 Reg 10:30-31).

17 Ἄνοιξον] + δη 98-379 | τὴν θυρίδα] τας θυρας 125 | κατ᾿ ἀνατολάς] sub * SyrH; *quae ab oriente est* Lat¹¹⁵ (apud 4 Reg 10:30–31) | om Ελισαιε – ἐτόξευσεν B | Ελισαιε V 127 64 55 158 372] ελισεαι 108; ελισσεαι 93; ελισσαιος 342 460 700; *Helisseus* Lat¹¹⁵ (apud 2 Kgs 10:30–31); ελισσαιε rel | Τόξευσον – εἶπεν] > *CII d* 246 *s*⁻⁴⁸⁸ *t*⁻³⁷⁰ *z*; om καὶ ἐτόξευσεν 245 | Τόξευσον] ρευξησον 245; ροιζησον A | ἐτόξευσεν] εροιζησεν A | εἶπεν³ B A *L* 460 700] + ελισαιε V 64 55 372; + ελισεε 158; + ελισσαιος 342; + ελισσαιε rel | Βέλος ∩ V; om καί⁶ 244 | om βέλος σωτηρίας 44 | ἐν] τω 460 | Ισραηλ *L CI*⁻²⁴³ᵗˣᵗ ⁷³¹ᵗˣᵗ 244 460 554 700] *Israel* Lat¹¹⁵ (apud 2 Kgs 10:30–31); Συρια rel | πατάξεις] παταξει B; επαταξεν 245 | τήν] εις γην 245 | om ἐν Αφεκ 236ᵗˣᵗ | Αφεκ] *Aseroth* Lat¹¹⁵ (apud 2 Kgs 10:30–31; = Ασηρωθ) | ἕως] pr και 460

18 αὐτῷ Ελισαιε] τω ιωας ελισσεαι *L* 460 700; om αὐτῷ *CII d*⁻¹⁰⁶ 245; sub ÷ SyrH | Ελισαιε Bᶜ V 64 55 158 372 Ra] *Ieu* Lat¹¹⁵ (apud 2 Kgs 10:30–319); ελεισαιε B*; ελισσαιος 342; ελισσαιε rel | Λαβέ] pr και 381* | πέντε βέλη *L* 460 700] *sagittas* Arm; τοξον *CI o* × 158 244 372 554 Aeth; το τοξον 247 121 488; τοξα rel | εἶπεν²] + ελισαιε 127; ελισσαιε 19′; + ελισσεαι 93 | om τῷ βασιλεῖ Ισραηλ *d*⁻¹⁰⁶ 381; om Ισραηλ 19′ | εἰς] εκ 245; > 158 |

γῆν] + και επαταξεν εις την γην 92 | ἐπάταξεν L 460 700 Lat[115] (apud 2 Kgs 10:30–31)]
εις την γην 106; *rex in terram* Sa; + ο βασιλευς rel | τρίς] τρεις 247 93 46–313 d[-106] 246
488 799 460 700;> 122*

19 om καὶ[1] – θεοῦ 246 | ὁ ἄνθρωπος τοῦ θεοῦ 460 Lat[115] (apud 2 Kgs 10:30–31)] post
αυτω tr rel | om ἐπ᾽ αὐτῷ 158 Aeth | εἶπεν] + αυτω 530 | ἐπάταξας[1]] -ξες 242 106;
percussiset Lat[115] (apud 2 Kgs 10:30–319) | om ἢ ἑξάκις CI[-243mg 731] | ἤ] και CII; ει V* |
ἂν – συντελείας] *percuttiebat Syriam totam usqu᾽ at fanem* Lat[115] (apud 2 Kgs 10:30–319)|
ἄν] εαν 247 488* | συντελείας] pr της 328 | τρίς] pr επι 71; τρεις V* 247 243 313 d[-106] 246
92-488-762* 244 372; τριτον L[-108] 460 700; τριτον τριον 108 | πατάξεις] -ξης 93; -ξον 342

20 ἀπέθανεν] post Ελισαιε tr L 460 700 | Ελισαιε B[c] M 127 64 130 55 158 372 Ra]
ελεισαιε B*; ελισσεαι 93; ελισεαι 108; ελισσαιος 700 342 460; *Helisseus* Lat[115] (apud 2 Kgs
10:30–319); ελισσαιε rel | θάπτουσιν L 460 700] εθαψαν rel | πειράται scripsi] *piratae*
Lat[115] (apud 2 Kgs 10. 30–319); μονοζωνοι om. mss | Μωαβ] μοαβ 313* | ἐλθόντος]
-τες 247 488* | om τοῦ 52* f

21 om ἐγένετο αὐτῶν 44 | αὐτῶν θαπτόντων] *cum sepelierunt piratae* Lat[115] (apud 2
Kgs 10. 30–319) | ἄνθρωπον ἕνα L 460 700] > 0; τον ανδρα rel; cf. *hominem unum*
Lat[115] (apud 2 Kgs 10. 30–319) | καὶ 2° – ἄνδρα 2] post Ελισαιε tr 246; > 74 | ἤγγισε
τὸ πειρατήριον αὐτοῖς L 460 700] *acceserunt ad monumentum* Lat[115] (apud 2 Kgs 10.
30–319); ιδου ειδον τον μονοζωνον rel | ἔρριψαν] εκρυψαν 799 | τὸν ἄνδρα 2] αυτου
71 | om τῷ 19 | Ελισαιε B[c] V 127 64 55 158 372] ελισσεαι 93; ελισεαι 108; ελεισαιε B*;
ελισσαιου 342 700; ελισσεαι 93; > 460; ελισσαιε rel | om καί 4° – Ελισαιε 2 52* | ἔφυγον
eds] *fugerunt* Lat[115] (apud 2 Kgs 10. 30–319); εφυγων 158; εφυγον και ηλθε L 460
700; επορευθησαν 71 342 Sa SyrH; ἐπορεύθη (+ ο ανος ο 372) rel | ἤψατο] + ο ανηρ ο
θαπτομενος L 460 700; + ο ανος 55 245 342 554 Sa; + *is vir* SyrH ↗; cf. + *homo* Lat[115]
(apud 2 Kgs 10:30–319) | Ελισαιε B[c] V 127 64 55 158 372 Ra] ελισσεαι 93 | ελισεαι 108;
ελεισαιε B*; ελισσαιου 342 460 700; ελισσαιε rel | ἔζησεν καί ἔστη] εστη και ανεζησε
125 | ἔζησε] + *homo* Aeth; + *homo* Lat[115] (apud 2 Kgs 10:30–319)| ἔστη L 460 700]
ανεστη rel; + *et stetit* Aeth | ἐπί] υπο 82 d[-106]

3. The Reconstruction of Elisha's Death and Burial for a Critical Edition of the Hebrew Bible (*HBCE*) (II Kings 10. 30–30a-i)

Edition A

30 וַיֹּאמֶר יְהוָה אֶל־יֵהוּא יַעַן אֲשֶׁר־הֱטִיבֹתָ לַעֲשׂוֹת הַיָּשָׁר בְּעֵינַי |וּ|כְכֹל אֲשֶׁר בִּלְבָבִי עָשִׂיתָ לְבֵית
אַחְאָב בְּנֵי רְבֵעִים יֵשְׁבוּ לְךָ עַל־כִּסֵּא יִשְׂרָאֵל:
30a וֶאֱלִישָׁע חָלָה אֶת־חָלְיוֹ אֲשֶׁר יָמוּת בּוֹ
וַיֵּרֶד אֵלָיו | מֶלֶךְ־יִשְׂרָאֵל וַיֵּבְךְ עַל־פָּנָיו
וַיֹּאמַר אָבִי אָבִי רֶכֶב יִשְׂרָאֵל וּפָרָשָׁיו:
30b וַיֹּאמֶר לוֹ אֱלִישָׁע קַח קֶשֶׁת וְחִצִּים וַיִּקַּח אֵלָיו קֶשֶׁת וְחִצִּים:

30c וַיֹּאמֶר לְ|יֵהוּ| מֶלֶךְ יִשְׂרָאֵל הַרְכֵּב יָדְךָ עַל־הַקֶּשֶׁת וַיַּרְכֵּב יָדוֹ |יֵהוּ| וַיָּשֶׂם אֱלִישָׁע יָדָיו עַל־יְדֵי |יֵהוּ|הַמֶּלֶךְ:

30d וַיֹּאמֶר פְּתַח הַחַלּוֹן קֵדְמָה וַיִּפְתָּח וַיֹּאמֶר אֱלִישָׁע יְרֵה וַיּוֹר וַיֹּאמֶר חֵץ־תְּשׁוּעָה לַיהוָה וְחֵץ תְּשׁוּעָה בְ|יִשְׂרָאֵל|וְהִכִּיתָ אֶת־אֲרָם בַּחֲצֵרוֹת אֲשֶׁר עַל פְּנֵי שֹׁמְרוֹן| עַד־כַּלֵּה:

30f וַיֹּאמֶר לְ|יֵהוּ|מֶלֶךְ־יִשְׂרָאֵל הַךְ־אַרְצָה וַיַּךְ שָׁלֹשׁ־פְּעָמִים וַיַּעֲמֹד:

30g וַיִּקְצֹף עָלָיו אִישׁ הָאֱלֹהִים וַיֹּאמֶר לְהַכּוֹת חָמֵשׁ אוֹ־שֵׁשׁ פְּעָמִים אָז הִכִּיתָ אֶת־אֲרָם עַד־כַּלֵּה וְעַתָּה שָׁלֹשׁ פְּעָמִים תַּכֶּה אֶת־אֲרָם:

30h וַיָּמָת אֱלִישָׁע וַיִּקְבְּרֻהוּ וּגְדוּדֵי מוֹאָב יָבֹאוּ בָאָרֶץ בָּא שָׁנָה:

30i וַיְהִי הֵם קֹבְרִים אִישׁ |וַיִּקְרְבוּ לַקָּבֵר| וַיַּשְׁלִיכוּ אֶת־הָאִישׁ בְּקֶבֶר אֱלִישָׁע |וַיָּנֻסוּ|וַיֵּלֶךְ וַיִּגַּע הָאִישׁ בְּעַצְמוֹת אֱלִישָׁע וַיְחִי וַיָּקָם עַל־רַגְלָיו: |

30 ₁ G S T V]> M (haplo) || **30a** Lat (*et helisseus infirmatus est infirmitatem suam qua mortus est et descendit ad eum rex israel et ploravit super faciem eius dicens pater pater rector israel et eques eius*) ed A] > (↓ 13:14) M G S T V ed B || * אֵלָיו Lat (*ad eum*) ed A] + יוֹאָשׁ M G S T V ed B || **30b** Lat (*et dixit ad eum helisseus accipe arcum et sagittas accepit arcum et sagittas*) ed A] > (↓ 13. 15) M G S T V ed B || אֵלָיו M G (προς αυτον) T V] > Lat S (gram; equal) || **30c** Lat (*et dixit ad Ieu regem israel impone manum tuam super arcum et imposuit manum suam Ieu et superimposuit manus suas helisseus super manus Ieu regis*) ed A] > (↓ 13:16) M G S T V ed B || *₁) יֵהוּ) Lat (*Ieu*) ed A]> M G S T V ed B || *₂) יֵהוּ) Lat (*Ieu*) ed A] > M S T V ed B Ιωας G^B ο βασιευς G^L (explic) || *₃) יֵהוּ) Lat (*Ieu*) ed A] > M G S T V ed B || **30d** Lat (*et dixit aperi fenestram quae ab oriente est et aperuit et dixit helisseus sagittare et sagittavit et dixit helisseus sagitta salutis domini et sagitta salutis in Israel et percuties Syriam in Aseroth quae est contra faciem Samariae usque ad finem*) ed A] > (↓ 13:17) M G S T V ed B || בְיִשְׂרָאֵל Lat (*in israel*) G^L (εν Ισραηλ) ed A] בָאֲרָם M G^{BO} (εν Συρια) S T V ed B || * בַּחֲצֵרוֹת אֲשֶׁר עַל פְּנֵי שֹׁמְרוֹן Lat (*in aseroth quae est contra faciem samariae usque ad finem*) ed A] בַּאֲפֵק M G S T V ed B || Lat + *et aperuit fenestram secundam et dixit sagittare et sagittauit sagittam salutis domini et sagittam saluti israel et dixit helisseus percuties syriam totam* (gloss + dbl translat *totam – usque ad finem*) (עַד־כַּלֵּה - כַּלֵּה) > M G S T V || **30f** Lat (*et iterum dixit helisseus ieu regi israel percute in terram et percussit ter et stetit*) ed A] > (↓ 13:18) M G S T V ed B || וַיֹּאמֶר Lat ed A] pr וַיֹּאמֶר קַח הַחִצִּים וַיִּקָּח M G S T V ed B || יֵהוּ Lat (*ieu*) ed A] > M G S T V ed B || **30g** Lat (*et contristatus est homo dei pro eo et dixit si percussisses quinquees aut sexies tunc percutiebas syriam totam usque ad finem et nunc percuties syriam ter*) > (↓ 13:19) M G S T V ed B || עַד־כַּלֵּה M G (εως συντελειας) S T V] *totam usque ad finem* Lat (gloss; dbl translat *totam – usque ad finem* 30 || (?) כַּלֵּה - עַד־כַּלֵּה **h** sim Lat (*et mortuus est Helisseus et sepelierunt eum et piratae Moab venerunt in terram illam*) ed A] > (↓ 13:20) M G S T V ed B || שָׁנָה בָּא M G S T V sim Lat^{95} (*post annum*)] > Lat^{Vind} (equal) || **30i** sim Lat (*et factum est cum sepelirent piratae hominem unum accesserunt ad monumentum et proicerunt hominem in monumentum helissei et fugerunt et adplicitus est homo ossibus helissei et vixit homo et surrexit super pedes eius*) ed A] > (↓ 13:20) M G S T V ed B || * וַיִּקְרְבוּ לַקָּבֵר Lat (*accesserunt ad monumentum*) sim G^L (και ηγγισε το πειραστηριον αυτοις) ed A] אֶת־הַגְּדוּד וְהִנֵּה רָאוּ M G^B S T V ed B || וַיָּנֻסוּ Lat G^L (και εφυγον) ed A] > M G^B S T V ed B ||

Textual Commentary

30a-i Lat. As detailed in the discussion above, the narrative of Elisha's death and burial has two different placements, as preserved, mainly, in Lat. Taking the Latin text as a witness of the OG, it has been proposed that the OG *Vorlage* constitutes Edition A and an older stage in the typology of 2 Kings. The main text reconstructs here a retroversion into Hebrew of the Greek underlying the Old Latin and is compared in the apparatus to the text of Edition B (13. 14–20) and differences with M of this passage are noted with the usual marks for interruptions in the copy-text. Each verse of 30a-i is thus first indicated in the apparatus as absent from Edition B and then particular variants between the two text-types are discussed.

30a *אֵלָיו **Lat** (*ad eum*) **ed A**] + יוֹאָשׁ **M G S T V ed B** || The addition of the name of the king in 13:14 Ed B is consequent with the adscription of the episode to the reign of Joash in this edition of the text. Edition A keeps an older form of the text where the 'king of Israel' is not specified (cf. e.g. the episode of Ahab's death in 1 Kgs 22).

30b *וַיִּקַּח **Lat G^L S**] + אֵלָיו **M G^B** (προς αυτον) **T V** (**gram; equal**) || In this case, it seems that Lat is not a reflection of OG in the omission of אֵלָיו / πρὸς αὐτόν, but a freer adaptation of the text. There are some Greek codices which also attest the minor omission, but, given the incidental nature of the omission, it has been preferable to defer to the copy-text of the edition in this case.

30c *יֵהוּ **x3 Lat** (*Ieu*) **ed A**]> **M G S T V ed B** || In this case, Ed A is the text which specifies the name of the king, in agreement with the placement of the unit within Jehu's reign. It is conceivable that these readings were a secondary development of Ed A and that an earlier form of the textual unit in the redaction phase of the book just kept a generic designation 'the king' or 'the king of Israel'. In this sense, it is remarkable that in the second instance of the name, both the *kai ge* text and *L* disagree with M in 13:16 in choosing different grammatical subjects to explicitate ('Joash' or 'the king', respectively). This seems to indicate that the inclusion of the episode in two different reigns produced parallel 'waves' of minor literary adaptations where the king in question was noted. Even though it is likely that an older form of the unit did not include mentions to any king in particular, the present forms deduced from the witnesses seem to indicate that the addition of names could have been part of the aforementioned process of integration of the literary unit into its respective position in each edition; therefore, the editorial choice has been to keep them in Ed A (as they appear in the only witness of that text-type in its position, Lat) and to defer to the copy-text (M) for their inclusion or exclusion in Ed B.

30d *בְּיִשְׂרָאֵל **Lat** (*in israel*) **G^L** (εν Ισραηλ) **ed A**] בַּאֲרָם **M G^{BO}** (εν Συρια) **S T V ed B** || The two editions differ in the interpretation of the 'arrow of salvation'. Whereas the testimony of OG (Lat + G^L in 13:17) understands it as salvation 'in Israel', M and related versions, including the *kai ge* Greek, interpret 'against Syria'. Both meanings are equally supported by the context of the narrative and seem to derive from a divergence in early developments of the unit. The version attested by OG seems to display a more logical literary structure, as it presents a double bipartite form, with two 'positive elements' (arrow of salvation by the Lord, and of salvation in Israel) followed by the negative one which includes the actual recipient of Elisha's ritual incantation (Syria) and the place of its military defeat. Despite this literary evaluation, the readings would be probably to be considered equal, except for the fact that each of them represents one of the two main text-types.

30d ‏אֲשֶׁר בַּחֲצֵרוֹת עַל פְּנֵי שֹׁמְרוֹן‎*‏ Lat (*in aseroth quae est contra faciem samariae usque ad finem*) ed A] ‏בָּאֲפֵק‎ M G S T V ed B || The Latin text has a unique reading for the toponym of the place where the king of Israel would defeat the Syrians. Whereas the rest of the textual tradition reads 'Aphek', Lat reads 'Hazeroth'. The geographical location of either place is anything but transparent and it would not be appropriate to choose a preferred reading based on the geographical layout as a primary argument. On the other hand, the *literary* arguments rouses suspicions on the usage of 'Aphek', as the location features prominently in the defeat of the Syrians by Ahab in 1 Kgs 20 (G 21). In this case, it is possible that 'Aphek' is a *lectio facilior*, influenced by the idea of Syrians being defeated by divine intervention takes place 'canonically' at Aphek. On the other hand, it is difficult to explain the ed A term as an adaptation: it probably has no relation with the Exodus station (Num 11. 35; 12. 6) and could be a corruption (it is suggestive to think of a deformation of Hazor, which fits geographically due to its proximity to the Golan) or witness the extra-biblical evidence already commented above. In any case, this variant would have taken place on the level of the Hebrew text (as OG as attested by Lat just transcribes) and it constitutes, in its present state, the oldest form of the toponym attainable in ed A.

30e-f. The text of these two verses is especially complicated as Lat is alone in attesting a quite strange reading, which may or may not be reflecting earlier (Greek and Hebrew) *Vorlagen*: it narrates the opening of a second window with the king firing a second set of arrows and Elisha pronouncing a second prophecy, this time on the victory over the totality of Syria. The text of Lat is redundant with the previous verse. Although this is not something strange to the narration of ritual actions, the Latin texts presents some problems here: 1) The parallelism is slightly awkward, as the direct speech and narrative clauses do not agree when compared with 30d: 'and he said, "fire"; and he fired an arrow of salvation…' vs. 'and he said, "fire" and he fired; and Elisha said, "it is an arrow of salvation…"'; 2) the command-fulfilment sequence is also lost: 'and he opened another window…' vs. 'and he said, "opened a window to the East", and he opened it'; 3) whereas 30d has a clear connection between the window chosen (eastward-facing, in the direction of Syria) and the ritual performed, one cannot but feel that the 'another window' of 30e is too generic. This seems to indicate that the text attested by Lat was amplified to include a second firing of arrows. This inclusion fits nicely in the boundaries of a *Wiederaufnahme* which, nevertheless, cannot be properly appreciated unless a hypothetical Hebrew *Vorlage* of Lat is reconstructed:

‏וְהִכִּיתָ אֶת־אֲרָם בַּחֲצֵרוֹת אֲשֶׁר עַל פְּנֵי שֹׁמְרוֹן עַד־כַּלֵּה‎
‏וַיִּפְתַּח חַלּוֹן שֵׁנִי וַיֹּאמֶר יְרֵה וַיּוֹר חֵץ־תְּשׁוּעָה לַיהוָה וְחֵץ תְּשׁוּעָה בְיִשְׂרָאֵל‎
‏וַיֹּאמֶר אֱלִישָׁע תַּכֶּה אֶת־אֲרָם כלה‎

The *Wiederaufnahme* is marked by the two oracles of destruction of Syria, which in turn end with very similar adverbial references using the element *klh*. Even if at some point in the history of the Hebrew text there were two different forms (‏עד כלה‎, 'unto the end/destruction' — ‏כלה‎, 'in its entirety'), they are so similar graphically, morphologically and semantically, that confusions would have been likely.

The reasons for adding a second ritual action parallel to the first is not easy to discern. It is possible that the construction led to a bipartite ritual, where the first action implies a victory against Syria in a particular battle, whereas the second leads to the victory over the totality of Syria. It is hard to speculate beyond what the textual materials include, but it is possible that an earlier (pre-Kings as such) literary unit just included a shorter victory oracle and that the modification (based on the ritual action and Elisha's interpretation in 30f-g) were later developed from it as a means of justifying the resurgence of the Syrians as an opponent in later passages of Dtr. This, of course, is beyond the possibilities of reconstruction within the framework of the books of Kings themselves. Nevertheless, it is remarkable that Edition B in chapter 13 is also quite rough and prone to difficulties of interpretation: 13. 18 reads in M (ed B) וַיִּקַּח הַחִצִּים קַח וַיֹּאמֶר, this is, a second instance of asking the king to take arrows, missing in 30 f. Ed B does not continue the narrative with a parallel reference to shooting but with the king being asked to 'strike the earth' (30f and 13:18), with the number of times he does so becoming the basis for Elisha's interpretation of a temporary victory against Syria (30g and 13:19). It is hard to determine whether the narrative here also refers to shooting against the ground with the bow (as the previous actions and the reference to getting arrows in ed B would suggest) or whether the king is asked to hit the ground without firing his bow (stamping with his foot or perhaps manually sticking the arrow-points into the ground). All in all, it feels that the passage underwent a series of developments and changes and it is also possible that different versions or traditions of the units co-existed for a time. The form attested by Lat is very uniform, perhaps too uniform (as later literary uniformization would be possible), but it seems to deepen on a contradictory statement: that Jehu's total victory is prophesized when two verses later Elisha states that his wins will be temporary only. Is it possible that the account of the king striking the ground and Elisha's interpretation were part of the development of the text in its process to become part of Dtr / proto-Kings and, as it happens repeatedly in the history of the books, these points of expansion of a section preserve some of the older and rougher forms of Kings' 'ancestors'. Nevertheless, it is difficult (or just impossible) to trace the history of the process in its entirety or even to reconstruct the two versions of the text in all details. In any case, from the point of view of the history of the *book* and of the preparation of a critical edition in particular, the following points can be made:

1. There could have existed a simple, short unit consisting of a ritual action followed by an oracle of victory, similar to other ritual-oracle correlations involving aggression and/or weapons (cf. 1 Kgs 22:11). Reaching this unit is quite beyond the scope of an editor of the book and, even if it can be envisaged, it should not be developed as part of the edition, as it could pre-date the redaction of the book proper.

2. At some point in the textual tradition this unit could have been expanded into two parallel actions/oracles (as attested by Lat). The time frame of this process is hard to determine, but the linguistic features around *klh* could indicate that it happened on the level of the Hebrew. It is, nevertheless, hard to vouch for its originality / antiquity (as it could involve harmonization) and the editor has deferred to the copy-text in this case as in others, as it is not fully clear that the expansion in 30e is part of ed A.

3. As the book took form, the materials of 30f / 13. 18 would be added in order to give a narrative reason for Jehu's temporary victory against the Syrians. It is noteworthy that, again, the text is framed by a possible *Wiederaufnahme*, עד כלה... עד כלה. Evidently, all textual witnesses include the text of 30f / 13:18 and its presence would be essential for the inclusion of the ritual-oracle episode into the book of 2 Kings, but the redaction development has left different traces in the different editions: the repetition of the command of taking arrows in ed B 13. 18, which is missing from ed A 30 f.

4. It is possible that this differing elements of redaction typology were connected to other variants in the passage: the lack of agreement in the choice of a place for the prophesized battle ('Hazeroth' vs. Aphek) could indicate a secondary nature in the notice or detailed reference of the battle itself (with a possible earlier oracle just stating something like 'it is an arrow of salvation by the Lord and an arrow of salvation in Israel, and you shalt beat Syria until its end'.) As the oracle became part of an announcement of temporary victory due to the king's falling short in the second ritual action, the need of specifying a particular place and battle for the first proclamation of victory would be required by narrative logic.

30g וַיִּקְרְבוּ לַקֶּבֶר M G (ἕως συντελείας) S T V] *totam usque ad finem* Lat (gloss; dbl?) || Here, in agreement with the previous verses, the Latin text here has what seems to be a double reading *totam / usque ad finem*. As commented above, the double translation can only derive from the Hebrew itself and thus Lat is attesting a lost Greek intermediary (even though in this passage the reading might not be original to OG but a harmonization with the two previous verses), *πᾶσαν τὴν Συρίαν ἕως συντελείας, thus including the two possible readings of כלה. As both readings are equally possible (though the double reading is clearly unlikely to be earlier), the editor has deferred to the copy-text (M).

30h בָּא שָׁנָה M G S T V sim Lat[95] (*post annum*)] > Lat[Vind] (equal) || The main Lat witness, *Codex Vindobonensis*, does not include the phrase, which is attested in the totality of the manuscript tradition and also in a different Old Latin testimony, the marginal gloss Lat[95]. The omission or addition of a temporal marker is a minor variant which could have taken place at different phases of the textual tradition, without being even certain to determine whether it happened in the Hebrew text or at the level of translation. Therefore, the edition has deferred to the copy-text of M.

30i *וַיִּקְרְבוּ לַקֶּבֶר Lat (*accesserunt ad monumentum*) sim G[L] (και ηγγισε το πειραστηριον αυτοις) ed A] וְהִנֵּה רָאוּ אֶת־הַגְּדוּד M G[B] S T V ed B ||This verse includes some of the most visible differences between the two proposed editions, which seem to indicate that they were actually two different versions of this episode or short miraculous notice. In both cases, the text is confusing to a certain level and some accidents of transmission may have taken place, but, to a certain extent, they can be reconstructed: in Edition A, the dead man is a member of the band of rovers, who just toss his corpse casually in Elisha's grave and hurriedly depart. In Edition B, there seems to be an anonymous group of people who are performing a burial and, as they see the band of rovers approaching, they hurry the procedure and throw the body in Elisha's grave. Thus, in Edition A, a dead Moabite rover is resurrected, whereas in Edition B it would be an Israelite. Even though it is likely that both versions of the legendary notice may be independent, the version of Edition A would be unlikely to have derived from Edition B, as it relates the miracle to a foreigner, whereas the change in the opposite direction (having the resurrected man be an Israelite, see above) would be more conceivable from a certain theological point of view. Also, the syntax in M is quite awkward, as the subject (performers of the burial) is not clearly defined and only when the band of rovers appears later in the verse it becomes clear that they are not the group reflected by הם, as the *nota accusativi* indicates that they are the object (the group that is seen). In this case, the agreements between G^L (chapter 13) and Lat are remarkable and define the Old Greek text, which, in turn, leads to the Hebrew text adapted in this edition.

30i *וַיָּנֻסוּ **Lat G^L** (και εφυγον) **ed A**]> **M G^B S T V ed B** || The reading appears in Lat and G^L and would constitute the Old Greek text. It is not, as it would seem by the Latin witness, a substitution of the more generic וַיֵּלֶךְ, but an additional verb. The problem seems to derive from a misunderstanding of the periphrastic construction וַיֵּלֶךְ וַיִּגַּע, 'and as he touched' (somehow reflected in the S text, ܘ‌ܐܬ‌ܐ ܠܘܬ ‌ܐܪܝ‌ܐ ܩ‌ܒ‌ܪ‌ܐ ܘܓ‌ܥ‌ܘ ‌ܒ‌ܗ, ‌ܘ‌ܐܪܝ‌ܐ) as the verb 'to go' (referred to the people performing the burial, see the secondary change of G^L to a plural or the also secondary elimination of the verb reflected in Lat, as it would be redundant with the more specific וַיָּנֻסוּ). Therefore, the text of Edition A has included both verbs, the narrative one expressing the flight of the band and the periphrastic וַיֵּלֶךְ which M preserved, although its meaning in Edition B shifted to a main-clause, non-periphrastic form.

All in all, this preliminary edition of the Edition A of II Kings 10. 30+ tries to show the problems and challenges of an eclectic edition of the Hebrew text of Kings. Even though the Latin text is easily retroverted into Hebrew considering the intermediating Greek, it is not always a simple (or possible) task to define clearly the boundaries of Edition A: some expansions may have taken place in the level of the Hebrew text (v. 30e), but they may be later developments, as both editions of the Hebrew, A and B, would have continued to grow and change and the moment that, as proposed, Edition A became the basis for the OG (and hence OL) translation, some of these changes would have already affected the text. Thus, the editor's choice has been to leave out v. 30e as suspicious of harmonization-expansion. On another level, some of the evidence points towards earlier stages of the text which must have coincided with earlier phases of redaction of the book. Although these are important to understand the process of textual growth through inclusion and development of literary units, which, in turn, led to two different editions or text-types according to choices taken, there is a red line which cannot be crossed in a critical edition, which is reconstructing into the text the pre-history of the text. Thus, the inclusions and *Wiederaufnahmen* have not been cleared unless there was supporting textual evidence and reconstruction of constituent independent units has been carried out in the textual commentary. Edition B would, of course, have no text here, as the episode appears in Chapter 13 under a different king. Textually speaking, the episode appears in that location in all textual witnesses. Nevertheless, the editor's policy will be to avoid the inclusion of duplicate text (so the episode will not appear in Chapter 13 of Edition A) when there are clear indications of repetition / transposition in the available evidence.

▼ ABSTRACT The present paper approaches a well-known problem often overlooked in textual studies of the Hebrew and Greek books of Kings: the different position of textual units of different lengths (from single phrases to long narrative episodes) when the Old Greek text (as attested by the Antiochene manuscripts and related evidence, saliently the Old Latin version) is compared both to MT and to the LXX kaige recension. Often, these changes of placement are related to issues regarding the history of redaction of the books, which can be (partially) glimpsed (and at times even reconstructed) when the evidence is examined. The methodology of reflecting these diverging editions/redactions of the text in modern ongoing critical editions (the Göttingen *Editio Maior* of LXX and the eclectic *HBCE* editorial project of the Hebrew text) poses numerous problems for editors in the construction of both eclectic text and apparatuses. Our research has therefore included both a text-historical discussion of a meaningful case study of placement changes around the episodes of Elisha's death and burial (in chapter 13 of II Kings as per MT order) which is then followed by full textual samples of the Greek and Hebrew editions with a detailed text-historical commentary and editors' reflections.

DANIEL PROKOP

Can We Understand the Pillars of the First Temple without the LXX?

Textual and Iconographic Perspective

Over the years, countless attempts have been made to explain, describe and comprehend the twin pillars flanking the entrance to the First Temple. Their structure, dimensions, placement, elaborate ornamentation and enigmatic names, as well as various kinds of archaeological data have added to the range and complexity of the scholarly discussion. Numerous reconstructions of the twin pillars emerged. However, the only evidence of their existence, the biblical descriptions, remained unchanged.

Among the voluminous literature dealing with the pillars Jachin and Boaz we discern different tendencies regarding the treatment of the basic literary sources. Those scholars who are mainly concerned with the study of traditions and editorial history of the biblical descriptions find little opportunity to discuss the relevant archaeological evidence. By way of contrast, a scholar like T. A. Busink, who strongly emphasizes the importance of archaeological evidence, fails to offer a penetrating exegesis of the ancient sources. Furthermore, most exegetes focus only on the MT while effectively ignoring the Greek textual witnesses of III Kingdoms.

The aim of this paper is to set the evaluation of the textual sources within a greater and more comprehensive set of approaches necessary for reconstructing the appearance and the meaning of the twin pillars. Thus, I Kings 7. 15–22 will be examined from various perspectives: text critical, redactional, and archaeological (especially iconographic). Using multiple approaches we will be able to not only present a more robust picture of the twin pillars but also to examine more appropriately the difficulties in the biblical texts.

1. Textual Witnesses

The most important textual witnesses of I Kings 7. 15-22 are: the Masoretic text of *Codex Leningradensis* (here identical with that of the Aleppo Codex); *Codex Vaticanus*; *Codex Alexandrinus* and the Lucianic text (identical with the marginal glosses of the OL from Spanish Vulgates). Unfortunately, the Dead Sea Scrolls have yielded extremely limited material from I Kings and so contribute little to our investigation.

New Avenues in Biblical Exegesis in Light of the Septuagint
ed. by Leonardo Pessoa da Silva Pinto and Daniela Scialabba, Turnhout, 2022 (*SEPT*, 1), pp. 93–103
© BREPOLS ❧ PUBLISHERS   DOI 10.1484/M.SEPT-EB.5.127713

In III Kingdoms 7. 3-9 the witnesses of the LXX are especially beneficial as textual traditions since they have not been affected by kaige revision and may, therefore, preserve readings which are closer to the Old Greek. Notably, the Greek witnesses of III Kingdoms 7. 3-9 are quite similar, and divergences among them do not change the image of the pillars, which in the LXX is practically the same.

However, the text of III Kingdoms 7. 3-9 is quite different from the corresponding I Kings 7. 15-22.[1] The most important differences concern both details and outline of the description.

A) Details

– Comparing III Kingdoms 7. 3b with MT-Jeremiah 52. 21b one finds a striking correspondence. The most important is the agreement as regards the thickness of the pillars (most probably the bronze was four fingers thick) and the information that they were hollow (נָבוּב/τὰ κοιλώματα). These two details are most probably omitted in I Kings 7. 15b through homoioteleuton (skipping from הָעַמּוּד to הָעַמּוּד):[2]

I Kings 7. 15b: יָסֹב אֶת־הָעַמּוּד הַשֵּׁנִי

III Kingdoms 7. 3b: **τὸ πάχος τοῦ στύλου τεσσάρων δακτύλων τὰ κοιλώματα** καὶ οὕτως ὁ στῦλος ὁ δεύτερος

MT-Jeremiah 52. 21b:יְסֻבֶּנּוּ וְעָבְיוֹ אַרְבַּע אַצְבָּעוֹת נָבוּב

The other possibility is contamination at the level of the Greek text: at some point in the Greek text transmission a scribe took the phrase from Jeremiah (as a consequence of the tendency to assimilate to Jeremiah 52. 21b).

– According to the LXX, the circumference of the pillars is fourteen cubits instead of the twelve stated in the MT. The difference is most probably linked with the last part of III Kingdoms 7. 3 mentioned above, which is absent in the MT.
– I Kings 7. 17 speaks of seven nets understood as 'wreaths of chain' for each capital, while according to the LXX there was only one net for a capital.
– I Kings 7. 20 and III Kingdoms 7. 9 are totally different. While the MT speaks of the capitals, the bulge, the net and the pomegranates, the LXX (even LXX[A] which in all other verses closely follows the MT) refers to μέλαθρον, ἐπίθεμα (τὸ) μέλαθρον, and πάχει (LXX[L])/πήχει (LXX[B]). LXX[A]-III Kingdoms 7. 9 tried to merge the *Vorlage* of the LXX with the MT by an addition at the end of the verse about the pomegranates around the second capital (unluckily with a rupture: LXX[A] has five rows instead of two-hundred pomegranates in the MT).

---

1 *Septuaginta Deutsch*, ed. by Wolfgang Kraus and Martin Karrer (Stuttgart: Deutsche Bibelgesellschaft, 2009), p. 395.
2 Mordechai Cogan, *1 Kings: A New Translation with Introduction and Commentary*, AB, 10 (New York: Yale University Press, 2000), p. 262.

– The names of the pillars in III Kingdoms 7. 7 are Ἰαχούμ (LXX^{B,L}); Ἰαχούν (LXX^A) and βαλαζ (LXX^B); βααζ (LXX^L); βοός (LXX^A) in comparison to Jachin and Boaz in I Kings 7. 21.

B)   Outline of the Description

Verses 19–20 are in a different place in the Greek and Hebrew textual traditions. It seems reasonable to assume that LXX^{B,L} (which are the best representatives of the OG of III Kingdoms 7. 3-9)[3] reflect the original order placing vv. 19–20 after v. 21. Verses 19–20 are most probably inserted before v. 21 in the MT because it wants to continue the description of the capitals presented in vv. 16–18. Verse 22 (present only in the MT and in LXX^A) is a clear redactional insertion. The first part of the verse is a doublet from v. 19a. The second part announces the completion of the construction. Verse 22a (absent in LXX^{B,L}) forms an *inclusio* with v. 19. Notably, the verse which constitutes the point of insertion (I Kings 7. 18) is corrupt only in the MT (with pomegranates, instead of capitals, on top of the columns). In this case the transposition of vv. 19–20 could have been made under the influence of the process of a ring composition or *Wiederaufnahme*:[4] lotus design of the capitals (v. 19), rounded projection, net-work, pomegranates (v. 20), names of the pillars (v. 21), lotus design of the capitals (v. 22).

How does the LXX contribute to our understanding of the pillars? Greek witnesses are especially valuable in order to understand the placement of the pillars,[5] which is inevitably connected with their meaning. Were they merely structural pillars or rather objects which conveyed a symbolic meaning, or both?

2. Placement of the Pillars

Generally speaking, there are two basic options about the exact location of the columns and their function. They were either free-standing or they supported a porch-roof.

---

3   The similarity of LXX^A-III Kingdoms 7. 3-9 with I Kings 7. 15-22 (a comparison of I Kings 7. 20 with LXX^B shows that *Codex Alexandrinus* has tried to merge its *Vorlage* with the MT; I Kings 7. 22 has its counterpart only in LXX^A; the same arrangement of the text is shared by LXX^A and the MT) is due to the fact that it is the Hexaplaric text, edited by Origen for the purpose of harmonizing the Old Greek with the (proto-)MT text.

4   The resumptive repetition proves to be of help in drawing the dividing lines between the respective units; see Baruch Halpern, 'Sacred History and Ideology: Chronicles' Thematic Structure - Indications of an Early Source', in *The Creation of Sacred Literature: Composition and Redactions of the Biblical Text*, ed. by Richard Elliott Friedman (Berkeley: University of California Press, 1981), p. 59.

5   See more in Adrian Schenker, 'Die Kapitelle der Säulen Jachin und Boas: Gestalt und Funktion. Eine textgeschichtliche Untersuchung von 1 Kön 7:16-22 und 3 Kgt 7:4-9', in *Tempel, Lehrhaus, Synagoge. Orte jüdischen Lernens und Lebens. Festschrift für Wolfgang Kraus*, ed. by Christian Eberhart and others (Paderborn: Verlag Ferdinand Schöningh, 2020), pp. 193-204

2.1. Textual Perspective

Both in the MT and in the LXX[6] we find several possibilities as to the position the pillars were intended to occupy:

I Kings 7. 19	בָאוּלָם	κατὰ τὸ αιλαμ	III Kingdoms 7. 8
I Kings 7. 21	לְאֻלָם הַהֵיכָל	τοὺς στύλους τοῦ αιλαμ τοῦ ναοῦ	III Kingdoms 7. 7
		τοὺς δύο στύλους τῷ αιλαμ τοῦ οἴκου	III Kingdoms 7. 3
II Chronicles 3. 15	לִפְנֵי הַבַּיִת	ἔμπροσθεν τοῦ οἴκου	II Paralipomenon 3. 15
II Chronicles 3. 17	עַל־פְּנֵי הַהֵיכָל	κατὰ πρόσωπον τοῦ ναοῦ	II Paralipomenon 3. 17

Yet at a first glance the location of the pillars in I Kings 7 seems to be different from that in the second book of Chronicles. In I–II Kings, neither the MT (בָאוּלָם and לְאֻלָם הַהֵיכָל) nor the Greek witnesses (κατὰ τὸ αιλαμ and τοῦ αιλαμ τοῦ ναοῦ) explicitly place the columns 'in front of' the *ulam*.[7] Nevertheless, a more precise analysis permits us to conclude that both Kings and Chronicles could speak about the same location of the pillars. Apart from the fact that in Chronicles *ulam* is a religious and not architectural term, the pillars are located 'in front of' the house and the *hekal*, but not 'in front of' the *ulam*. This detail is significant in the light of the fact that the Chronicler knows the term *ulam* and used it with respect to the temple (cf. I Chronicles 28. 11; II Chronicles 29. 7, 17; 8. 12; 15. 8). Namely, 'in front of the *ulam*' he placed an altar (II Chronicles 8. 12; 15. 8), not the columns. Furthermore, לִפְנֵי and עַל־פְּנֵי do not exclude the possibility that the pillars were part of the porch,[8] supporting a kind of a canopy that might have projected 'in front of' the *ulam*, just

---

6 Among the Greek witnesses there are small differences which change nothing in the meaning of the texts except two variants in III Kingdoms 7. 3 (LXX[B] has merely τὸ αιλὰμ τοῦ οἴκου; MS e (52) has τη εισοδω).

7 This is true also for Josephus who has τοῦ προπυλαίου παραστάδα, 'by the doorpost of the vestibule' (Josephus, *Ant.*, 8. 78).

8 The Hebrew terms לִפְנֵי and עַל־פְּנֵי often express that one object is in direct contact with another (II Kings 4. 29, 31; I Kings 6. 21) and can also express that one object is facing or opposite another, i.e. not directly attached to the second object (Genesis 23. 17, 19; Numbers 3. 4). Applied to the temple architecture, they specify the position of the *ulam* before the temple, but they do not indicate whether the structure was directly annexed to the temple building (I Kings 6. 3; II Chronicles 3. 4). Thus, it is impossible to infer from the text whether the *ulam* and the pillars were attached to the temple building or whether they stood at some distance opposite the temple.

as in the temple model which will be analyzed below. The traditions preserved in the MT and in the Greek witnesses permit the conclusion that both bronze columns were located in the *ulam* rather than outside of it. This also finds support from III Kingdoms 7. 9 stating that above the pillars there was a μέλαθρον. In this way they cannot be free-standing.

It is difficult to establish the meaning of בָּאוּלָם. The expression suggests that the pillars were in the front hall of the temple. The interior position of the pillars is implied by the manuscript c₂ which instead of αιλαμ reads στοά ('roofed colonnade'; cf. Ezekiel 40. 18).[9] In place of בָּאוּלָם the LXX reads κατὰ τὸ αιλαμ, supported by a Hebrew manuscript variant: כָּאוּלָם. Since ב and כ are similar, they could be easily confused (as one of Kennicott's manuscripts attests). Thus, either ב is an error in the MT, or כ is an error in the *Vorlage* of the LXX. Both readings make sense and there are no certain criteria to prefer one over the other. However, in the context of the description, בָּאוּלָם seems to be more understandable. In the case of כָּאוּלָם, the text could mean: '(מַעֲשֵׂה שׁוּשַׁן) like that in the porch'.[10] The writer wanted to express that the new information about the four cubits (possibly referring to the diameter of the capitals) and about the form (מַעֲשֵׂה שׁוּשַׁן), refers to the same columns as described in v. 21 and that they were made for the porch of the temple. Wolfgang Zwickel proposed that it is a noun to be derived from the root אלם II ('to bind'). In this sense the expression באולם would mean 'in a bound form'.[11] But it is unlikely that the same word (אולם) is used in the same description just a verse later with different sense. Only the meaning referring to the location of the pillars is coherent. Thus, a reader or copyist tried to say that the reference was to the pillars from the *ulam* of the temple and nothing else.

From the textual point of view, in all probability the twin pillars were not free-standing. Firstly, in Kings, neither the MT nor the LXX explicitly place the columns 'in front of' the porch. Secondly, in Chronicles it is the altar that is located 'in front of' the *ulam*, and not the columns, which are placed 'in front of' the house and the *hekal*. Thirdly, לִפְנֵי and עַל־פְּנֵי do not exclude the possibility that the pillars were attached to the temple building. Fourthly, according to III Kingdoms 7. 9 there was a beam (μέλαθρον) above the pillars. Now we will consider what information the material culture remains can provide about the possible position and meaning of the twin pillars.

2.2. *Archaeological/Iconographic Perspective*

In addition to the textual remains, the non-epigraphic evidence brought to light by archaeologists constitutes another major source for illuminating the phenomenon of the pillars flanking the entrance to the First Temple. We will look at a pair of pillars

---

9   Takamitsu Muraoka, *A Greek-English Lexicon of the Septuagint* (Louvain: Peeters, 2009), p. 637.
10   Otto Thenius, *Die Bücher der Könige* (Leipzig: S. Hirzel, 1873), p. 101.
11   Wolfgang Zwickel, *Der Salomonische Tempel*, KAW, 83 (Mainz: von Zabner, 1999), p. 114.

at the entrance to the holy place known from temples of the Iron Age II Levant.[12] In this way we will be able to explain the significance of the location of the columns.

A pair of columns is a well-known design element of temple façades in various temples excavated in or around the Land of Israel. Of particular significance for our study are two pillars found in front of the entrance to the Iron Age temples at Tel Motza, 'Ain Dara and Tell Ta'yinat:[13]

- Tel Motza: The Motza temple, located in the Judean Hills *c.* 5 km west of Jerusalem and dated to the ninth century BCE. The pillars were located slightly inside the entrance to the temple.
- 'Ain Dara: The temple at 'Ain Dara in northern Syria, dated to the tenth/eighth centuries BCE. The temple is approached by steps ascending to an entrance way flanked by two columns. The pillars are located inside the porch. The threshold at the entrance has been carved with a pair of *c.* meter-long footprints between the pillars. A second step with only one footprint completes the ascent into the next room. Probably the footprints represent a great deity striding in to take his place in the innermost room.[14]
- Tell Ta'yinat: Tell Ta'yinat temple, located in southern Turkey and dated to the ninth century BCE. Before the entrance several steps ascend to a portico in which stood two pillars, only one of which was preserved. As in the 'Ain Dara temple, the pillars were slightly inset, but whether they supported a roof it is impossible to say.

---

12 Unfortunately, we do not have enough comparative material from the Levant of the Persian and Greco-Roman periods that could help us to investigate how the motif was used after the destruction of the First Temple. Nevertheless, from the objects found outside Palestine we conclude that twin pillars at the entrance to a holy abode appear in the Second Temple period: e.g. stele from Monte Sirai, Sulcis (Ida Oggiano, 'Lo spazio fenicio rappresentato', in *Saturnia Tellus: Definizioni dello spazio consacrato in ambiente etrusco, italico, fenicio-punico, iberico e celtico. Atti del convegno internazionale svoltosi a Roma dal 10 al 12 novembre 204*, ed. by Xavier Dupré Raventós and others, MSPC (Rome: Consiglio Nazionale delle Ricerche, 2008), pp. 283–300 (p. 290), fig. 5:6-7), Carthage (Oggiano, 'Lo spazio fenicio', p. 292, fig. 6:6), Ghorfa (Oggiano, 'Lo spazio fenicio', p. 294, fig. 7:2); coin from Lixus (Oggiano, 'Lo spazio fenicio', p. 295, fig. 8:1). In all cases the pillars were not free-standing but were attached to the doorframes or supporting a porch roof. Notably, in the course of time, instead of two pillars flanking the entrance to the building of worship we frequently find four, five or even eight columns (Oggiano, 'Lo spazio fenicio', p. 295, fig. 8:2-5).

13 With respect to the Arad temple (Stratum X, dated to the eighth century BCE) Aharoni interpreted two stones as bases for two pillars at the sides of the entrance from the court to *hekal* and compared them to the twin pillars of the First Temple; see Yohanan Aharoni, 'Arad: Its Inscriptions and Temple', *The Biblical Archaeologist*, 31/1 (1968), 2–32 (p. 19). If these were indeed pillars, their position very close to the wall shows that they did not have an architectural function. However, according to Herzog there were no such pillars, and he does not show the stone bases in his plans; see Ze'ev Herzog, 'The Fortress Mound at Tel Arad: An Interim Report', *Tel Aviv*, 29/1 (2002), 3–109 (pp. 67–68); 'Perspectives on Southern Israel's Cult Centralization: Arad and Beer-Sheba', in *One God - One Cult - One Nation: Archaeological and Biblical Perspectives*, ed. by Reinhard Gregor Kratz and Hermann Spieckermann, BZAW, 405 (Berlin: de Gruyter, 2010), pp. 169–200 (p. 189).

14 Ali Abou-Assaf, *Der Tempel von 'Ain Dara*, DamF, 3 (Mainz am Rhein: Philipp von Zabern, 1990), pp. 15-16.

The three temples above (Tel Motza, 'Ain Dara and Tell Ta'yinat) are clearly in the same architectural tradition, having twin pillars flanking the entrance to the long-room tripartite temple, and can be considered as roughly contemporary with the First Temple building activities in Jerusalem.[15] In all cases columns were either inside or offset from the entrance towards the front. Judging from remains of the temples with columns *in antis*, it seems that they were not free-standing.

Notably, the temple models suggest that the pillars at the entrance could have been detached from the porch and at the same time connected with it by a porch-roof protruding from the doorway.

Pottery temple models assist us greatly in the attempt to reconstruct the appearance of ancient structures. In many cases they are the only evidence we have of certain aspects of façades or superstructures. Significantly, many of them are flanked by two pillars as in the case of the temple in Jerusalem. For the purpose of this study the most important are:

- Temple model found at Tell el-Far'ah North, probably biblical Tirzah, in the northern Samaria hills, dated to the eighth century BCE.[16] It has a temple façade that features two fluted, stylized palm-tree columns, which take the form of pilasters on the sides of a doorframe.
- 'Jordanian' shrine models:[17]

  A) An elaborately decorated model shrine from the Moussaieff collection, possibly originating from northern Transjordan, dated to the tenth/ninth centuries BCE. The opening is flanked by two large female drummers connected to the entablature and surmounted by double volute capitals.
  B) Shrine model, dated to the tenth/ninth centuries BCE, with two pillars detached from the doorframe supporting roof construction. The capitals are decorated with drooping lotus leaves.
  C) Shrine model dated to the tenth/ninth centuries BCE. A porch carries two round detached columns with large rectangular capitals that are joined to the fronton.

---

15 Wolfgang Zwickel, 'Solomon's Temple, Its Cultic Implements and the Historicity of Solomon's Kingdom', in *Solomon and Shishak: Current Perspectives from Archaeology, Epigraphy, History and Chronology: Proceedings of the Third BICANE Colloquium Held at Sidney Sussex College, Cambridge 26-27 March, 2011*, ed. by Peter James and Peter G. van der Veen (Oxford: Archaeopress, 2016), pp. 148–54 (pp. 150-51).
16 Alain Chambon, *Tell el-Far'ah 1. L'âge du Fer* (Paris: Recherche sur les Civilisations, 1984), pp. 77-78, 241, pl. 66; Beatrice Muller, *Les 'maquettes architecturales' du Porche-Orient Ancien: Mésopotamie, Syrie, Palestine du IIIe au milieu du Ier millénaire av. J.-C.*, BAH, 160 (Beyrouth: Institut Français d'Archéologie du Proche-Orient, 2002), II, p. 146, fig. 143a-d. There is also a similar shrine model from Tel Rekhesh: in the front are traces perhaps of columns flanking the entrance, but now lost; see Nehemia Zori, *The Land of Issachar: Archaeological Survey* (Jerusalem: Israel Exploration Society, 1977), pl. 33:3–5.
17 So-called 'Moabite' shrine models lack provenance. A few fragments were found in scientific excavations in Jordan; see Raz Kletter, 'A Clay Shrine Model', in *Yavneh II: The 'Temple Hill' Repository Pit*, ed. by Raz Kletter and others, OBOSA, 36 (Fribourg: Academic Press; Göttingen: Vandenhoeck & Ruprecht, 2015), pp. 28–84 (p. 41).

D) Shrine model (dated to the tenth/ninth centuries BCE). A porch has two pillars applied into a doorframe, decorated with drooping lotus leaves, supported by lion protomes.

E) Shrine model from Karak, dated to the eleventh/ninth centuries BCE with two naked female figurines flanking the entrance, holding small frame drums.[18] They could be goddesses or participants in a cultic rite, which could have been connected with fertility.[19]

F) Shrine model dated to the tenth/ninth centuries BCE. Round pillars that have capitals with drooping lotus leaves support the roof construction and are detached from the entrance. There are two oval openings in the niche between the pillars.

G) Shrine model dated to the tenth/ninth centuries BCE. There are two square columns beside the door.

- Temple model from the city Khirbet Qeiyafa. The site was most probably within the territory of the Kingdom of Judah, dated to the eleventh/tenth centuries BCE. The applied decoration at the front creates a narrow porch, with two attached pillars decorated by horizontal 'rope' designs and topped by round knobs with vertical incisions, possibly capitals. The pillars rest on lion-shaped bases (only one survives).
- Shrine model found at Yavneh, originated from a Philistine temple, dated to ninth/ eighth centuries BCE. The door is flanked by two square pillars, detached from the sides by thin openings. The roof extends above the pillars, curving upward sharply.

Another evidence is a cult stand from Ta'anach. The so-called 'Lampstand', dated to the tenth century BCE, was found in a cistern. This stand has four levels (which could be viewed as the entrance to the shrine). In the top register: four-legged animal (bovine or a horse) between two voluted columns and a sun disc above them.

---

18 See also the similar motif of women at the entrance to a model shrine of unknown provenance (probably from Syria or Jordan), dated to the Bronze Ages in Muller, *Les 'maquettes architecturales'*, p. 173, fig. 165a-d. The women are also placed within the temple: the two defaced figures (apparently naked fertility goddesses with their hands holding their breasts) shown standing inside the façade of a pottery temple model found lying on the floor of Temple 131 of Stratum X in Tell Qasile (Philistine port town on the northern bank of the Yarkon river), dated to the eleventh/tenth centuries BCE; see Joachim Bretschneider, *Architekturmodelle in Vorderasien und der östlichen Ägäis vom Neolithikum bis in das 1. Jahrtausend: Phänomene in der Kleinkunst an Beispielen aus Mesopotamien, dem Iran, Anatolien, Syrien, der Levante und dem ägäischen Raum unter besonderer Berücksichtigung der bau- und der religionsgeschichtlichen Aspekte*, AOAT, 229 (Neukirchen-Vluyn: Neukirchener Verlag, 1991), pp. 229–30, no. 79, fig. 74, pl. 85; Wolfgang Zwickel, 'Die Keramikplatte aus Tell Qasīle: Gleichzeitig ein Beitrag zur Deutung von Jachin and Boas', *Zeitschrift des deutschen Palästina-Vereins*, 106/1 (1990), 57–62 (p. 57); Amihai Mazar, *Excavations at Tell Qasile: Part One: The Philistine Sanctuary: Architecture and Cult Objects*, Qedem, 12 (Jerusalem: Institute of Archaeology of The Hebrew University of Jerusalem, 1980), p. 82; Yosef Garfinkel and Madeleine Mumcuoglu, *Solomon's Temple and Palace: New Archaeological Discoveries* (Jerusalem: Biblical Archaeology Society, 2016), pp. 109-11.

19 Sarit Paz, *Drums, Women, and Goddesses: Drumming and Gender in Iron Age II Israel*, OBO, 232 (Fribourg: Academic Press; Göttingen: Vandenhoeck & Ruprecht, 2007), pp. 76-77.

From the evidence above we conclude that the pillars at the entrance to the temple in the material culture remains from the Iron Age II Levant were either part of a doorframe or they were detached from the entrance supporting a porch-roof. The temple models show that the façade of the temple and the columns are the only visible elements from outside. The forms of the pillars as well as decorative elements which accompany them clearly indicate that the columns were meant to provide visual information about the deity and its powers. Based on the data above, now we will try to answer the question concerning the meaning of the placement of the pillars of the First Temple.

2.3. Symbolic Meaning of the Placement of the Pillars

The placement of the pillars at the entrance to the temple reveals a certain religious conception. In all probability they were intended neither as merely structural pillars nor as decorative elements. The temple remains and shrine models give us a certain clue about the meaning of the position of the pillars at the entrance to the temple:

a) The pillars could mark the entrance of Yhwh into the temple, as did the pair of footsteps from the 'Ain Dara temple, which were remarkably placed on the same line as the twin pillars. The columns of monumental dimensions at the entrance to the temple would give the impression of huge doorposts between which the superhuman sized God entered into his earthly dwelling place. Since at 'Ain Dara there are no return footprints, one could infer that the deity entered the sanctuary long ago without ever leaving, suggesting a continued divine presence.

b) The twin pillars located at the entrance to the temple form a mediating space between God's dwelling place and the world outside. The tendency to separate these spaces can be seen in miniature temple models. Here the pillars are frequently extended forward before the entrance and supporting a porch-roof. In this way they form an additional space, mediating and separating the interior of the temple from the space outside. Also the complex structures of the temples with indirect access, known from archaeological excavations, highlight the separation between the temple and the profane place.

c) The location of the pillars at the entrance makes them the most visible 'element' of the temple. In this way they may be perceived as an ancient 'information board' visually describing the object. Their measurements, bronze inlay, and abundantly decorated capitals testified about the 'dweller' of the structure. The pomegranates and the lotus flower design of the capitals conveyed the message of continuous blessing and prosperity offered by God.

Conclusions

Can we understand the pillars of the First Temple without the LXX? Yes, we can. However, our understanding of the columns without the LXX would be very limited. In order to properly understand the biblical description of the object, all textual data (not only the MT) need to be taken into account. The result should be confronted with archaeological/iconographic remains. Only in this way we can properly (i.e. basing on all available sources) interpret the appearance and the meaning of the artifact. On the one hand, there are some nuances that only a text can preserve and no archaeologist could ever unearth. On the other hand, archaeology and iconography reveal certain aspects of the cultural, religious and political background of the object that are beyond the realm of written sources.

As we have seen it is difficult to define the exact placement and the meaning of the position of the twin pillars at the entrance to the First Temple. Were they structurally functionless or did they serve as loadbearing pillars in the building? From a literary point of view, the biblical descriptions seem to indicate that the twin pillars did in fact belong to the vestibule of the temple and that they were not free-standing. None of the textual traditions in the book of Kings explicitly place the columns 'in front of' the portico. Furthermore, the position of the pillars in Chronicles is described as 'in front of' the house and the *hekal*, and not 'in front of' the *ulam* (this is the position of the altar). Moreover, לִפְנֵי and עַל־פְּנֵי do not exclude the possibility that the columns were attached to the porch. Finally, a μέλαθρον was placed above the pillars (III Kingdoms 7. 9), thus they cannot be free-standing. The comparison with the Iron Age II Levantine temples at Tel Motza, 'Ain Dara and Tell Ta'yinat, built according to the principle of a central axis with a tripartite division and a pair of pillars *in antis*, gives us no compelling reason for imagining a much different position for the First Temple pillars. Judging from the placement of the basis of the columns *in antis*, which were at the line of the side walls or slightly extended towards the front, we conclude that most probably they were not free-standing. The analysis of the temple models has shown that the pillars at the entrance could have been detached from the porch and at the same time connected with it by a porch-roof protruding from the doorway. This might have been the position of the pillars of the First Temple. The placement of the columns at the entrance was not accidental, but rather conveyed a symbolic message. They could have looked like huge gateposts between which the supersized God would have come into the temple. Thus, the pillars signal the entrance of God to his earthly abode. Being placed exactly at the entrance to the temple they form a mediating space between the house of God and the outside world. This tendency to separate the spaces can be noted in the extended porticos from the temple models and the elaborate indirect access to the temples known from archaeological remains. Finally, the location of the pillars makes them the most visible part of the temple informing bystanders about the character of the building. The shrine models reveal that the various architectural motifs on the pillars or in the immediate vicinity express an idea about God inside the temple in symbolic language.

▼ ABSTRACT The columns referred to as Jachin and Boaz are certainly among the most controversial features of the First Temple of Jerusalem. The issue is complicated by the fact that the pillars are presented differently in Hebrew and Greek textual traditions. The aim of this paper is to show that without the Septuagint as well as archaeological and iconographic evidence our understanding of the columns will be very selective. Greek witnesses and archaeological data are especially valuable in order to understand the placement and symbolic meaning of the pillars. The textual evidence and archaeological remains seem to indicate that the twin pillars did in fact belong to the vestibule of the temple. They announce a continued divine presence, highlight the separation between the temple and the profane place and inform bystanders in a symbolic language about continuous blessing and prosperity offered by God.

CAMERON BOYD-TAYLOR

Haman through the Looking Glass

The Refraction of Genre in Greek Esther

The present study looks at the Septuagint version of Esther (LXX-Esth) through the lens of generic analysis. Until recently the discussion of genre in the book of Esther was dominated by a single question: whether the various iterations of the story aimed at sober historiography or mere entertainment.[1] Scholarly opinion has in the main shifted from the former to the latter. If Esther was traditionally read as a contribution to Judean history, and with reference to a work such as Chronicles, the trend now is to view it as a carnavelesque fiction.[2] Whether or not the latter characterization proves persuasive, the underlying dichotomy is unsatisfactory, and needs to be nuanced.

Although Greek historiography will provide the primary orientation for the study, its initial point of reference is so-called novelistic literature, past and present. This choice is motivated only in part by the current stream of scholarship which construes the book of Esther as a type of novel.[3] For while this approach has proven fruitful, it remains decidedly problematic, as it risks assimilating Esther to a model of literary composition closely tied to early twentieth century sensibilities. Rather the impetus is genre theory. Taking a cue from the seminal work of Mikhail Bakhtin and his circle, one may define novelistic literature not as a genre *per se* so much as a refraction of other genres.[4] From this perspective, the comparison of LXX-Esth with the novel gains critical traction. Our attention is drawn not only to its sophisticated use of narration and dialogue to represent an emotionally charged incident, but to

---

1 Adele Berlin, 'The Book of Esther and Ancient Storytelling', *JBL*, 120 (2001), 3–14.
2 Catherine Vialle, *Une analyse comparée d'Esther TM et LXX: Regard sur deux récits d'une même historie*, BEThL, 233 (Leuven: Peeters, 2010), p. xlvi.
3 See notably W. Lee Humphreys, 'The Story of Esther and Mordecai: An Early Jewish Novella', in *Saga, Legend, Tale, Novella, Fable: Narrative Forms in Old Testament Literature*, ed. by George W. Coats, JSOTSS, 35 (Sheffield: JSOT, 1985), pp. 97–113; Lawrence M. Wills, 'The Jewish Novellas', in *Greek Fiction*, ed. by John Robert Morgan and Richard Stoneman (London: Routledge, 1994), pp. 223–38; and Lawrence M. Wills, *The Jewish Novel in the Ancient World* (Ithaca, NY: Cornell University Press, 1995). See also Cameron Boyd-Taylor, 'Esther's Great Adventure: Reading the LXX Version of the Book of Esther in Light of its Assimilation to the Conventions of the Greek Romantic Novel', *BIOSCS*, 30 (1997), 81–113.
4 See especially Mikhail Bakhtin, 'The Problem of Speech Genres', trans. by V. W. Mcgee, in *Speech Genres and Other Late Essays*, ed. by Caryl Emerson and Michael Holquist (Austin, TX: University of Texas Press, 1986), pp. 60–102.

New Avenues in Biblical Exegesis in Light of the Septuagint
ed. by Leonardo Pessoa da Silva Pinto and Daniela Scialabba, Turnhout, 2022 (*SEPT*, 1), pp. 105–127
© BREPOLS ❧ PUBLISHERS   DOI 10.1484/M.SEPT-EB.5.127714

the ways in which the Greek translation interacts with a wide range of literary forms. According to the reading of LXX-Esth here proposed, a crucial dimension of its meaning arises from this interaction.

The approach is, broadly speaking, philological. Thus whatever is said about the genre of LXX-Esth needs to be located against the background of its textual history. While admittedly the genetic relationship between the extant versions of Esther is not altogether clear, there is a growing consensus that they are all, in one way or another, the literary offspring of a self-contained Hebrew prose narrative with the basic shape of the Masoretic text (MT-Esth).[5] Since we are dealing with differing versions of a common source, one may distinguish between the Esther narrative as such, and the telling of that story in a particular way, on the understanding that a given telling may complicate and defamiliarize the narrative in various respects. Such transformations extend to genre, which, I suggest, is the case with LXX-Esth.

A comprehensive study of genre in LXX-Esth would warrant a monograph. Deferring to the conventions of the essay form, I shall focus on one aspect of the Greek version, its use of fictive epistolography, with a view to both the translator's engagement with his Hebrew source, and his creative appropriation of other models. Following a brief introduction to generic analysis, I take up the topic of generic complexity, a characteristic strategy of both novelists and historians, for which the embedded letter serves as an example. I turn next to the two royal letters recorded in LXX-Esth (Additions B and E), before engaging in a close reading of B (which · according to the narrator was dictated by Haman) with reference to its generic affiliations and communicative strategy. In the final section I situate Haman's letter within the overall narrative strategy of the Greek translation, a strategy indebted to certain Greek models, and congruent with a significant trend in late Hellenistic Jewish literature.

1.   Genre Matters

By literary genre one generally has in mind the classification of texts. Within the Western critical tradition, a tripartite distinction between epic, dramatic and lyric has long held sway,[6] though more elaborate schemes have been on offer. Thus Polonius divides drama into: 'tragedy, comedy, history, pastoral, pastoral-comical, historical-pastoral, scene individable, or poem unlimited'.[7] Yet to the extent that there is a common thread in contemporary genre theory, it is the movement away from

---

5   See Cameron Boyd-Taylor, 'Esther and Additions to Esther', in *T&T Clark Companion to the Septuagint*, ed. by James K. Aitken (London: Bloomsbury, 2015), pp. 203–21.

6   John Frow, *Genre*, The New Critical Idiom Series (London: Routledge, 2006), pp. 59–63.

7   William Shakespeare, *Hamlet*, ed. by Anne Thompson and Neil Taylor, Arden Shakespeare (London: Thompson, 2006), p. 262, 2. 2. 334–36. Polonius adds two further combinations in the Folio version: 'tragical-historical' and 'tragical-comical-historical-pastoral'. In this regard, it is worth noting that the title pages of the first two quartos of the play refer to *The Tragicall Historie of Hamlet*. Thompson and Taylor remark that the neoclassical critics deplored such mixed genres.

such taxonomic preoccupations (valid though they may be),[8] towards a functional analysis. One looks to the role of genre in the composition and interpretation of texts, not merely as so many descriptive labels, but constitutively. While there are other ways of thinking about genre, this approach is particularly congenial to philological investigation, a hallmark of which is its concern for historical contextualization.[9]

Adopting the formulation of Marko Juvan, genres are 'cognitive and pragmatic devices for intertextual pattern-matching'.[10] Such matching is to be understood in terms of family resemblance, and with reference to exemplars, 'such that texts or textual sets become generic prototypes by virtue of intertextual and meta-textual interaction'.[11] Genre thus represents a form of rule following.[12] The salient features of a genre are extrapolated by readers from exemplary instances, and then function as normative constraints in their subsequent dealings with texts.[13] Like all rules, their application involves practices of negotiation within a discursive community. Conventions emerge in the give and take of speech, and may then be codified in some manner, but need not be; they may simply be manifested in a shared inclination to match up texts one way rather than another, and to aim for some measure of consistency in so doing.[14]

Granted that readers engage in such intertextual pattern matching, and that they are inclined to extrapolate and negotiate rules, the question arises as to what sort of rules one is talking about. A way forward is offered by Umberto Eco, who, with an eye to semiotic analysis, likens them to intertextual frames.[15] Such frames schematize

---

8   See Benjamin G. Wright III, 'Joining the Club: A Suggestion about Genre in Early Jewish Texts', *DSD*, 17 (2010), 260–85 (p. 263): 'It does seem, however, that the tack taken by biblical scholars over the years — one that is primarily classificatory or definitional and that relies on lists of features — for the most part has been set aside in contemporary genre studies'.

9   James Turner, *Philology: The Forgotten Origins of the Modern Humanities* (Princeton, NJ: Princeton University Press, 2014), p. 164.

10 Marko Juvan, 'Generic Identity and Intertextuality', *Comparative Literature and Culture*, 7/1 (2005), 1–11.

11 Juvan, 'Generic Identity', pp. 1–11. See Wright, 'Joining the Club', p. 263: 'Among the different theories about genre, one that seems to me to offer the possibility of thinking fruitfully about the relationships among texts and genres is prototype theory, which begins from the position that we should look at literary categories along the same lines that people create other mental categories'.

12 For a discussion of rule following, see Philip Petit, *The Common Mind: An Essay on Psychology, Society, and Politics* (Oxford: Oxford University Press, 1996), pp. 65–66, 81–105.

13 See Frow, *Genre*, 10: 'In using the word "constraint" I don't mean to say that genre is simply a restriction. Rather, its structuring effects are productive of meaning; they shape and guide, in the way that a builder's form gives shape to a pour of concrete, or a sculptor's model shapes and gives structure to its materials'.

14 Boundaries are fuzzy; disagreement is possible; fallibility is assumed. Yet this is not to imply that genre is an arbitrary or subjective construct. Intersubjective agreement serves as a kind of regulative ideal; again, this is implicit in the idea of rule-following. One must also take into account the ostensive use of genre labels by speakers, and the place of such categories both in textual production as such, and in associated discourses.

15 Umberto Eco, *The Role of the Reader: Explorations in the Semiotics of Texts* (London: Hutchinson, 1981), p. 21. See also Boyd-Taylor, 'Esther's Great Adventure', pp. 95–96; Leroy Andrew Huizenga, *The New Isaac: Tradition and Intertextuality in the Gospel of Matthew*, NT.S, 131 (Leiden: Brill, 2009), pp. 56–57.

the reader's narrative and rhetorical knowledge, thereby guiding the inferences he or she makes in the course of reading a text, creating expectations which are then confirmed or disconfirmed as the case may be.[16] Understood thus, genre rules provide the generative matrix for 'the assumptions, the codes, and strategies operated by the writer and the audience he was addressing'.[17] Every text may be said to presuppose a 'model reader' (using Eco's terminology), who possesses the intertextual knowledge requisite to understanding. Catherine Vialle, *apropos* the book of Esther, aptly speaks of the 'pacte de lecture' between the narrator and the reader.[18]

Generic analysis, as Juvan observes, is inherently bifocal. From one perspective there is 'the working (influence) of semantic, syntactic, and pragmatic features of prototypical texts on their literary offspring'.[19] This orientation, which looks to the text's production, is especially relevant to a philologically motivated study, for one's sites are fixed squarely on historically situated authors and the repertoire of generic conventions available to them.[20] Insofar as the latter are drawn from exemplary texts and established performance practices, they are relatively stable; nevertheless they are actively negotiated and undergo transformation.[21] By situating the production of a text with reference to its generic precursors one may trace subtle shifts in authorial strategies, sensibilities, and habits of interpretation.[22]

Juvan's second focus of generic analysis is retrospective. From this stance one tracks the 'meta-textual descriptions and intertextual derivations or references,

---

16 A point nicely articulated by Christiane Sourvinou-Inwood, *'Reading' Greek Death: To the End of the Classical Period* (Oxford: Clarendon Press, 1996), pp. 3–4. Michael Caesar, *Umberto Eco: Philosophy, Semiotics and the Work of Fiction* (Oxford: Blackwell, 1999), delineates a possible hierarchy: i) *fabulae*, which script a sequence of events, and are typified by the folk tale; ii) motif frames, which specify certain recurrent elements but no fixed sequence, as with the Gothic; iii) typical situations like the shoot-out in a Western; and iv) tropes and rhetorical topoi. The configuration of a specific genre will depend upon the type of discourse in which it features.

17 Sourvinou-Inwood, *Greek Death*, p. 4.

18 Vialle, *Analyse Comparée*, p. xlvii.

19 Juvan, 'Generic Identity', pp. 1–11.

20 This need not imply a theory of genre. It always remains an open question to what extent authors and readers have recourse to explicit genre concepts. Yet to be culturally literate to any degree involves competence in the use of genre rules.

21 See Sune Auken, 'Genre and Interpretation', in *Genre and...* , ed. by Sune Auken, Palle Schantz Lauridsen and Anders Juhl Rasmussen, Copenhagen Studies in Genre, 2 (Copenhagen: Ekbátana, 2015), pp. 154–83 (p. 159): 'genres have a strong regulative influence on our interpretation of a given utterance or situation. This influence, however, is of a special nature, as regulations imposed by genre can be broken at a moment's notice or made the subject of manipulation or interpretation. Depending on the character of this break, it can lead either to an ingenious use of the genre, to a break between genre and utterance, or to a work that moves into, or even defines, an entirely different genre'.

22 This phenomenon is well illustrated by trends in so-called genre fiction. Taking the mystery novel as a prime example, one might, for instance, view the work of Agatha Christie as exemplary for English speaking authors of the 1930s. A writer such as Dorothy Sayers achieved specific literary effects in her novels precisely through establishing a strong family resemblance to such precursor texts. On the other hand, Philip Chandler's transposition of the genre to the back-alleys of San Francisco marks a more radical transformation. See Charles Brownson, *The Figure of the Detective: A Literary History and Analysis* (Jefferson, NC: McFarland & Co., 2014).

which establish or revise retroactively the hard core of genre pattern.[23] Within the reception of a text generic interventions can occur involving categories which, although unavailable to the author, bear significantly on interpretation. This may or may not involve cultural changes in reading practices. Either way the significance of the text may shift — together with its generic identity — resulting in new readings.[24] This is perhaps inevitable within a literary tradition, in which later texts influence the reading of earlier ones; so too it is a feature of the various learned discourses that attend such a tradition. No less relevant to philology, these classifications underscore the diachronic dimension of genre formation.[25]

The fact that LXX-Esth is a translation obviously has a decisive bearing on the present analysis, as it raises distinct interpretative problems. Translation may be regarded as a special case of textual reception given that it results in the production of a new text. In this respect it is akin to such practices as redaction, adaptation, quotation, plagiarism, and forgery. To what extent it differs categorically from other kinds of re-writing will depend upon the translator's methods and purposes, and the normative environment within which he or she is working.[26] Such factors will determine the degree, quality and cultural significance of transfer from the source.

With respect to its production and redaction, LXX-Esth has a number of intriguing features. Where the translation parallels MT-Esth, it tends to follow the phraseology of the Hebrew closely, and in this respect one might speak of textual transfer.[27] Yet

---

23 Juvan, 'Generic Identity', pp. 1–11.
24 A striking example of this sort of development is Film Noir. Initially used in reference to a handful of Hollywood films released during the Second World War, the impact of the term was negligible at first, yet it was taken up decades later, and would subsequently exert a decisive influence on the reception of a wide range of films from the 1940s and 1950s. A movie produced in accordance with the conventions of detective fiction, reclassified as Noir, is a work transformed: its family resemblance to exemplary works in the genre is now integral to its significance; the quality of attention it receives differs; it becomes subject to specific discursive practices, and commentary of various sorts attach to it; and, finally, as its status shifts, the material and social circumstances of its viewing change. See William Park, *What Is Film Noir?* (Lewisburg, PA: Bucknell University Press, 2011).
25 See Hindy Najman, 'The Idea of Biblical Genre: From Discourse to Constellation', in *Prayer and Poetry in the Dead Sea Scrolls and Related Literature: Essays in Honor of Eileen Schuller on the Occasion of Her 65th Birthday*, ed. by Jeremy Penner, Ken M. Penner and Cecilia Wassen (Leiden: Brill, 2012), pp. 307–21 (p. 313), *apropos* the retrospective classification of texts by readers through recourse to exemplars: 'This approach promises, I think, to be particularly fruitful for biblical and Dead Sea Scrolls studies, because it captures something central to Second Temple text production: namely, the process of producing new texts by rewriting, recasting and expanding pre-existing and already authoritative texts'.
26 Adapting a typology delineated by Gideon Toury, *Descriptive Translation Studies — and beyond* (Amsterdam: John Benjamins, 1995), pp. 170–71, we may distinguish between three types of transfer: linguistic, textual, and literary. All three may interact with the generic features of the text. For an application of this typology to ancient Jewish translation, see Cameron Boyd-Taylor, 'Toward the Analysis of Translational Norms: A *Sighting Shot*', BIOSCS, 39 (2006), 27–47.
27 The prose is relatively paratactic, which would likely have marked the text as a Greek-Hebrew translation: absent are some of the characteristic ways in which Greek literary prose is given cohesion. Yet this feature may well have been perceived by ancient readers as desirable. Parataxis in Greek prose narrative is suggestive of oral storytelling and communal tradition; at the same time, the foreignizing style that results perhaps enhanced the text's authority as a translation.

if there is a tendency in places towards formal representation of the source, there are also numerous occlusions and elaborations. Some of these changes deliberately approximate Greek prose conventions; others impact on the literary features of the text. Finally there are six extensive expansions or so-called Additions (comprising some 107 verses) with significant implications for its generic affiliations. In LXX-Esth one discerns both the working of the source text, and a process of retroactive revision.

Ideally one would want to contextualize these literary developments with some degree of historical precision. Unfortunately the date and provenance of LXX-Esth remain uncertain, and one must be content with scholarly conjecture.[28] A date in the late Persian or early Hellenistic period is probable for the original Hebrew narrative. The *terminus ad quem* of the Greek version is 93–94 CE, at which time it was paraphrased by Josephus (*Ant.*, 11. 184–296). There are indications of an earlier date for the translation, including most notably the colophon, which likely refers to the fourth year of the reign of Ptolemy XII Auletos and Cleopatra V (78/77 BCE). Hence I shall proceed on the assumption that the translation was undertaken at some point during the late second or early first century BCE. As to provenance, the colophon states Jerusalem, and this remains a possibility. Although Alexandria is widely mooted in the literature, the evidence cited is by no means conclusive, and a more complex history of translation and redaction involving both Coele-Syria and Egypt is possible.[29] Wherever it was undertaken, LXX-Esth is firmly situated in the literary culture of the late Hellenistic Greek speaking Near East, as will become apparent in the following sections.

2. Simple and Complex Genres

On the present view, the phenomenon of genre is bound up with our communicative purposes. This is due to the fundamental connection between genre and speech situation, such that a given genre mobilizes the specific package of background assumptions without which a successful speech act would be impossible.[30] Following Bakhtin, one may distinguish genres according to the complexity of the situations they evoke.[31] Whereas some are tied to particular speech acts and embedded in typical social exchanges, others comprise a multiplicity of different acts and arise in highly developed contexts.[32] Simple genres, which Bakhtin referred to as primary, are in a sense univocal: the 'I' of the speech act addresses his or her interlocutor as a unitary

---

28 See Boyd-Taylor, 'Esther and Additions', pp. 203–05.

29 Carey Moore, *Daniel, Esther and Jeremiah: The Additions*, AB, 44 (Garden City, NY: Doubleday, 1977), p. 191.

30 Frow, *Genre*, p. 30.

31 Bakhtin, 'The Problem of Speech Genres', pp. 61–62.

32 Bakhtin, 'The Problem of Speech Genres', p. 62: 'Secondary (complex) speech genres — novels, dramas, all kinds of scientific research, major genres of commentary, and so forth — arise in more complex and comparatively highly developed and organized cultural communication (primarily written) that is artistic, scientific, sociopolitical, and so on'. See also Frow, *Genre*, pp. 29–50.

subject.[33] When a primary genre is embedded within some larger speech situation, the result is a play of voices (or *heteroglossia*).[34] A favoured example is reported speech, which expresses the active relation of one message (that of the speaker, 'I') to another (that of the person who is quoted, 'he or she').[35]

For Bakhtin the modern European novel — in particular the work of Dostoyevsky — represents the exemplary model of a secondary genre, absorbing a range of voices from the larger culture, and thus activating different social realities; yet John Frow is right to ask whether any genre is inherently univocal, and, conversely, why the novel should be privileged, when there are obviously other literary forms that are multi-vocal.[36] He therefore prefers to speak in terms of relative complexity, such that a complex genre is one built out of references to other genres, whether through allusion, stylization or quotation. Any simple genre can become complex in this way, at least in principle, though the novel remains paradigmatic for its incorporation of diverse genres. With complexity comes the sort of displacement one associates with literature, since to incorporate one genre within another is to detach the former from its social moorings and render it a thematic object.[37]

The typical features of written correspondence nicely illustrate Bakhtin's concept of a simple genre. One may describe the primary speech situation of a letter as a mediated exchange between two spatially separated people, such that the speaker ostensibly addresses his or her interlocutor as a unitary subject.[38] The embedding of a letter within a narrative context, in turn, is a textbook example of how generic complexity gives rise to *heteroglossia*. The primary situation is retained but subordinated to a third-person speech situation in which it works *inter alia* as an expression of the speaker's character.[39] We are well reminded that the genealogy of the modern novel includes epistolary fiction, which given its interest in characterization, is telling.

---

33 Frow, *Genre*, p. 40.
34 David Lodge, *After Bakhtin: Essays on Fiction and Criticism* (London: Routledge, 1990), pp. 28–29, notes that an important point of reference for Bakhtin's analysis is Plato's discussion of poetics in the *Republic*, 3. 392d3–394c, where Socrates distinguishes between διήγεσις, which represents action in the poet's voice, and μίμησις, which represents it in the voices of the characters. The former is exemplified by dithyramb, the latter by drama. Epic represents a mixed form, alternating between the poet's speech and that of the characters. Plato illustrates this point by rewriting the opening scene of the Iliad as a διήγεσις, transposing quoted speech into reported speech. Lodge remarks that this exercise inadvertently demonstrates the potential within prose narrative for a mixing of the two modes, such that not only speech, but thoughts and feelings can be expressed, a potential fully realized in the technique of indirect narration mastered by authors such as Jane Austen, but not altogether absent in ancient prose narrative.
35 Frow, *Genre*, p. 43.
36 Frow, *Genre*, p. 45. It may be worth noting that an academic paper with direct quotation is multi-vocal.
37 From a semiotic point of view such complexity can be understood as a form of overcoding. See Eco, *Role of the Reader*, pp. 19–22. On the assumption that simple genres represent codes (carrying any of a range of cultural values, whether political, aesthetic, ethical), when one genre is embedded within another, its codes are selectively activated.
38 Frow, *Genre*, p. 47.
39 Frow, *Genre*, p. 47.

Generic complexity is exploited to varying degrees in ancient prose narrative and offers a useful vantage point on the production of LXX-Esth. It should be stressed at the outset that LXX-Esth shares many of the salient features of the other extant versions, including MT-Esth. Each is characterized by complexity, and this may be presupposed of the Hebrew source upon which LXX-Esth drew, which evidently contained both narrative exposition and reported speech. Viewed genetically, what LXX-Esth tends to do is elaborate upon this complexity; in this respect it likely continued a process already underway in its source material. This is obviously true of the so-called Additions, some of which may pre-date the Greek translation; others, such as the two letters, were perhaps introduced by a Greek redactor. Yet they are all part of a larger literary historical *Tendenz* which also includes the core of the Hebrew-Greek translation: LXX-Esth is more than the sum of its additions. Although looking specifically at the letters, I shall endeavour to keep this larger picture in view.

3. LXX-Esther and Greek Epistolography

The story of Esther, in the Hebrew version which comes down to us, turns on the promulgation of two royal commands. At MT-Esth 3. 12 the royal scribes are summoned to transcribe a document ordering the annihilation of the Judeans; it is translated into the various languages of the empire, and copies bearing the royal seal are duly sent out to the provincial officials by courier. The royal scribes are again summoned at MT-Esth 8. 9, and a document that effectively rescinds the order of the first is copied, translated, and sent out. While it is common to refer to these two documents as 'edicts' (*NRSV*), they are in fact the written conveyances (ספרים) of an inherently oral speech act, the king's instructions to his officials. One cannot be sure exactly what form they take within the narrative world of MT-Esth; in the world of LXX-Esth each text is specifically referred to as an ἐπιστολή, a term that would have evoked specific generic expectations for a Greek reader.

In Attic Greek the word ἐπιστολή (singular and plural) can denote anything sent by a messenger, whether oral or written.[40] Usage varies. Thus Thucydides extends the term to both oral and written messages, while Xenophon and the orators reserve it for the written form.[41] By the time LXX-Esth was translated it is regularly used in reference to the latter; ἐπιστολή and ἐπιστολαί occur frequently in the papyri for both private letters and official documents, including administrative orders. Letter writing had become a part of everyday life in certain spheres of Hellenistic society, and one sees the gradual development of a culture of letters, which, in turn, had an impact on

---

40 The form ἐπιστολή is derived from ἐπιστέλλειν, and the motivating background is evidently the sending of a communication over a certain distance. Compare the use of βύβλος or βυβλίον and δέλτος, motivated (metonymically) by writing materials; and γράμματα (alphabetic letters), from γράφειν (to write), motivated by the act of writing. See Martin Luther Stirewalt, *Studies in Ancient Greek Epistolography* (Atlanta: Scholars Press, 1993), pp. 67–87.

41 Rosenmeyer, *Epistolary Fictions*, pp. 19–20.

education.[42] The letter was thus not only a named genre (as one would expect), but a highly codified one; there were defined subgenres — the personal letter; judicial plea; administrative report; royal letter — each with its own conventions. It was an object of discourse (letter writing was analyzed and evaluated); moreover, the practice was institutionalized (knowledge of the genre was acquired within relatively formal settings).

The earliest normative reflections on letter writing that come down to us are those of Demetrius, *De elocutione*, 223–35, which probably dates to the middle of the second century BCE.[43] For Demetrius the letter is distinguished by a set of relatively fixed rules: undue length is to be avoided; it should be written in a mixed style combining the elegant and the plain, with a friendly tone and moderately free structure.[44] Manuals on letter writing circulated widely. Pseudo-Demetrius, *Letter Types*, which may date to as early as the second century BCE, offers examples of forms to be chosen according to occasion.[45] It would appear to have been addressed principally to public administrators. Paola Ceccarelli concludes that for ancient theorists and practitioners alike, the genre of epistolography encompassed writings of various types, and it was important to follow the rules specific to each.[46]

The narrator of LXX-Esth states that what is recorded in both instances are verbatim copies of original ἐπιστολαί: B.1 τῆς δὲ ἐπιστολῆς ἐστιν τὸ ἀντίγραφον τόδε; E.1 ὧν ἐστιν ἀντίγραφον τῆς ἐπιστολῆς τὰ ὑπογεγραμμένα. Within the narrative world of the Greek version, both B and E are presumably Aramaic-Greek translations. According to current scholarly consensus, however, they were actually produced in Greek. Carey Moore concludes that their literary style is such as to rule out the possibility of translation from a Semitic *Vorlage*, citing the 'florid and diffuse' character of the Greek in contradistinction to the language of Additions of A, C, D, and F, where the style is simple and straightforward.[47] Comparison with the letters of Ezra-Nehemiah underscores this point; more instructive still is a comparison with the parallels in Targum Sheni.[48] The highly artificial language of B and E, with its Atticistic pretensions, is aimed at a culturally literate Greek speaking audience; both letters likely come from the same author; each, in turn, has been specifically crafted for its place in the narrative. Prescinding from the matter of sources, we see

---

42   William Vernon Harris, *Ancient Literacy* (Cambridge, MA: Harvard University Press, 2009), pp. 127–28.

43   Paola Ceccarelli, *Ancient Greek Letter Writing: A Cultural History (600 BC – 150 BC)* (Oxford: OUP, 2013), p. 3.

44   Ceccarelli, *Ancient Greek Letter Writing*, p. 4.

45   Ceccarelli, *Ancient Greek Letter Writing*, p. 5. See Abraham Malherbe, *Ancient Epistolary Theorists* (Atlanta: Scholars Press, 1988), p. 2, for dating and authorship, as well as the text (pp. 31–41).

46   Ceccarelli, *Ancient Greek Letter Writing*, p. 6.

47   Moore, *Additions*, p. 193. This conclusion has been independently confirmed by Raymond A. Martin, 'Syntax Criticism of the LXX Additions to the Book of Esther', *JBL*, 94 (1975), 65–72, through detailed syntactical analyses.

48   Moore, *Additions*, p. 195. Charles V. Dorothy, *The Books of Esther: Structure, Genre and Textual Integrity*, JSOT.S, 187 (Sheffield: Sheffield Academic Press, 1997), p. 92, concurs. While the Greek and Aramaic versions of the letters share certain motifs, direct literary dependence may be ruled out.

the working of Greek prototypes in the semantic, syntactic, and pragmatic features of these texts. In a word, B and E are the literary offspring of Greek epistolography.[49] Erich Gruen stresses that they are marked as literary compositions, and, as such, adhere to an understood convention: 'No one was deceived'.[50]

What I shall call fictive epistolography is widely attested in ancient Greek literature.[51] Fictive here denotes a literary composition that is produced for a context external to the primary speech situation (here, the nexus between sender and recipient). The genre was deployed in various ways, but in Greek prose narrative prior to the imperial period (to the extent that it is known to us), such compositions are typically embedded within established non-fictive literary forms such as historiography.[52] With respect to the 'pacte de lecture', such texts are thus not fictional in the modern sense of make-believe. Rather, as Tim Whitmarsh suggests, their epistemic value appears to have been located in the liminal space between make-believe and public record, a space in which communal memory may figure. Arguably, it was only near the end of the Hellenistic age that one finds a distinct genre of extended Greek prose narrative emerging in which the characters and events, including letter writing, are pure inventions of the author, and communicated as such, namely, the Greek erotic novel, a genre that apparently flourished in the following centuries.[53]

Fictive letters are a salient feature of Jewish prose narrative from the period of the Second Temple.[54] Limiting our scope to original Greek compositions,[55] one sees a

---

49   L. Michael White and G. Anthony Keddie, *Jewish Fictional Letters from Hellenistic Egypt: The Epistle of Aristeas and Related Literature* (Atlanta: SBL, 2018), p. 322. It should be noted that while both letters have conventional prescripts, only E has the customary greeting (χαίρειν). Neither includes a final salutation (ἔρρωσο) and date. Dorothy, *Books of Esther*, p. 193, attributes this to the editorial process of embedding the letter in a narrative text. John Lee White, *Light from Ancient Letters* (Minneapolis, MI: Fortress, 1986), p. 200, notes that both the greeting and close are sometimes omitted in legal texts that appear in letter form.

50   Erich S. Gruen, *Heritage and Hellenism: The Reinvention of Jewish Tradition* (Berkeley, CA: University of California Press, 2002), p. 230.

51   For a comprehensive study of this genre, see Rosenmeyer, *Epistolary Fictions*.

52   Tim Whitmarsh, *Beyond the Second Sophistic: Adventures in Greek Postclassicism* (Berkeley, CA: University of California Press, 2013), p. 14.

53   Whitmarsh, *Second Sophistic*, pp. 11–34.

54   For an overview of this literature see White and Keddie, *Jewish Fictional Letters*. Doering, *Ancient Jewish Letters*, p. 167, documents a significant numerical increase in letters in the Greek versions as compared with the Hebrew bible.

55   Within the Hebrew-Aramaic tradition, there is of course Ezra-Nehemiah, which contains official correspondence with the Persian court (Ezra 1. 2–4; 4. 17–22; 6. 3–12; 7. 11–28). The question of its documentary status is vexed. See Lisbeth S. Fried, 'The Artaxerxes Correspondence of Ezra 4, Nehemiah's Wall, and Persian Provincial Administration', in *'Go Out and Study the Land' (Judges 18:2): Archaeological, Historical and Textual Studies in Honor of Anan Eshel*, ed. by Aren M. Maeir, Jodi Magness and Lawrence H. Schiffman, JSJ.S, 148 (Leiden: Brill, 2012), pp. 35–58. Levenson, *Esther*, p. 75, raises the possibility that this literature stimulated the creation of letters for Esther. Yet there are more proximal models. Closer in time to LXX-Esth is I Maccabees, which, while extant only in Greek, appears to be a Hebrew-Greek translation. The text features many references to written

strong family resemblance between LXX-Esth and a number of other Jewish texts.[56] The closest parallel is III Maccabees, a composition dating to the early Imperial period whose affinities with Esther are multiple.[57] It contains two royal letters attributed to Ptolemy IV Philopator (222/1–205/4 BCE) — one authorizing the destruction of the Jews; the other revoking it — written in a style sufficiently similar to B and E that some degree of literary dependence is not unlikely.[58]

It is often assumed that the use of fictive letters by Greco-Jewish authors approximates the genre of Greek historiography, and this may well be true. Greek speaking historians had two primary models, Herodotus and Thucydides, both of whom employ embedded letters (largely fictive, it seems).[59] Yet it does not follow from generic considerations that their use in later Jewish sources is primarily intended to achieve the effect of historical verisimilitude.[60] Quite simply, the use of verbatim documents is by no means a robust feature of Greek historiography.[61] If anything,

---

correspondence, as well as a number of embedded letters, likely fictive, which were evidently present in the *Vorlage*. For a discussion of the use of documents in this work, see John R. Bartlett, *1 Maccabees* (Sheffield: Sheffield Academic Press, 1998).

56 The Solomon letters of Eupolemus (*fl.* in mid-second century BCE) are of particular interest, insofar as they elaborate upon biblical sources. See G. Anthony Keddie, 'Solomon to His Friends: The Role of Epistolarity in Eupolemos', *Journal for the Study of the Pseudepigrapha*, 22/3 (2013), 201–37. Other significant points of reference include II Maccabees and the Letter of Aristeas, but also Josephus.

57 Levenson, *Esther*, p. 75. It has been tempting to group LXX-Esth and III Maccabees within an ethnically distinct genre, the so-called Jewish novel. There are doubtlessly important affinities between these texts, but to cordon off a handful of Greco-Jewish works from the larger cultural context begs a number of questions.

58 Noah Hacham, '3 Maccabees and Esther: Parallels, Intertextuality, and Diaspora Identity', *JBL*, 126/4 (2007), 765–85, makes a persuasive case for the literary dependence of Additions B and E on III Maccabees. For a succinct discussion of this issue, and the relevant secondary literature, see Doering, *Ancient Jewish Letters*, pp. 153–54, who concludes that despite the possibility of dependence the letters function quite differently in each book.

59 Regarding the use of letters by Herodotus, John Muir, *Life and Letters in the Ancient World* (London: Routledge, 2009), p. 85, concludes that, 'There seems little doubt that, where the texts of letters are quoted, Herodotus composed the letters himself'. As to Thucydides, Muir, *Life and Letters*, p. 86, writes, 'It is very unlikely that he saw the originals or copies of all the letters that he purports to quote, and it has been suspected on reasonable grounds that he must have adopted the same practice with letters as with the speeches he reports'. That is, Thucydides provides what, in his opinion, the speaker would have said on the occasion, while holding as far as possible to the sense of what was actually said.

60 Compare Sara Raup Johnson, *Historical Fictions and Hellenistic Jewish Identity: Third Maccabees in Its Cultural Context* (Berkeley, CA: University of California Press, 2005), p. 140.

61 A caveat is in order. Since Hellenistic historiography is extant for the most part only in a highly fragmentary form, secure conclusions cannot be drawn regarding its use of epistolography. Yet inferences may be framed with some degree of confidence from the two historians whose work is more or less preserved. As it happens, very few letters are quoted in full. For Polybius (*c.* 200–118 BCE), see Ceccarelli, *Greek Letter Writing*, p. 177, 'The content of most letters is not deemed important enough to be quoted but is usually summarized'. For Diodorus Siculus (*c.* 90–30 BCE), see Manuela Mari, 'Powers in Dialogue: The Letters and *diagrammata* of Macedonian Kings to Local Communities', in *Letters and Communities: Studies in the Socio-Political Dimensions of Ancient Epistolography*, ed. by Paola Ceccarelli and others (Oxford: Oxford University Press, 2018), pp. 121–46 (p. 124). Two notable exceptions include Diodorus Siculus, *Library of World History*, 18. 8. 2–7, which records Alexander's

Greek historians were disinclined to quote the documents available to them directly and or entirely.[62] They do not cite written correspondence where one would expect, and when they do record letters, the tendency, as Rosenmeyer has shown, is to use them less as a source of evidence, and more as part of a narrative strategy.[63] At the risk of generalization, letters tend to function as reported speech rather than as documentation. Hence their fictive character was acceptable. This appears to be the case with LXX-Esth, where the two royal letters, while in no respect modeled on historical Persian documents, significantly advance the rhetorical and thematic objectives of the translator. As I shall propose, the principal aim of Addition B — one served uniquely by its generic features — is to translate the existential threat posed by the figure of Haman into a political sphere recognizable to late Hellenistic Jews.

4. The First Royal Letter (Addition B)

The form and function of written correspondence in Greco-Roman antiquity is, as one might expect, closely bond up with social and political change. In Greece the practice of letter writing had its origins in private communication but was soon extended to military affairs. With the advent of Macedonian hegemony, and the trend towards courtly protocol and centralized bureaucracy, its use for official purposes became prevalent, and was taken up (along with other diplomatic instruments of the Macedonian court) by the Successors in the form of the royal letter.[64] Hellenistic chanceries developed formal patterns which were easily recognizable, providing a 'framework of mutual understanding for both officials and subjects'.[65] The political significance of this genre cannot be overestimated.[66] Within the Hellenistic social imaginary, the association of letter writing with the court is such that a punctilious attention to correspondence is part of the image of the ideal king.[67] A literary interest in royal letters appears early. According to Lucian, the grammarian Dionysodorus of Troezen (a student of Aristarchus and active in Alexandria in the second half of the second century BCE) is said to have edited the letters of Ptolemy I (367–283 BCE).[68]

---

letter announcing the recall of the Greek exiles read at the Olympic games of 324 BCE, and 18. 56, where he quotes Philip III's Diagramma on the liberation of the Greeks, which Polyperchon made known in 319 BCE.

62   Mari, 'Powers in Dialogue', p. 124.
63   Rosenmeyer, *Epistolary Fictions*, pp. 45–60.
64   Alice Bencivenni, 'The King's Words: Hellenistic Royal Letters in Inscriptions', in *State Correspondence in the Ancient World: From New Kingdom Egypt to the Roman Empire*, ed. by Karen Radner (Oxford: Oxford University Press, 2014), pp. 141–71 (p. 147).
65   Muir, *Life and Letters*, p. 83.
66   Muir, *Life and Letters*, p. 83: 'Monarchy was in the end a personal exercise of power and the king wrote to his subjects person to person in letter-form, the writer of the letters uttering the royal voice: the head of the royal chancery in Syria was known as the *epistolographos*, the Letter-Writer'.
67   Ceccarelli, *Ancient Greek Letter Writing*, p. 165.
68   Ceccarelli, *Ancient Greek Letter Writing*, p. 4.

Addition B conforms in structure (at least superficially) to known examples of letters from Hellenistic chancelleries.[69] The specific form of the text is well attested epigraphically for the Seleucid regime,[70] the ἐπιστολή-πρόσταγμα: a letter from a formal point of view, but a text bearing the illocutionary force of an order for those who received it, namely, the officials to whom it was addressed and their subordinates.[71] The word πρόσταγμα is attested in a number of epigraphic dossiers (groups of royal documents), where it is used by subordinate officials with reference to the king's orders, which are composed in the form of a letter, and consistently referred to as such (ἐπιστολή) by the monarch.[72] Such orders target a large audience; they may concern a specific administrative district, but are typically more wide ranging. In exceptional cases, the king might require that the letter be inscribed in stone, as appears to be the case in the narrative world of LXX-Esth, τὰ δὲ ἀντίγραφα τῶν ἐπιστολῶν ἐξετίθετο κατὰ χώραν (3. 14), 'Copies of the letters were posted in every land' (NETS).

Generally speaking a twofold distinction is made within royal correspondence on the basis of the recipient's identity: either 1) a political body with some degree of autonomy; or 2) a subordinate with injunctive powers, to whom administrative matters are referred.[73] This distinction is reflected in the language of the letter. While the first type is polite, elaborate, and marked by euergetism (the display of public benefaction) and friendship language, the second tends to be direct and laconic. In this respect, the ἐπιστολή-πρόσταγμα is a special case, as it combines the elaborate style with a more direct manner. For the purposes of the present analysis, I shall consider how these features, in particular the friendship language, advance the communicative strategy of the author.[74]

69 Claudine Cavalier, Esther, La Bible d'Alexandrie, 12 (Paris: Cerf, 2012), p. 164. The letter comprises four parts: i) the presentation of recipients (B.1); ii) a proclamation of benevolence (B.2); iii) an exposition of particular circumstances, and orders given in consequence (B.3–6); and iv) a general justification (B.7). For a detailed structural and stylistic analysis, see Dorothy, Books of Esther, pp. 92–102.
70 For the purposes of comparative analysis, I shall limit myself to the documented practices of the Seleucid chancery. A comprehensive study would obviously take into account the Ptolemaic evidence. A fundamental resource for comparative study remains C. Bradford Welles, Royal Correspondence in the Hellenistic Period: A Study in Greek Epigraphy (New Haven: Yale University Press, 1934).
71 Bencivenni, 'The King's Words', p. 151.
72 Bencivenni, 'The King's Words', p. 145.
73 Bencivenni, 'The King's Words', pp. 151–52. Compare Welles, Royal Correspondence, pp. xlii–xliii.
74 While the present analysis focuses on communicative strategy, it should be noted that the genre exhibits a number of distinctive stylistic features. See the discussion of Paola Ceccarelli, 'Image and Communication in the Seleucid Kingdom: The King, the Court and the Cities', in The Hellenistic Court: Monarchic Power and Elite Society from Alexander to Cleopatra, ed. by Andrew Erskine, Lloyd Llewellyn-Jones and Shane Wallace (Swansea: The Classical Press of Wales, 2017), pp. 231–56. One such feature evident in B is the shift in the king's self-reference from the 3rd person of the prescript to the 1st pl in the body of the letter.

This is nicely illustrated by a second century BCE inscription (SEG 57. 1838) which records a letter sent by Seleucus IV (187–75 BCE) to an official named Heliodorus.[75] The πρόσταγμα apparently concerns the appointment of Olympiodoros as ἀρχιερεύς in Coele-Syria and Phoenicia.[76] Of considerable interest is the manner of the opening section (ll. 13–18), in which Seleucus begins by expressing his concern that his subjects live in security and peace:

πλείστην πρόνοιαν ποιούμενοι περὶ τῆς τῶν ὑπο\τεταγμένων ἀσφαλείας καὶ μέγιστον ἀγαθὸ[ν] \ εἶναι νομίζοντες τοῖς πράγμασιν, ὅταν οἱ κατὰ \ τὴν βασιλείαν ἀδεῶς τοὺς ἑαυτῶν βίους διοικῶ\σιν, 'Taking the utmost consideration for the safety of our subjects, and thinking it to be of the greatest good for the affairs in our realm when those living in our kingdom manage their lives without fear'.[77]

Royal letters played an important role in promoting the Hellenistic monarch's political identity. A key aspect of this is an attitude of free benevolence towards his subjects.[78] In B the opening section of the letter we find the same motifs:

τοὺς τῶν ὑποτεταγμένων ἀκυμάτους διὰ παντὸς καταστῆσαι βίους, τήν τε βασιλείαν ἥμερον καὶ πορευτὴν μέχρι περάτων παρεξόμενος ἀνανεώσασθαί τε τὴν ποθουμένην τοῖς πᾶσιν ἀνθρώποις εἰρήνην, 'to secure lasting tranquility in the lives of my subjects and, in order to make my kingdom peaceable and open to travel throughout all its extent, to restore the peace desired by all people' (NETS).

The inclusion of such a text within an historical narrative invites the reader to locate the exercise of royal power against the crosshairs of idealized monarchic rule and the actual machinations of the royal court. On the one hand, the letter presents Artaxerxes 'as an idealistic, reasonable, and rather philosophical monarch'.[79] This is the model of kingship to which the narrator of LXX-Esth evidently subscribes,

---

75 Hannah M. Cotton and Michael Wörrle, 'Seleukos IV to Heliodoros: A New Dossier of Royal Correspondence from Israel', ZPE, 159 (2007), 191–205; Dov Gera, 'Olympiodoros, Heliodoros, and the Temples of Koilē Syria and Phoinikē', ZPE, 169 (2009), 125–55; Christopher P. Jones, 'The Inscription from Tel Maresha for Olympiodoros', ZPE, 171 (2009), 100–04; Alice Bencivenni, '"Massima considerazione": forma dell'ordine e immagini del potere nella corrispondenza di Seleuco IV', ZPE, 176 (2011), 139–53.

76 See Vasile Babota, The Institution of the Hasmonean High Priesthood (Leiden: Brill, 2013), pp. 44–46. The inscription appears on a stele five fragments of which have been recovered from Maresha (4 km southwest of Jerusalem). It contains three letters that are apparently genuine. The lower-most was sent by King Seleucus IV Philopator to Heliodorus. A second letter sent by Heliodorus to Dorymenes appears above (SEG 57. 1838 II. 7–12), as well as one sent by Dorymenes to Diophanes (II. 1–6). The letters are dated to the month Gorpiaios of the regnal year 134 (the summer of 178 BCE). The inscription was likely displayed in the most conspicuous of the sanctuaries of Coele-Syria and Phoenicia, including Jerusalem. For Heliodorus see II Maccabees 3.

77 Text and translation are derived from Jones, 'The Inscription'.

78 See James L. O'Neil, 'Royal Authority and City Law under Alexander and His Hellenistic Successors', The Classical Quarterly, 50/2 (2000), 424–31 (p. 430): 'The stress in royal edicts that the king's decisions (and those of his delegates) are in the interests of those for whom the edict has been issued clearly reflected a strong concern with Hellenistic ideas of kingship'.

79 Jon D. Levenson, Esther: A Commentary, OTL (Louisville: Westminster John Knox, 1997), p. 75.

and to which Artaxerxes ultimately conforms (Addition E).[80] Yet at this point in the narrative the king appears quite oblivious to what is happening.[81] The display of benevolence in the letter is thus deeply ironic, seeing that the πρόσταγμα promotes the agenda of an usurper.

As we have seen, the ideal Hellenistic monarch is committed to the welfare of his kingdom. This is underscored in the letter to Heliodorus. A priority of Seleucus is to ensure that the established sanctuaries receive the proper care (II. 18–22). Since Coele-Syria lacks someone to attend to this, the king announces his intention to appoint Olympiodoros (II. 23–27). What follows is in effect an embedded sub-genre, the letter of commendation:[82]

> Ὀλυμπιόδωρος, [τ]ὴν πίστιν ἡμῖν τῆς ὑπὲρ \ αὐτοῦ διαλήψεως ἐκ τῶν προγεγονότων χρόνων \ παρεισχημένος, [τρ]αφεὶς γὰρ <με>θ᾽ ἡμῶν καὶ τὴν ἀρίσ\την ἐν ἅπασιν ἀπενηνεγμένος διάθεσιν, κατὰ λόγον \ μὲν ἐπὶ τοῦ κοιτῶνος κατεστάθη τῆς τηλικαύτης \ πίστεως φανεὶς ἄξιος, δικαίως δὲ τῶν πρώτων <πρώ\των> φίλων ἀπεδείχθη, τῆς <τῆς> πρὸς ἡμᾶς φιλοστοργίας \ τὰς ἐκτενεστάτας [ἀπ]οδείξεις ποιησάμενος ἐν δὲ τῆι \ τοιαύτηι γενόμενος [τάξε?]ι, ʽ[he, who] has demonstrated his loyalty to us because of his attitude, from times gone by, as he had been raised with us and had gained for himself the best disposition in all things, he was, on the one hand, appointed chamberlain with reason, because he has proven himself worthy due to his longstanding loyalty, while on the other hand, he was justifiably introduced into the ranks of the first friends because of his love for us, having made the most assiduous demonstrations of loyalty while in such a [rank]ʼ.

Olympiodoros is identified as one who grew up in the royal court (I. 29, [τρ]αφεὶς γὰρ <με>θ᾽ ἡμῶν), had been first appointed chamberlain (ἐπὶ τοῦ κοιτῶνος), and subsequently First Friend (τῶν πρώτων φίλων), an honorific court title (II. 31–33). His standing rests on his character: his longstanding loyalty (τῆς τηλικαύτης \ πίστεως), and his love for the king (τῆς πρὸς ἡμᾶς φιλοστοργίας). Significantly, he shares the monarch's euergetism. Within B Haman is described in similar terms (B. 3):[83]

> ὁ σωφροσύνη παρ᾽ ἡμῖν διενέγκας καὶ ἐν τῇ εὐνοίᾳ ἀπαραλλάκτως καὶ βεβαίᾳ πίστει ἀποδεδειγμένος καὶ δεύτερον τῶν βασιλειῶν γέρας ἀπενηνεγμένος Αμαν,

---

80 O'Neil, 'Royal Authority', pp. 429–30, draws attention to the neo-Pythagorean views on kingship preserved in the fragments of Stobaeus's *Florilegium*. The ideal king 'considers the welfare of his subjects, showing goodwill to them like a father to his sons'. See for instance Diotogenes, 4. 7. 62, and Ecphantus, 4. 7. 64.

81 Levenson, *Esther*, p. 114.

82 Pseudo-Demetrius, *Epistolary Types*, pp. 20–25, illustrates the basic structure of such letters. See Malherbe, *Epistolary Theorists*, p. 33.

83 In accordance with the conventions that regulate Seleucid correspondence, individuals are identified by name only (the patronymic is absent, as is any indication of official title). Ceccarelli, 'Image and Communication', p. 238, observes that although this feature is in part due to the letter form, the fact that it was preserved by the royal chanceries suggests that it also served a rhetorical purpose, namely, that of presenting the king and the persons named as members of the same community who share the same interests. Yet compare E.17.

'Haman — who excels among us in sound judgment and is distinguished for his unchanging goodwill and steadfast fidelity and has attained the second place in the kingdom' (*NETS*).

Haman is here distinguished by the cardinal virtues of the model courtier, goodwill (τῇ εὐνοίᾳ) and fidelity (βεβαίᾳ πίστει). Later in the letter he is described as a 'second father' δευτέρου πατρὸς ἡμῶν (B.6).[84] Looking beyond B, we find that in the Greek version he is further identified as foremost among the king's 'Friends' (*NETS*), καὶ ἐπρωτοβάθρει πάντων τῶν φίλων αὐτοῦ (Esther 3.1); compare MT-Esth, שרים, 'officials' (*NRSV*). The φίλος was a recognizable political category within the context of Hellenistic monarchic rule.[85]

Bencivenni notes that to underscore the epistolary character of the ἐπιστολή-πρόσταγμα, 'the king usually expresses his orders by justifying them through a complex set of reasons'.[86] As a pretext for the genocide, Artaxerxes makes a lengthy and involved case against the nation targeted for destruction (B. 4–5). Remarkably the author of B employs this device to give vivid expression to an anti-Jewish polemic. This well illustrates an aspect of the text emphasized by Moore: 'the letter is a cleverly constructed piece of propaganda'.[87] Moore uses the word 'constructed' advisedly, for we find that the author of B is not relying upon his own imagination for the contents of the polemic, so much as adapting existing tradition, which he shapes according to the generic requirements of the ἐπιστολή-πρόσταγμα. In this respect there is nothing in the composition and embedding of B that is inconsistent with Greek historiography. The author's primary historical source is Esther 3. 8 (see MT-Esth), where, in a reported dialogue with King Artaxerxes, Haman brings two charges against a certain (unnamed) people (עם אחד): 1) their laws are different from all the nations; 2) they disobey the king's laws:

---

84   Compare the purported letter from Antiochus III (233–187 BCE) to Zeuxis, governor of Lydia, presented by Josephus (*c*. 37–100 CE), *Antiquities*, 12. 147–53, in which Zeuxis is addressed as a 'father' to the king. This text has the generic form of a contemporary ἐπιστολή-πρόσταγμα, though some of its stylistic features may post-date Antiochus III. See Lutz Doering, *Ancient Jewish Letters and the Beginnings of Christian Epistolography* (Tübingen: Mohr Siebeck, 2012), pp. 290–91. There is documentary evidence for correspondence between Antiochus and Zeuxis, though Zeuxis is not identified as a 'father' to Antiochus. See Hasan Malay, 'Letter of Antiochios III to Zeuxis with Two Covering Letters (209 BC)', *Epigraphica Anatolica*, 10 (1987), 7–15.

85   For the political significance of the term φίλος see Ioanna Kralli, 'Athens and the Hellenistic Kings (338–261 BC): The Language of the Decrees', *The Classical Quarterly*, 50/1 (2000), 113–32 (p. 127). In practical terms, a φίλος might have any of a range of responsibilities. Used both formally and informally in inscriptions, the term foregrounds the idea of a personal relationship with the king against the background of a strict hierarchical structure.

86   Bencivenni, 'The King's Words', p. 151. Ceccarelli, 'Image and Communication', p. 240, draws attention to some of the stylistic idiosyncrasies of these sections, notably the tendency to avoid a formal motivation clause (marked by ἐπειδή). He suggests that this particular feature presents the decision of the king as freely taken; it also cultivates a style of speech different from the city-decrees, which emphasize external motivation.

87   Moore, *Additions*, p. 194.

ויאמר המן למלך אחשורוש ישנו עם אחד מפזר ומפרד בין העמים בכל מדינות מלכותך
ודתיהם שנות מכל עם ואת דתי המלך אינם עשים ולמלך אין שוה להניחם,

'Then Haman said to King Ahasuerus, "There is a certain people scattered
and separated among the peoples in all the provinces of your kingdom; their
laws are different from those of every other people, and they do not keep the
king's laws, so that it is not appropriate for the king to tolerate them"' (NRSV).

Ὑπάρχει ἔθνος διεσπαρμένον ἐν τοῖς ἔθνεσιν ἐν πάσῃ τῇ βασιλείᾳ σου, οἱ δὲ νόμοι
αὐτῶν ἔξαλλοι παρὰ πάντα τὰ ἔθνη, τῶν δὲ νόμων τοῦ βασιλέως παρακούουσιν,
καὶ οὐ συμφέρει τῷ βασιλεῖ ἐᾶσαι αὐτούς, 'Then he spoke to King Artaxerxes,
saying, "There is a certain nation scattered among the nations throughout all
your kingdom; their laws are different from all the nations, and they disobey
the king's laws so that it is not expedient for the king to tolerate them"' (NETS).

While the king is vidently in the dark, the reader knows that Haman's target is the
Jewish nation.[88] The charges are in certain respects consistent with the worldview
of the implied author. Certainly, it is assumed that the Jews have distinct laws which
are of divine origin and binding; and while it is stressed that the Jewish subjects of
the king are basically law-abiding, fidelity to their own law might lead to behaviour
that could be misconstrued as disobedience. The royal letter takes up the two-fold
accusation of its source and elaborates upon it (B. 4). Notably the Judeans are not
identified by name:

ἐπέδειξεν ἡμῖν ἐν πάσαις ταῖς κατὰ τὴν οἰκουμένην φυλαῖς ἀναμεμῖχθαι δυσμενῆ
λαόν τινα τοῖς νόμοις ἀντίθετον πρὸς πᾶν ἔθνος τά τε τῶν βασιλέων παραπέμποντας
διηνεκῶς διατάγματα πρὸς τὸ μὴ κατατίθεσθαι τὴν ὑφ' ἡμῶν κατευθυνομένην ἀμέμπτως
συναρχίαν, '[Haman] pointed out to us that among all the tribes in the world there
is scattered a certain hostile people, who have laws contrary to those of every nation
and continually disregard the ordinances of kings so that the joint administration
of the kingdom that we honorably intend cannot be achieved' (NETS).

While the language is different, the force of the accusation remains basically the same,
though the reference to 'joint administration' (or better 'joint magistracy'), τὸ μὴ
κατατίθεσθαι τὴν ὑφ' ἡμῶν κατευθυνομένην ἀμέμπτως συναρχίαν, strikes a decidedly
political note.[89] Peculiar to the letter, however, is the further charge of misanthropy (B. 5):

διειληφότες οὖν τόδε τὸ ἔθνος μονώτατον ἐν ἀντιπαραγωγῇ παντὶ διὰ παντὸς ἀνθρώπῳ
κείμενον διαγωγὴν νόμων ξενίζουσαν παραλλάσσον καὶ δυσνοοῦν τοῖς ἡμετέροις
πράγμασιν τὰ χείριστα συντελοῦν κακὰ καὶ πρὸς τὸ μὴ τὴν βασιλείαν εὐσταθείας
τυγχάνειν, 'Therefore, whereas we understand that, since this nation stands constantly

88 Vialle, Analyse Comparée, p. 210.
89 Paul Cartledge, Hellenistic and Roman Sparta (London: Routledge, 2004), p. 134, apropos Sparta,
    observes that subsequent to 146 BCE the term συναρχία (singular) regularly denotes a joint-magistracy
    comprising the city's chief executive. In two documents it appears as the body that gives effect to
    the resolutions of other corporations. See IG v. 1. 480 and 448. Compare Strabo (c. 63 BCE – 24 CE),
    Geography, 15. 1. 52; and Polybius, History, 4. 4. 2.

all alone in opposition to all humanity, perversely following an estranging manner of life due to their laws and since it is ill–disposed to our interests, doing the worst harm and in order that our kingdom may not attain stability' (*NETS*).

The Jews are not only disobedient and possessed of a different set of laws, but they are opposed to all humanity (παντὶ διὰ παντὸς ἀνθρώπῳ), and, as such, pose a direct threat to the king's affairs (τοῖς ἡμετέροις πράγμασιν).[90] The accusation of misanthropy, while not in the translator's source, is by no means a product of make-believe. Here a further layer of intertextuality enters the narrative. The misanthrope was a well-established character type, of which the most notable figure is perhaps Timon of Athens (a contemporary of Pericles, *c.* 495–29 BCE).[91] The concept was adapted to the purposes of ethnography, however, and applied to the Jewish nation by Hecataeus of Abdera (*fl. c.* 300 BCE), best known for his *Aegyptica*. Hellenistic ethnography is characterized by its interest in causal connections, and Hecataeus attributes the distinctness of the Jewish way of life to their lawgiver, and the experience of exodus from Egypt, διὰ γὰρ τὴν ἰδίαν ξενηλασίαν ἀπάνθρωπόν τινα καὶ μισόξενον βίον εἰσηγήσατο, 'for, as a result of the expulsion of his people, he introduced a most inhuman and unsociable manner of life' (LCL).[92] The theme is taken up and given more sinister expression in an anecdote recorded by Posidonius (135–51 BCE).[93]

During the siege of Jerusalem by Seleucid forces in 134 BCE, we are told, certain courtiers (φίλοι) of Antiochus VII Sidetes (159–29 BCE) made a case for the total destruction of the Jewish nation: μόνους γὰρ ἁπάντων ἐθνῶν ἀκοινωνήτους εἶναι τῆς πρὸς ἄλλο ἔθνος ἐπιμιξίας καὶ πολεμίους ὑπολαμβάνειν πάντας, 'since they alone of all nations avoided dealings with any other people and looked upon all men as their enemies' (LCL). This misanthropy is due, the king's 'Friends' explain, to the national origins of the Jews, and (taking their cue from the ethnographic tradition) they proceed to relate a version of the Exodus narrative from an Egyptian perspective. They next remind Antiochus of the enmity towards the Jews of his illustrious forebear, Antiochus IV Epiphanes (*c.* 215–164 BCE), who is said to have discovered in the temple of Jerusalem the statue of a bearded man upon a donkey, whom they suppose was Moses, the lawgiver and founder of the nation, πρὸς δὲ τούτοις νομοθετήσαντος τὰ μισάνθρωπα καὶ παράνομα ἔθη τοῖς Ἰουδαίοις, 'the man, moreover, who had ordained for the Jews their misanthropic and lawless customs' (LCL). Epiphanes, shocked by the misanthropy of this nation, set about putting an end to their traditional practices (τὰ νόμιμα). Antiochus VII is now advised to either destroy this people, or, short of that, follow the precedent of Epiphanes. According to Diodorus, Antiochus proved magnanimous, dismissing the charges, and a massacre was avoided.

---

90 Cavalier, *Esther*, p. 98. White and Keddie, *Jewish Fictional Letters*, p. 322, note that the use of τὰ πράγματα in reference to the king's affairs is a characteristic feature of royal letters.

91 Lucian, *Timon, or The Misanthrope*. See Socrates's account of misanthropy in Plato, *Phaedo*, 89d3–e3.

92 *Apud* Diodorus Siculus, *Library of World History*, 40. 3. 1–9. For a thorough examination of the text, its attribution, and historical significance, see Bezalel Bar-Kochva, *The Image of the Jews in Greek Literature of the Hellenistic Period* (Berkeley: University of California Press, 2010), pp. 90–135.

93 *Apud* Diodorus Siculus, *Library of World History*, 34/35. 1. 3. The text comes down to us through an extract made by Photius, the ninth-century bishop of Constantinople. For a discussion of the attribution and significance of the extract, see Bar-Kochva, *Image of the Jews*, pp. 410–13, 440–57.

There are indications that this story reflects propaganda originating from Seleucid court historians. Remarkably, then, it seems that the author of B draws upon an actual anti-Jewish polemic (one rooted in Greek ethnography) that was likely still current at the time of the translation.[94] This not only contemporizes the letter but introduces a marked degree of intertextual complexity. As Claudine Cavalier observes, the anti-Jewish discourse of the royal letter gives a strictly political interpretation to the accusation of Esther 3. 8: 'Alors que dans le TM il est simplement question de particularisme, dans le grec il est question d'activisme politique contre la centralisation impériale'.[95] Yet to embed such discourse within a narrative is to expose its motives, and thus exorcise it.

5. Haman's Letter and the Narrative Strategy of LXX-Esther

Ancient Greek historians, it has been suggested, tend to use fictive letters not so much as putative sources of evidence, but rather as part of a larger narrative strategy. Certainly, the embedding of B within the narrative of LXX-Esth creates dramatic opportunities. For while the subject of speech is ostensibly the king, Arataxerxes, in a fascinating twist (taken up from the *Vorlage*, see MT-Esth 3. 12), the letter is actually dictated by Haman.[96] It is thus the distinct voice of Israel's opponent that addresses the Persian realm as a ventriloquist speaking through the mouth of the king. As Frow remarks *apropos* a scene in Jane Austen's *Mansfield Park*, 'it is precisely the generic characteristics of the letter which structures the scene's dramatic irony'.[97] The customary letter of commendation is used to promote the interests of the very one who has deceived the king. Moreover, it serves to further characterize Haman. In as much as the reader knows that Haman is the author, the list of exemplary attributes only underscores his vanity.[98]

According to Pseudo-Demetrius writing a letter is tantamount to drawing an image of one's soul.[99] B offers a privileged way of observing Haman; it gives a concrete

---

94 Yet compare Cavalier, *Esther*, p. 99, who explores the accusation of Jewish sedition in a Roman milieu. As she suggests, the discourse against the Jews in B likely draws upon numerous motifs from diverse sources. See, for instance, Cicero, *Pro Flacco*, 67, who accuses the Jews of organizing tumultuous assemblies: *huic autem barbarae superstitioni resistere severitatis, multitudinem Iudaeorum flagrantem non numquam in contionibus pro re publica contemnere gravitatis summae fuit*, 'But to resist this barbarous superstition were an act of dignity, to despise the multitude of Jews, which at times was most unruly in the assemblies in defence of the interests of the republic, was an act of the greatest wisdom' (LCL). See Anthony J. Marshall, 'Flaccus and the Jews of Asia (Cicero "Pro Flacco" 28.67–69)', *Phoenix*, 29/2 (1975), 139–54.
95 Cavalier, *Esther*, p. 98.
96 That the letter was dictated by an official rather than the king is not, in itself, exceptional within the context of a Hellenistic chancery. See Muir, *Life and Letters*, pp. 83–84.
97 Frow, *Genre*, p. 47.
98 Moore, *Additions*, p. 192.
99 For Ceccarelli, *Ancient Greek Letter Writing*, p. 4, this explains the frequent use of letters in novelistic fiction of the imperial period. Yet letter writing plays such a role in Greek historiography as well.

character to his menace.[100] Yet not only is the letter transparent to Haman's inner machinations, but, read in light of the Greek narrative, the motivation and scope of his anti-Jewish rhetoric are radically transformed. It is important to remember that in the first of the narrative expansions in LXX-Esth (A), which precedes the elevation of Esther, Mardochaios — identified as a courtier at the very outset — overhears a plot against the king and reports it personally, resulting in the execution of the perpetrators, two eunuchs, and the promotion of Mardochaios (A. 12–17), an episode without parallel in MT-Esth.[101] The Greek narrator then states that Haman sought to harm Mardochaios and his people on account of the two eunuchs (A. 17), implicating Haman in the initial plot, and presumably in the second one as well (Esther 2. 21–23), which LXX-Esth (over against MT-Esth) explicitly presents as a consequence of the first plot (2. 21).[102] Moreover he is later identified in the Greek text as a Macedonian (E. 10), and hence, as Levinson puts it, 'not only an alien but a secret agent of a nefarious foreign power to boot; a seditious alien'.[103]

Haman's self-identification as a model courtier in LXX-Esth is thus set against the background of his deception of Artaxerxes; his accusation against the Jews is part and parcel of his own his own complicity in regicide. In the second royal letter (Addition E), written by Esther and Mardochaios in the person of Artaxerxes (and evidently endorsed by the implied author), the reader is informed that Haman was endeavouring all along 'to transfer the power of the Persians to the Macedonians' (NETS), τὴν τῶν Περσῶν ἐπικράτησιν εἰς τοὺς Μακεδόνας μετάξαι (E. 14). This transformation has significant generic implications, insofar as the story of Esther and Mardochaios is now situated within a frame explicitly concerned with the economy of royal power.[104] This point is nicely observed by Cavalier: 'Tout le récit devant l'histoire d'une vaste machination contre l'empire perse de la part de Haman'.[105] The two plots of the eunuchs are thus part of a larger conspiracy that Mardochaios has twice blocked: Haman wishes to destroy the Jews in order to seize power.[106]

It is evident that the generic complexity of LXX-Esth, and specifically its use of fictive epistolography, not only complicates the discursive tissue of the narrative, bringing in distinct voices, but enriches its thematic texture as well. Within the narrative world of LXX-Esth the first royal letter is at once the expression and instrument of a complex

---

100 Vialle, *Une Analyse Comparée*, p. 209.
101 While the first narration of the plot in Addition A may at first blush appear to be a textual doublet of the second (paralleled in MT-Esth), or else a proleptic retelling of the same episode, there are in fact significant points of divergence. For a detailed commentary on the pericope, see Cameron Boyd-Taylor, 'A Tale of Two Eunuchs: A Commentary on Greek Esther 2.19–23 and A.12–17', in *The SBL Commentary on the Septuagint: An Introduction*, ed. by Dirk Büchner (Atlanta: SBL, 2017), pp. 169–206.
102 Boyd-Taylor, 'Two Eunuchs', p. 184.
103 Levenson, *Esther*, p. 114.
104 Meredith J. Stone, *Empire and Gender in LXX Esther* (Atlanta: SBL, 2018), p. 283, argues persuasively that the discourse of Addition E 'constructs Haman as an Other to stabilize the ideological narrative of Persia's supremacy'.
105 Cavalier, *Esther*, p. 106.
106 Cavalier, *Esther*, p. 106.

political deception. Such a narrative strategy aptly characterizes the use of fictive epistolary by Greek historians: 'The texts that mention letters seem fascinated with the connections between epistolary writing and deception'.[107] Rosenmeyer discerns a generic paradigm established in Homer, sustained in tragedy, and informing the status of letters in Herodotus and Thucydides, 'who continue to explore, although in a less overtly fictional format, the relationship between letter writing, political authority, and deception'.[108] This paradigm, I would offer, provides a key to understanding the significance of Haman's letter in LXX-Esth. We find that its inclusion is an integral part of a larger strategy aimed at recasting the story as an historical meditation on truth and power. The letter gives dramatic voice to the tension between God's law and the king's law. Yet the ensuing narrative shows not only that the law of Moses is congruent with legitimate authority, but ultimately supportive of it.

Thematically speaking the Greek narrative turns on the question of political loyalty. It asks, who is the true φίλος of the king? In this respect Mardochaios and Haman are foils. Whereas the former proves to be the king's most loyal servant, the latter is a seditious traitor, working against the king's interests; in Sarah Raup Johnson's succinct formulation, 'only the pious are loyal'.[109] Noah Hacham concludes that the author of the royal letters, perhaps taking his cue from III Maccabees, speaks to the anxieties of diaspora Jews living in uncertain times, encouraging them to place their hope in royal recognition of Judean loyalty and service.[110] The lawful Jew is the true φίλος of the king.[111]

Given its Persian court setting, and use of historical narrative as a means of political investigation, a potentially fruitful point of comparison for LXX-Esth are the Persica, a particular field of Greek historiography which developed throughout the fifth and fourth centuries BCE.[112] While its origins are in the late Archaic period, when Greek ethnographers began to take an increasing interest in Eastern societies, it was only after the Persian occupation of the Greek-speaking cities of Asia Minor

---

107   Rosenmeyer, *Epistolary Fictions*, p. 13.
108   Rosenmeyer, *Epistolary Fictions*, p. 14. For the letter as an instrument of death see Homer, *Iliad*, 6. 160–80.
109   Johnson, *Historical Fictions*, p. 157.
110   Hacham, '3 Maccabees and Esther', p. 784. See also Charles D. Harvey, *Finding Morality in the Diaspora: Moral Ambiguity and Transformed Morality in the Book of Esther*, BZAW, 128 (Berlin: de Gruyter, 2003), p. 226, who concludes that the conscientious loyalty of Mardochaios to the king is deliberately emphasized in the Greek version.
111   This theme, for which the royal letter is an admirable generic vehicle, is a preoccupation of late Hellenistic Jewish literature. See Johnson, *Historical Fictions*, p. 157, *apropos* texts such as Daniel, III Maccabees and Greek Esther: 'The moral of these stories is clear and consistent: faithful observance of the Jewish Law and loyal observance of the law of the land are two sides of the same coin, and no violation of the one can be justified by appeal to the other'.
112   The earliest Persica are attributed to Dionysius of Miletus, Hellanicus of Lesbos, and Charon of Lampsacus, whose work survives in fragments and epitomes. See Janett Morgan, *Greek Perspectives on the Achaemenid Empire: Persia Through the Looking Glass* (Edinburgh: Edinburgh University Press, 2016), pp. 193–94.

that Persia becomes the focus of intense historiographical study, such that a distinct form of literary expression emerges.[113]

To the extent that they are known to us, the later Persica are characterized by a high degree of hybridity, including the use of embedded texts, and feature both tragic and romantic motifs. The structuring principle is arguably novelistic, and in accordance with the conventions of the so-called Greek novella.[114] Following Lloyd Llewellyn and James Robson, this genre may be defined as a complex prose narrative concerned with ostensibly real-life characters in an identifiable historical setting; the plot typically turns on the reversal in fortunes of a central character; the exposition is of limited length, and the narrative is relatively self-contained.[115] The genetic connection between novelistic composition and historiography is particularly apparent in two authors with a noted interest in Persian settings, Ctesias of Cnidus (*fl.* 400 BCE) and Xenophon of Athens (*c.* 430–354 BCE).[116] Only the work of the latter is fully extant.

On the analysis of Llewellyn and Robson, Xenophon's *Cyropaedia*, a semi-fictional biography of Cyrus the Great, contains four distinct stories interwoven into the main historical narrative.[117] Each is interspersed with reported dialogue, which forms an important aspect of the way in which the stories are told; they feature stock characters associated with the world of the court (an indolent king; a cruel despotic figure; plotting eunuchs; a devoted servant; a beautiful but chaste woman); at the same time, and despite their brevity and formulaic character, 'they often contain scenes of emotional intensity'.[118] Xenophon's use of the novella was evidently anticipated by Ctesias, whose *Persica* appears to have been made of up a string of short and longer novellas intercalated within an historical framework.[119] Worthy of note are the parallels between the Zarinaea story in *Persica* and that of Panthea in *Cyropaedia*, especially in their depiction of the central female characters.[120] Like Esther, both are remarkably beautiful and strong women, who exert a profound influence over the course of events.

The *Persica* served an important political function in the Greek world by representing a threatening imperial entity as the 'other' over-against which a distinct

---

113   Lloyd Llewellyn-Jones and James Robson, *Ctesias' 'History of Persia': Tales of the Orient* (London: Routledge, 2009), p. 45.
114   Llewellyn-Jones and Robson, *Ctesias*, p. 69.
115   Llewellyn-Jones and Robson, *Ctesias*, p. 69.
116   Some of the embedded narratives of Herodotus (*c.* 484–25 BCE) exhibit strong novelistic characteristics. See the analysis of Henry R. Immerwahr, *Form and Thought in Herodotus*, Philological Monographs, 23 (Chico, CA: Scholars Press, 1996), pp. 69–71, of what he refers to as the *dramatic logos*, which bears a relation to Attic tragedy, and is structured on the basis of a strict distinction between speeches and action.
117   The stories of Panthea the Lady of Susa (*Cyropaedia*, 5. 1. 1–30; 6. 1. 30–55; 6. 4. 1–20; 7. 3. 3–17); Croesus (7. 2. 1–29); Gobryas (4. 6. 1–12; 5. 2. 1–14; 5. 4. 41–51); and Gadatas the chieftain (5. 3.15–4.51).
118   Llewellyn-Jones and Robson, *Ctesias*, pp. 70–71.
119   The work of Ctesias is available only in fragments. For text and translation, see Jan P. Stronk, *Ctesias' Persian History. Part I: Introduction, Text and Translation*, Reihe Geschichte, 2 (Dusseldorf: Wellem, 2010).
120   Llewellyn-Jones and Robson, *Ctesias*, p. 71.

Hellenic political identity could be constructed. Each generation produced its own Persica, which served to reconfirm Greek national self-consciousness, a tradition which continued until the advent of Alexander, and indeed beyond, as Greek speakers negotiated changing political realities.[121] On the present reading of LXX-Esth, the Greco-Jewish translator may be seen to have taken the Persica as a model in order to work through some of the ramifications of Jewish national identity within the imperial context of the Hellenistic world. In its Hebrew form the story of Esther already bears a strong resemblance to the Greek novella. These generic features are significantly heightened in LXX-Esth, likely under the influence of Greek exemplars. Significantly the action of the narrative is motivated by the threat of political insurrection; it then traces two classic reversal of fortune scenarios: the rise of Mardochaios, and the fall of Haman. The intervention of a strong and beautiful female character figures decisively, a pivotal scene the dramatic potential of which is fully exploited in LXX-Esth (Addition D). In this respect the generic term 'historical romance' (used long ago by Walter Miller *apropos* the *Cyropaedia*) seems a very apt description of the literary conventions at play in the Greek translation.[122]

▼ ABSTRACT   The present study investigates the use of fictive epistolography in Greek Esther (LXX-Esth). Following a brief introduction to generic analysis, it takes up Bakhtin's notion of generic complexity, for which the embedded letter is exemplary. It turns next to the two royal letters recorded in LXX-Esth (Additions B and E), and offers a close reading of B with reference both to its generic affiliations and communicative strategy. The letter is then situated within the overall narrative strategy of the Greek version, which, it is suggested, is indebted to certain Greek models, and congruent with a significant trend in late Hellenistic Jewish literature.

121 Llewellyn-Jones and Robson, *Ctesias*, p. 55.
122 Xenophon, *Cyropaedia, Books 1–4*, ed. by Walter Miller, LCL, 51 (Cambridge, MA: Harvard University Press, 1914), p. viii. For a discussion of LXX-Esth in relation to the conventions of romantic narrative (as delineated by Northrop Frye), see Boyd-Taylor, 'Esther's Great Adventure', pp. 102–13.

PETER DUBOVSKÝ

Rhetoric of Solomon's Speech in I Kings 8. 12–13 and III Kingdoms 8. 53a

Emanuel Tov reviewing the commentaries of the last three centuries pointed out various levels of scholars' engagement with the LXX (see his paper in this volume). The presence or the absence of the LXX in the commentaries depends not only on personal interest or the scholars' capacity to deal with complex textual problems, but also on methodologies the commentators adopted. In this paper I investigate rhetorical methodologies and how LXX studies can contribute to rhetorical analysis. The concept of rhetorical analysis varies significantly in scholarly writings. For some scholars, rhetorical analysis is a broad concept corresponding by and large to synchronic analysis. Thus, an analysis of poetics, structure or other literary dynamics of the biblical text can be considered rhetorical analysis. For other scholars, rhetorical analysis is applicable exclusively to discourses, their dynamic and persuasive power.[1] Since in this book narrative analysis and other synchronic methods are treated separately, I will focus on the rhetoric of direct speech in the Bible. By including direct discourse, the biblical writer stopped the narrative flow and forced the reader to listen to words put into the mouth of important heroes. Consequently, in a speech even a small change can make a big difference. An addition or elimination of one word can substantially change the dynamics of a speech and, consequently, its persuasive power and goal. From a rhetorical viewpoint, LXX constitutes a real 'problem', since, often, it not only varies the words, but also entire passages are placed in different places, changing the sequence of events. Thus, if the biblical scribes let a hero deliver his / her speech employing a rhetorical device, which is absent in LXX, then the rhetoric of the entire speech changes.

---

1 For some important studies in rhetorical analysis see, for example, Wilfred G. E. Watson, *Classical Hebrew Poetry: A Guide to Its Techniques* (Sheffield: JSOT Press, 1984); Samuel A. Meier, *Speaking of Speaking: Marking Direct Discourse in the Hebrew Bible*, VT.S, 46 (Leiden: Brill, 1992); Luis Alonso Schökel, *Manuale di poetica ebraica* (Brescia: Editrice Queriniana, 1989); Roland Meynet, *Traité de rhétorique biblique*, Rhétorique Sémitique, 4 (Paris: Lethiielleux, 2007); Ian Worthington, *A Companion to Greek Rhetoric*, Blackwell Companions to the Ancient World Literature and Culture (Oxford: Blackwell, 2007); Jeanne Fahnestock, *Rhetorical Style: The Uses of Language in Persuasion* (Oxford: Oxford University Press, 2011).

New Avenues in Biblical Exegesis in Light of the Septuagint
ed. by Leonardo Pessoa da Silva Pinto and Daniela Scialabba, Turnhout, 2022 (*SEPT*, 1), pp. 129–156
© BREPOLS ❦ PUBLISHERS   DOI 10.1484/M.SEPT-EB.5.127715

Consequently, whenever the Greek and Hebrew texts differ either in vocabulary, in syntax, or in sequence of narrated events, the rhetorical dynamic of a given passage changes. As the result, scholars would have instead of one rhetorical analysis several, often contradictory results. The choice of most scholars in studying the rhetorical devices of one text seems to be a pragmatic solution. A rhetorical analysis needs a fixed text that can be scrutinized, be it Hebrew, Greek, Latin, Syriac, Aramaic, Slavonic, etc.

The importance of the connection between rhetorical analysis and textual criticism has been noticed by textual critics as well. Scholars engaged in textual criticism have been fully aware that it is not sufficient to analyze the variants according to their typology such as omission, additions, transposition, but it is important to assess the role the variants play in a given text and manuscript.[2]

A further problem with LXX studies concerns the textual tradition of the Greek texts. The Greek texts had gone through a long and complex development that resulted in different types of Greek texts. Scholars have been debating for several decades regarding the Old Greek and its relation to the Hebrew text(s). Therefore, the most recent LXX studies urge scholars not to reduce their analysis of the Septuagint to Rahlfs's edition, but to take into consideration the developmental stages of the Greek Bible(s). The development of the Greek texts, their mutual relations and harmonization pose a further level of complication for scholars engaged in rhetorical analysis. Each Greek text, thus, has its own rhetorical dynamic. Consequently, a scholar engaged in rhetorical analysis should study the rhetoric of the MT but also that of a reconstructed Old Greek, the proto-Lucianic, Lucianic, Hexaplaric texts, etc. Since the multiplicity of variants, recensions, and editions of the LXX urge scholars to analyze several Hebrew and Greek texts from the rhetorical viewpoint and consequently, they may uncover other structures, rhetorical devices and dynamics. All this can lead to a labyrinth of rhetoric(s) in which not only beginners, but also well-trained scholars can easily get lost.

Keeping in mind the complexity of LXX studies, we can now return to the goal of this volume — the impact of LXX studies on exegetical methods. The question is whether the engagement of the LXX would require changes in the methodological principles of rhetorical analysis. The answer is negative. So, we can conclude that taking into consideration LXX studies does not change notably the nature of the rhetorical analysis, but as suggested by Siegfried Kreuzer, it significantly changes its application. Namely, how should a scholar committed to rhetorical analysis deal with different texts and consequently different, often diverging, rhetorical dynamics? The rhetorical analysis will need to make a step that has not been contemplated thus far: to compare the rhetoric of different textual traditions. Such a comparison can branch out into different studies such as a study of the development of rhetorical devices, an audience-oriented rhetoric, a reconstruction of theological background of different rhetorical strategies, etc.

---

2   Julio Trebolle Barrera, 'Textual Pluralism and Composition of the Books of Kings: 2 Kings 17,2–23: MT, LXX^B, LXX^L, OL', in *After Qumran: Old and Modern Editions of the Biblical Texts — The Historical Books*, ed. by Hans Ausloos, Bénédicte Lemmelijn and Julio Trebolle Barrera (Leuven: Peeters, 2012), pp. 213–26 (p. 213); see also Reinhard Gregor Kratz and Bernhard Neuschäfer, *Die Göttinger Septuaginta: Ein editorisches Jahrhundertprojekt* (Berlin: de Gruyter, 2013).

The following paper is an attempt to demonstrate the potential contribution of LXX studies to rhetorical analysis. Since such an endeavor cannot be done only on a theoretical level, a notoriously known example of an ancient hymn[3] in I Kings 8. 12–13 in the MT and in III Kingdoms 8. 53a serves as an example for illustrating a potential integration of two scholarly fields that have had little exchange. Let me summarize the steps of my analysis as well as the results I have reached. First, I will present Solomon's speeches in their literary context. Secondly, I will study the textual variants. This analysis will show that there were two different speeches inserted in two different places in Chapter 8. Thirdly, I will discuss important literary features of these speeches and their literary genres and show how the rhetoric and, consequently, the message of the texts changes depending on the content and the location of Solomon's speeches.

1. Solomon's Speeches and their Context

Solomon's speeches during the dedication of the Jerusalem temple easily qualify as the most impressive pieces of biblical rhetoric, be it in the Hebrew, Greek, Latin or other versions. A close comparison of I Kings 8 (the MT) and III Kingdoms 8 (Greek versions and partially also the Vetus Latina) shows that the Greek and Hebrew versions of these chapters by and large correspond to each other (Table 1). However, there are important textual differences.[4]

Section	MT	LXX[B]	LXX[L]	LXX[A]
Transportation of the ark	8. 1–11	8. 1–11	8. 1–11	8. 1–11
Speech n. 1 (Lord and deep darkness)	8. 12–13	absent	absent	8. 12–13
Speech n. 2 (Introductory blessing)	8. 14–21	8. 14–21	8. 14–21	8. 14–21
Speech n. 3 (Name theology)	8. 22–30	8. 22–30	8. 22–30	8. 22–30
Speech n. 4 (Petitions)	8. 31–53	8. 31–53	8. 31–53	8. 31–53
Speech n. 5 (Sun)	absent	8. 53(a)	8. 53(a)	8. 53(a)
Speech n. 6 (Concluding blessing)	8. 54–61	8. 54–61	8. 54–61	8. 54–61
Concluding ceremonial	8. 62–66	8. 62–66	8. 62–66	8. 62–66

Table 1. Sequence of events in I Kings 8 and III Kingdoms 8; for practical reasons I have listed only three Greek manuscripts.

Table 1 shows that the sequence of Solomon's speeches (I Kings 8. 12–61) is similar in all manuscripts and even a good part of the rhetorical devices occurs in both

---

3 Scholars generally recognized that verses 8. 12–13 contained an ancient tradition that was later reworked by the Deuteronomist; see Simon J. DeVries, *1 Kings*, WBC, 12, 2nd edn (Nashville: Thomas Nelson Publishers, 2003), pp. 122, 125.
4 It is beyond the purpose of this study to list all the differences between LXX and MT in Chapter 8; however, let me list at least some of them: 1. MT and LXX[B,L] disagree on the participants in the transportation of the ark in 8. 1; 2. Most textual differences are concentrated in verses 8. 27–33; 3. Another important group of important differences are in 8. 52 and 65.

the Hebrew and Greek texts. In sum, viewing Solomon's speeches from a larger perspective, it seems that the editors of these texts made their best to present them as similarly as possible, contrary to other chapters of the Books of the Kings.[5] Therefore, the differences between the Greek texts in III Kingdoms 8. 53a and Hebrew I Kings 8. 12–13 strikes an attentive reader (Table 2).

Section	MT	LXX[B,L]
Transportation of the ark	8. 1–11	8. 1–11
Speech n. 1 (Lord and deep darkness)	8. 12–13 Then Solomon said, 'The Lord has said that he would dwell in thick darkness. I have built you an exalted house, a place for you to dwell in forever'. (NRSV)	absent
Speech n. 2–4	8. 14–53	8. 14–53
Speech n. 5 (Sun)	absent	8. 53(a) 'A sun the Lord made manifest in the sky; he said that he should dwell in deep darkness: "Build my house, a remarkable house for yourself, to dwell in anew"'. (NETS)
Speech n. 6	8. 54–61	8. 54–61
Concluding ceremonial	8. 62–66	8. 62–66

Table 2. Position and the content of speeches n. 1 and 5.

Since the end of nineteenth century CE scholars have been arguing about the original Hebrew *Vorlage* of speeches n. 1 and 5, their mutual dependence, and their original position.[6] While scholars have been investigating the original version of Solomon's prayer and its location, they put aside the rhetoric of the different versions. Similarly, the scholars investigating the rhetoric of this chapter have not paid attention to the textual variants. In order to bring into dialogue these two fields it is necessary to start with an analysis of textual witnesses (Table 3).

---

5 See for example the article of Trebolle Barrera in this volume.
6 Three scenarios are plausible: 1. The poem(s) were inserted in two places; 2. The poem was originally after 8. 11 as in the MT and only later it was modified and placed after 8. 53 as in the LXX[B,L]; 3. the poem was originally after 8. 53 and then moved after 8. 11. Since the review of the scholarly opinions have been presented with great accuracy and erudition in two recently published articles, the reader is referred to them: Matthieu Richelle, 'How to Edit an Elusive Text? The So-Called Poem of Solomon (1Kgs 8:12–13 MT // 8:53a LXX) as a Case Study', *Textus*, 27 (2018), 205–28 (pp. 206–07, 224–25); Szabolcs-Ferencz Kató, 'Der Tempelweihspruch Salomos (1 Reg 8,12–12/ Lxx Iii Bas 8,53): Eine Neuer Vorschlag', *ZAW*, 131/2 (2019), 220–34 (pp. 220–21).

Rahlfs	LXX^B	LXX^L	LXX^A (8. 53)	OL	MT (8. 12–13)	LXX^A (8. 12–13)
Τότε ἐλάλησεν Σαλωμων ὑπὲρ τοῦ οἴκου, ὡς συνετέλεσεν τοῦ οἰκοδομῆσαι αὐτόν	Τότε ἐλάλησεν Σαλωμων ὑπὲρ τοῦ οἴκου, ὡς συνετέλεσεν τοῦ οἰκοδομῆσαι αὐτόν	τότε ἐλάλησε Σαλομων ὑπὲρ τοῦ οἴκου, ὡς συνετέλεσε τοῦ οἰκοδομῆσαι αὐτόν	Τότε ἐλάλησεν Σαλωμων ὑπὲρ τοῦ οἴκου, ὡς συνετέλεσε τοῦ οἰκοδομῆσαι αὐτόν	Tunc locutus est Solomon pro domo, quam consumavit aedificans	אָז אָמַר שְׁלֹמֹה	Τότε εἶπε Σαλωμών
Ἥλιον ἐγνώρισεν ἐν οὐρανῷ κύριος,	Ἥλιον ἐγνώρισεν ἐν οὐρανῷ κύριος,	Ἥλιον ἔστησεν ἐν οὐρανῷ κύριος,	Ἥλιον ἐγνώρισεν ἐν οὐρανῷ	Solem statuit in caelo Dominus		
εἶπεν τοῦ κατοικεῖν ἐν γνόφῳ	εἶπεν τοῦ κατοικεῖν ἐκ γνόφῳ	καὶ εἶπε τοῦ κατοικεῖν ἐν γνόφῳ	Κύριος εἶπε τοῦ κατοικεῖν ἐν γνόφῳ	et dixit commorare in dedicatione domus	יְהוָה אָמַר לִשְׁכֹּן בָּעֲרָפֶל	κύριος εἶπεν τοῦ σκηνῶσαι ἐν γνόφῳ
Οἰκοδόμησον οἶκόν μου, οἶκον ἐκπρεπῆ σαυτῷ,	Οἰκοδόμησον οἶκόν μου, οἶκον ἐκπρεπῆ σαυτῷ,	Οἰκοδόμησον οἶκόν μου, οἶκον εὐπρεπῆ σαυτῷ,	Οἰκοδόμησον οἶκόν μου, οἶκον εὐπρεπῆ σαυτῷ,	Aedifica mihi domum pulcherrimam	בְּנֹה בָנִיתִי בֵּית בֵּל לָךְ	ᾠκοδόμησα οἶκον κατοικητηρίου σοι
τοῦ κατοικεῖν ἐπὶ καινότητος.	τοῦ κατοικεῖν ἐπὶ καινότητος.	τοῦ κατοικεῖν ἐπὶ καινότητος.	τοῦ κατοικεῖν ἐπὶ καινότητος.	inhabitare in novitate	מָכוֹן לְשִׁבְתְּךָ עוֹלָמִים	ἔδρασμα τῆς καθέδρας σου αἰῶνας
οὐκ ἰδοὺ αὕτη γέγραπται ἐν βιβλίῳ τῆς ᾠδῆς;	οὐκ ἰδοὺ αὕτη γέγραπται ἐπὶ βιβλίου τῆς ᾠδῆς;	οὐκ ἰδοὺ αὕτη γέγραπται ἐν βιβλίῳ τῆς ᾠδῆς;	οὐχὶ αὕτη γέγραπται ἐν βιβλίῳ τῆς ᾠδῆς;	Nonne haec scripta sunt in libro Cantici?		

Table 3. Textual variants of speeches n. 1 and 5.

Thorough analyses of the variants presented by Trebolle Barrera and Richelle show that the Greek and Hebrew texts have several elements in common. Based on these similarities, scholars have argued that speeches n. 1 and n. 5 originally were one speech and they concluded that a text reconstructed on the basis of LXX^{B,L} represents the pre-Lucianic text.[7] Julius Wellhausen was one the first scholars who proposed a retroverted Hebrew text.[8] His proposal was then modified by numerous scholars, among whom are P. S. F. van Keulen, J. Trebolle Barrera, M. Richelle, and S. F. Kató (Table 4). The differences between their proposals depend on which text the authors preferred. Trebolle Barrera relied more on LXX^L and OL, whereas Richelle more on

---

7   See for example Julio Trebolle Barrera, 'From Secondary Versions through Greek Recension to Hebrew Editions. The Contribution of the Old Latin Version', in *The Text of the Hebrew Bible and Its Editions: Studies in Celebration of the Fifth Centennial of the Complutensian Polyglot*, ed. by Pablo A. Torijano Morales and Andrés Piquer Otero, Supplements to the Textual History of the Bible (Leiden: Brill, 2017), pp. 180–216 (p. 205).

8   Julius Wellhausen, *Die Composition des Hexateuchs un der historischer Bücher des Alten Testaments*, zweiter Druck mit Nachträgen (Berlin: Georg Reimer, 1889), pp. 268–69.

MT, and S. F. Kató combines both the Greek and Hebrew texts. These examples show that there is no consensus regarding the reconstruction of the *Vorlage* of the Hebrew text, nor on the variants of the Old Greek. Moreover, the reconstruction of the Hebrew *Vorlage* also depends on the theoretical models behind the scholarly discussion, namely, the precedence and importance of the Masoretic text (pre-Masoretic text), or the Old Greek (proto-Masoretic text), or even the Vetus Latina.[9]

Wellhausen[10]	Van Keulen[11]	Trebolle Barrera[12]	Richelle[13]	Kató[14]
			אז אמר שלמה על הבית ככלותו לבנות אתו	אז אמר שלמה על הבית ככלותו לבנות אתו
שמש הכין בשמים יהוה אמר לשכן בערפל בנה בניתי בית נוה לי לשבת לחדש	שמש הודע בשמים יהוה אמר לשכן בערפל בנה בית זבול לך לשבת בעולמים	שמש העמיד בשמים יהוה אמר לשכן בערפל בנה לי בית זבול לשבת לחדש	שמש הודע בשמים יהוה אמר לשכן בערפל בנה לי בית זבל לשבת לעולמים	שמש הודע בשמים יהוה אמר לשכן בערפל בנה בניתי בית זבל לשבת לעולמים
הלא־היא כתובה בספר הישר			הלא־היא כתובה על־ספר הישר	הלא־היא כתובה על־ספר הישר

Table 4. Reconstructions of the Hebrew *Vorlage*; the differences among the proposal are underlined.

In sum, even though the Greek and Hebrew texts share several similarities, the LXX contains important pluses.[15] Therefore, most scholars would agree with Juha Pakkala that 'the textual history of these verses may be even more complicated. It is probable

---

9 For a general review see *Textual History of the Hebrew Bible*, ed. by Armin Lange and Emanuel Tov (Leiden: Brill, 2016), 1B, pp. 362–446. See also Adrian Schenker, 'What Do Scribes, and What Do Editors Do? The Hebrew Text of the Masoretes, the Old Greek Bible and the Alexandrian Philological *Ekdoseis* of the 4th and 3rd Centuries b.c., Illustrated by the Example of 2 Kings 1', in *After Qumran: Old and Modern Editions of the Biblical Texts — The Historical Books*, ed. by Hans Ausloos, Bénédicte Lemmelijn and Julio Trebolle Barrera (Leuven: Peeters, 2012); Adrian Schenker, 'Die *Tiqqune Sopherim* im Horizont der biblischen Textgeschichte. Theologische Korrekturen, Literarische Varianten in alttestametlichen Text und Textvielfalt: Wie gehen sie zusammen?', in *Making the Biblical Text: Textual Studies in the Hebrew and the Greek Bible*, ed. by Innocent Himbaza, OBO, 275 (Fribourg: Academic Press, 2015), pp. 33–47; Anneli Aejmelaeus, 'Textual History of the Septuagint and the Principles of Critical Editing', in *The Text of the Hebrew Bible and Its Editions: Studies in Celebration of the Fifth Centennial of the Complutensian Polyglot*, ed. by Pablo A. Torijano Morales and Andrés Piquer Otero, Supplements to the Textual History of the Bible (Leiden: Brill, 2017), pp. 160–79.

10 Wellhausen, *Die Composition*, p. 269.

11 Percy S. F. van Keulen, *Two Versions of the Solomon Narrative: An Inquiry into the Relationship between MT 1 Kgs. 2–11 and LXX 3 Reg. 2–11*, VT.S, 104 (Leiden: Brill, 2005), p. 172.

12 Trebolle Barrera, 'From Secondary Versions', p. 206.

13 Richelle, 'How to Edit an Elusive Text?', p. 214.

14 Kató, 'Der Tempelweihspruch', p. 229.

15 See for example Kató, 'Der Tempelweihspruch'; for the pluses and their interpretation see Richelle, 'How to Edit an Elusive Text?', pp. 214–18.

that neither the MT nor the LXX preserves the oldest text in full'.[16] By comparing the content of speeches n. 1 and 5 in different manuscripts and in Chronicles, I argue that speech n. 1 and 5 were originally two independent speeches and only later were harmonized as it is now found in LXX.

2. Vetus Latina

A significant step forward in the investigation of Solomon's speeches n. 1 and 5 is Trebolle Barrera's study of OL. He showed that in this case OL indeed can contribute to the reconstruction of the textual history of Solomon's speeches.[17] Unfortunately, the Vetus Latina of I Kings 8 has not been entirely preserved; however, the marginal glosses to the Vulgate allow for reconstruction of the variants of the Vetus Latina (Table 5).[18] In the following paragraphs I compare the Vetus Latina with MT and the Greek manuscripts. Since a part of this comparison has already been done by Trebolle Barrera, this paper presents only the nuances that are important for grasping both the development of the textual tradition and the rhetorical dynamic of speeches n. 1 and 5.

Vetus Latina (L_{91-95})	Translation (author)	Retroverted text (author)[19]
Tunc locutus est Salomon pro domo, quam consumavit aedificans	Then Solomon said regarding the temple, when he had finished building (it):	אז אמר שלמה על הבית ככלותו לבנות (אתו)
Solem statuit in caelo Dominus et dixit Commorare in dedicatione domus,	'The Lord put the sun in the heaven and said (to it): "Sojourn in the dedication of the temple!	שמש העמיד (הכין) בשמים יהוה ו(י)אמר שב (שכן, לין) בחנכת הבית
aedifica mihi domum pulcherrimam inhabitare in novitate.	Build me a beautiful temple to live (in it) during the new month/moon!"'	בנה לי בית טוב לשבת לחדש
Nonne haec scripta sunt in libro Cantici?	Have not these been written in the Book of Song?	הלא־הם כתובים על־ספר השיר

Table 5. Vetus Latina, text, translation, and retroverted text.

---

16 Juha Pakkala, *God's Word Omitted: Omissions in the Transmission of the Hebrew Bible*, FRLANT, 251 (Göttingen: Vandenhoeck & Ruprecht, 2013), p. 225.

17 Trebolle Barrera, 'From Secondary Versions', pp. 204–07. His study presupposes a sophisticated model of mutual dependence of the manuscripts as presented in Pakkala and Mühler's book; See Julio Trebolle Barrera and Pablo Torijano Morales, 'From the Greek Recensions to the Hebrew Editions: A Sample from 1 Kgs 2:1–10', in *Insights into Editing in the Hebrew Bible and the Ancient Near East: What Does Documented Evidence Tell Us About The Transmission of Authoritative Texts?*, ed. by Reinhard Müller and Juha Pakkala, CBET, 84 (Leuven: Peeters, 2017), pp. 267–93 (p. 268).

18 Antonio Moreno Hernández, *Las glosas marginales de Vetus Latina en las Biblias Vulgatas Españolas 1–2 Reyes*, TECC, 49 (Madrid: CSIC, 1992), p. 105.

19 The translation and the reconstructed Hebrew *Vorlage* is proposed by the author. The author expresses his deep gratitude to his colleagues Augustinus Gianto and Luigi Santopaolo for their helpful comments. The author, however, bears responsibility for the possible questions and problems of the proposed translation.

First, all versions open speech n. 1 with an introductory statement 'Then Solomon said'. This phrase is shared by all the versions, including the MT. However, the OL has *pro domo* that corresponds to ὑπὲρ τοῦ οἴκου in LXX^{B,L}, but it does not occur in the MT.

Secondly, the phrase *quam consumavit aedificans* reflects the Greek, ὡς συνετέλεσεν τοῦ οἰκοδομῆσαι αὐτόν. The Greek versions correspond to OL, but the phrase is not in the MT.

Thirdly, the first words of Solomon's speech are rendered in OL in the past tense and refer to God's activity: *Solem statuit in caelo Dominus*. This phrase does not occur in MT but it corresponds to Ἥλιον ἔστησεν ἐν οὐρανῷ κύριος in LXX^L. However, the LXX^B has the verb ἐγνώρισεν instead of ἔστησεν. Despite all scholarly efforts, it is impossible to conclude that LXX^B is only a scribal mistake. The difference between the LXX^B and LXX^L has led scholars to different conclusions. Trebolle Barrera concludes that the reading of ἔστησεν represents the pre-Lucianic text, since it occurs in OL and in the Coptic translation.[20] Richelle noticed a growing preference for LXX^B (ἐγνώρισεν). But he cautiously concludes that there is no final solution.[21] Therefore we can conclude that there are two types of Greek texts (Table 6b): one preserved in LXX^B and the other preserved in LXX^L. As for the verbs in question, LXX^L is closer to OL. Similarly, the difference between LXX^L and LXX^B is noticeable in the position of the subject of the verb (the Lord).[22] While OL and LXX^L place the subject (the Lord) before the conjunction (*et*, καί), LXX^B has no conjunction καί and thus the subject (the Lord) can be the subject of the verb εἶπεν.[23] In sum, LXX^L is more similar to OL, whereas LXX^B is closer to MT (יהוה אמר לשכן בערפל), which has no *waw* conjunction.

Fourthly, another difference occurs with the phrase *dixit commorare*. An equivalent of this phrase is in LXX^{B,L}, which reads εἶπε τοῦ κατοικεῖν. OL employs the form *commorare*. This word can be either an infinitive of the active verb *commorare* or an imperative of the deponent verb *commoror*. There are several reasons to conclude that *commorare* is an imperative of the deponent verb. First, the Vulgate of I Kings 8. 12 has *tunc ait Salomon Dominus dixit ut habitaret in nebula*, without the infinitive.[24] This reflects normal Latin syntax, namely, that after *dixit* there is either direct speech or, if there is indirect speech, the clause is

---

20 Trebolle Barrera, 'From Secondary Versions', p. 205.
21 Richelle, 'How to Edit an Elusive Text?', pp. 209–11.
22 If the conjunction 'and' is missing then it makes sense to conclude that the Lord was the subject of the verb ἔστησεν/statuit or ἐγνώρισεν; see van Keulen, *Two Versions*, p. 165.
23 See Richelle, 'How to Edit an Elusive Text?', p. 211. Brooke's edition adds comma after the word κύριος and thus suggest that the κύριος is the subject of the verb ἐγνώρισεν. However, no comma is in the *Codex Vaticanus*.
24 Similarly, II Chronicles 6. 1 has the same structure both in Greek and Hebrew but the Latin translation is *tunc Salomon ait Dominus pollicitus est ut habitaret in caligine*.

introduced by *ut* or by the construction accusative plus infinitive.[25] Moreover, the investigation of the Latin texts of the Bible shows that the verb is mainly deponent.[26] Finally, a similar construction occurs a few times in OL or other texts.[27] Reading *commorare* as an imperative, the syntax of the OL changes radically. There are two imperatives: 'Dwell in the dedication of the house! [...] Construct me a beautiful house!' Whereas the first imperative refers to the sun, the second is addressed to Solomon. LXX^B,L correspond to MT, whereas OL has a different reading. The Hebrew retroverted texts of OL and LXX^B,L presuppose different consonants. The OL would have only the root (שב, שכ[ו]ן, לין), whereas LXX^B,L would have *lamed* (לשכן), as is the case in MT.

Fifthly, OL's *in dedicatione domus*[28] does not occur in the Greek manuscripts nor in MT (see Table 6b). LXX^L reads τοῦ κατοικεῖν ἐν γνόφῳ, which corresponds to MT' s לִשְׁכֹּן בָּעֲרָפֶל. Thus, both MT and LXX^L speak about God's decision/ intention to dwell in thick darkness. LXX^B is different from LXX^L because it reads ἐκ γνόφῳ 'out of darkness',[29] instead of ἐν γνόφῳ 'in the darkness'. Thus, LXX^B speaks about God's decision to no longer live in darkness. On the contrary, OL reads '[(Sun), dwell] in the dedication of the house [temple]!' A retroverted text based on OL would be: לין (שב) שכן בחנכת היבת. A similar phrase is in Psalm 29(30). 1 (*dedicatione domus*; cf. also II Chronicles 7. 9 and III Esdras 7. 7). Other ceremonies of such a dedication feast are: Numbers 7. 84, 88 (dedication of the altar); Nehemiah 12. 27 (dedication of the walls). God in OL commands the sun to dwell/stay in the dedication feast. It is impossible to reconstruct the details of this ceremony. It seems that it was connected with the sun and its rays entering the temple. A reference to the ceremony and the feast of the dedication of the temple is mentioned in II Chronicles 7. 9 (MT reads 'dedication of the altar'; Vulgate and Syriac read 'dedication of the temple').[30]

---

25 Another possible Latin construction would be *dixit se + commorare*. However, the OL does not have a subject in accusative (*se*).

26 There are several other reasons to buttress this claim. First, in Latin the verb *commorare in* as infinitive is often used after an auxiliary verb, if independent it is normally an imperative. Thus, for example: *Si cupis a Deo diligi, ama vulnera Christi, commorare in illis*. Cf. *Viator Christianus in Patriam tendens* (Rome: [n. pub.], 1709), p. 160.

27 Amos 7. 12 *et dixit Amasias ad Amos: Vada, discende in terram Iuda et ibi commorare et ibi prophetabis*. The OL does not follow here the MT. Other OL manuscripts read *ibi vive*. Other manuscripts follow the MT and read *comede ibi panem*, thus also the Vulgate. It can be also found in some quotations such as Genesis 35. 1 reads *Et dixit Deus ad Jacobum: surge, ascende Bethelem, et commorare ibi*; whereas the Vulgate reads *locutus est Deus ad Iacob surge et ascende Bethel et habita ibi*; Genesis 38. 8 *Rebeca* [...] *inquit, fuge mi fili, abi ad Labanum* [...] *et commorare apud eum*; Abbatis Lhomond, *Epitome Historiae Sacrae*, 59.

28 In some Latin manuscripts there is a version *in nebula edificationis domus meae*; cf. Moreno Hernández, *Las glosas marginales*, p. 105. This might be a harmonization with the Greek and Hebrew texts.

29 For possible interpretations see below.

30 Trebolle Barrera, 'From Secondary Versions', p. 205.

Sixthly, the command to build the house *aedifica mihi domum* in OL has its corresponding phrases in LXX[B,L], Οἰκοδόμησον οἶκόν μου. The word *mihi* can correspond to the Greek μου.[31] This phrase is different in MT. The forms of the Hebrew verbs are *qatal* 1st sg and infinitive absolute and not the imperative. Moreover, LXX[B,L] has two houses: οἶκόν μου, οἶκον εὐπρεπῆ (LXX[L]) / ἐκπρεπῆ (LXX[B]). The phrase οἶκον εὐπρεπῆ σαυτῷ, which corresponds literarily to MT's בֵּית זְבֻל לָךְ.[32] However, the pronoun has different meaning: in MT the לָךְ refers to God (to you), whereas the σαυτῷ in LXX[B,L] refers to Solomon. Two houses are juxtaposed in LXX, but the conjunction καί linking the two houses is found in no other manuscript. The absence of the conjunction according to van Keulen indicates that no Greek translator interpreted the verse as referring to two different houses.[33] Thus, if the expression οἶκον ἐκπρεπῆ σαυτῷ is understood as the apposition of οἶκόν μου, then God asked Solomon to build a beautiful house that will be God's house and, at the same time, the house of the king, which makes little sense. Therefore, it is more plausible to conclude that the expression οἶκον εὐπρεπῆ σαυτῷ is an insertion into the Greek text to harmonize it with MT, which has the exact same phrase בֵּית זְבֻל לָךְ. Thus, LXX[B,L] probably expanded the Latin *pulcherrimam* (see below) into οἶκον εὐπρεπῆ σαυτῷ. A similar difference between MT, OL, and LXX[B,L] continues in the following verse. The expression מָכוֹן לְשִׁבְתְּךָ in MT refers to God (suffix -ךָ), whereas LXX[B,L] do not have an equivalent to the Hebrew suffix -ךָ referring to God and, thus, the expression τοῦ κατοικεῖν in Greek can refer to either Solomon or God. No such ambiguity is found in OL since the verb *inhabitare* refers to God. Based on this observation, it is reasonable to accept Trebolle Barrera's suggestion that OG should be reconstructed on the basis of OL and it had only οἰκοδόμησον οἶκόν μου/μοι εὐπρεπῆ. LXX[B,L] has a plus (οἶκόν and σαυτῷ) that made LXX[B,L] harmonize the Greek text with MT.[34]

Seventhly, in LXX[B,L] Solomon's palace is qualified as εὐπρεπῆ (LXX[L]) / ἐκπρεπῆ (LXX[B]), while OL's reference to the temple qualifies it as *domum pulcherrimam* and MT describes it is as בֵּית זְבֻל. The term *domum pulcherrimam* does not correspond to the Hebrew phrase בית זבל, since the term זבל is never translated as *pulcher* or an equivalent in the Latin manuscripts. A normal equivalent of *pulcher* is טוב and an equivalent of זבל is *habitaculum*. The Greek translations in this case correspond to the Latin *pulcherrimum*, since both superlatives εὐπρεπῆ (LXX[L]) / ἐκπρεπῆ (LXX[B]) are derived from the verb πρέπω 'be fitting, be seemly/suitable', which corresponds well to the Hebrew טוב.

---

31 The Hebrew *Vorlage* would be either בנה לי בית, or בנה ביתי; see Richelle, 'How to Edit an Elusive Text?', p. 212 n. 17.

32 Several manuscripts read זבול; Benjamin Kennicott, *Vetus Testamentum Hebraicum cum Variis Lectionibus* (Oxonii: Typographeo Clarendoniano, 1776), p. 618.

33 van Keulen, *Two Versions*, p. 166.

34 Trebolle Barrera, 'From Secondary Versions', p. 205.

Eighthly, MT contains the expression מָכוֹן לְשִׁבְתְּךָ. Whereas the infinitive שבת has the equivalents in both LXX^{B,L} and OL, the substantive מָכוֹן does not occur in LXX^{B,L} or in OL.[35]

Ninthly, the phrase *in novitiate* has its equivalent in the Greek phrase ἐπὶ καινότητος, but MT has עוֹלָמִים.[36] Rendered in Hebrew as חדש, OL and the Greek texts link the presence of God with the celebration of a new month or a new moon (see below).

Tenthly, another harmonization of the Greek and Hebrew text of Solomon's speech n. 1 can be observed on Hexaplaric versions (Table 6a). According to the following table, text 'A[37] reads οἰκοδομῶν ᾠκοδόμησα οἶκον κατοικητηρίου σοι, which is a literal translation of the Hebrew בָּנֹה בָנִיתִי בֵּית זְבֻל. LXX^{A} does not have οἰκοδομῶν. The addition of the οἰκοδομῶν indicates that 'A made the Greek text even more similar to MT than LXX^{A}.

I Kings 8. 12–13 (MT)	III Kingdoms 8. 12–13 (LXX^{A})	III Kgdms 8. 12–13 (Hexaplaric; 'A)
אָז אָמַר שְׁלֹמֹה יְהוָה אָמַר לִשְׁכֹּן בָּעֲרָפֶל בָּנֹה בָנִיתִי בֵּית זְבֻל לָךְ מָכוֹן לְשִׁבְתְּךָ עוֹלָמִים	Τότε εἶπε Σαλωμών κύριος εἶπεν τοῦ σκηνῶσαι ἐν γνόφῳ ᾠκοδόμησα οἶκον κατοικητηρίου σοι ἕδρασμα τῇ καθέδρᾳ σου αἰῶνας	τότε εἶπεν Σαλωμών κύριος εἶπεν τοῦ σκηνῶσαι ἐν γνόφῳ *οἰκοδομῶν* ᾠκοδόμησα οἶκον κατοικητηρίου σοι ἕδρασμα τῇ καθέδρᾳ σου αἰῶνας,

Table 6a. Hexaplaric versions of Solomon's speech n. 1;
in italics a further harmonization/addition in Aquila.

Finally, the Greek texts and OL end Solomon's speech n. 5 with a reference to the Book of Song.[38] This reference is not in MT.

In light of these differences, it is possible to draw some conclusions. First, LXX^{B,L} are more similar to OL than to MT. Wherever there are differences between LXX^{B,L} and OL, the differences in LXX^{B,L} correspond to MT. Secondly, LXX^{L} is more similar to OL than LXX^{B}. LXX^{B} has some specific aspects that do not occur in any other text. Thirdly, the similarities between MT and OL are so few that it is difficult to speak about the same speech (Table 6b).

---

35 The LXX^{B,L} have only one verb for 'to dwell', κατοικεῖν, whereas the MT in 8. 12–13 has שכן and ישב. The Hexaplaric version as in LXX^{A} preserves this difference and translate לשכן as τοῦ σκηνῶσαι and לשבתך with the noun καθέδρας σου. The translations of שכן with (κατα)σκηνῶσαι is rather frequent; see Trebolle Barrera, 'From Secondary Versions', p. 204.

36 For possible retroverted Hebrew text see Richelle, 'How to Edit an Elusive Text?', pp. 211–13.

37 O' omits 8. 12–13; Frederick Field, *Origenis Hexaplorum Quae Supersunt: Sive Veterum Interpretum Graecorum in Totum Vetus Testamentum Fragmenta / Post Flaminium Nobilium, Drusium, Et Montefalconium, Adhibita Etiam Versione Syro-Hexaplari, Concinnavit, Enmandavit, Et Multis Partibus Auxit Fridericus Field*, 2 vols (Oxonii: E Typographeo Clarendoniano, 1875), I, p. 611.

38 Some scholars prefer to emendate the expression ἐν βιβλίῳ τῆς ᾠδῆς (retroverted as על-ספר השיר) to על-ספר הישר; Richelle, 'How to Edit an Elusive Text?', p. 213.

LXX^B (8. 53a; speech n. 5)	LXX^L (8. 53a; speech n. 5)	OL (Speech n. 5)	MT (8. 12–13; speech n. 1)
Τότε ἐλάλησεν Σαλωμων <u>ὑπὲρ τοῦ οἴκου, ὡς συνετέλεσεν τοῦ οἰκοδομῆσαι αὐτόν</u>	*τότε ἐλάλησε* Σαλομων <u>ὑπὲρ τοῦ οἴκου, ὡς συνετέλεσε τοῦ οἰκοδομῆσαι αὐτόν</u>	**Tunc locutus est Salomon** <u>pro domo, quam consumavit aedificans</u>	אָז אָמַר שְׁלֹמֹה
Ἥλιον ἐγνώρισεν ἐν <u>οὐρανῷ</u> **κύριος,** εἶπεν *τοῦ κατοικεῖν* ἐκ γνόφῳ	Ἥλιον ἔστησεν ἐν <u>οὐρανῷ</u> **κύριος,** *καὶ* εἶπε *τοῦ κατοικεῖν ἐν γνόφῳ*	<u>Solem statuit in caelo</u> **Dominus** <u>et</u> **dixit** commorare in dedicatione domus	יְהוָה אָמַר לִשְׁכֹּן בָּעֲרָפֶל
<u>Οἰκοδόμησον οἰκόν μου,</u> **οἶκον** *ἐκπρεπῆ σαυτῷ,*	<u>Οἰκοδόμησον οἰκόν μου,</u> **οἶκον** *εὐπρεπῆ σαυτῷ,*	<u>Aedifica mihi domum</u> pulcherrimam	בָּנֹה בָנִיתִי בֵּית זְבֻל לָךְ
τοῦ κατοικεῖν <u>ἐπὶ καινότητος.</u>	**τοῦ κατοικεῖν** <u>ἐπὶ καινότητος.</u>	**inhabitare** <u>in novitate</u>	מָכוֹן לְשִׁבְתְּךָ עוֹלָמִים
<u>οὐκ ἰδοὺ αὕτη γέγραπται</u> *ἐπὶ βιβλίου τῆς ᾠδῆς;*	<u>οὐκ ἰδοὺ αὕτη γέγραπται</u> *ἐν βιβλίῳ τῆς ᾠδῆς;*	<u>Nonne haec scripta sunt in libro Cantici?</u>	

Table 6b. OL, LXX^{B,L}, and MT. The words common in all versions are in bold; the words common in the OL and the LXX^{B,L} are underlined; the words in italics are in common in the MT and LXX^{B,L}, but not in the OL; the words in normal script occur only in a given version.

3. Chronicles

Before presenting the textual development of Solomon's speeches, it is necessary to compare them with the Books of Chronicles. The Hebrew text of Solomon's speech n. 1 is almost identical in both Kings and Chronicles (I Kings 8. 12–13//II Chronicles 6. 1–2). However, the Greek text of Chronicles changes the content of speech n. 1 significantly (Table 7).

I Kings 8. 12–13 (MT)	II Chronicles 6. 1–2 (MT)	II Paralipomenon 6. 1–2[39]
אָז אָמַר שְׁלֹמֹה יְהוָה אָמַר לִשְׁכֹּן בָּעֲרָפֶל בָּנֹה בָנִיתִי בֵּית זְבֻל לָךְ מָכוֹן לְשִׁבְתְּךָ עוֹלָמִים	אָז אָמַר שְׁלֹמֹה יְהוָה אָמַר לִשְׁכּוֹן בָּעֲרָפֶל: *וַאֲנִי* בָנִיתִי בֵית זְבֻל לָךְ וּמָכוֹן לְשִׁבְתְּךָ עוֹלָמִים:	τότε εἶπεν Σαλωμων Κύριος εἶπεν τοῦ κατασκηνῶσαι ἐν γνόφῳ· *καὶ ἐγὼ ᾠκοδόμηκα οἶκον τῷ ὀνόματί σου ἅγιόν σοι καὶ ἕτοιμον τοῦ κατασκηνῶσαι εἰς τοὺς αἰῶνας.*

Table 7. Speech n. 1; in italics the differences between the MT and the Greek texts of the Chronicles.

---

39   Some Greek versions of the Chronicles harmonize the text with the MT; *Paralipomenon liber II,* ed. by Robert Hanhart, Septuaginta Vetus Testamentum Graecum, VII 2 (Göttingen: Vandenhoeck & Ruprecht, 2014), p. 155.

In sum, Solomon's speech n. 1 in MT of II Chronicles 6. 1–2 closely follows MT of I Kings 8. 12–13. Similarly, the following speeches (n. 2–4) in II Chronicles 6. 3–40 closely follow MT of I Kings 8. 14–53. However, the contrary is true for speech n. 5. At this point the Chronicler introduced a different speech of Solomon that has the same form in both Hebrew and the Greek texts:

> Now rise up, O LORD God, and go to your resting place,
> you and the ark of your might.
> Let your priests, O LORD God, be clothed with salvation,
> and let your faithful rejoice in your goodness.
> O Lord, God, do not reject your anointed one.
> Remember your steadfast love for your servant David. (*NRSV*)

This new speech of Solomon in Chronicles substitutes speech n. 5. Thus, the Chronicler concludes Solomon's dedication of the temple with an invocation that is a form of a test: if God heard Solomon's prayer, then the temple was accepted by God (II Chronicles 6. 41–42). Only after this invocation does the fire consume the sacrifices (similar to Elijah and Abraham) and the temple is fill with the glory of God (II Chronicles 7. 1–2; cf. I Kings 8. 11).[40] The test has a positive result.

In sum, Chronicles, composed after the exile but before the Greek translations of the Books of Kings, indicate that already when the text was composed, speech n. 1 was fixed in its Hebrew form and it was faithfully transmitted in the Hebrew text of the Chronicles. On the contrary, the Chronicler felt free to substitute speech n. 5 with his own invocation. Later on, the Greek translators of Chronicles changed even speech n. 1.

4. A History of the Transmission of Solomon's Speeches n. 1 and 5

The comparison of the Greek, Latin and Hebrew texts of I Kings 8. 12–13 and III Kingdoms 8. 53a has shown that there are significant differences among the texts and, despite all scholarly efforts, it is not easy to establish a common *Vorlage* for LXX[B,L] (III Kingdoms 8. 53a) and MT (I Kings 8. 12–13). Notwithstanding this difficulty scholars have insisted that speech n. 1 and n. 5 can be traced down to one speech. Such a speech would be better preserved in the Old Greek[41] that can be reconstructed from LXX[B,L]. Such a reconstructed speech would represent a text older than the MT of I Kings 8. 12–13.[42]

---

40 Kató, 'Der Tempelweihspruch', pp. 222–23.
41 In fact it was Julius Wellhausen who proposed this idea and it was followed by all scholars; see Wellhausen, *Die Composition*, pp. 268–69.
42 Adrian Schenker, *Septante et Texte Massorétique dans l'histoire la plus ancienne du texte de 1 Rois 2–14*, Cahiers de la Revue Biblique (Paris: Gabalda, 2000), p. 134.

Before presenting a textual history of Solomon's speeches, let me summarize the results of the analysis presented above that serve as the basis for a reconstruction of the textual history of speeches n. 1 and 5.

First, only II Chronicles 6 and LXX^A of III Kingdoms 8 have both speeches (n. 1 and 5). Thus, Chronicles and LXX^A presented Solomon's speeches as a frame for speeches n. 2–4. Speeches n. 2–4 have been transmitted only with some minor differences in the Hebrew and Greek texts of I Kings 8 and II Chronicles 6. This core of speeches was introduced and concluded with speeches n. 1 and 5.[43] Consequently, the Chronicler and the composer of LXX^A understood Solomon's speeches n. 1 and 5 as two speeches that served different purposes.[44]

Secondly, a comparison of manuscripts showed that Solomon's speech n. 1 has been preserved in two forms: (1) The MT of I Kings 8. 12–13, II Chronicles 6. 1–2, the LXX^A of III Kingdoms 8. 12–13 and Aquila; (2) Greek translation of II Chronicles 6. 1–2. From this we can conclude that speech n. 1 was fixed in the time of the composition of the Chronicles and only later revised in the Greek translation of the Books of Chronicles.

Thirdly, while speech n. 1 was fixed in MT at the time of the composition of Chronicles, a comparison of manuscripts suggests that we can speak about three variants of speech n. 5: OL, LXX^{A,B,L},[45] and the Chronicler's invocation. Speech n. 5 in OL is a double command of the Lord. It was a combination of a command to build the temple with a declaration of God to dwell in the darkness in LXX^{B,L}. This was transformed into an invocation in II Chronicles 6. 41–42. While Chronicles' version of speech n. 5 is substantially different from OL and LXX^{B,L}, the one in OL is reflected in LXX^L and partially also in LXX^B, yet with important differences.

Based on these observations we can propose that Solomon's speeches n. 1 and 5 underwent complex redactional and editorial activities.

The **first stage** of the text represents one-insertion text, be it speech n. 1 or n. 5. Thus, we can distinguish the MT-insertion type and the LXX/OL-insertion type.

The MT-insertion served as an opening for Solomon's speeches: at this stage only verses 8. 12–13 were introduced. This text was quickly fossilized as seen in II Chronicles 6. 1–2 and reflected in LXX^A and Aquila.

The Greek and Latin insertions served as a conclusion of Solomon's speeches n. 2–4. A close comparison of 8. 53a in OL and LXX^{B,L} pointed out that the similarities between OL and MT of 8. 12–13 are very few. This suggests that OL presents speech n. 5 as a different speech than speech n. 1. Consequently, OL, by and large, may represent the Old Greek text. On the contrary, LXX^{B,L} are more similar to MT's

---

43 This understanding of the text can be seen in Origin's edition of Hexapla; cf. Field, *Origenis Hexaplorum*, p. 611.

44 In fact, most scholars agree that the insertions after 8. 11 and after 8. 53 took place in different stages: 'These two examples suggest that in each case the difference has been caused by the insertion of new material in two different places in the textual witnesses. […] It is no coincidence that in all cases the LXX represents a more original sequence than MT'; Emanuel Tov, *The Greek and Hebrew Bible: Collected Essays on the Septuagint*, V.T.S, 72 (Leiden: Brill, 1999), p. 414. See also van Keulen, *Two Versions*, p. 176.

45 The LXX^A follows closely the LXX^B, except the term εὐπρεπῆ that is similar to the LXX^L.

speech n. 1. Wherever LXX^{B,L} differ from OL, the versions in LXX^{B,L} followed MT. This observation suggests two possible solutions: 1) There were in fact two versions of speech n. 5: one preserved in LXX^{B,L} and the other preserved in OL; 2) LXX^{B,L} is a harmonization of the OG text as preserved in OL with the MT of I Kings 8. 12–13. The notes presented above urge us to opt for the latter.[46] The harmonization of LXX^{B,L} with MT can be observed on changing *in dedicatione domus* in OL into ἐν γνόφῳ in LXX^{B,L} ~ MT. Similarly, the imperative *commorare* in OL becomes an infinitive τοῦ κατοικεῖν in LXX^{B,L} ~ לִשְׁכֹּן in MT. Another sign of harmonization with MT is the addition of 'the second house' οἶκον εὐπρεπῆ/ἐκπρεπῆ σαυτῷ, which is a literal translation of בֵּית זְבֻל לָךְ of the MT.[47] Thus, LXX^{B,L} represent the harmonization of OG, as largely preserved in OL, with MT. This harmonization can be considered the **second stage** of the textual development of Solomon's speeches n. 1 and 5. The differences between LXX^B and LXX^L suggest that LXX^L follows more closely OL and wherever LXX^L is different from OL, the Greek text is similar to the MT of 8. 12–13. LXX^B has readings that, on the one hand, represent a further level of harmonization with the MT;[48] on the other hand, it contains the readings that cannot be explained as scribal mistakes.[49] In sum, the Old Greek as preserved in OL considered speech n. 5 distinct from speech n. 1. On the contrary, LXX^{B,L} considered speeches n. 1 and 5 as substantially similar.

---

46 Several scholars concluded that the LXX^{B,L} represent the texts that are closest to the OG; See Schenker, *Septante et Texte Massorétique*, pp. 134–35. Based on this reconstruction of the OG, some scholars developed a theory on the original text that spoke about sun-god. Thus, Pakkala's reconstruction of the text: 'Then Solomon said regarding the temple, when he had finished building it: "The Sun-god made (it) known in the heavens, Yhwh declared (he wants) to live in darkness. Build my temple, an exalted house for me, a new place to live in"'. Pakkala, *God's Word Omitted*, p. 230. So he concluded 'the Greek text implies that the Sun was an animate being, because Yhwh was able to address him. Since Judaism developed towards stricter monotheistic conceptions, it would be difficult to comprehend the addition of partially polytheistic ideas in later context'. Pakkala, *God's Word Omitted*, p. 225.

47 A harmonization with the MT is well-known in the LXX^{B,L}. In I Kings 8 there are several harmonizations of the Greek texts with the MT: the term 'all' in 8. 3 added in the LXX^L that corresponds to the MT but missing in the LXX^B; in 8. 5 the LXX^L has reversed order (oxen and sheep), whereas the LXX^B follows the MT (sheep and oxen); in 8. 6 the LXX^B reads 'The priests brought the ark to its place', whereas the LXX^L harmonizes the text according to the MT reading 'The priests brought the ark of the covenant of the Lord to its place'; in 8. 10–11 the LXX^B has only house, whereas the LXX^L follows the MT reading 'the house of the Lord'; in 8. 14 the MT and the LXX^L does not have king, while the LXX^B has the word king twice; in 8. 18 the LXX^L reflects the MT, whereas the LXX^B uses two different expressions 'Because it came upon your heart […] since it was upon your heart'. The harmonization is not restricted to Chapter 8, but it occurs in other parts of I Kings, thus for example the addition in III Kingdoms 6. 1: the LXX^L has the addition of καὶ ᾠκοδόμησεν τὸν οἶκον τῷ Κυρίῳ that corresponds to the MT וַיִּבֶן הַבַּיִת לַיהוָה that is missing in the LXX^B.

48 For the example the omission of *et*/καί.

49 The verb ἐγνώρισεν, instead of ἔστησεν. Scholars often consider the preposition ἐκ a corruption of the original text; see Richelle, 'How to Edit an Elusive Text?', p. 211 n. 16. However, it can be considered a theological correction suggesting that after the dedication of the temple God decided to leave the darkness.

The **third stage** of the textual development is the double insertion, one after verse 8. 11 and the other after 8. 53. This double insertion is preserved in LXX[A] (III Kingdoms 8. 12–13,[50] 53a) and in II Chronicles 6. 1–2, 41–42. At this stage of the text, speeches n. 1 and 5 form the frame for the rest of Solomon's speeches.

The **fourth stage** of textual development represents the Hexaplaric harmonization as in Aquila of III Kingdoms 8 and the Greek translation of II Chronicles 6. 1–2.

5. Rhetoric Analysis of the Versions

A reconstruction of the textual history as outlined above has shown that at some point the biblical authors and translators did consider speeches n. 1 and 5 to be two distinctive speeches and only in later stages these speeches were harmonized as in LXX[B,L]. In the following stages, i.e. in LXX[A] both speeches were preserved and finally both speeches were revised as in the Greek translations of Chronicles and in Aquila.[51] Therefore, for grasping the rhetoric of both speeches it is crucial to investigate the style and the meaning of both speeches in OL, LXX[B,L], and MT. In other words, the reconstruction of the textual history cannot be the end for an exegete. Rather, it should be a starting point. As argued in the introduction, a small change in the text can have a big significance in the rhetorical dynamics of a given passage. The rhetoric of a speech, the persuasive power of a discourse, and the meaning of a passage depend on the words chosen or omitted, the syntax, and the position of the phrases in the discourse. Since speeches n. 1 and 5 differ as to the wording, the literary genre, and their position in the chapter, it is only natural to expect that the rhetoric of MT, LXX[A,B,L] and OL would be different. To illustrate the impact of the different texts upon the rhetorical analysis this study will be divided into two parts — a study of the rhetoric of speeches n. 1 and 5 (micro-rhetoric) and a study of the rhetoric of the speeches within their context (macro-rhetoric).

5.1. *Micro-Rhetoric of the Versions*

The first task of rhetorical analysis is to understand the nature, structure and other peculiarities of the speeches. For this reason, each speech must be analyzed on its own.[52]

5.1.1. *Speech n. 1 (MT-I Kings 8. 12–13)*

One of the main differences between speech n. 1 (as in the MT of I Kings 8. 12–13; cf. also LXX[A]) and n. 5 (as in LXX[B,L] of III Kingdoms 8. 53a and the OL) is the

---

50   It is to be noted that 8. 13 is partially different in the LXX[A]. The MT reads בֵּית זְבֻל לָךְ, whereas the LXX[A] omits the words זְבֻל לָךְ.

51   This conclusion partially matches with the conclusions of Tov and Richelle who argued that the speeches were inserted at two different places and in different times (see above).

52   Some scholars reduced the differences between both speech to addition/omission of pious ideology; see DeVries, *1 Kings*, p. 117 n. 12.a.

form of the verb 'to build'. While the former has the verb in the indicative 1st sg (infinitive absolute and *qatal*, בנה בניתי), the latter has the verb in the imperative 2nd sg (οἰκοδόμησον).[53] Most scholars simply changed the indicative of the MT into an imperative, as in LXX[B,L] (cf. Table 4) and thus eliminated one of the most important differences between speech n. 1 and 5. However, no extant manuscript has the verb 'to build' in the imperative in speech n. 1, nor does any manuscript have the verb in the indicative in speech n. 5. While the change of the 1st sg *qatal* in speech n. 1 to an imperative is possible for textual critics, such a change causes serious problems for scholars studying the rhetoric of Chapter 8.

This might have been a reason why Wellhausen and others were cautious when retroverting the Greek into Hebrew and preferred to keep 1st sg (בנה בניתי בית נוה לי).[54] The literary genre of speech n. 1 and 5 depends, in fact, on the form of the verb 'to build'. Several scholars kept the infinitive absolute followed by a *qatal* (בנה בניתי). Wellhausen called the speech *eine Einweihungsrede Salomons* and Martin Noth called it *Hausweihesprüche*.[55] Oswald Loretz followed the same argumentative line and suggested a more radical solution, specifically, that the text as in the MT of I Kings 8. 12–13 should be kept as it is, including the 1st sg.[56] Based on the parallels from Ugarit he considered verses I Kings 8. 12–13 a poetic elaboration of the literary genre *Tempelweihespruch*.[57]

Burke O. Long built upon Loretz's proposal and presented further parallels, in particular, a Sumerian dedicatory inscription of Gudea.[58] According to Long, Gudea's inscription is a:[59]

very early and elaborate example of a rather stable literary genre: the dedicatory inscription. [...] these inscriptions are built on three essential elements: (1) the

---

53 The OL has two imperatives: *commorare* and *aedifica*.

54 Wellhausen, *Die Composition*, p. 269.; see also Martin Noth, *Könige* (Neukirchen-Vluyn: Neukirchener, 1968), I. Teilband IX/1, p. 168, 172; Kató, 'Der Tempelweihspruch', p. 229.

55 Wellhausen, *Die Composition*, p. 269; Noth, *Könige*, p. 181; Volkmar O. Fritz, *1 & 2 Kings*, Continental Commentaries (Philadelphia: Fortress Press, 2003), p. 90; DeVries, *1 Kings*, p. 113. It is important to notice that most scholars adopted the terminology, even though their retroverted text changed the indicative into the imperative.

56 Oswald Loretz, 'Der Torso Eines Kanaanäisch-Israelitischen Tempelweihspruches', *UF*, 6 (1974), 478–80 (pp. 479–80).

57 Loretz, 'Der Torso', pp. 478, 480; Other authors also recognized poetic nature of speech n. 1 and pointed out different rhetorical devices such as *parallelismus membrorum*; van Keulen, *Two Versions*, p. 177. A poetic nature of speeches was rarely taken into consideration by the authors who reconstructed the OG. An exception is Kató who based his reconstruction on the basis of the parallel structures; see Kató, 'Der Tempelweihspruch', p. 228–32.

58 'Oh, my king, Ningirsu, who turnest back the raging water; lord, whose word goes forth on high; O son of Enlil, thou warrior who commandest, my right hand has wrought for thee; I have built thy temple for thee; with joy I would bring thee into it. I will place my goddess Bau on thy left [?] side into a good dwelling ye shall go'. (Cylinder B, col. 2:16–3:1; Barton RISA, 239); see Burke O. Long, *1 Kings: With an Introduction to Historical Literature*, FOTL (Grand Rapids, MI: Eerdmans, 1984), pp. 97–98.

59 Long, *1 Kings*, p. 98.

address to a particular deity who is named and honored, (2) identification of the donor, and (3) a declaration that the donor has built, caused to be made [...] In form a dedicatory inscription is a 'prayer'; in function, both prayer and memorial to the king and his god(s)

Even though the parallels presented by Long can be rightly questioned, his basic point remained valid.[60] The verb 'to build' either in the 1st or 3rd sg refers to a past event. These forms of the verb were frequently used in literary genres, such as prayers, rituals; however, more frequently they occurred in royal inscriptions, dedicatory and commemorative texts, etc.[61] References to the construction of a temple completed by a king, especially in the historiographic compositions, was not only a mere reminiscence of the event, but it was part of royal propaganda. Such a speech was probably delivered[62] after edifices had been completed. These texts / speeches served primarily to exalt the builder. Seen in the prospective of the dedicatory inscriptions / speeches, speech n. 1 refers to a past event, in this case to Solomon's construction of the temple. In sum, the past tense ('I have indeed built') locates Solomon's speech in the category of dedicatory speeches / inscriptions.[63]

The second task of any rhetorical analysis is to capture the structure and the nature of the passage. Speech n. 1 is a direct speech of Solomon (first level of direct speech) within which is embedded a reference to God's speech (indirect speech):

I.	Narrator's introduction:		אָז אָמַר שְׁלֹמֹה
II.	Solomon's direct speech		
	1.	Solomon's introduction	יהוה אָמַר
	2.	God's indirect speech	לִשְׁכֹּן בָּעֲרָפֶל
	3.	Solomon's speech	בָּנֹה בָנִיתִי בֵּית זְבֻל לָךְ מָכוֹן לְשִׁבְתְּךָ עוֹלָמִים

This scheme shows that speech n. 1 has two parts: I. narrative introduction and II. Solomon's direct speech. Solomon's direct speech consists of three segments. In the first part Solomon indirectly reported God's speech (יהוה אמר + ל). This way of referring to someone's speech is not very frequent in the Bible, but when used it normally conveys the intention of the speaker to do something (Joshua 22. 33: אָמְרוּ לַעֲלוֹת עֲלֵיהֶם לַצָּבָא לְשַׁחֵת אֶת־הָאָרֶץ cf. also Exodus 17. 10). Thus, Solomon's speech combines God's speech and Solomon's action. While such a combination is not an

---

60   His examples from the Bible and from the ANE can hardly be considered the same literary genre.
61   For a ritual of dedication see SAA 12 87; for examples from the royal inscriptions see RIMA 1 A.0.33.1:4–18; RIMA 2 A.0.0.99.2:129–30; RINAP 4 104 iii 41–42; for dedicatory inscriptions see BE 01/1 38; RIME 3/2.01.03.14; RIME 4.01.10.05; 4.03.06.14.
62   Most text using the verb 'I have built/he has built' have survived in written form.
63   Long, 1 Kings, pp. 97, 247, 56.

unusual rhetorical device, the particularity of Solomon's speech is its poetic style, in particular *parallelismus membrorum*:[64]

לִשְׁכֹּן בָּעֲרָפֶל׃	יהוה אָמַר
מָכוֹן לְשִׁבְתְּךָ עוֹלָמִים	בָּנֹה בָנִיתִי בֵּית זְבֻל לָךְ

By means of this rhetorical device the scribes created a parallelism between לִשְׁכֹּן בָּעֲרָפֶל and מָכוֹן לְשִׁבְתְּךָ עוֹלָמִים, on the one hand, and the expressions יְהוָה אָמַר and בָּנֹה בָנִיתִי and בֵּית זְבֻל לָךְ, on the other hand.[65] Thus, the indirect speech presenting God's intention to dwell in thick darkness is counterbalanced by Solomon's action, his construction of the temple. God's dwelling (place), thick darkness, was transformed in the second sticho into a place in which God would live forever, the temple. The בֵּית זְבֻל (temple) becomes the מָכוֹן of God's dwelling. By means of this parallelism the scribes showed that God's decision to dwell in thick darkness was changed by Solomon's construction of the temple and from now on God would live in the temple.[66]

In sum, MT describes the passage from God-living in thick darkness to God-dwelling in the temple.[67] This shift can be better understood when inserted in the ANE context. In fact, darkness is one of the elements that linked biblical God[68] with other ANE gods.[69] The ANE gods were able to transform darkness into light.[70] As a result of this religious concept, a temple in the ANE became the physical structure that could transform darkness into light.[71] In view of these ancient traditions a construction of

---

64 This poetic style based on *parallelismus membrorum* is only partially preserved in the LXX[A]:
κύριος εἶπεν   τοῦ σκηνῶσαι ἐν γνόφῳ
ᾠκοδόμησα   οἶκον κατοικητηρίου σοι
ἕδρασμα τῆς καΘέδρας σου αἰῶνας.

65 Fritz, *1 & 2 Kings*, p. 90.

66 See Fritz, *1 & 2 Kings*, pp. 91–92. It is also possible that *parallelismus membrorum* has the opposite effect as well. The thick darkness suggests something otherworldly and mysterious whereas the temple is a concrete and human construction. The *parallelismus membrorum*, thus, suggests that the temple as place of encounter with God is both mysterious and concrete. God is both accessible and beyond human comprehension.

67 P. R. House formulates this shift as follows: 'Normally the Lord dwells "in dark cloud" or where human beings cannot see him. […] however, the Lord chooses to descend to earth and relate to Israel directly'. Paul R. House, *1, 2 Kings*, NAC, 8 (Nashville: Broadman & Holman, 1995), p. 139.

68 For more details see Martin Jan Mulder, *1 Kings*, HCOT (Leuven: Peeters, 1998), pp. 397–99.

69 For a more detailed study see Shiyanthi Thavapalan, 'Radiant Things for Gods and Men: Lightness and Darkness in Mesopotamian Language and Thought', *Colour Turn*, 6 (2018), 1–36. Some ANE texts can illustrate my argument: '[…] the most luminous lord among the gods, his master, an artfully wrought golden *šagan* bowl, whose decoration with bisons and snakes, and with the awe-inspiring dark raincloud attracts never-ending admiration […]' (RIME 3/2.01.05.02:19–20); see also a prayer to Nabu 'to show bright light to those who are in darkness' (STT 1 71:34).

70 See for example '[It is] you who illuminates their darkness like Shamash' (a collation BMS 12 + AOAT 034, 040 + OrNS 59, 487 + K.15430, 35:34; see ORACC website), '[Marduk] who illuminates the darkness' (BMS 58 o 4'), 'Šamaš, the great judge of the gods, the one who illuminates darkness' (RINAP 4 48:6), 'Illuminator [of darkness]' (SAA 20 31 r. 5), 'Dispeller of darkness' (SAA 20 31:21'), 'Lord whose opened face[?] brightens darkness[?]' (K 02860 o 1).

71 Referred to Iggi's temple: 'its great radiance, shining like Gira in the black darkness' (Sumer 04, 1–38 C).

the temple represented a shift from a god surrounded by darkness into a god who was light. A god living in the temple illuminated the people living in the darkness.

In the light of this brief study, speech n. 1 assumes a specific character. On the one hand, it bears features of dedicatory inscriptions rightly placed after the ceremony of dedication of the temple and whose purpose was to glorify King Solomon as a temple builder. On the other hand, ancient mythological traditions allowed the biblical scribes to elaborate an important theological argument: a god living in the darkness became a god living in the temple and thus illuminating his city and his people. This message is conveyed above all by means of the rhetorical device of *parallelismus membrorum*.

5.1.2.   Speech n. 5 (III Kingdoms 8. 53a, LXX[B,L] and OL)

There are four rhetorical devices employed in speech n. 5 that contradistinguish speech n. 5 from speech n. 1. First, speech n. 5 starts with a completion formula that does occur in MT. Secondly, speech n. 5 contains an imperative 'build!' (III Kingdoms 8. 53a) instead of the past tense as in MT (I Kings 8. 13). Thirdly, while both speeches refer indirectly to God's speech, speech n. 5 also reports a part of God's direct speech. Fourthly, speech n. 5 concludes with a reference to a source from which Solomon draws his speech (the Book of Song).[72]

Let us, first, present the technique of *Wiederaufnahme* (resumption) that the scribes adopted in LXX. The repetition of the verb συνετέλεσεν created a space into which the prayer could have been inserted. No such resumption is in MT.

[53]Τότε ἐλάλησεν Σαλωμων ὑπὲρ τοῦ οἴκου, ὡς **συνετέλεσεν** τοῦ οἰκοδομῆσαι αὐτόν

Ἥλιον ἐγνώρισεν ἐν οὐρανῷ κύριος,
εἶπεν τοῦ κατοικεῖν ἐκ γνόφῳ
Οἰκοδόμησον οἶκόν μου, οἶκον ἐκπρεπῆ σαυτῷ,
τοῦ κατοικεῖν ἐπὶ καινότητος.
οὐκ ἰδοὺ αὕτη γέγραπται ἐν βιβλίῳ τῆς ᾠδῆς;

[54]Καὶ ἐγένετο ὡς **συνετέλεσεν** Σαλωμων προσευχόμενος […] (LXX[B])

The differences between the MT and the Greek and Latin manuscripts have an impact on the structure of the passage as well. Let us start with the structure of speech n. 5 in LXX[L]:

I.   Narrator's introduction: τότε ἐλάλησε Σαλομων ὑπὲρ τοῦ οἴκου, ὡς
                                        συνετέλεσε τοῦ οἰκοδομῆσαι αὐτόν

II. Solomon's direct speech

    1.   Solomon's speech   Ἥλιον ἔστησεν ἐν οὐρανῷ κύριος, καὶ εἶπε
      A. God's intention   τοῦ κατοικεῖν ἐν γνόφῳ
      B. God's direct speech   Οἰκοδόμησον οἶκόν μου, οἶκον εὐπρεπῆ σαυτῷ,
      C. God's intention   τοῦ κατοικεῖν ἐπὶ καινότητος.
    2.   Solomon's reference to a source   οὐκ ἰδοὺ αὕτη γέγραπται ἐν βιβλίῳ τῆς ᾠδῆς;

---

72 Other differences will be discussed in the section 'Macro-rhetoric'.

While the general division (I. narrative introduction and II. Solomon's direct speech) is the same for speeches n. 1 and n. 5, the composition of part II is different. In contrast to speech n. 1 that has two different verbs for dwelling (יֵשֵׁב and שְׁכֹן), LXX[A,B,L] use only one verb τοῦ κατοικεῖν. The repetition of the same form of the same verb creates a space for the central part of the speech. i.e. the command to build the house(s). As a result, these segments are organized in a concentric structure:[73]

A Ἥλιον ἔστησεν ἐν οὐρανῷ κύριος, καὶ εἶπε
B **τοῦ κατοικεῖν** ἐν γνόφῳ
C Οἰκοδόμησον οἶκόν μου, οἶκον εὐπρεπῆ σαυτῷ,
B' **τοῦ κατοικεῖν** ἐπὶ καινότητος.
A' οὐκ ἰδοὺ αὕτη γέγραπται ἐν βιβλίῳ τῆς ᾠδῆς;

This concentric structure[74] highlights God's command (segment C). God's speech embedded into Solomon's speech adds weight to what is said. It was not Solomon who decided to build the temple and forced God to live in the temple, but it was God who decided it and commanded Solomon to carry out his decision. Some scholars noticed the importance of the imperative in the context of God's direct speech and called speech n. 5 *imperativische Hymnus*.[75] An investigation of similar cases in the ANE literature shows that the verb 'to build' in the imperative is normally a part of the divine command delivered in multifaceted forms such as visions, prophecies, omina, etc., contrary to the past tense of the verb that is mainly used in dedicatory inscriptions (see above).[76] Both the concentric structure of the speech and its ANE background highlight the divine command addressing a human being and the request to build a temple. This command speaks about a future temple, contrary to speech n. 1 that refers to a just completed temple.

This divine command is framed by a double repetition of the verbal form τοῦ κατοικεῖν. If these phrases are read together, then speech n. 5 contains God's two indirect speeches. The first presents God's intention to dwell in darkness while the second indicates his intention to live 'in newness'. God's direct speech is the turning point that radically changed God's dwelling on earth. In sum, it was not Solomon's

---

73 Parts A and A' represent speeches referring (εἶπε and γέγραπται) to God's works and to the source. Parts B and B' are linked by means of the same verb τοῦ κατοικεῖν.
74 Another feature to be noticed is the rhythm of Solomon's direct speech:
    Ἥλιον ἐγνώρισεν ἐν οὐρανῷ κύρι**ος**,
    εἶπεν τοῦ κατοικεῖν ἐν γνόφ**ῳ**
    Οἰκοδόμησον οἶκόν μου, οἶκον ἐκπρεπῆ σαυτ**ῷ**,
    τοῦ κατοικεῖν ἐπὶ καινότη**τος**.
75 Frank Crüsemann, *Studien zur Formgeschichte von Hymnus und Danklied in Israel*, WMANT (Neukirchen-Vluyn: Neukirchener, 1969), p. 19.
76 See for example 'At the time when Lugal-ayaĝu, the temple administrator of Iškur, ruled in Adab, Damgalnuna chose Ur-Imma in her holy heart and told him "Build my temple for me!"' (RIME 1.14.2001:1–4); command to Esarhaddon: 'He called his name for kingship to be the one who renovates Ešarra [and] makes [its] cult complete, [saying]: "Build lof[ty] Ešarra, the dais of my desire (and) make its design artful like the stars [lit. writing] of the firmament"'. (RIMA 4 76:5–8); cf. also RIMA 1 22:39–40; command to Nabonidus: 'During the night, he showed m[e] a dream, saying: "Quickly, build Eḫulḫul, the temple of the god Sîn of the city Ḫarrān"'. (Shaudig 3.1; Nabonidus 47 i 11).

construction of the temple that caused the change, but it was God who gave the command and Solomon only fulfilled the task.

Furthermore, even though speech n. 1 seems to convey a similar idea, the content is radically different. While speech n. 5 presents the temple as a permanent dwelling place of God, speech n. 1 only points to a radical shift in God's presence on earth, but it does not induce the reader to conclude that the temple is a permanent abode of God.

LXX^B has a different preposition ἐκ γνόφῳ instead of ἐν γνόφῳ, as in LXX^L. Even though most scholars consider the preposition ἐκ a scribal mistake, such a mistake can furnish a different interpretation of the passage. The preposition ἐκ indicates that God's intention was never to dwell in darkness, but God always wanted to come out of the darkness. However, the temple was needed to actuate God's desire to leave the darkness.

The rhetoric of speech n. 5 changes even more significantly in OL. The structure of the speech is not concentric but more linear, containing two parallel commands:

I.	Narrator's introduction:	Tunc locutus est Solomon pro domo, quam consumavit aedificans
II.	Solomon's direct speech	
	1. Solomon's speech	Solem statuit in caelo Dominus et dixit
	A. God's first command	commorare in dedicatione domus
	B. God's second command	Aedifica mihi domum pulcherrimam inhabitare in novitate
	2. Solomon's reference to source	Nonne haec scripta sunt in libro Cantici?

A difference important for our purposes are the variants in OL *in dedicatione domus* (בחנכת הבית) and *in novitiate* (חדש).[77] These expressions refer to a new month (חדש)[78] and the feast of the dedication of the temple (חנכת הבית), mentioned in the Latin and Syriac versions of (II Chronicles 6. 9).[79] The details of this celebration are far from being clear, but the text links the ritual with sun and the new moon.[80] Thus, OL reads that God gave two simultaneous commands, one to the sun to stay in the dedication of the temple and the other to Solomon to build the temple.

Comparing LXX^{B,L} with OL, it seems that the rhetoric of LXX^{B,L} is significantly different from that of OL. In LXX^{B,L} the description of God's work (sun in the heavens) creates a contrast between the created shining sun and God's intention to dwell in darkness. Thus, LXX^{B,L} puts the contrast between God creator of sun (light) and God linked to darkness.[81] This contrast was reconciled by Solomon's construction of the

---

77 In Greek the words 'to dedicate', ἐγκαινίζω, and the 'new(ness)', καινότης, have the same root and thus, the Greek translations would allow for a pun that cannot be reconstructed in Hebrew or in Latin.

78 Pakkala, *God's Word Omitted*, p. 229.

79 MT reads dedication of the altar; Vulgate and Syriac reads dedication of the temple. For more details see Trebolle Barrera, 'From Secondary Versions', p. 205.

80 The sun sojourning in the temple might refer to the rays of the sun that enter into the temple in a given moment of a year. But this is far from being a provable conclusion.

81 Schenker, *Septante et Texte Massorétique*, p. 134.

temple. No such rhetoric is in OL. OL's description of God's work (sun in the heavens) serves to demonstrate God's supremacy over the sun as well as over the king since God gives the commands to both of them. These two commands should find its full meaning during a celebration of the dedication of the temple, linked with the new moon.

Finally, the last sentence of speech n. 5 refers to a book in which God's command was written. Despite the fact that all manuscripts unanimously read *in libro Cantici*, ἐν βιβλίῳ τῆς ᾠδῆς (ספר השיר), most scholars prefer to read ספר הישר, based on a similar reference in Joshua 10. 13 and II Samuel 1. 18.[82] A similar expression occurs in Psalm 30. 1 (*psalmus cantici in dedication domus*, ψαλμὸς ᾠδῆς τοῦ ἐγκαινισμοῦ τοῦ οἴκου). If OL is read in connection with Psalm 30, then the author of speech n. 5 concludes the dedicatory speeches with Solomon quoting one of David's songs composed on the occasion of the dedication of the temple or its recurrences. Another possibility is to interpret the term song שיר as referring to one of Solomon's compositions, such as that mentioned in I Kings 4. 32; 5. 12.[83]

5.2. *Macro-Rhetoric of the Versions*

The rhetorical analysis cannot be confined to a few verses but the verses in question should be studied in their context. That speeches n. 1 and 5 are located in different places of Chapter 8 changes the rhetoric of the entire chapter and creates different intertextual links within MT, LXX[A,B,L], and OL. For this reason, it is not sufficient to analyze the rhetoric of speeches n. 1 and 5 on their own, but to see how these speeches influence the rhetoric of the whole chapter.

5.2.1. *Role of Speech n. 1 in I Kings 8*

While scholars still debate the original position and form of speeches n. 1 and 5, the rhetorical analysis shows that the decision to remove or to keep speech n. 1 after verse 8. 11 can significantly alter the meaning of the whole chapter.

The first question to be asked is what role speech n. 1 plays in I Kings 8. Is it the first speech in a long series of Solomon's speeches or is it a conclusion of the transferal of the ark so that the following speeches (n. 2–6) represent a separate unit? The difference between I Kings 8. 12–13 and the rest of Solomon's speeches becomes apparent when we look at the verbs introducing some of the speeches:

8. 12 אָז אָמַר שְׁלֹמֹה

8. 14 וַיַּסֵּב הַמֶּלֶךְ אֶת פָּנָיו וַיְבָרֶךְ

8. 22 וַיַּעֲמֹד שְׁלֹמֹה לִפְנֵי מִזְבַּח יְהוָה נֶגֶד כָּל קְהַל יִשְׂרָאֵל וַיִּפְרֹשׂ כַּפָּיו הַשָּׁמָיִם

8. 54–55 וַיְהִי כְּכַלּוֹת שְׁלֹמֹה לְהִתְפַּלֵּל אֶל יְהוָה אֵת כָּל הַתְּפִלָּה וְהַתְּחִנָּה הַזֹּאת קָם מִלִּפְנֵי מִזְבַּח יְהוָה מִכְּרֹעַ עַל בִּרְכָּיו וְכַפָּיו פְּרֻשׂוֹת הַשָּׁמָיִם: וַיַּעֲמֹד וַיְבָרֶךְ

---

82 See for example two latest articles: Richelle, 'How to Edit an Elusive Text?', p. 213; Kató, 'Der Tempelweihspruch', p. 229.

83 van Keulen, *Two Versions*, pp. 171–72.

A series of *wayyiqtols* structure Solomon's speeches n. 2–4 as a consecutive link of acts based on Solomon's movements. However, speech n. 1 does not have a verb of movement in the *wayyiqtol* form, but it starts with a particle אָז and a *qatal* form. Therefore, verses I Kings 8. 12–13 serve as a conclusion of verses 8. 1–11 and, at the same time, they function as the heading for the following speeches of Solomon.

First, let us explore speech n. 1 as the conclusion of verses I Kings 8. 1–11. After verse I Kings 8. 11 a reader remains with an unanswered question. The temple was built, the sacrifices were made, the ark was transferred, but the temple was filled with the cloud. Does this mean that God did not accept Solomon's temple? This pressing question is accentuated even more by the similarities between Exodus 40 and I Kings 8:

Exodus 40. 34–35	I Kings 8. 10–11
	וַיְהִי בְּצֵאת הַכֹּהֲנ־הַקֹּדֶשׁ
וַיְכַס הֶעָנָן אֶת־אֹהֶל מוֹעֵד	וְהֶעָנָן מָלֵא אֶת־בֵּית יְהוָה
וּכְבוֹד יְהוָה מָלֵא אֶת־הַמִּשְׁכָּן	
וְלֹא־יָכֹל מֹשֶׁה לָבוֹא אֶל־אֹהֶל מוֹעֵד כִּי־שָׁכַן עָלָיו הֶעָנָן	וְלֹא־יָכְלוּ הַכֹּהֲנִים לַעֲמֹד לְשָׁרֵת מִפְּנֵי הֶעָנָן כִּי
וּכְבוֹד יְהוָה מָלֵא אֶת־הַמִּשְׁכָּן	מָלֵא כְבוֹד־יְהוָה אֶת־בֵּית יְהוָה

The comparison of these two text shows that as the Lord accepted and consecrated the tabernacle, so the same Lord accepted and consecrated the temple. Therefore, the cloud and the glory of the Lord can be interpreted as the signs of God's presence. However, the differences between both narratives are even more important. The ark was transferred to the tabernacle by Moses in Exodus 45, whereas in I Kings 8 the priests, not Solomon, transferred the ark. Those who transferred the ark were unable to enter and communicate with God, namely Moses in Exodus 45. 35 and the priests in I Kings 8. 11. Even though Moses was able to approach God when the mountain was covered with the cloud in Exodus 19, he was not able approach God when the cloud and the glory of the Lord filled the tabernacle or the temple. However, in I Kings 8. 12–13 Solomon does speak with God. Thus, Solomon accomplished what Moses was not able to do, i.e. to speak with God when the temple was covered with the cloud and the glory of the Lord. Only after having finished speaking with God does he turn around and address the people (I Kings 8. 14).

Now let us insert speech n. 1 into its immediate context. The sequence of verses 8. 10–11 and 12–13 links the cloud עָנָן of v. 11 with the עֲרָפֶל of v. 12.[84] Thenceforth, the first sticho of Solomon's prayer n. 1 interprets the cloud filling the temple and prohibiting the priests from entering the temple as the Lord's decision to dwell in the darkness. J. Walsh concluded the following: 'the "thick darkness" in which he (the Lord) chooses to dwell is not only the windowless holy of holies deep within the Temple; it is also the obscurity of the cloud of glory in which Yahweh moves

---

84   The darkness is explained in the MT by the context not by the poem itself as in the LXX. In the MT the darkness is the cloud in the temple; see Schenker, *Septante et Texte Massorétique*, p. 134.

as he will, and it is, most of all, hiddenness of his mystery'.[85] The reader remains with an urgent question. The temple was built, the sacrifices were made, the ark was transferred, but the temple was filled with the cloud. Does this mean that God would remain in thick darkness?

The second sticho answers the dilemma employing the literary genre of dedicatory speeches. Solomon is the king who resolves the problem: 'I indeed built a lordly house for you' and this lordly house becomes the מָכוֹן לְשִׁבְתְּךָ עוֹלָמִים (see above). The rhetoric of MT is impressive: the first part of the dedicatory ceremony resulted in the fact that no one could access God, not even the priests. Nonetheless, through the temple and in the temple God became accessible. Thus, speech n. 1 represents the turning point of the narrative.

Moreover, I Kings 8. 12–13 not only concludes the dedicatory ceremony, but also sets the tone for the whole chapter. MT employs two different verbs שׁכן and ישׁב in speech n. 1. The former describes God's decision to dwell in the thick darkness while the latter refers to God's living in the temple. The root ישׁב occurs in 8. 27, 30, 39, 43, 49. It describes the place in which the Lord / his name / his glory dwells and from which and through which the Lord listens to the king's and people's petitions. The links between speech n. 1 and the rest of Solomon's speeches suggests that speech n. 1 serves as an interpretative clue for the following speeches, allowing an understanding of how it is possible that God can dwell in the temple. The following passages show the history of this gigantic jump in the divine-human relations.

In speech n. 2 Solomon outlines the history of the construction of the temple: God has chosen Israel and David to be his king; David wanted to build the temple (house) but was not allowed; his successor, Solomon, was able to accomplish it.

Speech n. 3 addresses a more fundamental question: Is it possible to build a house for God? The Deuteronomistic theology resolves it by means of a conditional promise and the name-theology.

Speech n. 4 builds upon the previous speeches. Once God became accessible through the temple, speech n. 4 illustrates which kind of petition could have been presented and heard by God. Seven petitions illustrate when, where, and how the king and the people can pray so that their prayers might be heard.

In sum, the introductory speech (I Kings 8. 12–13) starts with the 1st sg referring to Solomon, and this modality continues in the rest of the chapter. Adopting the dedicatory language, as argued above, Solomon presents himself not only as the king who constructed a temple as many other kings indeed did, but also as the one who made the inaccessible God accessible. Solomon, who was able to stand in front of God (I Kings 8. 22), was depicted as a priest contrary to the priests who were unable to stand in front of the cloud (I Kings 8. 11). Solomon was even greater than Moses. Moses dialogued with God on the mountain covered with the cloud (Exodus 19)

---

85 Jerome T. Walsh and David W. Cotter, *1 Kings*, Berit Olam. Studies in Hebrew Narrative & Poetry (Collegeville, MN: The Liturgical Press, 1996), p. 111; Albert Kamp, 'The Conceptualization of God's Dwelling Place in 1 Kings 8: A Cognitive Approach', *JSOT*, 40/4 (2016), 415–38 (pp. 425–26).

but was not able to enter the tabernacle when it was covered with the cloud and the glory of the Lord. Solomon, on the other hand, was able to speak to God when the temple was filled with the cloud and the glory of the Lord. Thus, the introduction of speech n. 1 determines the interpretation of the following speeches. Moreover, speech n. 1 presents Solomon not only as the king-builder (dedicatory inscription), but also as a new Moses.

5.2.2. The Absence of Speech n. 1 and the Role of Speech n. 5

According to MT the priests were unable to serve the Lord because of the cloud. However, in verse 8. 12–13 Solomon speaks directly with God and only after having finished speaking with God does he turn around and address the people. The absence of speech n. 1 in LXX^{B,L} alters the meaning of Solomon's gestures and speeches. MT presents the following sequence of events: (1) Temple is filled with the cloud and glory (I Kings 8. 10–11); (2) Solomon addresses God (I Kings 8. 12–13); (3) He turns around and addresses the people (I Kings 8. 14). Therefore, the gesture וַיַּסֵּב הַמֶּלֶךְ אֶת־פָּנָיו וַיְבָרֶךְ אֵת כָּל־קְהַל means that Solomon had his face, first, directed towards God while talking to him (I Kings 8. 12–13), and only then he turned it to the assembly. LXX^{B,L} agrees with MT that the priests were unable to serve the Lord because of the cloud and glory of the Lord. The following verse indicates that the king turns away his face and blesses the people. Therefore, the expression καὶ ἀπέστρεψεν ὁ βασιλεὺς τὸ πρόσωπον αὐτοῦ without the previous dialogue with God assumes a different meaning: when the temple is filled with the cloud, Solomon turns away his face. This gesture of Solomon can be interpreted in light of Exodus 3. 6, when the Lord appears to Moses '[a]nd Moses turned his face away, for he was afraid to look down before God' (NETS). Thereafter, Solomon was like Moses in Exodus 3. 6. In Exodus 3. 6 Moses turned away his face because he was afraid while in Exodus 40. 34–35, he cannot enter the sanctuary. In the Greek versions, the priests are unable to serve the Lord because of the cloud and Solomon, as Moses, turns away his face after seeing God's glory fill the temple.

Consequently, the meaning of speeches n. 2–4 changes. While in the MT speeches n. 2–4 serve as an explanation of a major shift in the history of the world, these speeches in LXX^{B,L} serve to build up momentum for the culmination that is reached in speech n. 5. Solomon's first speeches (n. 2) is about God. God is mentioned in the 3rd sg. Therefore, speech n. 2 serves as a sophisticated historical introduction. Solomon addresses God in the 2nd sg only in speeches n. 3 and 4, which present Solomon's supplications. Accordingly, Solomon's speeches are gradually building up momentum and speech n. 4 concludes with the exclamation: 'O my lord, O Lord!' A new section starts with τότε. The particle corresponds to אָז in I Kings 8. 12; in both cases it marks the turning point of the narrative. This speech represents Solomon's quotation of the divine speech as written in the Book of Song. It concludes a long journey starting with the construction of the temple, the dedicatory ceremony, and Solomon's speeches / prayers. As all Solomon's activities were the fulfilment of God's word (cf. III Kingdoms 8. 15), so God's words as written in the Book of Song were fulfilled at the dedication ceremony.[86] The terminology in LXX[B,L] of III Kingdoms 8. 53a creates intertextual links with the creation of the world in Genesis 1. 14–15, which describes God placing a great luminary in the sky, intended as the sun.[87] Moreover, the term γνόφος appears for the first time describing the deep darkness that fell as God's sign upon Egypt in Exodus 10. 22, that separated the Egyptians from the Israelites in Exodus 14. 20 and in which God was found (Exodus 20. 21). As such, it is the decisive moment in the fulfillment of God's word. The dedication ceremony not only represents the fulfilment of the words written in the Book of Song but also the fulfillment of two major moments described in the Scriptures — creation and exodus. Thus, the passage from a God living in darkness to the God present in the temple was foretold in the Scripture and completed in creation and the exodus.

Furthermore, speech n. 5 can also be interpreted as a big question mark. The imperative 'build me a remarkable house!' may assume a different meaning. The house built by Solomon was not remarkable enough and God required a new house to be built. Despite all Solomon's efforts, God decided to live in the darkness and even the offerings and prayers cannot make God change his mind. God still wanted to live in darkness, contrary to the sun that is known / placed in the sky. If this section was added and read in the context of the Second Temple, it could have been an invitation for the exiles to build a new and even grander temple than that of Solomon. So, speech n. 5 in LXX[B,L] indirectly suggests that Solomon himself concluded his solemn speeches stating that his temple was not sufficiently exalted and should have been substituted with another one.

Another rhetorical nuance can be derived from OL. Speech n. 5 in OL is focused on ceremonies that linked the sun and the dedication of the temple. OL suggests that Solomon's construction of the temple, his dedicatory ceremonies, and speeches were not sufficient and that the dedicatory feasts would be completed in a final ceremony that linked the dedication of the temple with the sun.[88] This interpretation moves attention from the physical building of the temple to liturgy, in particular, that of the (re)dedication of the temple as mentioned in II Chronicles 7. 9.

Conclusion

The example of Solomon's speeches illustrates that a small change inf the biblical text has an impact not only on the reconstruction of the Old Greek, but also on the meaning of the text. Each text has its own dynamic and leads a reader to radically

---

86 John Gray interprets the reference to ancient text as Solomon's legitimation of his claim to the throne; John Gray, *I & II Kings: A Commentary*, OTL, 2nd edn (Philadelphia: Westminster Press, 1976), p. 211.

87 The LXX[L] resumes more closely the vocabulary of LXX-Gen 1. 14–15.

88 James A. Montgomery, *A Critical and Exegetical Commentary on the Books of Kings*, ICC (Edinburgh: T&T Clark, 1951), p. 191.

or partially different conclusions. The rewording and the rearrangement of the text that can be irrelevant for one reader can be of great importance for another reader.

This paper also has pointed out another aspect to be kept in mind, namely, the difference between the reconstructed *Vorlage* and a manuscript. A given manuscript, even containing a mistake (cf. LXX^B) once in circulation functions as an artifact independent of its previous versions and carries its own persuasive power for the people reading it. The recent studies of LXX point out this double dimension of the text. On the one hand, it is of great importance to reconstruct the variants and their mutual relations; on the other hand, once the changes were introduced into the manuscripts, the manuscript assumes a new dynamic that should be explored on its own. LXX studies open a fascinating, yet intriguing, field in the constantly changing faces of biblical interpretation.

Finally, in this paper I have analyzed the MT, $LXX^{A,B,L}$ and OL of Solomon's speeches in I Kings 8. 12–13 and III Kingdoms 8. 53a. Even though the speeches seem very similar, small changes in the manuscripts altered the rhetorical dynamic of the whole chapter. The version in MT is concerned about the accessibility of God and Solomon's prayer represents a turning point in mediating the access to God. Solomon's princely temple marks a radical shift from the inaccessible God to the accessible God. The royal rhetoric exults the king and his deeds that become the center of the reader's attention.

OL and $LXX^{B,L}$ do not contain verses I Kings 8. 12–13 but have an addition after 8. 53. This addition creates a different rhetorical dynamic. OL introduces the importance of the ritual linked with the new month and the dedication of the temple, when God is present in the temple in a special way. Both LXX and OL may also contain a subtle critique of Solomon's temple and open a possibility for the construction of a new temple, an idea that might have been appealing during the Exile and even during Herod's reconstruction of the temple.

▼ ABSTRACT This paper investigates rhetorical methodologies and how Septuagint studies can contribute to rhetorical analysis. I Kings 8. 12–13 in the MT (III Kingdoms 8. 53a in the LXX) serves as an example for illustrating a potential integration of these two scholarly fields. This paper, first, presents Solomon's speeches in their literary context. Secondly, the analysis of textual variants shows that there were two different speeches inserted in two different places in Chapter 8. Thirdly, this paper discusses important literary features of these speeches and their literary genres and shows how the rhetoric and, consequently, the message of the texts changes depending on the content and the location of Solomon's speeches.

BENEDETTA ROSSI

Lost in Translation:
LXX-Jeremiah through the Lens of Pragmatics

The research around LXX-Jeremiah has been dominated mainly by text-critical analysis: as Georg Walser observes: 'The text has mostly (if at all) been used as a mere text-critical tool'.[1] In particular, the paramount divergencies between the shorter (LXX) and the longer (MT) texts have been usually considered in terms of *Vorlagen*, editions, and redactions.[2] This approach works on two main assumptions. The first is that LXX-Jeremiah provides a literal (or faithful[3]) translation of its Hebrew *Vorlage*. The second interpretive premise is that literal translation is a typical translation paradigm in Hellenistic times.

In the following, I shall offer some preliminary suggestions for slightly re-examining the two above mentioned assumptions by focusing on the role played by pragmatics in LXX-Jeremiah and in translations from the Hellenistic time. After illustrating the impact of pragmatics in studying LXX-Jeremiah (1.), I shall explore how pragmatic choices made by Greek translators provide reasons for variations, rearrangement, and omissions (2.; 3.). I shall then take a quick look at Latin translations of Greek classics to illustrate analogous pragmatic strategies at work (4.). Some provisional conclusions will then be drawn to consider problems and perspectives of the outlined approach (5.).

---

1 Georg A. Walser, *Jeremiah: A Commentary Based on Ieremias in Codex Vaticanus*, Septuagint Commentary Series (Leiden: Brill, 2012), p. 12.

2 See in this regard, Emanuel Tov, *Text-Critical Use of the Septuagint in Biblical Research: Completely Revised and Expanded Third Edition* (Winona Lake: Eisenbrauns, 2015), pp. 37–39.

3 For a clarification of the concept of literal or free translation in relation to the Septuagint, see Bénédicte Lemmelijn, 'Two Methodological Trails in Recent Studies on the Translation Technique of the Septuagint', in *Helsinki Perspectives on the Translation Technique of the Septuagint. Proceedings of the IOSCS Congress in Helsinki 1999*, ed. by Raija Sollamo and Seppo Sipilä, Publications of the Finnish Exegetical Society 82 (Helsinki: The Finnish Exegetical Society – Vandenhoeck & Ruprecht, 2001), pp. 43–63.

New Avenues in Biblical Exegesis in Light of the Septuagint
ed. by Leonardo Pessoa da Silva Pinto and Daniela Scialabba, Turnhout, 2022 (*SEPT*, 1), pp. 157–181
© BREPOLS ❧ PUBLISHERS   DOI 10.1484/M.SEPT-EB.5.127716

1. The Impact of Pragmatics in Studying LXX-Jeremiah

The importance of pragmatics for studying a translated text comes to the fore thanks to the new perspectives introduced in the 1970s by translation studies.[4] Translation studies focus on translated texts as a literary product within a specific literary system. This new paradigm explores the relationship between the translated text and the environment in which it is born, the circumstances that determine its production, the readers for whom it is intended, and the effects it is intended to produce.[5] Within this framework, focusing on pragmatics proves to be an essential and appropriate approach.

As Enrique Alcaraz highlights, pragmatics has opened 'new frontiers' in traductology and translation studies. In particular, the focus on pragmatics 'includes not only the analysis and comparison of the textual meaning of the same passage written in two different languages but of all the other textual categories (cohesion, thematization, etc.) that may affect their final perception by the receivers of the two languages, in the light of the theories and models of pragmatics'.[6]

Within this framework, Alcaraz distinguishes between transposition and modulation techniques in translation.[7] Transposition refers to everything related to the structures and components of meaning from a semantic (and morphological) point of view. The goal of transposition is 'semantic equivalence'.[8] Modulation, on the other, deals with 'categories of thought'; pragmatic equivalence is the goal of modulation.[9] Modulation, therefore, goes beyond the comparison of syntactic structures and

---

4   See in this regard, Theo Hermans, 'Introduction: Translation Studies and a New Paradigm', in *The Manipulation of Literature: Studies in Literary Translation*, ed. by Theo Hermans (London: Croom Helm, 1985), pp. 7–15. In particular, Hermans defines the new approach to literary translations as 'descriptive, target oriented, functional and systemic' (p. 10). See also Lawrence Venuti, 'Introduction', in *Rethinking Translation: Discourse, Subjectivity, Ideology*, ed. by Lawrence Venuti (London: Routledge, 1992), pp. 1–17. An overview on recent developments in translation studies is provided by Jacobus A. Naudé, 'It's All Greek. The Septuagint and Recent Developments in Translation Studies', in *Translating a Translation: The LXX and Its Modern Translations in the Context of Early Judaism*, ed. by Hans Ausloos and others, Bibliotheca Ephemeridum Theologicarum Lovaniensium, 213 (Leuven: Peeters, 2008), 229–50 (pp. 229–40).

5   See especially André Lefevere, *Translation, Rewriting and the Manipulation of Literary Fame*, Translation Studies (London: Routledge, 1992), p. vii, who considers translation as a 'rewriting' to 'reflect a certain ideology and a poetics and as such manipulate literature to function in a given society in a given way'. See also Edwin Gentzler and Maria Tymoczko, 'Introduction', in *Translation and Power*, ed. by Maria Tymoczko and Edwin Gentzler (Amherst: University of Massachusetts Press, 2002), pp. xi–xxviii; Peter Fawcett, 'Translation and Power Play', *The Translator*, 1 (1995), 177–92; Román Álvarez and M. Carmen-África Vidal, 'Translating: A Political Act', in *Translation, Power, Subversion*, ed. by Román Álvarez and M. Carmen-África Vidal, Topics in Translation, 8 (Clevedon: Multilingual Matters LTD, 1996), pp. 1–9.

6   Enrique Alcaraz, 'Translation and Pragmatics' in *Translation, Power, Subversion*, pp. 99–115 (p. 107).

7   Alcaraz, 'Translation', pp. 107–09.

8   Alcaraz, 'Translation', p. 108.

9   Alcaraz, 'Translation', p. 108.

semantic meaning in two different languages. Other linguistic categories come here into view, i.e., those related to pragmatics and discourse analysis, that may influence the final perception of the text by the recipient and produce a specific communicative effect on the addressee.[10]

The impact of translation studies has remained quite marginal to Septuagint study.[11] The Septuagint has been typically interpreted starting from its relation to the source text and its equivalence to it. Among the most prominent literary features of the Septuagint, undoubtedly, isomorphism stands out. As defined by Albert Pietersma, isomorphism is 'the replacement of a Hebrew word or morpheme with a Greek counterpart'.[12] Hence the Septuagint is described as an 'interlinear translation' aimed at bringing the Greek reader back to the Hebrew original.[13] As Pietersma highlights, in this kind of translation, the 'primary cognitive process is thus that Greek X is deemed a good match for Hebrew Y'.[14] The issue at stake is, therefore, the research of semantic and morphological equivalence. Relating the translated Greek words and phrases to the context seems to be a secondary concern.[15] These features are also ascribed to LXX-Jeremiah, where Pietersma and Saunders identify isomorphism with the 'basic norm' of the translator.[16]

Richard Weis recognizes three criteria that govern translation in LXX-Jeremiah: a) a 'consistent one to one sequential representation' of the form of its Hebrew source; b) formal equivalence should not sacrifice semantic equivalence; c) formal equivalence should not sacrifice the 'correct portrayal of figures in the text as figures from the past time'.[17] While Weis advocates an approach that is attentive to 'structure,

---

10   Alcaraz briefly expounds the relation between pragmatics and discourse: 'In pragmatics, language is no longer a group of structures or a set of sentences, as in structuralism or generativism. Language is discourse, and although this term can be intuitively understood, it has to be accounted for by means of a descriptive model' ('Translation', p. 105).

11   See in this regard, Naudè, 'It's All Greek'; see also Theo A. W. van der Louw, *Transformations in the Septuagint: Towards an Interaction of Septuagint Studies and Translation Studies*, CBET, 47 (Leuven: Peeters, 2007), pp. 1–92. The need to further integrate Septuagint and Translation Studies is also stressed by Dries de Crom, *LXX Song of Songs and Descriptive Translation Studies*, DSI, 11 (Göttingen: Vandenhoeck & Ruprecht, 2019), pp. 18–20.

12   See Albert Pietersma, 'Exegesis in the Septuagint: Possibilities and Limits (The Psalter as a Case in Point)', in *Septuagint Research: Issues and Challenges in the Study of the Greek Jewish Scriptures*, ed. by Wolfgang Kraus and R. Glenn Wooden, SBL.SCS, 53 (Atlanta: SBL, 2006), pp. 33–45 (p. 38).

13   See Albert Pietersma and Benjamin Wright, 'To the Reader of NETS', in *A New English Translation of the Septuagint. And the Other Greek Translations Traditionally Included Under that Title*, ed. by Albert Pietersma and Benjamin Wright (New York: Oxford University Press, 2007), pp. xiii–xx (pp. xiv–xv).

14   Pietersma, 'Exegesis', p. 38.

15   Pietersma, 'Exegesis', p. 38.

16   Albert Pietersma and Marc Saunders, 'Ieremias. To the Reader', in *A New English Translation*, pp. 876–81 (p. 876).

17   Richard D. Weis, '7.1 Textual History of Jeremiah', in *Textual History of the Bible: Volume 1B Pentateuch, Former and Latter Prophets*, ed. by Armin Lange and Emanuel Tov (Leiden: Brill, 2017), pp. 495–513 (p. 496).

intention and implied audience', nonetheless, the role of pragmatics in studying the LXX-Jeremiah has lingered in the shadows in the scholarly debate.[18]

To investigate how pragmatics impact a translated text, Alcaraz highlights the relevance of the following discourse categories, among others: cohesion, coherence, progressivity (thematization), and intentionality.[19] Cohesion deals with grammatical, syntactic, and lexical links that ensure the perception of a text as a textual unit, i.e., connections in the discourse/text itself. Coherence, on the other hand, focuses on the semantic cohesion of a text, as perceived by the reader/user, starting from extra-textual knowledge.[20] Progressivity (and thematization) refers to the information flow embedded in a text. Intentionality brings to the fore the strategies that highlight the goal pursued by the text and its author (or translator).

For evaluating the relation between LXX-Jeremiah and MT-Jeremiah through the lens of pragmatics, various strategies can be considered.[21] In the following, I shall highlight how the pursuit of discourse strategies can influence translation by bringing about specific and intentional changes of the source text. As test cases, I shall explore speech act in translation, communicative strategies at work, and the pragmatic relevance of a lexical coinage.

2. MT-Jeremiah 27. 5–11 (LXX-Jeremiah 34. 5–11): Speech Acts in Translation

MT-Jeremiah 27. 5–11 and LXX-Jeremiah 34. 5–11 show many differences, mostly quantitative, typically assessed one by one according to the criteria proper to textual

---

18 Richard D. Weis, 'Jeremiah Amid Actual and Virtual Editions: Textual Plurality and the Editing of the Book of Jeremiah', in *The Text of the Hebrew Bible and Its Editions: Studies in Celebration of the Fifth Centennial of the Complutensian Polyglot*, ed. by Andrés Piquer Otero and Pablo A. Torijano Morales, Supplements to the Textual History of the Bible, 1 (Leiden: Brill, 2016), pp. 370–99 (p. 383).

19 Alcaraz, 'Translation', p. 110.

20 For a definition and the meaning of categories in discourse analysis, see Jan Renkema, *Introduction to Discourse Studies* (Amsterdam: John Benjamins Publishing Company, 2004), pp. 103–20; Angela Ferrari, *Linguistica del testo: principi, fenomeni, strutture*, Manuali Universitari, 151 (Roma: Carocci, 2014), pp. 49–127.

21 Some contributions recently appeared that compare the structure of the communication in MT-Jeremiah and LXX-Jeremiah: e.g. Benedetta Rossi, 'Strategie comunicative in GerTM e GerLXX. Variazioni nella deissi e implicazioni interpretative a partire da Ger 9,9', in *Gottes Wort im Menschen Wort: Festschrift für Georg Fischer SJ zum 60. Geburtstag*, ed. by Dominik Markl and others, Österreichische Biblische Studien, 43 (Frankfurt a.M.: Peter Lang, 2014), pp. 153–70; Karin Finsterbusch and Norbert Jacoby, *MT-Jeremia und LXX-Jeremia 1–24: synoptische Übersetzung und Analyse der Kommunikationsstruktur*, Wissenschaftliche Monographien zum Alten und Neuen Testament, 145 (Neukirchen-Vluyn: Neukirchener Verlag, 2016); Karin Finsterbusch and Norbert Jacoby, *MT-Jeremia und LXX-Jeremia 25–52: synoptische Übersetzung und Analyse der Kommunikationsstruktur*, Wissenschaftliche Monographien zum Alten und Neuen Testament, 146 (Göttingen: Vandenhoeck & Ruprecht, 2017). In particular, the synoptic translation in two volumes provided by Finsterbusch and Jacoby visually displays some pragmatic strategies employed by MT and LXX, e.g. personal deixis, discourse deixis; divergences in discourse connectors. Focusing on the structure of communication brings to the fore strategies of textual cohesion.

criticism.[22] The most widespread interpretation ascribes the MT pluses as later additions to a shorter *Vorlage*, witnessed by the LXX.[23] Sometimes, scribal mistakes come into view to explain divergences between MT and LXX;[24] alternatively, the low exegetical value of some textual variants is highlighted.[25] Despite the fact that the translator is acknowledged to have a literal adherence to his *Vorlage*, one is nevertheless inclined to admit a certain freedom with respect to the source text.[26]

The usual interpretation of divergences between MT and LXX is based on a source-oriented approach, focused on the relationship between the Greek translation and its source. From this point of view, the way the translator works appears inconsistent, characterized by contradictory attitudes (i.e. adherence and freedom to the Hebrew original) apparent in a few verses. Attention to pragmatics and communicative intentionality of the translated text leads the way for a target-oriented analysis and helps to shed new light on the work of the translator.

2.1. Discourse Strategies in MT-Jeremiah

In MT-Jeremiah 27. 4b–11, Jeremiah sends a message to the lords of Edom, Moab, the Ammonites, Tyre, and Sidon (v. 3), by means of their ambassadors. In 27. 5–8, Yhwh provides the basis for the message: Nebuchadnezzar is given the full power and authority over creation and kingdoms.

The text makes the circumstances of the communication available to the reader:[27] the participants (i.e., speakers and recipients) and the discourse setting are made explicit. The outcome of the message, its contents as well as its tone, can be further inferred from the text itself.

---

22 See in this regard Emanuel Tov, 'Exegetical Notes on the Hebrew Vorlage of the LXX of Jeremiah 27 (34)', *ZAW*, 91 (1979), 73–93; William McKane, 'Jeremiah 27, 5–8, especially >Nebuchadnezzar, My Servant<', in *Prophet und Prophetenbuch, Festschrift für Otto Kaiser zum 65. Geburtstag*, ed. by Volkmar Fritz and others, BZAW, 185 (Berlin – New York: de Gruyter, 1989), pp. 98–110; Yohanan Goldman, *Prophétie et royauté au retour de l'exil: Les origins littérarires de la forme massorétique du livre de Jérémie*, OBO, 118 (Freiburg: Universitätsverlag Freiburg – Vandehoeck & Ruprecht, 1992), pp. 123–67; Anneli Aejmelaeus, '"Nebuchadnezzar, My Servant". Redaction History and Textual Development in Jer 27', in *Interpreting Translation: Studies on the LXX and Ezekiel in honour of Johan Lust*, ed. by Florentino García Martínez and Marc Vervenne, BETL, 192 (Leuven: Peeters, 2005), pp. 1–18.

23 A different overall interpretation of the variants is offered by van der Koij; he argues that the differences between MT and LXX are due to choices of the translator rather than due to a shorter *Vorlage*; see Arie Van der Kooij, 'Jeremiah 27:5–15: How do MT and LXX Relate to Each Other?', *JNSL*, 20 (1994), 59–78.

24 E.g. the absence of the phrase אֶת־הָאָדָם וְאֶת־הַבְּהֵמָה אֲשֶׁר עַל־פְּנֵי הָאָרֶץ (5.27) from the LXX, often ascribed to *homoioteleuton*; see Wilhelm Rudolph, *Jeremia*, HAT, 12 (J. C. B. Mohr [Paul Siebeck]: Tübingen, ³1968), p. 177.

25 See for instance Tov, 'Exegetical Notes', pp. 82–83; McKane, 'Jeremiah 27, 5–8', p. 99; Goldman, *Prophétie*, p. 131 on the lack of וְעַתָּה אָנֹכִי (MT 27. 6) from the Greek text.

26 See Aejmelaeus, 'Nebuchadnezzar', pp. 10–11.

27 A list of textual linguistic categories to describe discourse situation is provided by Jan Renkema and Christoph Schubert, *Introduction to Discourse Studies: New Edition* (Amsterdam: John Benjamins Publishing Company, 2018), pp. 49–52.

As regards discourse setting:[28] MT-Jeremiah 27. 3 makes clear that foreign messengers, 'who have come to Jerusalem to Zedekiah, king of Judah' (הַבָּאִים יְרוּשָׁלַם אֶל־צִדְקִיָּהוּ מֶלֶךְ יְהוּדָה) shall report the following message (vv. 5–8). Jerusalem and Zedekiah are the destination (יְרוּשָׁלַם, adverbial accusative; אֶל + צִדְקִיָּהוּ) of the movement (בוא) of the ambassadors. The syntax emphasizes the prominent position of the king of Judah. The expectation created by the situation described in v. 3 is that the ambassadors of the foreign rulers, who came to Zedekiah, will bring back a message from the ruler of Judah. Unexpectedly, the ambassadors will not bring back a word from Zedekiah, rather a message from Yhwh, to be spoken by them personally. The discourse setting renders the messengers of the foreign kings as bearers of Yhwh's message.

As regards the outcome: the message (vv. 5–8) does not aim to simply inform the recipients (i.e. a representative function of speech). Some illocutionary force indicating devices (IFIDs) point to a declarative linguistic act.[29]

a) *Performative verb*:
MT-Jeremiah 27. 6–7 express Nebuchadnezzar's appointment as follows:

> ⁶ וְעַתָּה אָנֹכִי נָתַתִּי אֶת־כָּל־הָאֲרָצוֹת הָאֵלֶּה בְּיַד נְבוּכַדְנֶאצַּר מֶלֶךְ־בָּבֶל עַבְדִּי וְגַם אֶת־חַיַּת הַשָּׂדֶה נָתַתִּי לוֹ לְעָבְדוֹ:
> ⁷ וְעָבְדוּ אֹתוֹ כָּל־הַגּוֹיִם וְאֶת־בְּנוֹ וְאֶת־בֶּן־בְּנוֹ עַד בֹּא־עֵת אַרְצוֹ גַּם־הוּא וְעָבְדוּ בוֹ גּוֹיִם רַבִּים וּמְלָכִים גְּדֹלִים:

> Now I give all these lands into the hand of King Nebuchadnezzar of Babylon, my servant, and I give him even the wild animals of the field to serve him. All the nations shall serve him and his son and his grandson until the time of his own land comes; then many nations and great kings shall make him their slave.

The initial וְעַתָּה followed by a *qatal* form (נָתַתִּי) indicates a performative speech act:[30] 'I give'. The following 1sg personal pronoun אָנֹכִי, as well as the repetition of the *qatal* נָתַתִּי לוֹ further reinforces the performative nuance of the phrase.[31]

b) *Discourse deixis*: the phrase אֶת־כָּל־הָאֲרָצוֹת הָאֵלֶּה is the object of the performative verb נָתַתִּי. The discourse indexical הָאֵלֶּה can be understood in reference to the speakers and recipients of the message, i.e., the messengers and their respective rulers (see v. 3). Against this backdrop, the indexical phrase 'all *these* lands' shows that Yhwh

---

28 I.e. *time, place*, or other *physical conditions* of the discourse (see Renkema – Schubert, *Discourse Studies*, pp. 50–52). Following Hymes's model, Renkema adds also the *scene*, considered 'the psychological counterpart to setting' (e.g. formal vs. informal).

29 According to Searle and Vanderveken, an IFID is 'Any element of a natural language which can be literally used to indicate that an utterance of a sentence containing that element has a certain illocutionary force or range of illocutionary forces', see John Searle and Daniel Vanderveken, *Foundations of Illocutionary Logic* (Cambridge: University Press, 1985), p. 2. Examples of IFIDs are word order, mood and modality, performative verbs, adverbs.

30 See in this regard, Ida Zatelli, 'Pragmalinguistics and Speech-Act Theory as Applied to Classical Hebrew', *ZAH*, 6 (1993), 60–74.

31 See in this regard also, Stipp, *Jeremia 25–52*, pp. 139–40.

hands over to Nebuchadnezzar the lands of the message recipients (i.e. the lords of Edom, Moab, the Ammonites, Tyre and Sidon). What may appear to be a syntactical inconsistency,[32] is actually clear if considered within the setting of the reported direct speech delivered by ambassadors to their rulers. The discourse indexical reinforces the declarative force of the message: Yhwh delivers *these* lands (i.e. the lands of the recipients' of the message) to Nebuchadnezzar.

c) *Noun in apposition*: Nebuchadnezzar is qualified as 'king of Babylon, my servant (עַבְדִּי)'. Within the framework of a declarative linguistic act, the epithet 'my servant' stresses for the recipients the proximity between Yhwh and Nebuchadnezzar; the king of Babylon comes to the fore as an agent of Judah's God (Yhwh), and Nebuchadnezzar's actions will mirror Yhwh's.[33] The epithet therefore reinforces the illocutionary force of the speech act.

d) *Adverbs and syntax*: the phrase וְגַם (v. 6) introduces a second sentence (וְגַם וְעַתָּה אָנֹכִי נָתַתִּי אֶת־כָּל־הָאֲרָצוֹת) coordinated with the first (אֶת־חַיַּת הַשָּׂדֶה נָתַתִּי לוֹ לְעָבְדוֹ הָאֵלֶּה בְּיַד נְבוּכַדְנֶאצַּר מֶלֶךְ־בָּבֶל עַבְדִּי). A second performative *qatal* נָתַתִּי לוֹ further stresses the declarative illocutionary force of the message. The phrase וְגַם precedes a second object: 'the wild animals of the field' (אֶת־חַיַּת הַשָּׂדֶה). Van der Merwe highlights a specific pragmatic force of the adverb גַם.[34] The adverb introduces an unexpected element, as well as a more specific and persuasive argument for the recipients. The mention of the 'the wild animals of the field' further restates the subjugation of the lands (and their inhabitants) to Nebuchadnezzar: if even the beasts, how much more the men! This function is also reinforced by the marked syntax (object – verb) with object in topicalized position.

In short: some IFIDs highlight the declarative illocutionary force of the message in MT-Jeremiah 27. 5–8. From the very moment the message is spoken, the subjugation of the lands (Edom, Moab, Ammon, Tyre and Sidon, v. 3) to Nebuchadnezzar is proclaimed and made effective. The declarative force of the message, combined with the discourse setting (v. 3), produces an effect of sarcastic irony: not only do the messengers not report a message from Zedekiah, but they themselves become heralds of their rulers' decree of submission to Yhwh.

The following v. 7 shows the expected and unavoidable consequences of Yhwh's declarative speech act and limits Nebuchadnezzar's power as well i.e. from the very moment of divine performative utterance until 'the time of his own land comes' (v. 7). Against this background, v. 8 unexpectedly shows the chance that a nation may refuse to serve Nebuchadnezzar. Preceded by a declarative linguistic act (v. 6), the sentence does not merely indicate an event, but describes an insubordination against Yhwh, followed by a sanction. The initial והיה (v. 8), functions as a discourse

---

32 See Stipp, *Jeremia 25–52*, p. 141.
33 See Stipp, *Jeremia 25–52*, p. 141.
34 See Christo H. J. van der Merwe and others, *A Biblical Hebrew Reference Grammar: Second Edition* (London: Bloomsbury T&T Clark, 2018), § 40.20.

marker and introduces a focus element i.e. the insubordinate 'nation or kingdom'.[35] If Nebuchadnezzar, Yhwh's servant, receives dominion over foreign countries, Yhwh himself appears as the ultimate agent on the scene of history. Rebellion against Nebuchadnezzar ends up to be rebellion against Yhwh, who shall punish the rebels. The transitive use of תמם (v. 8), rarely attested in the Hebrew Bible, further emphasizes this element.[36]

2.2. LXX-Jeremiah: Discourse Strategies Reconsidered

The Greek translator pursues a different communicative intentionality, starting from the explication of the discourse setting.[37] According to LXX-Jeremiah 34. 3, the messengers of the foreign kings go 'to their meeting (εἰς ἀπάντησιν αὐτῶν) in Jerusalem (εἰς Ιερουσαλημ), to Zedekiah king of Judah (πρὸς Σεδεκιαν βασιλέα Ιουδα)'. By means of the noun ἀπάντησις ('meeting, assembly'), the Greek text portrays a meeting of several ambassadors hosted by Zedekiah (πρὸς Σεδεκιαν) in Jerusalem.[38] The noun ἀπάντησις emphasizes the equal standing of the participants in the meeting.[39] What is expected is presumably joint decision-making. Through the phrase εἰς ἀπάντησιν αὐτῶν, the translator describes the discourse setting in different terms from that of MT.[40] The report the sovereigns expect from the ambassadors is likely to be that of joint concerted action.

As regards the content and goals of communication, LXX-Jeremiah 34. 6 states:

ἔδωκα τὴν γῆν τῷ Ναβουχοδονοσορ βασιλεῖ Βαβυλῶνος δουλεύειν αὐτῷ καὶ τὰ θηρία τοῦ ἀγροῦ ἐργάζεσθαι αὐτῷ

> I gave the earth to King Nabouchodonosor of Babylon to serve him, and the wild animals of the field to work for him.

MT-Jeremiah 27. 7 is absent from the Greek translation. Instead of the phrase וְעַתָּה אָנֹכִי נָתַתִּי (v. 6) the Septuagint has the aorist ἔδωκα.[41] As Tov highlights, the Hebrew וְעַתָּה is usually translated in LXX-Jeremiah as καὶ νῦν: 'In general, this word denotes that the speaker or author reached an important point in a speech or discourse. A priori, it is therefore unlikely that would have been missing from the translator's

---

35 See van der Merwe, *Grammar*, § 40.24.

36 See Tov, 'Exegetical Notes', p. 186. As Stipp, *Jeremia 25–52*, p. 139, highlights, since v. 5 the aim of the discourse is to show that Yhwh is the main agent of history.

37 For this preliminary survey, I have taken as a reference point for the LXX, Joseph Ziegler, *Jeremias, Baruch, Threni, Epistula Ieremiae*, Septuaginta. Vetus Testamentum Graecum Auctoritate Societatis Litterarum Gottingensis editum XV (Göttingen: Vandenhoeck & Ruprecht, 1957). Reconstruction of OG remains however necessary for a more in-depth study.

38 Different prepositions εἰς (+ ἀπάντησις and Ιερουσαλημ) and πρὸς (+ Σεδεκιας) stress the different functions of Jerusalem (the goal of movement, cf. vb. ἔρχομαι) and Zedekiah (the host of meeting).

39 See in this regard, *Diccionario Griego-Español*, ed. by Francisco Rodríguez Adrados (Madrid: CSIC, 1980–), II (1986), s. v. ἀπάντησις (p. 377): 'asamblea', 'reunion'.

40 Tov, 'Exegetical Notes', p. 82 considers εἰς ἀπάντησιν αὐτῶν as an addition by the translator.

41 According to McKane 'Jeremiah 27, 5–8', p. 99, the difference does not have great significance.

Vorlage. We must nevertheless accept this assumption [...] since elsewhere in Jer וְעַתָּה was rendered faithfully by καὶ νῦν.[42] The only exception is MT 40. 4 (= LXX 47. 4), where וְעַתָּה is rendered by ἰδοὺ.

From the point of view of pragmatics, the usual translation καὶ νῦν renders the usage of וְעַתָּה as a text connective that marks discourse cohesion. The only occurrence where וְעַתָּה does not appear in the translation, is MT-Jeremiah 27. 6. So far as I could verify, 27. 6 is the only instance where וְעַתָּה functions as a macro-syntactic sign, that introduces a performative speech act.[43]

The Greek rendering does not hint at the performative force of וְעַתָּה + *qatal* (נָתַתִּי). The aorist ἔδωκα expresses a past action.[44] Additional lexical markers that reinforce the declarative speech act (i.e. נָתַתִּי לוֹ [45];אָנֹכִי; עַבְדִּי), as well as v. 7 that elucidates the consequences of Nabouchodonosor's appointment by Yhwh, are consistently missing in the Greek text, as well as the temporal limit set to Nabouchodonosor's power.[46]

The accusative τὴν γῆν compared to MT אֶת־כָּל־הָאֲרָצוֹת הָאֵלֶּה (v. 6) reflects the same different communicative intentionality. MT gives Nebuchadnezzar authority (נָתַתִּי + *qatal*) over precise countries and territories (i.e. those ruled by discourse recipients), and reinforces the declarative speech act by means of the indexical phrase הָאֲרָצוֹת הָאֵלֶּה. In contrast the LXX suggests a generic and universal jurisdiction over 'the land' (τὴν γῆν). The object of God's creative action in v. 5 (ἐγὼ ἐποίησα τὴν γῆν), was handed over to Nabouchodonosor (v. 6: ἔδωκα τὴν γῆν). Indexical markers of a declarative speech act are consistently missing.

In summary, the consequences of a probable interpretive choice by the translator concerning the pragmatic force of the Hebrew phrase וְעַתָּה אָנֹכִי נָתַתִּי (27. 6) presumably led to a rearrangement of the translated text. The LXX does not convey God's investiture of Nabouchodonosor as ruler of foreign territories and servant of Yhwh. The assignment of universal power over the earth is recounted as a past event. A representative speech act comes into view (instead of the declarative illocutionary force conveyed by MT). The rebellion against Nabouchodonosor does not have religious connotations, but simply will be punished by the Babylonian sovereign himself (v. 6).

The comparison of MT and LXX based on discourse analysis and communicative goals shows that variations from the source text do not result from scribal errors, nor subsequent editorial reworking in MT, but of intentional choices made by the translator. The translator deliberately omitted certain parts of speech present

---

42 See Tov, 'Exegetical Notes', pp. 82–83.

43 See in this regard, Zatelli, 'Pragmalinguistics'.

44 See T. Muraoka, *A Syntax of Septuagint Greek* (Leuven: Peeters, 2016), § 28 da.

45 The 1ˢᵗ sg pronoun is lacking in S*.

46 As regards the difficulties in reconstructing v. 6 OG, see McKane, 'Jeremiah 27, 5–8', pp. 99–101; Aejmelaeus, 'Nebuchadnezzar', pp. 13–17, who argues rather for a short *Vorlage* underlying the Greek text and a number of targeted additions in a Palestinian edition of MT. The absence of δουλεύειν αὐτῷ and Ναβουχοδονοσορ in S (τῷ βασιλεῖ Βαβυλῶνος), Bo, Aeth, and the chance that S preserves the OG (see McKane, 'Jeremiah 27, 5–8', p. 100), does not preclude the possibility that the translator intentionally omitted the name Nebuchadnezzar and the epithet 'his servant'. The OG τῷ βασιλεῖ Βαβυλῶνος (S; Bo; Aeth) could have been later reworked to approximate the Hebrew original.

in the Hebrew text to change the communicative force of the source text in order to align the translation with a negative portrayal of Nabouchodonosor in the Hellenistic period.[47]

3. Problem Solving: Redactional versus Lexical-Pragmatic Strategies

MT-Jeremiah 26–29 (LXX-Jeremiah 33–36) focus on the struggle between authentic/authoritative prophecy and non-authentic/non-authoritative prophecy.[48] The first mention of prophets in the unit (עֲבָדַי הַנְּבִאִים 26. 5) conveys a positive sense: prophets are Yhwh's servants, sent by him. In v. 7, however, prophets are among those who accuse Jeremiah and sentence him to death (see vv. 7, 8, 11, 16). Hermann-Josef Stipp considers this awkward depiction of prophetic figures as one of the tensions (*Spannungen*) in Jeremiah 26, that discloses its complex redactional history.[49]

In the wake of scholars who stress the cohesion of the chapter,[50] the contrast between 'my servants the prophets' (v. 5) and their following behavior (vv. 7, 8, 11, 16) points to a narrative strategy. The recipient is puzzled: Jeremiah is sentenced to death by prophets, who are expected to be 'Yhwh's servants' (v. 5). The ambiguous depiction of prophets (and prophecy) runs through the account of Jeremiah's trial and sets the tone for the following chapters (chs. 27–29). A question is hanging in the air: how to discern between true and false prophecy?

Within Jeremiah 26–29, Jeremiah 28. 8–9 provides the only explicit criterion that reformulates Deuteronomy 18. 21–22.[51] Prophecy, and even more, announcements of

---

47 See in this regard, Stökl who ascribes the negative development of Nebuchadnezzar's portrayal to a late stage in the development of biblical texts; see Johnatan Stökl, 'Nebuchadnezzar: History, Memory, and Myth Making in the Persian Period', in *Remembering Biblical Figures in the Late Persian and Early Hellenistic Periods: Social Memory and Imagination*, ed. by Diana V. Edelman and Ehud Ben Zvi (Oxford: Oxford University Press, 2013), pp. 257–69 (pp. 268–69).

48 See among others, Anthony Chinedu Osuji, *Where is the Truth? Narrative Exegesis and the Question of True and False Prophecy in Jer 26–29 (MT)*, BETL, 214 (Leuven: Peeters, 2010); Morné Malan and Esias E. Meyer, 'Jeremiah 26–29: A not so Deuteronomistic Composition', OTE, 27 (2014), 913–29.

49 According to Stipp, the mention of prophets in vv. 7.8.11.16 is a later addition ascribed to the so called 'patrizische Redaktion'; see Hermann Josef Stipp, *Jeremia 25–52*, Handbuch zum Alten Testament, I 12, 2 (Tübingen: Mohr Siebeck, 2019), p. 26. For a detailed reconstruction of redactional levels in Jeremiah 26, see also, Hermann-Josef Stipp, *Jeremia im Parteienstreit: Studien zur Textentwicklung von Jer 26, 36–43 und 45 als Beitrag zur Geschichte Jeremias, seines Buches und judäischer Parteien im 6. Jahrhundert*, BBB, 82 (Frankfurt a.M.: Anton Hein, 1992), pp. 17–72.

50 See among others, Raimond Westbrook, 'The Trial of Jeremiah' in *Reading the Law: Studies in Honour of Gordon J. Wenham*, LBH.OTS, 461 (New York: T&T Clark, 2007), pp. 95–107; Georg Fischer, *Jeremia 26–52*, HThKAT (Freiburg i.B.: Herder, 2005), p. 23; Harald Knobloch, *Die nachexilischen Prophetentheorie des Jeremiabuches*, BZAR, 12 (Wiesbaden: Harrassowitz Verlag, 2009), pp. 45–72.

51 As for the link between Jeremiah 28. 8–9 and Deuteronomy 18. 21–22, see among others J. Todd Hibbard, 'True and False Prophecy: Jeremiah's Revision of Deuteronomy', *JSOT*, 35 (2011), 339–58 (pp. 344–49); Nathan Mastnjak, *Deuteronomy and the Emergence of Textual Authority in Jeremiah*, FAT, II 87 (Tübingen: Mohr Siebeck, 2016), pp. 71–75.

peace, need to be authenticated through accomplishment. Deuteronomy 18. 21–22 seems to play a crucial role in the dispute around true and false prophecy, especially when dealing with felicitous pronouncements. MT-Jeremiah and LXX-Jeremiah show different strategies for dealing with the fulfillment *criterion* (cf. Deuteronomy 18. 20–22) and consequently with the issue of true and false prophecy.

3.1. Strategies in MT-Jeremiah

MT-Jeremiah displays the following strategies:

a) Redactional Strategies

As previously shown, in Jeremiah 27. 12, 17 Jeremiah announces a chance of life, for those who submit to Nebuchadnezzar (הָבִיאוּ אֶת־צַוְּארֵיכֶם בְּעֹל מֶלֶךְ־בָּבֶל וְעִבְדוּ אֹתוֹ וְעַמּוֹ וִחְיוּ, v. 12). Against prophets who wish for a swift return of the temple vessels from Babylon to Jerusalem, Jeremiah contends that the remaining vessels shall be carried to Babylon; nonetheless they shall later return back to Jerusalem (vv. 19–22). Jeremiah's announcement of life (vv. 12. 17) and even more, his promise that the vessels will come back (vv. 19–22), need to be authenticated. The detailed list of the temple vessels in Jeremiah 27. 19–20 presumably serves the purpose of authentication.

Within 27. 19–22, an inverted resumptive repetition (*Wiederaufnahme*) (vv. 19.21) points to the redactional character of 27. 19–20: the detailed list of the vessels (אֶל־ הָעַמֻּדִים וְעַל־הַיָּם וְעַל־הַמְּכֹנוֹת וְעַל יֶתֶר הַכֵּלִים הַנּוֹתָרִים בָּעִיר הַזֹּאת) can be considered a later addition.[52] What is the goal of the addition? The list added in MT-Jeremiah 27. 19–20 probably pursues a double goal. Firstly, the list clarifies Jeremiah's announcement concerning the vessels left in Jerusalem (v. 22). A similar list of temple vessels occurs in Jeremiah 52. 17 (וְאֶת־עַמּוּדֵי הַנְּחֹשֶׁת אֲשֶׁר לְבֵית־יְהוָה וְאֶת־הַמְּכֹנוֹת וְאֶת־יָם הַנְּחֹשֶׁת), along with many other vessels (v. 18) used for service and brought to Babylon. The list of 52. 17, preceded by 27. 19, highlights that Jeremiah's words are accomplished.[53]

Secondly, the list further stresses the authenticity of Jeremiah's prophecy of return for a post-exilic audience.[54] Ezra 1. 7–11 shows a detailed list of temple vessels, that Sheshbazzar brings up from Babylon to Jerusalem. The precise meaning of this list is difficult to grasp. As Peter Acroyd highlights, the list hints probably at the 'totality of the vessels'.[55] In Ezra 1. 1, the return of temple vessels, and of the people themselves, is seen as foretold by Jeremiah, whose words are accomplished (v. 1): 'In the first year

---

52   See already Bernhard Duhm, *Das Buch Jeremia*, KHC.AT, XI (Tübingen – Leipzig: J. C. B. Mohr [Paul Siebeck], 1901), pp. 222–23.

53   See Fischer, *Jeremia 26–52*, 356.

54   See Thomas Bänzinger, 'Tempelgeräte als Prüfstein echter und falscher Prophetie. Die Erwähnung der Tempelgeräte in Esra 1,7–11 im Licht des Jeremiabuches', in *Die Königsherrschaft Jahwes: Festschrift zur Emeritierung von Herbert H. Klement*, ed. by Jacob Thiessen and Harald Seubert, STB, 13 (LIT: Wien, 2015), pp. 113–27.

55   Peter R. Acrkoyd, 'The Temple Vessels – A Continuity Theme', in *Studies in the Religion of Ancient Israel*, ed. by Pieter Arie Hendrik de Boer, VT.S, 23 (Leiden: Brill, 1972), pp. 166–75; see also Bob

of Cyrus king of Persia, that the word of Yhwh by the mouth of Jeremiah might be accomplished, Yhwh stirred up the spirit of Cyrus king of Persia so that he made a proclamation throughout all his kingdom and also put it in writing'. The reference to the 'totality of the vessels' in Ezra 1. 7–11 preceded by the mention of Jeremiah's words and their fulfillment (Ezra 1. 1) could have triggered the addition in Jeremiah 27. 19–20,[56] which mirrored 52. 17. According to Jeremiah 27. 19–20, the return of the vessels had been already announced by Jeremiah; as a result, he ends up being an authentic prophet, who aptly fits the fulfillment criterion of Deuteronomy 18. 20–22. Against this background, the list of Jeremiah 27. 19–20 could provide additional details to Jeremiah's words for post-exilic recipients, who can appreciate their fulfillment. The difference between Ezra 1. 7–11 and Jeremiah 27. 19 could be explained by the harmonization between 27. 19 and 52. 17.

b) Intertextual References

Jeremiah 28. 16 and 29. 32 hint at Deuteronomy 13. 6 for raising Hanania's and Shemaia's profiles: both prophets are sentenced to death for having spoken 'rebellion against Yhwh' (סרה + אל יהוה/על).

Deuteronomy 13. 6:

וְהַנָּבִיא הַהוּא אוֹ חֹלֵם הַחֲלוֹם הַהוּא יוּמָת כִּי דִבֶּר־סָרָה עַל־יְהוָה אֱלֹהֵיכֶם

> But that prophet or that dreamer of dreams shall be put to death, because he has spoken rebellion against Yhwh your God.

Jeremiah 28. 16:

לָכֵן כֹּה אָמַר יְהוָה הִנְנִי מְשַׁלֵּחֲךָ מֵעַל פְּנֵי הָאֲדָמָה הַשָּׁנָה אַתָּה מֵת כִּי־סָרָה דִבַּרְתָּ אֶל־יְהוָה

> Therefore, thus says Yhwh: Behold, I will remove you from the face of the earth. This very year you shall die, because you have spoken rebellion against Yhwh.

Jeremiah 29. 32:

לָכֵן כֹּה־אָמַר יְהוָה הִנְנִי פֹקֵד עַל־שְׁמַעְיָה הַנֶּחֱלָמִי וְעַל־זַרְעוֹ לֹא־יִהְיֶה לוֹ אִישׁ יוֹשֵׁב בְּתוֹךְ־הָעָם הַזֶּה וְלֹא־יִרְאֶה בַטּוֹב אֲשֶׁר־אֲנִי עֹשֶׂה־לְעַמִּי נְאֻם־יְהוָה כִּי־סָרָה דִבֶּר עַל־יְהוָה

> Therefore, thus says Yhwh: I am going to punish Shemaiah of Nehelam and his descendants; he shall not have anyone living among this people to see the good that I am going to do to my people, says Yhwh, for he has spoken rebellion against Yhwh.

Becking, 'Temple Vessels Speaking for a Silent God', in *Reflections on the Silence of God: A Discussion with Marjo Korpel and Johannes de Moor*, ed. by Bob Becking, OTS, 62 (Leiden: Brill, 2013), pp. 13–28.
56   The relation between Jeremiah 27. 19–20 and Ezra 1. 7 is already stressed by Bänzinger, 'Tempelgeräte', pp. 119–25.

The phrase 'to speak rebellion against Yhwh' (דבר + סרה + יהוה אל/על) labels Hananiah and Shemaiah as apostate prophets, while providing the reader an indisputable point of reference for discerning between authentic and non-authentic prophecy. On top of that, Jer 28. 17 confirms Hananiah's death in the same year (וַיָּמָת חֲנַנְיָה בַּשָּׁנָה הַהִיא בַּחֹדֶשׁ הַשְּׁבִיעִי, in that same year, in the seventh month, the prophet Hananiah died). The conclusion stresses a double kind of authentication: Jeremiah's words (הַשָּׁנָה אַתָּה מֵת :v. 16) fulfill (וַיָּמָת חֲנַנְיָה הַנָּבִיא בַּשָּׁנָה הַהִיא :v. 17); in addition, Hananiah dies and is debunked as a false and apostate prophet.

In summary, MT-Jeremiah employs redactional strategies (e.g. 27. 19–21), inter-textual references (e.g. Deuteronomy 18. 20–22 in Jeremiah 28. 8–9; Deuteronomy 13.6 in Jeremiah 28. 16 and 29. 32), as well as narrative strategies (e.g. accomplishment of Hananiah's death in 28. 17), for clarifying the thorny issue around true and false prophecy. These strategies pursue the goal of guiding the recipients in discerning the authentic prophet.

3.2. Strategies in LXX-Jeremiah

In LXX-Jeremiah, the neologism ψευδοπροφήτης plays a pivotal role for dealing with the issue at hand.[57] In their introduction to Jeremiah for the NETS, Pietersma and Saunders list the noun ψευδοπροφήτης among the 'variations at the word level'.[58] According to them, rendering נביא with ψευδοπροφήτης is a semantic variation 'due to context',[59] and ultimately a 'gloss' for נביא.

This explanation however does not fully elucidate the coinage ψευδοπροφήτης that can be reasonably ascribed to the Greek translator of Jeremiah. The neologism serves at least two main functions:

a) Lexicalizing the Fulfillment Criterion

According to Pietersma and Saunders '… when "pseudo-prophet" appears on the scene "prophet" by no means disappears […] it is not immediately clear how a prophet could become a pseudo-prophet'.[60] The coinage of ψευδοπροφήτης hints back to the noun ψευδόμαντις.[61] Sophocles (*Oedipus at Colonus*, 1096–97) and

---

57 For a definition of neologism within the Septuagint, and related *caveat*, see Katrin Hauspie, 'Neologisms in the Septuagint of Ezekiel', *JNES*, 27 (2001), 17–37 (pp. 17–19); Johann Cook, 'Translating the Septuagint. Some Methodological Considerations', in *Translating a Translation: The LXX and Its Modern Translations in the Context of Early Judaism*, ed. by Hans Ausloos and others, BETL, 213 (Leuven: Peeters, 2008), pp. 9–33 (pp. 30–31). According to Cook, creation of neologisms indicates 'the competence of the translator on a literary level' (p. 31).

58 See Pietersma – Saunders, 'Ieremias', p. 877.

59 Pietersma – Saunders, 'Ieremias', p. 877.

60 Pietersma – Saunders, 'Ieremias', p. 877.

61 The neologism ψευδοπροφήτης reflects a well attested paradigm of creating new words in Greek, through a 'productive prefix', see Hauspie, 'Neologisms', pp. 27, 33–34.

Euripides (*Orestes*, 1667–68) employ ψευδόμαντις in negative sentences for hinting at a prophetic pronouncement that does not come true.

Sophocles, *Oedipus at Colonus*, 1096–97

ὦ ξεῖν' ἀλῆτα, τὸν σκοπὸν μὲν <u>οὐκ ἐρεῖς</u>
<u>ὡς ψευδόμαντις·τὰς κόρας γὰρ εἰσορῶ</u>

O wandering stranger, you shall not say your guide
a false prophet; for I see the girls

The vision announced is not false, as the vision proclaimed by a ψευδόμαντις. The Chorus stresses that Theseus' promise (vv. 1040–1041: 'I shall not rest till I have placed your children in your hands') is reliable and comes true: Antigone and Ismene (the young women) are coming with Theseus.

Euripides, *Orestes*, 1667–68

ὦ Λοξία μαντεῖε, σῶν θεσπισμάτων
<u>οὐ ψευδόμαντις ἦσθ' ἄρ' ἀλλ' ἐτήτυμος.</u>

O, prophetic Loxias, for your oracles!
You were not a false prophet after all, but truthful

Orestes (who is speaking) recognizes the authenticity of Apollos' oracles, by contrasting the noun <u>ψευδόμαντις</u> with the adj. <u>ἐτήτυμος</u> 'reliable/true'.

The antonym ἀληθόμαντις 'true prophet' is used by Aeschylus, *Agamennon*, 1241 for prophecies which will happen; Cassandra is speaking:

τί γάρ;
τὸ μέλλον ἥξει. Καὶ σύ μ' ἐν τάχει παρὼν
ἄγαν γ' ἀληθόμαντιν οἰκτίρας ἐρεῖς.

What does it matter?
What's coming, comes. And soon you being present
grieving will unfortunately declare me a true prophetess.

Back to Jeremiah: it is reasonable to argue that the coinage ψευδοπροφήτης implies a reference to prophetic pronouncements that do not fulfill. The neologism therefore conveys information on the fulfillment requirement (see MT-Jeremiah 28. 8–9; LXX-Jeremiah 36. 8–9). From LXX-Jeremiah 33 to Jeremiah 36, Jeremiah's adversaries are labeled as ψευδοπροφῆται, i.e. prophets whose words are not accomplished. Confronted with ψευδοπροφῆται, Jeremiah on the contrary ends up being the reliable and authentic prophet; if ψευδοπροφῆται's words will not happen, Jeremiah's words on the contrary are trustful and will become true.

As previously shown, the list of temple vessels in MT-Jeremiah 27. 19–20 seems to answer the fulfillment criterion, and indicates that Jeremiah is an authentic prophet to post-exilic recipients. LXX-Jeremiah, resolves issues around fulfillment of prophecies by means of a lexical coinage; the list of vessels, which apparently solves the same issue within MT, does not appear in LXX-Jeremiah.

In summary, LXX-Jeremiah lexicalizes the conflict between true and false prophecy. The neologism ψευδοπροφήτης, that mirrors the classical Greek ψευδόμαντις, serves the purpose of disambiguating, while providing recipients with an interpretive key. The noun prompts the expected answers by the recipients; in addition, the noun provides a lexical solution for discerning true prophecy according to the *fulfillment criterion*. Deuteronomy 18. 21–22, turns out to be embedded in the semantic nucleus of ψευδοπροφήτης; redactional strategies (e.g. list of vessels in 27. 19–20) or references to other authoritative texts (e.g. Deuteronomy 13. 6 in Jeremiah 28. 16 and 29. 32) end up being redundant.

b) Disambiguating and Orienting Interpretation

As previously shown, MT-Jeremiah 26 confronts the reader with an ambiguous portrayal of prophets. The ambiguity is resolved by LXX-Jeremiah 33 (= MT-Jeremiah 26) by means of the noun ψευδοπροφήτης, which occurs 4 times in the whole chapter (33. 7, 8, 11, 16). From the very first time Jeremiah's adversaries take the floor (v. 7), the narrator labels them as 'false prophets' (οἱ ψευδοπροφῆται).

An external and authoritative voice, i.e. the narrative voice, provides the necessary information for entering the prophetic arena: Jeremiah is accused by ψευδοπροφῆται; in contrast, the prophet from Anathot, who survives the trial and escapes the death sentence, can safely be recognized as authentic prophet.

The coinage ψευδοπροφήτης orients the reader's interpretation. In 35. 1 (= MT-Jeremiah 28. 1) Hananiah comes into view: Ανανίας υἱὸς Αζωρ ὁ ψευδοπροφήτης ὁ ἀπὸ Γαβαων ('Hananiah the son of Azur, the pseudo-prophet from Gabaon'). From the beginning, the addressees of the narrative know that Hananiah is a false prophet. The same happens with regard to prophets in Babylon (Ahab, Zedekiah, v. 21; and Shemaiah, v. 31), who are defined ψευδοπροφῆται already in 36. 1: 'these are the words of the letter, which Jeremiah sent from Jerusalem to the elders of the exile and to the priests and to the pseudo-prophets (καὶ πρὸς τοὺς ψευδοπροφήτας)'.

The noun ψευδοπροφήτης is used for characterizing prophets from their very first mention (e.g. Jeremiah 34. 7; 35. 1; 36. 1, 8). References to Deuteronomy 13. 6 (see MT-Jeremiah 28. 17 and 29. 32), that offer recipients a clear interpretive key, are provided by MT at the end of the narratives. These hints are (consistently) missing in the LXX, where the noun ψευδοπροφήτης provides recipients with a clear interpretive tool from the very beginning.

In summary, to a certain extent, the coinage ψευδοπροφήτης mirrors the principle of economy that regulates linguistic changes.[62] A lexical strategy, able to provide clear and effective answers to the reader, preserves the maximum economy within a textual system.

---

62 The principle of economy or principle of least effort, 'consists in tending towards the minimum amount of effort that is necessary to achieve the maximum result, so that nothing is wasted'; see Alessandra Vicentini, 'The Economy Principle in Language. Notes and Observations from Early Modern English Grammars', *Mots Palabras Words*, 3 (2003), 37–57 (p. 38). The principle was firstly described as regards phonetics and syntax (by Martinet) but gradually extended to semantics; as

c) Searching for Textual Coherence

Among the nine occurrences of the noun ψευδοπροφήτης in Jeremiah, eight of them appear in chs. 26–29. Consequently, these chapters are identified as narrative about true and false prophecy, and are tied together by a clear lexical hinge (33. 7; 34. 7; 35. 1; 36. 1).

Besides lexical repetitions, a pivotal strategy at work in MT to link together chs. 26–29 is provided by superscriptions with their chronological framework.[63] Jeremiah 27. 1 with the mention of Jehoiakim, however, is fraught with difficulties and usually emended.[64] Chronological strategies for coordinating LXX-Jeremiah 33–36 do not seem relevant for the Greek translator. In LXX-Jeremiah 33–36, textual coherence is provided by a lexical thread, i.e. the noun ψευδοπροφήτης. Quite curiously, the awkward mention of Jehoiakim (27. 1 MT) is (consistently) absent in LXX-Jeremiah 34. 1. The translator could have easily skipped a strange chronological reference, as thematic coherence was secured by means of the coinage ψευδοπροφήτης.

4. Translating in Hellenistic Time: Provisional Suggestions

As Tessa Rajak rightly points out, 'the Greek Bible translation was a major step in a new direction and yet was not altogether a novelty'.[65] Translating was not unfamiliar in the Hellenistic time, and texts were not translated only for practical purposes.[66] The Roman world offers empirical evidence that provides suggestions for reconsidering *translations* in Hellenistic time. Latin literature starts with Latin translations of Greek classics: in third century BCE, Livius Andronicus translates parts of Homer's *Odyssey*: the *Odusia*.[67] In addition, Roman dramatists such as Plautus, Terence, or Caecilius Statius, among others, translated plays from the Greek originals.[68]

Vicentini highlights, 'words are constantly being shortened, permuted, eliminated, borrowed and altered in meaning, but, thanks to the *Principle of Least Effort*, an equilibrium with a maximum of economy is always preserved' (p. 40).

63   See in this regard Stipp, *Jeremia 25–52*, p. 26.

64   See Stipp, *Jeremia 25–52*, p. 134. Stipp ascribes to Jeremiah 27. 1 also the function of synchronizing the prophetic announcement with oracles against Edom, Moab, Amnon, etc. (see also pp. 135–36).

65   Tessa Rajak, *Translation and Survival: The Greek Bible of the Ancient Jewish Diaspora* (Oxford: Oxford University Press, 2009), p. 24.

66   See Rajak, *Translation*, p. 25.

67   For introductory issues, see Enrico Flores, 'Introduzione', in *Livi Andronici Odvsia: Introduzione, edizione critica e versione italiana*, Forme materiali e ideologie del mondo antico, 39 (Napoli: Liguori Editore, 2011), pp. xi–xxiii. For critical editions of the fragments of Andronicus's Odusia, see Lucius Livius Andronicus, *Odvsia*, in *Fragmenta Poetarum Latinorum Epicorum et Lyricorum Praeter Ennivm et Lvcilicm. Post W. Morel Novis Cvris Adhibitis edidit Carolvs Buechner*, ed. by Jürgen Blänsdorf, Bibliotheca Scriptorum Graecoruum et Romanorum Teubneriana (Stutgardiae: Teubner, ³1995), pp. 21–32; Flores, *Odvsia*.

68   For an overview on translating and translation in ancient Rome, see Maurizio Bettini, *Vertere: Un'antropologia della traduzione nella cultura antica*, Piccola Biblioteca Einaudi Nuova Serie, 573 (Torino: Einaudi, 2012), pp. 32–87.

To be clear: I do not want to stress here any direct influence from the Roman world on the Greek translation of Jeremiah.[69] I shall just provide some suggestions, that hopefully clarify some translating techniques at work in Hellenistic time. In addition, the following will show that the paradigm of interlinear translations within a school setting is not the only translation paradigm available in the Hellenistic time.

a) Variation in Discourse deixis

Andronici, *Odusia* (XXVIII Flores; 4 Blänsdorf):[70]

Neque tamen te oblitus sum Laertie noster

Nor yet have I forgotten you our own Laertes' son.

The fragment is recognized as the translation of ξ 144:[71]

ἀλλά μ᾽ Ὀδυσσῆος πόθος αἴνυται οἰχομένοιο

but it is longing for Odysseus, who is gone, that seizes me

Eaumaeus is talking with Odysseus, whom he hosted. Odysseus' identity is unknown to Eumaeus, who expresses his longing for him. Andronicus' translation changes discourse deixis: Odysseus is addressed by 2nd sg (*te*), and by means of a vocative (*te… Laertie noster*). The shift in discourse deixis intensifies the pathos of the scene, while at the same time enhancing the narrative tension for the recipient who knows that Eumaeus is talking to Odysseus.[72]

b) Additions and Omissions

Andronici, *Odusia* (XVII Flores; 15 Blänsdorf):[73]

ibi manens sedeto donicum uidebis
me carpento uehentem domum uenisse <parentis>

there sit and wait until you shall see that,
driving in my carriage, I have come to <paternal> home

---

69 As Rajak points out, 'It is a fanciful but pleasing idea that inspiration could have come from the West, percolating somehow from Rome' (*Translation*, p. 24).

70 A commentary on the fragment is provided by Simona Manuela Manzella, 'Commento ai Frammenti XVII-XXXII', in Livio Andronico, *Odissea: Commentario*, ed. by Mariantonietta Paladini and Simona Manuela Manzella, Forme materiali e ideologie del mondo antico, 45 (Napoli: Liguori Editore, 2014), pp. 87–198 (pp. 166–74).

71 See Manzella, 'Commento', pp. 167–69. For the *Odyssey*, see Homerus, *Odyssea*, ed. by Martin L. West, BSGRT, 2026 (Berlin: de Gruyter, 2017). Blänsdorf considers the fragment a translation of α 65 (πῶς ἂν ἔπειτ᾽ Ὀδυσῆος ἐγὼ θείοιο λαθοίμην), cf. Andronicus, *Odvsia*, in *Fragmenta Poetarum Latinorum*, pp. 22–23. See also the discussion in Karl Büchner, 'Livius Andronicus und die erste Künstlerische Übersetzung der Europäischen Kultur', *Symbolae Osloenses*, 54 (1979), 37–70 (pp. 53–54).

72 See Manzella, 'Commento', pp. 170–71, who traces the increasing *pathos* to the demands of oral performance.

73 See Flores, *Odvusia*, p. 19; Büchner, 'Livius Andronicus', pp. 50–51; Manzella, 'Commento', pp. 89–96.

The fragment translates ζ 295–97:[74]

ἔνθα καθεζόμενος μεῖναι χρόνον, εἰς ὅ κεν ἡμεῖς
ἄστυδε ἔλθωμεν καὶ ἱκώμεθα δώματα πατρός.
αὐτὰρ ἐπὴν ἡμέας ἔλπηι ποτὶ δώματ᾽ ἀφῖχθαι
[…]

> sit down there, and wait for a time, until we
> come to the city and reach the house of my father.
> But when you think that we have reached the house […]

According to the *Odyssey*, Nausicaa invites Odysseus to wait until she reasonably could have reached home from the washing pools, with her maidens. The translation is overall shorter than the Greek original. Andronicus reshapes the scene, by means of slight variations.[75] Among them, he introduces two connected details. The first is *videbis*. According to Andronicus, Odysseus can look at Nausicaa until she reaches her father's house. The second is *carpento vehentem*: Nausicaa travels back home on a wagon.

According to ζ 36–38 Athena suggests to Nausicaa to ask her father for a wagon and mules (ἡμιόνους καὶ ἄμαξαν) 'to take the girdles, garments and shining rugs' (ζῶστρά τε καὶ πέπλους καὶ ῥήγεα σιγαλόεντα) (v. 38). Nausicaa's wagon is repeatedly mentioned through ζ (ἄμαξα: ζ 37, 72, 260: ἀπήνη: ζ 57, 69, 73, 75, 78, 88, 252). Andronicus probably picks up the wagon from the former narrative, and adds this detail to the scene. The addition seems therefore to pursue textual coherence.

Moreover, as Odysseus can see Nausicaa all the while until she arrives home, it can be argued that Andronicus probably skipped the following vv. 298–99, where Odysseus is invited to enter the city and to ask for Alcinoo's house (καὶ τότε Φαιήκων ἵμεν ἐς πόλιν ἠδ᾽ ἐρέεσθαι | δώματα πατρὸς ἐμοῦ, μεγαλήτορος Ἀλκινόοιο, 'then go to the city of the Phoeacians and ask | for the house of my father, great-hearted Alcinous', vv. 298–99).[76] Asking for Alcinoo's house is made redundant by the chance Odysseus has to see Nausicaa until she reaches her father's house.

Omissions happen also in Latin translations of Greek plays. In the prologue of *Adelphoe*,[77] Terentius defends himself from those accusing him of having stolen a scene from Plautus' *Commorientes*. He answers as follows:

---

74 See Andronicus, *Odvsia*, in *Fragmenta Poetarum Latinorum*, p. 26; Manzella, 'Commento', pp. 90–91.

75 A detailed list of variations, additions, and omissions in *Odusia*, XVII Flores is provided by Manzella, 'Commento', p. 91–96; see also Alfonso Traina, *Vortit barbare: Le traduzioni poetiche da Livio Andronico a Cicerone* (Roma: Edizioni dell'Ateneo, 1970), pp. 24–26; Mario Zambarbieri, *L'Odissea com'è: lettura critica: 1: Canti I–XII* (Milano: LED, 2002), pp. 493–94.

76 So Manzella, 'Commento', pp. 92–93: 'questa "interpretazione visiva" […] della scena omerica, non dà solo ragione di una traduzione che è ben lungi dall'essere imprecisa, ma può aver comportato altresì […] l'eliminazione dei versi 298–99 e 300–02 di Omero, dove Nausicaa invita l'eroe, una volta giunto in città, a chiedere dove si trovi la casa di Alcinoo'.

77 See Terentius A. Publius, *Adelphoe*, in *Térence: Hécyre. Adelphes*, Tome III, texte établi et traduit par J. Marouzeau (Paris: Les Belles Lettres, 1949), pp. 93–188.

Synapothnescontes Diphili comoediast;
eam Commorientes Plautus fecit fabulam;
in graeca adulescens est, qui lenoni eripit
meretricem in prima fabula; eum Plautus locum
reliquit integrum; eum hic locum sumpsit sibi
in Adelphos, uerbum de uerbo expressum extulit (Terentius, *Adelphoe*, 6–11).

> Synapothnescontes is a comedy by Diphilus;
> this Plautus rendered in his play the Commorientes.
> In the Greek play there is a young man who carries off from a pimp
> a prostitute, in the first scene; this part Plautus
> has left out entirely; the present author has taken that part over for himself
> in the *Aldelphoe*, and has rendered it word for word.

Terentius informs his audience that Plautus, while translating Diphilus' comedy *Synapothnescontes*, leaves out entirely from his translation a scene (*locum reliqui integrum*). Terence picks up for his *Adelphoe* the *locum* Plautus omits.

In summary, omissions do not seem alien to Hellenistic translation practices, and happen due to pragmatic choices of the translators.

c) Changing Titles and Images

Plautus' prologues to his comedies, often witness the habit of renaming the Greek originals:

Huic Graece nomen est Thensauro fabulae:
Philemo scripsit, Plautus uortit barbare,
Nomen Trinummo fecit. Nunc hoc uos rogat
Vt liceat possidere hanc nomen fabulam (Plautus, *Trinummus*, 18–21).[78]

> The name of this play in the Greek is *Thesaurus*;
> Philemon wrote it, Plautus translated it into the barbarian language
> and gave it the name 'The Three Pieces of Money'. Now, he asks you,
> that this play may keep this name.

Changing the titles of the Greek originals conveys a precise interpretive choice; at the same time, the identity of the play is transformed: e.g. a *Thesaurus* becomes a *Trinummus*, i.e. three pieces of money.[79]

---

78 See Titus Maccius Plautus, *Trinummus*, in Plaute, *Comédies: Trinummus. Truculentus. Vidularia. Fragmenta*, Tome VII, texte établi et traduit par Alfred Ernout (Paris: Les Belles Lettres, 1940), pp. 7–89.

79 See on this regard Bettini, *Vertere*, pp. 37–49.

Aulus Gellius (*Noctes Atticae*, II, XXIII) compares Caecilius Statius' *Plocium* and Menander's Greek original play.[80] Here is the beginning of a dialogue between two men (*Noctes Atticae*, II, XXIII, 12–13):[81]

Ἔχω δ'ἐπίκληρον Λάμιαν· οὐκ εἴρηκά σοι
Τοῦτ; — εἶτ' ἄρ' οὐχί; — κυρίαν τῆς οἰκίας
καὶ τῶν ἀγρῶν καὶ * πάντων ἀντ' ἐκείνης
ἔχομεν, Ἄπολλον, ὡς χαλεπῶν χαλεπώτατον·
ἅπασι δ'ἀργαλέα 'στίν, οὐκ ἐμοὶ μόνῳ,
υἱῷ, πολὺ μᾶλλον θυγατρί. — Πρᾶγμ' ἄμαχον λέγεις,
εὖ οἶδα.

> I have (to wife) an heiress Lamia! I did not tell you
> that? — What, really? No? — A mistress of the house
> and lands, of all that's hereabout. And in return
> I have, by Apollo, the most unbearable evil of evils.
> She is unpleasant with everyone, not only with me,
> but her son, her daughter, most of all — An irresolvable problem, you tell me,
> I know it well.

Sed tua morosane uxor, quaeso, est? — Quam rogas?
Qui tandem? — Taedet mentionis, quae mihi,
Vbi domum adueni, adsedi, extemplo sauium
Dat ieiuna anima. — Nil peccat de sauio.
Vt deuomas uult, quod foris potaueris

> But tell me, is your wife captious? — How can you ask?
> In what manner then? — I am ashamed to tell;
> when I came home as soon as I sat down, she straight gives me a kiss
> with fasting breathe — She doesn't lack wit.
> She wants you to spew up what you've drunk abroad.

The Greek Lamia is a female demon who devours human flesh. Caecilius changes the reference to this Greek monster with the adjective *morosus* that means captious, hypercritical, hard to please, peevish.

On the one hand, Caecilius' rendering conveys a different tone; on the other, the adjective is familiar to the audience and perfectly fits the setting of a Latin comedy. The same applies to the change in the description of the woman's behavior. Menander stages a shrew but Caecilius changes the woman's portrait, introducing the unpleasant detail of her bad breath (*ieiuna anima*, fasting breath, i.e. the unpleasant breath of the morning).[82]

---

80 See Bettini, *Vertere*, pp. 47–48.
81 See Aulu-Gelle, *Les nuits attiques. Livres I–IV*, texte établi et traduit par René Marache (Paris: Les Belles Lettres, 1967).
82 Mention of bad breath suits the tone of the Roman comedy; see Bettini, *Vertere*, p. 48; see also Traina, *Vortit barbare*, pp. 40–53.

In summary, the examples illustrated above show how pragmatic needs lead the translator to rework the source text through additions, omissions, and significant lexical changes. The possibility of reworking the source text for pragmatic needs is not alien to the Hellenistic time.

5. LXX-Jeremiah through the Lens of Pragmatics: Problems and Perspectives

The examples above illustrated that some variations and omissions in LXX-Jeremiah are due to the translator's pragmatic goals. Evidence from Latin literature has shown that relevant qualitative and quantitative variation from source texts, due to the translator's communicative goals, are common in the Hellenistic time in Latin translations as well. Some problems come into view, however.

The isomorphism of LXX-Jeremiah seems to bring evidence against the possibility that the translator alters the source-text by changes and omissions. As Tov highlights, due to the relatively literal character of LXX-Jeremiah 'its translator would not be expected to abbreviate his *Vorlage* drastically'.[83] A virtual shorter *Vorlage* seems to account better for macro-level variations.[84] The relation between isomorphism and pragmatic/communicative goals pursued by translators is here at stake. In particular, are translator's pragmatic choices subordinated or superordinated to the linguistic and textual make-up of the text?

Within a source-oriented interpretation, isomorphism is considered in terms of equivalence or fidelity to the source text. This feature defines the character of a translation, to such an extent that the translator's pragmatic choices would be subordinate to it.[85] A target-oriented interpretation, typical of translation studies, prompts reconsidering the issue at hand.

I give here two examples:

a) Intralinguistic translations of the *Iliad*, from Homeric to Hellenistic Greek, come into view as an empirical model for isomorphic features of the Septuagint. They are a likely school product, whose goal would be to bring the reader to the original and not to offer the reader an independent text.[86] A consequence

---

83   Emanuel Tov, *The Text-Critical Use of the Septuagint in Biblical Research: Completely Revised and Expanded Third Edition* (Winona Lake: Eisenbrauns, 2015), pp. 19–20. So again Tov: 'the main criterion for the text-critical evaluation of any short text in the LXX […] is the character of the translation unit in which that short text is found. In general, if a certain book is rendered literally, it is not to be assumed that the translator omitted large sections that were found in his *Vorlage*' (p. 19).

84   See in this regard, Weis, 'Jeremiah amid Actual and Virtual', pp. 383–84.

85   As Pietersma highlights, determining whether the translator acts as author (maximum involvement) or as medium (minimum involvement) hangs on the 'textual linguistic make-up' of a translated text; see Pietersma, 'Exegesis', pp. 35–37.

86   See Albert Pietersma, 'A New Paradigm for Assessing Old Questions. The Relevance of the Interlinear Model for the Study of the Septuagint', in *Bible and Computer. The Stellenbosch AIBI-6 Conference. Proceedings of the Association Internationale Bible et Informatique 'From Alpha to Byte'. University of Stellenbosch 17–21 July, 2000*, ed. by Johann Cook (Leiden: Brill, 2002), pp. 337–64

can be drawn: interlinear and isomorphic style of translation does not serve the preservation of the integrity of the source-text, rather, mainly the communicative purpose of the translation itself. The educational setting is of primary importance for explaining the isomorphic, interlinear character of Homer's translations in Hellenistic Greek.

b) Andronicus' *Odusia*, as well as Latin translations of Greek plays, show how the translator's communicative priorities can change the source text. The desire to make texts born and represented in a Greek environment accessible to the public of Ancient Rome involves a series of adaptations by the translator, which substantially obey pragmatic reasons.[87] Again, the target-oriented goals determine the translation style, which serves specific purposes.

In summary, the Hellenistic world testifies that different translation styles (isomorphic or 'free') serve different purposes. Both intralingual translations of Homeric poems and Latin translations of Greek plays show how pragmatics' choices are superordinate to morphological and syntactic ones. Isomorphism, therefore, mirrors a deliberate communicative choice on behalf of the translator. Consequently, a translation's isomorphic nature does not preclude the chance that the translator makes changes based on clear pragmatic and communicative choices. As White emphasizes, isomorphism alone cannot determine the character of a translation.[88]

A last question comes here into view. The isomorphism of the Septuagint and the literal rendering of the Hebrew original is sometimes traced back to the authority of the source text. Adherence to an authoritative and normative source-text would have prevented substantial variations by the translator.[89] Examples of ancient translations show however that the normativity of a text does not always imply a literal adherence to it by translators.

(pp. 348–49); Martin Rösel, 'Schreiber, Übersetzer, Theologen. Die Septuaginta als Dokument der Schrift-, Lese-, und Übersetzungskulturen des Judentums', in *Die Septuaginta — Texte, Kontexte, Lebenswelten*, ed. by Martin Karrer and Wolfgang Kraus, WUNT, 219 (Tübingen: Mohr Siebeck, 2008), pp. 83–102 (pp. 94–96).

87   According to Traina Andronicus' aim in translating Homer is: 'avvicinare il testo più che possibile ai lettori latini, sia spiegando sia romanizzando Omero. Spiegando, cioè ora ampliando ora semplificando il testo là dove era oscuro o prolisso [...] romanizzando, cioè operando una continua sostituzione di espressioni, concezioni, istituzioni greche con romane', see Traina, *Vortit barbare*, p. 12. Büchner, 'Livius Andronicus', pp. 61–65 show the extent to which recipients of the translation ('das Publikum') and the communicative goals impact the Andronicus' translation style.

88   See Wade A. White, 'A Devil in the Making. Isomorphism and Exegesis in OG Job 1:8b', in *Septuagint Research: Issues and Challenges in the Study of the Greek Jewish Scriptures*, ed. by Wolfgang Kraus and R. Glenn Wooden, SBL.SCS, 53 (Atlanta: SBL, 2006), pp. 145–56 (pp. 146–47), who shows that in OG Job an isomorphic approach combines with interpretive renderings of the translator.

89   So Aejmelaeus: 'My impression is that the reverence felt by the first Bible translators towards their source text was too great to allow conscious, manipulation of its meaning', see Anneli Aejmelaeus, 'Levels of Interpretation. Tracing the Trail of the Septuagint Translators', in *On the Trail of the Septuagint Translators: Collected Essays*, CBET, 50 (Leuven: Peeters, 2007), pp. 295–312 (p. 307).

Darius' Behistun trilingual inscription presents itself as an authoritative and normative text.[90] Nonetheless, its rendering in different languages entails variations, omissions, and interpolations as well. The best-known omission is that of DB § 70 in the Babylonian version carved on the Behistun relief. In all probability, the omission is due to communicative and pragmatic reasons.[91] Further variations and omissions are due to adaptations to the cultural context,[92] e.g. the addition of stereotypical formulas to bring the style of the inscription closer to that of Mesopotamian royal annals, dating of events according to the Babylonian calendar, and terminology and phrases that describes Darius' kingship.[93]

Adaptation to a new cultural context provide reasons also for the addition of the epithet 'god of the Iranians' (*nap arianam*) in the Elamite version of DB §§ 62; 63. The intentional addition pursues communicative goals, i.e. to adapt the epithet to Elamite recipients.[94]

The Aramaic version of Behistun inscription, thought to closely correspond to the Babylonian version, shows remarkable divergences from the source text. Greenfield and Porten, enumerate different types of variants: e.g. additions; scribal omissions due to homoioteleuton; variant expressions or variant formulations of the same expressions. Several abridgements come also into view.[95] The Aramaic version of DB in § 13 rearranges the order of the Babylonian text, and interpolates DB with the Aramaic translation of DNb § §10–11 (ll. 50–60).[96] Nonetheless, as Greenfield and

---

90   The inscription features the *topoi* of authoritative official documents in ANE: e.g. DB § 56e-h; § §60–61 (blessing and curse); § 65 (invitation not to destroy the inscription) and § § 66–67 (following blessing and curse); see Rüdiger Schmitt, *Die altpersischen Inschriften der Achaimeniden: Editio minor mit deutscher Übersetzung* (Wiesbaden: Reichert Verlag, 2009).

91   See Francesco Aspesi, 'La versione aramaica su papiro dell'iscrizione monumentale trilingue di Dario a Behistun', *ACME: Annali della Facoltà di Lettere e Filosofia dell'Università degli studi di Milano*, 58 (2005), pp. 15–27 (pp. 19–20); see also Florence Malbran-Labat, 'La trilingue de Behistun et les singularités de la version babylonienne', *Semitica*, 48 (1998), 61–74.

92   See in this regard, Malbran-Labat, 'Trilingue'.

93   See Malbran-Labat, 'Trilingue', pp. 66–69.

94   Gian Pietro Basello, 'Le unità amministrative dell'impero achemenide (satrapie): il potere percepito dai popoli sottomessi e le immagini di ritorno', in *Ciro chiamato per nome (Is 45,4): l'epoca persiana e la nascita dell'Israele biblico tra richiamo a Gerusalemme e diaspora perenne. Atti del XVII Convegno di Studi Veterotestamentari (Assisi, 5–7 Settembre 2011)*, ed. by Gian Luigi Prato, Ricerche Storico Bibliche, 25 (Bologna: EDB, 2013), pp. 37–97 (pp. 74–77).

95   See Jonas C. Greenfield and Bezalel Porten, *The Bisitun Inscription of Darius the Great Aramaic Version: Text, Translation and Commentary*. Corpus Inscriptionum Iranicarum: Part I Inscriptions of Ancient Iran. Vol. V The Aramaic Versions of the Achaemenian Inscriptions. Texts I (London: Lund Humphries, 1982), pp. 5–16. The Aramaic version shows close resemblance to a shorter Babylonian version of Behistun relief, found in Babylon (see Greenfield and Porten, *Bisitun Inscription*, p. 16). This however does not invalidate the comparison with the original Babylonian relief, see Jan Tavernier, 'An Achaemenid Royal Inscription: The Text of Paragraph 13 of the Aramaic Version of the Bisitun Inscription', *JNES*, 60 (2001), 161–77 (p. 162).

96   See Bezalel Porten and Ada Yardeni, *Textbook of Aramaic Documents from Ancient Egypt: Volume III Literature, Accounts, Lists* (Winona Lake: Eisenbrauns, 1993), pp. 59–71 (p. 71). Greenfield and Porten number the same paragraph as § 10 (Greenfield and Porten, *Bisitun Inscription*, pp. 47–51), due to a different paragraph division of the Aramaic text (eleven instead of fourteen paragraphs in

Porten highlight, the Aramaic translation of DB shares syntactic features and word order with the Babylonian source text; one Akkadian loanword comes also into view.[97] As a matter of fact, the syntactic adherence of a translation to its original can go together with essential variations such as omissions, interpolations, or shifts in the source text's order. The normativity of a text does not prevent communicative and pragmatic reasons from determining variations within the translation.[98]

In summary, the authority of the source text does not necessarily entail isomorphism and literalism of the translated text. Assuming literalness of a translation on the basis of the normativity of the source-text does not seem to consider once again the prevalence of pragmatic and communicative reasons which cause important variations in translation.

As Lefevere highlights, 'on every level of the translation process, it can be shown that, if linguistic considerations enter into conflict with considerations of an ideological and/or poetological nature the latter tend to win out'.[99] Between isomorphism and pragmatic choices, that serve ideological concerns, the latter have the upper hand. Adherence to the morphological and syntactic form of the source text ends up to subordinate to them.

Something ends up lost in translation; the alleged grandson of Ben Sira is aware of that: '… for what was originally expressed in Hebrew does not have the same force when it is in fact rendered in another language (οὐ γὰρ ἰσοδυναμεῖ αὐτὰ ἐν ἑαυτοῖς Εβραϊστὶ λεγόμενα καὶ ὅταν μεταχθῇ εἰς ἑτέραν γλῶσσαν)' (Sirach, Prolog 1. 21–22). Looking at LXX-Jeremiah through the lens of pragmatics could provide a useful window for re-evaluating LXX-Jeremiah and its relation to MT-Jeremiah, while further enlightening context, purposes and interests of the potential translators and readers.

▼ ABSTRACT   Divergencies between MT- and LXX-Jeremiah have been typically considered in terms of *Vorlagen*, editions, and redactions. A well-established assumption in the field is that LXX-Jeremiah is a literal translation of a Hebrew *Vorlage*. This essay reconsiders the issue by focusing on the role played by pragmatics in LXX-Jeremiah.

Porten and Yardeni). In § 13 (= § 10 according to Greenfield and Porten) Aramaic ll. 64–65 combines Babylonian ll. 97–98 with ll. 105–06; Aramaic ll. 66–70 interpolates old Persian DNb (ll. 50–60); then Aramaic ll. 71–74 corresponds to Babylonian ll. 101–03. See also Schmitt, *Inschriften*, pp. 110–11; Tavernier, 'Achaemenid Royal Inscription'.

97   See Greenfield – Porten, *Bisitun Inscription*, p. 21.

98   As Adriano Valerio Rossi highlights: 'In culture dove la comunicazione orale, in condizioni di plurilinguismo intensivo, è la forma prevalente di comunicazione, bisogna fare i conti con continui riaggiustamenti che contestualizzano culturalmente il dato nuovo che altrimenti non sarebbe compreso dal destinatario, abituato ad un diverso sistema di valori (*competenza comunicativa*)'; see Adriano Valerio Rossi, 'Competenza multipla nei testi arcaici: le iscrizioni di Bisotun', *ΑΙΩΝ: Annali del dipartimento di studi del Mondo Classico e del Mediterraneo Antico Sezione Linguistica*, 7 (1985), pp. 191–210 (p. 208).

99   Lefevere, *Translation*, p. 39.

In particular, I highlight how the pursuit of discourse strategies can influence translation by bringing about specific and intentional changes of the source text. As test cases, I explore speech act in translation, communicative strategies at work, and the pragmatic relevance of a lexical coinage. In terms of empirical evidence, a fresh look at Latin translations of Greek Classics shows that relevant qualitative and quantitative variation from source texts, due to the translators' communicative goals, are common in the Hellenistic time. Additional evidence from ancient translations finally points out that the normativity of a text does not always imply a literal adherence to it by translators. The examples provided in this essay show that commitment to the source text's morphological and syntactic form subordinates to pragmatic choices that serve communicative and/or ideological concerns. Eventually, considering the impact of pragmatics in translation seems crucial for opening new avenues in reading LXX-Jeremiah.

LEONARDO PESSOA DA SILVA PINTO

Narratological Approaches
to the LXX of the Books of Samuel

The title of this paper recalls and dialogues with van der Louw's article of 2013 entitled 'A Narratological Approach to the Septuagint?'.[1] There are two main differences between the two titles. The first and more evident is that van der Louw's title ends with a question mark, for, in his article, he deems some attempts at a narratological approach to the Septuagint questionable, namely, those of John Beck and Helmut Utzschneider which tend to exaggerate the translator's role as a storyteller. Van der Louw's warnings are important and will be dealt with later in the discussion of some methodological traps that must be avoided, and I shall also refer to the problems with the works of Beck and Utzschneider. However, I am convinced that the sensible application of narratological approaches to the Septuagint is not only a possibility but, already, a reality, and this paper will focus on the successful attempts that have been made and on the principles that must be observed in this kind of research. The second difference between the two titles is that I prefer to talk about narratological approaches in the plural, for there are different applications of narrative analysis to the Septuagint in current scholarship, as I shall try to make clear below.

The book of Samuel is an interesting testing ground for the study of narrative in the Septuagint since it has been one of the favourite books in the Bible for the application of narrative analysis. This has been true since Robert Alter's classic work, *The Art of Biblical Narrative*,[2] and every manual of narrative analysis of the biblical stories contains numerous examples taken from the books of Samuel, even if these are almost always limited to the analysis of the Hebrew of the Masoretic text. The stories about David seem to have fascinated students of narratology, and much literature has been produced in this regard. Therefore, apart from occasional examples taken from other biblical books, the discussion will privilege the situation in I–II Samuel.

As is well known, narrative analysis focuses on problems related to characterization, plot, narrator, the relationship between reader and narrator and so on. It is generally counted among the so-called synchronic approaches, but I hope it will become

---

1   Theo A. W. van der Louw, 'A Narratological Approach to the Septuagint?', *ZAW*, 125/4 (2013), 551–65 (pp. 561–65).
2   Robert Alter, *The Art of Biblical Narrative*, Revised and Updated (New York: Basic Books, 2011).

New Avenues in Biblical Exegesis in Light of the Septuagint
ed. by Leonardo Pessoa da Silva Pinto and Daniela Scialabba, Turnhout, 2022 (*SEPT*, 1), pp. 183–197
© BREPOLS ❧ PUBLISHERS   DOI 10.1484/M.SEPT-EB.5.127717

clear in the following discussion that it cannot be practiced in Septuagint studies successfully without attention to diachrony.

1. Two Different Uses of Narrative Analysis in Septuagint Studies

There are at least two different uses of narrative analysis in the study of the Septuagint. In these two uses, the goal of the analysis is different, and, therefore, some method-ological steps are also adapted.

1.1. Narrative Analysis as a Mean for Elucidation of the Textual History

In one approach, the narrative features of the Septuagint are studied as a step in the reconstruction of the history of the text in order to understand its formation and transmission. This method was applied by Adrian Schenker in his book *Älteste Textgeschichte der Königsbücher*, and by his pupil, Philippe Hugo, in his doctoral thesis titled *Les deux visages d'Élie*, both discussing texts of the books of Kings. Schenker and Hugo have published numerous papers applying their methodology not only to the books of Kings,[3] but to the books of Samuel as well.[4]

---

3 Adrian Schenker, 'Un cas de critique narrative au service de la critique textuelle (1 Rois 11,43–12,2–3.20)', *Biblica*, 77/2 (1996), 219–26; 'Jéroboam et la division du royaume dans le texte massorétique et la Septante ancienne', in *IX Congress of the International Organization for Septuagint and Cognate Studies, Cambridge, 1995*, ed. by Bernard E. Taylor, SBLSCS, 45 (Atlanta: SBL, 1997), pp. 171–76; 'Die zwei Erzählungen von Joabs Tod (1 Kon 2:28–34) im Massoretischen Text und in der LXX', in *X Congress of the International Organization for Septuagint and Cognate Studies, Oslo 1998*, ed. by Bernard E. Taylor, SBLSCS, 51 (Atlanta: SBL, 2001), pp. 27–35; 'Junge Garden oder akrobatische Tänzer? Das Verhältnis zwischen 1 Kön 20 MT und 3 Regn 21 LXX', in *The Earliest Text of the Hebrew Bible: The Relationship between the Masoretic Text and the Hebrew Base of the Septuagint Reconsidered*, ed. by Adrian Schenker, SBLSCS, 52 (Leiden: Brill, 2003), pp. 17–34; 'L'iconoclasme de Jéhu. Comparaison du TM et de la LXX ancienne en 2 R 10,18–28', in *L'enfance de la Bible hébraïque: L'histoire du texte de l'Ancien Testament à la lumière des recherches récentes*, ed. by Adrian Schenker and Philippe Hugo, Le monde de la Bible, 52 (Genève: Labor et Fides, 2005), pp. 170–84; Philippe Hugo, 'Text and Literary History: The Case of 1 Kings 19 (MT and LXX)', in *Soundings in Kings: Perspectives and Methods in Contemporary Scholarship*, ed. by Mark Leuchter and Klaus-Peter Adam (Minneapolis, MN: Fortress Press, 2010), pp. 15–34.

4 See Philippe Hugo, 'Die Septuaginta in der Textgeschichte der Samuelbücher: Methodologische Prinzipien am Beispiel von 2Sam 6,1–3', in *Die Septuaginta — Texte, Kontexte, Lebenswelten: Internationale Fachtagung veranstaltet von Septuaginta Deutsch (LXX.D), Wuppertal 20.-23. Juli 2006*, ed. by Martin Karrer and Wolfgang Kraus, WUNT, 219 (Tübingen: Mohr Siebeck, 2008), pp. 336–52; 'The Jerusalem Temple Seen in 2 Samuel According to the Masoretic Text and the Septuagint', in *XIII Congress of the International Organization for Septuagint and Cognate Studies, Ljubjana 2007*, ed. by Melvin K. H. Peters, SBLSCS, 55 (Atlanta: SBL, 2008), pp. 187–200; 'Abner der Königsmacher *versus* David den gesalbten König (2Sam 3,21.39): Die Charakterisierung Abners und Davids als Merkmale der literarischen Abweichung zwischen dem Massoretischen Text und der Septuaginta', in *Die Septuaginta — Texte, Theologien, Einflüsse: 2. internationale Fachtagung veranstaltet von Septuaginta Deutsch (LXX.D), Wuppertal 23.-27.7. 2008*, ed. by Wolfgang Kraus and

According to Hugo, the methodological steps to be followed in this kind of research are: 1) critical reconstruction of the oldest text of the Septuagint; 2) synoptic reading of the Masoretic text and the Septuagint (and 4QSam, where extant); 3) text critical analysis; 4) literary comparison; 5) historical ordering of the texts or editions.[5] In his thesis, Hugo spoke of a sixth step, a summary on the history of the text and the discussion of the characteristics of the revised edition.[6] The first step is self-evident; if one wishes to study the Old Greek, it is necessary to ascertain that the Greek text under consideration is the closest possible to the original translation, and not a later revision or recension. The synopsis, though not strictly necessary, is a convenient provision of an easy and fast way to see the differences between the texts and to compare them. The third step, the text critical analysis, is necessary to eliminate scribal errors and textual corruptions present in each version, including translational and inner-Greek mistakes. The fourth step, the literary comparison, allows the emergence of the literary patterns or features of each text; if a narrative text is our focus, the tools of narrative analysis are especially adequate for this task, though other methods or approaches can certainly contribute. The use of literary analysis for the comparison of the Septuagint and the Masoretic text is not something new in scholarship, but here we are talking about a systematic analysis according to contemporary narratology. Once the different literary features of each version have emerged from the analysis, the fifth step is to give an estimation of the direction of the textual development according to criteria of plausibility. The sixth step, as I understand it, does not add anything new to the analysis but represents a summary of the most important aspects treated in steps four and five and provides a general conclusion based on the previous discussion of specific cases.

One example of this approach to the books of Samuel is Hugo's study of Abner's characterization in II Samuel 3. 6–39, particularly vv. 21 and 39. Hugo suggests that there are two literary versions of the story of Abner in this chapter, the Septuagint version being the oldest.[7] In the Masoretic text's version of v. 21, Abner is the instigator of a bond between David and Israel whereas, in the Septuagint, it is Abner that would stablish a bond with either the people of Israel or the king of Judah. In this case, the text of the Septuagint is more problematic because it raises the questions of Abner's authority to make a covenant and of the identity of the other partner. According to Hugo, Abner seems to have more power and authority in the Greek version; he is practically a king maker. This portrait of David is more complicated than the one found in the Masoretic text for, in the Septuagint, David depends on Abner to establish the covenant for him. In v. 39, while David speaks of himself as weak in relation to Joab and Abishai in the Masoretic text, in the Septuagint, David's

---

Martin Karrer, WUNT, 252 (Tübingen: Mohr Siebeck, 2010), pp. 489–505; 'The Unique Messiah: A Tendency in Favour of David's Kingship in the MT of Samuel', in *In the Footsteps of Sherlock Holmes: Studies in the Biblical Text in Honour of Anneli Aejmelaeus*, ed. by Kristin de Troyer, Timothy Michael Law and Marketta Liljeström, CBET, 72 (Leuven: Peeters, 2014), pp. 331–51.

5 See Hugo, 'Die Septuaginta', pp. 336–37.
6 See Hugo, *Les deux visages*, pp. 120–25.
7 See Hugo, 'Abner der Königsmacher', pp. 489–505.

eulogy of the deceased Abner underscores his good qualities by contrast with the wickedness of the sons of Zeruiah. For Hugo, David's portrait in the MT is designed to underscore his innocence: he is powerless, in comparison to Joab and his brother, and cannot be blamed for the murder of Abner. Furthermore, the Masoretic text's version reminds the reader that David is the anointed one. In Hugo's opinion, the MT displays a secondary, pro-Davidic edition of the story. In other articles, Hugo proposes that the MT has a secondary and more pronounced pro-Temple bias compared with the Septuagint, and that it also underscores David's kingship *vis a vis* Saul. An anti-Saulide tendency would be the other side of the coin of the pro-Davidic tendency in the MT.[8]

The studies of Schenker and Hugo have tended to show that the Septuagint of Kings (and of Samuel) reflects a Hebrew *Vorlage* that is more ancient than the Masoretic, or proto-Masoretic, text, which would represent an already edited or secondary form.[9] In a more recent paper, however, Schenker concluded that in II Kings 1. 17–18 and 8. 6, both the MT and the Septuagint display secondary literary features which have developed in divergent directions. In this case, the textual development of the MT and the Septuagint are parallel, and none of them has a better claim to originality; both depend on an archetype that needs to be reconstructed.[10] This conclusion is closer to my own opinion on the text of Samuel in general.

1.2. *Narrative Analysis for Elucidating the Story in Greek*

In the other approach, narrative analysis is used for the sake of understanding the stories of the Septuagint in themselves. An example of this approach is found in Benjamin Johnson's *Reading David and Goliath in Greek and Hebrew: A Literary Approach*. This author begins his study confessing that the discussion about the differences between the David and Goliath stories in the Septuagint and the Masoretic text achieved no consensus among scholars, and that it might not be possible to decide which one is the oldest version. Thus, Johnson studies the literary and narrative features of both texts for their own sake, refraining from a decision about the priority of one of the two versions.

Some of the steps used by Schenker and Hugo are also useful for those who want to study the narrative in Greek text for its own sake. Of course, the comparison of the story in the Septuagint with the narrative in the MT is necessary, for the peculiarities of the Septuagint version are made evident through the contrast with the Hebrew text. In this sense, the synopsis can be a very useful tool, though not a mandatory one.

---

8 See Hugo, 'The Jerusalem Temple', pp. 187–200; 'The Unique Messiah', pp. 331–51.

9 Though not always. For example, MT is considered to have preserved the oldest version in Schenker, 'Un cas', pp. 219–26.

10 See Adrian Schenker, 'Archetype and Late Literary Developments in 2 Kings 1:17–18 and 8:16', in *Die Septuaginta — Orte und Intentionen: 5. Internationale Fachtagung veranstaltet von Septuaginta Deutsch (LXX.D), Wuppertal 24.-27. Juli 2014*, ed. by Siegfried Kreuzer and others, WUNT, I 361 (Tübingen: Mohr Siebeck, 2016), pp. 326–36.

In fact, in order to highlight the differences in the Greek narrative, Johnson systematically compares the MT version of the story with the Septuagint in the fifth chapter of his book, the last before the conclusions, though references to specific differences between the Septuagint and the MT are found in the previous chapters as well. In my doctoral dissertation, I chose to present a narrative reading of the MT first, before discussing the Septuagint version.[11] Given that the Septuagint account of the David and Goliath story is the shorter one, Johnson's choice seems adequate for his study, but I believe that starting with the study of the narrative in the MT is to be recommended in most cases.

Obviously, the first step of verifying that the Greek text being used is the Old Greek and not something else cannot be omitted in any approach. Some of the other steps, however, need to be adjusted for this different kind of enquiry. The third step, text critical study, used by Hugo and Schenker to eliminate scribal mistakes and textual corruptions from the analysis, does not have the same goals in this kind of research. In fact, readings derived from mistakes can be significant from the point of view of an approach that is strictly narratological. Scribal errors can generate readings that change the plot or the characterization in a meaningful way. The notion of intentionality is not as central for this kind of study as it is for those interested in the history of the text's development or in the textual priority of one version. Johnson also considers that changes can be literarily significant whether they are intentional or not.[12] In any case, the issue of intentionality may be very important to evaluate the quality of the translator as an author or as a storyteller, but not to evaluate the narrative itself. Although I approve of Johnson's observation here and many of his insights regarding the two versions of the story, I am less fond of his relegating the text critical discussion to the footnotes in his book. Furthermore, despite the practicality of the procedure, I also think it is problematic simply to take *Codex Vaticanus* as 'the' representative of the Septuagint text without evaluating the other Greek witnesses, even in the non-kaige sections of Samuel.

Clearly, in order to discuss the narratives in the Septuagint of Samuel and secure the access to the OG as required by the first step mentioned above, it is paramount to understand the state of the Greek text of this book. This is a principle that should be observed in the study of any text in the Septuagint, but it is important to notice that the Greek text of each book or section of the Septuagint might be different in this respect.

After presenting the varied goals and applications of narrative analysis to the Septuagint of Samuel, a word about the nature and extent of the differences between the stories in MT and LXX is in order.

---

11 Leonardo Pessoa da Silva Pinto, *Different Literary Editions in 2 Samuel 10–12: A Comparative Study of the Hebrew and Greek Textual Traditions*, TECC, 81 (Madrid: CSIC, 2019).

12 See Benjamin J. M. Johnson, *Reading David and Goliath in Greek and Hebrew: A Literary Approach*, FAT, II 82 (Tübingen: Mohr Siebeck, 2015), pp. 16, 20–21.

2. The Scale and the Quality of the Differences

In some books, the narrative can be changed dramatically according to the version. Consider, for example, the book of Esther, which is longer in Greek than in Hebrew, with consequences for the characterization of Esther and the king, for the reader's response and for the theology of the book. For example, in the Greek narrative, God is more present in the plot and in control of human affairs. Furthermore, a clearer path to interpretation is given to the reader of the Greek version.[13] Even the literary genre of the story is often considered different in the Greek version.[14]

In Samuel, however, we do not find such large-scale differences between the shape of the whole book in the MT and in the Septuagint, though the narrative of specific episodes might differ considerably. At least in two places, the narrative of the Septuagint has been considered to be radically different from the MT: the story of David and Goliath that was mentioned above, and the story of the birth of Samuel along with Hannah's Psalm (I Samuel 1–2). In this last case for example, it has been argued that Hannah's role in the story is diminished in the Septuagint version whereas her husband Elkanah is more active than in MT,[15] though it has also been pointed out that the MT removes the references to Hannah's entering the temple in Shiloh and presenting herself before the Lord.[16] These can be considered large-scale differences, configuring different editions of those stories. In my thesis, I suggested that, in II Samuel 11, the differences between the Septuagint and the MT regarding the references to the battle against Rabbah of the Ammonites are not due to scribal mistakes but the result of intentional editing with a narrative aim.[17] More often, however, the differences will be on a smaller scale.

The scale of the differences is described by Emanuel Tov in the following way:

A difference involving one or two words, and sometimes an isolated case of a single verse, is considered a small difference, while a discrepancy involving a whole section or chapter indicates a substantial difference, often relevant to literary

---

13 Catherine Vialle, 'La problématique du pouvoir dans Esther hébreu (TM) et Esther grec (LXX)', *ZAW*, 124/4 (2012), 568–82. For a thorough study of the plots, characters, and narrative strategies of each version, see Catherine Vialle, *Une analyse comparée d'Esther TM et LXX: Regard sur deux récits d'une même histoire*, BEThL, 233 (Leuven: Peeters, 2010).

14 Cameron Boyd-Taylor, 'Esther's Great Adventure: Reading the LXX version of the Book of Esther in Light of its Assimilation to the Conventions of the Greek Romantic Novel', *BIOSCS*, 30 (1997), 81–113 (p. 81). See also Boyd-Taylor's contribution in this volume.

15 See Stanley D. Walters, 'Hannah and Anna: The Greek and Hebrew Texts of 1 Samuel 1', *JBL*, 107/3 (1988), 385–412; Jürgen Hutzli, *Die Erzählung von Hanna und Samuel: Textkritische und literarische Analyse von 1. Samuel 1–2 unter Berücksichtigung des Kontextes*, ATANT, 89 (Zürich: Theologischer Verlag, 2007).

16 See the discussion in Juha Pakkala, *God's Word Omitted: Omissions in the Transmission of the Hebrew Bible*, FRLANT, 251 (Göttingen: Vandenhoeck & Ruprecht, 2013), pp. 200–10.

17 Pessoa da Silva Pinto, *Different Literary Editions*, pp. 123–202.

criticism. However, a group of seemingly unrelated small differences might also display a common pattern, pointing to a more extensive phenomenon.[18]

Small-scale changes can happen in both directions but, for the books of Samuel, Tov suggested that more small theological changes are found in the MT than in the Septuagint.[19]

These distinctions and considerations regarding the scale of the differences are valid but bear more impact on the study of textual formation and transmission than on the narrative analysis *per se*. A small-scale difference may have a deeper effect on the narrative than a more extensive change.

Connected with the problem of the scale of the differences is the question about the nature of a different literary edition. Different literary editions are generally recognized when full-scale changes are detected. Small-scale changes, which could be described as sporadic or isolated, should not be taken as proof of intentional and systematic editing, unless there is accumulation of small changes pointing in the same direction (take, for example, the Baal names in Samuel). However, as explained, even isolated changes might be relevant for a narratological study.

As for the nature of the variants, Schenker distinguishes two kinds of variants, textual and literary, the latter referring to voluntary corrections or reformulations that change the meaning of the original text for a reason.[20] Although this is defensible conceptually, I would rather recommend caution with distinctions of this sort, for the separation between the two kinds of variants often gets blurred. In some cases, we simply cannot decide whether the variant originated from an error in copying or from an intentional change with a specific purpose. Considerations of narrative analysis may suggest that a variant traditionally attributed to phenomena concerning textual transmission is actually of a literary nature. In other cases, modifications introduced by copyists can shape the story in a literarily way. For example, Schenker considers harmonization a phenomenon of textual nature.[21] However, since harmonizations tend to improve the coherence of a text and even to eliminate contradictions, they can have implications for the story, reinforcing the connection between elements of the plot, or reducing the number or the level of ambiguities in the narrative. They can also create connections with other parts of the book or with other works, generating intertextuality. These changes influence the reader's understanding of the story. When speaking about harmonizations, Tov explains that 'some such changes were inserted unconsciously, but most were inserted because of a theological concern

---

18 Emanuel Tov, 'The Septuagint as a Source for the Literary Analysis of Hebrew Scripture', in *Exploring the Origins of the Bible: Canon Formation in Historical, Literary, and Theological Perspective*, ed. by Craig A. Evans and Emanuel Tov, Acadia Studies in Bible and Theology, 31 (Grand Rapids: Baker Academic, 2008), pp. 31–56 (p. 31).

19 Emanuel Tov, 'Theological Tendencies in the Masoretic Text of Samuel', in *After Qumran: Old and Modern Editions of the Biblical Texts — The Historical Books*, ed. by Hans Ausloos, Bénédicte Lemmelijn and Julio Trebolle Barrera, BEThL, 246 (Leuven: Peeters, 2012), pp. 3–20.

20 Adrian Schenker, 'Der Ursprung des massoretischen Textes im Licht der literarischen Varianten im Bibeltext', *Textus*, 23 (2007), 51–67.

21 See Schenker, 'Der Ursprung', p. 54.

for perfection, especially harmonizing pluses'.[22] I would just like to point out that the concern for perfection does not always need to be theological but could also be simply related to literary interest in the completion of a form, in the smoothing of the narrative and in the improvement of the story's coherence.

One last point is that many of the studies in this field have tried to determine the differences between biblical stories in the MT and the LXX in a somewhat narrow way, at times overstressing the interest in text formation and transmission, at times focusing too much, for example, in characterization or in elements with theological implications. For narratology, however, many other elements can be significant.

I shall now discuss the core principles for the application of narratology to the Septuagint stories, especially for the books of Samuel.

3. Principles for Narrative Analysis of the Septuagint of Samuel

Some of the following principles are important for all work of interpretation of the Septuagint, not only narrative analysis, whereas others are specific to the study of narrative technique. Finally, some principles apply only to the narrative analysis of the LXX of I–II Samuel.

3.1. *Knowledge of the State of the Greek Text*

The first principle has already been mentioned; it regards the need for a good knowledge of the textual situation of the Septuagint of the book under analysis, especially for the books where the Göttingen edition is not yet available.

For Samuel, the edition of the Göttingen Septuagint is still being prepared by Finnish scholars, I Samuel by Anneli Aejmelaeus, II Samuel by Tuukka Kauhanen. Therefore, one must appeal to the Cambridge edition (Brooke-McLean) or that of Rahlfs. Some of the Greek manuscripts witnessing the text of Samuel have been identified as Lucianic, and, therefore, the Lucianic or Antiochene text constitutes a textual tradition that must be taken into consideration in the study of Greek Samuel. For I Samuel and II Samuel 1–9, the textual witnesses of the Septuagint can be divided into three main groups, the B-text, the Lucianic text and the Hexaplaric text, while other manuscripts witness to a hybrid form. From II Samuel 10 on, we find the kaige text that supplanted most textual traditions and which was identified thanks to the preliminary work of Thackeray on the translators of Samuel-Kings, and more clearly through the work of Barthélemy. Without entering into details, this means that the textual situation of the Septuagint of Samuel is very complex,

---

22 Emanuel Tov, 'The Septuagint of Numbers as a Harmonizing Text', in *Die Septuaginta — Geschichte, Wirkung, Relevanz: 6. Internationale Fachtagung veranstaltet von Septuaginta Deutsch (LXX.D), Wuppertal 21.–24. Juli 2016*, ed. by Martin Meiser and others, WUNT, 405 (Tübingen: Mohr Siebeck, 2018), pp. 182–201 (p. 182).

and it is not enough to study the text offered by Rahlfs in his manual edition as if it were 'the' Septuagint or the OG.

The Antiochene or Lucianic text is of great importance, especially in the kaige section. However, it has its own peculiarities. Many of its textual and stylistic features in Samuel-Kings-Chronicles have been studied by Rahlfs, Brock and Allen.[23] Furthermore, Fernández Marcos has pointed out a series of principles of a literary nature followed by this text in the historical books such as: completing the unsaid in the scheme prediction-fulfilment (stronger changes than, for example, the simple explicitation of a subject); addition of sentences to clarify or smooth the narrative; stylistic rewriting including elimination of Semitisms and change of hyperbaton; theological corrections; and the presence of double or alternative readings.[24] Knowledge of these features is necessary in order to distinguish between its oldest substratum, a text that is close to the OG, and its later developments with recensional aspects. The same applies to the kaige witnesses in II Samuel 10–24: one must learn the features of the kaige revision or recension in order to separate the recensional features from the OG that formed its base-text.

To sum-up: finding the oldest text of the Septuagint of Samuel is, in itself, a difficult task that is still being carried out. Since the narratologists must first decide which text is going to be exegeted, even on this level, that of the definition of the text that is to be analyzed, a narratological study of the Septuagint meets a great challenge, and textual criticism of the Greek text becomes necessary.

3.2. Study of Translation Technique

It is inevitable that considerations regarding translation technique play a role in the analysis. As Johann Cook puts it, it is a consensus that 'one of the premises of Septuagintal studies, including attempts to determine its "theology/exegesis", is the need to determine in detail the translation technique followed by the translator.'[25] This means that not only the general approach of the translator, often classified simply as free or literal, has to be taken into consideration, but also the specific issues attaching to his use of vocabulary and syntax *vis a vis* his *Vorlage*. Therefore, the second principle is the need for studying the translation technique for the book or the section analyzed. Otherwise, there is a risk of attributing too much creativity

---

23 Alfred Rahlfs, *Septuaginta-Studien*, 3 vols (Göttingen: Vandenhoeck & Ruprecht, 1904–11), III: Lucians Rezension der Königsbücher (1911); Sebastian Brock, *The Recensions of the Septuagint Version of I Samuel*, Quaderni di Henoch, 9 (Torino: Silvio Zamorani, 1996); Leslie C. Allen, *The Greek Chronicles: The Relation of the Septuagint of I and II Chronicles to the Massoretic Text*, VT.S, 25 and 27, 2 vols (Leiden: Brill, 1974), I: The Translator's Craft.

24 See Natalio Fernández Marcos, 'Literary and Editorial Features of the Antiochian Text of Kings', in *VI Congress of the International Organization for Septuagint and Cognate Studies, Jerusalem 1986*, ed. by Claude E. Cox, SBLSCS, 23 (Atlanta: SBL, 1987), pp. 287–304.

25 See Johann Cook, 'Interpreting the Septuagint — Exegesis, Theology and/or Religionsgeschichte?', in *Die Septuaginta — Texte, Theologien, Einflüsse: 2. internationale Fachtagung veranstaltet von Septuaginta Deutsch (LXX.D), Wuppertal 23.-27.7. 2008*, ed. by Wolfgang Kraus and Martin Karrer, WUNT, 252 (Tübingen: Mohr Siebeck, 2010), pp. 590–606 (p. 591).

to the translator. This risk can be seen in the approach of John Beck in his book *Translators as Storytellers: A Study in Septuagint Translation Technique*,[26] a work much criticized by van der Louw in the article mentioned above. Van der Louw reproaches Beck's tendency to attribute every deviation of the Septuagint from the source text to intentional changes of the translator.[27] Another application of narrative analysis criticized by van der Louw is Utzschneider's paper 'Die LXX als Erzählerin',[28] where some arguments in favour of the translator's role in shaping the narrative are forced and do not stand up to a close examination.

Some interpretation is presupposed by the act of translating, for the translator must decode the source text, and therefore understand it, and then encode the message in the target text by making it understandable in the target language. Therefore, before finding ways to express the message in the target language, the translator carries out an operation of interpretation.[29] This is the reason why Tov called this sort of interpretation, inherent to the act of translating, 'linguistic exegesis',[30] though I believe this terminology is prone to generate some confusion (all exegesis is on some level 'linguistic') and is better avoided. There is, of course, a degree of interpretation in the act of decoding, and the translator must transmit his understanding of the source;[31] however, this does not make 'translation' a synonym for 'exegesis' and calling the translator a storyteller strikes us as an exaggeration, at least in the case of Samuel. There are signs of the translator's literary sensibility, as we shall see below, but that should not be overstated.

In what concerns the translator's role as an exegete, theologian or, in our case, a storyteller, there are two competing views among scholars, what we may call the minimalist *versus* the maximalist approach. The maximalists are those who tend to give a more important role to the translator, and Martin Rösel is one of the authors often associated with this maximalist approach. The followers of the interlinear

---

26   John A. Beck, *Translators as Storytellers: A Study in Septuagint Translation Technique*, Studies in Biblical Literature, 25 (New York: Peter Lang, 2000).

27   See van der Louw, 'A Narratological Approach', pp. 555–56. The book received much criticism from reviewers that pointed out, among other problems, the lack of a proper treatment of text critical issues; see Martin Rösel, 'Review of Beck, John A. Translators as Storytellers: A Study in Septuagint Translation Technique', *ZAW*, 113/3 (2001), 459; Alison Salvesen, 'Review of Beck, John A. Translators as Storytellers: A Study in Septuagint Translation Technique', *JTS*, 52/2 (2001), 755–56.

28   Helmut Utzschneider, 'Die LXX als Erzählerin. Beobachtungen an der LXX-Fassung der Geburts- und Kindheitsgeschichte des Mose (Ex 2,1–10)', in *Die Septuaginta — Texte, Theologien, Einflüsse: 2. internationale Fachtagung veranstaltet von Septuaginta Deutsch (LXX.D), Wuppertal 23.-27.7. 2008*, ed. by Wolfgang Kraus and Martin Karrer, WUNT, 252 (Tübingen: Mohr Siebeck, 2010), pp. 462–77.

29   Umberto Eco, *Dire quasi la stessa cosa: Esperienze di traduzione* (Milano: Bompiani, 2013), pp. 244–53.

30   See Emanuel Tov, 'The Composition of 1 Sam 16–18 in the Light of the Septuagint Version', in *Empirical Models for Biblical Criticism: With a New Foreword by Richard Elliott Friedman*, ed. by Jeffrey H. Tigay, Dove Studies in Bible, Language, and History (Eugene, OR: Wipf & Stock, 2005), pp. 97–130 (p. 107).

31   See Martin Rösel, 'Translators as Interpreters: Scriptural Interpretation in the Septuagint', in *Tradition and Innovation: English and German Studies on the Septuagint*, ed. by Martin Rösel, SBLSCS, 70 (Atlanta: SBL, 2018), pp. 57–86 (p. 69).

model, like Albert Pietersma, are among those considered minimalists.[32] I believe that these tags are misguided, and that the positions of the two authors mentioned are not so distant; for example, Rösel actually criticizes Beck's monograph for the same reasons as those mentioned above. The real question behind the different positions concerns the criteria for identifying the cases where the translator intentionally added a different nuance of theological or ideological importance; in other words, for determining when and how the translator's ideas may have affected individual renderings. I believe that the study of translation technique is the first and better way to answer that question, even if, in some cases, the doubt will remain whether the translator intentionally gave the text a different nuance or meaning. The point made by Aejmelaeus is relevant, especially for translations like Greek Samuel:

> The translators surely showed their particular intentions at times, but the intention of the translator cannot always be asked, especially not in the case of standard renderings [...] As a matter of fact, it is only through the translated text that we know anything about the intentions of the translator.[33]

In this sense, I believe that, in cases where the translator's rendering is the expected translation of the source text but implies some degree of semantic shift, we should not talk about the translator's intention or creativity, for he is just doing his job in the most straightforward manner possible,[34] even if the shift in meaning might be significant from the point of view of narratology.

Lack of attention to translation technique can mislead the interpreter. One could wrongly presuppose the presence of variants in the *Vorlage* of the Septuagint in cases where the differences are simply the result of translational phenomena or even simply typical features of Hellenistic Greek. Many of the 'deviations' or differences from the Hebrew of MT can be explained through appeal to the translation technique applied by the Greek translator.

Unawareness of the more literalistic approach of the translator of Samuel may lead scholars to exaggerate the role of the translator. It is generally accepted, and with good reason, that the Septuagint of Samuel is a fairly literalistic translation of its *Vorlage*. For books where the translation is more of a formal correspondence, which is the case with Samuel, exegesis by the translator is something that must be

---

32 Albert Pietersma, 'Exegesis in the Septuagint: Possibilities and Limits (The Psalter as a Case in Point)', in *Septuagint Research: Issues and Challenges in the Study of the Greek Jewish Scriptures*, ed. by Wolfgang Kraus and R. Glenn Wooden, SBLSCS, 53 (Atlanta: SBL, 2006), pp. 33–45 (p. 36) speaks of the different emphasis on the translator as a medium in the minimalist approach vs. the translator as an author in the maximalist approach.

33 See Anneli Aejmelaeus, 'Translation Technique and the Intention of the Translator', in *On the Trail of the Septuagint Translators: Collected Essays*, ed. by Anneli Aejmelaeus, CBET, 50, Revised and Expanded Edition (Leuven: Peeters, 2007), pp. 59–69.

34 Examples of over-interpreting what is simply a literal rendering of the source text can be found in LaMontagne's article about the LXX of the book of Ruth where even the translation of לֵב with καρδία is seen as a sign of the translator's special understanding of the story; see Nathan LaMontagne, 'LXX Ruth: Translation, Interpretation, Characterization', in *XIV Congress of the IOSCS, Helsinki, 2010*, ed. by Melvin K. H. Peters, SBLSCS, 59 (Atlanta: SBL, 2013), pp. 59–71.

demonstrated, not presupposed.[35] In the past, scholars like Henry Gehman and John Wevers tended to attribute too many differences in the Septuagint of Samuel to the translator,[36] but, since they wrote before the Qumran findings, it was easier for them to dismiss the possibility of a different *Vorlage* behind the Greek translation. For Samuel we cannot forget that the source text was a *Vorlage* that differed from the MT, and most distinct features of the Septuagint of Samuel are due to that *Vorlage*. Therefore, what may look like deviation from the MT is often faithfulness to the Hebrew *Vorlage* used by the translator.

There are, however, a few areas where the Greek translator had to make decisions, for example, in the use of verbal tenses. Since the verbal systems of the two languages are so different, the translator could not avoid introducing new nuances to the text. If the translation of the Hebrew narrative into Greek occasionally resulted in losses of meaning, sometimes the Greek language adds distinctions that either cannot be seen in Hebrew or operate differently. In the Septuagint of the books of Samuel, for example, the perfect tense often occurs in direct speech when characters describe what they know, see or hear as present for them. When talking about the translation technique of the Septuagint of I Samuel, Aejmelaeus states that the Greek translator had a good eye for verbal tenses. He used the imperfect to mark repetition and duration, but also in subordinate clauses or direct discourse (non-narrative parts) to express the point of view of a character rather than the narrator.[37] That would be an interesting sign of the translator's literary sensibility.

The simple fact that LXX is a translation also accounts for some losses in the narrative, such as verbal irony and wordplays that are only possible in the source language, though the translator could also have created new wordplays in Greek, intentionally or not. The handling of the vocabulary can even reinforce the link with other stories in biblical and non-biblical literature. An interesting example from the book of Judges was found by Natalio Fernández Marcos. Even though the OG of Judges is basically a faithful translation of the Hebrew text, sometimes the translator's choice of vocabulary creates effects of intertextuality with other biblical stories or even with Greek literature. According to Fernández Marcos, the Greek translator of Judges 11, the story of Jephthah's daughter, uses lexical choices to establish a connection with the story of the *Aqedah* in Genesis, but also with Iphigenia's sacrifice in Euripides' tragedy.[38]

---

35   See Pietersma, 'Exegesis in the Septuagint', p. 45.
36   See Henry Snyder Gehman, 'Exegetical Methods Employed by the Greek Translator of 1 Samuel', *JAOS*, 70 (1950), 292–96; John William Wevers, 'A Study in the Exegetical Principles Underlying the Greek Text of 2 Sm 11:2–1 Kings 2:11', *CBQ*, 15/1 (1953), 30–45 (pp. 35–45). Also, for the γδ section, see John William Wevers, 'Principles of Interpretation Guiding the Fourth Translator of the Book of the Kingdoms (3 K. 22:1–4 K. 25:30)', *CBQ*, 14/1 (1952), 40–56 (pp. 55–56).
37   See Anneli Aejmelaeus, 'The Septuagint of 1 Samuel', in *VIII Congress of the International Organization for Septuagint and Cognate Studies, Paris 1992*, ed. by Leonard Greenspoon and Olivier Munnich, SBLSCS, 41 (Atlanta: SBL, 1995), pp. 109–29 (pp. 120–22).
38   Natalio Fernández Marcos, 'Jephthah's Daughter in the Old Greek (Judges 11:29–40)', in *Die Septuaginta — Texte, Theologien, Einflüsse: 2. internationale Fachtagung veranstaltet von Septuaginta Deutsch (LXX.D), Wuppertal 23.-27.7. 2008*, ed. by Wolfgang Kraus and Martin Karrer, WUNT, 252 (Tübingen: Mohr Siebeck, 2010), pp. 478–88.

Van der Louw also reminds us that the 'reading experience' of the Greek text of the Septuagint is generally worsened, not improved, by the translator's strict adherence to the source text. For example, by contrast with most Septuagint translations, contemporary Greek narrative made wide use of particles and participles and avoided repetition.[39] In agreement with van der Louw's observation, it can be said that many syntactic structures in the Septuagint of Samuel strike the reader as unidiomatic Greek. The overwhelming use of parataxis would be a case in point. I also endorse van der Louw's conclusion that narratologists cannot avoid serious linguistic work.[40]

Another point deserving commentary has been raised by Zipora Talshir who criticizes a fundamental assumption prevailing in studies focused on the meaning of the Greek text, namely, that the translation necessarily has a logical meaning. Talshir discusses examples of awkward translations from First Esdras, cases where the Greek does not seem to make sense.[41] Despite Talshir's observation and although we can find cases where the translator produced nonsensical texts, I believe that it is a good principle to start with the assumption that the translation might have made sense to those who produced it and to those who read it. The fact that the Greek translation often offers a text more coherent and harmonized than its source is enough proof that the goal of the translators was to offer something comprehensible. There are cases where we might have to admit that the translator could not produce a reasonable text, but that is the exception, not the rule.

3.3. *Knowledge of the Method of Narrative Analysis*

The third principle regards the knowledge of the narrative approach in general, the method for analyzing stories. This principle is quite straightforward and can be presented more briefly. The interpreter must have a good knowledge of the principles of the narrative approach, especially as applied to biblical stories. Since no method works independently of its user, the scholar's intuition and sensibility play a significant role. Furthermore, every caution required by narrative analysis as applied to the biblical text in general applies to the work with the Septuagint as well. Therefore, overreading and imposition of artificial meanings or structures are risks that the interpreter should also avoid in the work with the Septuagint. In any case, every method or approach can be misused, and this is not an argument against the legitimacy of a narratological approach to the Septuagint.

3.4. *Knowledge of the Narrative in the Masoretic Text*

The fourth principle regards the knowledge of the story in the MT. Since the Septuagint is a translation, most elements of the stories in the Greek version are a reflex of the

---

39 See van der Louw, 'A Narratological Approach', pp. 553–54.
40 See van der Louw, 'A Narratological Approach', p. 564.
41 See Zipora Talshir, 'Synchronic and Diachronic Approaches in the Study of the Hebrew Bible: Text Criticism within the Frame of Biblical Philology', *Textus*, 23 (2007), 1–32 (pp. 4–6).

narrative in the source text. Therefore, it is not only useful but very important to have a good idea about the features of the narrative in the MT in order to identify better what is peculiar to the Septuagint version of the stories. In the end, in order to analyze the Septuagint version of a narrative, it is strongly recommended that one first analyzes its version in the MT. It is better not to detach the exegesis of the Septuagint from the exegesis of the Hebrew text.

It might be useful to remind narratologists interested in the Septuagint of another point that concerns narrative analysis of the Bible in general. It is unwise to ignore all the work done by diachronic research in the past, as well as the issues still being discussed. In this regard, I agree with Talshir that pretending that biblical stories are modern fiction can lead the interpreter to impose very artificial structures.[42] One example regards the problem of defining the literary unit, the beginning and the end of the text to be interpreted. This is a question that occupied diachronic research for centuries, and it would be naïve to disregard its contribution and insights, though it is also true that, in some cases, narrative analysis can help to correct false results of diachronic approaches by showing, for example, that some contradictions in the stories are just apparent and belong to the same narrative unit instead of constituting signs of different literary layers.

Conclusion

I conclude quoting Hendel: 'close reading of the biblical (or any) text is a multilayered activity, requiring various skills and competences'.[43] For our subject, a sound application of a narratological approach to the Septuagint requires several skills. Apart from being skilled in narratology, the researcher will need good knowledge of textual criticism of the book or section under scrutiny, of the narrative in the MT, of the state of the Septuagint for that text, including questions of translation technique and of linguistics. This is a demanding challenge, requiring an impressive set of skills. Nevertheless, I believe that it is not only possible, but a challenge worth accepting.

The relevance of the Septuagint for our understanding of the biblical narratives cannot be stressed enough. I quote Tov: 'The MT is often considered the major textual source for the study of Hebrew Scripture, but actually the LXX is equally important, the only problem being that its Hebrew parent text cannot be reconstructed easily'.[44] Furthermore, the Septuagint is also a text worth studying for its own sake, not just for its value for textual criticism of the Hebrew Bible. As explained above, the Septuagint was not completely absent from literary approaches in the past, but it is undeniable that the focus of former generations was not the Greek version. The difference we notice more recently is a greater interest in the Septuagint as a text worth studying in itself, an effort to study its features systematically, a change that is most welcome in our field.

---

42   See Talshir, 'Synchronic and Diachronic', p. 13.
43   See Ronald Hendel, 'Plural Texts and Literary Criticism: For Instance, 1 Samuel 17', *Textus*, 23 (2007), 97–114 (p. 98).
44   Tov, 'The Septuagint as a Source', p. 54.

▼ ABSTRACT The application of narratological approaches to the Septuagint versions of biblical stories is legitimate but requires from the researcher several skills and much caution. Narrative analysis may be practiced in order to understand a story in the LXX for its own sake or as a step in the study of textual development. Apart from attention to general principles of narrative analysis, the scholar engaged in this kind of study must take into consideration questions concerning textual criticism and textual transmission of the book under scrutiny, especially of its Septuagint version, translation technique of the Greek version and linguistics, and the narrative feaures of MT's version of the story. This is a promising field of research that might reveal several interesting aspects of the biblical text, particularly of its Greek version.

MARTIN KARRER

Septuagint and New Testament in Papyri and Pandects

Texts, Intertextuality and Criteria of Edition

Interest in the material transmission, coherence and intertextuality between Septuagint and New Testament Scriptures has increased in the last decades. The question has arisen: Does the evidence known today from manuscripts influence the methodological and hermeneutical perspectives on the Bible and biblical exegesis?[1] Two issues can be considered in order to answer this question: the characteristics of manuscripts combining Septuagint and New Testament texts and the textual history of the New Testament quotations.

The second perspective is well-studied, but the first perspective is unwonted. Even synopses of manuscripts combining Septuagint and New Testament texts are rare.[2] The material, therefore, promises unexpected insights. The present contribution addresses this subject. It looks for manuscripts containing Septuagint and New Testament scriptures and asks: Are there intertextual interests manifesting themselves in these material units, and can a development be recognized from antiquity to the end of the Byzantine time?

I will first consider the papyri (second to fifth centuries; § 1). Then, I will examine the so-called full Bibles of the Byzantine time, the pandects of the fourth to fifteenth centuries (§ 2; the term πανδέκτης / 'pandect' originated in the fifth or early sixth

---

1 Peter Dubovsky prepared the conference 'New Avenues in the Exegesis of the Bible in the Light of the Septuagint' held at the *Pontificio Istituto Biblico* in Rome 2019 and asked: How does an intertextual approach influence the methodological and hermeneutical perspectives on the whole Bible and on the New Testament 'if the Septuagint studies are taken into consideration?' (emails to Martin Karrer on 8 November 2018 and 31 March 2019).

2 The best available overviews are provided by Dirk Jongkind, 'Manuscripts of the Greek Bible', in *The New Testament in Antiquity and Byzantium: Traditional and Digital Approaches to its Texts and Editing. A Festschrift for Klaus Wachtel*, ed. by H. A. G. Houghton and others, ANTF, 52 (Berlin: de Gruyter, 2019), pp. 189–201; Patrick Andrist, 'Au croisement des contenus et de la matière: les structures des sept pandectes bibliques grecques du premier millénaire. Étude comparative sur les structures des contenus et de la matérialité des codex Vaticanus, Sinaiticus, Alexandrinus, Ephraimi rescriptus, Basilianus, "Pariathoniensis" et de la Biblia Leonis', *Scrineum Rivista*, 17/2 (2020), 3–106. I will augment the material in the following.

New Avenues in Biblical Exegesis in Light of the Septuagint
ed. by Leonardo Pessoa da Silva Pinto and Daniela Scialabba, Turnhout, 2022 (*SEPT*, 1), pp. 199–277
© BREPOLS 🕮 PUBLISHERS   DOI 10.1484/M.SEPT-EB.5.127718

century).[3] Afterwards, I will look for some consequences (§ 3) and summarize the results (§ 4).[4]

1. Combinations of Septuagint and New Testament Texts in the Papyri

Fragments of the Septuagint exist from Hellenistic times,[5] fragments of the New Testament from the middle of the second century CE onwards. But the production of documents combining Septuagint and New Testament texts in material units started dilatorily and in a complicated process.

1.1. The Use of Biblical Texts in the Second Century

According to Justin, writings of the prophets (συγγράμματα τῶν προφητῶν) were read alongside recollections of the apostles (ἀπομνημονεύματα τῶν ἀποστόλων)[6] in meetings of Christian congregations. The texts were read from different scrolls or codices as long as the time allowed (ἀναγινώσκεται, μέχρις ἐγχωρεῖ; Justin, I apol., 67. 3).[7] That way, subsequent readings of biblical books are recorded in the middle of the second century; but Justin does not refer to manuscripts holding old and new texts in a material unit.

---

3   The term 'pandect' traces back to the Latin loanword *pandectes* rendering the Greek word πανδέκτης, '[collection] containing everything'. The most famous πανδέκτης of late antiquity was the collection of laws compiled under the emperor Justinian. The Latin loanword is used for a full Greek Bible by Cassiodorus in the sixth century (*inst.*, I. 14. 4; cf. fn. 105) and, maybe, was transferred to the concept of a full Latin Bible already in the fifth century as Hugh Houghton, *The Latin New Testament: A Guide to Its Early History, Texts, and Manuscripts* (Oxford: Oxford University Press, 2016), pp. 87–88 concludes from a notice in the *Codex Sangermanensis* I (BNF Lat. 11553, VL 7 / Vg G; fol. 69ʳ). One may speculate, therefore, that πανδέκτης was the oldest Greek designation for the full Bible and early transferred from there to Latin descriptions of the Bible. Immediate evidence in Greek, however, is missing.

4   The second issue mentioned will concentrate on the reception of Septuagint texts in the quotations of the New Testament (textual history, reception and theology). The matter is stimulating, as well; I integrated it into the paper held in Rome 24 October 2019 but the subject needs a separate contribution.

5   See Siegfried Kreuzer and Marcus Sigismund, 'Overview of Textual Witnesses to the Septuagint', in *Introduction to the Septuagint*, ed. by Siegfried Kreuzer (Waco: Baylor University Press, 2019), pp. 57–63.

6   That means texts related to our later New Testament, perhaps the Gospels.

7   See Mogens Müller, 'Justin und die Septuaginta. Benutzung und Bedeutung', in *Die Septuaginta — Themen, Manuskripte, Wirkungen: 7. Internationale Fachtagung veranstaltet von Septuaginta Deutsch (LXX.D), Wuppertal 19.-22. Juli 2018*, ed. by Eberhard Bons and others, WUNT, 444 (Tübingen: Mohr Siebeck, 2020), pp. 740–52. Cf. Jan Heilmann, *Lesen in Antike und frühem Christentum*, TANZ (Tübingen: Francke, 2021), pp. 512–14 (Heilmann analyzes the practices of ancient reading comprehensively).

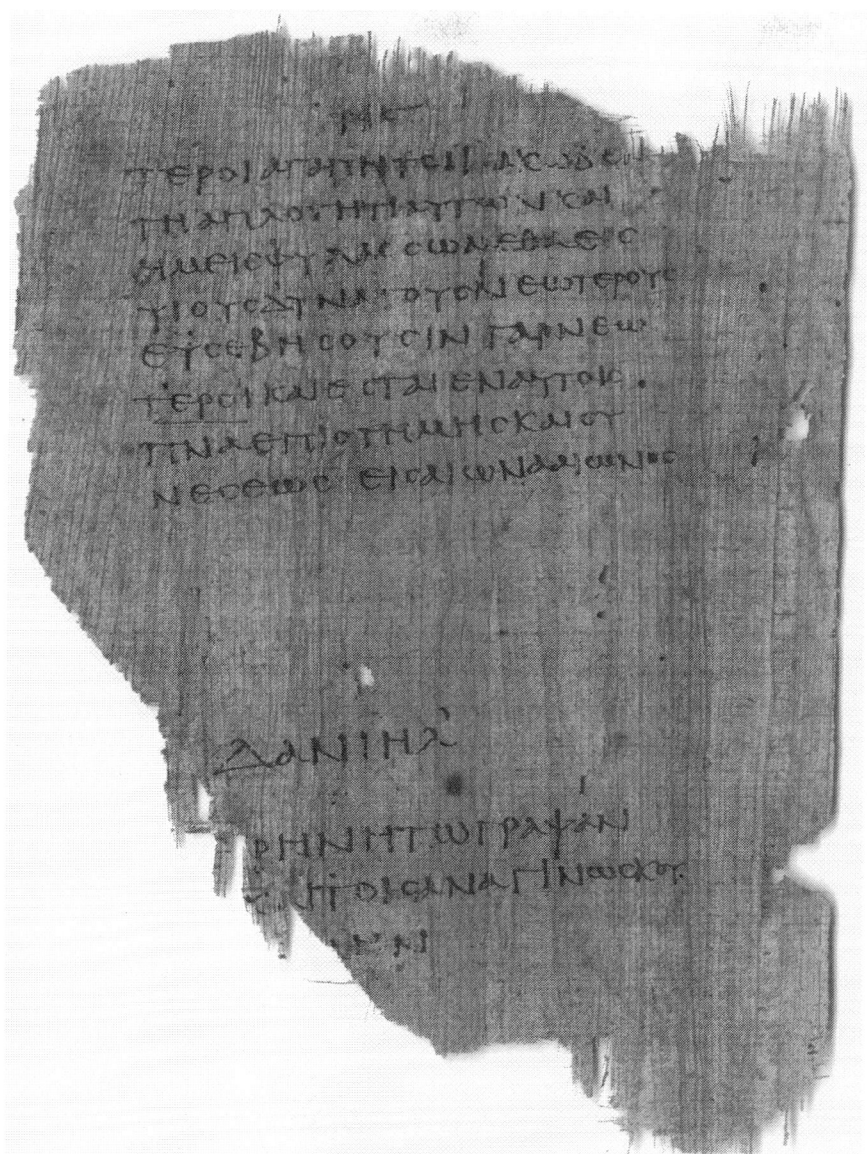

Fig. 3. Susanna 62a–62b and 'subscriptio' of the book Daniel in Pap. 967 Ra.;
P. Köln Theol. fol. 37ᵛ (p. 196 of the whole papyrus).[8]

---

8   Fig.: Papyrussammlung Köln; cf. <http://www.uni-koeln.de/phil-fak/ifa/NRWakademie/
papyrologie/PTheol/PT37v.jpg> [accessed 12 April 2020].

The communities needed manuscripts for the readings. Collections of parts of the Septuagint and the New Testament (Pauline letters; Gospels) grew until the end of the second century. Codex Chester Beatty VI (963 Ra.; second or third century)[9] evidences a Pentateuch-collection; preserved are folios of Numbers and Deuteronomy.[10]

Papyrus 967 Ra. (written about or shortly after 200) accounts for the prophets mentioned by Justin. The preserved folios first contain Ezekiel, then Daniel and after the 'subscriptio' of the book Daniel (Δανιηλ) a greeting to the readers: '[P]eace to the scrib[e] and to the reade[rs]', [εἰ]ρήνη [...] τοῖς ἀναγινώσκου[σιν] (see fig. 3). The verb ἀναγινώσκειν means reading aloud in public and corresponds to the information on readings (ditto ἀναγινώσκειν) in Justin's apology. It seems that we get an impression of the συγγράμματα τῶν προφητῶν (writings of the prophets) Justin spoke of.

Strikingly, Pap. 967 Ra. attaches the non-prophetical book Esther after Daniel. This alignment makes sense if we think of a greater collection beginning with the 'Former' Prophets of the Jewish tradition (the today's Historical Books were subsumed into the Prophets in old references[11] since the Prophets were thought as giving orientation in Israel's history). If this was the case, the collection started with the Former Prophets (the Historical Books), and Esther was separated from them as an appendix since it was disputed in Christianity as in Judaism (Esther was late accepted into the Hebrew scriptures as well).

Siegfried Kreuzer goes one step further and not only assumes that Pap. 967 Ra. indicates a stratification of Scriptures. He also proposes that the codex belonged to a series of volumes containing all (or nearly all) Septuagint writings which were recognized analogously to the Tanach.[12] The idea of an overall collection is attractive[13] without being provable. The correlation to Justin carries weight at any rate. Justin's

---

9 A date in the second century was common opinion for a long time. Brent Nongbri, *God's Library: The Archaeology of the Earliest Christian Manuscripts* (London: Yale University Press, 2018), pp. 146–50, opened the date; the end of the second or the third century are possible too.

10 P. Heid. Inv. G 8+1020a (= Ra. 970), in addition, holds fragments of Exodus 8 and Deuteronomy, but it is difficult to say if the manuscript contained the books in their entirety; see Alfred Rahlfs and Detlef Fraenkel, *Verzeichnis der griechischen Handschriften des Alten Testaments* (Göttingen: Vandenhoeck & Ruprecht, 2004), pp. 140–41, 513.

11 See Sirach, prologue 1, 8–10, 24–25 and Josephus, *Ap.*, I. 37–42 (quoted in section 2.4, below). Cf. 4QMMT C and Luke 24. 44, too; for 4QMMT, see Reinhard G. Kratz, 'Mose und die Propheten: Zur Interpretation von 4QMMT C', in *From 4QMMT to Resurrection: Mélanges qumraniens en hommage à Émile Puech*, ed. by Florentino García Martínez and others (Leiden: Brill, 2006), pp. 151–76.

12 Siegfried Kreuzer, 'Papyrus 967: Bemerkungen zu seiner buchtechnischen, textgeschichtlichen und kanongeschichtlichen Bedeutung', in *Geschichte, Sprache und Text: Studien zum Alten Testament und seiner Umwelt*, ed. by Siegfried Kreuzer, BZAW, 479 (Berlin: de Gruyter, 2015), pp. 437–56 (pp. 452–56).

13 See Rahlfs and Fraenkel, *Verzeichnis*, p. 468.

prophets in *I apol.*, 67. 3 possibly cover the 'Former' and the 'Latter' Prophets (Historical and Prophetic Books).

Nevertheless, the hiatus between collections of the Septuagint and the New Testament is neither bridged by the mentioned manuscripts nor by any other sample of early papyrological material. The decisive fact stays: The collections of Septuagint and New Testament writings were distributed disjointedly up to the beginning of the third century. The thesis of a Christian second-century edition connecting both, Septuagint and New Testament writings, which was conceived by David Trobisch,[14] is not evidenced by the extant sources.[15]

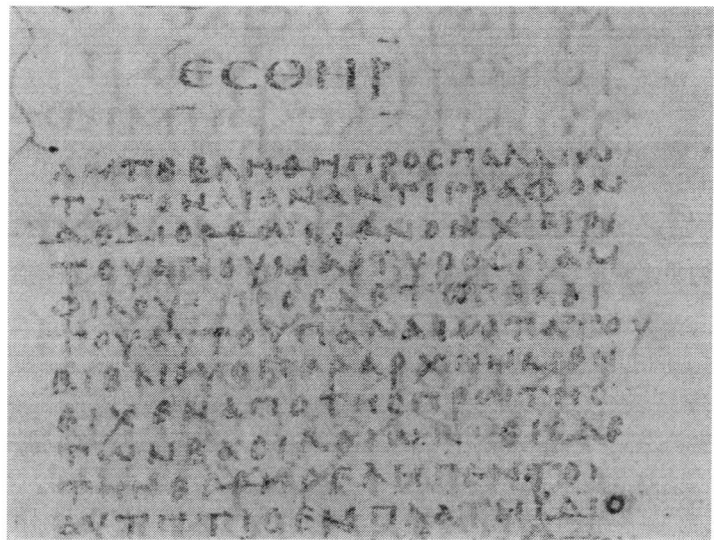

Fig. 4. Colophon to Esther in the Codex Sinaiticus, fol. XIX (= quire 37, fol. 3ʳ), lines 1–10.[16]

1.2. The Developments of the Third Century

The third century is marked by an increasing number of NT and LXX papyri and an intensive progress in the transmission of the Septuagint; the Hexaplaric text originated by the work of Origenes.

---

14 David Trobisch, *The First Edition of the New Testament* (Oxford: University Press, 2012); for the Septuagint, see pp. 62–64, 104.
15 See the criticism of Trobisch's thesis in *The Reliability of the New Testament: Bart Ehrman and Daniel Wallace in Dialogue*, ed. by Robert B. Stewart (Minneapolis: Fortress Press, 2011), pp. 62–65.
16 Fig.: Universitätsbibliothek Leipzig <http://www.codex-sinaiticus.net/de/manuscript. aspx?book=9&chapter=10&lid=de&side=r&verse=3l&zoomSlider=0> [accessed 13 April 2020].

The decisive point for our theme results from the huge material used by Origenes: The better knowledge of the Septuagint and other textual forms of the Greek writings of Israel did not accelerate a juncture to New Testament writings. The Hexaplaric text rather was published for its own and partitioned in volumes for its transmission. Old codices of the Septuagint were corrected in themselves.

The colophon to Esther in the *Codex Sinaiticus* (fig. 4) gives a color to these incidents. The fourth-century scribe points to an early manuscript (ἀντίγραφον, line 2) holding the books from I Kingdoms to Esther (ἀπὸ τῆς πρώτης τῶν βασιλείων εἰς δὲ τὴν Εσθηρ, lines 8–10). This manuscript was corrected in the third century by Pamphilus (δεδιορθωμένον χειρὶ τοῦ ἁγίου μάρτυρος Παμφίλου, lines 4–5) according to the Hexapla (διορθώθη πρὸς τὰ ἑξαπλᾶ ᾿Ωριγένους, line 16), as he tells. Then it was transmitted in the corrected form; the fourth-century scribe used it for collations (and did not accept some writings of proper names).[17]

That way, we can reconstruct a history of the used text. In the beginning stood a pre-Hexaplaric codex holding the LXX text of I–IV Kingdoms and Esther. IV Kingdoms ended in the time of Jehoiachin (25. 27; IV Kingdoms is lost in ℵ), and Esther followed immediately since Esther 1. 1c remembers the time of Jehoiachin (ℵ Ιεχονιου). This is a fine linkage and means that Esther increased in value against Pap. 967 Ra. (whereas Chronicles were separated as it was usual in the Hebrew tradition). The initial codex was somewhat younger than Pap. 967 Ra., as it seems, or written in another region.

That codex with the books I Kingdoms to Esther carried around half the pages of the foregoing books from Genesis to Judges or Ruth; maybe the codex was the third volume of a greater collection.[18] Hence, we find a second evidence for the late pre-Hexaplaric tendency to collect essential parts or the whole Septuagint sequentially. The distribution of the Hexapla in several volumes tied up there. It used existing samples of Septuagint books and added comparable codices (mirrored up to the Syrohexapla). In appropriate cases, the Septuagint was presented as the main text, and variants of the other columns were quoted in the margins.

At the same time, any hint of an expansion of these collections into full Bibles is lacking. The report of the colophon to Esther (ℵ) is concerned only with the Septuagint. The surrounding papyrological material of the third century corresponds; it does not show any gathering of a Septuagint Book together with Matthew, which would bridge the gap to the Gospels. Collections of akin genres (Historical Books of LXX and Acts, letters in LXX and apostolic letters, Prophetic Books and Revelation) are missing as well, and even Christological 'testimonia' combining 'messianic' passages from the LXX and NT are absent in the papyri of the second and third centuries.

---

17 Line 16 is not depicted in fig. 2. Full transcription and interpretation in Peter J. Gentry, 'Origen's Hexapla and Tetrapla', in *Handbook of the Septuagint*, ed. by Alison G. Salvesen and Timothy Michael Law (Oxford: Oxford University Press, 2021), pp. 553–71 (p. 559).

18 More cannot be said. It is impossible to decide, whether the assumed two first volumes of the collection were divided into Nomos and Joshua-Ruth, or if they thought of Genesis to Ruth already as Octateuch.

Surely, sources have been lost due to the state of preservation. It must be expected at least that a smaller collection preceding the Odes (containing songs from Jewish and early Christian scriptures) will be found; I will mention the growth of the Odes below. Nonetheless, the great number of papyrus-fragments rules out pure chance in the reported facts.

I will sketch the small evidence for textual combinations in the papyrological material up to the fourth century in the following. I summarize, in advance, and record the result as

> *thesis 1*: Combinations of Septuagint and New Testament writings in material units were neither mandatory for the eldest biblical readings in the communities nor enhanced by the Hexaplaric impulses of the third century. They present a subsequent, not the first step of biblical transmission.

An additional hint may be helpful: Many sources mentioned in the following were decomposed in the history of research according to the disciplines; they are numbered separately in the lists of LXX and NT manuscripts (Ra. or GA). I am reversely interested in the unity of the old documents and look for the interrelation between old and new texts; I combine Ra. and GA numbers in the identification of the manuscripts.

1.3. *Exodus and Revelation in PapOxy VIII 1075 / 1079*

The oldest document pertinent to our subject is PapOxy VIII 1075 (Exodus) /1079 (Revelation) (see figs 5 & 6). The recto holds lines of the last chapter of Exodus (40. 26[29]-finis; Ra. Sigel 909), the verso lines of the first chapter of Revelation (1. 4–7; GA p[18]).[19] That the lost part of the papyrus showed the whole text of Exodus, is indicated by the 'subscriptio' on the fragment ('Exodos'; recto, last line). Analogously, Revelation was most likely complete too.

The text of Exodus has been dated to the third century (probably the first half) since Hunt's edition.[20] The hand of Revelation is a little younger but still dated into the third century by a majority of researchers as well.[21] A debate arose as to whether we have to do with a section of a scroll[22] or the page of a codex.[23] The debate is

---

19 The inscriptio and verses 1. 1–3 of Revelation have been destroyed.
20 Arthur S. Hunt, *The Oxyrhynchus Papyri: Part VIII*, Egypt Exploration Fund, 1075 (London: The Egypt Exploration Fund, 1911), pp. 5–6.
21 Hunt did not exclude the fourth century. Present researchers find strong indications for the middle of the third century; see David P. Barrett and Philip Wesley Comfort, *The Text of the Earliest New Testament Greek Manuscripts*, 3rd edn, 2 vols (Grand Rapids, MI: Kregel, 2019), II. Papyri 75–139, pp. 360–61. Pasquale Orsini and Willy Clarysse, 'Early New Testament Manuscripts and Their Dates. A Critique of Theological Palaeography', *EThL*, 88 (2012), pp. 443–74 (p. 469), propose 200–300 CE.
22 So, the consensus from Hunt up to Rahlfs and Fraenkel, *Verzeichnis*, p. 295.
23 The codex-form is proposed by Brent Nongbri, 'Losing a Curious Christian Scroll but Gaining a Curious Christian Codex: An Oxyrhynchus Papyrus of Exodus and Revelation', *NT*, 55 (2013), pp. 77–88; *God's Library*, p. 343 n. 49; cf. Nongbri's Internet post (more literature can be found there).

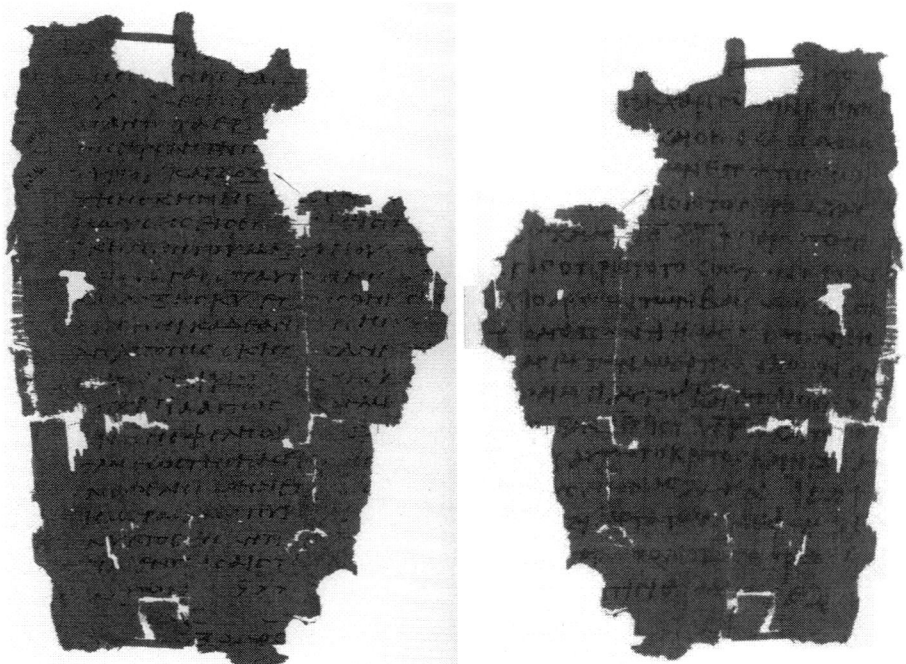

Figs 5 & 6. Papyrus Oxyrhynchus VIII 1075/1079. Left: British Library Papyrus 2053^r (Exodus 40. 26[29]-finis);[24] right: British Library Papyrus 2053^v (Revelation 1. 4–7)[25].

going on[26] and a decision hardly possible although the question is of relevance. The book Exodus is much longer than Revelation; therefore, the second scribe would have been able to add more than Revelation to the verso if our manuscript was a scroll. Moreover, a scroll of Exodus might have served primarily for liturgical and in addition for private interests; a codex written in two steps such as ours would have been primarily in private use.[27]

---

24 Fig.: <https://commons.wikimedia.org/wiki/Category:British_Library_Papyrus_2053#/media/File:Papyrus_Oxyrhynchus_1075_-_British_Library_Papyrus_2053_recto_-_Book_of_Exodus_40.jpg> [accessed 05 April 2020].

25 Fig.: <https://commons.wikimedia.org/wiki/File:Papyrus_18_POxy1079.jpg> [accessed 05 April 2020].

26 Peter Malik, 'P.Oxy. VIII.1079 (p18): Closing on a "Curious" Codex?', NTS, 65 (2019), pp. 94–102 renewed the thesis of a scroll (against Nongbri).

27 See Thomas J. Kraus, '"When Symbols and Figures Become Physical Objects": Critical Notes about Some of the "Consistently Cited Witnesses" to the Text of Revelation', in Book of Seven Seals: The Peculiarity of Revelation, its Manuscripts, Attestation, and Transmission, ed. by Thomas J. Kraus and Michael Sommer, WUNT, 363 (Tübingen: Mohr Siebeck, 2016), pp. 51–69 (pp. 57–59); Giovanni

As matters stand, we must abstain from specifying the form (scroll or codex) although slightly preferring the scroll.[28] But we can limit the content; there are no indications for more text than Exodus and Revelation. Moreover, the papyrus may have been supplemented with Revelation for a private owner, yet, that does not exclude the owner's having loaned it for the service of a community of modest means.[29] We can imagine both, private and public use even in the case that our document was a codex.

The combination of Exodus and Revelation is surprising since Revelation was controversial in third-century Alexandria (see Dionysus of Alexandria according to Eus., *h.e.*, VII. 25). Can it be explained tentatively? A consensus is lacking.[30] Some observations, however, are noteworthy:

In our papyrus, the book Exodus was written first. The existing page occupies the preferred side (the recto) of the papyrus. Revelation was attached, starting on the verso; it took the second place. Though, the script is clear and readable. The page with Exodus was not affected by the re-use.[31] That purports that the writer and owner were interested in perceiving both the famous Septuagint book of Exodus and the controversial Revelation.

Exodus was of central relevance for Jewish communities. A scroll (if our document was a scroll) would fit well to Jewish Torah tradition, and the idiom 'children of Israel' (οἱ υἱοὶ Ισραηλ) is found unabbreviated in the preserved fragment honoring Israel (line 15). It would go too far to conclude a Jewish provenance of the Exodus text from these indications.[32] The writer of Exodus was more probably a Christian (see, e.g. the common abbreviation KY for the genitive of the nomen sacrum 'kyrios' in lines 7 and 12).[33] In that case, our papyrus indicates good Christian-Jewish contacts; conflicts did not overshadow the neighborhood of Jews and Christians in Egypt at that time.

How did the scribe, then, accentuate Christian identity? Eldon Epp points to the quoted texts in the fragment: Exodus 40 speaks of Israel's priests and the cloud being on the holiest place (especially 40. 31, 38). Revelation 1 vice versa calls the people addressed priests (ἱερεῖς 1. 6) and honors Christ as the Son of Man coming with the clouds (cf. Daniel 7. 13).[34] If the correspondence of the texts is created intentionally, the owner of the manuscript envisaged a community which was priestly-oriented in using

---

Bazzana, '"Write in a Book What You See and Send It to the Seven Assemblies". Ancient Reading Practices and the Earliest Papyri of Revelation', in *Book of Seven Seals*, ed. by Thomas J. Kraus and Michael Sommer, WUNT, 363 (Tübingen: Mohr Siebeck, 2016), pp. 11–31 (pp. 16–17).

28 So, too, Jongkind, 'Manuscripts', p. 196.
29 See Malik, 'P.Oxy. VIII.1079', p. 101.
30 The majority of scholars thinks of a *non liquet*; cf. Bazzana, 'Book', p. 17.
31 See Jongkind, 'Manuscripts', p. 127: 'Though the roll was intentionally produced as an Exodus roll, its empty verso received the additional purpose of containing the text of Revelation and that without retiring the use of the Exodus text on the recto'.
32 But we cannot strictly exclude a Jewish pre-owner: see Kurt Treu, 'Die Bedeutung des Griechischen für die Juden im Römischen Reich', *Kairos*, 15 (1973), pp. 123–44 (p. 142).
33 See Rahlfs and Fraenkel, *Verzeichnis*, p. 295.
34 Eldon Jay Epp, 'The Oxyrhynchus New Testament Papyri: "Not without Honor Except in Their Hometown?"', in *Perspectives on New Testament Textual Criticism: Collected Essays, 1962–2004*, ed. by Eldon Jay Epp, NT.S, 116 (Atlanta: SBL, 2008), pp. 743–801 (pp. 758–59).

Figs 7 & 8. Papyrus Amherst I 3 = Morgan Library Pap. Gr.3. Left: extract of the recto with Hebrews 1. 1 (above in the middle);[35] right: extract of the verso with Genesis 1. 1–5 LXX and Aquila[36].

Exodus tradition (cf. Exodus 19. 6) and followed Jesus whom they saw elevated in the clouds of God's presence. We would say today, the document belonged to a Jewish-Christian community or at least a community with sympathy for Jewish traditions.

Moreover, Exodus is a main reference work for the plagues and visions of Revelation.[37] Revelation 15. 3 reminds of the Song of Moses (ᾠδὴ Μωϋσέως), the famous victory song of Exodus 15 (ᾠδή Exodus 15. 1). Revelation 18. 4 combines a motif of Deutero-Isaiah (Isaiah 48. 20) and the theme of the book of Exodus when saying ἐξέλθατε ὁ λαός μου, 'go out, my people' (ἐξέρχεσθαι is found about forty times in Exodus). This theme is put in a nutshell by the 'subscriptio' ἔξοδος which replaced the older title 'exagôgê'[38] of the book Exodus successively from the late second century onwards;[39] and indeed, our papyrus is the oldest manuscript witnessing that 'subscriptio' (recto, line 24). Thus, the theme of the Exodus builds a bridge between the texts. An 'Exodus' (ἔξοδος) marked the formation of God's people in the time of Moses. Now, the Exodus characterizes the way of God's people in the dangerous times of the late third century; ἐξέλθατε (Revelation 18. 4) gives the impulse 'leave a hostile environment that ignores God's will'.

35 Fig.: Morgan Library; cf. <https://commons.wikimedia.org/wiki/File:Papyrus_Amherst_3a. png> [accessed 08 April 2020].

36 Fig.: Morgan Library; cf. <https://commons.wikimedia.org/wiki/File:Papyrus_Amherst_3c_-_ Morgan_Library,_Pap._Gr._3_-_Book_of_Genesis_1,1–5.jpg> [accessed 08 April 2020].

37 The references are investigated by Michael Sommer, *Der Tag der Plagen: Studien zur Verbindung der Rezeption von Ex 7–11 in den Posaunen- und Schalenvisionen der Johannesoffenbarung und der Tag des Herrn-Tradition*, WUNT, 387 (Tübingen: Mohr Siebeck, 2015).

38 For ἐξαγωγή see Aristobul (Eus., *praep.ev.*, XIII. 12. 1) and Philo (*migr.*, 14, etc.).

39 The name ἔξοδος is found from Justin (*dial.*, 59. 1. 2, etc.) onwards. Details in Anna Mambelli, 'Le prime attestazioni di Ἔξοδος come titolo del secondo libro del Pentateuco', in *Exodos: Storia di un vocabolo*, ed. by Eberhard Bons and others, Fonti, ricerche, testi, 62 (Bologna: Società Editrice Il Mulino, 2020), pp. 167–77.

A last idea may be added. The noted controversy which devalued Revelation in Alexandria was caused by chiliastic speculations (cf. Eus., *h.e.*, VII. 25. 1–3). Hence, the question arises: Did the owner esteem Revelation chiefly because of his hope for a chiliastic new Jerusalem? The line old Exodus — new Exodus — heavenly Jerusalem forms a tempting and perhaps chiliastic-sensuous train of thoughts.

The scanty papyrus fragment sounds a note of caution. The mentioned train of thoughts is hypothetic. Nevertheless, the combination of Revelation and Exodus is interpretable and fascinating. It is certain, at least, that the book of Revelation which seems marginal in the New Testament today holds an important role in the history of combinations of New Testament and Septuagint, and that the combination expresses a positive relation to the Jewish roots of Christianity.

PapOxy VIII 1075 / 1079 (Exodus/Revelation) is the only document of the third century combining whole Scriptures of LXX and NT.

1.4. Hebrews 1. 1 and Genesis 1. 1–5 in Papyrus Amherst I 3b / c

The next witness which can be mentioned, Papyrus Amherst I 3b (Hebrews 1. 1) and c (Genesis 1. 1–5), is of a different character (figs 7 & 8). The initial text on its recto is non-biblical, namely a Christian letter written from Rome between 250 and 285 CE. An early reader (second hand) added Hebrews 1. 1 on the top of col. 2 (late third century).[40] The entry holds only the three lines πολυμερῶς καὶ πολυτρόπως / πάλαι ὁ θεὸς λαλήσας τοῖς πατρά/σιν ἡμῶν ἐν τοῖς προφήταις, 'God spoke to our fathers[...]' (GA p¹²; I normalize the orthography) and was perhaps not more than an occasional note.[41] Nevertheless the text of the New Testament quotation is precious (the ἡμῶν after τοῖς πατράσιν is found in p⁴⁶ᶜᵒʳʳ· too).

A third hand turned the folio and inserted Genesis 1. 1–5 (LXX and Aquila) on the verso (Ra. Sigel 912). The purpose of this addendum which was made in the end of the third or beginning of the fourth century[42] is contentious.[43] A maximalistic explanation will look for intertextual relations to Hebrews and find them. Hebrews 1. 1 goes on in 1. 2, namely, and culminates in the declaration: God 'created the times' (ἐποίησεν τοὺς αἰῶνας). Vice versa, Genesis 1. 1 LXX states 'God created in the beginning' (ἐν ἀρχῇ ἐποίησεν ὁ θεός). God created — as is told in the papyrus Amherst according to Genesis 1. 3–4 — the light and divided light from darkness.

---

40 The text was edited in Bernhard P. Grenfell and Arthur S. Hunt, *The Amherst Papyri: Being an Account of the Greek papyri in the Collection of the Right Hon. Lord Amherst of Hackney* (London: H. Frowde, 1900), I, pp. 28–31. They proposed a date in the end of the third or beginning of the fourth century (p. 30). Orsini and Clarysse, 'Early New Testament Manuscripts', p. 469 date the lines of Hebrews 1. 1 on 250–300 CE.

41 See Kurt Aland and Barbara Aland, *The Text of the New Testament* (Grand Rapids: Eerdmans, 1995), p. 85.

42 See *Genesis*, ed. by John W. Wevers, Septuaginta Vetus Testamentum Graecum, I (Göttingen: Vandenhoeck & Ruprecht, 1974), p. 24.

43 The text is seldom discussed in younger times; see the short notes in Barrett and Comfort, *The Text of the Earliest New Testament*, I. Papyri 1–72, p. 69; Tobias Nicklas, 'Zur historischen und theologischen Bedeutung der Erforschung neutestamentlicher Zeitgeschichte', *NTS*, 48 (2002), 145–58 (pp. 154–55); Epp, 'Oxyrhynchus Papyri', p. 759 n. 49.

If the Christian writer of Genesis 1. 1–5 thought so, he or she was stimulated by Hebrews 1. 1–2 and searched for a kind of biblical theology (if the modern term is allowed). Even an astonishing omission in the Papyrus Amherst may be elucidated that way: Genesis 1. 5a lacks in both, the LXX and the Aquila quotation. The omitted text described how God gave the name to the special time of day and night (καὶ ἐκάλεσεν ὁ θεὸς τὸ φῶς ἡμέραν καὶ τὸ σκότος ἐκάλεσεν νύκτα LXX-Genesis 1. 5a). Our theologian who was guided by the opening of Hebrews looked for God's creating word and the creation of the times in the sense of the 'aeons' (epochs and infinite periods) as it seems in that case. He could neglect the notice concerning day and night.

A minimalistic interpretation, on the contrary, will deny any conscious intertextuality. It will assume that we find nothing more than a writing exercise. That would mean that our scribe quotes Genesis 1 simply because the text was well acquainted to him. Yet, a theological feature must be added even then: The scribe cites Genesis 1. 1–5 according to Aquila behind the Septuagint version. Thus, the translation ἐν κεφαλαίῳ ἔκτισεν θεός (Aquila) appears aside to ἐν ἀρχῇ ἐποίησεν ὁ θεός (Septuagint). Did the scribe merely want to show his knowledge of different textual forms in a time when the Hexapla spread? Or did he pen the verses for ongoing studies ('Studienzwecke[n]')?[44] In any case, he knew the Aquila text that was preferred in the Jewish communities and quoted it, apart from 1. 5a, properly. His lines are the oldest witness for the Septuagint text and the best witness for the Aquila text of our verses.

All in all, a conscious intertextuality can be doubted in the Papyrus Amherst. One point, however, agrees with the observations to the Exod-Rev-Papyrus (PapOxy VIII 1075 / 1079): The writer of the Genesis lines was attentive to Jewish traditions.

The minimum we can and must say, therefore, as a result of sections 1.3 and 1.4, is a

thesis 2: The combination of Septuagint and New Testament Scriptures developed slowly in the third century. The innovation was triggered by interests of single communities or single learned readers. It originated in Christianity but reminds Christianity of its Jewish roots.

1.5. The Sections from Matthew and Daniel in Oslo Univ.-Bibl., P. Inv. 1661

Oslo Univ.-Bibl., P. Inv. 1661 (Ra. 994; GA p⁶²) broadens the perspective. It covers fragments of thirteen leaves of a bilingual miniature codex. The first part of the codex contains text from Matthew (surviving are fragments of 11. 25–30, Greek and Achmimic), the second part a section of Daniel 3 Θ (surviving are Greek fragments of 3. 51–53).

No reconstruction of the codex allows for more content than half a chapter of the New Testament and the Septuagint (e.g. Daniel 3. 51–56 and a second short section of Θ). But, remarkably, the piece of Daniel transcends Odes 8 (which begins in Daniel 3. 52). Therefore, the small codex was perhaps a kind of private lectionary of biblical scenes

---

44 See Rahlfs and Fraenkel, *Verzeichnis*, p. 260. Fraenkel reports the thesis of a writing exercise too (doubting it).

praising the one God who gives wisdom and deep knowledge (Matthew 11. 25–27), is gracious (Matthew 11. 28–29) and exalted beyond measure (Daniel 3. 52; Odes 8).[45] Or it was used as an amulet (the small format permitted to be worn on the body).[46]

The private owner of the codex did not combine whole Scriptures of the Septuagint and New Testament. This differs from PapOxy VIII 1075/1079 (cf. 1.3). Though, an interest in private, perhaps apotropaic lessons combining extracts from the New Testament (in our case, a Gospel) and the Septuagint or Theodotion (in our case: Daniel) becomes obvious. Moreover, the purchaser of that codex presented the New Testament texts first. His perception started in the New Testament and went from there to the Septuagint (again a counterpart to PapOxy VIII 1075/1079).

1.6. Disputed and Younger Examples for Textual Combinations

Other examples fell by the wayside in the last decades, are younger or only remotely belong to our theme.

1.6.1. The Bodmer Miscellaneous Codex (LDAB 2565)

The *Bodmer Miscellaneous Codex* gathered texts of diverse provenance in the fourth century (the collected material was written in the third to fourth century) but was not preserved in its originally assembled form. Reconstructions were indispensable. The research tested if both, LXX and NT texts, could be assigned to the codex. Most of the contents were identified with certainty; an important New Testament part definitely belonged to it, the today's p[72] GA (I–II Peter, Jude).[47] Though, was it the same with a smaller Old Testament counterpart containing LXX-Psalms 33. 2–34. 16 (P. Bodmer IX)? The efforts to integrate this part into the codex failed as we will see. Nevertheless, the material is important; I will sketch it briefly:

The pages with the Psalms originally belonged to a document which contained the 'Apology of Phileas' *ex ante* (P. Bodmer XX);[48] the Psalms begin on the last verso of P. Bodmer XX. The text of the Psalms probably continued on following folios;

---

45 See Rahlfs and Fraenkel, *Verzeichnis*, pp. 270–71; *Susanna, Daniel, Bel et Draco*, ed. by Olivier Munnich (after Joseph Ziegler), Septuaginta Vetus Testamentum Graecum, XVI 2, 2nd edn (Göttingen: Vandenhoeck & Ruprecht, 1999), pp. 195–97; Pinakes, diktyon 76007.

46 The use of the codex as an amulet cannot be excluded; see Theodore S. de Bruyn and Jitse H. F. Dijkstra, 'Greek Amulets and Formularies from Egypt Containing Christian Elements: A Checklist of Papyri, Parchments, Ostraka, and Tablets', *Bulletin of the American Society of Papyrologists*, 48 (2011), 163–216 (p. 214). Hans J. Sagrusten, *Pergamente und Papyri: Das grosse Puzzle der ältesten Bibelhandschriften* (Witten: SCM R. Brockhaus, 2018), pp. 73–76, votes for the use as amulet surmising a historical context in or shortly after the Diocletianic persecution.

47 That part has an own history: see Tommy Wasserman, *The Epistle of Jude: Its Text and Transmission*, CBNT Series, 43 (Stockholm: Almqvist & Wiksell International, 2006), pp. 30–50; Brent Nongbri, 'The Construction of P. Bodmer viii and the Bodmer "Composite" or "Miscellaneous" Codex', *Novum Testamentum*, 58 (2016), 394–410.

48 For the older research see Tommy Wasserman, 'Papyrus 72 and the Bodmer Miscellaneous Codex', *NTS*, 51 (2005), 37–154.

Psalms 34. 16 breaks in the verse. A parallel is preserved in P. Chester Beatty XV; there the apology is told and followed by Psalms, too, now starting with Psalm 1 (fragments of Psalms 1–4 are preserved). The Phileas narrative undeniably drew upon the Psalms in Christianity.

Phileas was put to death as a martyr in 305 and became widely known in the fourth century (cf. Eus., *h.e.*, VIII. 9–10).[49] His martyrdom gave a date to the papyrus; P. Bodmer XX/IX must have been written after 305. In addition, the combination of the martyrdom-narrative (the apology) with the Psalms became theologically significant: A martyr attracted veneration; he had the reputation of being righteous and having suffered under his enemies as described in the Psalms (see the praise of the righteous in LXX-Psalms 1 and 33 and cf. the contrast to enemies in LXX-Psalms 1–2; 33–34).

If P. Bodmer XX/IX was to be integrated into the Miscellaneous Codex, the question followed: was the collector pursuing theological interests, too (now in the later fourth century)? A skeptical view *eo ipso* did not exclude coincidences; the connection between the Psalms and the Catholic Letters was not necessarily the primary intent of the potential collection.[50] On the other hand, a Christological or martyrological motif cluster connecting the Psalms and the Letters is easily found.[51] Wolfgang Wiefel postulated the strongest reference in the history of research; according to him the compiler maybe thought of I Peter as a kind of homily on the Psalms since LXX-Psalms 33. 13–17 is quoted in I Peter 2. 3; 3. 10–12.[52]

The longstanding discussion and the impressive assumptions failed in the last years.[53] The examination by Brent Nongbri in 2015 caused reasonable doubts 'that there is sufficient evidence to claim that P. Bodm. XX+IX was bound to the texts of the "Miscellaneous" or "Composite" codex'.[54] Today it is held that the Septuagint Psalms were not part of the Bodmer Miscellaneous Codex.[55]

Nevertheless, one point of the discussion is still relevant for our subject: The text critical examination did not detect any clear-cut harmonization between the text of quotations in the New Testament letters and the text of the LXX-Psalms.[56] That

---

49 Hans Reinhard Seeliger and Wolfgang Wischmeyer, *Märtyrerliteratur: Herausgegeben, übersetzt, kommentiert und eingeleitet* (Berlin: de Gruyter, 2015), pp. 223–71 (pp. 268–70 and passim).

50 See Tobias Nicklas and Tommy Wasserman, 'Theologische Linien im "Codex Bodmer Miscellani"?', in *New Testament Manuscripts: Their Texts and Their World*, ed. by Tobias Nicklas and Thomas J. Kraus, TENT, 2 (Leiden: Brill, 2006), pp. 161–88 (pp. 170–71).

51 See David G. Horrell, *Becoming Christian: Essays on 1 Peter and the Making of Christian Identity*, Library of New Testament Studies (London: Bloomsbury, 2013), pp. 54–66, especially pp. 63–66.

52 Wolfgang Wiefel, 'Kanongeschichtliche Erwägungen zu Papyrus Bodmer VII/VIII (P⁷²)', APF, 22/23 (1974), 289–304 (p. 299).

53 I thank Tommy Wasserman, Lund, and Peter Malik, Wuppertal, for important hints in April 2020.

54 Brent Nongbri, 'Recent Progress in Understanding the Construction of the Bodmer "Miscellaneous" or "Composite" Codex', *Adamantius*, 21 (2015), 171–72 (p. 172).

55 See Nongbri's blogpost <https://brentnongbri.com/2018/03/31/p-bodmer-xxix-and-the-bodmer-composite-codex/> [accessed 07 April 2020].

56 See Wasserman, *Epistle*, pp. 40–41.

observation was confirmed by a detailed analysis[57] and stays even if the material unit of the Miscellaneous codex must be abandoned. The result shows that the transmission of the Septuagint and New Testament writings happened independently in our centuries in spite of the first textual combinations.

1.6.2.   Cairo, Eg. Mus., P. Inv. 88747

Another genre of text is represented by the strips of parchment used for the binding of *Cairo, Eg. Mus., P. Inv. 88747*. The strips carry fragments of Hebrews 12. 22–23; Genesis 31. 8 and Psalm 26. 4 (fourth century), but did not belong to a biblical manuscript. They display divergent instructions for a life in the presence of God (Hebrews 12. 22–23; Psalm 26. 4) and on earth (Genesis 31. 8). Their origin was perhaps a 'theological treatise'.[58]

1.6.3.   P. Oslo Inv. 1644

I return to the amulets (cf. 1.5). *P. Oslo Inv. 1644* (fragments of a folio; Ra. 2115) carries the Our Father (Matthew 6. 9–13), the apostolic greeting II Corinthians 13. 13 and lines of LXX-Psalm 90. 1–4 (P. Schøyen 1.16; fourth century).[59] The grouping of prayer, greeting and Psalm assures of God's help and protection (cf. βοήθεια and σκέπη LXX-Psalm 90. 1). Interestingly, the sequence from the New Testament to the Septuagint is marked; LXX-Psalm 90 is separated by an ornament. One may doubt, however, if the ornament marks the combination of NT and LXX; the rhetorical crescendo to the motifs of help is the primary intent of the invocation and, therefore, the Psalm is emphasized.[60]

1.6.4.   P. Mich. Inv. 6427

P.Mich. Inv. 6427 (fragments of a folio; Ra. 2154) contains remnants of a prayer on the recto (early fourth century); the prayer quotes motifs from Isaiah 40. 14; 66. 1 and Hermas, *Mand.*, I. 1. Sometime later, Ode 8 (Daniel 3. 52–53, 58–68,

---

57 Patrick T. Egan, 'The Manuscript Tradition of Greek Psalms 33–34 and 1 Peter 3:10–12', in *Die Septuaginta — Entstehung, Sprache, Geschichte: 3. Internationale Fachtagung veranstaltet von Septuaginta Deutsch (LXX.D), Wuppertal 22.-25. Juli 2010*, ed. by Martin Meiser and others, WUNT, 286 (Tübingen: Mohr Siebeck, 2012), pp. 505–28, did not find more than 'six points of agreement in the 24 unique readings' of p[72] (P. Bodm. IX), an agreement which is to be expected randomly (quotation p. 524).

58 See Rahlfs and Fraenkel, *Verzeichnis*, pp. 163–64 and oS-29, pp. 464, 471, 563; Jongkind, 'Manuscripts', pp. 198–99.

59 Rahlfs and Fraenkel, *Verzeichnis*, p. 270. Amulets do not have GA-numbers; the number will be GA T16 probably (following Brice Jones), if the document will get a number in the future.

60 The combination of the Our Father and LXX-Psalm 90 is more frequently preserved later on (e.g. PGM P17 = P.Iand. 1.6): see Thomas J. Kraus, *Ad Fontes: Original Manuscripts and Their Significance for Studying Early Christianity — Selected Essays*, Texts and Editions for New Testament Studies (Leiden: Brill, 2007), p. 54; de Bruyn and Dijkstra, 'Greek Amulets', pp. 172, 188.

77–84) was added onto the verso (late fourth century).[61] The papyrus touches our attention insofar, as the prayer combines motifs of the Septuagint and Hermas, an early Christian writing which is included in the *Codex Sinaiticus*. The verso demonstrates the early transmission of one of the Odes showing an old textual form (variants can be correlated to Pap. 967 Ra., B and R).[62] We encounter the piety of two generations of early Christians living with the scriptures, no more, no less.

1.6.5.   P. Mich. Inv. 1574

The fragment *P.Mich. Inv. 1574* (one folio, text only on the recto; Ra. 895)[63] was written in the fifth century and is therefore the latest witness to be mentioned here. It combines beatitudes for someone who is suffering (Matthew 5. 11; 5. 6; Psalm 118. 2a) with the consolation in Lamentations 3. 27–31. The sequence of quotations is explained best if the fragment was part of a letter of consolation.[64]

All in all, the fragments (sections 1.6.2 to 1.6.5) demonstrate that passages from the Septuagint and New Testament were readily combined in the daily life and thought of Christians in late antiquity and early Byzantine times — a fact which is known from tractates of the church fathers as well. A textual adaptation between the quoted wordings of New Testament and Septuagint cannot be observed, as far as one can say in face of the mutilations.

So, a second convergence comes up in the papyri: The text of Exodus was not touched by the Christian who added Revelation in PapOxy VIII 1075 /1079. Papyrus Amherst I 3c recorded the differences between the Septuagint and the Aquila text of Genesis 1 besides Hebrews 1. Papyrus Oslo 1661 documented biblical texts bilingually. The Bodmer Papyri indirectly support the independent transmission of New Testament and Septuagint Scriptures. Private letters, tractates or amulets are less significant but confirm that quotations are altered no more than tangentially.

I summarize these observations in a

thesis 3: The correlation of New Testament and Septuagint texts did not set off a ponderable textual harmonization in pre-Constantinian times.

---

61 Digitized in <https://quod.lib.umich.edu/a/apis?type=boolean;view=reslist;rgn1=apis_inv;select1=phrase;q1=P.Mich.inv.%25206427> [accessed 9 May 2020].

62 See Michael Gronewald, 'Ein liturgischer Papyrus: Gebet und Ode 8: P. Mich. Inv. 6427', *Zeitschrift für Papyrologie und Epigraphik*, 14 (1974), 193–200.

63 Digitized in <https://quod.lib.umich.edu/cgi/i/image/image-idx?view=entry&subview=detail&cc=apis&entryid=X-1473&viewid=1574r.TIF> [accessed 9 May 2020].

64 See Rahlfs and Fraenkel, *Verzeichnis*, pp. 8–9. The full list of sigla is presented in <https://rep.adw-goe.de/bitstream/handle/11858/00-001S-0000-0022-A30C-8/Rahlfs-Sigeln_Stand_Dezember_2012.pdf?sequence=1&isAllowed=y> [accessed 25 Aprile 2020].

2. Septuagint and New Testament in the So-Called Full Bibles

The Christian communities lost many manuscripts in the Decianic and Diocletianic persecutions.[65] Then, the times of oppression ended. Any constraint upon the production of codices was overruled by the approval of Christianity in the Constantinian era.[66] The Christian communities became able to create great codices and, now indeed, connected Septuagint and New Testament Scriptures voluminously. The history of the Greek pandects started in the fourth and fifth centuries. It went on throughout the Byzantine times; I give an overview up to the end of the fifteenth century.

2.1. The Known Greek Pandects (Fourth to Fifteenth Centuries)

Greek pandects are rare. I list the known manuscripts:
Three of the 'full Bibles' of the fourth and fifth (or beginning of the sixth) centuries have survived, the codices:
– *Vaticanus* (B),
– *Sinaiticus* (ℵ) and
– *Alexandrinus* (A).[67] These codices were used for a long time as is shown, e.g., by the work of correctors.

A fourth old codex, the *Codex Ephraemi rescriptus* (C), is heavily damaged.

After the early sixth century, the Byzantines seldom created full Bibles.[68] Liturgical needs and collections of parts of the Bible dominated the material transmission of the

---

65 See, e.g., Eus., *h.e.*, VIII. 8, the so-called minutes of Cirta (mentioned in Augustine, *Contra Cresconium*, III. 26–27; CSEL 52, p. 435) and the hints to the 'traditores' (the ones who had handed down scriptures) in Augustine, *De baptismo*, libri VII, here V. 1. 1 (CSEL 51, p. 262).

66 Constantine charged the production of fifty codices with divine Scriptures (Eus., *vit.Const.*, IV. 36). But it is disputed if these books were full Bibles; cf. Martin Wallraff, *Kodex und Kanon: Das Buch im frühen Christentum*, Hans-Lietzmann-Vorlesungen, 12 (Berlin: de Gruyter, 2013), pp. 39–41.

67 Information on B in Patrick Andrist (ed.), *Le manuscrit B de la Bible (Vaticanus graecus 1209): Introduction au fac-similé, Actes du Colloque de Genève (11 juin 2001), Contributions supplémentaires*, Histoire du texte biblique, 7 (Lausanne: Éditions du Zèbre, 2009); Pietro Versace, *I Marginalia del Codex Vaticanus*, Studi e Testi, 528 (Vatican City: Biblioteca Apostolica Vaticana, 2018). For ℵ, see David Parker, *Codex Sinaiticus: Geschichte der ältesten Bibel der Welt* (Stuttgart: Deutsche Bibelgesellschaft, 2012).

68 The famous purple manuscripts of the sixth century did not strive for a continuum of LXX and NT Scriptures, but focused on parts of the Bible. Two must be mentioned here: a) *Codex Purpureus Rossanensis* contains Matthew and Mark plus twelve folios of additional material, inter alia forty quotations from the Septuagint; see Elijah Hixson, *Scribal Habits in Sixth-Century Greek Purple Codices*, New Testament Tools, Studies and Documents, 61 (Leiden: Brill, 2019), p. 19, etc.; though, the Septuagint quotations are non-continuous. b) Two folios of Luke were secondarily attached to the 'Wiener Genesis' (folios of LXX-Genesis; ÖNB Cod. Theol. gr. 31, fol. XXV–XXVI); they must be separated as folios of the New Testament Codex N (GA 022).

biblical texts.[69] Only a few Middle-Byzantine pandects are preserved, often damaged or in part. I list the known manuscripts, shortly annotated:[70]

- The uncial *Codex Venetus* (V, eight century) or *Codex Basiliano-Vaticanus* (so called, if the Venetian MS Bibl. Marc. Gr. 1 is combined with MS gr. 2106 from the Vatican Library) lost the New Testament portion.[71]
- The 'queen' of the minuscules, Paris, BnF Gr. 14 (Ra. 198, NT GA 33; late ninth or better beginning of the tenth century), called *codex Pariathoniensis*, is incomplete (great parts of LXX and single folios of Mark and Luke are lost), and the order of the existing leaves is confused.[72]
- *Codex Vaticanus Reginensis* gr. 1A–1B, called also *Biblia Leonis patricii* (Ra. 55; probably first half of the tenth century, at latest eleventh century) lost the second portion of the Septuagint and the New Testament part.[73]
- The *Greek pandect of Vienna* (Codex Wien, ÖNB Theol. gr. 23; Ra. 130 / NT GA 218) therefore is the first of the younger complete codices. It was written in the last decades of the Middle-Byzantine period (late twelfth century) or after the end of the Middle-Byzantine Empire (thirteenth century; that date is more probable).[74]

The Byzantine Empire was renewed in the second half of the thirteenth century. But the production of pandects remained small.

---

69 See the hints concerning the Old Testament in James Miller, 'The Prophetologion: The Old Testament of Byzantine Christianity?', in *The Old Testament in Byzantium*, ed. by Paul Magdalino and Robert Nelson, Dumbarton Oaks Byzantine Symposia and Colloquia (Washington, DC: Dumbarton Oaks Research Library and Collection, 2013), pp. 55–76, and the overview on the New Testament transmission in Derek Krueger and Robert S. Nelson, 'New Testaments of Byzantium. Seen, Heard, Written, Excerpted, Interpreted', in *The New Testament in Byzantium*, ed. by Derek Krueger and Robert S. Nelson (Washington, DC: Dumbarton Oaks, 2016), pp. 1–20.

70 See the overview in Jongkind, 'Manuscripts', pp. 189–201 and Andrist, 'Au croisement'. I add Zittau Stadtbibl. A 1 (NT GA 664; fifteenth century) to the pandects listed by Andrist and Jongkind. Besides, I will have a look on the evidence for a lost manuscript of the Septuagint in Vivarium (Cassiodorus, *inst.*, I. 14. 1.4; see sections 2.4.1 and 2.4.4 and table 2).

71 See Sidney Jellicoe, *The Septuagint and Modern Study* (Winona Lake: Eisenbrauns, 1993), pp. 197–99; Andrist, 'Au croisement', pp. 45–55.

72 Pinakes, diktyon 49574 and diktyon 30090. Precious information in Irmgard Hutter, 'Eine verspätete Bibelhandschrift (Paris, BNF, gr. 14)', *Palaeoslavica*, 10 (2000), 159–74. According to Hutter, the manuscript dates to the early tenth century and was written in Constantinople (pp. 162–63). In addition, see Andrist, 'Au croisement', pp. 53–62.

73 Pinakes, diktyon 66171. Facsimile: Paul Canart and Suzy Dufrenne (ed.), *Die Bibel des Patricius Leo: Codex Reginensis Graecus 1B*, Codices e Vaticanis Selecti, 75, (Zürich: Belser, 1988). Information in *La Bible du Patrice Léon: Codex Reginensis Graecus 1: commentaire codicologique, paléographique, philologique et artistique*, ed. by Paul Canart, Studi e testi, 463 (Città del Vaticano: Biblioteca apostolica vaticana, 2011); Andrist, 'Au croisement', pp. 63–70.

74 Description in Herbert Hunger and Otto Kresten, *Katalog der griechischen Handschriften der Österreichischen Nationalbibliothek, Teil 3, 1: Codices Theologici 1–100*, Museion NF, IV, 1, 3, 1 (Wien: B. Hollinek, 1976), pp. 39–40. Literature in <https://ntvmr.uni-muenster.de/liste?docID=30218> and <https://pinakes.irht.cnrs.fr/notices/cote/71690/> [accessed 31 May 2020]. Four hands worked in the Bible. The style of writing differs from hand to hand; that is a significant divergence from the old pandects.

- The *Bible of Ferrara* (Bibl. Com. Cl. II, 187, I–III) is the only preserved pandect of the fourteenth century. The scribe did not mention his name in a colophon but can be identified as Nikodemos Xenos (it is the same scribe as in Ferrara, Bibl. Com. Cl. II, 188; for that manuscript see below). Therefore, the pandect can be dated into the second quarter of the fourteenth century (1334 plus/minus some years). It was brought to the West for the use at the council of Ferrara and Florence and is complete (three volumes; Ra. 106, NT GA 582).[75]
- The second manuscript of a great part of the Septuagint in the library of Ferrara is not a pandect, but may be compared (Bibl. Com. Cl. II, 188; Ra. 107). That codex is signed by the scribe Nikodemos Xenos and dated by him; it was written within less than six weeks, 8 June to 15 July 1334 (fol. 241^{r-v}; Nikodemos is also the scribe of the pandect Bibl. Com. Cl. II, 187). The manuscript contains the first part of the Septuagint, i.e. the Octateuch, I–IV Kingdoms, I–II Paralipomena, I–II Esdras, I–IV Maccabees, Esther, Judith and Tobit. The origin of that collection can be traced back to the twelfth century.[76] The 'inscriptio' of the codex designates the collection as ἱστορίαι πᾶσαι ('all historical narratives').[77]

The interest in Greek pandects increased in the fifteenth century thanks to ecumenical contacts and endeavors for preserving the Greek biblical heritage after the fall of Constantinople (1453).

- *Codex Vaticanus* (B) must be mentioned a second time here. For, the lost folios of Genesis 1. 1–46. 28a; Psalms 105. 27–137. 6b; Hebrews 9. 14–13. 25 and Revelation were supplemented probably before 1450 (fol. 1519–1536 with Hebrews and Revelation are tagged as GA 1957 today). The *Vorlage* for the supplement of Genesis is identified (Chisianus IV 38; Ra. 19).[78] Studies on the scribing hand are going

---

75 Description of the codex in E. Martini, *Catalogo di manoscritti greci esistenti nelle biblioteche italiane* (Milano: U. Hoepli, 1896), I.II, pp. 351–52 <https://archive.org/details/catalogodimanoso1martgoog/page/n.136/mode/2up> [accessed 25 April 2020]. Martini printed the number of manuscript Bibl. Com. Cl. II, 187 mistakenly as 187–88. Hence, many mentions in the literature are tangling, even the description by Alfred Rahlfs, *Verzeichnis der griechischen Handschriften des Alten Testaments, für das Septuaginta-Unternehmen aufgestellt*, MSU, 2 (Berlin: Weidmannsche Buchhandlung, 1914), pp. 59–61. For the rectification see Alexander Turyn, *Dated Greek Manuscripts of the Thirteenth and Fourteenth Centuries in the Libraries of Italy* (London: University of Illinois Press, 1972), I, pp. 183–84. Cf. also <https://ntvmr.uni-muenster.de/liste?docID=30218 and https://pinakes.irht.cnrs.fr/notices/cote/71690/> [accessed 31 May 2020].

76 Manuscripts containing the Octateuch, I–IV Kingdoms, Paralipomena, Esdras, I–IV Maccabees, Esther, Judith, Tobit are:
- Ra. 71 Paris BNF Gr. 1, twelfth century;
- Ra. 74 Florence Bibl. Laur., S. Marco 700, thirteenth century;
- Ra. 107 Ferrara Bibl. Com, Cl. II, 188, written 1334;
- Ra. 610 Paris BN, Suppl. gr. 609, fourteenth century;
- cf. Ra. 125 Moskau Staatl. Hist. Mus., Syn. gr. 30 (containing the collection Genesis to Tobit plus Proverbs, Ecclesiastes, Canticles, Wisdom), fourteenth century.

77 The codex is described in Martini, *Catalogo*, pp. 352–53, and Turyn, *Dated Greek Manuscripts*, p. 184; for the 'Inscriptio' see Wevers, *Genesis*, p. 75 and cf. below section 2.8.

78 See Wevers, *Genesis*, pp. 9 and 13; Janko Šagi, 'Problema historiae codicis B', *Divus Thomas. Commentarium de philosophia et theologia*, 75 (1972), 3–29 (pp. 13–17).

on promisingly.[79] The Pastoral Letters and Philemon were not supplemented; whether they were ignored by chance or intentionally, is an open question.[80]

- The *Bibles of Bessarion*, Bibl. Marc. Gr. Z. 5 (= 420; Ra. 68; NT GA 205) and 6 (Ra. 122; NT GA 2886) were produced in the West after the council of Ferrara and the fall of Constantinople.[81] They became important for the print of the Septuagint in the beginning of the sixteenth century (see section 3.4.3).
- The last manuscript to be mentioned here is *Codex Zittau Stadtbibliothek A 1* (Ra. 44; NT GA 664).[82] A prospection of the nearly unknown codex showed that it is written on the island Crete (which was Venetian at that time) in the end of the fifteenth or the first years of the sixteenth century.[83] It combines the books from Genesis to Tobit — a collection as in Ferrara, Bibl. Com. Cl. II, 188 — with the New Testament. The New Testament part is not entitled separately. Fol. 1ʳ of the Septuagint part picks up the motif ἱστορίαι πᾶσαι ('all historical narratives'; cf. section 2.8.2) which is known already by the mentioned 'inscriptio' of the second LXX manuscript in Ferrara (Ra. 107). That means that the history of the pandects must take into regard the development of part-collections within the transmission of the Septuagint.[84]

---

79 Daniele Bianconi, *Cura et studio: Il restauro del libro a Bisanzio*, Hellenica, 66 (Alessandria: Edizione dell' Orso, 2018), pp. 56–57, compares the hand to one of the scribes working at the manuscript BNF Grec 2501.

80 Cf. section 2.4.3 below. It is also an open question whether Pastoral Letters and Philemon were originally contained in B; see Stephen Pisano, 'The *Vaticanus Graecus 1209*: A Witness to the Text of the New Testament', in *Le manuscrit B de la Bible (Vaticanus graecus 1209): Introduction au fac-similé, Actes du Colloque de Genève (11 juin 2001), Contributions supplémentaires*, ed. by Patrick Andrist, Histoire du texte biblique, 7 (Lausanne: Éditions du Zèbre, 2009), pp. 77–97 (p. 77). Cf. Martin Karrer, 'Die alte Überlieferung des Hebräerbriefs / The Ancient Textual Tradition of the Epistle to the Hebrews', prepared for publication in: Marcus Sigismund and Darius Müller (ed.), *Prolegomena to the Project of an Editio Critica Maior of Hebrews*, SBL Text-Critical Studies (SBL: Atlanta, 2022), § 3.3.

81 For the date, see Alan T. Farnes, *Simply Come Copying: Direct Copies as Test Cases in the Quest for Scribal Habits*, WUNT, 481 (Tübingen: Mohr Siebeck, 2019), pp. 124–37. The relation between the two Bessarion-Bibles is discussed controversially. 2886 (= 205abs) was understood as being a copy of 205 in earlier times. Alan Welsby, *A Textual Study of Family 1 in the Gospel of John*, ANTF, 45 (Berlin: de Gruyter, 2014), pp. 84–85, reversed the dependence and classified 205 as copy of 2886. Farnes, *Copying*, argues that the two Bessarion-Bibles are not copies of one another (pp. 162–65).

82 A reworking of the older description of the codex which is given in the Handschriften-Katalog of the Christian-Weise-Bibliothek (Lisa-Tetzner-Str. 11, 02763 Zittau, Mscr. A 1 Biblia graeca) is in progress. Herman Charles Hoskier, *Concerning the Text of the Apocalypse: Collations of All Existing Available Greek Documents with the Standard Text of Stephen's Third Edition* (London: Bernard Quaritch, 1929), I, pp. 330–37, proposed a date at the beginning of the sixteenth century (p. 330).

83 The examination of the manuscript (24–25 August 2020) was done by Martin Karrer (the author of that contribution), Dr Beate Noack (Zittau) and Dr Patrick Andrist (LMU Munich). We could identify the scribe, Thomas Bitzimanos, who worked on Crete in the last decades of the fifteenth and perhaps the first years of the sixteenth century. The codex came from there to the West. Rahlfs, *Verzeichnis*, p. 325, assumed that the manuscript was used for the reprint of the Aldine in Strasbourg 1526; see below section 3.4.4. The codex was donated to the library of Zittau by Johann Fleischmann in 1620.

84 Collections of the whole Septuagint without New Testament part (esp. Ra. 46; whole Septuagint without Psalms) and secondary bindings of LXX writings (Ra. 52 Florence Bibl. Laur., Acquisti 44; Genesis to Tobit) are evidenced.

The second part of the Septuagint (Psalms, Wisdom Books and Prophetic Books) is excluded in the pandect of Zittau, perhaps due to the beginnings of the print.[85] Nevertheless, the Cretian manufacture interpreted the selection of the 'histories' and New Testament writings as a kind of full Bible. The layout of the LXX and NT folios in the codex is identical (every page has thirty lines, the same frame, etc.) and the preserved original binding covers all the books (LXX and NT) in one volume.

I will consult the younger pandects alongside the old ones in order to delineate the characteristic features concerning our theme. Future research may broaden the material by looking at the lemmata of commentaries, lectionaries[86] and multi-text manuscripts[87] combining LXX and NT writings (I do not treat these additional manuscripts in the present contribution).

2.2. The Use of the Greek Language for All Biblical Writings

A first aspect of all the mentioned pandects is obvious and, nonetheless, essential: the dominance of the Greek language. That dominance was self-evident for the New Testament but not *eo ipso* for Israel's Scriptures. For the Jewish custom to use Greek translations and nevertheless to hand down the Hebrew scriptures was fairly known through the centuries.

Indeed, Origen took into regard both languages in his Hexapla. He presented the Hebrew text (square script and transliteration) along with the Septuagint and the other Greek versions current in the Jewish communities of the Roman and Parthian empires (Aquila, Symmachus, Theodotion).[88] Sure, the Hebrew columns of the Hexapla were less widely read and distributed.[89] The Christian communities basically lived with the Greek texts of the Jewish Scriptures.[90] But it would be a mistake to forget the Jewish neighborhood in the decisive times up to the sixth century: The Septuagint was read publicly by Jewish communities on Sabbaths up until the early third century according

---

85 A Greek-Latin Psalter was edited by Johannes Crastonus in Milan 1481 (incunable M36246). Greek Psalters were printed by Alexandros of Crete in Venice 1486 (incunable M36247) and by Aldus Manutius in Venice 1497 (ed. by Justinos Dekadyos; incunable M36248); cf. Felix Albrecht, 'Report on the Göttingen Septuagint', *Textus*, 29 (2020), 201–20 (pp. 205–07). Perhaps an early print of the Prophets was expected but did not happen.

86 Jongkind, 'Manuscripts', identifies the following lectionaries and Byzantine commentary manuscripts combining parts of LXX and NT: Codex Sancti Symeonis, Domschatz Trier (lectionary from the tenth century; no Ra. number; GA ℓ 179); P.Mich. Inv. 3718 (commentary of the seventh century quoting Proverbs and Gospels; Ra. 890, no GA number); cf. London, Lambeth Palace, Sion College, Arc L 40.2/ G1 (GA ℓ 234 from eleventh to twelfth century, prophetologion of the eight century in underwriting).

87 Multi-text-manuscripts of the New Testament sometimes hold extracts from the Septuagint, e.g. GA 792. I thank Darius Müller, Wuppertal, for that hint.

88 For the complex genesis and distribution of the Hexapla / Tetrapla see Gentry, 'Origen's Hexapla'.

89 Only fragments survived; cf. John D. Meade, *A Critical Edition of the Hexaplaric Fragments of Job 22–42* (Leuven: Peeters, 2020).

90 The correction of Jerome came later and did not affect the Greek transmission of the Bible.

to Tertullian.[91] It was only slowly superseded by the so called 'younger' translations, again translations, as must be remarked here, and Greek textual forms persisted besides the Hebrew text (up to the middle Byzantine era and later on; cf. § 2.8.1). A peculiar interest in the Greek language, therefore, must be noted in both, the Jewish and the Christian contexts of the late Roman or early Byzantine era, respectively; I sum up in a

> *thesis 4*: Whoever reads the full Bibles of the fourth to sixth centuries, will place himself or herself back to Greek Judaism and Greek Christianity and will use Hebrew parallel texts only in a second step for recognizing intertextual relations.

2.3. The Absence of the Term 'Septuagint' in the 'inscriptiones'

The pre-Constantinian manuscripts sometimes envisaged a collection of the whole Septuagint (as we saw in sections 1.1 and 1.2). But the scribes did not realize that idea. Moreover, they did not introduce the term 'Septuagint' into the 'inscriptiones' of the Pentateuch or any other collection. The consequences are remarkable:

The beginning of Genesis is destroyed in ℵ and B. Though, there is no indication that we should insert a denomination for the whole collection into the manuscripts. A scribe added the 'inscriptio' 'Genesis' in codex A (before Genesis 1. 1) without introducing a title for a greater collection of the 'Septuagint' at that place.

Central element	Main manuscript	Correlated forms	Hint
παλαιὰ ἁγία γραφή	Ra. 131 (11th cent.)	short form: ἡ παλαιά Ra. 76 (13th cent.)	young development: πᾶσα παλαιὰ γραφὴ καὶ νέα B supplement
βιβλίον λεγόμενον παλαιόν	Ra. 527 (14th cent.)	ἀρχὴ - τοῦ παλαιοῦ (scl. βιβλίου) Ra. 125 (14th cent.) and Ra. 53 (from 1439) - παλεῶν (= παλαιῶν, scl. βιβλίων) Ra. 707 (late?)	
συνθήκη ἡ παλαιά	Ra. 319 (MS from 1021, but the 'inscriptio' may be younger)	variant: ἡ παλαιὰ διαθήκη (Ra. 346; 17th cent.)	other examples with the 'inscriptio' διαθήκη are not known
cf. ὀκτάτευχος	Ra. 59 (15th cent.)		collection of the books Genesis – Ruth
cf. ἱστορίαι πᾶσαι	Ra. 107 (from 1334) and Ra. 44 (about 1500)		collection of the books Genesis – Tobit

Table 1. Motifs in the 'inscriptiones' of Genesis-manuscripts indicating collections of the Septuagint or of parts of the Septuagint.[92]

---

91 Tertullian, *apol.*, 18, narrates the legend on the publication of the translation by the seventy under Ptolemy and adds: 'sed et Iudaei palam lecitant […] vulgo aditur sabbatis omnibus'; 'but the Jews, too [and implicitly not only Christians] read (scl. the Greek texts) publicly […] all have access on the Sabbaths'.

92 The 'inscriptiones' of the manuscripts which were used in front of the book Genesis up to the fifteenth century are listed in Wevers, *Genesis*, p. 75.

Indeed, all the 'inscriptiones' of manuscripts listed in table 1 are younger. These younger 'inscriptiones' allow for some variety but prefer the idioms 'Old Scripture' (παλαιὰ γραφή or similar) and 'Old Book' or 'Old Books' (βιβλίον παλαιόν or similar; see table 1). I will return to these expressions later on. One observation, however, must be mentioned already here:

The term 'Septuagint' belongs to the old narratives on the translation of the Tora (see the legend of the Septuagint since Aristeas) and is used by the Church Fathers for additional books successively. Justin refers οἱ ἑβδομήκοντα ('the Seventy') also to the Prophets (dial., 68. 7; besides αἱ γραφαί dial., 68. 8). Irenaeus (adv.haer., III. 21. 2) and Augustine (Aug.civ., XVIII. 42–44) mean the most or all the pre-Christian biblical books when speaking of 'the Septuagint'.[93] Nevertheless, the term is not introduced into the textual transmission in itself. An 'inscriptio' like οἱ ἑβδομήκοντα ('the Seventy') is missing in the pandects and the Greek Genesis manuscripts up to the end of the Byzantine time. We must be conscious of this peculiarity when speaking of the manuscripts (despite the fact that we cannot avoid the term).

2.4. The Arrangement of the Books Used by Jews and Christians

The scribes of the pre-Constantinian time did not constitute an unanimously accepted overall order of the old writings which should be collected in the pandects. The Byzantine scriptoria, therefore, had to master the arrangement of the Septuagint books.

2.4.1. Old Groupings of the Scriptures

The frame for the possible decisions stretches back to the pre-Constantinian times. Three groups of scriptures had crystallized in Judaism up to the first century and were acknowledged in Christianity: the Torah / Nomos or Μωϋσῆς (cf. Acts 15. 21), the Prophets — understood in the wide sense of the today's historical and prophetical books — and the other Writings, i.e. the poetical and sapiental books. These were all in all twenty-two or twenty-four books (Josephus, Ap., I. 37–42;[94] IV Esdras 14. 44–46).[95]

The long portion of 'the prophets' included so many divergent and long writings that it was divided now and then in the second century. It seems that Justin and the earliest Christian manuscripts (up to Pap. 967 Ra.) did not yet participate

---

93 For the use by Cassiodorus see fn. 143.
94 See the comments in John M. G. Barclay, *Flavius Josephus: Translation and Commentary* (Leiden: Brill, 2007), X. Against Apion, pp. 28–33.
95 See Emanuel Tov, *Textual Criticism of the Hebrew Bible*, 3rd edn (Minneapolis: Fortress Press, 2012), pp. 129–31. The ideal number twenty-two or twenty-four of the books is embedded into the Hellenistic world: Guy Darshan, 'The Twenty-Four Books of the Hebrew Bible and Alexandrian Scribal Methods', in *Homer and the Bible in the Eyes of Ancient Interpreters*, ed. by Maren Niehoff, JSRC, 16 (Leiden: Brill, 2012), pp. 221–44 (p. 227), compares the number of the Homeric books (twenty-four) and of the letters of the Hebrew alphabet.

in such a separation (see section 1.1). But it is explicitly attested to in a letter of Melito from Sardes (died *c*. 180) which is quoted in Eus., *h.e.*, IV. 26. 13–14: Melito narrates there that he travelled to the East (i.e. to the Eastern centers of Judaism and early Christianity) to get information on 'the books of the old covenant' (τὰ τῆς παλαιᾶς διαθήκης βιβλία), their number and order (τάξις). He recorded the data he obtained in a list using the book titles of the Greek tradition (Genesis, Exodos, etc.)[96] and separating the Historical Books from the Prophets. Only the Historical Books (the first part of the Prophets in the older perspective) follow the Torah in his arrangement (Joshua, Judges, Ruth, I–IV Kingdoms, I–II Chronicles). The Psalms, the Proverbs, etc. come after the Chronicles, and the end of the list (after Job) is formed by the Prophets (Isaiah, Jeremiah, Dodekapropheton, Daniel and Ezekiel). Esdras (maybe Esra-Nehemia) is appended to the Prophets. Esther is not mentioned.

Melito did not disclose if he found this order in Jewish or in Christian communities and how far he himself was active in the rearrangement of the books. The perspective on the 'old covenant' is surely Christian. Nevertheless, the splitting of the prophets was perhaps already established in Jewish communities and only filled up by him,[97] for Melito's order does not agree with the preserved Christian manuscripts of his time. I mentioned the other system of the 'Prophets' in Pap. 967 Ra.[98] and can add at least one aspect of the manuscript cited in the colophon of Esther (‎א; see section 1.2); it appended Esther to Kingdoms whereas Melito excluded Esther from his list.[99]

Thus, Melito is presenting nothing more than a possible order, although the splitting of the Historical and Prophetic Books and the intermediate placement of the Wisdom Books was successful later on:

---

96 His order of the Pentateuch is unique: Arithmoi (Numbers) follows Exodos, and Levitikon is becoming the fourth book.

97 See for the discussion Peter Brandt, *Endgestalten des Kanons: Das Arrangement der Schriften Israels in der jüdischen und christlichen Bibel* (Berlin: Philo, 2001), pp. 73–77; Edward Earle Ellis, *The Old Testament in Early Christianity: Canon and Interpretation in the Light of Modern Research*, WUNT, 54 (Tübingen: Mohr Siebeck, 1991), pp. 10–12; Edmon L. Gallagher, *Hebrew Scripture in Patristic Biblical Theory: Canon, Language, Text*, Supplements to Vigiliae Christianae, 114 (Leiden: Brill, 2012), pp. 21–24.

98 The Historical Books were included in the 'Prophets', the order of Ezekiel and Daniel differs from Melito, etc.

99 Moreover, the scriptorium of *Codex Sinaiticus* which used the old codex, does not insert Wisdom Books between the historical narratives and the Prophetic Books; see below.

Codex Vaticanus[100]	Codex Sinaiticus[101]	The order of the Greek Bible according to Cassiodorus, *inst.* I. 14. 1
Genesis to Deuteronomy	Genesis to Deuteronomy (w/o Exodus)	Genesis to Deuteronomy
Historical Books (Joshua to II Chronicles and II Esdras)	Historical Books (only Joshua, Judges, I Chronicles, II Esdras)	Joshua, Judges. Ruth I–IV Kingdoms, I–II Paralipomena
Psalms	Esther, Tobit, Judith, I Maccabees,	Psalms
Wisdom Books (Job between	IV Maccabees	Wisdom Books
Canticles and Wisdom, Sirach at	Isaiah, Jeremiah and Lamentations	Prophets: Isaiah, Jeremiah, Ezekiel,
the end)	(Ezekiel and Daniel are missing)	Daniel, Dodekapropheton
Esther, Judith, Tobit	Minor Prophets (Joel to Malachi)[103]	Job
Minor Prophets	Psalms	Tobit, Esther, Judith, I–II Esdras, I–II Maccabees
Isaiah, Jeremianic literature, Ezekiel, Daniel[102]	Books of Wisdom (Proverbs to	
(not included: I–IV Maccabees, Odes, Psalms of Solomon)	Sirach and — at the close — Job)	
Gospels	Gospels	Gospels
Acts	Pauline Letters (including Hebr)[104]	Acts
Catholic Letters	Acts	Catholic Letters (without Jude)
Pauline Letters up to Hebrews 9. 14	Catholic Letters	
(lost or not included: last chapters of Hebrews, Pastorals, Revelation)	Revelation Barnabas and Hermas	Pauline Epistles (Hebrews is not mentioned) Revelation

Table 2. The arrangement of scriptures in the so-called full Bibles from 4th century (Codices Vaticanus and Sinaiticus) and the transfer of the Greek Bible to the Latin West (Cassiodorus).[105]

---

100 Details of the arrangement, the structure of collections and the quires of B are described by Andrist, 'Au croisement', pp. 17–22.
101 Details of the arrangement, the structure of collections and the quires of ℵ are described by Andrist, 'Au croisement', pp. 23–29.
102 Daniel would not be counted with the Major Prophets in the Hebrew text.
103 Aside from Amos and Hosea, Micah is also lacking.
104 Hebrews follows Paul's letters to the churches. This means that 1–2 Timothy, Titus, and Philemon are found after Hebrews.
105 Cassiodorus founded the Monasterium Vivariense in 554 CE and established a library there. A 'Graecus pandectes' was present in the library at the time when Cassiodorus wrote his *Institutiones*. The codex was written totally in Greek, was divided into seventy-five books and was consulted when the Latin Bible (which was preferably used) needed some clarification (*inst.*, I. 14). Three Latin pandects existed in Vivarium. See Cassiodorus Senator, *Einführung in die geistlichen und weltlichen Wissenschaften (Institutiones divinarum et saecularium litterarum): Eingeleitet, übersetzt und erläutert von Andreas Pronay*, Spudasmata, 163 (Hildesheim: Olms, 2014), especially the introduction, pp. 18–20.

2.4.2. Codex Vaticanus

The line starting with Melito was refined up until Athanasius (39th Easter Letter, 367 CE) and Amphilochius (c. 380).[106] The arrangement in Codex Vaticanus (B) accords: The Psalms and Wisdom Books take their place after the Historical Books and before the Prophets. Insofar, Codex Vaticanus leads into the middle of the Christian textual history.[107]

Nonetheless, the open provenance of Melito's order stays,[108] and the text of Vaticanus shows a remarkable interaction to the Jewish textual development in the following special instance:

Hebrew manuscripts from that time are lost. But the Medieval Masorah indicates corrections in some cases by presenting a supralinear letter. One of these corrections pertains to the narration how the Danites set up an idol (Judges 18. 30): The earlier Hebrew reading 'ascribed the erecting of the idol in Dan to one of the descendants of Moses'.[109] The Hebrew correction added one letter in the (unvocalized) name and thus replaced Moses with the despised Manasseh (מנשׁה). The correction was done before the fifth century as b.Baba Batra 109b proves. It disburdened the memory of Moses.

Intriguingly, Vaticanus is the first textual witness for this correction. The codex transliterates the Hebrew alteration and carries the corrected name (Μανασση) in Greek whereas the Vetus Latina and the mainstream of the Septuagint transmission (especially A[110]) confirm the older reading Moses. The scribe of Vaticanus in Judges 18. 30 must have had Jewish contacts.

---

106 Amphilochius Iconisensis, Iambi ad Seleucum, ed. by E. Oberg, Patristische Texte und Studien, 9 (Berlin: de Gruyter, 1969), lines 251–320. See also E. Oberg, 'Das Lehrgedicht des Amphilochios von Ikonion', JbAC, 16 (1973), 67–97; Edmon L. Gallagher and John D. Meade, The Biblical Canon Lists from Early Christianity: Texts and Analysis (Oxford: Oxford University Press, 2017), pp. 149–57.

107 See Heinz-Josef Fabry, 'The Biblical Canon and Beyond. Theological and Historical Context of the Codices of Alexandria', in Textcritical and Hermeneutical Studies in the Septuagint, ed. by Johann Cook and Hermann-Josef Stipp, VT.S, 157 (Leiden: Brill, 2012), pp. 21–36 (pp. 26–27) and Patrick Andrist, 'Le milieu de production du Vaticanus graecus 1209 et son histoire postérieure: le canon d'Eusèbe, les listes du IVᵉ siècle des livres canoniques, les distigmai et les manuscrits connexes', in Le manuscrit B de la Bible (Vaticanus graecus 1209): Introduction au fac-similé, Actes du Colloque de Genève (11 juin 2001), Contributions supplémentaires, ed. by Patrick Andrist, Histoire du texte biblique, 7 (Lausanne: Éditions du Zèbre, 2009), pp. 227–56 (pp. 227–47).

108 Moreover, that order allowed for influences from the Jewish tradition as the mentioned Amphilochius demonstrates: He organizes the Scriptures in Nomos, Historical Books, Wisdom Books and Prophets but restricts the number of books according to the Hebrew tradition. His 'list is the closest of any early Christian author to the Jewish scriptural corpus' as Eugen J. Pentiuc, The Old Testament in Eastern Orthodox Tradition (Oxford: Oxford University Press, 2014), p. 121 writes. Interestingly enough, his poem doubts Esther still (l. 288; cf. Pap. 967 Ra. and Melito); was Esther not only in Christianity but also in Judaism longer controversial than it is normally thought?

109 Tov, Textual Criticism, p. 53.

110 Judges 18 is lost in א.

2.4.3. Codex Sinaiticus

Codex Sinaiticus, on the other hand, roughly conforms to the older tripartite structure of the Septuagint and Tanach known by Josephus (cf. above, section 2.4.1). The Historical and Prophetic Books (i.e. the Prophets in the wider sense) follow the Pentateuch, and the Psalms and Wisdom Books come at the end. Furthermore, the Minor Prophets follow the Major Prophets — an order opposed to *Codex Vaticanus*, but in accordance with the Hebrew Bible.

Thus, elements of both, *Codex Sinaiticus* and *Codex Vaticanus* interact with Jewish traditions. Perhaps, the scriptorium of ℵ reacted to anti-Christian polemics under Julian the Apostate (Heinz-Josef Fabry assumes this). In any case, the old order supported the Christian use of scripture in the sense of a 'presbyteron kreitton'. The knowledge of the Jewish textual order and Jewish variants (cf. B) demonstrated education and continuity to the Jewish tradition. Seen in our sketch of history, the arrangement of ℵ was not due to a 're-Judaization'.[111] Rather, it underscored contacts which had never been lost in the history of textual transmission.[112]

Hence, it is no surprise that the tripartite scheme and the placement of the Sapiential writings in the end of the collection went on in the fifth century. *Codex Alexandrinus* took it up (see fig. 12), and the final place of the Sapiential writings can also be reconstructed in the damaged *Codex Ephraemi*.[113]

2.4.4. Ongoing Divergences

Divergences remained in the order of books after the Pentateuch and Historical Books. I mention the different places of writings like Job within the overall structure of ℵ, B and Cassiodorus's literary description of his Septuagint (see table 2). Evidently, the Christian scriptoria and scholars went on working on questions of order within the blocks of Nebiim and Ketubim in the sixth century and later on.[114]

One aspect is of special interest: Analog discussions are, *mutatis mutandis*, exposed by the Jewish reports in b. Baba Batra 14b (fifth or sixth century).[115] The research on

---

111 But cf. Fabry, *Biblical Canon*, pp. 29–31.
112 The special situation following the persecutions must be taken into consideration, too: The Christian communities needed pre-texts for the replacements of their manuscripts lost in the time of persecution. Jewish manuscript loans facilitated Jewish influences.
113 Rahlfs and Fraenkel, *Verzeichnis*, p. 468 attribute a 'deutliche Orientierung am hebr. Kanon' to *Codex Venetus* too.
114 The transfer of the Septuagint into a Latin context by Cassiodorus needs more attention than it can be given here: Cassiodorus describes his arrangement of the biblical books in *inst.*, I. 1–9 and the order of the Septuagint in *inst.*, I. 14 (see table 2). The arrangements differ; the Psalms follow to the Historical Books in Cassiodorus's Septuagint, but to the Prophets in his own arrangement (I. 4), etc. A comparison to the *Codex Amiatinus* may be added; cf. Bonifatius Fischer, 'Codex Amiatinus und Cassiodor', *BZ*, 8 (1962), 57–79; Karen Corsano, 'The First Quire of the Codex Amiatinus and the *Institutiones* of Cassiodorus', *Scriptorium*, 41 (1987), 3–34.
115 Text with translation in <https://www.sefaria.org/Bava_Batra.14b?lang=bi> [accessed 9 April 2020].

contacts between Christianity and Judaism in the transmission of biblical texts which has started in the 1980s[116] must go on.[117]

I add an eye-catching variant in the corrections of *Codex Sinaiticus*. The most prominent stream of the Septuagint transmission transposed Malachi 3. 22, a verse speaking of Moses, and the prospect of the day of the Lord. That made the memory of Moses the last word of the Dodekapropheton, against the Hebrew text of Malachi 3. 22–24 (4. 4–6 in LXX[B,A]).[118] Yet, not only so-called Lucianic manuscripts disagree; a later corrector of *Sinaiticus* (cb2) reestablishes the Hebrew order too (correcting signs on fol. 87[b] ad loc.). We do not know whether the corrector claimed an acquaintance with the Hebrew text, but in effect his correction matches the mainstream of the Jewish textual transmission.

---

116 See for the discussion on the 'Wiener Genesis' (sixth century) Karl Clausberg, *Die Wiener Genesis: Eine kunstwissenschaftliche Bildergeschichte* (Frankfurt: Fischer, 1984), pp. 7–10 (concerning the story of Joseph on fol. 13, 31 and 32); Barbara Zimmermann, *Die Wiener Genesis im Rahmen der antiken Buchmalerei: Ikonographie, Darstellung, Illustrationsverfahren und Aussageintention* (Wiesbaden: Reichert, 2003) and Pınar Serdar Dinçer, 'The Vienna Genesis in the Light of Early Byzantine Illuminated Theological Manuscripts', in *The Bible in Byzantium: Appropriation, Adaptation, Interpretation*, ed. by Andreas Külzer and Claudia Rapp (Göttingen: Vandenhoeck & Ruprecht, 2019), pp. 47–67 (pp. 51–52).

117 Cf. section 2.8. The theory that Judaism abandoned and refused the Septuagint in Byzantine times has been challenged by recent research: see Jonas Leipziger, *Lesepraktiken im antiken Judentum: Rezeptionsakte, Materialität und Schriftgebrauch*, Materiale Textkulturen, 34 (Berlin / Boston: De Gruyter, 2021), esp. pp. 222-229.

118 Old Greek according to Alfred Rahlfs and Robert Hanhart, *Septuaginta: Editio altera* (Stuttgart: Deutsche Bibelgesellschaft, 2006), II, p. 565 ad loc. and *Duodecim prophetae*, ed. by Joseph Ziegler, Septuaginta Vetus Testamentum Graecum, XIII (Göttingen: Vandenhoeck & Ruprecht, 1984), p. 339 ad loc.

Basilianus (resp. Venetus; Ra. V)	Pariathoniensis (Ra. 198, NT GA 33)	Biblia Leonis (Ra. 55; vol. II reconstructed according to the miniatures)	Vienna ÖNB Cod. Theol. gr. 23[119]
Pentateuch	Fragments of	Pentateuch	Genesis to Deuteronomy
Joshua, Judges, Ruth		Joshua, Judges, Ruth	Historical Books (Joshua
I–IV Kingdoms	III Kingdoms	I–IV Kingdoms	to II Chronicles and II
I–II Paralipomena		I–II Paralipomena	Esdras)
(Psalms and Odes?)	and II–III Maccabees	III Esdras and II Esdras	Esther, Judith, Tobit, I–III
Job and Wisdom Books		Judith, Esther, Tobit, I–IV	Maccabees
Dodekapropheton	Dodekapropheton	Maccabees, Job	Psalms
Isaiah, Jeremiah, Ezekiel,	Prophetae maiores (parts	Psalms and Odes	Wisdom Books (Job and
Daniel	lost)	(lost vol. II:	Proverbs to Sirach)
Hagiographs (Tobit – IV		Wisdom Books	Isaiah, Jeremianic
Maccabees)	(Psalms?)	Dodekapropheton	literature, Ezekiel, Daniel
		Prophetae maiores	Minor Prophets (Hosea
(NT lost)			to Malachi)
	Gospels	Gospels	Gospels
	Acts	Acts	Acts (inscriptio + 1,1–13)
	Catholic Letters	Catholic Letters	Act-Hypothesis, etc.
probably in the end:	Pauline Epistles	Revelation	Praxapostolos (Acts 1
Esther, I–II Esdras	(end is lost)	Pauline Epistles)	iterum)
			Pauline Epistles
			Revelation

Table 3. The reconstructed arrangement of scriptures in the pandects of the 8th to 10th century (parts of all these pandects are lost)[120] and the arrangement of the Bible of Vienna (end of 12th or 13th century).

2.4.5. The Middle Byzantine Period and the Bible of Vienna

The arrangement of the Prophets, Hagiographs and Wisdom Books remained fluid in the Middle Byzantine Period. For some centuries, the Major Prophets followed to the Dodekapropheton preferentially (V; Ra. 198; Ra. 55; see table 3). Then, the Dodekapropheton was postponed to the end of the Septuagint as is shown by the Bible of Vienna (ÖNB Codex Theol. gr. 23; late twelfth or thirteenth century).

---

119 <https://search.onb.ac.at/primo-explore/fulldisplay?docid=ONB_alma21395498920003338& context=L&vid=ONB&lang=de_DE&search_scope=ONB_gesamtbestand&adaptor=Local%20 Search%20Engine&tab=default_tab&query=any,contains,Cod.%20Theol.%20gr.%2023&offset=0> [accessed 12 April 2020].

120 See the more detailed data in Andrist, 'Au croisement', p. 29.

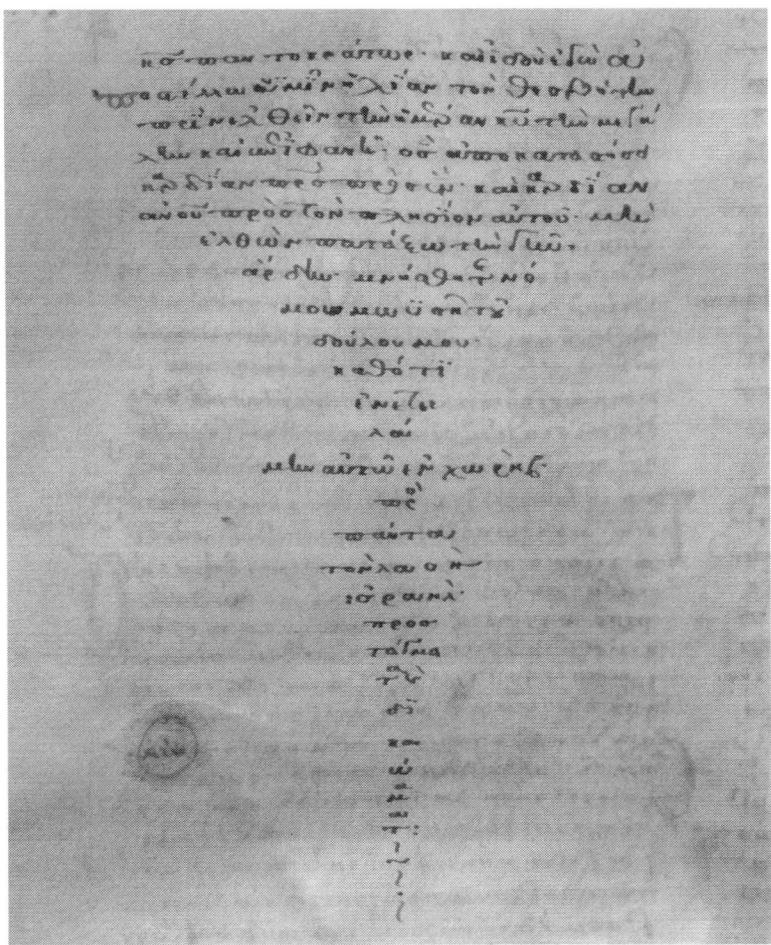

Fig. 9. LXX-Malachi 4. 3–6 (par. MT-Malachi 3. 23–24, 22) in
Codex Theol. gr. 23, Österreichische Nationalbibliothek Wien, fol. 485ᵛ.[121]

Moreover, the Bible of Vienna contains the important transposition of the last
verses of Malachi contrary to the Hebrew Bible and contrary to the corrector of *Codex
Sinaiticus*. Nevertheless, it would be wrong to read an anti-Jewish affect here. The
scribe puts into sharp relief just LXX-Malachi 4. 6 (3. 22 in MT): μνήσθητε νόμου
Μωυσῆ τοῦ δούλου μου καθότι ἐνετειλάμην αὐτῷ ἐν Χωρηβ πρὸς πάντα τὸν Ισραηλ
προστάγματα καὶ δικαιώματα, 'remember the law of Moses [...] as I commanded

---

121   Fig. 9: Österreichische Nationalbibliothek Wien; cf. <https://ntvmr.uni-muenster.de/manuscript-
workspace> [accessed 11 April 2020] ad loc. (via GA min. 218).

him […] for all Israel' (fig. 9, lines 8–29). The last word of the Septuagint cherishes Moses and the words of God given to Israel.

This observation will disappoint everyone who expects a great gesture in the Greek Christian pandects connecting the hope for Elijah (Malachi 3) with John the Baptist (Matthew 1). The Septuagint in the Greek Bible is, so to speak, more obliged to Moses in all phases of its development than the modern Western Bible translations are.[122]

All in all, our observations result in

thesis 5: Jewish-Christian contacts concerning the biblical texts outlasted the parting of the ways. The Jewish roots of the Septuagint remain sustainably relevant throughout time.

2.5. The Place of the New Testament in the Pandects

What place should be given the New Testament in the overall order of the collection? The pre-Constantinian sources used the sequence older Scripture — younger Scripture (PapOxy VIII 1075/1079) as well as the way from a New Testament quotation to the older text (P. Oslo 1661; p. Amherst I 3; cf. P. Oslo Inv. 1644). The full Bibles of the fourth and fifth century, however, only pondered the first possibility. The scriptoria unanimously decided to place the Septuagint first.

As a consequence, all the Byzantine scriptoria became obliged by the criterion 'presbyteron kreitton' ('what is older, requires the higher respect'). The Greek pandects respected — as Amphilochius records in his poem on the Scriptures — that the New Testament was 'written second';[123] the praxis is going on up to the supplement of *Codex Vaticanus* and the Bible of Zittau.

Hence, the ancient Scriptures of Israel form the access point to the Scriptures of Christianity until today, not the other way around. All Christian full Bibles proceed from the Jewish to the Christian Scriptures thanks to a decision which prevailed in the fourth century.

That aspect is so evident that it is normally overlooked. I underscore it and state in

thesis 6: Hermeneutically, the Septuagint requires priority in the overall order and intertextuality of the Bible.

2.6. The Interest in the Unity of the Whole Bible

The Greek Bibles intended a great unity of the overall collection which is divided today into the Septuagint and the New Testament. They are less imbued by the categories 'Old' and 'New Testament' as we would think today.

---

122 The Western tradition and modern translations like the sequence Malachi-Matthew but they use the Hebrew text (closing with the prospect of Elijah's return) and often ignore the so-called Apocrypha. See Thomas Hieke, 'Jedem Ende wohnt ein Zauber inne: Schlussverse jüdischer und christlicher Kanonausprägungen', in *Formen des Kanons: Studien zu Ausprägungen des biblischen Kanons von der Antike bis zum 19. Jahrhundert*, ed. by Thomas Hieke, SBS, 228 (Stuttgart: Katholisches Bibelwerk, 2013), pp. 225–52 (pp. 245–48).

123 *Iambi ad Seleucum*, 188 (ed. Oberg; cf. fn. 106): καινὴ [scl. διαθήκη] γάρ ἐστι δευτέρον γεγραμμένη.

2.6.1. The Old Pandects

The matter becomes evident in the old pandects, even if the front pages and parts of Genesis or the whole book Genesis are lost (as it is the case in ℵ, B and C):

The scriptorium of *Codex Vaticanus* (B) did not introduce an interleaf carrying the title 'New Testament' (ἡ καινὴ διαθήκη) nor a *titulus initialis* 'New Testament' above the title of the first Gospel. Codicologically, the cut between Daniel (the last book of LXX) and Matthew is comparable to the cut between II Ezra (the last of the Historical Books) and the Psalms in the *Vaticanus*. The scriptorium marks the end of the foregoing part of the collection by two blank columns in both times (pp. 624 and 1234); and the new part of the overall collection starts analogously on a new page displaying the actual title (Psalms or Matthew, respectively), ornamentation and initial at the first verse (pp. 625 and 1235).[124]

In *Codex Sinaiticus* (ℵ), a quire (qu. 73) is absent after the last book of the Septuagint (Job).[125] But the first page of Matthew is preserved (p. 200r = quire 74, fol. 1ʳ), and again a foregoing line with a *titulus initialis* 'New Testament' lacks.[126]

The same is valid for *Codex Ephraemi Rescriptus* (C). Matthew begins on a new folio (106ʳ) and names only the title of the Gospel (no *titulus initialis* 'New Testament' besides).

All in all, the subtitle 'New Testament' is not used in the internal text of the old pandects. Vice versa, the beginning of the New Testament is lost in *Codex Alexandrinus* (A). The first page of Genesis is preserved, however, and holds the title γένεσις κόσμου ('Genesis of the inhabited world') without a foregoing page or line 'Old Testament' (BL MS 1 D V fol. 5ᵃ).[127]

---

124   The major discontinuity of the codex is found between Tobit and the Prophets (fol. 944ᵛ / 945ʳ) as Andrist, 'Au croisement', p. 22 shows. Maybe, the scriptorium planned two volumes and the beginning of the second volume with fol. 945.

125   It cannot be excluded that it was planned to divide the texts of ℵ into two or three volumes. The volume with the New Testament would have opened with the Prophetic Books if two volumes were planned, or with the Poetic Books if three volumes were planned: Andrist, 'Au croisement', p. 28.

126   Quire 73 was perhaps assigned to the Eusebean Canon-Tables; cf. Jack Finegan, *Encountering New Testament Manuscripts: A Working Introduction to Textual Criticism* (Grand Rapids: Eerdmans, 1974), p. 134. It is not permitted to posit a folio containing the title 'New Testament' into the quire, against Martin Karrer, 'Von den Evangelien bis zur Apk. Die Ordnung der Schriften in der Edition des Neuen Testaments', in *The New Testament in Antiquity and Byzantium: Traditional and Digital Approaches to its Texts and Editing. A Festschrift for Klaus Wachtel*, ed. by H. A. G. Houghton and others, ANTF, 52 (Berlin: de Gruyter, 2019), pp. 249–64 (p. 256). But the interest in a more visible marker at the end of the Septuagint is not modern. A certain Theophylakt will introduce a mention of the New and the Old Testament at this place in Middle-Byzantine times; he adds the prayer after Job: 'O God of the Old and the New Testament […] receive the repentance of […] Theophylakt and make him worthy to obtain of your kingdom' (ὁ παλαιᾶς καὶ καινῆς διαθήκης θς […] δέξαι τὴν μετάνοιαν τοῦ […] θεοφυλάκτου καὶ ἀξίωσον αὐτὸν τυχεῖν τῆς βασιλείας σου […]; ℵ fol. 199ᵇ = quire 72 fol. 8ᵛ).

127   Details of the arrangement, the structure of collections, the quires and paratexts of A are described in Andrist, 'Au croisement', pp. 30–39.

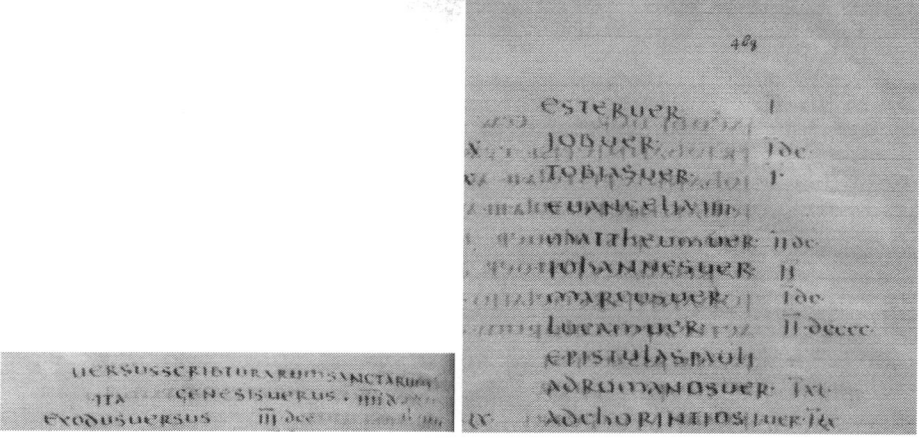

Figs 10a & 10b. Excerpts from the list of verses for the Holy Scriptures in Codex 06 (*Claromontanus*): a (left). from fol. 467ᵛ; b (right). from fol. 468ʳ Col. 2.[128]

2.6.2. The Stichometrical List in Codex Claromontanus

The stichometrical list of books which is inserted between Philemon and Hebrews in *Codex Claromontanus* (06, sixth century) confirms the observations. The list probably utilized a Greek *Vorlage* from the fourth century.[129] It names all the texts from Genesis (cf. fig. 10a) to Revelation equally 'holy Scriptures'. The 'EUANGELIA IIII' follow directly after Job and Tobit (cf. fig. 10b). An organization according to 'New' and 'Old' Testament is lacking.

2.6.3. The Middle- and Late-Byzantine Pandects

Scriptoria keep traditions. Most Middle- and Late-Byzantine pandects are damaged (comparably to the old pandects). Though, the existing evidence is clear:

An interleaf bearing the title ἡ παλαιά διαθήκη ('the Old Testament') is missing up to the supplementation of *Codex Vaticanus* and the Bible of Zittau. Beyond the pandects, the idiom συνθήκη ἡ παλαιά is witnessed in middle Byzantine manuscripts. Though, that idiom signalizes an 'old compound' of Scriptures (see the 'inscriptio' to Genesis in Ra. 319, a manuscript containing the Octateuch, Esther, Tobit and Judith). It must be distinguished from the idiom ἡ παλαιά διαθήκη ('Old Covenant / Old Testament') which occasionally comes into use in a Greek manuscript of early modern times (see the 'inscriptio' foregoing Genesis in Ra. 346; cf. table 1).

---

128 Figs: Bibliothèque nationale de France, Paris.
129 'Genesis' transliterates a Greek title, etc.

Analogously, an interleaf or line with the *titulus initialis* 'New Testament' in Greek before Matthew 1. 1 is missing in Middle Byzantine manuscripts[130] as well as in the Bibles of Vienna,[131] Ferrara and Zittau.[132] The supplementator of *Codex Vaticanus* follows the convention, too, and does not add a note as 'New Testament' (or similar) in front of Matthew 1 (p. 1235).

Nevertheless, the cultural contacts of the fifteenth century bring over some complexity. The supplementator of *Codex Vaticanus* indicates in his 'inscriptio' to the book of Genesis that the codex contains πᾶσαν τὴν παλαιὰν γραφὴν καὶ τὴν νέαν ('the whole old and new scripture'; B p. 1, cf. table 1), and a Latin title page 'Novum Testamentum' is inserted in the Bible of Ferrara (Ra. 106 / GA 582).[133] But these influences are secondary. Even the young hand which adds the table of contents in B lists the biblical books (from Genesis to Revelation) without a partition into the collections 'Old and New Testament' / 'Old and New Scripture' (B page III[134]). Ensuing from the material evidence of the great codices,

thesis 7 results: The New Testament is understood as the last of the inner-biblical collections in the arrangement of the full Greek Bibles. It is less sharply separated from the preceding collections than in the modern editions.

Fig. 11. Excerpt from the table of contents of Codex Alexandrinus BL MS 1 D V, fol. 4[r].[135]

---

130 I mention the indirect evidence of *Codex Venetus* (Ra. V): The last preserved page (Venice p. 163b) contains the *ep. ad Carpianum* of Eusebius and the beginning of the Canon Tables (following on IV Maccabees and a Chronographion). That means that paratexts, not an interleaf New Testament, separated the parts of the Bibles. Andrist, 'Au croisement', pp. 45–55 reconstructs the structure of the whole codex in a plausible way.

131 ÖNB Theol. gr. 23, fol. 485[v] (Malachi) / 486[r] (Matthew).

132 Stadtbibl. Zittau A 1, fol. 543, 545 (Matthew). The Latin 'ordo librorum Biblicorum' in the Bible from Zittau (p. i) consequently neither notes 'Vetus' nor 'Novum Testamentum' (before Genesis and Matthew respectively).

133 That Bible was divided in three volumes. The entry 'Novum Testamentum' is written secondarily in Latin on fol. 1 of vol. III (GA min. 582).

134 For an image see <https://digi.vatlib.it/view/MSS_Vat.gr.1209> [accessed 1 October 2020].

135 Fig. from: *The Codex Alexandrinus: facsimile edition, published by British Library*, Vol. I-IV, 1879-1883, detail fol. 4r; cf. <http://www.csntm.org/Manuscript/View/GA_02> [accessed 6 September 2019].

2.7. The Table of Contents in Codex Alexandrinus (A)

Codex Alexandrinus (A) incorporates a table of contents for the first time (BL MS 1 D V, fol. 4ʳ). The uncial script is roughly from the same period as the hands within the codex (perhaps a little younger[136]); and an important motif is new (end of the 5th, beginning of the 6th cent.):

2.7.1. The Collection of the New Testament

The list uses the subheading 'The New Testament' (ἡ καινὴ διαθήκη) before the Gospels (fig. 11). This seems to be an exception to the noted rule. Yet, the equivalent heading 'Old Testament' is still lacking. The Septuagint Scriptures are placed at the outset and begin immediately with the book of Genesis, without an overarching title (fig. 12). The ongoing list is structured by a series of collections, as we know it from the other pandects. Hence, we have to look at the whole structure, before returning to the New Testament (in section 2.7.3).

Interestingly, not only the New Testament is marked in the table of contents. Other collections are also designated:

2.7.2. The Idea of an Octateuch

The sequence starts with the first mention of the idea of an Octateuch: The writings from Genesis to Ruth are summed up as 'together 8 books' (ὁμοῦ βιβλία η´; fig. 12). The term 'Octateuch' (ὀκτάτευχος) rises in about the same time[137] and will sometimes be used in Byzantine codices (see the 'inscriptio' of Genesis in Ra. 75 and Ra. 59).[138] But the idea of an Octateuch does not cut down the prominence of the Pentateuch (Israel's law) in the Greek pandects. The next table of contents in a pandect, fol. 4ᵛ of the Biblia Leonis (Ra. 55) will, rather, combine the two conceptions. The books

---

136 See Andrew Smith, *A Study of the Gospels in Codex Alexandrinus: Codicology, Palaeography, and Scribal Hands*, NTTS, 48 (Leiden: Brill, 2014), pp. 64, 117. Smith allows for the possibility that the hand may be even 'the personal script of one of the original scribes' (p. 117).

137 The idea of an Octateuch did not have relevance before: Cyril marked Ruth as part of Judges and hence quoted five books of the Nomos, seven books up to Judges in *cat.*, IV. 35. Amphilochius used the term 'Pentateuch' (πεντάτευχος) in his *Iambi ad Seleucum*, 264. The Old Latin tradition liked the Heptateuch; see Pierre-Maurice Bogaert, 'Eptaticus: le nom des premiers livres de la Bible dans l'ancienne tradition chrétienne grecque et latine', in *Titres et articulations du texte dans les oeuvres antiques: Actes du colloque international de Chantilly 1994*, ed. by Jean-Claude Fredouille and others, Collection des études Augustiniennes, 152 (Paris: Institut d'études Augustiniennes, 1997), pp. 313–37.

138 The word ὀκτάτευχος is first recorded by Prokopios of Gaza (+ 538) — see John Lowden, 'Illustrated Octateuch Manuscripts. A Byzantine Phenomenon', in *The Old Testament in Byzantium*, ed. by Paul Magdalino and Robert Nelson, Dumbarton Oaks Byzantine Symposia and Colloquia (Washington, DC: Dumbarton Oaks Research Library and Collection, 2013), pp. 107-52 (p. 107) — and in Latin transcription by Cassiodorus, *inst.*, I. 1. 1: 'Primus Scripturarum divinarum codex est Octateuchus'. The famous illustrated Octateuchs (LXX text with catenae) mainly originated from the eleventh to the thirteenth century; Kurt Weitzmann and Massimo Bernabò, *The Byzantine Octateuchs*, 2 vols (Princeton: Princeton University Press, 1999).

[ΓΕ]ΝΕϹΙϹΚΟϹΜΟΥ·	✝ΑΛΤΗΡΙΟΝΜΕΤΩΔΩΝ
Ε[Ξ̅Ο]ΔΟϹΑΙΓΥΠΤΟΥ·	ΙΩΒ
ΛΕΥΙΤΙΚΟΝ·	ΠΑΡΟΙΜΙΑΙ·
[Λ]ΡΙΘΜΟΙ·	ΕΚΚΛΗϹΙΑϹΤΗϹ·
ΔΕΥΤΕΡΟΝΟΜ[Ι]ΟΝ·	ΑϹΜΑΤΑΑϹΜΑΤΩΝ·
ΙΗϹΟΥϹΝΑΥΗ·	ϹΟΦΙΑΗΠΑΝΑΡΕΤΟϹ
ΚΡΙΤΑΙ·	ϹΟΦΙΑΙΗϹΟΥΓΙΟΥϹΙΡΑΧ
ΡΟΥΘ· ΟΜΟΥΒΙΒΛΙΑ Η̅	ΗΚΑΙΝΗΔΙΑΘΗΚΗ
ΒΑϹΙΛΙΩΝ Α̅	ΕΥΑΓΓΕΛΙΑ Δ̅
ΒΑϹΙΛΙΩΝ Β̅	ΚΑΤΑΜΑΤΘΑ[ΙΟΝ]
ΒΑϹΙΛΙΩΝ Γ̅	ΚΑΤΑΜΑΡΚ[ΟΝ]
ΒΑϹΙΛΙΩΝ Δ̅	ΚΑΤΑΛΟΥΚΑΝ
ΠΑΡΑΛΙΠΟΜΕΝΩΝ Α̅	ΚΑΤΑΙΩΑΝΝΗΝ
ΠΑΡΑΛΙΠΟΜΕΝΩΝ Β̅	ΠΡΑΞΕΙϹΑΠΟϹΤΑΛΩΝ
ΟΜΟΥΒΙΒΛΙΑ Ϛ̅	ΚΑΘΟΛΙΚΑΙ Ζ̅
ΠΡΟΦΗΤΑΙ Ι̅Ϛ̅	ΕΠΙϹΤΟΛΑΙΠΑΥΛΟΥ Ι̅Δ̅
ΩϹΗΕ Α̅	ΑΠΟΚΑΛΥΨΙϹ[ΙΩΑ]ΝΝΟΥ
ΑΜΩϹ Β̅	ΚΛΗΜΕΝΤΟϹΕ[ΠΙϹΤΟ]ΛΗ Α̅
ΜΙΧΑΙΑϹ Γ̅	ΚΛΗΜΕΝΤΟϹΕ[ΠΙϹΤΟ]ΛΗ Β̅
[Ι]ΩΗ[Λ] Δ̅	
[Λ]Β[ΔΕΙ]ΟΥ Ε̅	ΟΜΟΥ ΒΙΒΛΙΑ [......]
ΙΩ[ΝΑ]Ϲ Ϛ̅	
[ΝΑΟΥ]Μ Ζ̅	✝ΑΛΜΟΙϹΟΛΟΜΩΝΤΟϹ
ΑΜΒΑΚΟΥΜ Η̅	Ι̅Η̅
ϹΟΦΟΝΙΑϹ Θ̅	
ΑΓΓΑΙΟϹ Ι̅	
ΖΑΧΑΡΙΟϹ Ι̅Α̅	
ΜΑΛΑΧΙΑϹ Ι̅Β̅	
ΗϹΑΙΑϹ Ι̅Γ̅	
[Ι]ΕΡΕΜΙΑϹ Ι̅Δ̅	
[Ι]ΕΖΕΚΙΗΛ Ι̅Ε̅	
[Δ]ΑΝΙΗΛ Ι̅Ϛ̅	
[Ε]ϹΘΗΡ	
ΤΩ[Β]ΙΤ	
[ΙΟ]Υ[Δ]ΕΙΘ	
ΕϹΖ[Ρ]ΑϹ Α̅ ΙΕΡΕΥϹ	
ΕϹΖ[ΡΑ]Ϲ Β̅ ΙΕΡΕΥϹ	
ΜΑΚΚΑΒ[Α]ΙΩΝΛΟΓΟϹ Α̅	
ΜΑΚΚΑΒΑΙΩΝΛΟΓΟϹ Β̅	
ΜΑΚΚΑΒΑΙΩΝΛΟΓΟϹ Γ̅	
ΜΑΚΚΑΒΑΙΩΝΛΟΓΟϹ Δ̅	

Fig. 12. The table of contents in *Codex Alexandrinus* (BL MS 1 D V, fol. 4ʳ); transcription by Andrew Smith.[139]

of Moses get the first place there (τοῦ Μωυσέως is the first line of content) and are explicitly counted; they are 'together five' (ὁμοῦ βιβλία ε'; line after Deuteronomy). The hint on the 'Octateuch' (ἡ ὀκτάτευχος) is inserted afterwards (after Ruth; see fig. 13).

---

139   The table is taken from Smith, *Study*, p. 67. The original is too heavily damaged for presenting a photo here; but see <http://www.csntm.org/Manuscript/View/GA_02> [accessed 17 April 2020].

2.7.3. The Other Collections of Pre-Christian Books
and the Place of the New Testament

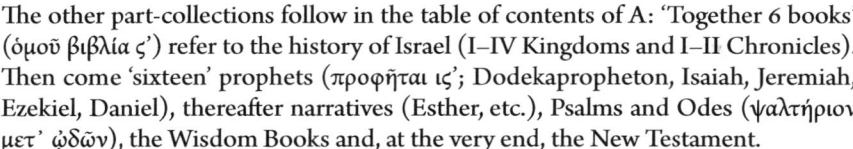

The other part-collections follow in the table of contents of A: 'Together 6 books' (ὁμοῦ βιβλία ϛ') refer to the history of Israel (I–IV Kingdoms and I–II Chronicles). Then come 'sixteen' prophets (προφῆται ιϛ'; Dodekapropheton, Isaiah, Jeremiah, Ezekiel, Daniel), thereafter narratives (Esther, etc.), Psalms and Odes (ψαλτήριον μετ' ᾠδῶν), the Wisdom Books and, at the very end, the New Testament.

The headline of the New Testament collection, therefore, signalizes nothing more than a well-known collection and does not need correspondence in the running text of the Bible. One may compare the handling of the collection of the 'Prophets' (προφῆται). The beginning of the Prophets within the codex is preserved; it holds no more than the headline Hosea (Ωσηε) and the text from Hosea 1. 1 onwards (λόγος κυρίου ὃς ἐγενήθη πρὸς Ωσηε κτλ.; fol. 277ᵃ). It must be assumed, hence, that the interior of the *Codex Alexandrinus* analogously abstained from an interleaf and a headline 'New Testament' on the lost pages of Matthew 1–24. That means that the classification 'New Testament' merely belongs to the table of contents. The running text of *Codex Alexandrinus* did it without the intertitle 'New Testament', analogously to the other old codices.

2.7.4. The Psalms of Solomon

The list does not end with the New Testament. The table of contents uses two systems for counting the books in a collection. The prophets are counted in the headline, the Octateuch, Historical Books and New Testament in final remarks. We find the formula ὁμοῦ βιβλία ('together... books') behind the Christian texts (the numeral is destroyed but the constituent element of the formula is visible). Then, however, a controversial pre-Christian collection is added, the 18 (ιη') Psalms of Solomon.

That indicates an important development of the hermeneutical perspective. All acknowledged texts of Septuagint and New Testament are listed before the controversial Psalms of Solomon. We can say in

> *amplifying thesis 6*: The Septuagint has a hermeneutical priority over the New Testament in the Old Bible Codices, and the Septuagint and New Testament together have hermeneutical priority over disputed books.[140]

---

140 It is difficult to say if the codex V (*Venetus, Basiliano-Vaticanus*) shows a similar phenomenon: Esther and Esdras A/B come after the New Testament (according to the most probable reconstruction). The acknowledgement of these books is not doubted in the time when the codex was written (eighth century). But perhaps the orderer of our codex wished to devaluate Esther and Esdras A/B. An alternative explanation is proposed by Patrick Andrist; he thinks of 'une erreur de fabrication'; Andrist, 'Au croisement', pp. 53–54.

2.8. The Names 'Bible' and 'Divine Scripture' and the Hesitancy to Use the Category 'Old Testament'

A next question emerges from our observations: What will become the best name for the Bible and its parts in the history of the pandects?

2.8.1. The Abstention from the Category 'Old Testament' in the Old Codices

We discovered the hesitancy to use the category 'Old Testament' in the old codices. And yet, the classification Old / New Testament was established in reflections of the Old Church. Melito spoke of the Old Testament (παλαιὰ διαθήκη; see section 2.4), and the combination of 'Old' (παλαιά) and 'New Testament' (καινὴ διαθήκη)[141] was instituted from about 200 CE onwards.[142] In the time of the great codices, the partition is documented, e.g. in the Catechetical Lectures of Cyril of Jerusalem, *cat.*, IV. 33(–37), in Canon 59 of the so-called council of Laodicea and in the mentioned poem of Amphilochius, *Iambi in Seleucum*, 263, 289. Therefore, the abstention from the category 'Old Testament' in the material transmission of the Greek pandects needs an explanation.

One aspect is known already: The Greek scriptures of Israel were mainly transmitted in partial collections, as we saw (Law, Historical Books, Prophets, etc.). Evidently, the notion of a series of collections remained stronger than the overall classification. That aspect, however, does not suffice alone as explanation; the Christian Scriptures formed a collection of collections no less and yet are summarized in the meta-term 'New Testament' in *Codex Alexandrinus*'s table of contents.[143]

A second reason must be taken into consideration, too: The Greek Scriptures of Israel were transmitted not only in Christianity, but also in Judaism. The Christians preferred the Septuagint translation, their contemporary Jewish neighbors favored other versions (Aquila, etc.). Nonetheless, both referred to the same biblical writings, and the classification 'Old Testament' existed only in Christianity (resonant with theological connotations).[144] The Jewish transmission denied it. Said otherwise, the

---

141 For the complex genesis of the term 'New Testament', see Wolfram Kinzig, 'Καινὴ διαθήκη: The Title of the New Testament in the Second and Third Centuries', *JThS*, 45 (1994), 519–44.

142 See, e.g., Clemens Alex., *strom.*, V. 85 and Origenes, *comm. Ioh.*, V. 4.

143 Moreover, Cassiodorus infers the division Old Testament / New Testament into his description of the Septuagint in *inst.*, I. 14. That chapter is of special interest for a second reason, too: It refers the term Septuagint to the whole collection beginning with Genesis and ending in Revelation. Did Cassiodorus use the name 'Septuaginta' for the whole Bible at this place and 'Vetus / Novum Testamentum' for the division which became common in the Latin world? The text of Cassiodorus is not entirely clear (he knows that only the Old Testament books are translated according to the legend of the seventy translators). The Latin development of the term 'Septuaginta' in Medieval times also needs further exploration; first hints in Cornelia Linde, *How to Correct the Sacra Scriptura? Textual Criticism of the Bible between the Twelfth and Fifteenth Century*, Medium Aevum Monographs, 29 (Oxford: Society for the Study of Medieval Languages and Literature, 2012), pp. 8–13.

144 The connotation 'God's old disposition related to Christ' is present from Clemens Alex., *strom.*, V. 85 onwards.

overall structure of the pandects and the restraint against the category 'Old Testament' in the codices implicitly recommit to the Jewish background of the Septuagint Scriptures.

The clarification corresponds to the observations in the preceding paragraphs: Undoubtedly, the Septuagint became a Christian collection in antiquity. But that did not mean, that the Jewish background of the included texts was forgotten. The transmission respected the double inner address of the Septuagint scriptures to Judaism and Christianity.

It may be noted that this implication of the full Bibles does not necessarily request an ongoing interchange with the Jewish neighbors in questions of textual transmission during the Middle and Late Byzantine times. Those contacts, however, existed[145] at least at certain points.[146] It would be wrong to forget them.[147]

2.8.2. The Title 'Biblia'

An unpretentious title shines up in the second preserved table of contents in a pandect. The fol. 4^v in *Vaticanus Reginensis* gr. 1 ('Biblia Leonis patricii', tenth or at latest eleventh century) calls the twenty-five scriptures from Genesis to Psalms 'books' in themselves (see the last line of fig. 13: βιβλία: κε΄)[148] and simultaneously the 'First Book' of the collection in total (τὸ πρῶτον βιβλίον in the headline and πρώτη βίβλος in the 'subscriptio' of the list, respectively; fig. 13). We expect the plural 'Biblia' in the sense of 'the holy Books' as a name for the greater collection from Genesis to Revelation.

Originally, the 'Biblia Leonis patricii' consisted of two volumes. For the list on fol. 4^v does not mention the Wisdom Books, the Prophets, Gospels, etc. Indeed, the miniatures which opened the Scriptures of the second volume are preserved (and famous for their high quality). These miniatures allow the reconstruction of volume II: It extended from the Wisdom Books and the Prophets (Daniel in the end) to the Gospels, the Praxapostolos,

---

145 Some evidence for contacts is collected in section 2.4 above (for the so-called Wiener Genesis) and in 3.5 below (Codex Vat. Gr. 752). Barbara Crostini, 'The Greek Christian Bible', in *The New Cambridge History of the Bible*, ed. by Richard Marsden and E. Ann Matter (Cambridge: Cambridge University Press, 2012), II. From 600 to 1450, pp. 41–55 (pp. 46–48) gives hints on a 'multifaith *Sitz im Leben*' of some manuscripts in Middle and Late Byzantine times. The material evidence for Byzantine Jewish manucripts of holy scriptures in Greek language is rare and fragmentary, but present research assumes that more Greek Biblical manuscripts of Jewish provenance existed: see Leipziger, *Lesepraktiken*, pp. 299-308.

146 Codex F of the Septuagint is of special interest. *Exodus*, ed. by John W. Wevers, Septuaginta Vetus Testamentum Graecum, II 1 (Göttingen: Vandenhoeck & Ruprecht, 1991), pp. 7–8 introduced the siglum F^h for a Medieval corrector using the text form of the MT. Mariachiara Fincati, *The Medieval Revision of the Ambrosian Hexateuch: Critical Editing between Septuaginta and Hebraica Veritas in MS Ambrosianus A 147 inf.*, DSI, 5 (Göttingen: Vandenhoeck & Ruprecht, 2016), proves that the text of codex F was compared to the MT in juncture with the restoration of the codex in the eleventh century. Natalio Fernández Marcos, 'Greek Sources of the Complutensian Polyglot', in *Jewish Reception of Greek Bible Versions: Studies in their Use in Late Antiquity and the Middle Ages*, ed. by Nicholas de Lange and others (Tübingen: Mohr Siebeck, 2009), pp. 302–15 (p. 310), speaks of a 'Jewish corrector'.

147 On the other hand, anti-Jewish polemics must be taken into regard, too: see for the ninth century Kathleen Corrigan, *Visual Polemics in the Ninth-Century Byzantine Psalters* (Cambridge: Cambridge University Press, 1992), pp. 43–61.

148 Cf. section 2.7.2 for the Pentateuch and the Octateuch in the table.

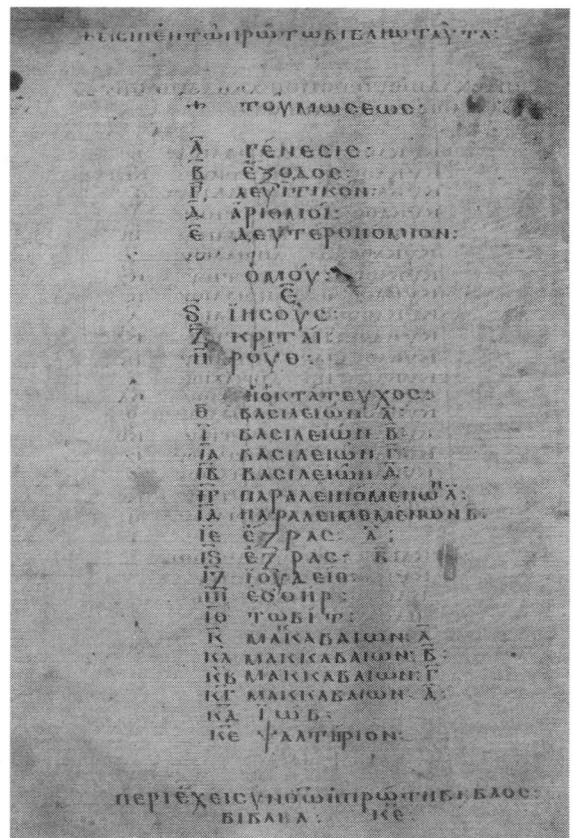

Fig. 13. The table of contents in the 'Biblia Leonis patricii', Vatican Library Reg. gr. 1A (Ra. 55), fol. 4ᵛ.[149]

Revelation and the Pauline Letters. Revelation was placed between Jude and Romans (Reg. gr. 1B, fol. Iʳ; see table 3 and cf. section 2.9).[150] Insofar, the pandect consisted of two βιβλία, and the New Testament was a sub-collection in volume II.

The characteristic usage of the plural βιβλία ('Books') must have started before the ninth century since it spread to the West in late Carolingian or Ottonian times and became the Latin loanword 'biblia' (Bible).[151] The term designated the two-, three- or multi-volume work of the whole Bible consisting of the single biblical

---

149   Fig.: <https://digi.vatlib.it/view/MSS_Reg.gr.1.pt.A> [accessed 17 April 2020].
150   Details in Andrist, 'Au croisement', pp. 64–67.
151   A summary of the difficult etymological discussion for the word 'Bible' is given by Eric Ziolkowski, *The Bible in Folklore Worldwide: A Handbook of Biblical Reception in Jewish, European Christian, and Islamic Folklores* (Berlin: de Gruyter, 2017), pp. 1–3.

writings (which could be called 'books' as well).[152] The fuller term 'bibliotheca' is merely witnessed as a Latin loanword;[153] it reflected the old Latin pandects via the case ('thêkê') holding two, three or more codices. Maybe the word was now and then used for Greek pandects between the sixth and eighth century; but the preserved sources do not prove that aspect.

The extent of the Greek volumes was fluid. A group of Septuagint manuscripts which got relevance for the pandects (see section 2.1) contained Genesis to Tobit (Octateuch, I–IV Kingdoms, Paralipomena, Esdras, I–IV Maccabees, Esther, Judith, Tobit).[154] This volume is shorter than the preserved part of the 'Biblia Leonis patricii'. However, a second book containing the rest of the Septuagint Scriptures (Psalms, Wisdom Books, Prophets) did not gain ground in the Byzantine Period.[155] The collection from Genesis to Tobit was called per se 'the book called the old one' in the colophon of the manuscript from Ferrara (Ra. 107, written 1334). There the scribe notes 'completed is [...] the present book called the old one', ἐτελειώθη [...] τὸ παρὸν βιβλίον τὸ ἐπονομαζόμενον παλαιόν;[156] 'old Book' explicitly means the first part of the Septuagint (the ἱστορίαι / 'historical narratives'),[157] not the whole Septuagint or the Old Testament in the sense of the Latin 'Vetus Testamentum'. Nevertheless, the idea of a whole Bible is implicated; the scribe speaks of the 'present' book evoking that there can be written a second and perhaps a third book (resulting in 'biblia' / the 'Bible').

As a consequence, it was imaginable to combine the great parts of the Bible differently up to the fifteenth century. The Bible of Zittau (Ra. 44; NT GA 664), our youngest pandect, will make it do with the collection from Genesis to Tobit and the New Testament only; Psalms, Wisdom Books and Prophets are missing (as noted in section 2.1). The 'inscriptio' of the first part implies the double notion of 'book'; we read παλαιὸν (scl. βιβλίον) σὺν θ(ε)ῷ ἔχον τὰς[158] ἱστορίας πάσας / [new line] γένεσις βιβλίον α´ (in free translation: 'old [book], written with God and holding all the historical narratives / Genesis, book 1 within the collection'). The New Testament part is not characterized by an own title (fol. 543ʳ [545ʳ] starts with Matthew immediately) but marked as an own entity by the numbering of the quires (see the entry quire α on folio 543ʳ [545ʳ]).

---

152 See for example Chrysostomos, *hom. in ep.Col.*, IX. 1, PG 62:361. The writings of the inner-biblical collections were called 'books' (βιβλία) already in the table of contents of *Codex Alexandrinus* (fig. 8).

153 See Isidore of Seville, *etym.*, VI. 6. 1 and the material evidence, registered in Houghton, *Latin New Testament*, pp. 87–88.

154 That shorter (and nevertheless voluminous) collection spread from the twelfth century onwards: see the list of manuscripts in fn. 76. One may deliberate if there are predecessors in the tenth and eleventh centuries which were even shorter (Ra. 120 and 121).

155 The Prophets (Dodekapropheton and the four Major Prophets Isaiah / Jeremiah / Ezekiel / Daniel) were often combined in manuscripts (Q; Ra. 22, 26, 36, 43, 48, 51, 96, etc.). But the Psalms were usually transmitted separately.

156 Ra. 107 (Ferrara Bibl. Com. Cl. II, 188), fol. 241; transcription by Martini, *Catalogo*, p. 353.

157 See the 'inscriptio' of Ra. 107, quoted above in section 2.1.

158 Wevers, *Genesis*, p. 75, mistakenly proposes the reading εχοντας (lectio continua).

2.8.3. The Title 'Scripture'

The phrase βιβλία / 'Bible' could be combined with γραφή, 'scripture'. The fuller idiom θεία γραφή ('divine scripture')[159] was introduced by the Greek fathers[160] and spread in Latin contexts too.[161] It distinguished the 'Bible' as 'divine Scripture' from the books of daily life. But the short notion was thought sufficient as well.

The explication παλαιὰ ἁγία γραφή is first found in the Middle Byzantine codex Wien ÖNB, Theol. gr. 57 (Ra. 131, eleventh century) and designates the Octateuch there.[162] Insofar, the development may be compared to the use of 'biblion / biblia': The first part of the Septuagint is an 'old scripture' or an 'old book'; it would be wrong to confound the narrower Greek meaning of the idiom with the wide sense of the expression 'Old Testament'.

Yet, the cultural contact of the fifteenth century transforms the perspective. The supplementator of *Codex Vaticanus* who works in that time sums up the pre-Christian writings as πᾶσα ἡ παλαιὰ γραφή ('the whole [!] old scripture') and combines that great collection with the 'new scripture' (νέα γραφή). That way, he understands *Codex Vaticanus* as βιβλίον περιέχον πᾶσαν τὴν παλαιὰν γραφὴν καὶ τὴν νέαν ('book containing all the old scripture and the new'; 'inscriptio' in front of Genesis 1, p. 1).

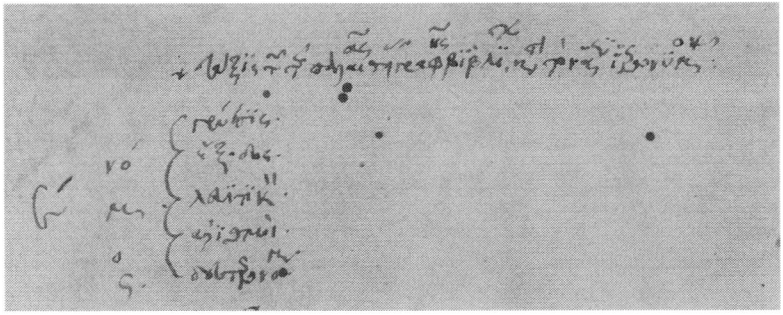

Fig. 14. The reference to Jerome's order of the biblical books in *Codex Vaticanus*, p. iv (detail; image: Bibliotheca Apostolica Vaticana).

The wide sense of παλαιὰ γραφή as 'old scripture' resembling the avoided title 'Old Testament' wins priority from then on. That is shown by a later addendum of the *Codex*

---

159 For example, Athanasius, *de incarnatione*, III. 5 (ed. by F. L. Cross, p. 6); *oratio*, IV. 27 contra Arianos (ed. by W. Bright, p. 244); Theodoret, *de curatione*, 49 (= p. 64 / p. 114 R; ed. by C. Scholten, p. 340); Johannes Damascenus, exp. fidei 92 (IV 19; ed. by B. Kotter, p. 218).

160 See the plural γραφαὶ θεῖαι, too. That plural is used in Origenes, *princ.*, IV. 1. 1 where the Latin version holds 'divinae scripturae'. The Greek version of Origenes, *princ.*, IV. 1. 1 explicates the contents of Scripture as Old and New Testament; that explication is often assessed as a gloss.

161 See, e.g., Cassiodorus, *inst.*, I. 12–14.

162 That codex is of interest also by its marginalia (numerous Greek and some Hebrew annotations): see the codicological data in Hunger and Kresten, *Katalog*, p. 101.

Vaticanus which is less known: A Greek scribe of the sixteenth century[163] introduces the order of the pre-Christian books 'according to Jerome' on the page foregoing the first folio of Genesis. He uses the title τάξις τῶν τῆς παλαιᾶς θείας γραφῆς βιβλίων, κατὰ τὸν ἅγιον Ιερωνυμον ('order of the books of the old divine scripture according to Jerome'; p. iv). The Greek terminology (θεία γραφή, βιβλία) and a Latin perspective (the reference to Jerome) merge (see fig. 14).

2.8.4. The Titles of the First Prints

The first published print of the whole Greek Bible (Septuagint and New Testament), the Aldine (Venice 1518), will nevertheless prioritize the Greek tradition. The printer creates the title πάντα τὰ κατ᾽ ἐξοχὴν καλούμενα βιβλία θείας δηλαδὴ γραφῆς παλαιᾶς τε καὶ νέας, 'All [the books] called quintessential books of the Manifestly Divine Old and New Scripture'. At the same time, Aldus avoids the word 'testamentum' even in the Latin paraphrase of the title 'Sacrae Scriptvrae Veteris Novaeque Omnia', 'All [scl. books] of the Old and New Holy Scripture'.[164] The Bible is, so to speak, the archetypical book. The long Septuagint consists of two parts, called μέρη in Aldus's table of contents (first part Genesis — Psalms, second part Wisdom Books and Prophets), and the New Testament is the 'third part' (the name 'New Testament' is neither used in the table of contents nor in the folio of the print before Matthew 1. 1).

Erasmus will try to put forward a third form of title for the printed New Testament. He calls it 'Novum Instrumentum' in his first edition (1516). But that title flops. Erasmus will correct it and choose 'Novum Testamentum' from 1519 onwards. The Complutensian Polyglot (printed up to 1517, publicly distributed not before 1520) will prefer the Latin titles 'Vetus' and 'Novum Testamentum' from the start.

Thus, via Erasmus and Complutensis the Latin idiom of the Western tradition will become the common name for the parts of the Bible. In consequence, the peculiarity of the Greek Bibles is nearly forgotten today but worth a revival. I summarize the result as

> *thesis 8*: The designations 'Old' and 'New Testament' are avoided in the continuous text of the Old Bibles and used as sparingly as possible in their tables of contents. The Greek textual development recommends speaking unpretentiously of the one Bible (βιβλία) or Divine Scripture (θεία γραφή). That one Bible contains a sequence of internal collections (sometimes called μέρη, 'portions') consisting of single writings (often called βιβλία, 'books' too).

All our observations forbid to promote a sharp separation between the initially Jewish and the initially Christian parts of the Bible. Contacts between Judaism and

---

163   For the image (fig. 14) see <https://digi.vatlib.it/view/MSS_Vat.gr.1209> [accessed 4 November 2020]. The hand (B[36]) is dated by Versace, *Marginalia*, p. 66; see also his transcription (p. 306).
164   The title is digitized, e.g. in <https://www.e-rara.ch/zuz/content/structure/19146217> [accessed 24 April 2020].

Christendom demand more attention in the material transmission of the Greek Jewish scriptures than was thought in previous research.

2.9. The Inner Order of the New Testament

The inner order of the New Testament raised questions, too. The place of the Pauline Letters, the Praxapostolos and Revelation varied.

2.9.1. A Controversial Book: Revelation

The Book of Revelation was controversial in the East from the third century onwards (see above, § 1.3). After the Constantinian shift, Athanasius advocated the book in his famous 39th Easter Letter. *Codices Sinaiticus* (א), *Alexandrinus* (A) and *Ephraemi Rescriptus* (C) included it into the Bible. They always began the book on a new page; *Alexandrinus*, moreover, split Revelation by an empty page (fol. 149^v) from the preceding writing (Philemon). The scriptoria evidently appreciated Revelation and yet marked it as a separated text.

Cyril (cat. 36) and Canon 66 of the so-called council of Laodicea, on the other hand, did not mention Revelation; and Amphilochius had his doubts about it (*Iambi in Seleucum*, 316–19). The doubts increased in the sixth to ninth centuries and even prevailed for a time (what is less known). Nikephoros, patriarch of Constantinople at the beginning of the ninth century, ranged Revelation in the 'antilegomena'.[165] The NT majuscule 044 (a New Testament collection from the ninth to tenth century) ignored it; and the most famous Middle Byzantine pandect, Paris, BnF Gr. 14 (the *Pariathoniensis* or New Testament minuscule GA 33), probably did not contain the work (ninth or early tenth century).[166]

The doubts did not carry the day. But Revelation did not find entry into the Greek liturgy, and the arrangement of the book in the New Testament was less determined than is known today. The next of the pandects, the Biblia Leonis (Vat. Reg. gr. 1, tenth or at the latest eleventh century) placed Revelation among the Epistles, between the Catholic Letters (Praxapostolos) and Romans (cf. table 3). The same order is chosen by the New Testament minuscules GA 1424 (ninth to tenth century) and GA 1870 (eleventh century).[167] By that way, the surrounding letters which were read in the liturgy valorized the book of Revelation. It seems that the scriptoria of these codices were thinking of the epistolary opening in Revelation 1. 4–6 and of the seven letters

---

165   PG 100, 1057–59.
166   Andrist, 'Au croisement', pp. 58–62, reconstructs the order of the codex in two volumes. He does not exclude that Revelation was placed at the end of volume II (containing Prophets, Gospels, Praxapostolos and Pauline Letters). But the structure of quires makes good sense without Revelation, as well as a paratextual hint to Revelation is missing (whereas fol. 73^r–76^v include prologues to the Epistles).
167   GA 1424 contains the whole New Testament, GA 1870 Praxapostolos, Revelation and Pauline Letters. In both manuscripts Revelation is placed between Jude and Romans. Prologues to the Pauline Letters and the martyrion of Paul separate Romans from Revelation.

in Revelation 2–3 and weighted the epistolary aspects of Revelation higher than the generations before them and later on.

2.9.2. The Order of Septuagint and New Testament Books in Later Byzantine Times

In later Byzantine times, Revelation was accepted more and more.[168] The interest in the book increased. A cross-influence between New Testament and Septuagint supported placing Revelation in the end of the Bible, the order which was initiated in the old pandects and prevails today:

- The Septuagint presented the Historical Books after the Nomos. The order of the Wisdom Books and the Prophets varied for a time; but in the Middle and Late Byzantine Period, the Prophets moved to the end successively (cf. section 2.4).
- The New Testament, vice versa, began with the Gospels. The historical book (Acts) took the second place according to imperative old pandects (B A) and the great number of the Byzantine manuscripts. The arrangement Gospels–Acts, hence, corresponded to the arrangement Law–Historical Books of the Septuagint.[169] The Catholic and Pauline Letters (normally in this order in Byzantine times) became the equivalent to the Wisdom Literature.

The parallel structure of Septuagint and New Testament was perfected if Revelation was identified as a Prophetic Book in correspondence to the Prophetic Books of the Septuagint and placed at the end. That was done in the next of our pandects, the Bible of Vienna (Ra. 130; NT GA 218; twelfth/thirteenth century). The order from the Law to the Prophets and from the Gospels to Revelation is found there (see table 3). Said otherwise: The search for an analog order of the Septuagint and the New Testament asserted the acknowledgement of Revelation and helped secure its place at the end of the Greek Bible.

2.9.3. The Medieval Order of the Latin Bibles

Remarkably enough, a similar development occurred in the Latin Bibles. The manuscripts of the Vulgate differed for a long time.[170] Then, in late Middle Ages, the idea of a parallel structure of Old and New Testament evolved. The idea outlived the change to the print medium. We find the parallel structure, therefore, explicated in a table included in a renowned early print, the Vulgate of Lyon

---

168   See Stephen J. Shoemaker, 'The Afterlife of the Apocalypse of John in Byzantium', in *The New Testament in Byzantium*, ed. by Derek Krueger and Robert S. Nelson, Dumbarton Oaks Byzantine symposia and colloquia (Washington, DC: Dumbarton Oaks, 2016), pp. 301–16 (pp. 302–06).

169   The name πράξεις ('acts') which was introduced for the 'acts' of individuals in Israel's history (II Chronicles 12. 15; 13. 22; 27. 7, etc.) had become the title of Acts.

170   See Robert Weber and Roger Gryson, *Biblia sacra iuxta Vulgatam Versionem*, 5th edn (Stuttgart: Deutsche Bibelgesellschaft, 2007), p. xiii. An old list (going back to the 4th century) is preserved in the so-called Cheltenham canon (ed. by Erwin Preuschen, *Analecta* [Leipzig: Mohr, 1893], pp. 138-40). Rev is mentioned there after Acts and followed by 1-3 John. The list is (secondarily?) divided into "indiculum veteris" and "indiculum novi testamenti" in the manuscripts keeping it in the 9th and 10th century.

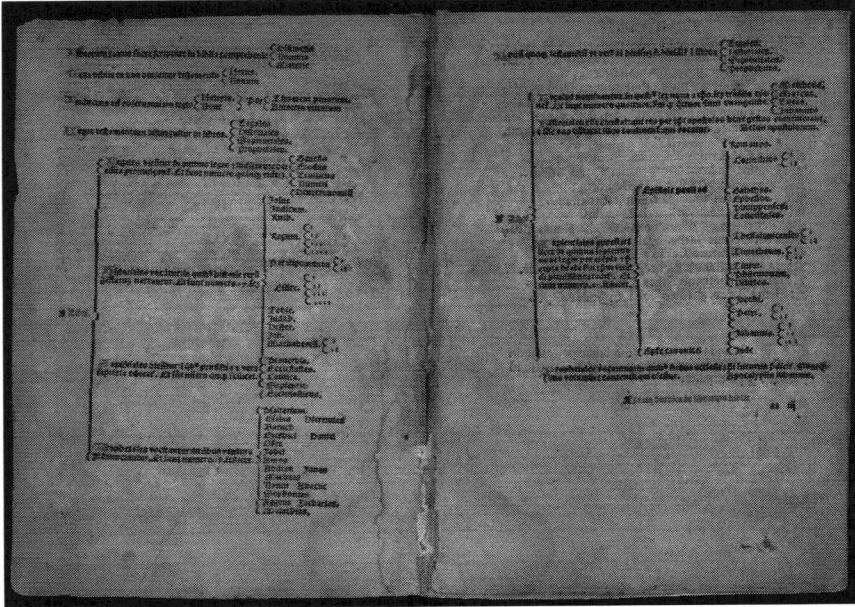

Fig. 15. The 'divisiones' in the Vulgata Lyon 1519, pp. 4–5
(photo from the so-called Stuttgarter Vulgata).[171]

(fig. 15): Both parts of the Bible, the 'Vetus Testamentum' (to the left) and the 'Novum Testamentum' (to the right) contain 'Legales' ('Law' and, respectively, the Gospels which are called 'nova lex'), 'Sapientiales' (Wisdom Books and New Testament Letters, respectively) and 'Prophetales' (Prophets and Revelation, respectively; see fig. 15). [172]

At a glance, the corresponding arrangement from the Law to the Prophets and from the Gospels to Revelation united the Christian Greek and Latin Bibles over and against the order of the Hebrew Bible which ends in the Wisdom Books and the Chronicles. But the arrangement of the Greek Bible paid less attention to the terminology of the Old and New Testament than the Latin Bible; and full Bibles were used so seldom in the East that a continuous production regulating the order of the Bible did not emerge. Hence, the order of the Greek Bible remained fragile, as we will see in the following.

---

171 Fig.: Württembergische Landesbibliothek Stuttgart; cf. <https://www.wlb-stuttgart.de/bibel/01_GENES/0004_005.JPG> [accessed 11 April 2020].

172 The scheme was transferred into the Sistine edition of the Vulgate 1590: see the page between the table of contents and page 1 of Genesis in <https://ia902903.us.archive.org/24/items/vulgatasixtina/Vulgata%20Sixtina.pdf> [accessed 2 May 2020].

2.9.4. The Council of Basel and John of Ragusa

The exchange between East and West expanded in the fifteenth century. The biblical Scriptures were not a matter of dispute at the councils of Basel, Florence, and Ferrara held in the face of Ottoman expansion. But the Greek Scriptures were needed for biblical references, conversations, prayers and worships of the guests. Humanists, in addition, liked the language which was also used by the Greek Fathers and philosophers.[173]

It is no surprise, therefore, that Ivan Stojković (John of Ragusa) who travelled to Constantinople on behalf of the council of Basel (1435–37) also bought manuscripts. He was not able to acquire a full Bible; pandects were rare. But he succeeded in purchasing manuscripts of the main parts of the Septuagint and the whole New Testament. Some of these manuscripts were Greek commentaries holding the biblical text in the 'lemmata'; the only manuscript of Revelation, e.g., contained the commentary of Andrew of Caesarea (min. 2814 GA).

Ivan Stojković brought these manuscripts and codices of the classical authors to Basel.[174] However, the council, which was dominated by conciliarists, had lost its relevance when he returned (1437–38). The manuscripts came to the monastery of the Dominicans due to his estate and stayed in Basel.

Erasmus used the manuscripts obtained by Ivan Stojković in preparing his edition of the New Testament (printed by Froben in Basel 1516). Thus, the Byzantine text collected for the council in Basel provided the potential for Erasmus's New Testament. Yet, Erasmus changed the perspective, as is immediately visible by the print of Revelation: Erasmus neglected the peculiarity of the commentary-manuscript, extracted the 'lemmata' (assisted by a team of the printing house) and printed the text like a Western book (using the Latin *capitula*, etc.) following to the Catholic Letters; the character of the *Vorlage* — being a separate commentary beside the New Testament writings used in the liturgy — was lost.[175]

Erasmus's arrangement of the New Testament became common sense, and the Septuagint manuscripts in Basel are less known. The purchase of Ivan Stojković failed in making the great line of the Greek pandect tradition known to the West.

---

173 An outlook to the end of the fifteenth century is of interest here: The youngest of our pandects, the Bible of Zittau, will be acquired together with a codex containing the works of Plato; the two codices, Bible and Plato are preserved as a twin in Zittau (Stadtbibliothek A1 and A2).

174 See the list of the manuscripts in Andre Vernet, 'Les manuscrits grecs de Jean de Raguse', *Basler Zeitschrift für Geschichte und Altertumskunde*, 61 (1961), 75–108. It is often forgotten that an important part of the manuscripts contains Scriptures of the Septuagint or the text of Septuagint Scriptures in Greek commentaries.

175 See Martin Karrer, *Der Codex Reuchlins zur Apokalypse: Byzanz – Basler Konzil – Erasmus*, Manuscripta Biblica, 5 (Berlin: de Gruyter, 2020), pp. 29–39, 75–87.

2.9.5. The Council of Ferrara-Florence

The Latin-Greek negotiations went on in Ferrara and Florence. There, the council was shaped by papal interests.[176] A full Greek Bible was brought over by the orthodox delegation. The pandect which is preserved in Ferrara contains the Septuagint and the New Testament in three volumes (Ra. 106, GA 582). Latin *capitula* are inserted showing that some Latin readers were expected. The order of the Septuagint is disturbed (the Psalms are added in volume II secondarily).[177]

Surprisingly, the last two lines of II Maccabees have been moved from the end of volume II (the end of the Septuagint) to fol. 1ʳ of the New Testament volume (volume III). Was that juncture from II Maccabees to Matthew caused by an error in the binding? The last words between Septuagint and New Testament rather fit to a special idea of continuous text. For we read: '(anything) of a skilfully prepared text delights the ears of those who read according to the *sequence*. Let here be the end' (τῆς κατασκευῆς τοῦ λόγου, τέρπει τὰς ἀκοὰς τῶν ἐντυγχανόντων τῇ συντάξει. ἐνταῦθα δὲ ἔσται / ἡ τελευτή II Maccabees 15. 39). II Maccabees, the book finishing the last collection of scriptures from the Septuagint,[178] indicates the interest in a sequential reading. The words are used as closing and as transition to the next collection, the Gospels.[179]

Bible of Vienna GA 218	Bible of Ferrara GA 582	cf. NT in GA 209	Bibles of Bessarion: GA 205 and 2886	Bible of Zittau GA 664
Gospels	Gospels	Praxapostolos	Gospels	Gospels
Praxapostolos[180]	Pauline Letters	Pauline Letters	Praxapostolos	Praxapostolos
Pauline Letters	Praxapostolos	Gospels	Revelation	Pauline Letters
Revelation	Revelation	Revelation (added in the 15ᵗʰ cent.)	Pauline Letters	Revelation

Table 4. The Order of the New Testament books in the younger pandects.

Within the New Testament, manuscripts from *Vaticanus* onwards had connected Acts and the Catholic Epistles (as 'Praxapostolos'); the Pauline Letters followed (see table 2 and the Bible of Vienna in table 4). The Bible of Ferrara retained the Praxapostolos yet inserted it after the Pauline Letters. Revelation took the last place as it did in

---

176   See Sebastian Kolditz, *Johannes VIII. Palaiologos und das Konzil von Ferrara-Florenz (1438/39)*, Monographien zur Geschichte des Mittelalters, 60/1–2 (Stuttgart: Hiersemann, 2013/2014), II.

177   See Martini, *Catalogo*, pp. 351–52.

178   The codex was interested in the collections; see the note between Psalms 150 and 151, reacting to the different extent of the Psalter (transcription in Martini, *Catalogo*, p. 352).

179   That intention was broken later on when the Latin title 'Novum Testamentum' was inscribed below the verse from II Maccabees (cf. fn. 133).

180   First verses of Acts two times: see table 3.

the Bible of Vienna (GA 218) and will do it in the edition of Erasmus. The scribe of the pandect justified the presence of the book in the Bible by the inscription 'of the evangelist, the virginal Theologos / the venerable Revelation exists' (εὐαγγελιστοῦ παρθένου θεολόγου / ἀποκάλυψις ἡ σεβασμία πέλει III fol. 106ᵛ; prefixed to the text and formed metrically as an epigram).[181] That way, the worth of Revelation was claimed and the inner order of the New Testament followed the convention (whereas Erasmus will arrange Acts before Romans).

2.9.6. GA 209 and Bessarion

The pandect of Ferrara presents Revelation as part of the New Testament. But another codex, brought to Ferrara by the renowned Greek scholar Bessarion,[182] member of the orthodox delegation, evidences the remaining complexity. This codex (GA 209; see table 4) originally held Praxapostolos, Pauline Epistles (Hebrews at their end, separated from Philemon by a folio) and Gospels in that order which corresponded to the system of lessons in the liturgy (first Epistles, then Gospels). Revelation was lacking, reminiscent of its missing liturgical relevance.

Interestingly, Revelation was added before the council or shortly afterwards. The ecumenical contacts demanded the integration of Revelation in the New Testament collection. The supplementator chose the most common place, the end of the New Testament.[183]

However, that was not the end of the story. Bessarion sustained the vision of a church union after the council and the fall of Constantinople. He became cardinal in the West and titular Latin Patriarch of Constantinople, collected manuscripts[184] and studied their text and arrangement. Finally, he made his own decision. He proposed the order Gospels-Praxapostolos-Revelation-Pauline Letters in the full Bibles which were produced under his direction (GA 205 and 2886). That renewed the order indicated by the Biblia Leonis (cf. above, § 2.9.1).

2.9.7. Emmanuel of Constantinople

Another Greek humanist, Emmanuel of Constantinople, went into exile in England. He constructed the order Pauline Letters-Praxapostolos-Revelation-Gospels around the same time in a New Testament manuscript (GA 69; the so-called Leicester-

---

181 The same epigram is used later in GA 1626 (addition by a younger hand). Emmanuel van Elverdinghe, Munich, is working on that subject.
182 For the biography of Bessarion, see Farnes, *Copying*, pp. 127–28. It is possible that Bessarion and Ivan Stojković (John of Ragusa) knew one another; Welsby, *Textual Study*, p. 9.
183 See Ulrich B. Schmid, 'Die Apokalypse, überliefert mit anderen neutestamentlichen Schriften — eapr-Handschriften', in *Studien zum Text der Apokalypse*, ed. by Marcus Sigismund, Martin Karrer and Ulrich Schmid (Berlin: de Gruyter, 2015), pp. 421–42 (pp. 427–28).
184 One of these manuscripts was the mentioned *Codex Venetus* (V); see Rahlfs and Fraenkel, *Verzeichnis*, p. 372.

codex).[185] His arrangement of the New Testament has one aspect in common with Bessarion's: The book of Revelation which was not accepted in the Greek liturgy is surrounded by the prominent writings used in the liturgical lessons. In other words, the last doubts about the canonical status of Revelation vanished in the fifteenth century (the Western estimation of Revelation did not allow for anything else). But the parallel structure of the Septuagint and the New Testament (which is delineated in sections 2.9.2 and 2.9.3) was not convincing the exiled Greek scholars. They thought a liturgical embedding of Revelation to be of greater relevance than a tying together Greek and Latin Bibles via the same order of books.

2.9.8. The Prints of the Sixteenth Century

The proposals of the Greek humanists died away. The printed full Bibles of the sixteenth century did not concede more than a placement of the Maccabean books between Malachi and Matthew adding III Maccabees against the Vulgate (the Aldine and the Complutensian have the order Malachi-I–III Maccabees-Matthew).[186] All the prints consolidated the place of Revelation at the end of the Bible, and the alternatives of the fifteenth century are forgotten today.

Nonetheless, the discussion makes aware of the differing dynamics in the Greek and Latin transmission of the Bible and the liturgical interest of Orthodox Christianity. At least, one effect of the Greek tradition becomes visible in the *Editio Critica Maior* of the New Testament: Revelation follows the Pauline letters there, as it does in the majority of those Greek pandects which placed Revelation at the end of the Bible (GA 218; 664 and the supplement of *Codex Vaticanus*, min. GA 1957).

I sum up the facts in

> *thesis 9*: The tangencies and differences between the Greek and the Latin Bibles in the late Byzantine time and Western Middle Ages, respectively, exhibit cultural contacts and discussions. Ecumenical endeavors arose but did not supersede the pursuit of an own structure of the Greek Bible fitting to the liturgical interest of Greek Christianity.

Thesis 9 is all the more important as it explains the rare occurrence of Greek pandects *per se*: Full Bibles were not needed in the liturgy.

3. Consequences

The arrangement of the pandects, their titles and development convey significant contributions to our theme. The Christian transmission understood pandects as

---

185 The original order of that manuscript was reconstructed by J. Rendel Harris, *The Origin of the Leicester Codex of the New Testament* (London: C. J. Clay, 1887), pp. 12–16 (using the numbering of the quires). The Gospels were transposed to the beginning of the codex in later times.
186 Both, Aldine and Complutensian have the order Malachi-I–III Maccabees-Matthew.

great collections consisting of parts (or internal collections). The parts followed one another, but nevertheless formed a consistent unit which started with the Penta- or Octateuch and went on in varying order to the Historical Books, the Psalms, Wisdom Books, Prophets and, finally, on to the early Christian writings.

Material transmission avoided the separation of 'Septuagint' or 'Old Testament' scriptures versus 'New Testament'. Indeed, the pandects used neither the title 'Old Testament' nor the title 'New Testament' in the continuous Greek text. Moreover, they ignored the title 'Old Testament' also in the tables of contents and inserted the line 'New Testament' into a table of contents only once (in *Codex Alexandrinus*). The idea of a unified whole Bible was stronger than the theological differentiation between Old and New Testament.

This idea of a union of all the books preceding and following to Christ's incarnation is a Christian theologumenon. Yet, the pandects maintained the pre-Christian Scriptures as such; the material transmission took into regard the Jewish provenance of the Scriptures of the Septuagint as we saw. The textual and theological correlation of Jewish and Christian Scriptures characterizes the pandects.

Do these observations demand consequences in methodology and hermeneutics? I single out some aspects.

3.1. Christian Influences on the Septuagint?
Psalms of Solomon and the 'anointed lord' as a Test Case

Christian add-ons to the Septuagint and alterations in Septuagint writings are less imperative than it was once thought as can be shown in many cases.[187] I take the Psalms of Solomon as an example.

3.1.1. The Psalms of Solomon: A Disputed Book

These psalms belong to the Wisdom Books in most manuscripts which have survived. All the manuscripts are young (tenth to sixteenth century). The only mention of Psalms of Solomon in an old pandect is the table of contents in *Codex Alexandrinus*.[188] This table confirms the title (ψαλμοὶ Σολομῶντος) but separates Psalms of Solomon from the writings of the Septuagint and New Testament (see § 2.7).

The younger manuscripts contain Psalms of Solomon besides the Hexasophion (Proverbs, Ecclesiastes, Canticles, Job, Wisdom, Sirach) or Wisdom and Sirach. The main witnesses are Ra. 253 (twelfth century) and Ra. 260 (tenth century; part

---

187 See the Wuppertal research on the New Testament quotations from the Septuagint summed up in Martin Karrer and Johannes de Vries, *Textual History and the Reception of Scripture in Early Christianity: Textgeschichte und Schriftrezeption im frühen Christentum*, SBLSCS, 60 (Atlanta: SBL, 2013).

188 The text of the Psalms of Solomon itself stood at the end of the codex and is lost.

of the illuminated 'Bible of Niketas'[189]).[190] From there, research deduced the idea of an old collection of Wisdom Books. This conception allowed for the integration of Psalms of Solomon into modern editions of the Septuagint. Therefore, the Psalms of Solomon count today as part of the Septuagint. Alfred Rahlfs placed them at the end of the Hexa- or, respectively, Heptasophion (after Sirach) in his hand edition.[191]

This place of Psalms of Solomon has become controversial in the last decades. The widely read English translation in NETS followed Rahlfs's order (Psalms of Solomon at the end of the Poetic and Wisdom Books).[192] The Septuaginta Deutsch, on the other hand, called into question the old Wisdom Collection (which is not documented in old manuscripts) and appended Psalms of Solomon onto the Psalmistic Literature.[193] Finally, Felix Albrecht (Göttingen LXX, 2018) kept the idea of an old collection of Wisdom Books including Psalms of Solomon, but preferred to place Psalms of Solomon after Wisdom (in agreement with the majority of textual witnesses).[194]

What is the best way for a future edition? Codex Vaticanus breaks off in Hebrews, and Sinaiticus in Hermas. Of course, it cannot be completely ruled out that one of these codices held Psalms of Solomon as an appendix, comparable to Codex Alexandrinus.[195] Nevertheless, the inclusion is very improbable, and what is more: If the inclusion was done, it took place after the last of the included Christian writings (the last book of the New Testament or Hermas). All of the early pandects (B, א, A) exclude Psalms of Solomon from the Wisdom or the Psalmistic Books of the Septuagint. In short, Psalms of Solomon are shown to be a disputed writing and must be separated from the series of collections forming the heart of the Bible, if we follow the early pandects.

The matter becomes even clearer when the younger manuscripts are consulted. These manuscripts prove that Psalms of Solomon obtained the interest of high society in the Middle Byzantine Period. Especially the court liked Solomon's royalty and

---

189 The so-called Bible of Niketas (Ra. 90; Ra. 719+260; Turin, Florence, Copenhagen) contained greater parts of the Septuagint; Hans Belting and Guglielmo Cavallo, Die Bibel des Niketas: Ein Werk der höfischen Buchkunst in Byzanz und sein justinianisches Vorbild, Veröffentlichung der Heidelberger Akademie der Wissenschaften (Wiesbaden: Ludwig Reichert Verlag, 1979). John Lowden, 'An Alternative Interpretation of the Manuscripts of Niketas', Byzantion, 53 (1983), 559–74, set 'the euphonious title "Bible of Niketas"' aside (p. 568) since the manuscript held neither the full Septuagint nor the New Testament.

190 Psalmi Salomonis, ed. by Felix Albrecht, Septuaginta Vetus Testamentum Graecum, XII 3 (Göttingen: Vandenhoeck & Ruprecht, 2018), pp. 236–37.

191 Rahlfs and Hanhart, Septuaginta, II, pp. 471–89.

192 Albert Pietersma and Ben Wright, A New English Translation of the Septuagint and the Other Greek Translations Traditionally Included under that Title (New York: Oxford University Press 2007), pp. 763–76; the Psalms of Solomon are translated by Kenneth Atkinson.

193 Wolfgang Kraus and Martin Karrer (ed.), Septuaginta Deutsch: Das griechische Alte Testament in deutscher Übersetzung, 2nd edn (Stuttgart: Deutsche Bibelgesellschaft, 2010), pp. 915–31, transl. by Klaus Scholtissek and Georg Steins. The Codex Athonensis Lavra Θ 70 can be compared: The core of the collection of miscellanea (today split and damaged) is formed by a Psalms catena and the Psalms of Solomon (Ra. 769); cf. the description of the codex in Albrecht, Psalmi Salomonis, pp. 17–23.

194 That is the place in Ra. 253, 260 and younger manuscripts: see Albrecht, Psalmi Salomonis, pp. 236–37, 237 n. 2.

195 Thus Albrecht, Psalmi Salomonis, pp. 240–41.

wisdom; the 'Bible of Niketas' (the most famous witness) is an imperial manuscript. But noble interest did not prevail in the material transmission as a whole. None of the younger pandects understood Psalms of Solomon to be an integral element of the Bible. The contrary, all pandects exclude them. The development of the pandects depreciates the value of Psalms of Solomon and favors altering the order of the hand edition of the Septuagint.

Said as

> *proposal 1*: The younger pandects should be taken into regard in the edition of the Septuagint besides the old pandects.

As a consequence, the Psalms of Solomon should be excluded from the continuous text of the Septuagint.[196] One may deliberate either to append Psalms of Solomon at the end of the Septuagint — after the acknowledged Scriptures — or to present them in an attachment behind the New Testament Scriptures as the table of contents in *Codex Alexandrinus* recommends.

3.1.2.   The 'anointed lord' in Psalms of Solomon 17–18

Psalms of Solomon 17–18 culminate in messianic hopes. All Greek manuscripts read χριστὸς κύριος in 17. 32.[197] The phrase is used without article, χριστός therefore an attribute to κύριος; the meaning 'anointed lord' results. The same phrase, however, is found in Luke 2. 11 and customarily translated as 'Christ the Lord' there (King James Version, etc.). Hence, the question arose as to whether the Christian idiom influenced the reception and transmission of Psalms of Solomon.

The critique prevailed in the late nineteenth century. An alternative base text was conjectured from a reconstructed Hebrew *Vorlage* משיח יהוה ('anointed of the Lord'): the Greek idiom χριστὸς κυρίου, 'the anointed of the Lord'.[198] Rahlfs accepted the conjecture in his hand edition of the Septuagint (ad loc.). It became common sense for more than a century. The *Novum Testamentum Graece* noted the parallel in the margin to Luke 2. 11 up to and including the twenty-seventh edition; but the twenty-eight edition of the *Novum Testamentum Graece* deleted the reference.[199]

Paradoxically, the alteration of the marginal note in the New Testament happened just as the edition of Psalms of Solomon began to doubt the conjecture which postulated an inner-Greek alteration of the phrase: Robert Wright (2007) included manuscripts which were unknown to Rahlfs (Ra. 655, 659, 3004) as well as the Syriac version, and all manuscripts confirmed χριστὸς κύριος in 17. 32. The preponderate

---

196 See the cautious deliberation of Scholtissek and Steins in Kraus and Karrer, *Septuaginta Deutsch*, p. 915.
197 See also the genitive χριστοῦ κυρίου / χριστοῦ αὐτοῦ in Luke 18. 1, 5, 7.
198 The conjecture was introduced by Augustus Carrière, *De Psalterio Salomonis disquisitionem historico-criticam scripsit* (Strasbourg: Heitz, 1870), ad loc. (17. 32).
199 A second reference was deleted, too: the reference to χριστὸς κύριος in Threni 4. 20 (discussed below; see the end of section 3.1).

evidence for the phrase 'anointed lord' could no longer be ignored, he stated.[200] Felix Albrecht took the next step in 2018 and challenged the longstanding thesis of a misunderstood Hebrew pattern. According to him, Psalms of Solomon are written in Greek from the beginning. All evidence considered, χριστὸς κύριος is the oldest text ('ursprünglich').[201] The idea of an 'anointed lord' (= an eschatological king legitimized by God) witnessed in Psalms of Solomon and Luke is a facet of Jewish messianism, no Christian innovation (the reference in the margin to Luke 2. 11 must be renewed).

That critical inversion of previous research fits well to our observations in sections 1 and 2. The early Christians transmitted Greek Jewish writings all in all correctly, as we have seen.

Two subsequent matters should be mentioned. First, the reception of Psalms of Solomon is small in all ancient literature, Jewish and Christian.[202] That explains the hesitations of the old and the younger pandects. Said in other words: The theologically fascinating sketch of the time of the Messiah in Psalms of Solomon 17–18 did not suffice for justifying the full admission of a book into the biblical pandects. The acknowledgement of a Jewish Scripture as part of the Septuagint and full Bible demanded acceptance by Jews and Christians.

Secondly, the Septuagint manuscripts (B, A, etc.) carry the phrase χριστὸς κύριος ('anointed lord') in Lamentations 4. 20, too. Here the Hebrew pattern משׁיח יהוה is preserved. At first glance, the conjecture χριστὸς κυρίου seemed even more plausible than in Psalms of Solomon 17.[203] Rahlfs (in the hand edition) and Joseph Ziegler (in the Göttingen LXX) corrected the Greek text consistently (against the manuscripts).[204] But another explanation makes more sense after the re-correction of Psalms of Solomon 17. 32: The translation of Lamentations is older than the formulation in Psalms of Solomon. It seems that the translation of Lamentations created the idiom χριστὸς κύριος ('anointed lord') looking back to the ill-fated history of Judah (the king = anointed lord was captured). Messianic hopes which spread afterwards picked up the new idiom. Read in this way, the expression in Luke 2. 11 takes root in a century-old development of Jewish thought and language.

---

200 Robert B. Wright, *Psalms of Solomon: A Critical Edition of the Greek Text*, Jewish and Christian texts in contexts and related studies (New York: T&T Clark, 2007), pp. 48–49.

201 See Albrecht, *Psalmi Salomonis*, p. 34, for the Greek origin of Psalms of Solomon, pp. 70–76 for the discussion of the evidence, and p. 356 (ad loc.).

202 See Albrecht, *Psalmi Salomonis*, pp. 255–59.

203 See the discussion in the commentaries, e.g. Ulrich Berges, *Klagelieder*, Herders theologischer Kommentar zum Alten Testament (Freiburg: Herder, 2002), pp. 263–64; Johan Lust, 'Messianism and Septuagint', in Johan Lust, *Messianism and the Septuagint: Collected Essays*, ed. by K. Hauspie, BEThL, CLXXVIII (Leuven: Leuven University Press, 2004), pp. 9–26 (pp. 14–15 = pp. 179–80); Holger Gzella, 'Verheißung: Die Zukunft angesichts Gottes', in *Die Theologie der Septuaginta / The Theology of the Septuagint*, ed. by Hans Ausloos and Bénédicte Lemmelijn, Handbuch zur Septuaginta, 5 (Gütersloh: Gütersloher Verlagshaus, 2020), pp. 503–53 (pp. 552–53).

204 Rahlfs and Hanhart, *Septuaginta*, II, p. 764; *Ieremias, Baruch, Threnei, Epistula Ieremiae*, ed. by Joseph Ziegler, Septuaginta Vetus Testamentum Graecum, XV, 2nd edn (Göttingen: Vandenhoeck & Ruprecht, 1976), pp. 490–91; Ziegler cites a part of old versions for the reconstruction of κυρίου.

Whether the proposed modification of the history of messianic terminology will succeed, stays open. But one point can clearly be noted as

proposal 2: All text critical decisions postulating a strong Christian influence on the transmission of the Septuagint should be examined once more. Conjectures which are based on the thesis of a Christian influence on the text of the Septuagint are uncertain.

3.2. Jewish and Christian Texts in the Septuagint: The Arrangement of the Odes

In the fourth and the fifth century, traditions stood in high esteem, as we have seen. Hence, an undercurrent from old to new texts instigated the order of the Bible. The Septuagint collections came first in the great pandects, then the Christian writings. This arrangement set the standard for all of the following full Bibles.

The principle prohibited the introduction of Christian texts into the collections of the Septuagint if it was consequently exerted. There is one exception, however, in Rahlfs's edition: The Odes combine Jewish and Christian Songs and are inserted into the Septuagint.[205] We must therefore control Rahlfs's disposition:

---

205 Rahlfs and Hanhart, *Septuaginta*, II, pp. 164–83; *Psalmi cum Odis*, ed. by Alfred Rahlfs, Septuaginta Vetus Testamentum Graecum, X, 3rd edn (Göttingen: Vandenhoeck & Ruprecht, 1979), pp. 78–80, 341–65.

Codex Alexandrinus	P. Vindob. K 8706 (= Ra. 2036)[206]	Edition by A. Rahlfs[207]
No overall inscription for the collection[208]	No overall inscription for the collection[210]	The title 'Odes' is added[212]
1 Exodus 15. 1–19	1 Exodus 15 (preserved vv. 1–8)	1 Exodus 15. 1–19
2 Deuteronomy 32. 1–43	2 Deuteronomy 32 (pres. vv. 5–43)	2 Deuteronomy 32. 1–43
3 LXX I Kingdoms (MT I Samuel) 2. 1–10	3 LXX I Kingdoms (MT I Samuel) 2. 1–10	3 LXX I Kingdoms (MT I Samuel) 2. 1–10
4 Isaiah 26. 9–20	4 Jonah 2. 3–10	4 Habacuc 3. 2–19
5 Jonah 2. 3–10	5 Isaiah 25. 1–10a	5 Isaiah 26. 9–20
6 Habacuc 3. 2–19	6 Isaiah 26. 1–4	6 Jonah 2. 3–10
7 Isaiah 38. 10–20	7 Isaiah 26. 11–20 (vv. 9–10 omitted)	7 Daniel 3. 26–45
8 Oratio Manasse	8 Isaiah 38. 9 (= inscriptio) and	8 Daniel 3. 52–88
9 Daniel 3. 26–45	10–20	9 Luke 1. 46–55, 68–79
10 Daniel 3. 52–88	9 Oratio Manasse	10 Isaiah 5. 1–9
11 Luke 1. 46–55 (Rahlfs: Od 9a)	10 Daniel 3. 26–45	11 Isaiah 38. 10–20
12 Luke 2. 29–32	11 Daniel 3. 52–61	12 Oratio Manasse
13 Luke 1. 68–79 (Rahlfs: Od 9b)	12 Luke 1. 54–55	13 Luke 2. 29–32
14 Concluding hymn	13 Luke 2. 29–32	14 Concluding hymn
Subscriptio ΩΔΑΙ ΙΔ΄ (= 14 Odes)[209]		
	(The end of the manuscript is lost).	
	Odes 5 and 6 (Isaiah 25. 1–10a; 26. 1–4) are added.[211] The following Odes are missing: A Od 4 / Ra. Od 6 (Habacuc 3, perhaps an omission by chance) A Od 13 / Ra. Od 9b (Luke 1. 68–79) A Od 14 / Ra. Od 14 (Gloria)	Ode 10 Ra. (Isaiah 5. 1–9) is missing in A and Ra. 2036 (P. Vindob. K 8706). It is sometimes integrated into the collection from the Greek-Latin codex R onwards.

Table 5. The Order of the Odes.

The papyrus-fragments show no more than the reception of single Odes.[213] Hence, the development of the collection seems to be young. A small Jewish compendium of famous songs which were not integrated into the book of Psalms (the today's Psalms 1–150/51) probably stood at the beginning. The transformation into a Christian

206 Digital photographs in <https://digital.onb.ac.at/RepViewer/viewer.faces?doc=DOD_%2BZ194671804&order=1&view=SINGLE> [accessed 3 May 2020]; description in Rahlfs and Fraenkel, *Verzeichnis*, pp. 434–35.

207 Rahlfs, *Psalmi*, lists the order of the Psalms on pp. 79–80.

208 The inscriptio of Ode 1 serves as beginning of the collection: (α) ᾠδὴ Μωυσέως ἐν τῇ ἐξόδῳ (*Codex Alexandrinus*, fol. 565ʳ).

209 *Codex Alexandrinus*, fol. 569ᵛ; Rahlfs and Hanhart, *Septuaginta*, II, p. 164 n. 8.

210 The inscription for Ode 1 can be read: α ᾠδὴ Μωυσέ[ως].

211 Isaiah 25. 1–10a and 26. 1–4 are well attested in the Coptic tradition of Odes (often expanded to Isaiah 25. 1–12 and 26. 1–8); see Rahlfs and Fraenkel, *Verzeichnis*, p. 434.

212 Rahlfs and Hanhart, *Septuaginta*, II, p. 164: 'Inscriptionem ωδαι ego addidi; non est in mss'.

213 See especially P.Mich. Inv. 6427, described above in § 1.5.4. The fragmentary transmission in papyri is going on in the seventh or eighth century: see P.Mich.inv. 1572 (lines of the ode Isaiah 26. 9–10 in form of an amulet).

collection happened tardively and did not become widespread before the fourth century; *Codex Sinaiticus* (ℵ) and *Vaticanus* (B) ignore the Odes.

Codex Alexandrinus (A), on the other hand, uses the phrase 'psalter with odes' (ψαλτήριον μετ᾽ ᾠδῶν; cf. fig. 12) in the table of contents as though it were a fixed and well-known formula. This is best explained, if the preceding Jewish collection was already connected to the Psalter in a loose form and thereupon was expanded and broader accepted in the Christian use of the late fourth and the beginning of the fifth century.

The connection is still loose in the interior text of the *Alexandrinus*. For, the 'inscriptio' of the Psalms disregards the expansion in the table of contents; alone the title 'psalter' is placed before Psalm 1 (ψαλτήριον fol. 533ʳ). The 'subscriptio' follows after Psalm 151; the notion 'psalms and autographs' (ψαλμοὶ καὶ ἰδιόγραφοι fol. 564ᵛ) uses a motif of the last Greek psalm (Psalm 151. 1) and separates Psalms and Odes. Thus, the Odes are marked as an own collection.

The originally Jewish and then Christian base of the Odes is formed by the two songs of Moses and the song of Hannah (see A and Ra. 2036 in table 5 plus R and Ra. 55). The first of the songs of Moses, the 'Song of Moses in the Exodos' ([α] ᾠδὴ Μωυσέως ἐν τῇ ἐξόδῳ) opens the collection (A fol. 565ʳ). After growing up, the collection contains fourteen Odes in A (see the 'subscriptio' quoted in table 5), respectively thirteen Odes in the Coptic-Greek P. Vindob. K 8706 = Ra. 2036.[214] Ra. 2036, the oldest witness for a transmission separated from the Psalms (sixth century), adds two songs to *Codex Alexandrinus* and, vice versa, omits three Odes recorded in A (see table 5 again).

Thus, the extent of the collection is still flexible in the fifth and sixth century. Though, one feature is in common: *Codex Alexandrinus* and Ra. 2036 present the Jewish Odes first. Not only Odes 1–3 but also Odes 4–10 (A), or Odes 4–11 (P. Vindob. K 8706 = Ra. 2036), respectively, echo the priority of the pre-Christian songs and the Jewish origins of the collection. Moreover, the 'Oratio Manasse' — the only text not included in another Septuagint writing — is inserted after the prayer of Hezekiah (Isaiah 38) and followed by the prayer of Azariah (Daniel 3. 26–45) both times; the Prayer of Manasseh belongs to a series of prayers and especially corresponds to the prayer of Hezekiah. This evidence indicates a second, younger stage of the Jewish collection and supports our observations concerning a longstanding interchange of venerated texts between Christian and Jewish communities.

P. Vindob. K 8706 (= Ra. 2036) merely adds the 'Magnificat' and 'Nunc dimittis' in the end. *Codex Alexandrinus* enlarges the collection with the 'Benedictus' and a Christian hymn, too. The main witnesses, hence, apply the aforementioned hermeneutical principle of biblical collections (cf. thesis 6). They start with Israel's Greek texts and demand to read the younger songs in the perspective of the older ones. Indeed, the 'Magnificat', 'Benedictus' and 'Nunc Dimittis' are Christian, but

---

214 Digital photographs in <https://digital.onb.ac.at/RepViewer/viewer.faces?doc=DOD_%2BZ194671804&order=1&view=SINGLE> [accessed 3 May 2020]; description in Rahlfs and Fraenkel, *Verzeichnis*, pp. 434–35.

explicitly performed in Israel and for the praise of Israel (Odes 9. 54, 68 Ra.). That way, the Odes combine the light coming to the Gentiles and the glory of Israel (Odes 13. 32b Ra.). They inspire the idea of a Christian Bible obliged to Israel.

Alfred Rahlfs, however, did not follow *Codex Alexandrinus* and P. Vindob. K 8706 (= Ra. 2036). He preferred the order evolving in the later centuries ('In jüngerer Zeit', as he writes)[215] and integrated Jewish and Christian Odes. He placed Isaiah 5. 1–9 (missing in A and Ra. 2036), Isaiah 38. 10–20 and Prayer of Manasseh after Luke 1. 46–55, 68–79 (see table 5). His interest in younger developments and Greek-Latin contacts rouses respect; the Greek-Latin bilingual *Codex Veronensis* R (sixth century) marks the starting point for the transpositions within the collection.[216] Nevertheless, the principles of edition collide here.[217] *Codex Alexandrinus* and P. Vindob. K 8706 (= Ra. 2036) claim priority.

I, therefore, state as

> *proposal* 3: The Christian Odes belong to the full Greek Bible, as the development of the pandects proves. But a revitalization of the oldest order (*Codex Alexandrinus*) should take place and show the Jewish core of the collection. The Christian amplification at the end of the Odes then builds a bridge from Israel's scriptures to Christianity.

The proposal balances the orientation towards the Jewish origin of the Odes and the orientation on the amplified Christian collection. That balance allows for the enduring inclusion of the Odes into the Septuagint and avoids banishing them into an appendix of the Septuagint.[218]

3.3. The Order of the Biblical Books: Textual History and Critical Editions

The Septuagint and New Testament were successively formed in the Late Roman and Early Byzantine Periods. The Pentateuch, Prophets and Historical Books, the Psalms and the heart of the other Septuagint collections (Wisdom Books, Hagiographa) as well as the part-collections of the New Testament (Gospels, Pauline Letters, Acts and Catholic Letters) were broadly acknowledged in the post-Constantinian Era, as we saw (sections 1 and 2). But Revelation remained disputed (see § 2.9). Peripheral writings

---

215 Rahlfs, *Psalmi*, p. 79.

216 The codex contains eight Odes. The seventh is Luke 1. 46–55, the eighth Daniel 3. 52–88.

217 Eastern Christianity which used the Odes extensively experimented in the order and added further texts; the Bible of Vienna (ÖNB Theol. gr. 23; late twelfth or thirteenth century), e.g., confirms the arrangement Psalms/Odes, but differs from Rahlfs's order within the Odes and appends three post-biblical prayers (the prayer of Eustratios, etc.): see Hunger and Kresten, *Katalog*, p. 39. The Odes in the Bible of Vienna have a tripartite structure (examination 2021/06/20): praises from different LXX-books (from Exodus 15 up to Daniel 3) – hymns from the Gospel (Mary and Zachariah) – prayers of kings (Manasseh, Hezekiah) and saints (Eustratios etc.).

218 The proposal also allows to document the textual plus of younger manuscripts. An appendix to the Odes could hold the additional Odes of the bilingual manuscripts (Ra. 2036 and R) and the postbiblical prayers added in the Bible of Vienna (cf. fn. 217). Rahlfs prepared the differentiation by setting apart his Odes 10–14. A future electronic edition will have more possibilities.

(Psalms of Solomon, Hermas, Barnabas, I–II Clement) were not yet excluded from biblical collections in the time of the old pandects, and other works were not finally included (III–IV Maccabees). The order of the part-collections and the place of some books within the pandects were not definitely fixed up till the end of the Byzantine Era. As a consequence, different views were held even in the time of transition into the print medium (end of fifteenth century), and some clearings concerning the order of the Septuagint and the New Testament stand open until this day.

Biblia Leonis (Ra. 55)	Vienna ÖNB Cod. Theol. gr. 23[219]	Ferrara, Bibl. Com. Cl. II, 187 (Ra. 106)	Venice, Bibl. Marc. Gr. Z. 5 and 6 (Bessarion)[220]	Zittau A 1 (and Ferrara, Bibl. Com. Cl. II, 188)	Aldine	Rahlfs volume I
Genesis, Exodus, Leviticus, Numbers, Deuteronomy, Joshua, Judges, Ruth (counted as 8 Books in the table of contents of A and called octateuch in the table of contents of Ra. 55), I–IV Kingdoms, I–II Paralipomena					Genesis, Exodus, Leviticus, Numbers, Deuteronomy, Joshua, Judges, Ruth I–IV Kingdoms, I–II Paralipomena	
I–II Esdras Judith Esther Tobit I–IV Maccabees (followed in the volume by Job and Psalms)	I–II Esdras Esther Judith Tobit I–III Maccabees (followed by Psalms, orations, Job, etc. up to the IV and XII Prophets)	I–II Esdras Tobit Judith Esther (then Wisdom Books and IV+XII prophets), in the end I–II Maccabees (Psalms-Odes are inserted secondarily)	IV + XII Prophets, Job, Psalms, Proverbs, Ecclesiastes, Canticles, I–II Esdras, Esther Wisdom, Sirach Judith Tobit I(-III) Maccabees	I–II Esdras I–IV Maccabees Esther Judith Tobit	Esdras (Esra-Nehemia) Esther Tobit Judith *Job, Psalms Wisdom Books Prophets* I–III Maccabees	I–II Esdras Esther Judith Tobit I–IV Maccabees

Table 6. Octateuch, historical books and narratives of the Septuagint in the younger pandects (columns 1-5) and the prints (columns 6-7).

219 <https://search.onb.ac.at/primo-explore/fulldisplay?docid=ONB_alma21395498920003338&context=L&vid=ONB&lang=de_DE&search_scope=ONB_gesamtbestand&adaptor=Local%20Search%20Engine&tab=default_tab&query=any,contains,Cod.%20Theol.%20gr.%2023&offset=0> [accessed 12 April 2020].

220 For the content of Venice, Bibl. Marc. Gr. Z. 5 and 6, cf. Offizielles Verzeichnis der Rahlfs-Sigeln. Stand: Dezember 2012, numbers 68 and 122 <http://hdl.handle.net/11858/00-001S-0000-0022-A30C-8> [accessed 7 October 2020]. Ra. 68 contains I–III Maccabees, Ra. 122 only fragments of I Maccabees.

3.3.1.   The Order of the Septuagint

The order of the Septuagint in Rahlfs's hand edition performed a kind of consensus in the twentieth century despite some unavoidable tensions. I retell that Israel's Historical Books were understood as former Prophets in the Greek transmission up to the second century (cf. 2.4.1). Then the Prophets were more and more set apart. As a consequence, the early and Middle-Byzantine pandects tested different orders of the part-collections within the Septuagint:[221]

3.3.1.1. Octateuch, Historical Books and Greek Narratives

The Octateuch, Historical Books and Greek narratives were linked gradually. In the late Byzantine epoque, a collection of ἱστορίαι πᾶσαι ('all historical narratives') evolved ranging from the Pentateuch over the Historical Books to the Hagiographs (Ra. 107 and Bible of Zittau).[222] But that collection did not achieve a consensus. The affiliation of III–IV Maccabees and the place of the Maccabean books remained disputed. The pandects written after the eleventh century (after the Biblia Leonis patricii) excluded IV Maccabees with the only exception of the Bible of Zittau (Ra. 44). The Bible of Ferrara, e.g., contained not more than I–II Maccabees and separated these books from the Hagiographs.

Bessarion accepted I–III Maccabees (see Ra. 68; the corresponding folios in Ra. 122 are damaged), but proposed an alternative overall order of the Septuagint earning attention (see tables 6 and 7). He placed the Prophets after the Historical Books, disagreeing with the mainstream of the younger pandects (cf. §§ 2.4 and 2.9.2). That proposal renews the old 'Hebrew' order and is best explained by an ecumenical interest: The famous Latin translator Jerome had preferred the 'Hebrew' order (as was reported, e.g., by Cassiodorus, *inst.*, I. 12. 1–2). It seems that Bessarion tried to build a bridge between the Greek and Latin tradition in returning to the oldest tradition preceding the Greek and Latin translations.[223]

---

221   See table 2 for the codices B and א, fig. 8 for A, table 3 for the pandects of the Middle-Byzantine Period.

222   See section 2.1 and table 1.

223   Interestingly, a Greek scholarly interest in the order of Jerome is explicitly evidenced sometime later by the entry inserted into *Codex Vaticanus*, p. iv. A Greek scribe of the sixteenth century inserted a table of the LXX books according to Jerome there (see fig. 10 and the quotation in § 3.8.3). The overall order corresponds to Cassiodorus and Bessarion, but a noteworthy detail differs: Bessarion's Bibles (Ra. 68 and 122) present Historical Books, Prophets and Hagiographs (Job, Psalms, etc.) in the sequence recorded as Jerome's position by Cassiodorus. But Cassiodorus, *inst.*, I. 1. 12, did not mention Daniel, and Bessarion placed Daniel under the Prophets (after Ezekiel). The scribe of *Vaticanus*, p. iv, on the contrary, ranges Daniel in the Wisdom Books, between Canticles and I–II Paralipomena. He must have read Jerome, *prol. Dan*: 'admoneo [...] haberi Danihelem apud Hebraeos [...] inter eos qui Agiographa conscripserunt', *Biblia Sacra iuxta vulgatam versionem*, ed. by Robert Weber and Roger Gryson, 5th edn (Stuttgart: Deutschebibelgesellschaft, 2007), p. 1342; and, perhaps, he also knew a Jewish Bible print.

The Bible of Vienna (Ra. 130) represented the mainstream concerning the overall order of the Septuagint (Prophets in the end) and combined the Hagiographs with the Historical Books in a kind of middle way. It inserted I–III Maccabees after Tobit and excluded the youngest of the Maccabean books which was disputed since the fourth century: IV Maccabees was included in *Codex Sinaiticus*, but not in *Codex Vaticanus*; it was included in *Codex Alexandrinus* and Biblia Leonis, but not in the late Byzantine Bibles (for the one exception, the Bible of Zittau, cf. § 3.4.4).

Thereupon, the first published prints of the Septuagint, the Aldine (see table 6) as well as the Complutensian Polyglot, restricted the presentation of the Maccabean books. They excluded IV Maccabees and separated I–III Maccabees from the Hagiographs by placing them at the end of the Old Testament (cf. the place of I–II Maccabees in the Latin tradition).

Rahlfs, on the other hand, appreciated the text of IV Maccabees since it was presented in two old pandects (*Codices Sinaiticus* and *Alexandrinus*). He included IV Maccabees into volume I of his hand edition of the Septuagint and placed I–IV Maccabees after the Hagiographs. That way, he preferred the order developing in the Middle Byzantine Period after the beginnings in *Codex Sinaiticus*. In effect, the little-known Bible of Vienna best prepares the order of volume I of the modern critical edition of the Septuagint; the only difference in order from Pentateuch to Maccabees is the inclusion / exclusion of IV Maccabees.

Bible of Vienna (Ra. 130)	Bible of Ferrara (Ra. 106)	Bibles charged by Bessarion (Ra. 68 + 122)	Codex Vaticanus	cf. Rahlfs
		IV + XII Prophets		
		Job		
Psalms, Odes (+		Psalms (no Odes)	Psalms (no Odes)	Psalms, *Odes*,
tres orationes)	Job, Proverbs,	Proverbs,	Proverbs,	Proverbs,
Job, Proverbs,	Ecclesiastes,	Ecclesiastes,	Ecclesiastes,	Ecclesiastes,
Ecclesiastes,	Canticles,	Canticles,	Canticles,	Canticles,
Canticles,	Wisdom, Sirach,	I–II Esdras,	Job, Wisdom,	Job, Wisdom,
Wisdom, Sirach,	IV + XII proph	Esther,	Sirach	Sirach,
IV + XII Prophets	(Psalms-	Wisdom, Sirach	*Esther, Judith,*	*Psalms of Solomon,*
	Odes inserted		*Tobit*	XII + IV Prophets
	secondarily)		XII + IV Prophets	

Table 7. Psalms, Wisdom Books and Prophets in the younger pandects.

3.3.1.2. Psalms, Wisdom Books and Prophets

The order of Psalms, Wisdom Books and Prophets held some flexibility, too.

Psalms: The old codices appended a psalm telling David's beheading of the 'allophyle' (i.e. Goliath) to the collection of Psalms 1–150. The 'inscriptio' characterized that psalm as being 'outside the number' (ἔξωθεν τοῦ ἀριθμοῦ, inscriptio LXX-Psalms 151. 1). Consistently, the 'subscriptio' to the psalter in *Codex Vaticanus* (written by another hand than the Psalms themselves) counted Psalms 1–150 alone ('subscriptio' ρν' = 150 psalms, p. 713; Psalm 151, p. 714). *Codex Alexandrinus* differentiated '150 psalms and one written in own hand' (ψαλμοὶ ρν' καὶ ἰδιόγραφος; subscriptio fol. 564ᵛ). *Codex Sinaiticus*, however, fully included Psalm 151 into the psalter; there, the 'subscriptio' counts ρνα' = 151 psalms and follows to Psalm 151 (qu. 64, fol. 1ʳ).

The Bible of Ferrara (Ra. 106; psalms written by a second hand) tried a middle way in the fifteenth century. It rendered Psalm 151 but noted the number of the psalms contained by the main collection (ρν' = 150) in front of it.[224] Bessarion looked for a comparability to the Hebrew tradition and Jerome, as we saw; and Psalm 151 and Odes were not transmitted in Hebrew collections and the Vulgate. Therefore, Bessarion excluded Psalm 151 as well as the Odes from the pandect Bibl. Marc. Gr. Z. 6 (Ra. 122), somewhat surprising today.

Rahlfs, on the contrary, harks back to the oldest Greek codices. He prefers *Codex Sinaiticus* in that case (and *Codex Alexandrinus* concerning the Odes; cf. section 3.2). He gives the additional psalm the number 151 and relegates the 'subscriptio' of *Codex Vaticanus* (cut between Psalms 150 and 151) to the apparatus.

Prophets: The Minor Prophets preceded the Major Prophets in *Codices Vaticanus* and *Alexandrinus* but followed to the Major Prophets in *Codex Sinaiticus* (see table 2). The younger pandects (Bibles of Vienna and Ferrara; cf. Bessarion) aligned themselves with the order of *Sinaiticus*; Rahlfs, however, gets back to *Vaticanus* (table 7).

Job: The place of Job differed in *Codices Vaticanus* (after Canticles), *Sinaiticus* (at the end of the Wisdom Books) and the table of contents of *Alexandrinus* (at the beginning of the Wisdom Books; see table 2 and fig. 12). Rahlfs, again, gets back to *Vaticanus*. Though, the majority of younger pandects prefer the order of *Alexandrinus* (Bibles of Vienna and Ferrara). Bessarion proposes a third way, separates Job from the Wisdom Books and additionally divides the Wisdom Books by Esdras-Esther (table 7).

Evidently, Rahlfs rates *Codex Vaticanus* highest and *Codex Sinaiticus* second. Nevertheless, he drifts from *Codex Vaticanus* concerning the numbering of Psalm 151 (with *Sinaiticus*), Odes (with younger witnesses), Psalms of Solomon (see section 3.1.1), Esther, Judith and Tobit (see 3.1.1.1). Rahlfs's arrangement is often taken for granted and, yet, not self-evident.

---

224 Transcription in Martini, *Catalogo*, p. 352.

	place of Hebrews in NT	inscriptio	subscriptio	additions to the subscriptio	notes
ℵ	following to II Thessalonians	προς εβραιουc	προc εβραιουc	cτιχοι ψν = 750 stichoi	The stichoi of II Thessalonians are counted, too: cτιχων ρπ = 180 stichoi
A	following to II Thessalonians	προc εβραιουc	προς εβραιους	εγραφη απο ρωμης	
B	following to II Thessalonians	first hand: no inscriptio; corrector: προc εβραιουc	(lost)		
C		(lost)	προς εβραιους		Tischendorf proposed a place of Hebrews after the lost II Thessalonians
min. 33	following to II Thessalonians	προc εβραιουc	προc εβραιουc		
Ra. 55 (Biblia Leonis patricii)	probably following to Philemon;[225] cf. § 2.9.1				Revelation is placed between Catholic and Pauline Epistles; hence, Hebrews becomes the last book of the Bible (cf. GA 1424 and 1870)
min. 218 (Bible of Vienna)	following to II Thessalonians	προc εβραιουc επιστολη του αγιου Παυλου	-	εγραφη απο Ιταλιας κτλ.	

225 The medaillon for Hebrews is destroyed in Vat. Reg. gr. 1 B, fol. I^r, but can be supplemented; see Paul Canart, 'Notice codicologique et paléographique', in *La Bible du Patrice Léon: Codex Reginensis Graecus 1: commentaire codicologique, paléographique, philologique et artistique*, ed. by Paul Canart, Studi e testi, 463 (Città del Vaticano: Biblioteca apostolica vaticana, 2011), pp. 3–57 (p. 4).

	place of Hebrews in NT	inscriptio	subscriptio	additions to the subscriptio	notes
min. 582 (Bible of Ferrara)	following to Philemon	η προς εβραιους επιστολη του Παυλου	-		Hebrews stands at the end of the Pauline Epistles and before the Praxapostolos; Rev marks the end of the Bible
min. 1957 (B suppl.)	(see above)	-			Pastorals and Philemon are not supplemented; Hebrews stands before Revelation, and Revelation marks the end of the Bible
min. 2886 (and min. 205; both charged by Bessarion)	following to Philemon	-	η προς εβραιους επιστολη	1. εγραφη απο Ιταλιας κτλ. 2. στιχοι ψν = 750 stichoi	Revelation is placed before Romans, and Hebrews stands at the end of the Bible
min. 664 (Zittau)	following to Philemon	προς εβραιους επιστολη	η προς εβραιους επιστολη	1. εγραφη απο Ιταλιας κτλ. 2. στιχοι ψγ (= 703; GA 1424 and 1870 have the same number of stichoi)	1. Hebrews stands before Revelation 2. The stichoi of II Thessalonians are counted, too: στιχοι ρπ = 180 stichoi

Cf. the order of writings in the first print editions:

Erasmus and Aldine (influenced by Erasmus): Philemon – Hebrews – Catholic Epistles

Complutensian Polyglot: Philemon – Hebrews – Praxapostolos (Acts and Catholic Epistles)

Table 8. The place of Hebrews in the New Testament.

3.3.2. The Order of the New Testament

The order of the New Testament has become controversial within the last years. I look back for a moment:

Erasmus not only printed Revelation without commentary in 1516 (cf. § 2.9.4); he also separated Acts from the Catholic Letters (against the majority of the Byzantine manuscripts) and arranged the Catholic after the Pauline Epistles in the end. This arrangement differed from the Complutensian Polyglot which was printed before but published after Erasmus's *Novum Instrumentum*; the Polyglot maintained the Praxapostolos (Acts and Catholic Epistles followed after the Pauline collection). Nevertheless, the Polyglot held one point in common with Erasmus; both conceptualized Hebrews as an appendix to the Pauline Epistles and inserted it behind Philemon (table 8).

The latter decision corresponded to a young development in the Greek pandects. Hebrews followed to Philemon in the Greek Bibles from the fourteenth century onwards (see the Bibles of Ferrara, Venice [Bessarion] and Zittau in table 8).[226] Vice versa, the old pandects had inserted Hebrews after Paul's epistles to communities (II Thessalonians). That placement claimed the same respect for the ambitious anonymous writing (which became assigned to Paul) as for Paul's community writings.

The late Byzantine change of order did not wish to diminish the relevance of Hebrews. The scriptoria rather worked conservatively. They understood the anonymous homily as a Pauline Epistle and added old editorial marks (see the notes on the provenance of Hebrews from Rome or Italy and the 'stichoi' in table 8). Yet, they regarded the deviations from Paul in style and theology and placed Hebrews after all the Pauline Epistles.

Erasmus's proposal of order prevailed in the sixteenth century and persisted for half a millennium. Then, the *Editio Critica Maior* (ECM) of the New Testament challenged Erasmus's assumptions. The editorial team decided in 2017 to retrieve the combination of Acts and Catholic Epistles which is delineated in the old pandects. The so-called Praxapostolos follows the Gospels and is placed before the Pauline Epistles in the ECM.[227] The Complutensian which was overshadowed by Erasmus for centuries is becoming rehabilitated.

---

226 Perhaps, the dynamics of that development even explain the unusual supplementation of *Codex Vaticanus*: Evidently, the supplementator did not want to break up the old and venerable sequence II Thessalonians-Hebrews (p. 1512) by inserting Pastoral and Philemon. But an appendix of individual letters after Hebrews was outdated (see the other young pandects). As a consequence, the supplementator ignored Paul's Epistles to individuals (Timotheus, Titus, Philemon); they are not supplemented, and Hebrews becomes the last Epistle of the Pauline collection, foregoing Revelation.

227 *Editio Critica Maior*, ed. by Holger Strutwolf and others (Stuttgart: Deutsche Bibelgesellschaft, 2017), III.1.1. Die Apostelgeschichte. Text. Kapitel 1–14, p. 1*, against the first published part of the ECM, *Editio Critica Maior*, ed. by Barbara Aland and others (Stuttgart: Deutsche Bibelgesellschaft, 1997), IV.1. Die Katholischen Briefe, p. 1*.

3.3.3. The Place of Hebrews

Where will Hebrews[228] be placed in that new situation, behind II Thessalonians or Philemon or in a third position? The decision stands open at present and must be done when the edition of Hebrews will start (in about 2023). The old pandects (*Codices Sinaiticus, Vaticanus* and *Alexandrinus*) and important Middle-Byzantine Bibles (*Codex Pariathoniensis*, min. 33, and Bible of Vienna, min. 218 GA) recommend inserting the writing amidst the Pauline Epistles, behind II Thessalonians (table 8). That is a strong argument, and yet, not the oldest available conception for the place of Hebrews; the alternative arrangement Romans-Hebrews-I Corinthians is witnessed already by the letter collection in p[46] which is older than the presentation in the pandects.

ms.	century	inscriptio	remark
D 06	5th	προϲ εβραιουϲ	Hebrews was originally separated from Philemon by empty pages (fols 467^v–469^r). A stichometrical list is inserted there (467^v–468^v; see fig. 6) not mentioning Hebrews.
020	9th	του αγιου [...] Παυλου επιστολη προϲ εβραιουϲ	The foregoing fol. 174^v–175^r contain a hypothesis to Hebrews.
044	9th–10th	προϲ εβραιουϲ (subscriptio ditto)	Hebrews begins on a new page (as every Pauline letter).
056	10th	no inscriptio	The hypothesis to Hebrews (fol. 340^v–341^r) serves as inscriptio.
0142	10th	προϲ εβραιουϲ	A short hypothesis (τοις ευσεβουσι Εβραιοις Παυλος ταδε) foregoes on fol. 341^r.

The mentioned collections contain Praxapostolos and Pauline Epistles (044 also Gospels). Revelation is never included.

Table 9. New Testament-manuscripts of the 1st millennium placing Hebrews after Philemon.

The matter changes if we consult manuscripts of New Testament collections from the 5th century onwards (table 9) and the younger pandects. The bilingual *Codex Claromontanus* (fifth century) presents Hebrews following to Philemon (separated by leaves with other text), and Middle-Byzantine collections support this sequence (Philemon-Hebrews in 020, 044, 056, 0142; ninth to tenth centuries). The conservative tendency of the pandects retards the reception of that arrangement. But the Late-Byzantine Bible of Ferrara and the post-Byzantine pandects (Bessarion and Zittau) take it over (see table 8 and § 3.3.2).

The younger arrangement fits better to the peculiarity of Hebrews. p[46] (Romans-Hebrews) and the old pandects (II Thessalonians-Hebrews) ignore the objections

---

228 See William H. P. Hatch, 'The Position of Hebrews in the Canon of the New Testament', *HTR*, 29 (1936), 133–51.

against the Pauline provenance of Hebrews which were allowed in the Old Church[229] and have become common sense since the sixteenth century. The findings of historical criticism definitely recommend the place of Hebrews behind Philemon according to the young pandects and supported by relevant New Testament majuscules.

3.3.4. The Arrangement of Revelation

The place of Revelation was even more controversial than Hebrews. The New Testament collection of majuscule 044 (cf. table 9) and, probably, *Codex Pariathoniensis* (min. 33) ignored the work because of the Middle-Byzantine doubts reported in section 2.9.1. The late pandects put it in different places indicating its peculiarity (cf. the notes in table 8). The strongest line of development favors a place of Revelation in the end of the Bible (cf. §§ 2.9.2 and 2.9.5), but its special status should be highlighted in the edition. That could be done, e.g. by inserting an empty folio before Revelation in the hand edition of the New Testament (cf. the empty page 149^v in *Codex Alexandrinus*).[230] All in all, it seems best

> to give Hebrews a place after Philemon (with the younger pandects) and before Revelation[231] in the *Editio Critica Maior* (*proposal 4*).

A special hint may be added: Every arrangement of the New Testament collections is remote from the textual prototype,[232] and none of the sketched arrangements has become universally accepted in an epoque of textual transmission. Erasmus's order Acts-Pauline Epistles-Catholic Epistles-Revelation is prepared in manuscripts from the eleventh century onwards (min. 241, 367, 1704 GA),[233] and the sequence Acts-Pauline Epistles-Catholic Epistles is shown as well by one of the manuscripts which were brought to Basel by John Stojcovic (UB Basel AN IV 5 = min. 2816 GA). Again, the pandects are more conservative than the selections of New Testament writings (no pandect supports the Erasmian order in total). Therefore, the editors can make another choice in the hand edition than in the *Editio Critica Maior*; the Erasmian order is not yet given up in the Nestle-Aland (twenty-eighth edition).[234]

3.3.5. Barnabas, Hermas and I–II Clement

If the critical edition of the Septuagint allows for an integration of the Psalms of Solomon, as is done by the Göttingen LXX and is accepted above in a modified way (see section 3.1), an analogy for the New Testament must be discussed. Barnabas and

---

229 Tertullian, *pud.*, 20. 2, ascribed Hebrews to Barnabas.
230 See Karrer, 'Von den Evangelien bis zur Apk', p. 263.
231 See the arrangement of the Bible of Zittau and — *mutatis mutandis* since Philemon and Pastorals are omitted — in the supplement of *Codex Vaticanus*.
232 The collection of the Catholic Epistles remained fluid up to the sixth or seventh century; Wolfgang Grünstäudl, 'Was lange währt … : Die Katholischen Briefe und die Formung des neutestamentlichen Kanons', *Early Christianity*, 7 (2016), 71–94.
233 min. 367 and 1704 GA show the sequence Philemon-Hebrews, too.
234 More details in Karrer, 'Von den Evangelien bis zur Apk'.

Hermas are included in *Codex Sinaiticus*, I–II Clement in *Codex Alexandrinus*, and I–II Clement even forego the appendix of Psalms of Solomon in the table of contents of *Codex Alexandrinus*. The critical editions of the New Testament disagree from the old codices in that case. They follow the younger pandects and exclude Barnabas, Hermas, and I–II Clement. They confirm the delimitations of the New Testament which became stronger in the history of canon than the delimitations of the Septuagint.

Nevertheless, an inner tension of the editorial work comes out into view: New Testament textual criticism rates the old pandects higher than younger ones, but the content of the New Testament is delimitated as in the young pandects. Perhaps, a distinction between the extensive critical edition and the smaller hand edition of the New Testament opens more possibilities. The *Editio Critica Maior* of the New Testament would become better comparable to the critical edition of the Septuagint in the Göttingen LXX, if both editions would cover all writings presented in the old pandects and/or mentioned in the table of contents of *Codex Alexandrinus*.

3.3.6. A Great Wish: Cooperation between the Editions of the Septuagint and New Testament

In the end, a question results concerning both the edition of the Septuagint and the New Testament: The editors have developed different concepts in history, and some of the differences are inevitable (e.g., the Septuagint needs an Hexaplaric apparatus). But relevant issues are in common. The arrangement of both editions, for example, reflects the interest in the old pandects as well as developments of younger pandects, but in different ways. Nevertheless, the edition of the Septuagint records all writings contained in the old pandects or mentioned in the table of contents of *Codex Alexandrinus* and arranges the books in some aspects comparably to the Middle Byzantine Period; the present edition of the New Testament records only the books of the later canon (influenced by Western developments as can be seen in the Latin *capitula* and in the rendition of Revelation without accompanying commentary) and prefers an Early Byzantine arrangement at the moment (perhaps with exception of the place of Hebrews). Has the time not come for an interdisciplinary discourse looking for more convergences? I say it as

> *proposal 5*: The cooperation of the great editorial projects should be intensified. Common work on the old and young Greek pandects promises new insights into the textual history and will open common perspectives on the extent and the inner order of the Greek Bible.

The scientific exchange has started.[235] Conferences on textual forms and on the biblical texts in the Prophetologion and New Testament lectionaries, i.e. the text used in

---

235 The conference (2018) on the so-called Antiochean text, which is high-rated in LXX-, but given up in NT-textual criticism, has resulted in the volume *Trifaria varietas?: Entstehung, Entwicklung und Problematik des Konzepts von Rezensionen des biblischen Textes*, ed. by Siegfried Kreuzer and Martin Karrer, BN.NF, 184 (Herder: Freiburg, 2020).

liturgy through the centuries, took place in 2018 and 2021.[236] The textual history gains in importance for both editions besides the reconstruction of the archetype. I add that the younger pandects are to be seen in the context of the Greek-Latin contacts of twelfth/thirteenth and the fifteenth century. The relevance and complexity of the matter, therefore, transcends editorial discussions; the debate should be opened to the neighboring disciplines (Byzantine studies, History and Philology) and held ecumenically.

3.4. The Younger Pandects: Notes, 'kephalaia', Text-Types and Influences on the Early Prints

The study of the *Codices Vaticanus* (old parts), *Sinaiticus, Alexandrinus, Ephraemi Rescriptus* and *Basiliano-Vaticanus* is well established in textual criticism. The younger pandects escaped a comparable attention. The Bibles of Vienna, Ferrara, Venice and Zittau and the supplement of *Codex Vaticanus* are, so to speak, a sleeping beauty which must be awakened.

3.4.1. Hexaplaric and Other Notes in the Margins

Some aspects are known, for example, the Hexaplaric notes in parts of the Pentateuch of the Bible of Vienna (Ra. 130). Other pandects, such as the Bible of Ferrara, display short Greek and Latin notices in the margins. Thus, they give hints to the understanding and reception of the biblical books in the Byzantine Era and to Greek-Latin contacts.

3.4.2. The kephalaia

A second aspect is long recognized, but demands consequences: The younger pandects insist on the Greek *kephalaia* ('chapters') of the New Testament. The contacts to Latin Bibles evidently increased in the era around and after the Council of Ferrara and Florence; and yet, not even the youngest pandect, the Bible of Zittau (Ra. 44), or the supplement of the *Codex Vaticanus* which may be written in a Latin context (min. 1759)[237] hint to the Latin *capitula* of the New Testament.

Hence, the pandects remind us that the priority of the Latin *capitula* which was introduced by Erasmus is questionable. At present, the Greek *kephalaia* are presented

---

236 The 2021 conference on the lectionaries will result in the volume *Liturgische Traditionen: Ihr Nutzen und Stellenwert für die biblische Editionswissenschaft / Liturgical Traditions: Their Use and Value for Critical Editions of the Bible*, ed. by F. Albrecht, F. Feder and M. Karrer, Reihe Antike Schriftauslegung / Ancient Scriptural Interpretation (Göttingen: Vandenhoeck & Ruprecht, 2022).

237 Theodore C. Skeat, 'The Codex Vaticanus in the Fifteenth Century', *JThSt*, 35 (1984), 454–65, stimulated the idea that the supplementation of the codex was made in Constantinople for the purposes of the orthodox delegation travelling to the Council of Ferrara and Florence (p. 463). The discussion is still going on; see Paul Canart, 'Le Vaticanus graecus 1209: notice paléographique et codicologique', in *Le manuscrit B de la Bible (Vaticanus graecus 1209): Introduction au fac-similé, Actes du Colloque de Genève (11 juin 2001), Contributions supplémentaires*, ed. by Patrick Andrist, Histoire du texte biblique, 7 (Lausanne: Éditions du Zèbre, 2009), pp. 19–43 (p. 27, 40 n. 58). The supplement can be written in Rome or Italy too, as Patrick Andrist takes into consideration; Andrist, 'milieu', pp. 248–50.

only in the inner margin of the critical edition of the New Testament (Nestle-Aland[28]). They deserve more attention. I submit as

proposal 6: The Greek *kephalaia* should be given greater value in the edition of the New Testament.

This could be done in the headlines or a special apparatus of the *Editio Critica Maior*[238] and by a bold, better visible print of the *kephalaia* in the inner margin of the hand edition of the New Testament.

3.4.3. The Younger Pandects and the Textual History of the Bible

The younger pandects are witnesses for the development of the biblical text and deserve more attention in this regard. Only the older pandects (B, א, A, C, V) are intensively studied up to now due to the interest in the prototypes and early developments of the biblical text.

The *Codex Pariathoniensis* (Ra. 198, NT GA 33) may be ranked at the end of this series. The scriptorium exhibited the high claim of the Bible in the Middle-Byzantine period by an archaizing tendency.[239] That is why this codex presents a text near to the old prototypes and is comprehensively used in the critical editions.

The younger pandects changed the perspective. They prioritized forms of the standard text of their time, the twelfth to fifteenth centuries. A perception of that development seemed of less relevance in the old conventions of textual criticism. Though, the awareness for the Byzantine sources is increasing within the last generations. The manuscripts transmit old readings in an own manner and additionally highlight textual characteristics of the finishing-off Middle Byzantine and Late Byzantine Period. Some indications are known; more must be explored:

The Bible of Vienna (Ra. 130, GA 218) represents group *s* of the Pentateuch text (a textual form influenced by the recension of Origenes)[240] and the main form of the Byzantine text in the scriptures of the New Testament which are analyzed, namely the Byzantine majority text (Byz) in Acts, K(oine) in Revelation.[241]

The Bibles of Ferrara (Ra. 106, GA 582) and Zittau (Ra. 44, GA 664) draw upon the text of the Pentateuch according to the prominent Byzantine 'd-group' (a main group of Byzantine textual transmission).[242]

---

238 The *Editio Critica Maior* of Revelation introduces an apparatus of segmentations into the edition.
239 Hutter, 'Bibelhandschrift', p. 169, assumes that the scriptorium worked in Constantinople within a context characterized by 'antiquarisch-wissenschaftlichen Interessen'.
240 See Wevers, *Genesis*, p. 58; Wevers, *Exodus*, p. 42.
241 Cf. *Editio Critica Maior*, ed. by Holger Strutwolf and others (Stuttgart: Deutsche Bibelgesellschaft, 2017), III. Die Apostelgeschichte. Teil 2: Begleitende Materialien, p. 8; *Text und Textwert der griechischen Handschriften des Neuen Testaments*, ed. by Markus Lembke and others, ANTF, 49 (Berlin: de Gruyter, 2017), VI. Die Apokalypse: Teststellenkollation und Auswertungen, p. 24.
242 Wevers identified this 'd-group'. The group is best represented by codices containing the great collection Octateuch, I–IV Kingdoms, Paralipomena, Esdras, I–IV Maccabees, Esther, Judith and Tobit, i.e. Ra. 44 (the Bible of Zittau), 106 (the full Bible of Ferrara), 107 (the collection of LXX-'historiai' in Ferrara) and in addition Ra. 125 and 610; *Leviticus*, ed. by John William Wevers,

The supplement of Genesis in *Codex Vaticanus* refers to the text of *Codex Chisianus* IV 38 (Ra. 19; twelfth century).[243] This textual form is closely related to MS Ra. 108[244] which was sent later from Rome to Spain for the preparation of the Complutensian Polyglot.[245] The supplement of lost Psalms shows the so-called Antiochean text, i.e. the textual form dominating the transmission of Psalms throughout the Byzantine time.

The supplement of Hebrews stands near to the K^r-group (fam. 35, a highly standardized text spreading from eleventh or twelfth century onwards).[246] And interestingly, the textual form used for the supplement of Revelation (GA 1759)[247] is related to the textual form witnessed by the Complutensian Polyglot, again; the NT manuscripts consulted for the print in Alcalá are lost, but the textual form is reconstructed and got the name 'Complutensian text'.[248]

All in all, the restoration of *Vaticanus* proofs the interest of the fifteenth century in standardized textual forms. It prepares the tendency which is later pursued by the print of the Complutensian Polyglot.

Bessarion highly appreciates the Septuagint text of *Codex Vaticanus*.[249] For the Gospels, he prefers a text related to the widespread family 1 of the Testament in his Bibles.[250]

Again, the textual preference becomes relevant for the early prints of the Bible. A copy of Bibl. Marc. Gr. Z. 5 (Ra. 68) will be made and sent by the Venetian Senate to cardinal Cisneros in Spain; that manuscript (Ra. 442; heavily damaged in the Spanish Civil War) will be used as one of the *Vorlagen* for the Historical Books (from Kingdoms onwards) and for the Wisdom Books in the Complutensian Polyglot.[251] And the Venetian printing house of Aldus will preferentially draw upon Venetian

---

Septuaginta Vetus Testamentum Graecum, II 2 (Göttingen: Vandenhoeck & Ruprecht, 1986), p. 27; for the collations see John William Wevers, *Text History of Greek Numbers*, MSU, 16 (Göttingen: Vandenhoeck & Ruprecht, 1982).

243 Cf. above with fn. 78. Ra. 19 contains Octateuch, I–IV Kingdoms, Paralipomena, Esdras, Judith, Esther, I–II Maccabees.

244 Ra. 108 is a collection containing the Octateuch, I–IV Kingdoms, Paralipomena, Esdras, Judith, Esther (*L*- and o'–Text) and Tobit. Codices holding a collection are evidently preferred in the fifteenth century.

245 See Wevers, *Genesis*, p. 53 and the overview on the manuscripts used for the Complutensian Polyglot by Fernández Marcos, 'Greek Sources'.

246 I thank E. Gerke, Wuppertal, for the collations of the supplemented text of Psalms and Hebrews in B (GA 1759); I name min. 18 GA for the related manuscripts which were found by E. Gerke in 2020.

247 The immediate *Vorlage* for GA 1759 is lost; Šagi, 'Problema', pp. 25–28, could not identify it.

248 See Marcus Lembke, 'Der Apokalypsetext der complutensischen Polyglotte und sein Verhältnis zur handschriftlichen Überlieferung', in *Studien zum Text der Apokalypse*, ed. by Marcus Sigismund, Martin Karrer and Ulrich Schmid (Berlin: de Gruyter, 2015), pp. 33–133.

249 Bibl. Marc. Gr. Z. 6 (Ra. 122) is a copy of B in great parts: see Farnes, *Copying*, p. 39.

250 The Gospel text of Bibl. Marc. Gr. Z. 5 (NT GA 205) and 6 (NT GA 2886) as well as of the New Testament minuscule GA 209 (known to Bessarion and mentioned in table 4) belong to this family.

251 Séamus O'Connell, *From Most Ancient Sources: The Nature and Text-Critical Use of the Greek Old Testament Text of the Complutensian Polyglot Bible*, OBO, 215 (Fribourg: Academic Press; Göttingen: Vandenhoeck & Ruprecht, 2006), p. 167; Natalio Fernández Marcos, 'Un manuscrito complutense redivivo: MS griego 442 = Villa-Amil 22', *Sefarad*, 65 (2005), 65–83.

manuscripts; the manuscripts of Bessarion, therefore, will carry weight for the text of the Septuagint in the Aldine Bible from 1518 (besides other manuscripts).[252]

Regarding the text of Revelation (the book excluded from Byzantine liturgy), the Bible of Ferrara (NT GA 582; belonging to fam. 104 of Revelation) shows influences from Andrew of Caesarea (the most famous commentator of the book) and Arethas (the second renowned Byzantine commentator).[253] The Bibles of Bessarion (counted as GA 205 and GA 2886 for the NT parts) represent the text of Andrew of Caesarea;[254] and the Bible of Zittau follows the text of Arethas.[255]

That way, the pandects confirm the relevance of the commentaries (Andrew and Arethas) in the transmission of Revelation. The textual form of min. 2814 (Revelation) which was bought by Ivan Stojković in Constantinople and used by Erasmus for his print of the New Testament (text of Andrew; see section 2.9.4) agrees to the mainstream textual development. The text of the Koine (K; Bible of Vienna) and the so-called Complutensian text (witnessed by the supplement to B), on the other hand, show that standardized texts of Revelation existed besides the commentaries and were appreciated as well.

Two tendencies shine through the long development. On the one hand, the scriptoria of the pandects use *Vorlagen* of prominent textual groups and enforce the preferred textual form; they strive for a standard text. On the other hand, textual forms compete. A strict standardization fails.

3.4.4. An Outlook: The First Prints

The traversing trends go over into the time of the first prints. I mention two aspects:

The worth of the codices was assessed differently by the humanists. Even the relevance of *Codex Vaticanus* was controversial. None other than Erasmus will underestimate the value of that today's most prominent codex. He will not take into regard the relevant variants of *Vaticanus* which were communicated to him when preparing the reprints of his New Testament edition.[256]

The overall content of the Septuagint was not finally fixed even in the early sixteenth century. IV Maccabees was excluded from the Bibles of Vienna and Ferrara as well as from the Bibles of Bessarion. It was not supplemented in *Codex Vaticanus* and neither printed in Alcalá (Complutensian) nor in Venice 1518 (Aldine),

---

252 See Rahlfs, *Verzeichnis*, pp. 306–07, and Jellicoe, *Septuagint*, pp. 351–52. The Psalms were already printed by Aldus Manutius in 1497 according to the main textual tradition, the so-called Lucianic text (M36248). The Greek manuscript used in 1497 is not yet identified. The Aldine of 1518 will be based on the text of 1497 (incunable M36248); see Albrecht, 'Report', p. 207.

253 Josef Schmid, *Studien zur Geschichte des griechischen Apokalypse-Textes*, MThS, I 1, 2 vols (München: Zink, 1955–56), II. Die alten Stämme (1956), p. 28.

254 See Lembke and others, *Text*, p. 24.

255 The text is next related to GA 175, a manuscript of the tenth/eleventh century: cf. Lembke and others, *Text*, p. 638.

256 See Jan Krans, 'Erasmus and Codex Vaticanus. An Overview and an Evaluation', *ASE*, 37 (2020), 447-470.

as we saw (3.3.1). Though, Johannes Lonitzer (Lonicerus) and Wolfgang Köpf(f)el (Cephaleus) working in Strasbourg discovered the work in a Greek codex and incorporated IV Maccabees into their Greek Bible of 1526. The provenance of their manuscript stood open for a long time.[257] Eberhard Nestle proposed that the Bible of Zittau, the youngest of our pandects (Ra. 44), was used in Strasbourg.[258] Indeed an alternative manuscript containing IV Maccabees is not known in the region, and the title corresponds. The manuscript and the print attribute the work to Josephus (Ἰωσίππου εἰς τοὺς Μακκαβαίους βιβλίον; Ra. 44, fol. 497ᵛ or 499ᵛ, respectively). They quote a widespread Greek conviction as we know today; but the reference to a 'book of Josephus' surprises in a Bible. Therefore, Nestle's thesis is valuable. A study confirming Nestle's thesis by the detailed comparison of the text is in progress (in Wuppertal).

All the mentioned data recommend detailed studies on the younger pandects, based on collations and transcriptions. As a consequence, I request in my

proposal 7, to collate the full text and the paratexts of the younger pandects.

The collations will reveal relevant new aspects for the research on the textual history, theological discussions and the transition from handwritten manuscripts to the printed media.

3.5. *The Unity of the Bible and Theological Reflection*

So far, I have spoken of texts; now I pick up the theological question: How was it possible to think of a unity of the Bible while knowing that the biblical Scriptures were originally written in different languages, perceiving that the primordial collections of these scriptures were set up in distinct religious communities, recognizing that the overall collection was assembled successively, and experiencing that the arrangement of the late overall collection was still fluid?

Origen developed the crucial idea in the beginning of the third century. He illustrated it by a renowned scene of Revelation: A scroll is seen in Revelation 5. 1–5, written on both sides and sealed; only Christ can open it. Origen transmitted this image to the Scripture. The text in front of the scroll is visible, as is the text of the biblical writings; that text can be read by everybody and holds an obvious meaning. The corresponding text on the back, however, is sealed and perceivable only when being opened by Christ (*comm. Ioh.*, V. 4).

Seen from this perspective, the visible text of the Scripture may be composed out of different books, may be read and used from outsiders and sinners as well as from insiders. They do not find the pivotal, non-obvious meaning. The instruction

---

257 Moses Hadas, *The Third and Fourth Books of Maccabees, Edited and Translated* (New York: Harper & Bros., 1953), p. 136, spoke of the use of a 'single poor manuscript'. He found out that the Septuagint of Strasbourg 'was the basis of the numerous 16th century editions' (p. 136).

258 Eberhard Nestle, 'Bibelübersetzungen, griechische', *TRE*, 3 (1897), 2–24 (p. 5 lines 11–13) (Ho. 44 = Ra. 44). Most parts of the Bible ΤΗΣ ΘΕΙΑΣ ΓΡΑΦΗΣ ΠΑΛΑΙΑΣ ΔΗΛΑΔΗ ΚΑΙ ΝΕΑΣ ΑΠΑΝΤΑ. Divinae scripturae veteris novaeque omnia, Strasbourg 1526 are a reprint of the Aldine.

by Christ is needed for becoming aware of the decisive meaning of the theological point that the many books are really one book.[259]

Origen's approach was developed further in the following centuries (e.g. by Jerome, *comm. Is.*, 29. 9–12[260]). Cyril of Alexandria topped off the thoughts on the unity of the Bible.[261] He took up Origen's motif of the Scripture (γραφή) sealed by God 'as one book' (καθάπερ βιβλίον ἓν) and added the often-quoted sentence 'For the whole Scripture is a unity (ἓν γὰρ ἡ πᾶσά ἐστι) and spoken through one, the holy Spirit' (λελάληται δι' ἑνὸς τοῦ ἁγίου πνεύματος, *comm. Is.*, 29. 11–12).[262] Hence, the Spirit opens the Christological understanding of the Scripture (of all the different scriptures). The Scripture becomes a unity in a profound theological sense (ἓν) through the Spirit who is 'one' (δι' ἑνός; a reflection of trinitarian monotheism).[263]

This line of thought often attracted anti-Jewish effects. In the eyes of Cyril, the Jews failed up against the Christological message of the Spirit and the one Scripture (*comm. Is.*, 29. 11–12). But the central point is valid in abstraction from anti-Jewish notes. The fundamental idea explains the peculiarities of the Byzantine pandects:

- The holy Scripture consists of books and collections and, yet, forms a continuous text and a unity now in theological perspective. For the Spirit speaks through all the Scriptures. It would be wrong, therefore, to separate parts of the Bible within the current text. The division into Old and New Testament was not only historically banned from the interior of the pandects. The ban made theological sense, too.
- The theological aim directs the exegesis. Nevertheless, the literal text of the Scriptures is not at all arbitrary. In contrary, the Spirit lightens and decodes just the literal text. Hence, the literal text needs care and accurateness. Thus, the theological argument protects the old literal texts. Efforts looking for the best texts of the old Scriptures are justified, and contacts to the Jewish neighbors who have good old texts become very plausible.

In this way, the inner dynamics of the textual development crystallizing in the pandects and the theological argument complement and support one another.

---

259 See Matthew R. Crawford, 'Scripture as "One Book": Origen, Jerome and Cyril of Alexandria on Isaiah 29:11', *JTS*, 64 (2013), 137–53.
260 CCSL 73.373–74.
261 Cyril has come across already as one of the Fathers framing the terminology of Old and New Testament and listing the canonical books: see sections 2.7 fn. 138, 2.8 and 2.9.
262 PG 70, 656A.
263 See Matthew R. Crawford, *Cyril of Alexandria's Trinitarian Theology of Scripture*, Oxford Early Christian Studies (Oxford: Oxford University Press, 2014), pp. 112–13; Robert Louis Wilken, 'Cyril of Alexandria as Interpreter of the Old Testament', in *The Theology of St Cyril of Alexandria: A Critical Appreciation*, ed. by Daniel A. Keating and Thomas Weinandy (London: T&T Clark, 2007), pp. 1–21 (pp. 14–15).

Fig. 16. Aquila (to the left) and Symmachus (to the
right) in Codex Vat. Gr. 752, fol. 187ʳ
(at LXX-Psalm 59. 1–3).[264]

An intriguing manuscript of the Psalms illustrates the matter. The Codex
Vat. Gr. 752 (written in about 1059)[265] reminds every user of the old translations by

264 Fig.: Bibliotheca Apostolica Vaticana; cf. <https://digi.vatlib.it/view/MSS_Vat.gr.752.pt.1> [accessed
     4 May 2020].
265 General information in *A Book of Psalms from Eleventh-Century Byzantium: The Complex of Texts
     and Images in Vat. Gr. 752*, ed. by Barbara Crostini and Glenn Peers, Studi e Testi, 504 (Città del
     Vaticano: Biblioteca Apostolica Vaticana, 2016).

an own chapter of the Prolegomena (fol. 8ᵛ–9ᵛ; called 'De Interpretibus VI' in the description of the manuscript[266]). The description there starts with the Septuagint (using that term explicitly): Πρώτη ἐστιν ἡ τῶν Ἐβδομήκοντα […]', 'the first [most important and oldest translation] is the one of the Seventy […]' (fol. 8ᵛ). Then the paragraph goes on to the so-called younger translations (Aquila, Symmachus, etc.).[267] Long-living traditions of the Hexapla become visible (cf. sections 1.2 and 1.4). Other prolegomena follow (fol. 9ᵛ–17ᵛ).

Thereupon, two miniatures lead over to the biblical text in showing the crucified and exalted Christ (fol. 18ʳ⁻ᵛ). The readers learn that the Psalms are to be read Christologically; and the catena of the Fathers (especially Hesych of Jerusalem) accompanies the lemmata of the LXX-Psalms (fol. 19ʳ–250ᵛ).

From time to time the text gives relevant hints to the old translators. The most prominent case, fol. 187ʳ, enlists Aquila (the preferred translator of the Byzantine Jews[268]) and Symmachus for the understanding of LXX-Psalm 59. 3 (ὁ θεός ἀπώσω ἡμᾶς, 'O God, you have rejected us'). Furthermore, a miniature depicts both translators in conversation about their translations and with a halo[269] — even Aquila who was criticized in the prolegomena for having left the Christian community[270] (see the miniature in fig. 16).[271] The artist may have worked independently from the compiler of the prolegomena and perhaps only knew the catenae. But if we could ask him for

---

266 <https://digi.vatlib.it/mss/detail/225684> [accessed 5 May 2020].

267 Two miniatures inserted on fol. 9ʳ show Aquila and Hadrian or three translators, respectively. The inscription on the second miniature (depicting the three translators) reads κάστρον ἡ σινόπης. [ἑρ]μηνείσαν καὶ αὐτοὶ τὴν θείαν γραφήν, 'the fort of Sinope (the home of Aquila); they translated the divine Scripture, too'.

268 Justinian had articulated a strong preference for the Septuagint in his Novel 146 (February 8, 553) but permitted that Jews also used the translation of Aquila (*Corpus Iuris Civilis III Novellae*, 146. I. 1; <https://droitromain.univ-grenoble-alpes.fr/> [accessed 5 May 2020]). See Nicholas de Lange, 'Jewish Greek Bible versions', in *The New Cambridge History of the Bible*, ed. by Richard Marsden and E. Ann Matter (Cambridge: Cambridge University Press, 2012), II. From 600 to 1450, pp. 56–68 (p. 63); Jenny R. Labendz, 'Aquila's Bible Translation in Late Antiquity: Jewish and Christian Perspectives', *HTR*, 102 (2009), 353–88 (pp. 374–76).

269 Detailed description in Glenn Peers, 'Process and Meaning: Penitence, Prayer and Pedagogy in Vat. Gr. 752', in *A Book of Psalms from Eleventh-Century Byzantium: The Complex of Texts and Images in Vat. Gr. 752*, ed. by Barbara Crostini and Glenn Peers, Studi e Testi, 504 (Città del Vaticano: Biblioteca Apostolica Vaticana, 2016), pp. 437–65 (pp. 439–44).

270 Aquila had a bad name in Christianity; see Epiphanius, *De mensuris et ponderibus*, 14–15, PG 43, 260–61 and other sources; Natalio Fernández Marcos, *The Septuagint in Context: Introduction to the Greek Versions of the Bible* (Leiden: Brill, 2000), p. 111; Labendz, 'Aquila's Bible Translation', pp. 376–86. Our codex (Vat. Gr. 752 fol. 9ʳ col. 1) tells: 'the second (translation) is the one of Aquila; he, who comes from Sinope in Pontus and is a Greek, was baptized in Jerusalem; the wretched, who has become godless in selling Christ (scl. by his involvement by astrology expressed in some forms of the legend) and went on to the Jews, translated the divine Scripture under the Emperor Hadrian, who had leprosy; (he made his translation) 44 periods of time after the translation of the 72 (= the Septuagint)' (δεύτερα ἡ τοῦ ἀκύλα· οὗτος / ἀπὸ σινώπης τοῦ πόν/του ὑπάρχων· καὶ ἕλλην ὤν / ἐβαπτίσθη ἐν ἱεροσολύ/μοις· καὶ πώλων / τὸν χ̅ν̅ ἀθείκας / ὁ ἄθλιος καὶ / τοῖς ἰουδαίοις / προδραμὼν ἠρ/μήνευσε καὶ αὐτὴν τὴν θείαν / γραφὴν ἐπὶ ἀδριανοῦ βα/σιλέως· τοῦ λεπρωθέντος· / μετὰ χρόνους· μ̅δ̅· τῆς τῶν / ο̅β̅· ἑρμηνείας: Transcription by Peter Malik, Wuppertal, 5 May 2020).

271 The astonishing fact is noted, e.g., by Crostini, 'Greek Christian Bible', pp. 47–48.

his intention, he probably would concede 'Aquila was alienated to Christianity, as is told' and, nevertheless, insist: 'Aquila and Symmachus help in understanding the Scripture; both must be perceived via their translation and hence earn the halo'.[272]

Hermeneutics have changed after the Byzantine Period. According to the historical criticism (used in this contribution), research on the historical progress in itself allows for explaining the unity of the Bible. But the history of the pandects and biblical manuscripts cannot be fully understood without envisaging their theological contexts. Greek thoughts correlate to the Greek transmission of the Scriptures and are mirrored, e.g. in the catena manuscripts. Therefore, I dare to make an

> *eighth proposal*: Exegetical commentaries on the Greek Scriptures should include hints to the interpretations of the Greek Fathers and their theology of Scripture.

4. Conclusion

The Greek manuscripts combining texts from the Septuagint and the New Testament tell a long and fascinating story. A few papyri give color to the beginnings (section 1). They display the use of biblical texts in private studies, in Christian piety and in communities which sometimes deviated from the ecclesial mainstream.[273]

After the Constantinian shift, full Bibles appear (section 2). The old pandects (א, A, B, C) are famous and well examined, the younger pandects nearly unknown and yet of high interest, too. The title 'Bible' ('biblia') arises (§ 2.8). The order of the biblical texts develops, reaches something like a first finale in the Bible of Vienna (twelfth to thirteenth century)[274] and turns up again surprisingly in the discussions and endeavors for a Latin-Greek church union in the fifteenth century (Bibles of Ferrara and Venice; sections 2.4, 2.6, 2.9 and 3.3).[275] The scriptoria endeavor for a standardized text, and yet, textual forms compete (§ 3.4.3). Even the prints which will supersede the pandects (Erasmus, the Aldine and Complutensian) can be better understood by comparisons to the pandects in some respect (§§ 2.8.4, 2.9.4, 3.4.3, and 3.4.4).

If we look into the Greek pandects, all of them understand the Bible as a unity and avoid the division of their interior text into Old and New Testament. That phenomenon has its roots in the textual history but is supported by theological reflections on the

---

272 Barbara Crostini and Glenn Peers, 'Introduction', in *A Book of Psalms from Eleventh-Century Byzantium: The Complex of Texts and Images in Vat. Gr. 752*, ed. by Barbara Crostini and Glenn Peers, Studi e Testi, 504 (Città del Vaticano: Biblioteca Apostolica Vaticana, 2016), pp. 21–40 (p. 30), look to the historical context (e.g. Karaite communities within Byzantium) and consider the possibility that the peculiarities of the codex intended 'a dialogue across otherwise-perceived divides' between Christian and Jews.

273 I could not exclude chiliastic influences on the most fascinating of the pertinent papyri, PapOxy VIII 1075 (Exod) /1079 (Rev); see section 1.3.

274 Wien, ÖNB Theol. gr. 23 (Ra. 130; NT GA 218).

275 Ferrara, Bibl. Com. Cl. II, 187, I–III (Ra. 106, NT GA 582; fourteenth century); Venice, Bibl. Marc. Gr. Z. 5 (= 420; Ra. 68; NT GA 205) and 6 (Ra. 122; NT GA 2886), both fifteenth century (the Bibles of Bessarion).

efficacy of the one Spirit in the one Scripture as we saw (§ 3.5). Moreover, textual transmission's obligations to Jewish traditions are stronger than was thought previously (§§ 2.4, 2.8.1, and 3.5); some pertinent corrections are recommended against older conventions of biblical editions (§§ 3.1 and 3.2).

The results open up a wide field for future research. The textual history of the Greek pandects deserves ongoing exploration. The investigation of Jewish and Christian contacts in the textual transmission of the Septuagint Scriptures which has started should go on. Connections to the genesis and history of the old Latin pandects are little-known.[276] The use of the Greek pandects in the cultural conflicts of the late Middle Ages demands attention.[277] The route of the manuscripts from their previous Greek owners to the present libraries is of interest for their reception history, etc.

The present contribution has given an overview on the manuscripts and articulated outcomes in the form of theses. I repeat the main theses:

1) The coordination of Septuagint and New Testament texts in material units started in the third century.[278] Not an overall tendency, but interests of single communities and learned readers triggered the early development.
2) The full Bibles belong to the time after the Constantinian shift. The scriptoria of the fourth and fifth (or early sixth) century produced the celebrated great codices. Afterwards the attention to full Bibles declined. In sum not more than a dozen Byzantine pandects are preserved, and many of them are incomplete.[279]
3) The correlation of New Testament and Septuagint texts did not set off a ponderable textual harmonization. The established textual forms possessed dignity. Textual criticism must take into regard that stability of transmission.
4) The full Bibles originated in Christianity. But the use of the Septuagint and the other Jewish translations (or revisions; Aquila, etc.) reminded Christianity of its Jewish roots. The Jewish-Christian contacts concerning the biblical texts outlasted the parting of the ways. The Jewish roots of the Septuagint therefore remain sustainably relevant.
5) The pandects understand the Bible as a unit consisting of a series of collections. The New Testament became the last collection in the arrangement. Hermeneutically, the Septuagint requires priority in the overall order and intertextuality of the Bible.
6) None of the pandects separated the New Testament from the foregoing collections in building a contrast between Old and New Testament. The idea of a unity of all the biblical Scriptures prevailed and was supported by orthodox theology.

---

276 Cf. the etymology of the term pandect in fn. 3 and the hints to the library of Cassiodorus in section 2.4.4 (with fn. 114) and table 2. A correlation of the development of Greek and Latin pandects is needed.
277 The text and margins of the Bible of Ferrara, e.g., can be surveyed in the context of the discussions held on and following to the council of Ferrara and Florence.
278 I rejected the thesis of a biblical collection combining Septuagint and New Testament already in the second century: see § 1.1.
279 See the list in § 2.1.

7) Revelation was controversial in Greek Christianity for a long time but became an integral part of the pandects, all in all.[280] The Psalms of Solomon, in contrary, were not fully integrated. They were understood as an appendix (*Alexandrinus*) or excluded (so the younger pandects).[281]

As a consequence, I made some proposals. I repeat them here:

1) The younger pandects should be taken into regard in the edition of the full Bible and of the Septuagint besides the old pandects. The young manuscripts, their taxonomy and collations of their text are worth care and attention.

2) The Greek pandects recommend avoiding a division of the Bible into 'Old' and 'New Testament' in favor of a sequence of μέρη ('portions'), altogether forming the one Bible (βιβλία).[282] Subsequently, an intensified exchange between the editorial teams of the Göttingen LXX and the *Editio Critica Maior* of the New Testament on extent, arrangement and criteria of the editions is desired.

3) Text critical decisions postulating a strong Christian influence on the transmission of the Septuagint should be reconsidered. Conjectures which are based on the thesis of a Christian influence on the text of the Septuagint are unsure (e.g. the conjecture χριστὸς κυρίου in Psalms of Solomon 17. 32).[283]

4) The 'One Bible' lives in the orthodox Christianity via the liturgy. The Christian Odes belong to the full Greek Bible, in this respect. But a revitalization of the oldest order of the Odes (according to *Codex Alexandrinus*) should turn out the Jewish core of the collection.[284]

5) The Greek structuring of the biblical books into *kephalaia* must be valorized in the edition of the New Testament. The place of Hebrews in the *Editio Critica Maior* is not yet settled; I prefer the established place after Philemon with the young pandects (against the arrangement II Thessalonians-Hebrews of the old pandects).[285]

6) The biblical manuscripts recall their use in Orthodox Christianity and motivate ecumenical encounters. Exegetical commentaries on the Greek Scriptures should include information about the interpretations by the Greek Fathers.[286]

▼ ABSTRACT The writings of the Septuagint and of the first Christians were transmitted separately for generations. The first combination of biblical books is witnessed in the third century (PapOxy VIII 1075 / 1079). From the fourth century onwards, the inner-biblical collections were combined into full Bibles. The old uncials א, B, A, C and the LXX-part

---

280 Cf. §§ 2.9 and 3.3.4.
281 Details in § 3.1.1.
282 See § 2.8, etc.
283 See § 3.1.2.
284 See § 3.2.
285 See § 3.3.3.
286 I thank Tim Germund, Benjamin Blum and Marybeth Hauffe for their help in preparing the print.

in codex Venetus, the great minuscule Ra. 198/GA 33, the LXX-part of the Biblia Leonis patricii, the pandect of Vienna, the Bible of Ferrara, the Bibles of Bessarion and the Bible of Zittau are preserved. These manuscripts (originating up to about 1500) normally do not divide the βιβλία / ἁγία γραφή into Old and New Testament. This essay analyzes the samples of books in the overall collection, their titles and their order, possible Christian-Jewish contacts and the place of disputed books (Rev; PsSal). It proposes the order of A for the Odes (against Ra). It doubts the influence of New Testament quotations on the textual transmission of the Septuagint. If reflects the theological interest in the unity of the Bible which is claimed from Origen and Cyril of Alexandria onwards. The observations recommend stronger contacts between the editions of the Septuagint and New Testament.

LUCIANO BOSSINA

The Litter of Solomon

Textual and Exegetical Problems in Canticles 3. 6–11

οὐκ ἐκ τῆς ἱστορίας ὁ περὶ τῆς κλίνης λόγος

Gregory of Nyssa

1. Pompey and the Temple of Jerusalem

In the summer of 63 BCE, at the height of his eastern campaign, Pompey storms Jerusalem:[1] on the Sabbath, while the Jews observe their day of rest, Roman soldiers build embankments so as to conquer the sturdy walls defending the Temple. A breach opens and allows the besiegers to enter: 12,000 Jews will perish in the conflict. Pompey enters the Temple, 'whither it was not lawful for any to enter but the high priest', and sees what lies inside.[2] Josephus provides the list: 'the golden table, the holy candlestick, and the pouring vessels, and a great quantity of spices; and besides these there were among the treasures two thousand talents of sacred money'.[3] 'Yet did Pompey touch nothing of all this' — Josephus assures us — 'on account of his regard to religion'. This news, which the Flavian historian repeats with similar words in both the *Bellum* and the *Antiquitates*, served to exalt the magnanimous figure of Pompey. Josephus speaks of εὐσέβεια, Cicero of *pudor*, demonstrating in the midst of one of his legal orations how this news circulated in Rome and what its use was in the political debate of the time (*Pro Flacco* 28,

---

1 Sources about Pompey's campaign in Syria and Judea: Cic. *pro Flacco* 67; Diod. Sic. *Biblioth.* XL. 4G; Liv. *Perioch.* 102; Strab. XVI. 2. 40; Plin. *Hist. nat.* XXXIII. 136; Jos. Fl. *Ant.* XIV. 34–79; *Bellum* I 131–58; Plut. *Pomp.* 39. 3–42. 3; *Moral.* 168C; Flor. *Epit.* III. 5. 29–30; Appian. *Bell. civ.* V. 40; *Bell. mitr.* 506; 557; *Bell. syr.* 250–54; 367, Tac. *Hist.* V. 9. 1; Tert. *Apol.* XVI. 2–3; Cass. Dion. *Hist. rom.* XXXVII. 7. 1; 15. 1–16; 20. 1. Iust. *Epit.* XL. 2. 3–5; Eutrop. *Brev.* VI. 14. 2; Fest. *Brev.* 16. 2–3; Amm. Marc. *Hist.* XIV. 8. 12; Oros. *Hist.* VI. 6. 1–4; Sulp. Sev. *Cron.* II. 26. 5–6; Zonar. *Epit.* X. 5.
2 Jos. Fl. *Bellum* I. 152.
3 Jos. Fl. *Ant.* XIV. 72.

New Avenues in Biblical Exegesis in Light of the Septuagint
ed. by Leonardo Pessoa da Silva Pinto and Daniela Scialabba, Turnhout, 2022 (*SEPT*, 1), pp. 279–302
© BREPOLS ❧ PUBLISHERS   DOI 10.1484/M.SEPT-EB.5.127719

67–68). Yet Cassius Dio presents a completely different version of the facts, and reports crudely that after the conquest of Jerusalem and the Temple πάντα τὰ χρήματα διηρπάσθη (XXXVII 16, 4).[4]

This contradiction within the sources as to the sacking of the Temple in 63 BCE corresponds to the more general attitude of ancient historiography, which tried to mitigate, or deny entirely, the ferocity of Pompey's conquest of Jerusalem. The witnesses that transmit the most vivid memory are essentially Jewish: the *Pesher of Habakkuk* discovered in Qumran (*1QpHab*), very close to the events — which laments the arrival of the 'Kittim', who 'come from far off, from the islands of the sea, to devour all the nations, like an eagle, insatiable', 'to destroy and pillage the cities of the country'[5] – and the *Psalms of Solomon* that mention the 'Gentiles', 'coming up to the altar' and 'brazenly trampling around with their sandals on'.[6] But this tradition was overwhelmed by powerful opposing forces: the case of Josephus, benevolent and conciliatory, is the most evident, but it was certainly not the only one.

In fact, the Romans, the Jews and the Christians were all interested in erasing the memory of Pompey's sacking of Jerusalem. On the Roman front, the Flavian era had an unconditional admiration for Pompey, and took advantage of the complacent pen of Josephus to expressly deny the despoliation of the Temple, depicting the warlord

---

4   Tacitus (*Hist.* V. 9, 1) offers a rather simplifying account: 'The first Roman to subdue the Jews and set foot in their temple by right of conquest was Gnaeus Pompey: thereafter it was a matter of common knowledge that there were no representations of the gods within, but that the place was empty and the secret shrine contained nothing [*nulla intus deum effigie vacuam sedem et inania arcana*]. The walls of Jerusalem were razed, but the temple remained standing' (transl. by C. H. Moore). This account does not consider the distinction between the 'Holy', which contained the treasury, and the 'Holy of Holies', which was in fact empty.

5   *1QpHab* coll. II–III (on Abacuc 1. 6–9): text and translation: Florentino García Martínez and Eibert J. C. Tigchelaar, *The Dead Sea Scrolls Study Edition* (Leiden: Brill, 1999), vol. 1, pp. 12–13. See Karl Elliger, *Studien zum Habakuk-Kommentar vom Toten Meer* (Tübingen: Mohr, 1953); William Hugh Brownlee, *The Text of Habakkuk in the Ancient Commentary from Qumran* (Philadelphia: SBL, 1959); William Hugh Brownlee, *The Midrash Pesher of Habakkuk* (Missoula, Mont.: Scholars Press, 1979); John Glyndwr Harris, *The Qumran Commentary on Habakkuk* (London: A. R. Mowbray, 1966).

6   Psalm of Solomon 2. 2: Robert B. Wright, *The Psalms of Solomon: a Critical Edition of the Greek Text* (London: T&T Clark, 2007); *Psalmi Salomonis*, ed. by Felix Albrecht, *Septuaginta. Vetus Testamentum Graecum auctoritate Academiae Scientiarum Gottingensis editum*, vol. XII, pars 3 (Göttingen: Vandenhoeck & Ruprecht, 2018). For the historical context and the multiple references to Pompey in the *Psalms of Solomon*, see Benedikt Eckhardt, 'The Psalms of Solomon as a historical source for the late Hasmonean Period', in *The Psalms of Solomon. Language, History, Theology*, ed. by Eberhard Bons and Patrick Pouchelle (Atlanta: SBL, 2015), pp. 7–29 (but all the essays in the volume are of prime interest). See also Kenneth Atkinson, *I Cried to the Lord: a Study of the Psalms of Solomon's Historical Background and Social Setting* (Leiden: Brill, 2004); Kenneth Atkinson, *A History of the Hasmonean State. Josephus and Beyond* (London: T&T Clark, 2016), pp. 147–57; Kenneth Atkinson, *The Hasmoneans and their Neighbors: New Historical Reconstructions from the Dead Sea Scrolls and Classical Sources* (London: T&T Clark, 2018), pp. 113–42.

as a kind of gentleman, unable to steal. On the Jewish front, posthumous memory preferred to direct anti-Roman accusations towards other and more resounding targets: the expedition of Titus and Vespasian a century later, with the apocalyptic destruction of the Temple, and the still later persecution of Hadrian — historical events which, compared to the sacking by Pompey, seemed decidedly more serious and symbolic. Christian historians acted in similar terms, with the additional aggravating circumstance of the charge of deicide: the punishers of the Jewish infidels could not be *ante Christum*, and therefore the Roman power that crushes Jerusalem is not that of Pompey, but that of Titus and Vespasian, moved by the avenging hand of God. These forces — different in their ways, but similar in their results — marginalized the memory of the sacking by Pompey, placing the manifestation of Roman violence in a later period.

Yet, thanks to the powerful impression provoked by the triumph celebrated by Pompey in 61 BCE, the memory of his sacking of Jerusalem is also documented by other sources. Both Plutarch and Appian have left quite detailed descriptions, and their reports undoubtedly show that in the magnificent spoils of war exhibited through the streets of Rome during that extraordinary triumph, not a few came directly from Jerusalem.[7]

Among these sources, the list provided by the *Chronicon Paschale*, a historical work of primary importance and mostly based on excellent documentation, is particularly striking. In the year 61 BCE (under the consulship of Marcus Pupius Piso Frugi Calpurnianus and Marcus Valerius Messalla Niger) the *Chronicon* records the following information (*Chron. Pasch.* 350. 19–351. 11: ιζ'. ὑπ. Πίσωνος καὶ Μεσσάλα):

> Πομπήιος ὁ μέγας ἑλὼν τὰ Ἱεροσόλυμα καὶ τὸν ναὸν συλήσας, καὶ ἀφελόμενος τὰς ἁγίας γραφὰς καὶ τοὺς κανθάρους καὶ χαρακτῆρας χρυσοῦς καὶ ἄλλα πολλὰ ἅγια σκεύη καὶ τὴν ἄμπελον τὴν χρυσῆν καὶ τὴν κλίνην Σολομῶνος, Ὑρκανῷ τὴν ἀρχιερωσύνην τῷ υἱῷ Ἀλεξάνδρου καὶ Ἀλεξάνδρας τῆς Σαλίνας παραδίδωσι, καὶ Ἀντίπατρόν τινα Ἀσκαλωνίτην τῆς Παλαιστίνης ἐπιμελητὴν καθιστᾷ· τό τε πᾶν ἔθνος Ἰουδαίων ὑπόφορον Ῥωμαίοις καταστήσας πολλοὺς αὐτῶν αἰχμαλώτους εἰς Ῥώμην ἤγαγεν τῇ συγκλήτῳ.
>
> Ὑρκανὸς τὰ ὑπὸ Πομπηίου καθαιρεθέντα τείχη τῆς Ἱερουσαλὴμ ἀνίστησιν.

According to the *Chronicon*, when the spoils of war were paraded, the people of Rome could also admire the 'litter of Solomon' (κλίνη Σολομῶνος), directly stolen from the Temple (τὸν ναὸν συλήσας). But which κλίνη was it? And what do we know about it?

---

7 Plut. *Pomp.* 42, 2–5; Appian. *Bell. mitr.*, 116–17.

It is not difficult to ascertain that the only document attesting a specific κλίνη Σολομῶνος is to be found in the Septuagint translation of the Song of Songs, within a scene with an evident nuptial character (Canticles 3. 6–11):[8]

⁶ Τίς αὕτη ἡ ἀναβαίνουσα ἀπὸ τῆς ἐρήμου
ὡς στελέχη καπνοῦ τεθυμιαμένη
σμύρναν καὶ λίβανον ἀπὸ πάντων κονιορτῶν
μυρεψοῦ;

⁷ ἰδοὺ ἡ κλίνη τοῦ Σαλωμων,
ἑξήκοντα δυνατοὶ κύκλῳ αὐτῆς
ἀπὸ δυνατῶν Ισραηλ,
⁸ πάντες κατέχοντες ῥομφαίαν
δεδιδαγμένοι πόλεμον,
ἀνὴρ ῥομφαία αὐτοῦ ἐπὶ μηρὸν αὐτοῦ
ἀπὸ θάμβους ἐν νυξίν.
⁹ φορεῖον ἐποίησεν ἑαυτῷ ὁ βασιλεὺς Σαλωμων
ἀπὸ ξύλων τοῦ Λιβάνου,
¹⁰ στύλους αὐτοῦ ἐποίησεν ἀργύριον
καὶ ἀνάκλιτον αὐτοῦ χρύσεον,
ἐπίβασις αὐτοῦ πορφυρᾶ,
ἐντὸς αὐτοῦ λιθόστρωτον,
ἀγάπην ἀπὸ θυγατέρων Ιερουσαλημ.
¹¹ ἐξέλθατε καὶ ἴδετε
ἐν τῷ βασιλεῖ Σαλωμων
ἐν τῷ στεφάνῳ, ᾧ ἐστεφάνωσεν αὐτὸν ἡ μήτηρ αὐτοῦ
ἐν ἡμέρᾳ νυμφεύσεως αὐτοῦ
καὶ ἐν ἡμέρᾳ εὐφροσύνης καρδίας αὐτοῦ.

⁶ Who is this coming up from the wilderness,
like columns of smoke,
perfumed with myrrh and frankincense,
of all the perfumer's powders?

⁷ Look, it is the litter of Salomon!
Around it are sixty mighty men
of Israel's mighty men,
⁸ all holding a sword
and expert in war —
a man, his sword at his thigh
because of terror by night.
⁹ King Salomon made himself a sedan chair
from Lebanon's trees.
¹⁰ He made its posts silver,
its back gold,
its step purple;
its interior was inlaid with stone,
love from Ierousalem's daughters.
¹¹ Come out, and look
at King Salomon,
at the crown with which his mother
crowned him on the day of his wedding
and on the day of his heart's gladness.

Did this κλίνη really end up in Rome? The issue concerns not only Pompey's triumph and the sacking of the Temple of Jerusalem, but the history itself of the Song of Songs.

---

8 The Song of Songs is not yet edited in Göttingen's *editio critica maior*: I therefore quote the text of Rahlfs: *Septuaginta, id est Vetus Testamentum graece iuxta LXX interpretes*, ed. by Alfred Rahlfs, editio altera, quam recognovit et emendavit Robert Hanhart (Stuttgart: Deutsche Bibelgesellschaft, 2006). The translation (with small modifications) is by Jay C. Treat: *A New English Translation of the Septuagint and the Other Greek Translations Traditionally Included under that Title*, ed. by Albert Pietersma and Benjamin G. Wright (New York: Oxford University Press, 2007), p. 663. Two contributions of primary importance have recently been published on the Septuagint translation of the Song: Jean-Marie Auwers, *Le Cantique des Cantiques*, La Bible d'Alexandrie, 19 (Paris: Cerf, 2019); Dries de Crom, *LXX Song of Songs and Descriptive Translation Studies* (Göttingen: Vandenhoeck & Ruprecht, 2019). Anyone who wants to study LXX Song of Songs cannot ignore these two relevant works.

2. Character and Importance of the Section 3. 6–11

It is acknowledged that the Song presents innumerable historical, linguistic and literary problems, starting from the difficulty of recognizing a unitary project among its different sections. On this fundamental aspect there are diametrically opposed hypotheses in the history of its exegesis: some scholars attribute to the work a basic unity, and also a specific theology, while others instead consider it only an unsuccessful juxtaposition of 'songs' or 'epigrams' of different origins.

From this point of view, section 3. 6–11 has its own recognizable cohesion,[9] and shows two features that make it particularly important in the overall structure of the work. Firstly, the most explicit references to 'King Solomon' are concentrated in these verses: the Solomonic authorship of the Song (accepted by all ancient exegesis) and therefore its entry in a well-structured triptych (with Proverbs and Qohelet) essentially depends on these verses, which therefore played a crucial role also in the difficult process of canonization of the text, both in the Jewish and in the Christian sphere.[10] Today, of course, no scholar would still be willing to confirm the authorship of Solomon, and there is also a widespread awareness that the dating of the work must be later by many centuries: this is proved by linguistic analysis,[11]

---

9   However, there is no lack of opposing opinions: Gillis Gerleman, *Ruth / Das Hohelied* (Neukirchen-Vluyn: Neukirchener Verlag, 1963), pp. 134–43 hypothesizes two different compositions (vv. 6–8 and 9–11). Othmar Keel, *Das Hohelied* (Zürich: Theologischer Verlag, 1986), pp. 118–29 e Günter Krinetzki, *Kommentar zum Hohelied. Bildsprache und theologische Botschaft* (Frankfurt am Main: Lang, 1981), pp. 118–36 even three: vv. 6–8; 9–10d; 10e–11. See Gianni Barbiero, *Song of Songs. A Close Reading*, transl. by Michael Tait (Leiden: Brill, 2011), pp. 142–45.

10 John Barton, 'The Canonicity of Song of Songs', in *Perspectives on the Song of Songs — Perspektiven der Hoheliedauslegung*, ed. by Anselm C. Hagedorn (Berlin: de Gruyter, 2005), pp. 1–7 denies that the canonization of the Song has ever been problematic: 'It is hard to discuss supposed Christian opposition to the acceptance of the Song, since I am not aware of any evidence for it whatever' (p. 1); 'None of the Fathers argues that the book is of doubtful status' (p. 2); 'there is no evidence at all that any serious interpreters in antiquity ever read the Song "literally" anyway' (p. 5). These statements leave one astonished: Barton evidently ignores the various testimonies on the Christian opposition to the Song, both in the East (Didym. Alex. *Comm. in Eccl.* 5, 30–6, 23) and in the West (Filastr. *Div. Her. Lib.* CXXXV, CL); he also ignores that in the Antiochene context the Song has never found full acceptance until Theodoret. It is surprising that the explicit and well-known opposition to the Song of Theodore of Mopsuestia (who interpreted the Song 'literally' and certainly was a 'serious interpreter') is also overlooked. But this topic cannot be covered here: see Luciano Bossina, 'Il prezzo della pace. Il Cantico dei cantici ad Antiochia tra Teodoro e Teodoreto (con l'edizione del Prologo dell'Explanatio in Canticum canticorum)', *Rivista di Storia del Cristianesimo*, 18 (2021, forthcoming); Luciano Bossina, 'Teodoreto, Abisak e i "calunniatori del Cantico dei cantici"', *Vetera Christianorum*, 59 (2022, forthcoming).

11 After the studies of Giovanni Garbini, *Cantico dei cantici* (Brescia: Paideia 1992), summary overview pp. 296–99; and of F. W. Dobbs-Allsopp, 'Late Linguistic Features in the Song of Songs', in *Perspectives on the Song of Songs*, pp. 27–77, there can no longer be any doubt that the language of the Song is (very) late Hebrew. Certainly, there is no shortage of eccentric positions: in 2006 Gary A. Rendsburg argued that the Song should be linguistically dated to the Persian era, cf. Gary A. Rendsburg, 'Israelian Hebrew in the Song of Songs', in *Biblical Hebrew in Its Northwest Semitic Setting. Typological and Historical Perspectives*, ed. by Steven E. Fassberg and Avi M. Hurvitz (Jerusalem: Hebrew University Magnes Press, 2006), pp. 315–23. In 2009

and finally also by relevant historical and archaeological arguments.[12] However, the problem remains of explaining the Solomonic 'fiction' of the text and the evocative role of the famous king in these verses.

Rendsburg himself, together with Scott B. Noegel, *Solomon's Vineyard. Literary and Linguistic Studies in the Song of Songs* (Atlanta: Society of Biblical Literature, 2009), instead argued that 'the Song of Songs was written circa 900 b.c.e. [*sic*], in the northern dialect of ancient Hebrew, by an author of unsurpassed literary ability' (p. 184). Fortunately, these theses do not seem to have enjoyed much success: in a recent Handbook the Song is considered and studied as an example of Late Biblical Hebrew: Matthew Morgenstern, 'Late Biblical Hebrew', in *A Handbook of Biblical Hebrew, Volume 1: Periods, Corpora, and Reading Traditions*, ed. by W. Randall Garr and Steven E. Fassberg (Winona Lake, Indiana: Eisenbrauns, 2016), pp. 43–54. More cautious are Ian Young, Robert Rezetko, Martin Ehrensvärd, *Linguistic Dating of Biblical Texts. An Introduction to Approaches and Problems*, 2 vols (London/New York: Routledge, 2014), I, p. 138: 'other books like Jonah, Ruth and Song of Songs, cannot be assigned to a particular historical period on the basis of their linguistic profiles'; I, p. 197: 'Song of Songs cannot be placed anywhere in a linear history of B[iblical] H[ebrew]. The dialect of Song of Songs is not A[rchaic] B[iblical] H[ebrew]. Nor is it E[arly] B[iblical] H[ebrew] or L[ate] B[iblical] H[ebrew]. Following the end of the biblical period, the dominant literary language was a form of BH, i.e. Q[umran] H[ebrew]. It cannot be later than this, since manuscripts of the Song of Songs turn up at Qumran. Song of Songs fits nowhere in a linear history of BH. Whatever period we date it to, we must explain its language as evidence of another variety of Hebrew than that of the rest of the Hebrew Bible. Once we realise that Song of Songs' Hebrew was, according to our current knowledge, never the normal sort of literary Hebrew in any age, we no longer have any firm peg to date its composition'. There is also to consider that the Song presents a 'heavily Mishnaising' Hebrew, cf. *A Handbook of Biblical Hebrew*, I, p. 230; p. 244: 'Probably the biblical book whose language is most commonly linked with M[ishnaic] H[ebrew] is the Song of Songs'; see also e.g. Michael V. Fox, *The Song of Songs and Ancient Egyptian Love Songs* (Madison: University of Wisconsin Press, 1985), p. 187: 'The language of the Song resembles Mishnaic Hebrew in many ways'; Miguel Pérez Fernández, *An Introductory Grammar of Rabbinic Hebrew*, trans. by John F. Elwolde (Leiden: Brill, 1999), pp. 30–33 quotes exactly Canticles 3. 7: '"the litter of Solomon"; literally: "his litter which belongs to Solomon"'. Yet, there is disagreement among scholars on the consequences that Aramaisms entail in dating a biblical text: cf. Avi Hurvitz, 'The Chronological Significance of "Aramaisms" in Biblical Hebrew', *Israel Exploration Journal* 18 (1968), 234–40; Avi Hurvitz 'Hebrew and Aramaic in the Biblical Period: The Problem of "Aramaisms" in Linguistic Research on the Hebrew Bible', in *Biblical Hebrew: Studies in Chronology and Typology*, ed. by Ian Young, (London: T&T Clark, 2003), pp. 24–37; Gary A. Rendsburg, 'Hurvitz Redux: On the Continued Scholarly Inattention to a Simple Principle of Hebrew Philology', in *Biblical Hebrew*, pp. 104–28.

12   See the well-argued considerations of Torleif Elgvin, *The Literary Growth of the Song of Songs in the Hasmonean and Early-Herodian Periods* (Leuven: Peeters, 2018), who links the undeniable Hellenistic imprint of the Song with the historical, urban and cultural development of Jerusalem, reaching the conclusion that only an author of the Hasmonean era could have composed a work of this kind. The dating suggested by Elgvin ('the book reflects an ongoing editorial process across the first century b.c.e.': p. 195), is perhaps the latest that has ever been proposed, but must be taken seriously. Instead, I would be more cautious about the stages of the 'editorial growth' he proposes; in fact there is the risk of overinterpreting the fragments on the Song found in Qumran. See the reviews of Ian Young in *Australian Biblical Review*, 6 (2019), pp. 107–09; Mika Pajunen in *Dead Sea Discoveries*, 27 (2020), 156–59; Matthias Hopf, in *Journal for the Study of Judaism*, 51 (2020), 583–605.

Another feature of this section is its performative and theatrical dimension:[13] compared to the general static nature of the Song, which largely contains only a description ('diegetic' and not 'dramatic', to quote Aristotle) of the two lovers, vv. 3.6–10 develop one of the few representable scenes, through the entrance of a double wedding procession, with the bride and groom respectively accompanied by two different escorts. These verses are therefore crucial to reflect on a possible 'theatrical' dimension of the work (that the Song was a *drama* is already expressly stated by Origen[14]) and on its potential fruition.

Certainly, ancient exegesis posed other and more important questions: both in the Christian and in the Jewish sphere, these verses were also subjected to the necessarily allegorical interpretation which conditioned the entire exegetical history of the Song, if only for the need to discipline and legitimize the strong erotic charge of the text within a religious context.

In patristic exegesis the Christological interpretation dominate:[15] Hippolytus identified in the κλίνη the image of Christ;[16] according to Didymus of Alexandria and Nilus of Ancyra the κλίνη represents the body of Christ;[17] according to Philo of Carpasia τὸ μνῆμα τοῦ Ἰησοῦ.[18] Otherwise, Theodoret recognizes it as a symbol of the Holy Scriptures.[19]

Nonetheless, beyond the allegorical solutions, the patristic tradition shows also a perfect awareness of the historical unreliability of the story. A theologian like Gregory of Nyssa affirms this with unusual frankness. According to an argumentative scheme certainly derived from Origen, Gregory bases his spiritual and allegorical interpretation

---

13 The dramatic and performative dimension of the Song is at the centre of the essay by Matthias Hopf, *Liebesszenen. Eine literaturwissenschaftliche Studie zum Hohenlied als einem dramatisch-performativen Text* (Zürich: Theologischer Verlag, 2016); Matthias Hopf, 'The Song of Songs as a Hebrew "counterweight" to Hellenistic drama', *Journal of Ancient Judaism* 8 (2017), 208–21.

14 Orig. *Comm. in Cant.*, *Prol.*, p. 61, 5–8 Baehrens: 'Epithalamium libellus hic, id est nuptiale carmen, dramatis in modum mihi videtur a Salomone conscriptus, quem cecinit instar nubentis sponsae et erga sponsum suum'.

15 A significant collection of interpretations on Canticles 3. 6–11 is to be found in Procopius' *Epitome*: *Procopii Gazaei Epitome in Canticum canticorum*, edita a Jean-Marie Auwers, CCSG, 67 (Turnhout: Brepols, 2011), scholia 143–59. See Jean-Marie Auwers, *L'interprétation du Cantique des cantiques à travers les chaines exégétiques grecques* (Turnhout: Brepols, 2011), pp. 68–74. Precise references to the patristic exegesis of the passage also in Auwers, *Le Cantique des cantiques*, pp. 238–45.

16 Hipp. *In Cant. Paraphr.* 27 Richard: Κλίνη τοῦ Σολομῶντος οὐκ ἄλλη τρανὴ ἐκηρύττετο, ἀλλ᾽ ἢ ὁ Χριστός.

17 Didym. Alex. *Comm. in Ps. 40–49*, 281, 28–29: περὶ τ[ὴν] κλίνην οὖν τοῦ Σολομῶντος οὗτοι οἱ ἑξήκοντα δυνατοί εἰσιν, περὶ τ[ὸ σ]ῶμα τὸ κυριακόν, [κυκ]λοῦντες αὐτό. Nil. Ancyr. *Comm. in Cant.* 35, 1 Rosenbaum: κλίνην εἶναι τὸ σῶμα τὸ κυριακόν (the wording is so similar that a direct dependence is probable).

18 Phil. Carp., *Enarr. in Cant.*, PG 40, 80–81, 46: Κλίνην μοι νόει, τὸ μνῆμα τοῦ Ἰησοῦ (in Procopius' *Epitome*, schol. 147 Auwers, the wording is slightly different: Κλίνην τὸ μνῆμα Χριστοῦ λέγει). Previously Philo had interpreted it as an image of the Church: Ἀπεικάζεται ἡ κλίνη τοῦ Σαλομὼν τῇ Ἐκκλησίᾳ τοῦ Θεοῦ (PG 80, 40–41).

19 Theod. Cyr. *Explan. in Cant.*, PG 81, 121, 42–43: Κλίνην τοῦ νυμφίου τὰς θείας νοήσωμεν Γραφάς.

on the impossibility of understanding the text in a historical sense. His argument, which we have already referred to in the epigraph, deserves to be quoted in full:

Now what is said about the 'litter' does not derive from any history, and this ought to be evident to everyone from the data that have been recorded about Solomon. With perfect accuracy the scriptural text described his palace and his table and the rest of his way of life in the palace. But concerning his bed it said nothing novel or special, and hence there is compelling reason why in this case interpretation should not stick with the letter but, by a more deliberate and laborious way of understanding, transpose what is said to the level of spiritual comprehension, after distancing the mind from the literal sense.[20]

Unfortunately, we cannot compare Gregory's text with the corresponding Origenian model, because the exegesis of Origen on these verses has not been preserved, neither in the Latin translation of the *Commentary*, nor in the *Homilies*, nor in the fragments of the *catenae*:[21] but everything suggests that Gregory depends on Origen in observing the unreliability of the ἱστορία.[22] Notoriously, it was Origen himself who affirmed the need to provide an accurate examination of the literal meaning ('expositio historica') before moving on to the spiritual interpretation

---

20   Greg. Nyss. *Hom. VI in Cant.*, GNO VI, 190, 9–18 Langerbeck: ὅτι μὲν οὖν οὐκ ἐκ τῆς ἱστορίας ὁ περὶ τῆς κλίνης λόγος ἐστί, παντὶ δῆλον ἂν γένοιτο διὰ τῶν σωματικῶς περὶ τοῦ Σολομῶνος ἱστορηθέντων, οὗ καὶ τὰ βασίλεια καὶ τὴν τράπεζαν καὶ τὴν λοιπὴν ἐν τῇ βασιλείᾳ διαγωγὴν μετὰ πάσης ἀκριβείας ὁ λόγος ὑπέγραψεν. καινὸν δέ τι καὶ παρηλλαγμένον εἶπε περὶ τῆς κλίνης οὐδέν, ὡς πᾶσαν ἀνάγκην εἶναι μὴ παραμεῖναι τῷ γράμματι τὴν ἐξήγησιν, ἀλλὰ διά τινος ἐπιμελεστέρας κατανοήσεως μεταλαβεῖν τὸν λόγον εἰς πνευματικὴν θεωρίαν τῆς ὑλικῆς ἐμφάσεως τὸν νοῦν ἀποστήσαντας; transl.: Gregory of Nyssa, *Homilies on the Song of Songs*, translated with an Introduction and Notes by Richard A. Norris Jr. (Atlanta: Society of Biblical Literature, 2012), p. 203.

21   As is known, the *Commentary*, in Rufinus's translation, is preserved up to v. 2, 15: *Origenes Werke 8: Homilien zu Samuel 1., zum Hohelied und zu den Propheten Kommentar zum Hohelied in Rufins und Hieronymus' Übersetzung*, hrsg. von Wilhelm Adolf Baehrens (Leipzig: Hinrichs 1925). Two homilies are then preserved in the translation of Jerome: Origene, *Omelie sul Cantico dei Cantici*, ed. by Manlio Simonetti (Milano: Fondazione Lorenzo Valla, 1998). For the fragments from the *catenae* see Origene, *Commentario al Cantico dei cantici. Introduzione, testo, traduzione e commento* a cura di Maria Antonietta Barbàra (Bologna: EDB, 2005). In the section we are interested in, only a fragment of Procopius *Epitome* is preserved (on Canticles 3. 6: fr. 33 Barbàra = 144 Auwers).

22   The exegetical and theological influence of Origen on Gregory's interpretation of the Song is recognized since the time of Ambrogio Traversari: see Matthieu Cassin, 'D'Origène à l'édition de 1615: sources et postérités des Homélies sur le Cantique de Grégoire de Nysse', in *Gregory of Nyssa, In Canticum Canticorum. Analytical and Supporting Studies. Proceedings of the 13th International Colloquium on Gregory of Nyssa (Rome, 17–20 September 2014)*, ed. by Giulio Maspero and others (Leiden: Brill, 2018), pp. 77–118 (pp. 78–80; in this essay, pp. 109–11, Cassin also publishes the exegesis of James of Kokkinobaphos on the 'litter of Solomon', which depends, with few variations, on that of Gregory). However, the influence of Origen should not be reduced only to allegorism, which in the Song is almost inevitable and therefore not indicative: see Manlio Simonetti, 'Gregorio di Nissa interprete del Cantico dei cantici', in *Gregory of Nyssa, In Canticum Canticorum. Analytical and Supporting Studies*, pp. 137–54 (pp. 141–42).

('spiritalis intelligentia'), according to the Pauline distinction between 'letter' and 'spirit' applied to the biblical text.[23] Gregory, for his part, not only affirms that the words on the 'litter of Solomon' do not find confirmation διὰ τῶν σωματικῶς […] ἱστορηθέντων, but also offers a close analysis of the ἱστορίαι that contradicts the story of the Song: it is therefore highly probable that his entire discussion is inspired by a lost Origenian model.

In any case, the argument is conducted in an impeccable manner. I Kings (in particular chapters 5 and 11) describes in great detail the luxury of Solomon's life: his royal palace (βασίλεια), his τράπεζα and in general all his sumptuous διαγωγή. Not to mention the extraordinarily detailed description of the construction of the temple and the palace, which takes up two large chapters (I Kings 6–7). Yet not a single word is dedicated to its alleged κλίνη. If Solomon had really possessed the κλίνη that the Song attributes to him, it would not have gone unnoticed in such a careful description. This is enough for Gregory to deny historical credibility to Solomon's κλίνη (and thus to legitimize the allegory).

The argument is not trifling, especially if we consider the fragments of Eupolemus (*FGrHist* 723), who likewise describes the construction of the temple by Solomon, elaborating on its details and size, and even reporting the official correspondence with the Egyptian pharaoh Uaphres and with the 'king of Tyre and Sidon' Souron. It is an emphatic exaltation of Solomon's greatness and wealth: yet not even here is there a single reference to the κλίνη.

The later Jewish exegesis does not offer more tangible results, but the *Targum* (not earlier than the sixth century CE) is significant precisely for what it does not say.[24] After quoting verse 7, the Targumist immediately devotes himself to the 'sixty warriors armed with swords'; but produces not a single word on the litter. The silence perhaps reveals an embarrassment: the comment is all historical-symbolic, with cross references to every possible support offered by the Old Testament, but the Targumist found nothing useful on the 'litter of Solomon'.

The historical problems raised by Gregory must be taken seriously even today. Yet the issue is even more critical. Anyone who reads the entire scene without prejudice and excessive devotion to the *Textus Receptus* must recognize a logical flaw in the whole narration, a flaw that the Greek translator has inherited from an already corrupted Hebrew *Vorlage*. To understand the intrinsic illogicality of the text, it is necessary to dwell in particular on three crucial points: the φορεῖον of v. 9, the female subject of v. 6 and finally the κλίνη of v. 7.

23 Orig. *Comm. in Cant.* I, p. 89, 9–13 Baehrens: 'Haec ergo erit totius libelli species et secundum hanc pro viribus historica a nobis aptabitur expositio. Spiritalis vero intelligentia secundum hoc nihilominus, quod in praefatione signavimus, vel de ecclesia ad Christum sub sponsae vel sponsi titulo vel de animae cum Verbo Dei coniunctione dirigitur'. On the methodical assumptions of this *Commentary* see Bernhard Neuschäfer, *Origenes als Philologe* (Basel: Reinhardt, 1987), pp. 77–84.
24 *Il Cantico dei cantici. Targum e antiche interpretazioni ebraiche*, ed. by Umberto Neri (Roma: Città Nuova, 1993), pp. 119–23.

3. The 'sedan chair' of Solomon (3. 9)

At v. 9 Solomon enters the scene in a 'sedan chair': φορεῖον. The Hebrew word underlying the Greek translation (אפריון) has been the subject of many studies, not only because it is a *hapax legomenon* in the whole of the Old Testament, but also because its understanding has important consequences for dating (and interpreting) the entire book.[25] Since 1829 (A. Th. Hartmann),[26] the view has been that אפריון is borrowed from Greek φορεῖον, that is to say from the same term later used by the Septuagint. This interpretation (which dates back even to Jerome[27]) found acceptance especially among scholars who stressed the need to interpret the Song in the light of the Greek literature of the Hellenistic period, with inevitable effects on its dating.[28] Predictably enough, an alternative was sought in possible (though implausible) Semitic roots.[29] Other scholars have looked to Sanskrit (*paryāna / paryanka*), but with unsatisfactory results.[30] Still others have sought for an answer in Iranian (**upari-yāna*[31]) or in the Egyptian world.[32] Not surprisingly, there have been attempts to circumvent the problem by modifying the term through conjecture, transforming the 'litter' into a 'palace'.[33]

---

25 Detailed analysis of the problem in Luciano Bossina, 'Once again on אפריון <φορεῖον (Canticles 3, 9). Some historical remarks', *Henoch* 42/2 (2020), 396-408.

26 A. Th. Hartmann, 'Über Charakter und Auslegung des Hohelieds mit besonderer Rücksicht auf die neueste Bearbeitung desselben von Ewald, Döpke und Umbreit', *Wiener's Zeitschrift für wissenschaftliche Theologie* (1829), p. 425, n. 27, who immediately deduced chronological consequences: 'Was liegt Unwahrscheinliches darin, dass während der seleucidischen Periode, in welche das Hohelied frühestens gesetzt werden kann, das Wort φορεῖον, womit die Juden zuerst in Syrien bekannt wurden, […] in die hebr. Sprache eingebürgert wurde?'.

27 *Commentary on Isaiah* 7, 14: *Sancti Hieronymi presbyteri Commentariorum in Esaiam. Libri I–XI*, cura et studio Marci Adriaen (Turnholti: Brepols, 1963).

28 Eduard Isidor Magnus, *Kritische Bearbeitung und Erklärung des Hohen Liedes Salomo's* (Halle: J. F. Lippert, 1842), p. 156; Heinrich Graetz, *Schir ha-schirim oder das salomonische Hohelied* (Wien: W. Braumüller, 1871), pp. 54–55.

29 See e.g. F. Delitzsch, *Das Hohelied, untersucht und ausgelegt* (Leipzig: Döprffling & Franke, 1851), pp. 24–26.

30 Ferdinand Hitzig, *Das Hohelied erklärt* (Leipzig: Hirzel, 1855), p. 51: 'parjâna ist im Sanskrit *Sattel, Reilsattel*, also begrifflich dem *Tragsessel* nahe verwandt'; see also *Das Hohelied und der Prediger. Theologisch-homiletisch bearbeitet* von O. Zöckler (Bielefeld: Velhagen und Klasing, 1868), p. 53; R. Gordis, 'A Wedding Song for Solomon', p. 270, n. 21. Against the borrowing from Sanskrit see W. Rudolph, *Das Buch Ruth, Das Hohe Lied, Die Klagelieder* (Gütersloh: Gerd Mohn, 1962), pp. 139–40.

31 Geo Widengren, *Sakrales Königtum im AT und im Judentum* (Stuttgart: Kohlhammer, 1955), p. 112, n. 80, a hypothesis proved to be completely unreliable: see Frithiof Rundgren, 'אפריון "Tragsessel, Sänfte"', *Zeitschrift für Alttestamentliche Wissenschaft* 74 (1962), 70–71.

32 Gillis Gerleman, *Ruth / Das Hohelied* (Neukirchen-Vluyn: Neukirchener Verlag, 1963), pp. 140–43; Manfred Görg, 'Die "Sänfte Salomos" nach HL 3,9f', *Biblische Notizen* 18 (1982), 15–25.

33 Hugo Winckler, *Altorientalische Forschungen* (Leipzig: Eduard Pfeiffer, 1905), III / 2, pp. 236–38, who transforms the sedan chair (אפריון) into a palace (אפדן). Hypothesis also supported by Alfred Jeremias, *Das Alte Testament im Lichte des alten Orients* (Lipzig: Hinrichs, 1930), p. 670. Yet Winckler (and Jeremias) did not consider that the term אפריון is also attested in the *Mishna* (exactly in wedding context): see below.

This debate — which some have judged 'not edifying'[34] – testifies to the difficulty of accepting, beyond the linguistic questions, a historical fact that requires moving the chronology of the text to many centuries later, with direct and not always welcome consequences for its interpretation.[35] However, even scholars who do not doubt the late linguistic character of the Song have recently expressed a degree of scepticism as to the interpretation of אפריון as a Grecism, which is finally deemed 'unlikely' (Dobbs-Allsopp)[36] or 'tempting but perhaps deceptive' (de Crom).[37]

To pose the question correctly, one must begin with two assumptions: (a) there is unanimous agreement that אפריון is a loanword; (b) no alternative proposal to a Greek origin is considered convincing.[38] Nevertheless, linguistic and historical arguments are still raised against the hypothesis of a calque from Greek. The former[39] seem to be perfectly surmountable on the basis of the observations made many years ago by Frithiof Rundgren.[40] From a purely linguistic point of view, there seems to be no argument against the hypothesis that אפריון is a loanword from Greek φορεῖον.[41]

---

34 Garbini, *Cantico dei cantici*, p. 212.

35 See Giovanni Garbini, 'Calchi lessicali greci nel *Cantico dei Cantici*', *Rendiconti dell'Accademia Nazionale dei Lincei*, 39 (1984), 149–60 (pp. 151–52); Giovanni Garbini, *Note di lessicografia ebraica* (Brescia: Paideia 1998), pp. 20–22. One can compare the well-informed and balanced analysis by Rudolph, *Das Buch Ruth, Das Hohe Lied, Die Klagelieder*, pp. 139–40 (who also notes that even the word the Midrash uses to explain אפריון is in turn a Grecism: *pirjûma* [*porjôma*] = φόρημα) with the extensive but inconclusive discussion by André Robert and others, *Le Cantique des cantiques. Traduction et commentaire* (Paris: Librairie Lecoffre & J. Gabalda Éditeurs, 1963), pp. 147–50, who provide the translation 'trône'.

36 In rejecting all other hypotheses, Dobbs-Allsopp, 'Late Linguistic Features', p. 68 states that 'from a purely linguistic perspective the equation of Hebrew *'appiryôn* with Greek *phoreion* remains problematic'.

37 De Crom, *LXX Song of Songs*, p. 104.

38 De Crom, *LXX Song of Songs*, p. 104: 'In conclusion, the status of אפריון as a loanword is unmistakable, but its parent language cannot be identified with any certainty'.

39 The major linguistic problems concern the 'addition of the prothetic *'aleph'* and the vocalization: see, e.g., André Robert and others, *Le Cantique des cantiques*, pp. 147–50; Dobbs-Allsopp, 'Late Linguistic Features', p. 68; De Crom, *LXX Song of Songs*, p. 102.

40 Rundgren, אפריון '"Tragsessel, Sänfte"', pp. 70–72: 'Die Verbindung *ph* oder *p* + Konsonant mußte entweder durch ein prosthetisches Alef mit Vokal + *p* = *f* wiedergeben oder mittels eines Hilfsvokals aufgelöst werden [...] Ein frikativisches *p* = *f* konnte im Anlaut durch Alef mit Vokal + *p* wiedergeben werden. Ein אפריון kann also an sich sowohl ein *phoreion* als ein *foreion* reflektieren, z. B. אפטנא <φάτνη'. Further corroboration is provided by other possible examples, such as אפירסטא <πειράτης and אפרדוכסוס <παραδόξως. See S. Krauss, *Griechische und lateinische Lehnwörter im Talmud, Midrasch und Targum*, mit Bemerkungen von I. Löw (Berlin: Calvin & Co., 1898) Teil. 1., p. 140, § 269 B: 'Prothese bei einem einzelconsonantigem Anlaut', who also cites אפריון and other cases. As for vocalization: 'Die Vokalisation *'apiryōn, 'appiryōn* dürfte man am besten als eine Kreuzung von *piryōn* mit '*ªfiryōn* betrachten können. Dadurch wurde ja auch die klassische Aussprache des φ restituiert. In solchen Fällen ist jedoch auf Verschiedenheiten der Vokalisation nicht allzu viel zu geben'.

41 See again Rundgren, אפריון '"Tragsessel, Sänfte"', p. 72: 'Aus dem Obenstehenden ergibt sich, daß אפריון als ein greichisches Lehnwort im Spät hebräischen anzusprechen ist'.

On the other hand, the historical aspect is more insidious. Indisputably, the sedan chair is an object imported from the East,[42] and for some scholars this constitutes a serious argument against the Greek origin of the word אפריון.[43] Yet a detailed analysis of the Greco-Roman sources leads to different conclusions. In fact, all the texts in which φορεῖον / *lectica* occur converge in considering it (a) a luxury item; (b) an exotic asset, connected with the East; (c) a status symbol denoting a manifestation of power.

The fashion for using sedan chairs was widely embraced in both the Hellenistic and the Roman age; the Hellenistic monarchies, adopting a strongly orientalizing ceremonial, displayed it as an emblem of royalty and luxury: kings,[44] politicians,[45] ambassadors,[46] philosophers with ambitions of power,[47] matrons,[48] impostors[49] and false prophetesses[50] began to be transported on sedan chairs, which even in their material structure perfectly resemble that of Solomon, as described by the author of the Song — a full description taking up two complete verses.[51] Even Roman legislation had to deal with it: various *leges sumptuariae*, from the First Punic War up to Julius Caesar, began to prohibit its use so as to limit excessively ostentatious luxury.[52]

All this helps to contextualise the lexical choice of the author of the Song. For his wedding procession, the bridegroom wishes to assume the appearance of a king (indeed, the most famous and sumptuous king of Israel, Solomon) and he has therefore made himself a luxurious and regal sedan chair. The adoption of a Grecism alludes to the display of a fashionable object of outlandish taste, representing a status symbol in the Hellenistic monarchies. As already pointed out, all scholars — even those who do not accept the hypothesis of a calque from Greek — agree in considering אפריון a

---

42 See the excellent discussion by H. Lamer, *Lectica, -icula, -icarius (lectus, -ulus)*, in: Pauly-Wissowa, *Realencyclopädie der classischen Altertumswissenschaft*, 23. Halbband (Stuttgart: Metzlersche Verlagsbuchhandlung, 1924), coll. 1056–1108.

43 De Crom, *LXX Song of Songs*, p. 103: 'This suggests that the word, like the practice it refers to, did not have a long-standing tradition in the Greek world, further reducing its viability as the source for Hebrew אפריון'. This opinion is widespread: see also Gerleman, *Ruth/Das Hohelied*, p. 141.

44 Cf. Polyb. *hist.* XXX. 25.18 = Athen. V.23 (195c).

45 Dinarch. *in Demosth.* 36.

46 Aul. Gell. *Noct. Att.* X.3.5.

47 Posid. fr. 247 Theiler = Athen. V.49 (214 a–b).

48 Plut. *Arat.* 17.

49 Flav. Jos. *Bell. Iud.* II.105.

50 Posid. fr. 199 Theiler = Plut. *Mar.* 17, 1–5.

51 Canticles 3. 9–10: the אפריון is built 'from wood of Lebanon', 'its post is of silver', 'its headboard of gold', 'its seat of purple'. The many φορεῖα mentioned by Polibius, Posidonius and Plutarch are χρυσόποδα or ἀργυρόποδα, covered with purple blankets. It is a royal object ('King Solomon') exactly like the φορεῖον κεκοσμημένον βασιλικῶς used in Corinth by Alexander's widow to go to the theatre (Plut. *Arat.* 17). See also Curt. Ruf. *Hist. Alex.* VIII. 9. 24.

52 Liv. XXXIV. 1–8 (*Lex Oppia*); Suet. *Iul.* XLIII.2 (Caesar 'denied the use of litters and the wearing of scarlet robes or pearls to all except those of a designated position and age, and on set days'; see also Eus. *Chron.* anno 46). On the *leges sumptuariae* see Ernst Baltrusch, *Regimen morum: Die Reglementierung des Privatlebens der Senatoren und Ritter in der römischen Republik und frühen Kaiserzeit* (München: Beck, 1989); Anna Bottiglieri, *La legislazione sul lusso nella Roma repubblicana* (Napoli: Edizioni Scientifiche Italiane, 2002).

linguistic loan.[53] But no one seems inclined to ask *why* the author of the Song wanted to take a word from another language. Both in the ancient and modern world, luxury is regularly connected with imported items.[54] In designating the bridegroom's sedan chair, the author of the Song of Songs expressly avoided using a Semitic term because he wanted to indicate something exotic: an object used by *foreigners* in exhibiting their luxury and their power. And at that time the foreigners who dominated the world spoke Greek.

The term then — perhaps also due to the influence of the Song — firmly entered the Hebrew lexicon, so much so that the *Mishna* explicitly attests the nuptial use of אפריון in Hadrian's era and beyond.[55]

The analysis of the historical context, therefore, does not invalidate, but, conversely, corroborates the hypothesis of a Greek origin for the term אפריון.

4. The Female Character of v. 6

The Septuagint helps to correctly set up the discussion on one of the most controversial passages of the text. V. 3. 6 opens with the following question:

מִי זֹאת עֹלָה מִן־הַמִּדְבָּר

Τίς αὕτη ἡ ἀναβαίνουσα ἀπὸ τοῦ ἐρήμου

Actually, there should be no doubt that the Hebrew interrogative pronoun is feminine. There are indeed some rare cases in which מי refers to a thing and not a person:[56] however, the feminine of the demonstrative זאת remains unavoidable. Also, the other ancient versions understood the text in this way (*Vetus Latina*: 'Quae est haec quae ascendit'; *Vulgata*: 'Quae est ista quae ascendit'; *Peshitta*: 'mn hy hd'). In addition, if needed, there are at least two other arguments that certify the female gender: (a) In the Song this same expression occurs twice more — 6. 10 (מי זאת: Τίς αὕτη) and 8. 5 (מי זאת: Τίς αὕτη) — and in both cases it announces the bride's entry onto the scene. (b) Even the *Targum* understood the text as feminine, so as to apply the image

53 Cf. De Crom, *LXX Song of Songs*, p. 104.
54 Useful remarks in G. Nenci, 'Tryphé e colonizzazione', in *Modes de contacts et processus de transformation dans les sociétés anciennes. Actes du colloque de Cortone (24–30 mai 1981)* (Roma: École Française de Rome, 1983), pp. 1019–31.
55 See *Das Evangelium nach Matthäus erläutert aus Talmud und Midrash*, von Hermann L. Strack, Paul Billerbeck (München: Beck, 1926), p. 509 (on Mt 9, 15): 'Soṭa 9, 14: Im letzten Kriege (gegen Hadrian 132–35 n. Chr.) erließ man die Verordnung, daß die Braut nicht in einer Sänfte (אפריון HL 3, 9 φορεῖον) durch die Stadt getragen werden sollte (wörtlich: ausgehn oder ihren Auszug halten sollte). Unsre Lehrer aber haben es (in der Folgezeit) erlaubt, daß die Braut in einer Sänfte durch die Stadt getragen werde'.
56 Paul Joüon, *Grammaire de l'hébreu biblique* (Rome: Institut Biblique Pontifical, 1996 [1923¹]), § 144b. Whoever interprets Canticles 3. 6 in this way appeals to Joüon, but the difference in the wording is symptomatic: Joüon observed that 'on trouve *rarement* מי pour les choses'. In Robert and others, *Le Cantique des cantiques*, p. 140, 'rarement' becomes 'plusieurs fois'.

of the bride to the feminine Israel.[57] The question returns cyclically in the medieval Jewish interpretation: the Karaite commentator Yefet ben'Eli (tenth century CE) has no doubts about the feminine, and interprets it as a reference to Israel returning from the desert to the promised land.[58]

Yet, many modern scholars prefer to interpret the expression as neutral, translating: '*What is this* coming up from the wilderness' (Exum[59]); '*Qu'est-ce là qui monte du desert*' (Robert-Tournay-Feulliet[60]); '*Che cos'è* che sale dal deserto' (Ravasi[61]). Whoever does not erase the feminine by interpretation, erases it by conjecture. Karl Budde already believed that מי זאת was an 'Ausgleichung' with v. 8. 5, and should therefore be corrected in מה זאת . [62] Carl Siegfried was of the same opinion, accepting Budde's conjecture, and consequently translating '*Was ist's* den'.[63] Kittel's BH (Gustav Dalman) also accepted the correction, expressly quoted in the apparatus.[64]

---

57   *Il Cantico dei cantici. Targum e antiche interpretazioni ebraiche*, pp. 116–17. On the interpretation of the Song in early rabbinic literature, see Jonathan Kaplan, *My Perfect One. Typology and Early Rabbinic Interpretation of Song of Songs* (Oxford: Oxford University Press, 2015); Michael Fishbane, 'Excursus: A History of Jewish Interpretation of the Song of Songs', in *The JPS Bible Commentary — Song of Songs* (Philadelphia: The Jewish Publication Society, 2015), pp. 245–310.

58   Joseph Alobaidi, *Old Jewish Commentaries on the Song of Songs I, The Commentary of Yefet ben Eli* (Bern: Peter Lang, 2010), p. 212: 'Thus, the scribe, in the name of the Lord of the universe, says: *Who is this woman!* (Canticles 3:6). Nevertheless, it is not an interrogation. It is about expressing the joy of coming back and their arrival [in the land of Israel]'.

59   Jo Cheryl Exum, *Song of Songs. A Commentary* (Louisville: Westminster / John Know Press, 2005), p. 138, who, however, provides no justification.

60   Robert and others, *Le Cantique des cantiques*, p. 140.

61   Gianfranco Ravasi, *Il Cantico dei cantici. Commento e attualizzazione* (Bologna: EDB, 1992), pp. 312–13. The same solution already in Gianfranco Nolli, *Cantico dei cantici* (Torino: Marietti, 1968), p. 95: 'La espressione ebraica *mî zo't* = *chi è questa*, fu interpretata dagli antichi come riferentesi alla Sposa, perché *zo't* è di genere femminile: la Vg traduce: *Chi è costei?* Rettamente i moderni, contro le traduzioni antiche, preferiscono il neutro al femminile'.

62   Karl Budde, 'Das Hohelied', in Karl Budde and others, *Die fünf Megillot*, KHAT, 17 (Freiburg: Mohr [Siebeck], 1898), pp. 16–21 (p. 16).

63   Carl Siegfried, *Prediger und Hoheslied*, übersetzt und erklärt (Göttingen: Vandenhoeck & Ruprecht, 1898), pp. 105–06.

64   This conjecture is absent in BHS (cur. F. Horst). Here is a list (certainly not exhaustive) of exegetes who interpret (or modify) the pronoun as neuter: Heinrich Ewald, *Die salomonischen Schriften* (Göttingen: Vandenhoeck & Ruprecht, ²1867), p. 361; Graetz, *Schir Ha-Schirim*, p. 150; Paul Joüon, *Le Cantique des Cantiques* (Paris: Beauchesne, 1909); René Dussaud, *Le Cantique des cantiques: essai de reconstitution des sources du poème attribué à Salomon* (Paris: Leroux, 1919); Wilhelm Wittekindt, *Das hohe Lied und seine Beziehungen zum Istarkult* (Hannover: Lafaire, 1925); Denis Buzy, *Le Cantique des Cantiques* (Paris: Letouzey et Ané, 1949), p. 110; Krinetzki, *Kommentar zum Hohelied*, p. 118; Roland Edmund Murphy, *The Song of Songs* (Minneapolis: Fortress Press, 1990), p. 148; Anne-Marie Pelletier, *El Cantar de los Cantares* (Estella/Navarra: Editorial Verbo Divino, 1995), p. 15; Tremper Longman III, *Song of Songs* (Grand Rapids, MI: William B. Eerdmans, 2001), p. 133; P. W. T. Stoop-Van Paridon, *The Song of Songs: A Philological Analysis of the Hebrew Book* (Leuven: Peeters, 2005), p. 157. For a good refutation of this solution see Piet B. Dirksen, 'Song of Songs 3, 6–7', *Vetus Testamentum*, 39 (1989), 219–25; Garbini, *Cantico dei cantici*, pp. 59, 211–12.

The reason why this interpretation was suggested is that 'the litter of Solomon' enters the scene immediately after,[65] and there does not seem to be any relationship between the entry of a *female* person (מי זאת) and an object on which a *man* is seated. The narration therefore appears 'illogical':[66] some scholars have recognized an overall 'Unklarheit des Textes', which even led them to judge it 'beschädigt und unvollständig'.[67]

The translation of the *Septuagint*, while remaining literal, has managed to circumvent these difficulties, because the correlation between the first feminine αὕτη ἡ ἀναβαίνουσα and the successive ἡ κλίνη τοῦ Σαλωμων maintains in Greek at least a semblance of grammatical legitimacy, even if it forces to relate a pronoun with an evident personal value to an inanimate object: a 'litter'.

This escamotage may have prevented the patristic exegetical tradition from raising objections to the passage. However, it must be recognized that even this solution is insufficient to provide an overall meaning to the scene: both in Hebrew and in Greek the expression of v. 6 necessarily requires the entry of a female figure.[68]

It should be noted that this is not just a question of grammar: it is a question of common sense. The person who enters the scene is wrapped in perfumes (ὡς στελέχη καπνοῦ τεθυμιαμένη | σμύρναν καὶ λίβανον ἀπὸ πάντων κονιορτῶν μυρεψοῦ), and it is rather difficult to believe that these perfumes, about which the author is very insistent, are suitable for Solomon.[69]

The outcome is very clear: whoever cancels the feminine, cancels the entry of the Sulamite, and immediately focuses attention on the King and his φορεῖον / אפריון.

But here another problem opens up: where is Solomon?

---

65 See e.g. Gerleman, *Das Hohelied*, p. 134: 'Was Erstaunen erregt [...], ist die Erscheinung des Festzuges'.
66 Ravasi, *Il Cantico dei cantici*, p. 313.
67 Rudolph, *Das Buch Ruth, Das Hohe Lied, Die Klagelieder*, p. 141.
68 As Rudolph says (*Das Buch Ruth, Das Hohe Lied, Die Klagelieder*, p. 141), the text 'weist [...] unverkennbar auf eine weibliche Person'. The problem was also addressed in medieval Jewish exegesis. Yefet ben'Eli expressly discusses the hypothesis that the mention of the *miṭṭâ* may represent the answer to the question '*who is this [woman]*', but he prefers to think that the periphrastic expression of the possessive ('*this is his bed, that belongs to Solomon*') intends to emphasize the privileged relationship between God and Israel, who 'belongs to *the lover*': Alobaidi, *Old Jewish Commentaries on the Song of Songs I*, p. 214: 'Some scholars have advanced that the expression: *Behold, this is his bed, that belongs to Solomon* (Canticles 3:7) is the answer to *who is this [woman] who rises from the desert* (Canticles 3:6) We think it is rather an explanation to the expression: *who is this [woman] ...* (Canticles 3:6) and that it belongs to *the lover*. He said to the one who is rising from *the desert*: "this is the bed for Solomon". The meaning is that the Messiah reigns over this community'.
69 In the Song the reference to perfumes and fragrant spices is very frequent. The most mentioned one is 'myrrh', which 'emphasizes female attraction' and is 'generally an attribute of the woman' (with the exception of 1. 13 and 5. 13: Gianni Barbiero, *Cantico dei cantici. Nuova versione con introduzione e commento* (Milano: Paoline, 2004), pp. 477–78. 'Incense' always refers to the woman. In the description of the female protagonist, the olfactory aspect is dominant: see for example the comparison of the female body with the garden (4. 13–14): 'henna', 'nard', 'saffron', 'sweet cane', 'cinnamon', 'with all trees of incense', 'myrrh', 'aloes', and 'all the finest spices'. Myrrh and incense also have a cultic meaning, and this aspect also helps to recognize the female identity of the person who comes up from the desert (see below).

5. The Litter of Solomon (v. 7)

The term denoting the litter in v. 7 is מטה (*miṭṭâ*: κλίνη): a word widely attested in the Old Testament and unequivocal.[70] Two objects therefore appear on stage: *miṭṭâ* and *'appiryôn*. Yet they seem to be hosting the same person, namely Solomon. The absurdity continues: if Solomon is on a 'litter', why does he appear, immediately after, on the 'sedan chair'? We have two persons and two objects, but the narration is manifestly incongruous: the bride is announced (v. 6), but she does not arrive; the bridegroom is on a 'litter' (v. 7) and at the same time on a 'sedan chair'˙(v. 9).

To find a plausible sense, scholars have come up with various hypotheses.

(a) Most believe that *miṭṭâ* and *'appiryôn* refer to the same object. According to this interpretation, the author of the Song would have indicated the same litter with two different words.[71] This hypothesis, predictably assumed also in the patristic tradition, is not acceptable. From the point of view of the narrative unfolding, it would require imagining that the groom / Solomon has 'built for himself' the sedan chair and sent it to the bride to pick her up (!). From a rhetorical point of view, it would also be necessary to suppose a ὕστερον-πρότερον: the sedan chair is built and described in v. 9, but in v. 7 is already in use by the bride!

Furthermore, a very serious linguistic problem remains: this hypothesis requires accepting not only that the author, within two verses, adopts two different words for the same object, but also that in the second case he has recourse to an eccentric and mysterious *hapax legomenon*. The question is unavoidable: why should he have used the unattested *'appiryôn* to designate a simple and already mentioned *miṭṭâ*? Surprisingly enough, this problem is never addressed. The singularity of the term *'appiryôn* and the statement that Solomon expressly wanted to 'build' it 'for himself' (the Greek translation emphasizes this value very well: φορεῖον ἐποίησεν ἑαυτῷ ὁ βασιλεὺς Σαλωμων) show, on the contrary, that the author had in mind a particular item, quite distinct from the previous 'litter'. And indeed vv. 9–10 are entirely intended for the description of a precious and uncommon object, which cannot in any way coincide with the *miṭṭâ* of v. 7.

(b) A more sophisticated variant of this hypothesis is that the duplication of the term is not due to the author, but to a subsequent redactor, who would have inserted a gloss to explain a *hapax legomenon* such as *'appiryôn*. The hemistich of 'Solomon's *miṭṭâ*' would therefore be an extravagant and non-original element, introduced in the text later, in order to explain what the unusual *'appiryôn* was. This is, for example, the

---

70 See Andreas Angerstorfer, "*ereś*", in *Theologisches Wörterbuch zum Alten Testament* (Stuttgart: W. Hohlhammer, 1989), VI, pp. 406–10. It should be noted that in v. 1, 16 the Septuagint adopts κλίνη also to render ערש, indicating the real bed of lovers.

71 See e.g. Gianni Barbiero, *Song of Songs. A Close Reading*, p. 153: 'Generally the term [*'appiryôn*] is unterstood as a synonym of *miṭṭâ*'. However, Barbiero himself acknowledges an 'inconsistency' in the meaning of the two terms: 'Perhaps the author was not familiar with these objects of luxury, or perhaps he made use of different sources. In any case, at the level of the final redaction, the reference of v. 9a to 7a is unquestionable: it is the same object' (p. 153, n. 55). I believe instead that it is 'questionable'.

hypothesis of Wilhelm Rudolph, according to which all the words of hemistich 7a 'sind offenbar an falscher Stelle in den Text geratene Glosse zu dem hapax legomenon אפריון V. 9'.[72] Of course, anyone who does not have an unmotivated devotion to the Masoretic text must seriously consider the hypothesis that the text has been altered through a redactional process, and that false inserts may have been produced. But in this case, it would be difficult to explain why the gloss should have infiltrated *two verses earlier*. Why build *ex nihilo* a hemistich, and invent a 'litter of Solomon' as an explanatory gloss in v. 7, if the *hapax legomenon* appears only in v. 9? Moreover, there is an additional insurmountable difficulty: in v. 7, as we have seen (and Rudolph himself is firmly and rightly convinced of this), the entry into the scene of a woman is presupposed. Why then would the gloss, conceived to explain *Solomon's* 'sedan chair' of v. 9, be introduced in the context in which *the bride* acts? It is no coincidence that Rudolph must immediately assume a much wider textual corruption, namely the loss of an entire strophe after v. 10, which should have described the bride in her own litter and the welcome reserved for her by the groom.[73] The hypothesis of the explanatory gloss, as is evident, does not solve the problem, and rather risks enlarging it.

(c) This is demonstrated by another and more daring variant of the same hypothesis, which extends the suspicion of a large number of glosses to the entire section 3. 6–11, in order to resolve the textual inconsistencies of the scene and of the overall 'Königstravestie'.[74] Oswald Loretz starts from the assumption that in vv. 3. 6–11 all references to an explicit historical and geographical reality are a later insert, the product of a 'redaktionelle Hand', that would attempt 'den jugendlichen Liebenden durch König Salomo zu ersetzen und das geliebte Mädchen in eine Freundin der "Mädchen von Jerusalem" zu verwandeln'. This leads him to remove all references to Solomon, the desert and Jerusalem as 'glosses'. The text comes out profoundly disfigured: in v. 6 the reference to the desert is expunged (the female figure, therefore, 'comes up', but it is not known where from); in v. 7 both the 'litter of Solomon' and the 'mighty men of Israel' are erased; in v. 9 'King Solomon' disappears (therefore the 'sedan chair' remains without owner); in v. 10 both 'King Solomon' and 'the daughters of Jerusalem' are expunged. As regards the difficult coexistence of 'litter' and 'sedan chair', Loretz takes therefore a radical position: he completely deletes the first, and keeps only the latter (but taking it away from Solomon).[75]

---

72 Rudolph, *Das Buch Ruth, Das Hohe Lied, Die Klagelieder*, p. 139.
73 Rudolph, *Das Buch Ruth, Das Hohe Lied, Die Klagelieder*, p. 141: 'hinter V. 10 war in einer weiteren Strophe gewiß ursprünglich gesagt, daß die Braut in dem Tragsessel saß und daß der bräutigam in der Hochzeitskrone sie erwartete oder ihr entgegenging'.
74 Oswald Loretz, 'Enjambement, versus und "salomonische" Königstravestie im Abschnitt Canticum canticorum 3, 6–11', in *Gott und Mensch im Dialog. Festschrift für Otto Kaiser zum 80. Geburtstag*, ed. by M. Witte (Berlin: De Gruyter, 2004), pp. 805–16.
75 This is the text resulting from Loretz's critique (the square brackets indicate the expunctions): 3. 6 'Wer ist die, die da herankommt [aus der Wüste] wie eine Palmettensäule umräuchert von Myrrhe und Weihrauch von allen Würzen des Händlers? 7 [Siehe, das Bett Salomos!] Sechzig Helden sind rings um sie her: [Von Israels Helden!] 8 Alle sind schwertgewohnt, kundig des Krieges. Jeder hat sein Schwert an der Hüfte gegen nächtlichen Schrecken / 9 Eine Sänfte machte erfür>sie<[sich der König Salomo] aus Libanonhölzern: 10 Ihre Säulen machte er aus Silber, ihre Lehne aus Gold,

Undoubtedly, after this drastic censorship, the text has a proper meaning, and Loretz must be credited with having posed two serious problems: the need not only to re-establish the logic of the story, but also to give a satisfactory explanation to the Solomonic fiction. Nevertheless, the solutions he suggests do not seem acceptable: the intervention in the text is too radical and rewrites it almost entirely. The same applies to the presence of Solomon: references to the famous king are not to be expunged, but to be interpreted. In other words, one must assume the point of view of a Hellenistic author who constructs a wedding scene attributing to the bridegroom the evocative and symbolic role of the greatest seducer in the history of Jewish kings.

6. Towards a Possible Solution: The Sulamite and the Queen of Sheba

The analysis of the text has revealed a series of inconsistencies which have not gone unnoticed by critics, but which have mostly remained unresolved:

(a) At v. 6 a female figure is announced, but actually does not appear.

(b) At v. 7 then a 'litter (*miṭṭâ*) of Solomon' enters the scene: but Solomon (v. 9) is on a 'sedan chair' (*'appiryôn*), which he had expressly 'built for himself'. The two terms (*miṭṭâ* / *'appiryôn*) are different, and cannot designate the same object. Where then is Solomon? On the litter or on the sedan chair? And why should he 'build himself a sedan chair' if he has already entered the scene on the litter?

(c) The person on the litter is 'perfumed with myrrh and frankincense', which certainly do not suit Solomon. Moreover, the text speaks of 'exotic powders', which come from abroad: a detail that makes the reference to the king even more improbable.

(d) The person on the litter comes up 'from the desert': but Solomon is not in the desert, and he is waiting for his bride in Jerusalem.

There is only one way, philologically very simple, to resolve all these inconsistencies with a single and minute correction. As Giovanni Garbini pointedly proposed, in v. 7 it is sufficient to introduce 'Sulamite' in place of 'Solomon'.[76] It is she, then, the female protagonist of the Song, who is seated on the litter that comes up from the desert: it is she who is 'perfumed' in (exotic) fragrances. The name Solomon and the word Sulamite have the same root, and therefore the retouching in the consonant text is

---

ihren Sitz aus Purpurwolle, ihr Inneres ist ausgeschmückt mit Liebe [von den Töchtern Jerusalems]. 11 Kommt heraus und seht [Töchter Zions den König Salomo] den Kranz, mit dem ihn bekränzt seine Mutter am Tag seiner Hochzeit und am Tag seiner Herzensfreude!'.

76 Garbini, *Cantico dei cantici*, p. 212. It is a clearly effective solution, and it is surprising that it has not been accepted (or even discussed) by critics. Indeed, this is not the only example of Garbini's findings which has not been given due credit: 'italicum est, non legitur'.

minimal (שלמה / שולמית). By substituting 'Sulamite' for 'Solomon', the development of the narrative becomes clear and logical:

v. 6:   A female figure (מי זאת: τίς αὕτη) comes up from the desert, exhaling the scent of myrrh and incense, with many exotic powders.

v. 7:   It is the *litter* [מטה: κλίνη] *of the Sulamite* [שולמית]. Around it are sixty mighty men.

v. 8:   All holding a sword and expert in war.

v. 9:   King Solomon made himself a sedan chair [אפריון: φορεῖον] from Lebanon's trees [...]

v. 10:   Jerusalem's daughters come out, and look at King Solomon

It is hard to deny that this small correction is of huge benefit in the understanding of the text.

It is evident that the scene presupposes a double wedding procession, the meeting of the two spouses, each accompanied by their own escort. The deep understanding of the passage, with all its allusive elements, clarifies not only the real intentions of the author, but also the reason why the text was subsequently and purposefully altered. It is necessary to return to the insistence on perfumes: this element has a crucial exegetical value, and would not have escaped the ancient reader. Also, in this part the text is rather controversial, as evidenced by the systematic contradictions between the ancient translations.[77]

Two details help to better define the identity of the female figure: the fragrances surrounding the woman who comes up from the desert are imported products (לכור: μυρεψοῦ), and 'exotic powders'. Incense (לבונה: λίβανος) was also imported, and came in particular from Sheba, along the caravan routes (see Jeremiah 6. 20: 'What does it matter to me that incense comes from Sheba?'; Isaiah 60. 6: 'all come from Sheba, carrying gold and incense').[78]

---

77 Especially in 3. 6b: LXX: ὡς στελέχη καπνοῦ τεθυμιαμένη; Aquila: ὡς ὁμοίωσις καπνοῦ ἀπὸ θυμιάματος; Vetus Latina: sicut vitis propago, fumo incensa; Vulgata: sicut virgula fumi ex aromatibus; Peshitta:'yk 'tr' dtnn'). See Garbini, *Cantico dei cantici*, pp. 60–61, who reconstructs Hebrew on the basis of the Vetus Latina ('sicut vitis propago'), assuming it as a different (and more correct) variant of the Septuagint. The presence of the 'vitis' is actually quite curious, and requires an explanation. However, it has been proposed to relate it to the use of στέλεχος in Ezekiel 19. 11: if this were the case, the translation of the Vetus Latina would not testify to a different Greek *Vorlage*, but would depend on a free interpretation of the translator, starting from ὡς στελέχη of the Septuagint. For these and similar problems of the Vetus Latina see Eva Schulz-Flügel, 'Interpretatio. Zum Wechselwirkung von Übersetzung und Auslegung im lateinischen Canticum canticorum', in *Philologia Sacra*, ed. by Roger Gryson (Freiburg i.B.: Herder, 1993), pp. 131–49; Giovanni Battista Bazzana, 'La *Vetus Latina* del *Cantico dei Cantici*. Traduzione interpretazione', in *Il Cantico dei Cantici nel Medioevo*, ed. by Rossana E. Guglielmetti (Firenze: SISMEL, 2008), pp. 91–108 (pp. 94–96). Even the ancient exegetes found it difficult to understand this image: it is enough to refer to Auwers, *Le Cantique des cantiques*, pp. 239–40.

78 See also Ezekiel 27. 22 and Diether Kellermann, 'lᵉbōnâ', in *Theologisches Wörterbuch zum Alten Testament* (Stuttgart: W. Hohlhammer, 1984), IV, pp. 455–61; Fabrizio Pennacchietti 'The Queen of Sheba, the glass floor and the floating tree-trunk', *Henoch*, 22 (2000), 223–46 (= Fabrizio Pennacchietti, *Three Mirrors for Two Biblical Ladies. Susanna and the queen of Sheba in the eyes of*

The perfumed and foreign woman who comes up from the desert to meet Solomon is an allusive but transparent image of the Queen of Sheba.[79] Chapter 10 of the I Kings tells of the Queen's arrival at Solomon's court with an insistent reference to scented essences: 'She came to Jerusalem with a very great retinue, with camels bearing spices and very much gold and precious stones' (10. 2); 'Then she gave the king 120 talents of gold, and a very great quantity of spices and precious stones. Never again came such an abundance of spices as these that the queen of Sheba gave to King Solomon' (10. 10).

The scene of the Song therefore evokes a nuptial procession. The two protagonists are about to celebrate their wedding, and their meeting is ritualized in the image of the famous couple Solomon and the Queen of Sheba, the most seductive and controversial royal couple that the history of Israel has known.

The allusive presence of the Queen of Sheba did not escape patristic exegesis, even if the reactions of individual commentators were different. The ancient exegetes tried to give a historical identity to the Sulamite, seeking among the many women loved by Solomon the one who could be being reflected in the description of a beautiful, young, dark-skinned foreign woman. Some identified her as the daughter of the Pharaoh, others in Abisagh, still others, inevitably, as the Queen of Sheba.[80] Yet a purely historical interpretation posed serious difficulties.

The first problem was that some details were not reflected in the pages dedicated to Solomon in the rest of the Old Testament: Gregory of Nyssa, as we have seen, could not explain why elsewhere there was never any mention of the magnificent 'litter' that the Song attributed to Solomon, and he deduced from this that the text had to be interpreted allegorically. In his homilies and in other patristic commentaries the litter was therefore subjected to an essentially Christological exegesis, while the evocation of the Queen of Sheba and her encounter with Solomon — according to an interpretation already present in the Gospels (cf. Matthew 12. 42; Luke 11. 31) — became an allegorical image of the recognition of Christ by the pagans.

The second and more serious problem was that a purely historical-literal reading would have crushed the Song under the weight of its eroticism, and could have led to the denial of the spiritual value of the text. As is notoriously well known, some Christian exegetes came to this express conclusion. The image of the woman coming up from the desert, 'black and beautiful' (Canticles 1. 5), convinced for example Theodore of Mopsuestia that the Song was a profane work, composed by Solomon to justify his marriage to an Egyptian princess ('Aegyptiacum convivium'). This interpretation, as is known, embarrassed Theodoret, who dedicated the entire Prologue of his *Commentary* to defending the sacred nature of the Song and to rejecting Theodore's thesis, even without explicitly mentioning him. This theme

---

Jews, Christians, and Muslims (Piscataway: Gorgias Press, 2006), pp. 78–119; Fabrizio Pennacchietti, 'La via dell'incenso e la regina di Saba', in *Andata e ritorno dall'antico Oriente. Cultura e commercio nei bagagli degli antichi viaggiatori. Atti del Convegno internazionale, Milano, 16 marzo 2002* (Milano: Centro Studi del Vicino Oriente, 2002), pp. 123–35.

79   See again Garbini, *Cantico dei cantici*, pp. 59–60.

80   See Bossina, 'Il prezzo della pace'; Bossina, 'Teodoreto, Abisak e i «calunniatori del Cantico dei cantici».

was also raised in conciliar context (Council of Constantinople in 553 CE): thirty years later, Western witnesses reported that Theodore 'per hunc librum Aethiopissae reginae Salomonem blanditum fuisse professus est'.[81]

The allusive presence of the Queen of Sheba therefore risked casting a rather sinister and certainly less than spiritual light on the whole text. Whoever has altered v. 3. 7, attributing to Solomon 'the litter of the Sulamite', was moved by similar scruples. The scene evokes one of the least edifying episodes in Solomon's biography: the relationship with the foreign 'concubine', the most famous among the extramarital affairs of a king who, precisely because of his sexual incontinence and his weakness for exotic women, has led the kingdom to ruin.

The original readers of the ancient Jewish text would all have remembered Solomon's excessive passion for foreign women (I Kings 11. 1: 'Solomon loved *many foreign women*, along with the daughter of Pharaoh: Moabite, Ammonite, Edomite, Sidonian, and Hittite women'); the introduction, to please these foreign women, of pagan cults (I Kings 11. 4: 'his wives turned away his heart after other gods'); and the large amount of 'incense' that those women burned in sacrifices to their foreign divinities (I Kings 11. 8). To the ancients, then, this memory would have projected onto the scene of the Song an image too similar to that of the Queen of Sheba, and would consequently have made the reference to a perfumed woman, 'coming up from the desert' on a 'litter', unwelcome.

To delete this scene, a small scribal tweak of the name was sufficient: the litter changed from being the litter of the 'Sulamite' to being the litter of 'Solomon'. Never mind if the king in this way, with miraculous ubiquity, manages to be at the same time on a 'litter' that comes up from the desert *and* on a 'sedan chair' that comes out from Jerusalem.

7. Conclusions

As we reach the end of this investigation, we can therefore draw the following conclusions.

(a) The 'litter of Solomon' never existed. It did not exist either in historical reality or in the literary fiction of the Song. The original text was about a litter 'of the Sulamite', not 'of Solomon'.

---

81 Theodore's interpretation of the Song was discussed during the Constantinopolitan Council of 553, whose acts are the only information available. We also know this debate from three letters of Pelagius. In the third it is expressly stated: 'Nam cum Theodorus canticorum canticum uellet exponere et non ad commenta, sed potius ad deliramenta laboretur, per hunc librum Aethiopissae reginae Salomonem blanditum fuisse professus est' (*Concilium uniuersale Constantinopolitanum sub Justiniano habitum*, ed. by Eduard Schwartz, in ACO, 4 vols (Berlin: de Gruyter, 1927–82): IV. 2:131. 7–9). On the authorship of these letters, and in particular of the third, see however Paul Meyvaert, 'A Letter of Pelagius II Composed by Gregory the Great', in *Gregory the Great. A Symposium*, ed. by John C. Cavadini (Notre Dame, Indiana: University of Notre Dame press, 1995), 94–116.

(b) The Hebrew text was altered to hide the obvious allusion to the Queen of Sheba, evoking as it did one of the least edifying episodes in the biography of a king too weak to resist the charms of foreign women: from that moment on the 'litter of the Sulamite' became the 'litter of Solomon'.

(c) This textual correction predates the Septuagint, which translated an already altered text.

(d) A separate case are the fragments from Qumran, four different witnesses of the Song: 4QCant^a (4Q106); 4QCant^b (4Q107); 4QCant^c (4Q108); 6QCant (6Q6), all dating from 30 BCE and 50 CE.[82] Fr. 2 of 4QCant^a (dated to the 'Early Herodian Period') contains Canticles 3. 7–4. 6, but the first part of v. 7 is missing due to a lacuna in the manuscript, and therefore it cannot be ascertained whether the litter was attributed to 'Solomon' or to the 'Sulamite'. This check is instead possible in 4QCant^c (Canticles 3. 7–8): the text is very damaged, but on the first line one can read the letters למה, which allow the integration of the name 'Solomon' (למה[שלש]). This fragment is dated to the 'mid-to-late Herodian period' (Elgvin). The dating is uncertain because the fragment is very small in size. We can however affirm that around the beginning of the Christian era the correction had already been practised. Still different, but no less interesting, is 4QCant^b, dated around the 'second half of the first century BCE' (Elgvin): the second column contains an abbreviated version of 3. 2–4. 1 but the fragment is so damaged that it is not easy to understand if vv. 3, 6–8 are omitted altogether (Tov, Flint, Gauls) or if they appear in a shorter form (Elgvin)[83]. If we accept the hypothesis of voluntary omission,[84] we must deduce that whoever copied this manuscript (or its antigraph)

---

82   Editions: Emanuel Tov, 'Three Manuscripts (Abbreviated Texts?) of Canticles from Qumran Cave 4', *Journal of Jewish Studies* 46 (1995), 88–111; Emanuel Tov, 'Canticles', in *Discoveries in the Judaean Desert, Qumran Cave 4: XI: Psalms to Chronicles*, ed. by Eugene Ulrich and others (Oxford: Clarendon Press 2000), pp. 195–219; Émile Puech, 'Le Cantique des Cantiques dans les manuscripts de Qumrân: 4Q406, 4Q407, 4Q408 et 6Q6', *Revue Biblique*, 123 (2016), 29–53. First evaluations in G. Wilhelm Nebe, 'Qumranica I: Zu Unveroffentlichten Handschriften aus Hohle 4 von Qumran', *Zeitschrift für die Alttestamentliche Wissenschaft* 106 (1994), 310–12. See also Ian Young, 'Notes on the Language of 4QCant^b', *Journal of Jewish Studies*, 52 (2001), 122–31; Peter W. Flint, 'The Book of Canticles (Song of Songs) in the Dead Sea Scrolls', in *Perspectives on the Song of Songs*, pp. 96–104; Brian P. Gault, 'The Fragments of "Canticles" from Qumran: Implications and Limitations for Interpretation', *Revue de Qumrân*, 24 (2010), 351–71. A new edition of the Canticles scrolls, with 'no small difference' from the previous ones, is to be found in Elgvin, *The Literary Growth*, pp. 5–99.

83   Elgvin, *The Literary Growth*, 47–50; 89: '4QCant^b II not only jumps from 3:2a [...] to 3:6, but also contains a much shorter version of vv. 6–11'. However, the reconstruction of Elgvin is extremely conjectural. The difference between 'abbreviated version' and 'shorter version' is essential. The abbreviated version is the result of a selection by a copyist who voluntarily omits some verses. The existence of a 'shorter version', as Elgvin understands it, would instead demonstrate that the Qumran fragments derive from 'an early stage of transmission' (p. 89), in which the text of the Song had not yet reached its final development.

84   Emanuel Tov, 'Excerpted and abbreviated biblical texts from Qumran', *Revue de Qumrân*, 16 (1995), 581–600: 'While the texts of *Exodus, Deuteronomy*, and *Psalms* probably presented liturgical anthologies, the *Canticles* texts contain abbreviated versions of an undetermined nature, probably reflecting the excerptors' literary taste [...]. The shorter text of the two scrolls was created consciously by the scribes or their predecessors, who shortened the content of the biblical book,

intentionally skipped the entrance of the woman (v. 6), the arrival of the litter (v. 7) and the mighty men who accompanied her (v. 8). The text would restart with the entrance of Solomon's sedan chair. One would think that the whole scene of the 'perfumed' woman who 'comes up from the desert' created several difficulties, which led to its complete omission.

Finally, the testimony of the *Chronicon Paschale*, from which we started, remains to be explained. It is quite evident that a κλίνη Σολομῶνος certainly did not parade during Pompey's triumph, but this does not exempt us from asking ourselves how this story could have come about. The most plausible explanation is that the author of the *Chronicon* reconstructed the triumph by juxtaposing the detailed description of the historian Appian and the memory of the Song.

In his book on the *Mithridatic Wars* Appian wrote as follows:

[Pompey] was awarded a triumph exceeding in brilliancy any that had gone before, being now only thirty-five years of age. It occupied two successive days, and many nations were represented in the procession [...]. In the triumphal procession were two-horse-carriages and *litters laden with gold* (φορεῖα χρυσοφόρα) or with other ornaments of various kinds, also *the couch of Darius*, the son of Hystaspes (Δαρείου τοῦ Ὑστάσπου κλίνην), the throne and sceptre of Mithridates Eupator himself, and his image, eight cubits high, made of solid gold, and 75,100,000 drachmas of silver coin; also an infinite number of wagons carrying arms and beaks of ships, and a multitude of captives and pirates, none of them bound, but all arrayed in their native costumes.[85]

Probably the author of the *Chronicon* identified the κλίνη Σολομῶνος, which he knew from the Song, in one of the φορεῖα χρυσοφόρα reported by the historian. The presence of the κλίνη Δαρείου will have persuaded him that, next to the litter of the Persian king Darius, there should also be the litter of the Jewish king Solomon. Thus Pompey's self-identification with Alexander would have been perfectly accomplished: the 'Great' who had defeated the Persians was now succeeded by the 'Great' who had defeated the Jews.

In this way, thanks to the translation of the Septuagint and a skilful blend of Song of Songs and Appian's history, the never-existing 'litter of Solomon' even managed to parade through the streets of Rome.

---

and not by scribal negligence. [...] The assumption that no scribal negligence is involved is based on the fact that in the three instances of a shorter text in the two different manuscripts, complete literary units are lacking (p. 591). I prefer quoting the original version of the article, and not the reprint in Emanuel Tov, *Hebrew Bible, Greek Bible and Qumran: Collected Essays* (Tübingen: Mohr Siebeck, 2008), pp. 27–41, because in this second print the wording is unclear. Flint, "The Book of Canticles", p. 101 believes that the abbreviated version was intended to limit the erotic dimension of the text. Against this hypothesis: Gault, in "The Fragments", is sceptical about the possibility of understanding the function of the fragments and therefore the purpose of the abbreviation'.

85   Appian. *Hist.* XII: *Bell. Mitr.* 116 (transl. by H. White) pp. 464–67 (the italics are mine).

▼ ABSTRACT The *Chronicon Paschale* (350. 19–351. 11) reports that during Pompey's triumph the 'litter of Solomon', stolen from the Temple of Jerusalem, paraded through the streets of Rome. The only Greek source of this 'litter' is the Septuagint translation of the Song of Songs (3. 6–11): however, a careful analysis of the text reveals a series of inconsistencies which can only be resolved by correcting the name of 'Solomon' in that of the 'Sulamite'. The original text of the Song, which rather mentioned a 'litter of the Sulamite', was later altered, in order to avoid a clear allusion to the controversial relationship between Solomon and the Queen of Sheba. The textual correction predates the Septuagint, which translated an already altered text. From that moment on, thanks to the extraordinary diffusion of the Septuagint, the never-existing 'litter of Solomon' has earned a place in history.

GEORG GÄBEL

Reading 'According to the Revelation Shown to Moses'

A Study of the Influence of the LXX Text on Patristic Biblical Interpretation

This article seeks to contribute to the study of the influence of the Greek text of Israel's Scriptures on patristic biblical interpretation. How did the wording that early Christian exegetes found in their Greek text make possible, prompt, or contribute to their exegesis? Needless to say, '[t]he subject is too large to be adequately handled in a single chapter'.[1] I discuss a select group of texts. Most of them interpret the revelation of a 'pattern', 'model', or 'plan' for Israel's sanctuary that Moses received on mount Sinai (LXX-Exodus 25. 9, 40; 26. 30); a smaller number of texts refers to Aaron's high priesthood, to the tabernacle, or to details of its furnishings.

In his *Commentary on Romans*, Origen writes that the law for the sacrificial rites on Yom Kippur (cf. Leviticus 16) should be understood *secundum illam revelationem, quae Moysi in monte demonstrata esse dicitur* (*Comm. Rom.*, 3. 8).[2] For Origen, the revelation of the 'pattern', 'model', or 'plan' that Moses was shown is a hermeneutical key that unlocks the understanding of the law, which should therefore be read 'according to that revelation said to have been shown to Moses on the mountain'. Consequently, early exegetes seek to ascertain what kind of knowledge Moses gained in the revelation shown to him, and they seek to bring that insight to bear on their interpretations of the instructions for the tabernacle and for the cult, but also of the law more generally. I therefore focus on two questions:

First, how do early exegetes use the Greek text to understand what it was that Moses was shown? Concentrating on the 'pattern', 'model', or 'plan' for Israel's sanctuary, I contend that the Greek terminology used especially in LXX-Exod 25. 40 (the verse most frequently cited in the examples discussed), but also in LXX-Exod 25. 9; 26. 30 provides a reference point for interpretations informed by ancient Greek philosophy, allowing exegetes to read Scripture in dialogue with contemporaneous

---

1 Henry Barclay Swete, *An Introduction to the Old Testament in Greek* (Cambridge: Cambridge University Press, 1902), p. 476.

2 More precisely, Origen argues that the sequence of sacrificial rites prescribed in Leviticus 16, each for the benefit of a specific group of recipients, indicates the differentiated order in which different groups of recipients will benefit from the salvation wrought by Christ. See Origenes, *Römerbrief-Kommentar*, trans. by T. Heither, FC, 2, 6 vols (Freiburg: Herder, 1990–99), II, p. 128.

New Avenues in Biblical Exegesis in Light of the Septuagint
ed. by Leonardo Pessoa da Silva Pinto and Daniela Scialabba, Turnhout, 2022 (*SEPT*, 1), pp. 303–326
© BREPOLS ❧ PUBLISHERS   DOI 10.1484/M.SEPT-EB.5.127720

epistemology and cosmology. This prompts some exegetes to identify the 'pattern' shown to Moses with the intelligible world, or to reject that identification, or to develop an interpretation of their own, yet on the basis of such philosophically informed approaches.

Second, how do early exegetes use the Greek text to find connections between diverse biblical passages, the better to understand them in light of the 'revelation shown to Moses?' One important device in patristic exegesis is the interpretation of one verse or passage in light of one or more others, or the uncovering of correspondences between biblical characters or circumstances. Widening my focus to include texts that refer to Aaron's high priesthood, to the tabernacle, or to details of its furnishings, I contend that the Greek biblical text exhibits a range of features that allow early exegetes to find the connections and correspondences they require to support their interpretations.[3]

1. Hebrew and Greek Terminology in Exodus 25. 9, 40; 26. 30 MT/LXX and Textual Variation in Manuscripts and Patristic Citations

1.1. Terminology

In Exodus 25–30, we read the instructions for the building of Israel's desert tabernacle. Moses, staying on mount Sinai for forty days and nights (Exodus 24. 18), was told that the tabernacle, together with its furnishings and accoutrements, should be made according to instructions he received. The MT of Exodus 25. 9 speaks of a תַּבְנִית shown to Moses, a 'pattern' according to which the tabernacle and its furnishings were to be made.[4] The same Hebrew word occurs again in MT-Exod 25. 40, where Moses is told to make them 'according to the pattern' that he was shown on the mountain.

---

3 I do not aim in this article to give an overview of the early history of interpretation of the verses cited, nor do I claim to present a selection of texts that represent the views of the various early Christian schools of thought or their different approaches to biblical hermeneutics. Translations from the Greek or Latin are my own unless otherwise noted. Wherever possible, I have used the abbreviations suggested in *The SBL Handbook of Style: For Ancient Near Eastern, Biblical, and Early Christian Studies*, ed. by Patrick H. Alexander and others (Peabody: Hendrickson, 1999). Where this was not feasible, I have additionally used abbreviations suggested in Lampe's *Patristic Greek Lexicon* for the titles of works of early Christian authors, and abbreviations suggested in Schwertner's *IATG* for the names of scholarly publications; see *A Patristic Greek Lexicon*, ed. by Geoffrey William Hugo Lampe (Oxford: Clarendon Press, 1961); Siegfried M. Schwertner, *Internationales Abkürzungsverzeichnis für Theologie und Grenzgebiete: International Glossary of Abbreviations for Theology and Related Subjects*, 2nd edn (Berlin: de Gruyter, 1992).

4 I cite the Masoretic text of this and the following verses as edited in *Biblia Hebraica Stuttgartensia*, ed. by Karl Elliger and Wilhelm Rudolph, 2nd edn (Stuttgart: Deutsche Bibelgesellschaft, 1984): כְּכֹל אֲשֶׁר אֲנִי מַרְאֶה אוֹתְךָ אֵת תַּבְנִית הַמִּשְׁכָּן וְאֵת תַּבְנִית כָּל־כֵּלָיו וְכֵן תַּעֲשֹוּ׃, 'In accordance with all that I show you concerning the pattern of the tabernacle and of all its furniture, so you shall make it' (*NRSV*).

תַּבְנִית[5] is derived from בנה, 'to build', but is mostly translated in these verses as 'model', 'archetype', 'design', 'image', or even 'architect's plan'.[6] A different Hebrew word, מִשְׁפָּט, is used in MT-Exod 26. 30, where Moses is told to 'erect the tabernacle according to the plan'[7] (*NRSV*) that he had been shown.[8]

In the LXX, παράδειγμα is the translation of the Hebrew תַּבְנִית in Exodus 25. 9 (counted as v. 8 in Wevers's edition).[9] In Exodus 25. 40, תַּבְנִית is translated as τύπος.[10] Finally, in Exodus 26. 30, εἶδος is used to render מִשְׁפָּט.[11] The *Greek-English Lexicon of the Septuagint* by Lust, Eynikel and Hauspie[12] suggests 'model, plan, pattern' as translations of παράδειγμα in Exodus 25. 9, 'archetype, pattern, model' for τύπος in Exodus 25. 40, and 'pattern' for εἶδος in Exodus 26. 30. This is broadly in agreement with the (considerably wider) range of possible meanings of these words listed in the *Greek-English Lexicon* by Liddell and Scott.[13]

1.2. Citations and Textual Variants

I note selected textual variants in the texts of the above verses, restricting myself to such as may be relevant to the thematic focus of this article. I pay special attention to LXX-Exod 25. 40, a verse frequently cited in the passages of patristic works I discuss.

LXX-Exod 25. 9 and LXX-Exod 26. 30 are cited in only one of the passages of patristic works discussed in this article (Ps.-Justin, *coh. Gr.*, 29). Differences between the texts of these citations and the texts edited by Wevers will be mentioned in the relevant section of this article, as they are mainly due to problems of the textual tradition of the *Cohortatio ad Graecos*.

---

5 וּרְאֵה וַעֲשֵׂה בְּתַבְנִיתָם אֲשֶׁר־אַתָּה מָרְאֶה בָּהָר׃, 'And see that you make them according to the pattern for them, which is being shown you on the mountain' (*NRSV*).

6 See *Lexicon in Veteris Testamenti Libros*, ed. by Ludwig Koehler and Walter Baumgartner (Leiden: Brill, 1985), s.v.; S. Wagner, 'בָּנָה', in *Theologisches Wörterbuch zum Alten Testament*, ed. by G. Johannes Botterweck, Helmer Hinggren and Heinz-Josef Fabry, 10 vols (Stuttgart: Kohlhammer, 1973–2016), I (1973), pp. 689–706 (pp. 704–06).

7 See *Lexicon in Veteris Testamenti Libros*, s.v.; B. Johnson, 'מִשְׁפָּט', in *Theologisches Wörterbuch zum Alten Testament*, ed. by G. Johannes Botterweck, Helmer Hinggren and Heinz-Josef Fabry, 10 vols (Stuttgart: Kohlhammer, 1973–2016), V (1986), pp. 93–107 (pp. 104–05).

8 וַהֲקֵמֹתָ אֶת־הַמִּשְׁכָּן כְּמִשְׁפָּטוֹ אֲשֶׁר הָרְאֵיתָ בָּהָר׃, 'Then you shall erect the tabernacle according to the plan for it that you were shown on the mountain' (*NRSV*).

9 καὶ ποιήσεις μοι κατὰ πάντα, ὅσα ἐγώ σοι δεικνύω ἐν τῷ ὄρει, τὸ παράδειγμα τῆς σκηνῆς καὶ τὸ παράδειγμα πάντων τῶν σκευῶν αὐτῆς· οὕτω ποιήσεις. I cite the text of this and the following verses as edited in *Exodus*, ed. by John William Wevers, Septuaginta Vetus Testamentum Graecum, II 1 (Göttingen: Vandenhoeck & Ruprecht, 1991).

10 ὅρα ποιήσεις κατὰ τὸν τύπον τὸν δεδειγμένον σοι ἐν τῷ ὄρει.

11 καὶ ἀναστήσεις τὴν σκηνὴν κατὰ τὸ εἶδος τὸ δεδειγμένον σοι ἐν τῷ ὄρει.

12 Johan Lust, Erik Eynikel and Katrin Hauspie, *Greek-English Lexicon of the Septuagint*, Revised Edition (Stuttgart: Deutsche Bibelgesellschaft, 2003).

13 Henry George Liddell and Robert Scott, *A Greek-English Lexicon*, 9th edn (Oxford: Clarendon Press, 1996).

Wevers's apparatus notes variants for both of the two instances of παράδειγμα in LXX-Exod 25. 9; I restrict myself to the replacements:[14]

τὸ παράδειγμα 1°] το (> 15) υποδ. (-διγμα 58) 15-58^mg-72-376-767 19' (sed hab Compl)
τὸ παράδειγμα 2°] το υποδειγμα 15-376 19' (sed hab Compl)

The citation of this verse in Ps.-Justin, *coh. Gr.*, 29, reads παράδειγμα.[15]

No textual variation is noted in Wevers's apparatus[16] for the word εἶδος in LXX-Exod 26. 30.

For Exodus 25. 40, the following Greek and Latin text forms are adopted in critical editions[17] of Philo's *Legum Allegoriae*, 3. 102, the Göttingen LXX (ed. by Wevers) and the LXX ed. by Rahlfs, of Hebrews 8. 5 and of works of Ps.-Justin, Eusebius of Caesarea and Origen discussed in this article:

Philo, *Leg.*, 3. 102	κατὰ τὸ παράδειγμα τὸ δεδειγμένον σοι ἐν τῷ ὄρει <u>πάντα</u> ποιήσεις				
LXX ed. Wevers; Rahlfs	ὅρα	ποιήσεις	κατὰ τὸν τύπον	τὸν δεδειγμένον	σοι ἐν τῷ ὄρει.
Hebrews 8. 5	ὅρα **γάρ φησιν**,	ποιήσεις <u>πάντα</u>	κατὰ τὸν τύπον	τὸν δειχθέντα	σοι ἐν τῷ ὄρει
Ps.-Just., *coh. Gr.*, 29. 1	Ὅρα,	ποιήσεις	κατὰ τὸν τύπον	τὸν δεδειγμένον	σοι ἐν τῷ ὄρει
Eus., *Praep. ev.*, 12. 19. 1	Ὅρα,	ποιήσεις <u>πάντα</u>	κατὰ τὸν τύπον	τὸν δειχθέντα	σοι ἐν τῷ ὄρει
Eus., *Dem. ev.*, 4. 16. 53		ποιήσεις <u>πάντα</u>	κατὰ τὸν τύπον	τὸν δειχθέντα	σοι ἐν τῷ ὄρει
Eus., *Hist. eccl.*, 1. 3. 2	ὅρα,	ποιήσεις <u>πάντα</u>	κατὰ τὸν τύπον	τὸν δειχθέντα	σοι ἐν τῷ ὄρει
Or., *Hom. Num.*, 17. 4. 7	vide **inquit**	facies <u>omnia</u>	secundum typum,	qui ostensus est	tibi in monte

I add a simplified excerpt of the apparatus of Wevers's edition (restricting myself to variants that are relevant to the comparison of the above texts):[18]

before ποιήσεις] *add* πάντα 707^c
before κατὰ τὸν τύπον] *add* πάντα F *b* 129-246 127 *s* 126 509 Hebr 8:5 Phil I 136 Bo (sed hab Compl)
τὸν τύπον τόν] το παραδειγμα το Phil I 135s
δεδειγμένον] υποδεχθεντα 46; δειχθεντα (διχθ. 376; δεχθ. 130) O^-767-15 *f*. *s* 126-28 426 799 Hebr 8:5 = Compl

---

14 See Wevers (ed.), *Exodus*.
15 I will not comment below on Gregory of Nyssa's *De Vita Moysis*, 1. 51, but I note that there seems to be an allusion to LXX-Exod 25. 9 in that passage, where he reads ὑπόδειγμα, not παράδειγμα. Gregory may allude to a text of Exodus 25. 9 reading ὑπόδειγμα, but it seems more likely that he alludes to the majority text of this verse, using ὑπόδειγμα in a play on παράδειγμα (for editions, cf. section 4.3 below).
16 See Wevers (ed.), *Exodus*.
17 For Philo: *Philo*, trans. by F. H. Colson and G. H. Whitaker, LCL, 226 (Cambridge: Harvard University Press, 1929; repr. 1991), I, p. 370. For Hebrews: *Novum Testamentum Graece*, ed. by Barbara and Kurt Aland and others, 28th edn (Stuttgart: Deutsche Bibelgesellschaft, 2012). For the editions of the patristic works used, see the citations in subsequent parts of this article.
18 See Wevers (ed.), *Exodus*.

The citation of LXX-Exod 25. 40 in Hebrews 8. 5 differs from the text in the LXX editions in that it adds πάντα after ποιήσεις, reads δειχθέντα instead of δεδειγμένον, and includes the words γάρ and φησίν that seem to have been added by the author. Numerous witnesses, including Hebrews, add πάντα and read δειχθέντα, whereas (γάρ and) φησί/*inquit* are found only in Hebrews and in one citation of Origen (in Latin). Philo's citation adds πάντα, though in a position different from that of the addition in Hebrews and the others and in the context of an otherwise peculiar text that reads παράδειγμα instead of τύπον. Hebrews may have read πάντα (and perhaps δειχθέντα) in a LXX *Vorlage*, although the relevant LXX variants could be due to harmonization with the text of Hebrews. The citation in Origen's *Hom. Num.*, 17. 4, extant in Latin, includes *inquit* and *omnia*. The text of this citation seems to be influenced by the text of the citation in Hebrews 8. 5. The three citations of Eusebius read πάντα and δειχθέντα, but do not include γάρ or φησίν. It is possible that they, too, were harmonized to the text of the citation in Hebrews 8. 5, though this is uncertain.[19]

The addition of πάντα/*omnia* after ποιήσεις in some witnesses, including nearly all of the patristic citations mentioned above, underlines that the divine command not only refers to the tabernacle narrowly understood, but may be read as including the priesthood and indeed the totality of the cult to be instituted. This is conducive to interpretations that find in the 'revelation shown to Moses' the hermeneutical key for the individual provisions of cultic law and, by implication, for the law or even for Scripture more generally. Once the citation is used in the wider context of epistemological and cosmological discourses, the command to make 'all things' according to the pattern shown resonates with the notion that the world of intelligible ideas contains the forms for the entirety of the sense-perceptible world.

2. Septuagint Terminology as a Bridge between Biblical Tradition and Late Antique Epistemology and Cosmology

2.1. Reading LXX-Exodus 25. 9, 40; 26. 30 in Hellenistic-Roman Times

What exactly was the 'pattern' or 'model' that Moses was shown? To what kind of reality did he gain access? How should the relationship between that reality and the desert tabernacle be described, and what does this reveal about the proper understanding of Israel's cult, of the law, and of Scripture? Early Jewish parabiblical

---

19 For discussions, see Gert J. Steyn, '"On Earth as it is in Heaven…": The Heavenly Sanctuary Motif in Hebrews 8:5 and its Textual Connection with the "Shadowy Copy" (ὑποδείγματι καὶ σκιᾷ) of LXX Exodus 25:40', *HvTSt*, 67 (2011) <http://www.hts.org.za/index.php/HTS/article/view/885> [accessed 07 January 2021] (pp. 3–6 of 6); Florenc Mene, 'Scribal Harmonization in Codex Alexandrinus? The Pentateuchal Quotations in the Corpus Paulinum', *TC: A Journal of Biblical Textual Criticism*, 25 (2020), 1–35 (pp. 15–16) <http://jbtc.org/v25/TC-2020-Mene.pdf> [accessed 07 January 2021].

writings mention ascents to a sanctuary in heaven[20] such as that famously described in *1 En.*, 14. The *Songs of the Sabbath Sacrifice*[21] describe the worship of the angels in the heavenly sanctuary and cite the hymns sung by them in the heavenly liturgy.[22] To be sure, such ideas go far beyond the biblical account of the revelation granted to Moses. But once they gained acceptance, they were bound to influence readers and exegetes of biblical texts. Moreover, readers conversant with Hellenistic-Roman culture sought to develop an understanding of biblical texts that was consistent with epistemological and cosmological concepts prevalent at the time. It was in this context that the Greek terminology used in the verses cited came to play an important role. Whatever the translators of the LXX thought that Moses had been shown on the mountain, some early interpreters used the words they found in the LXX as bridges between the biblical tradition and Greek philosophical discourses.

2.2. *Greek Terminology: Philosophical Usage*

Plato uses the words παράδειγμα and εἶδος (among others) to refer to the archetypal, intelligible realities: In the *Timaeus*, we are told that the world is an image (εἰκών) of a παράδειγμα since it was made in accordance with that which is reasonable and unchangeable, whereas the copy (τὸ μίμημα) is visible and changeable (*Tim.*, 28c–29b, 48e–49a). Also in the *Timaeus* (*Tim.*, 51b–c), the question is asked whether there is such a thing as, for instance, fire as such, and whether there exists an intelligible form of everything (εἶδος ἑκάστου νοητόν).[23]

Similarly, Philo, the Alexandrian Jewish exegete and Middle Platonic philosopher, writing in Alexandria in the first half of the first century CE,[24] speaks about the intelligible world of ideas as the παράδειγμα for the creation of the visible world (*Opif.*, 16, 19). Philo's understanding of creation is determined by his Middle-Platonic philosophy. According to this school of thought, the ideas are within the divine mind; they are God's thoughts. Philo compares the world of ideas according to which the visible world was made to a mental plan made by an architect before the inception of the actual building work. He receives in his soul τύποι, 'outlines', of buildings and streets ('as in wax', referring apparently to a writing tablet) before actually building them according to that plan. Similarly, when God was about to found the 'great city' that is the visible world, he, too, had τύποι in his thoughts out of which he put together

---

20 For an introduction, see Marta Himmelfarb, *The Apocalypse: A Brief History*, Wiley Brief Histories of Religion (Malden: Wiley-Blackwell, 2010), pp. 15–30, 75–95.

21 For an introduction, see Daniel Stökl Ben Ezra, *Qumran: Die Texte vom Toten Meer und das Antike Judentum*, Jüdische Studien, 3, UTBW, 4681 (Tübingen: Mohr Siebeck, 2016), pp. 370–75.

22 For an interpretation, see Peter Schäfer, *Die Ursprünge der jüdischen Mystik* (Berlin: Verlag der Weltreligionen, 2011), pp. 187–206.

23 On the realm of the intelligible realities, see Plato, *Resp.*, 509d.

24 According to Kamesar, Philo lived '*c.* 15 BCE – 45 CE'; Adam Kamesar, 'Introduction', in *The Cambridge Companion to Philo*, ed. by Adam Kamesar (Cambridge: Cambridge University Press, 2009), pp. 1–5, especially p. 1.

an intelligible world and then completed the visible world, using the intelligible one as the pattern, παράδειγμα (*Opif.*, 17–20, 24).[25]

The relevant terminology, used in philosophical contexts, acquires a surplus of meaning. The 'paradigms', 'patterns', or 'plans' are here to be understood as intelligible ideas; the 'outlines', as outlines within the mind of the creator.

3. The Intelligible Tabernacle

The Greek terminology in LXX-Exod 25. 9, 40; 26. 30 can serve as a bridge connecting the biblical tradition and the Greek philosophical tradition. This prompted or contributed to philosophically informed interpretations, and more specifically to interpretations that understand the revelation of the παράδειγμα, τύπος, or εἶδος shown to Moses as providing access to the world of intelligible ideas that he contemplated (in one example, the interpreter rejects this understanding). Before I turn to works of early Christian exegetes, it will be useful to look at Philo's understanding of the relevant terminology in the context of his understanding of the making of the tabernacle.

3.1. *Philo of Alexandria: Moses, the Tabernacle, and the Intelligible Ideas*

Philo gives an interpretation of the building of the desert tabernacle in his *Life of Moses* (*Mos.*, 2. 74–76):[26]

σκηνὴν οὖν, ἔργον ἱερώτατον, δημιουργεῖν ἔδοξεν, ἧς τὴν κατασκευὴν θεσφάτοις λογίοις ἐπὶ τοῦ ὄρους Μωυσῆς ἀνεδιδάσκετο, τῶν μελλόντων ἀποτελεῖσθαι σωμάτων ἀσωμάτους ἰδέας τῇ ψυχῇ θεωρῶν, πρὸς ἃς ἔδει καθάπερ ἀπ᾽ ἀρχετύπου γραφῆς καὶ νοητῶν παραδειγμάτων αἰσθητὰ μιμήματα ἀπεικονισθῆναι. […] ὁ μὲν οὖν τύπος τοῦ παραδείγματος ἐνεσφραγίζετο τῇ διανοίᾳ τοῦ προφήτου διαζωγραφούμενος καὶ προδιαπλαττόμενος ἀφανῶς ἄνευ ὕλης ἀοράτοις εἴδεσι· τὸ δ᾽ ἀποτέλεσμα πρὸς τὸν τύπον ἐδημιουργεῖτο, ἐναποματτομένου τὰς σφραγῖδας τοῦ τεχνίτου ταῖς προσφόροις ἑκάστων ὑλικαῖς οὐσίαις.[27]

---

25 Further on Philo, see George Boys-Stones, *Platonist Philosophy 80 BC to AD 250: An Introduction and Collection of Sources in Translation*, Cambridge Source Books in Post-Hellenistic Philosophy (Cambridge: Cambridge University Press, 2018; repr. 2019), pp. 158–59, 183.

26 Text: Philo, *Moses (De Vita Mosis)*, trans. by F. H. Colson and G. H. Whitaker, LCL, 289 (Cambridge: Harvard University Press, 1935; repr. 1994), VI, pp. 484–86.

27 'It was determined, therefore, to fashion a tabernacle, a work of the highest sanctity, the construction of which was set forth by Moses on the mountain by divine pronouncements. He saw with the soul's eye the immaterial forms of the material objects about to be made, and these forms had to be reproduced in copies perceived by the senses, taken from the original draught, so to speak, and from patterns conceived in the mind. […] So the shape of the model was stamped upon the mind of the prophet, a secretly painted or moulded prototype, produced by immaterial and invisible forms; and then the resulting work was built in accordance with that shape by the artist impressing the stampings upon the material substances required in each case'. Translation by Colson and Whitaker: Philo, *Moses*, pp. 485–87.

This interpretation is entirely in agreement with the (Middle-)Platonic theory of ideas: Moses saw intelligible ideas which left an imprint in his own mind, and this in its turn served as a blueprint for the material tabernacle to be made. The philosophical terminology in this text is unmistakeable: ἀσωμάτους ἰδέας τῇ ψυχῇ θεωρεῖν, νοητὰ παραδείγματα, αἰσθητὰ μιμήματα, τύπος, παράδειγμα, εἶδος. Although Philo does not cite LXX-Exod 25. 9, 40; 26. 30, the terminology found in those verses (τύπος, παράδειγμα, εἶδος) is clearly in evidence here. Similarly, in *Leg.*, 3. 102, Philo, citing LXX-Exod 25. 40, explains that Moses made τὰ ἀρχέτυπα of the tabernacle and its furniture, whereas Bezalel, the builder of the desert tabernacle, made τὰ μιμήματα, and the former claim must refer to the contemplation of the intelligible ideas that Moses had seen, forming these archetypes, as it were, in his own mind, so that the archetypes in Moses' mind then served as the pattern that Bezalel copied in his work.[28]

Beyond the making of the desert tabernacle, Philo can also interpret the Exodus texts cited in the context of more general philosophical questions. In *QE*, 2. 90, commenting on LXX-Exod 26. 30, Philo says that this verse has in view 'the paradigmatic essences of the ideas by saying "according to the appearance [LXX: εἶδος] which was shown to thee on the mountain". But the prophet did not see any corporeal thing there but all incorporeals'.[29] According to Philo, Moses was shown the incorporeal, intelligible ideas. According to *QE*, 2. 52, what LXX-Exod 25. 9 means is that Moses was shown 'the forms of intelligible things and the measures of all things in accordance with which the world was made'.[30] This goes far beyond the immediate concern of the biblical text. When Moses contemplated the archetypal forms of the tabernacle, he saw the world of intelligible ideas. This cosmological and epistemological interpretation is possible because, for Philo, the cosmos is a temple (cf. *Spec.*, 1. 66; *Plant.*, 48–50). The sanctuary on earth represents the cosmic temple. Moses saw the blueprint, as it were, of the cosmic temple that is creation and of the desert tabernacle.[31]

Philo interprets the revelation granted to Moses in terms of Middle Platonic cosmology and epistemology. To be sure, his Middle Platonic interpretation of Scripture was not prompted by the wording of the relevant verses (LXX-Exod 25. 9, 40; 26. 30). His interpretation is embedded in Philo's wider effort to discern and expound systematically the true meaning of the Scriptures, so that its essential agreement with Middle Platonic philosophy becomes evident. But the Greek wording of the verses cited is immediately relevant to Philo's understanding of Israel's desert tabernacle. This wording makes possible or significantly facilitates his understanding of the revelation Moses received on the mountain as granting insight into the intelligible ideas, the patterns for the creation of the material cosmos. Moreover, this wording

28 Cf. further *Somn.*, 1. 206; *Congr.*, 8.
29 The text is extant in Armenian. English translation: Philo, *Questions and Answers on Exodus*, trans. by Ralph Marcus, LCL, 401 (Cambridge: Harvard University Press, 1953), p. 139.
30 Translation: Philo, *Questions and Answers on Exodus*, pp. 99–100.
31 The same notion seems to underlie Philo's exegesis of Exodus 25. 8 in his *QE*, 2. 51: God orders the construction of a sanctuary 'so that I may appear among you'. God, Philo explains, appears in his works, that is, in the world, but also in the human mind that has sanctified itself.

also allows Philo to inscribe his philosophical understanding of Scripture into the text of specific biblical verses.

3.2. Ps.-Justin: Plato and Moses

Not everyone was willing to subscribe to the notion that Moses had seen the world of intelligible ideas, even though — or, in the following case, precisely because — the interpretive possibilities inherent in the Greek terminology of LXX-Exod 25. 9, 40; 26. 30 were not lost on readers. In his *Cohortatio ad Graecos*, Ps.-Justin[32] aims to show the superiority of Christianity over Greek religion, and this includes, among other claims, the contention that Plato derived his philosophy from the teaching of Moses. Ps.-Justin writes (*coh. Gr.*, 29. 1–2):[33]

> Καὶ Πλάτων δέ, μετὰ τὸν θεὸν καὶ τὴν ὕλην τὸ εἶδος τρίτην ἀρχὴν εἶναι λέγων, οὐκ ἄλλοθέν ποθεν, ἀλλὰ παρὰ Μωϋσέως τὴν πρόφασιν εἰληφὼς φαίνεται, τὸ μὲν τοῦ εἴδους ὄνομα ἀπὸ τῶν Μωϋσέως μεμαθηκὼς ῥητῶν, οὐ διδαχθεὶς δὲ τηνικαῦτα παρὰ τῶν εἰδότων, ὅτι οὐδὲν ἐκτὸς μυστικῆς θεωρίας τῶν ὑπὸ Μωϋσέως εἰρημένων σαφῶς γινώσκειν ἐστὶ δυνατόν. Γέγραφε γὰρ Μωϋσῆς ὡς τοῦ θεοῦ περὶ τῆς σκηνῆς πρὸς αὐτὸν εἰρηκότος οὕτως· Καὶ ποιήσεις μοι κατὰ πάντα, ὅσα ἐγὼ δεικνύω σοι ἐν τῷ ὄρει, τὸ παράδειγμα τῆς σκηνῆς [cf. LXX-Exod 25. 9]. Καὶ αὖθις μικρὸν ὕστερον οὕτως· Ὅρα, ποιήσεις κατὰ τὸν τύπον τὸν δεδειγμένον σοι ἐν τῷ ὄρει [cf. LXX-Exod 25. 40]. Καὶ πάλιν· Καὶ ἀναστήσεις τὴν σκηνὴν κατὰ τὸ εἶδος τὸ δειχθέν σοι ἐν τῷ ὄρει [cf. LXX-Exod 26. 30], οὕτω ποιήσεις αὐτό. Τούτοις οὖν ἐντυχὼν ὁ Πλάτων καὶ οὐ μετὰ τῆς προσηκούσης θεωρίας δεξάμενος τὰ γεγραμμένα ῥητά, ᾠήθη εἶδός τι χωριστὸν προϋπάρχειν τοῦ αἰσθητοῦ· ὃ καὶ παράδειγμα τῶν γενομένων ὀνομάζει πολλάκις, ἐπειδὴ τὸ Μωϋσέως οὕτω περὶ

---

32 He was an otherwise unknown early fourth or third century author, identified by some as Marcellus of Ancyra. See Michael Fiedrowicz, *Apologie im frühen Christentum. Die Kontroverse um den christlichen Wahrheitsanspruch in den ersten Jahrhunderten*, 3rd edn (Paderborn: Schöningh, 2006), pp. 93–94. Riedweg thinks that the *Cohortatio* was written roughly between 312–22 CE or perhaps before 303 CE: Christoph Riedweg, *Ps.-Justin (Markell von Ankyra?), Ad Graecos de Vera Religione (bisher 'Cohortatio ad Graecos'): Einleitung und Kommentar*, SBA, 25/1–2, 2 vols (Basel: Friedrich Reinhard, 1994), I, p. 52.

33 Text: *Ps.-Justin*, II, p. 570. Cf. other editions: Pseudo-Iustinus, *Cohortatio ad Graecos. De Monarchia. Oratio ad Graecos*, ed. by M. Marcovich, PTS, 32 (Berlin: de Gruyter, 1990), p. 65; *Corpus Apologetarum Christianorum Saeculi Secundi*, ed. by J. C. T. Otto, 2nd edn (Jena: Fischer, 1879), III.2, pp. 100–03. Riedweg carries out emendations on the basis of Marcovich's text (see Riedweg, *Ps.-Justin*, II, pp. 451–52 and II, p. 570 n. 151–54). The words καὶ τὸ παράδειγμα πάντων τῶν σκευῶν αὐτῆς· οὕτω ποιήσεις are omitted in the citation of LXX-Exod 25. 9, but the words καὶ κατὰ τὸ παράδειγμα πάντων τῶν σκευῶν αὐτῆς, καὶ οὕτως ποιήσεις are added, according to Riedweg's edition, at the end of *coh. Gr.*, 29. 2, and the words οὕτω ποιήσεις αὐτό are added after LXX-Exod 26. 30. The citation of LXX-Exod 26. 30 differs from the text edited by Rahlfs and Wevers in that it reads τὸ δειχθέν instead of τὸ δεδειγμένον. The text in Marcovich's edition differs on the position in the text of καὶ τὸ παράδειγμα πάντων τῶν σκευῶν αὐτῆς· οὕτω ποιήσεις and on the order of the citations of LXX-Exod 25. 40 and LXX-Exod 26. 30. Cf. Pseudo-Iustinus, *Cohortatio ad Graecos*.

τῆς σκηνῆς σημαίνει γράμμα· καὶ κατὰ τὸ παράδειγμα πάντων τῶν σκευῶν αὐτῆς, καὶ οὕτως ποιήσεις.[34]

According to Ps.-Justin, Plato learned his theory of ideas from Moses, specifically, from LXX-Exod 25. 9, 40; 26. 30. But, says Ps.-Justin, Plato failed to understand the 'mystical' meaning of these words. Ps.-Justin does not tell us here what that meaning is, nor does he give us his own interpretation of the biblical text. It is more important to him to criticize Plato for his inadequate understanding of it, which resulted in his belief that there is such a thing as a separate idea (εἶδός τι χωριστόν) that precedes sense-perceptible reality (προϋπάρχειν τοῦ αἰσθητοῦ) and that Plato calls the παράδειγμα of the things to have come into existence. The Platonic concept of ideas is thus the result of Plato's failure to understand properly the relevant passages of Scripture. That Greek literature, culture, and wisdom were derived from biblical sources and indeed from the writings of Moses is not a contention peculiar to Ps.-Justin.[35] But he is the only early Christian author, to my knowledge, to claim that the text of LXX-Exod 25. 9, 40; 26. 30 specifically was the source of Plato's (allegedly) misguided philosophy.

As Riedweg argues, Plato's misunderstanding of Scripture (alleged by Ps.-Justin) would seem to be very similar to the interpretation of Scripture actually advocated by Philo of Alexandria, viz. that Moses contemplated the world of ideas. Indeed, the misunderstanding that Ps.-Justin alleges seems to depend on Philo's exegesis.[36] But while Ps.-Justin fully understands the 'Platonic' implications of the Greek terminology (τύπος, παράδειγμα, εἶδος) used in LXX-Exod 25. 9, 40; 26. 30, he emphatically rejects the interpretation of it in Platonic terms. It would hardly have been possible for Ps.-Justin to comment on these verses in the way he did had he not read them in the Greek version of the LXX. It is this Greek text that allows the interpreter to

---

34 'And Plato, saying that, in addition to God and Matter, the Idea is the third principle, seems to have taken the suggestion from none other but from Moses, having learned the designation of the Idea from the words of Moses; but he had not learned at the time from those who know that it is not possible, without the mystical contemplation, to understand clearly any of the things said by Moses. For Moses wrote that God spoke to him about the tent, thus: And you will make for me according to all the things that I have shown you on the mountain, the pattern of the tent. And again, a little later, thus: See, you will make [it] according to the pattern shown to you on the mountain. And again: And you will erect the tent according to the form shown to you on the mountain; so will you make it. Now, having encountered these things, and not having received the written words with the adequate contemplation, Plato supposed that there exists, before what is visible, a separate idea [εἶδος], which he also frequently calls the pattern [παράδειγμα] of the things that came into existence, since the writing of Moses declares concerning the tent thus: and according to the pattern [παράδειγμα] of all its implements; and so you will make [it/them]'.

35 See Arthur J. Droge, *Homer or Moses? Early Christian Interpretation of the History of Culture*, HUTh, 26 (Tübingen: Mohr Siebeck, 1989). On the belief in the priority of Moses over Plato, see pp. 59–65 (on Justin Martyr) and pp. 157–67 (on Origen).

36 Riedweg, *Ps.-Justin*, II, pp. 448–50. Daniélou argues that Philo was the source of Ps.-Justin's remarks on the creation of man in *coh. Gr.*, 30. See Jean Daniélou, *Histoire des Doctrines Chrétiennes avant Nicée*, BT (Tournai: Desclée, 1961), II. Message Évangélique et Culture Hellénistique aux IIᵉ et IIIᵉ Siècles, p. 114.

read LXX-Exod 25. 9, 40; 26. 30 in light of the writings of Plato, even if this results, in the case of Ps.-Justin, in an uncompromising rejection of Plato's philosophy and, by implication, of interpretations of the biblical text inspired by Middle Platonism.

3.3. Eusebius of Caesarea (i): Moses and Political Philosophy

In his *Praeparatio Evangelica*, Eusebius of Caesarea[37] purports to show that biblical religion is superior to Greek mythology and philosophy.[38] He uses passages taken from works of ancient authors to prove his point. In one passage (*Praep. ev.*, 12. 19. 1), he cites LXX-Exod 25. 40 (and Hebrews 8. 5), with a brief explanation:[39]

> Τοῦ θείου χρησμοῦ φήσαντος Μωσεῖ· Ὅρα, ποιήσεις πάντα κατὰ τὸν τύπον τὸν δειχθέντα σοι ἐν τῷ ὄρει τοῦ τε ἱεροῦ λόγου σαφέστερον εἰπόντος· Οἵτινες ὑποδείγματι καὶ σκιᾷ ἐλάτρευον τῶν ἐπουρανίων εἰκόνα τε ἄντικρυς τῶν ἐν νοητοῖς θειοτέρων τὰ παρὰ Μωσεῖ σύμβολα περιέχειν διδάσκοντος, ἐπάκουσον ὅπως καὶ ὁ Πλάτων τὰ ὅμοια διερμηνεύει ἐν ἕκτῳ τῆς Πολιτείας ὧδε γράφων.[40]

There follows a lengthy citation of Plato's *Republic* (*Resp.*, 500d–501c). In the context, Plato's Socrates speaks about a philosopher who focuses the mind on that which is (τοῖς οὖσι) and who attempts to become similar to what he sees there (*Resp.*, 500b). Philosophers will also wish to make public life more just and virtuous. In so doing, they are painters (ζωγράφοι) using a divine pattern (τῷ θείῳ παραδείγματι χρώμενοι, *Resp.*, 500e). Like artists, they will have to draw a sketch of the state's constitution (ὑπογράψασθαι τὸ σχῆμα τῆς πολιτείας, *Resp.*, 501a), taking their design from that in man which is of divine form and godlike (θεοειδής τε καὶ θεοείκελον, *Resp.*, 501b).

Eusebius thinks that the comparison of Moses and Plato reveals a profound agreement. Similarly to Philo, he does not restrict the meaning of the biblical texts he cites to the revelation of a pattern for the construction of the tabernacle (as noted above, Eusebius's text of LXX-Exod 25. 40 includes πάντα, and this may facilitate his generalizing interpretation).[41] According to Eusebius, LXX-Exod 25. 40 indicates that the 'symbols' described by Moses contain an image (εἰκών) of 'more divine things' ἐν

---

37   He was born around 263 CE and died in 339 CE according to Berthold Altaner and Alfred Stuiber, *Patrologie: Leben, Schriften und Lehre der Kirchenväter*, 8th edn (Freiburg: Herder, 1978), p. 217. According to the same authors, the *Praeparatio Evangelica* was written between 312 and 322 CE (p. 221).
38   On Eusebius's approach to apologetics in the *Praeparatio Evangelica*, see the chapter entitled, 'Eusebius: The History of Culture as Praeparatio Evangelica', in Droge, *Homer or Moses?*, pp. 168–93.
39   Text: Eusebius, *Werke*, ed. by Karl Mras, GCS, 43.2 (Berlin: Akademie-Verlag, 1956), VIII. Die Praeparatio Evangelica, Zweiter Teil, p. 109.
40   'Since the divine oracle spoke to Moses: See, you will make all things according to the pattern shown to you on the mountain, and since the sacred word said more clearly, who served an outline and shadow of the heavenly things, [thus] teaching that the symbols of Moses plainly contain an image of the more divine realities in the intelligible world: hear[, then,] how Plato, too, expounds similar things in the sixth [book] of the Republic, writing thus'.
41   Cf. section 1.2 above.

νοητοῖς, in the intelligible world.[42] Eusebius cites Hebrews 8. 5, where the word σκιά, 'shadow', is used to describe the representation on earth of the τύπος revealed to Moses. Attridge notes that the use of σκιά 'as an image for components of the phenomenal or material world is Platonic'.[43] 'Shadow' plays an important role in Philo's interpretation of the making of the tabernacle. Philo says that Bezalel, the craftsman who oversaw the making of the tabernacle, apprehended God from a shadow (Leg., 3. 101–02). Moses was instructed by God himself (Philo cites LXX-Exod 25. 40), and Bezalel was instructed by Moses (Leg., 3. 102–03). Therefore, Bezalel, as it were, traced shadows, whereas Moses produced the archetypal patterns (Somn., 1. 206). In the context of Praep. ev., 12. 19. 1, Eusebius seems to use σκιά in his citation of Hebrews 8. 5 similarly to denote the inferiority of the sense-perceptible representation of the intelligible 'pattern'. Eusebius, then, understands LXX-Exod 25. 40 (read with Hebrews 8. 5) in terms of the distinction between the intelligible and the sense-perceptible worlds, and he explicitly refers to Plato who, he says, 'expounds similar things'.

Eusebius does not discuss the terminology of παράδειγμα and εἶδος in LXX-Exod 25. 9; 26. 30 (he cites LXX-Exod 25. 40), and unlike Philo, he does not comment here on cosmology. The word παράδειγμα occurs in the passage he cites, Resp., 500e, but Eusebius does not cite LXX-Exod 25. 9 where it also occurs. He could certainly have selected other passages from Plato's works where his doctrine of ideas is more clearly in evidence (together with its cosmological implications). But this is not his concern here. Eusebius chooses to cite the above passage from Plato's Republic no doubt because he wishes readers to see that Plato's ideal of the philosopher as lawgiver has been realized in Moses: The constitution and the laws that he gave were indeed grounded in an intelligible pattern shown to him 'on the mountain'. Eusebius, similarly to Philo and Ps.-Justin, is not much interested here in the building of Israel's desert tabernacle as such. He uses the biblical citation to argue that divine revelation as understood in the passage cited is in full agreement with, even superior to, Platonic philosophy, fulfilling its aspirations.

The contention that Moses and Plato are in profound agreement was admittedly not prompted by the exegesis of a few verses in Exodus. It was due first and foremost to Eusebius's intention to give an apology for Christianity as the true religion in the context of the Graeco-Roman culture of late antiquity. But the argument that Eusebius presents nevertheless amounts to a claim that this agreement can be demonstrated on

---

42 On the sense-perceptible as an image of the intelligible, see Plutarch, Quaest. plat., 3. 1001E (commenting on Plato's analogy of the line): [...] κατὰ τὸν Πλάτωνα παραδείγματα καὶ ἰδέας τὰ νοητὰ τῶν αἰσθητῶν ὥσπερ εἰκόνων ἢ ἐμφάσεων ὑποτιθέμενον. Text: Plutarch, Moralia, trans. by Harold Cherniss, LCL, 427 (Cambridge: Harvard University Press, 1976), XIII.1. Platonic Questions, p. 36. '[...] according to Plato, who makes the intelligibles paradigms and forms of perceptibles, which are as it were images and impressions'. Translation: Boys-Stones, Platonist Philosophy 80 BC to AD 250, p. 390.

43 Harold W. Attridge, The Epistle to the Hebrews, Hermeneia (Philadelphia: Fortress Press, 1989), p. 219. He refers to Plato, Resp., 515a–b. Further on εἰκών and σκιά in philosophical discussions of the relationship between the intelligible and sense-perceptible realms, see Scott D. Mackie, Eschatology and Exhortation in the Epistle to the Hebrews, WUNT, II 223 (Tübingen: Mohr Siebeck, 2007), pp. 106–13.

the basis of a comparison between specific biblical and philosophical sources. Clearly such a claim is possible only on the basis of the LXX text. The Greek terminology of the LXX serves as a bridge between biblical tradition and philosophy, making possible the foundational exegetical decision to identify the 'pattern' of the tabernacle and the intelligible ideas.[44]

3.4. Eusebius of Caesarea (ii): Moses and Christ

In his *Demonstratio Evangelica*, Eusebius of Caesarea again comments on LXX-Exod 25. 40. His approach presupposes philosophically informed interpretations, but also transforms them: Eusebius now claims that Moses had seen Christ. Eusebius writes (*Dem. ev.*, 4. 16. 53):[45]

> Ἐπὶ τούτοις ἅπασιν καὶ τὰ Μωσέως αὖθις παραθετέον, ὃς κατὰ τὸν δειχθέντα αὐτῷ τύπον τὸν ἴδιον ἀδελφὸν τὸν Ἀαρὼν ἀρχιερέα καταστησάμενος, ἀκολούθως τῷ φήσαντι πρὸς αὐτὸν χρησμῷ ποιήσεις πάντα κατὰ τὸν τύπον τὸν δειχθέντα σοι ἐν τῷ ὄρει, δῆλός ἐστιν ὡς τοῖς τῆς διανοίας ὄμμασιν καὶ τῷ θείῳ πνεύματι συνιδὼν τὸν μέγαν τῶν ὅλων ἀρχιερέα, τὸν ἀληθῆ Χριστὸν τοῦ θεοῦ, [οὗ] μετὰ τῆς ἄλλης σωματικῆς καὶ τυπικῆς λατρείας τὴν εἰκόνα διαγράφων τὸν δηλωθέντα τῇ τοῦ ἀληθοῦς Χριστοῦ προσωνυμίᾳ τετίμηκεν.[46]

According to the text of LXX-Exod 25. 40 cited by Eusebius, Moses was to make 'all things' (πάντα) according to the pattern shown to him.[47] Eusebius assumes that the instructions Moses received included provisions for the high priesthood. He interprets the words of LXX-Exod 25. 40 as indicating the relationship between a revealed 'pattern' (τύπος) and the high priest and cult as its representation. The words

---

44 This raises the fascinating, but (in my view) open question of whether the translators of the LXX chose to use the relevant terminology precisely in order to facilitate interaction with Greek philosophical thought in ways such as those of Philo, Ps.-Justin, and Eusebius. See the discussion in Ann Conway-Jones, *Gregory of Nyssa's Tabernacle Imagery in its Jewish and Christian Contexts*, Oxford Early Christian Studies (Oxford: Oxford University Press, 2014), p. 88. Karrer discusses other passages where the Greek text of the LXX was at least open to interpretation in philosophical terms: Martin Karrer, 'Septuaginta und Philosophie', in *Die Septuaginta — Orte und Intentionen: 5. Internationale Fachtagung veranstaltet von Septuaginta Deutsch (LXX.D)*, Wuppertal 24.–27. Juli 2014, ed. by Siegfried Kreuzer and Martin Meiser, WUNT, 361 (Tübingen: Mohr Siebeck, 2016), pp. 3–35.

45 Text: Eusebius, *Werke*, ed. by Ivar A. Heikel, GCS, 23 (Leipzig: Hinrichs, 1913), VI. Die Demonstratio Evangelica, p. 194.

46 'With all this we should again compare the records of Moses, who when he established his own brother as High Priest, according to the pattern that had been shown to him, in accordance with the oracle which said to him: You will make all things according to the pattern shown to you on the mountain, plainly shows that he had perceived with the eyes of the mind and by the Divine Spirit the great High Priest of the Universe, the true Christ of God, Whose image he delineated together with the rest of the corporeal and figurative worship, and honoured the person indicated with the name of the real Christ'. Translation (with slight alterations): *The Proof of the Gospel, Being the Demonstratio Evangelica of Eusebius of Caesarea*, trans. by William John Ferrar, Translations of Christian Literature, Series I, 2 vols (London: SPCK, 1920), I, pp. 214–15.

47 Cf. section 1.2 above.

τοῖς τῆς διανοίας ὄμμασιν […] συνιδών are reminiscent of the words used by Philo in his description of the same event, τῇ ψυχῇ θεωρῶν (*Mos.*, 2. 74). This is in continuity with the philosophically informed interpretations of that verse previously discussed: What is seen with the 'eyes of the mind' is then represented in a sketch, as it were, in the sense-perceptible realm. There is a decisive difference, however. Whereas Philo speaks of the contemplation of the intelligible ideas, Eusebius says that it was (the pre-existent) Christ whom Moses saw 'with the eyes of the mind'. Since Moses had been instructed to 'make all things according to the pattern' shown to him, and since he established his brother as high priest, Eusebius concludes that Moses had seen the high priest of the universe. According to early Christian belief, the 'great high priest' is Christ (Hebrews 4. 14; cf. 8. 1).

Exegetical traditions[48] may have contributed to this interpretation. In John 12. 41, the evangelist asserts that Isaiah saw 'his', i.e. Christ's, 'glory' and that he 'talked about him'.[49] Indeed Eusebius (citing John 12. 37–41) explicitly says in his *Dem. ev.*, 9. 16. 1–4 that Isaiah's vision was a vision of Christ. He seems to import the notion that a revelatory experience ascribed to a character in the Hebrew Bible may in fact have been an encounter with the pre-existent Christ into his interpretation of the revelation given to Moses on mount Sinai. Indeed Josephus claims that Moses had seen the throne of God with the cherubim, since (according to him) Moses said that he saw the cherubim 'sculptured upon the throne of God', Χερουβεῖς […] ζῷα δέ ἐστι […], Μωυσῆς δέ φησι τῷ θρόνῳ τοῦ θεοῦ προστυπεῖς ἑωρακέναι (*Ant.*, 3. 6. 137).[50] If Moses saw the throne with the cherubim, this would have been the 'pattern' shown to him, and the desert tabernacle (especially the ark with the cherubim) was a representation of what he had seen. Josephus uses the words 'throne' (θρόνος) and 'living beings' (ζῷα) that do not occur in LXX-Exod 25–40, indicating that he probably has in mind Ezekiel's vision of the throne with the 'living beings' (cf. LXX-Ezek 1. 5, 26).[51] If indeed Moses saw a vision similar to those of Ezekiel or Isaiah, and if those prophetic visions were in fact visions of the pre-existent Christ, it seems to follow that Moses, too, saw a vision of Christ.

Eusebius's exegesis of LXX-Exod 25. 40 remains indebted to philosophically informed interpretations of the τύπος shown to Moses. But he integrates such interpretations into his Christological understanding of the revelation Moses received. If Christ, then, is the 'pattern' represented by Aaron's high priesthood, does Scripture

48 On the identification of the God of Israel seen in Isaiah's vision with the pre-existent Christ in early Christian exegesis, see Bogdan G. Bucur, '"I saw the Lord": Observations on the Christian Reception History of Isaiah 6', *ProEccl*, 23 (2014), 309–30 (pp. 309–12).
49 Rudolf Schnackenburg, *Das Johannesevangelium, Zweiter Teil, Kommentar zu Kapitel 5–12*, HTKNT, 4.2 (Freiburg: Herder, 1971; repr. 2000), p. 520, comments: 'Wahrscheinlich setzt der Evangelist das jüdische Verständnis, daß Jesaja Gottes Herrlichkeit sah, voraus; aber er deutet die δόξα betont auf die Herrlichkeit Jesu, die dieser nach 17,5 schon vor Grundlegung der Welt beim Vater besaß. Dann aber liegt es nahe, daß der Evangelist bei der Schau des Propheten den präexistenten Christus meint'.
50 Text and translation: Josephus, *Jewish Antiquities, Books I–IV*, trans. by Henry St John Thackeray, LCL, 242 (London: Harvard University Press, 1930; repr. 1967), IV, pp. 380–81.
51 In Ezekiel 1, the description of the four 'beings' (ζῷα v. 5 and others) in vv. 5–25 is followed in vv. 26–27 by the description of a throne and of 'one who looked like a human being' on a throne.

provide further clues as to the correspondence between these characters? Eusebius thinks that it does. He claims that Moses 'honoured the person indicated [i.e. Aaron] with the name of the real Christ'. This claim (which I explain in section 4.1 below) leads us to the question of how early exegetes use the Greek text in their search for correspondences and connections between biblical texts, characters, or circumstances.

4. Interpreting Scripture with Scripture

Early exegetes use insight gained in LXX-Exodus 25. 40 to interpret other passages of Scripture and vice versa, or they cite that verse in support of a correspondence they see between biblical characters and circumstances, or they include LXX-Exod 25. 40 in a web of citations and allusions that helps them to support their interpretations. They further use references to other biblical contexts to corroborate details of their own interpretation of the tabernacle and its furnishings. In so doing, they apply a method widely used in patristic exegesis, viz. to elucidate the meaning of one biblical verse or passage, or of a character or circumstance, by reference to another. Several features in their Greek text guide them in finding the correspondences and the connections they require for that purpose.

4.1. Eusebius of Caesarea (iii): The Names of Christ

Greek forms of Hebrew names or designations may be used in more than one context, naming or designating different characters. The Greek text of the LXX allows the exegete to find correspondences between different characters mentioned in the LXX and in the NT on the basis of their shared Greek names or designations.

Eusebius of Caesarea avails himself of this feature of the Greek text: In one passage of his *Ecclesiastical History*,[52] he claims that correspondences exist between Jesus Christ and two characters mentioned in the LXX, Aaron and Joshua. Remarkably, Eusebius appeals to the revelation granted to Moses on mount Sinai and cites LXX-Exod 25. 40 to substantiate this contention. He claims that Moses was well aware of the names 'Christ' and 'Jesus' and of their implications (*Hist. eccl.*, 1. 3. 1–5).

In *Hist. eccl.*, 1. 3. 2, Eusebius writes:[53]

> σεπτὸν ὡς ἔνι μάλιστα καὶ ἔνδοξον τὸ Χριστοῦ ὄνομα πρῶτος αὐτὸς γνωρίσας
> Μωυσῆς τύπους οὐρανίων καὶ σύμβολα μυστηριώδεις τε εἰκόνας ἀκολούθως χρησμῷ
> φήσαντι αὐτῷ ὅρα, ποιήσεις πάντα κατὰ τὸν τύπον τὸν δειχθέντα σοι ἐν τῷ ὄρει

---

52 Written between 290 and 325 CE according to J. Ulrich, 'Eusebius', in *Lexikon der Antiken Christlichen Literatur*, ed. by Siegmar Döpp and Wilhelm Geerlings, 3rd edn (Freiburg: Herder, 2002), pp. 240–45 (p. 242).

53 Text: Eusebius, *Werke*, ed. by Eduard Schwartz and Theodor Mommsen, GCS, 9.1 (Leipzig: Hinrichs, 1903), II. Die Kirchengeschichte: Erster Teil, p. 28.

παραδούς, ἀρχιερέα θεοῦ, ὡς ἐνῆν μάλιστα δυνατὸν ἄνθρωπον, ἐπιφημίσας, τοῦτον Χριστὸν ἀναγορεύει [...].[54]

Eusebius claims that Moses made Aaron known as 'anointed/Christ' (Χριστός).[55] This claim is possible on the basis of the Greek text of the LXX which indeed speaks of the 'anointed priest' (ὁ ἱερεὺς ὁ χριστός). The high priest and the priests of Israel were anointed. Thus, when Moses is instructed to anoint Aaron (and his sons) in Exodus 28. 41; 29. 7; 30. 30; 40. 13, the verb משׁח in the MT is rendered as χρίω in the LXX. Leviticus 4. 3, 5, 16; 6. 15 speak of the 'anointed priest' (MT: הַכֹּהֵן הַמָּשִׁיחַ), using 'the title of the high priest in preexilic times',[56] and this is rendered as ὁ ἀρχιερεὺς ὁ κεχρισμένος in LXX-Lev 4. 3 and as ὁ ἱερεὺς ὁ χριστός in LXX-Lev 4. 5, 16; 6. 22(15). The LXX text thus applies the designation 'the anointed' (ὁ χριστός) to Aaron, allowing Eusebius to claim that Moses made Aaron known as Χριστός.

Eusebius further claims (Hist. eccl., 1. 3. 3–4, not cited above) that the name of Joshua and its significance were also known to Moses. This claim, too, is possible on the basis of the Greek text: Joshua's Hebrew name, יְהוֹשֻׁעַ, is rendered as Ἰησοῦς in the Greek text of the LXX, and this, of course, is also the name of Jesus in the Greek NT. But Eusebius is not content merely to ground his claim in the identity of Greek names or designations. Regarding Joshua, he further notes that he was to lead his people, similarly to Jesus. There is thus a real analogy between these characters and their functions.

A similar analogy also exists between Christ and Aaron, Eusebius asserts. He presents a longer and more theologically sophisticated version[57] of the argument found in Hist. eccl., 1. 3. 2 in his Demonstratio Evangelica, 4. 15. 10–18. Eusebius notes that the tabernacle and its furnishings were to be anointed (Dem. ev., 4. 15. 11; cf. Exodus 30. 22–33, in MT and LXX). Anointing with oil, Eusebius contends, represents the anointing with the Holy Spirit who may be called the oil of God. Christ is the only one truly anointed with the Spirit (Dem. ev., 4. 15. 13–15). Referring to the 'pattern' shown to Moses on mount Sinai (Dem. ev., 4. 15. 11; 4. 15. 17), Eusebius again mentions that Moses called the man set apart for priestly service 'anointed/Christ' (χριστός) and that this designation was given to other anointed leaders, too (Dem. ev., 4. 15. 18;

---

54 'Moses himself was the first to recognize how peculiarly august and glorious is the name of Christ. Having imparted the types of heavenly things, and symbols, and the mysterious images, in accordance with the oracle which said to him, See, you will make all things according to the pattern shown to you on the mountain, he declared High Priest of God as able as possible a man [and] made him known as anointed/Christ [...]'. Translation (with slight alterations): Eusebius, The Ecclesiastical History, trans. by Kirsopp Lake, LCL, 153, 2 vols (London: William Heinemann; New York: G. P. Putnam's Sons, 1926), I, p. 29.

55 His text of LXX-Exod 25. 40 includes the addition of πάντα, and he must assume that 'all things' includes the high priesthood, cf. section 1.2 above.

56 Jacob Milgrom, Leviticus 1–16: A New Translation with Introduction and Commentary, AB, 3 (New York: Doubleday, 1991), p. 231.

57 For theological implications, see Holger Strutwolf, Die Trinitätstheologie und Christologie des Euseb von Caesarea: Eine dogmengeschichtliche Untersuchung seiner Platonismusrezeption und Wirkungsgeschichte, FKDG, 72 (Göttingen: Vandenhoeck & Ruprecht, 1999), pp. 174–77.

cf. 4. 15. 6; 4. 16. 53).[58] A range of persons designated as 'anointed/Christ' in the LXX (especially Aaron) thus represent Christ as the one truly anointed with the Spirit.

For Eusebius, attention to identical Greek names or designations in different biblical contexts is not a mere play with words. The identity of their names and designations can indicate real analogies between the persons so named, and the exegete can uncover those analogies and use them in theological argumentation.

4.2. Origen: 'The Tents that the Lord has Pitched'

The LXX sometimes uses one Greek word to translate different Hebrew words. This allows the exegete to pursue the occurrences of the relevant Greek word across a range of biblical passages. Sometimes the Greek translation of a Hebrew word is prompted by an alternative vocalization (relative to the MT) of the Hebrew consonant text. This may also allow the exegete to connect the relevant passage with other passages where the same Greek word occurs. If this word also occurs in the NT, this further allows the exegete to find connections with relevant NT passages.

In his *Homilies on Numbers* (*Hom. Num.*, 17. 4, extant in Latin translation), Origen,[59] commenting on LXX-Num 24. 5–6,[60] reads a word connecting these two verses: They both mention 'tents' (σκηναί). This is not the case in the MT, however. The Greek translation of one Hebrew word in v. 6 not only allows Origen to understand v. 5 and v. 6 as referring, in different ways, to 'tents'. It also prompts him to create a web of additional biblical references that (in Greek) in one way or another also refer to 'tents'. Origen uses the mention of 'tents' in diverse biblical contexts to unfold his understanding of the Christian life and its eschatological goal.

Numbers 24. 5, in the Masoretic and LXX texts, reads:

מַה־טֹּבוּ אֹהָלֶיךָ יַעֲקֹב מִשְׁכְּנֹתֶיךָ יִשְׂרָאֵל׃   Ὡς καλοί σου οἱ οἶκοι, Ιακωβ, αἱ σκηναί σου, Ισραηλ.

Levine translates the MT: 'How lovely are your tents, oh Jacob, your dwellings, oh Israel!'[61] LXX-Num 24. 5 mentions σοῦ οἱ οἶκοι, 'your houses', and αἱ σκηναί σου, 'your tents', where the MT has אֹהָלֶיךָ, 'your tents', and מִשְׁכְּנֹתֶיךָ, 'your dwellings'. The Hebrew word מִשְׁכָּן is used elsewhere to denote the desert tabernacle (Exodus 25. 9; 26. 1 and others), where the LXX also has σκηνή. In *Hom. Num.*, 17. 4. 1–3, Origen discusses diverse possible interpretations of this verse. The difference between 'houses' and

58 See Eusebius, *Werke*, VI, pp. 174–76, 194.
59 Origen, born around 185 CE, lived in Alexandria until his departure for Caesarea. He died around 253 CE. Origen's homilies on the Pentateuch were preached in Caesarea after his departure from Alexandria according to H. J. Vogt, 'Origenes', in *Lexikon der Antiken Christlichen Literatur*, ed. by Siegmar Döpp and Wilhelm Geerlings, 3rd edn (Freiburg: Herder, 2002), pp. 528–36 (pp. 528–30).
60 While the homilies are extant in Latin translation, Origen must have read a Greek biblical text.
61 Baruch A. Levine, *Numbers 21–36: A New Translation with Introduction and Commentary*, AB, 4A (New York: Doubleday, 2000), pp. 188–89, 196.

'tents' that he sees in the Greek text allows him to find in these words references to different groups of people, including those who, living in stable buildings, are perfect in their works ('houses'), whereas others are on an endless journey, ever striving for greater wisdom and insight ('tents') (*Hom. Num.*, 17. 4. 2). He then proceeds to give an interpretation of the 'tents' mentioned in LXX-Num 24. 6. The Masoretic and LXX texts of that verse read:

כִּנְחָלִים נִטָּיוּ ὡσεὶ νάπαι σκιάζουσαι

כְּגַנֹּת עֲלֵי נָהָר καὶ ὡσεὶ παράδεισοι ἐπὶ ποταμῶν

כַּאֲהָלִים נָטַע יְהוָה καὶ ὡσεὶ σκηναί, ἃς ἔπηξεν κύριος,

כַּאֲרָזִים עֲלֵי־מָיִם ὡσεὶ κέδροι παρ᾽ ὕδατα.

The Hebrew word אהלים is vocalized as אֲהָלִים in the MT, meaning 'aloewood'.[62] Levine translates the MT: 'They stand high like palm groves, like gardens beside the river; Like aloes planted by YHWH, like cedars near the water'.[63] The LXX translators, however, took אהלים to mean 'tents', σκηναί: ὡσεὶ σκηναί, ἃς ἔπηξεν κύριος. For Origen, therefore, v. 6 continues to speak about 'tents', and this allows him to juxtapose the 'tents' that the Lord has pitched, mentioned in v. 6, and the 'tents' of the Israelites, mentioned in v. 5. But what are these 'tents that the Lord has pitched'? Origen writes (*Hom. Num.*, 17. 4. 7):[64]

> Extra hunc mundum me progredi convenit, ut videam, quae sint tabernacula, quae fixit Dominus. Illa nimirum sunt, quae ostendit Moysi, cum tabernaculum construeret in deserto, dicens ad eum: vide inquit facies omnia secundum typum, qui ostensus est tibi in monte. Ad imitationem ergo istorum tabernaculorum, quae fixit Dominus, Istrahel debet facere tabernacula [...].[65]

Origen's reasoning is probably influenced here by other texts, though he does not cite them: Hebrews 9. 11 mentions a tent 'not made by hands, that is, not of this creation'. This is the true tent, ἣν ἔπηξεν ὁ κύριος, οὐκ ἄνθρωπος Hebrews 8. 2 (cf. σκηναὶ ἃς ἔπηξεν κύριος LXX-Num 24. 6). The Greek text of LXX-Num 24. 6 may well have reminded Origen of Hebrews 8. 2, thus providing a first intra-biblical connection. Only a few verses later, in Hebrews 8. 5, the author of Hebrews cites the same verse that Origen also cites in the above passage, LXX-Exod 25. 40. Origen's text of LXX-Exod 25. 40 agrees with the citation of that verse in Hebrews 8. 5. It includes *omnia* and *inquit*,

---

62 See *Lexicon in Veteris Testamenti Libros*, s.v. I אֲהָלִים.

63 Levine, *Numbers 21–36*, pp. 188–89, 196–97.

64 Text (extant in Latin translation): Origenes, *Werke*, ed. by Wilhelm Adolf Baehrens, GCS, 30 (Leipzig: Hinrichs, 1921), VII. Homilien zum Hexateuch in Rufins Übersetzung. Zweiter Teil, p. 162. Cf. Origène, *Homélies sur les Nombres*, ed. by Louis Doutreleau, SC, 415, 442, 2 vols (Paris: Cerf, 1996–99), II, pp. 294–97. The paragraph numbers are those of Doutreleau's edition (Baehrens does not further subdivide *Hom. Num.*, 17. 4).

65 'It is fitting that I proceed outside this world, so that I may see of what kind the tents may be that the Lord has pitched. They are doubtless those that he showed to Moses when he built the tabernacle in the desert, saying to him: see (he said), you will make all things according to the pattern shown to you on the mountain. In imitation, therefore, of those tents that the Lord has pitched, Israel must make tents [...].'

the translation of φησίν, a word likely to have been added by the author of Hebrews.[66] Assuming, then, that Origen is aware of the citation of Scripture in Hebrews 8. 5 and of its context within Hebrews (8. 2), we may understand his argument in the above passage as follows:

In Hebrews 8. 5, the 'pattern' shown to Moses is set over against a 'likeness and shadow', and LXX-Exod 25. 40 is cited in support. Origen thinks that God showed Moses the 'tents that the Lord has pitched'. Similarly to what he sees in Hebrews, Origen sets the 'tents that the Lord has pitched' in LXX-Num 24. 6 over against Israel's tents on earth (LXX-Num 24. 5) and cites LXX-Exod 25. 40 in support. It follows that LXX-Exod 25. 40 must be understood to mean that Moses was shown heavenly tents, and the tents of Israel would then seem to be their representation on earth.

Origen continues (*Hom. Num.*, 17. 4. 7):[67]

[…] Paulus […] arte faber tabernaculorum [sc. inveniebatur]. […] Paulus […] a faciendis tabernaculis terrenis ad coelestia tabernacula construenda translatus sit. Construit enim coelestia tabernacula docens unumquemque viam salutis et beatarum in coelestibus mansionum iter ostendens. Facit tabernacula Paulus et cum ab Hierusalem in circuitu usque ad Illyricum replet Evangelium Dei ecclesias construendo; et hoc modo facit et ipse tabernacula ad similitudinem tabernaculorum coelestium, quae ostendit Deus in monte Moysi.[68]

The use of the word σκηναί in LXX-Num 24. 5–6 allows Origen to connect these verses with the mention of Paul's trade in Acts 18. 3. Paul was a 'tentmaker' (σκηνοποιός). He built 'heavenly tents' by building churches and teaching everyone the way of salvation. Origen concludes that the church built by the apostle, in analogy to the tents of Israel, is a representation on earth of the heavenly tents.

In addition to this ecclesiological interpretation, he then turns to the life of the believer (*Hom. Num.*, 17. 4. 8):[69]

Sed et unusquisque nostrum, si qui tamen exivit de Aegypto et habitat in deserto, in tabernaculo debet habitare et diem festum in tabernaculis agere. […] commorationis in deserto fit memoria per tabernacula; in tabernaculis enim habitaverunt patres nostri in deserto […].[70]

---

66 Cf. section 1.2 above.

67 Origenes, *Werke*, VII.2, pp. 162–63; cf. Origène, *Homélies sur les Nombres*, II, pp. 294–97.

68 'Paul [was found to be] by trade a tentmaker. Paul […] was transferred from the making of earthly tents to the building of heavenly tents. For he builds heavenly tents in that he teaches everyone the way of salvation and in that he points out the way of the happy abodes in the heavens. Paul also makes tabernacles when, beginning from Jerusalem and on all sides as far as Illyricum, he fully proclaims the Gospel of God by building churches; and in this way, he himself, too, makes tents in the likeness of the heavenly tents that God has shown to Moses on the mountain'.

69 Origenes, *Werke*, VII.2, pp. 163; cf. Origène, *Homélies sur les Nombres*, II, pp. 296–97. For *commorationis*, Doutreleau reads *commemorationis*, which seems to be an error.

70 'But each of us, too — if anyone has gone out of Egypt and lives in the desert, he must live in a tent and must celebrate the feast in tents. The sojourn in the desert is remembered by tents, since our fathers lived in tents in the desert'.

Origen sees connections with yet more biblical texts that, once again, he finds in the LXX. According to MT-Lev 23. 34–36, 42–43, the Israelites were required to dwell 'in booths' (בַּסֻּכֹּת, Leviticus 23. 42) during the feast called the 'feast of booths' (חַג הַסֻּכֹּת) in MT-Lev 23. 34; Deut 16. 13, 16; 31. 10. This is rendered as ἑορτὴ σκηνῶν ('feast of tents') in LXX-Lev 23. 34; Deut 16. 13 (and as ἑορτὴ τῆς σκηνοπηγίας, 'fest of the setting up of tents', in LXX-Deut 16. 16; 31. 10). The 'booths' (סֻכֹּת) are called σκηναί, 'tents', in LXX-Lev 23. 42–43. This allows Origen to speak about the command to live in 'tents' during the feast in his discussion of the 'tents' mentioned in LXX-Num 24. 5–6, although different Hebrew words are used in the MT of the relevant verses, סֻכָּה in Leviticus 23. 42–43, אֹהֶל and מִשְׁכָּן in Numbers 24. 5, אֹהָלִים in Numbers 24. 6. 'We', too, must dwell in 'tents' when we celebrate 'the feast'. For Origen's audience, this makes good sense since he has explained in a previous paragraph (referred to, but not cited above) that, in his understanding, the 'tents' of Israel mentioned in LXX-Num 24. 5 may be interpreted as referring to those who are ever striving to proceed in the quest for wisdom and understanding and who live, as it were, in tents.[71]

Origen introduces yet another biblical reference (*Hom. Num.*, 17. 4. 8):[72]

> Vide autem, si non sunt tabernacula, quae fixit Deus, etiam illa, quae Salvator commemorat in evangelio dicens: facite vobis amicos de mammona iniquitatis, ut, cum defeceritis, recipiant vos in aeterna tabernacula.[73]

According to Luke 16. 9, Jesus told his audience that they should make friends for themselves, 'so that [...] they may receive you into the eternal tents (εἰς τὰς αἰωνίους σκηνάς)'. Again, the connection is made possible by the use of σκηναί in LXX-Num 24. 6 and of the same word in Luke 16. 9. The eternal σκηναί of Luke 16. 9, Origen suggests, are the same as those mentioned in LXX-Num 24. 6, that is, the 'tents that the Lord has pitched' are the future abode of believers; the implication being that the 'tents' of this future abode are the same 'heavenly tents' that were shown to Moses on mount Sinai.

The connections between all of the biblical verses and passages cited and alluded to — including those that refer to the 'tents' of the feast of tabernacles, the 'tents' built by Paul, and the 'eternal tents' mentioned by Jesus — would probably not have occurred to an exegete on the basis of the MT. The Greek text of the LXX allows

---

71 '[I]dcirco eorum, qui iter sapientiae Dei incedunt, non domos laudat — non enim pervenerunt ad finem —, sed tabernacula miratur, in quibus semper ambulant et semper proficiunt, et quanto magis proficiunt, tanto iis proficiendi via augetur et in immensum tenditur, et ideo istos ipsos profectus eorum per spiritum contuens tabernacula ea nominat Istrahel'; *Hom. Num.*, 17. 4. 2; Origenes, *Werke*, VII.2, p. 160; cf. Origène, *Homélies sur les Nombres*, II, pp. 288–89. To go out into the desert and to live in 'tents' is therefore tantamount to setting out and to proceeding on the way of wisdom: *Hom. Num.*, 17. 4. 9, Origenes, *Werke*, VII.2, pp. 163–64; cf. Origène, *Homélies sur les Nombres*, II, pp. 298–99. For eschatological implications, see Brian E. Daly, *The Hope of the Early Church: A Handbook of Patristic Eschatology* (Cambridge: Cambridge University Press), p. 50.

72 Origenes, *Werke*, VII.2, p. 163; cf. Origène, *Homélies sur les Nombres*, II, pp. 296–97.

73 'See, however, whether the tents that God has pitched are not also those that the Savior mentions in the Gospel, saying: make friends for yourselves with the mammon of injustice, so that, when you are wanting, they may receive you into the eternal tents'.

Origen to combine what would seem to modern readers various and diverse biblical material, and he masterfully uses the opportunities this provides for his biblical interpretation.

4.3. Gregory of Nyssa: 'Our True Bearers'

The Greek text of the LXX contains translations of Hebrew words that allow exegetes to find a surplus of meaning in, e.g. the designation of a physical object. In the context of the exegete's interpretation, a Greek word used may support his understanding in ways that the Hebrew text would not. This understanding may then allow the exegete further to refer to other passages that now turn out to be thematically related, and this correspondence may be used to corroborate the exegete's interpretation.

In his *Life of Moses*, Gregory of Nyssa[74] comments extensively on Moses' ascent to mount Sinai (he cites LXX-Exod 25. 40 in *v. Mos.*, 2. 170) and develops his own interpretation of the tabernacle in Christological, angelological and ecclesiological terms (*v. Mos.*, 2. 170–88).[75] Gregory claims that the tabernacle 'would be Christ' (*v. Mos.*, 2. 174), but he adds an angelological interpretation, asserting that the pillars, the cherubim and the other accoutrements of the tabernacle are the heavenly powers, since they were all created 'in him' (*v. Mos.*, 2. 179; cf. Colossians 1. 16).[76] In the context of this interpretation, Gregory goes on to suggest explanations of the various furnishings of the tabernacle. I focus on one detail.

In Exodus 25. 13–15, Moses is instructed to make staves or poles that will be used to carry the ark of the covenant. They are called בַּדִּים ('sticks', 'staves') in the MT.[77] Josephus calls them σκυταλίδες, 'sticks', in *Ant.*, 3. 6. 136, a translation closer in meaning to the Hebrew word than the Greek word used in the LXX, ἀναφορεῖς. The *Greek-English Lexicon of the Septuagint* suggests 'bearer' as a translation of ἀναφορεύς (in addition to 'carrying pole, stave').[78] The *Lexicon Gregorianum Online* similarly suggests 'Träger' ('bearer') as the basic meaning[79] (cf. ἀναφορέω, ἀναφέρω 'to bring up', 'to carry up').

---

74 Gregory was born between 335 and 340 CE and seems to have died before 400 CE. He probably wrote his *De Vita Moysis* around 390 CE according to F. Dünzl, 'Gregor von Nyssa', in *Lexikon der Antiken Christlichen Literatur*, ed. by Siegmar Döpp and Wilhelm Geerlings, 3rd edn (Freiburg: Herder, 2002), pp. 299–304.

75 See Conway-Jones, *Gregory of Nyssa's Tabernacle Imagery*.

76 As Daniélou and Conway-Jones argue, where earlier interpreters thought that Moses had seen the intelligible tabernacle, Gregory thinks that he had seen the world of angels, and the contemplation of the latter (αἱ ὑπερκόσμιοι δυνάμεις […] αἱ ἐν τῇ σκηνῇ θεωρούμεναι, *v. Mos.*, 2. 179) has replaced the contemplation of the intelligible ideas. See Jean Daniélou, *Platonisme et Théologie Mystique: Essai sur la Doctrine Spirituelle de Saint Grégoire de Nysse*, Theol, 2 (Paris: Aubier, 1944), pp. 170–74; Conway-Jones, *Gregory of Nyssa's Tabernacle Imagery*, pp. 134–37, 145–48.

77 See *Lexicon in Veteris Testamenti Libros*, s.v. I בד.

78 See Lust, Eynikel and Hauspie, *Greek-English Lexicon of the Septuagint*, s.v.

79 *Lexicon Gregorianum Online*, ed. by F. Mann and K. Savvides <https://referenceworks.brillonline.com/browse/lexicon-gregorianum-online> [accessed 07 January 2021].

In *v. Mos.*, 2. 179, Gregory claims that the heavenly powers of which the tabernacle consists support the universe. Given the traditional analogy between cosmological and anthropological tabernacle symbolism, it may seem plausible to him that the function of the angels *vis à vis* the cosmos would have an analogy in their service rendered to humans. He does claim that they render such service in *v. Mos.*, 2. 180, where he gives a more specific interpretation of the ἀναφορεῖς:[80]

> ἐκεῖ οἱ ἀληθινοὶ ἀναφορεῖς ἡμῶν, οἱ Εἰς διακονίαν ἀποστελλόμενοι διὰ τοὺς μέλλοντας κληρονομεῖν σωτηρίαν, οἱ καθάπερ δακτυλίοις τισὶ ταῖς ψυχαῖς ἡμῶν ἐνειρόμενοι τῶν σῳζομένων, δι᾿ ἑαυτῶν πρὸς τὸ ὕψος τῆς ἀρετῆς τοὺς κειμένους ἐπὶ γῆς ἀναφέροντες.[81]

Reading the Greek text of LXX-Exod 25. 13–15 and the mention of the ἀναφορεῖς in the context of his angelological interpretation of the tabernacle, Gregory concludes that the ἀναφορεῖς are angels who 'carry up […] those lying upon the earth' (τοὺς κειμένους ἐπὶ γῆς ἀναφέροντες).

Gregory quotes Scripture in support of this interpretation. An important authority for him is Paul who, he thinks (*v. Mos.*, 2. 178), must have seen the tabernacle in his ascent to the third heaven (cf. II Corinthians 12. 1–4). In *v. Mos.*, 2. 178, Gregory refers to the epistle to the Hebrews (believed to have been written by Paul) in support of one detail of his interpretation. In *v. Mos.*, 2. 180, Gregory's understanding of the ἀναφορεῖς allows him to see a correspondence between the instructions for the tabernacle in LXX-Exod 25. 13–15 and Hebrews 1. 14. According to this verse, the angels are 'sent for service for the sake of those who are to inherit salvation'. Gregory thinks that his understanding of the ἀναφορεῖς is in agreement with the information provided by the *auctor ad Hebraeos*.

In summary, Gregory finds a surplus of meaning in the Greek word ἀναφορεῖς that allows him to integrate the mention of the 'bearers' used to carry the ark into his angelological interpretation of tabernacle symbolism and to find a thematic correspondence with Hebrews 1. 14 that he uses to support his interpretation.

Conclusion

This article has discussed texts that interpret the revelation of a 'pattern', 'model', or 'plan' for Israel's sanctuary (LXX-Exod 25. 9, 40; 26. 30) or that refer to Aaron's high priesthood, to the tabernacle, or to details of its furnishings.

---

80 Text: *De Vita Moysis Pentecosten* in *Gregorii Nysseni Opera Online*, ed. by E. Mühlenberg and G. Maspero <https://referenceworks.brillonline.com/browse/gregorii-nysseni-opera> [accessed 07 January 2021]. Cf. Grégoire de Nysse, *La Vie de Moïse ou Traité de la Perfection en Matière de Vertu*, trans. by Jean Daniélou, SC, 1, 2nd edn (Paris: Cerf, 1955), p. 88.

81 'There are our true bearers, sent for service for the sake of those who are to inherit salvation. They are slipped through the souls of those being saved as through rings and by themselves carry up to the height of virtue those lying upon the earth'. Translation (with slight alterations): Gregory of Nyssa, *The Life of Moses*, trans. by Abraham J. Malherbe and Everett Ferguson, CWS (New York: Paulist Press, 1978), p. 100.

In the interpretations studied, the influence of the Greek text was evident in two respects. First, for some readers in late antiquity, the Greek terminology used in LXX-Exod 25. 9, 40; 26. 30 serves as a bridge connecting biblical tradition and philosophical discourses. While some interpreters see profound agreement between biblical tradition and (Middle-)Platonic philosophy, one exegete rejects the Platonic theory of ideas on the grounds that Plato had allegedly read, but misunderstood LXX-Exod 25. 9, 40; 26. 30, whereas another develops a Christological interpretation that nevertheless presupposes a philosophically informed understanding of the verses cited. In each case, it is the Greek terminology in these verses that serves as reference point for such interpretations and debates.

Second, a range of textual features facilitate the interpretation of one verse or passage by reference to one or more other verses or passages. Such features are Greek key words occurring in more than one context; identical Greek names or designations used for different biblical characters in different contexts; Greek translations due to alternative vocalizations of the Hebrew consonant text (relative to the MT) that may serve to connect the passage containing the word so translated with other texts where the relevant word also occurs; identical Greek translations of diverse Hebrew words, allowing the exegete to pursue the occurrences of the relevant word across a range of passages; Greek translations of Hebrew words that create a surplus of meaning, prompting or supporting the exegete's interpretation and allowing him or her to find thematic correspondences with other passages. Exegetes avail themselves of these features to find connections between two or more passages in the LXX and in the NT or within the LXX, or correspondences between biblical characters or circumstances.

The Greek terminology and the textual features mentioned are present in the texts, but they would remain latent would exegetes not read these texts in interaction with other factors. In the wider context of Hellenistic-Roman culture, it is the encounter of early Judaism and early Christianity with Greek philosophy that prompts exegetes to find reference points in Scripture for philosophically informed interpretations. Early Christian interpreters of Scripture are influenced by exegetical traditions and Christological beliefs. They further regard the entirety of their Christian Scriptures (the LXX and the NT) as one unified whole within which diverse passages may be related one to another for mutual elucidation. Their interpretations rest on the assumption that the language of Scripture, including the Greek text of the LXX, is meaningful even in its details and will guide the exegete in his or her quest for understanding.

▼ ABSTRACT How did the Greek text of the LXX influence early exegesis? This article discusses texts by Philo of Alexandria, Origen, Ps.-Justin, Eusebius of Caesarea, and Gregory of Nyssa that interpret the revelation of a 'pattern', 'model', or 'plan' for Israel's sanctuary (LXX-Exod 25. 9, 40; 26. 30) or that refer to Aaron's high priesthood, to the tabernacle, or to details of its furnishings. In these texts, the influence of the Greek text is evident in two respects. First, the Greek terminology used in LXX-Exod 25. 9, 40; 26. 30 allows exegetes to read Scripture in dialogue with contemporaneous epistemology and cosmology. Second, a range of textual features help exegetes to find connections and correspondences between biblical texts, characters, and circumstances, thus facilitating the interpretation of one verse or passage in light of one or more others.

LUCA MAZZINGHI

The Importance of the LXX for Biblical Theology

Some Notes on Method

In this paper I have been given a task that seems peripheral in the context of a conference organised by the Pontifical Biblical Institute: what is the importance of the LXX for biblical theology? I say 'peripheral' because, for many exegetes, biblical theology is something of a Cinderella among the biblical sciences, even though one always wishes to recognize it as really belonging to the world of exegesis. It is precisely the Bible which provides us with an interesting suggestion: Luke's Gospel closes with a picture of Jesus opening the minds of his disciples so that they understand the Scriptures (Luke 24. 45), something he had already done with the two on the road to Emmaus (Luke 24. 18). Luke mentions explicitly the Law of Moses, the prophets and the psalms (Luke 24. 17). It is this comprehensive interpretation of the Scriptures, placed on the mouth of Jesus himself, that lies at the heart of what we call 'biblical theology'.

In this paper, I intend to touch on three aspects in a summary way: first of all, I want to recall what it is we understand by 'biblical theology'; secondly, to clarify the currently much debated problem concerning a possible theology of the LXX; thirdly, I would like to suggest a possible concrete way of understanding the relationship between biblical theology and the theology of the LXX, looking at this also from the methodological point of view. As is clear, the first two aspects touch on themes that have been much discussed on which we cannot claim to be saying anything new; the third aspect, however, has been studied much less.

Fundamentally, the relationship between biblical theology and the LXX is a very old problem. Augustine writes a well-known letter to Jerome (*Ep.*, 71) asking him to concentrate on the translation of the text of the LXX rather than on that of the Hebrew text, and he concludes his letter thus:

> I would like you to explain to me why, in many passages, the text of the Hebrew manuscripts of sacred Scripture is so different from the Greek text, known as the LXX. In fact, the latter text has not a little importance in view of its widespread diffusion and the fact that it was used by the apostles. That is attested not only by the facts, but I recall that you have attested it yourself. Thus, you would be performing a very useful role if you were to re-establish the Latin text on the basis of the Greek version of the LXX; because the one which we have, in its

New Avenues in Biblical Exegesis in Light of the Septuagint
ed. by Leonardo Pessoa da Silva Pinto and Daniela Scialabba, Turnhout, 2022 (*SEPT*, 1), pp. 327–340
© BREPOLS PUBLISHERS
DOI 10.1484/M.SEPT-EB.5.127721

various codexes, offers such notable variants that it can only be tolerated with difficulty [...].[1]

In the same letter, Augustine defends the value of the LXX and the need for a correct translation starting out from a secure textual basis. Moreover, he affirms the apostolic nature of the LXX and its constant use in the Oriental Church.

1.   The Nature of Biblical Theology: A Discussion in Progress

What do we understand by 'biblical theology'? I must immediately preface my remarks by saying that I am tackling this subject from the perspective of a Christian reader who considers Scripture as made up of two Testaments. One of the most interesting advocates of biblical theology, Paul Beauchamp, wrote: 'biblical theology has its own role: to give a reasonable account of the way in which the Christian faith as expressed today is faithful to its biblical basis, and to bring this fidelity up to date'.[2]

In a study of fourteen years ago, the Italian biblical scholar Roberto Vignolo described the role of biblical theology as the attempt to respond critically to the *intentio profundior* of the Scripture, understood as memory of and witness to a salvific revelation.[3] Thus, biblical theology is different from a religious-historical study of the different beliefs of Israel, of Jesus and of the early church but is also different from a conceptual system, like the old dogmatics, which seeks to prescind from the historical and literary dimensions of the biblical texts. Biblical theology stands as a kind of sentinel at the border between exegesis, understood as an objective scientific activity, and systematic theology as the study of the religious meaning of the biblical texts.

Thus understood, biblical theology entered the field of biblical studies with the famous programmatic discourse of Philipp Gabler which took place on 30 March 1787. It is well aware of the diversity of theologies present in the Bible — a good example would be a recent book of Georg Fischer on the theologies (in the plural!) of the Old Testament[4] — but it is equally aware of the unity of Scripture as a whole. This is the perspective which we adopt or try to adopt in the department of Biblical Theology in the Gregorian University.[5]

I would underline the fact that, considered from this perspective, biblical theology presupposes a believing view of the Scriptures even if it is possible in itself to write a biblical theology that is written from a perspective that is correct methodologically

---

1   Cf. PL XXXIII, 241–43.

2   Paul Beauchamp, 'Biblique (Théologie)', in *Dictionnaire critique de théologie*, ed. by Jean-Yves Lacoste (Paris: Presses Universitaires de France, 1998), pp. 169–73.

3   Roberto Vignolo, 'Teologia biblica, teologia della Bibbia e dintorni', *RivBibIt*, 56 (2008), 129–55 (pp. 131–55), with an extensive bibliography. See also Guido Benzi, 'Teologia biblica', in *Temi teologici della Bibbia*, ed. by Romano Penna, Giacomo Perego and Gianfranco Ravasi (Cinisello Balsamo: San Paolo, 2010), pp. 1383–95.

4   Georg Fischer, *Theologien des Altes Testaments* (Stuttgart: Verlag Katholisches Bibelwerk, 2012).

5   Cf. <https://www.unigre.it/it/ua/facolta/teologia/dipartimenti/teologia-biblica/> [accessed 09 January 2021].

and which, nevertheless prescinds from faith. In one of his articles in 1956, 'À propos de la théologie biblique', Roland de Vaux wrote provocatively:

> It has sometimes been claimed and recently said again that only the absence of a religious commitment can guarantee the objectivity of this research. This is a sophism or a paradox. It would be like saying that one has to be colour-blind to be a good critic of art or that one must be deaf to be a good critic of music.[6]

On the other hand, biblical theology must never seek to exercise control over the other biblical disciplines or claim superiority in the face of the various exegetical methods. Rather, it must position itself alongside them with great humility and well aware of having an absolute need of them.[7]

In this twofold identity, biblical and theological, lie, simultaneously, both the challenge and the principal difficulty of biblical theology. To give one example, which I take from Roberto Vignolo,[8] biblical theology is not a noble princess who is surrounded by the exegetical sciences as handmaids ready to help her in her most noble tasks; she is not even an old lady who is now unfashionable, wholly controlled by a carer (scientific biblical exegesis proper) who takes her where the carer wishes. Still to be built, and this is a task which no one has yet attempted, perhaps because it is too much for a single person, is a biblical theology of the whole of the Bible, understood as a salvific-historical revelation, which lets the Bible speak for itself along with its different and necessary theological perspectives. Here, we come across an aspect to which we shall have to return: the indispensable coexistence, in biblical theology, of a necessary plurality and of a profound search for unity.

Already in 1967, in his book *Wort und Glaube*, Gerhard Ebeling wrote:

> In biblical theology, the theologian who devotes himself specifically to studying the relationship between the Old and New Testaments must indicate the sense which he attributes to the Bible as a whole, that is, he must, above all, resolve the theological problems which derive from the analysis of the multiplicities of the biblical testimonies considered in their reciprocal relationship [...] In the theology of the Old and New Testaments, the theologian who devotes himself to the study of the one or the other in particular must give an overall account of his understanding of the one and the other: that is to say, he must pay particular attention to the theological problems which arise from the fact he is seeking to explain the reciprocal relationship between the numerous witnesses of the Old Testament and of the New.[9]

It is within this reciprocal relationship between the numerous witnesses of the two Testaments that we also find the testimony of the LXX.

---

6   Roland de Vaux, 'À propos de la théologie biblique', *ZAW*, 68 (1956) 225–27 (p. 226). See also Franco Festorazzi, 'Il problema del metodo nella teologia biblica', *La Scuola cattolica*, 91/4 (1963), 253–76.
7   In this connection, see also the introductory reflections to biblical theology made by James Barr, *The Concept of Biblical Theology: An Old Testament Perspective* (London: SCM Press, 1999), pp. 3–17.
8   Vignolo, 'Teologia biblica', p. 136.
9   Gerhard Ebeling, *Wort und Glaube*, 3rd edn (Tübingen: Mohr Siebeck, 1967), p. 88.

2. The Question of the Theology of the LXX

If we wish to tackle the question of the importance of the LXX for biblical theology, we must first of all deal with a preliminary problem: does a theology of the LXX actually exist? As all know well, this is a subject which is much discussed today and on which there does not seem to be any consensus. However, in the conferences and in the publications which circulate today in an ever-increasing quantity about the LXX, there is also an increasing interest in the study of its theology. I shall limit myself here to a summary of the basic considerations.

In a speech made at Würzburg in 1962, Joseph Ziegler expressed his hope thus: 'It is a welcome and fruitful task to prepare materials so that finally a long-awaited and desired theology of the LXX can be written by someone'.[10] It must be remembered that, in those years, the influence of authors such as Georg Bertram was powerful. Bertram believed that he had found a *Septuaginta-Frömmigkeit* different from and (for him) superior to that of the Masoretic text,[11] something maintained also by Ziegler himself. It is an idea often reflected in the *Theologisches Wörterbuch zum Neuen Testament*, alongside the belief of authors, like Bertram and Martin Hengel, that the LXX should be considered as an authentic preparation for Christianity. Consequently, there is a clear risk of approaching the LXX from latent anti-Jewish perspectives (perhaps not by chance, Bertram sympathised with National Socialism).[12]

Sixty years have passed since Ziegler expressed his hope, and this task has still not been carried out. More recently, Jonathan Cook has coined the distinction between the 'minimalists' (Albert Pietersma, for example) and the 'maximalists', the latter represented by those scholars favourable to the possibility of writing a theology of the LXX. Among these, I recall Martin Rösel and Jan Joosten, but also the Italian, Mario Cimosa.[13] In this brief space, it is impossible to enter into a debate which is still raging.[14] In my opinion, however, there are good arguments which have to be taken into account in favour of a possible theology of the LXX, albeit with all methodological caution.

In a fundamental study, 'Theologically Motivated Exegesis Embedded in the Septuagint',[15] Emmanuel Tov recognises a clear theological dimension present in many texts of the LXX but notes that the greater difficulty is represented by the

10 Joseph Ziegler, 'Die Septuaginta: Erbe und Auftrag', in Joseph Ziegler, *Sylloge: Gesammelte Aufsätze zur Septuaginta* (Göttingen: Vandenhoeck & Ruprecht, 1971), pp. 590–614 (p. 613).

11 See Georg Bertram, 'Praeparatio Evangelica in der Septuagint', *VT*, 7 (1957), 225–49.

12 See Martin Rösel, 'Towards a "Theology of the Septuagint"', in *Septuagint Research: Issues and Challenges in the Study of the Greek Jewish Scriptures*, ed. by Wolfgang Kraus and R. Glenn Wooden, SBLSCS, 53 (Atlanta: SBL, 2006), pp. 239–52.

13 See Johann Cook, 'Toward the Formulation of a Theology of the Septuagint', in *Congress Volume: Ljubljana 2007*, ed. by André Lemaire (Boston: Brill, 2010), pp. 621–37.

14 See Alex Douglas, 'Limitations to Writing a Theology of the Septuagint', *BIOSCS*, 45 (2012), 10–117 (p. 104, n. 1), with a good bibliography.

15 Emanuel Tov, 'Theologically Motivated Exegesis Embedded in the Septuagint', in *Translation of Scripture: Proceedings of a Conference at the Annenberg Research Institute May 15–16, 1989*, ed. by David M. Goldenberg (Philadelphia: Annenberg Research Institute, 1990), pp. 215–33.

plurality and heterogeneous nature of the LXX.[16] Thus, the question posed by Gert Steyn remains true: of which LXX are we speaking?[17] More basically, of what are we speaking when we speak of the LXX? Strictly speaking, in fact, the LXX should be reduced to the Pentateuch alone; in the broader sense, we end up embracing the entire span of the books of the Hebrew Bible, but, broader still, we also include the non-translated texts, as, for example, the book of Wisdom, a book of undoubtedly high theological value. Alex Douglas reminds us that a theology of the LXX is possible only when we have defined what we understand by the 'LXX'.[18]

However, I do not think that this difficulty ought to constitute an insurmountable obstacle in the way of a theology of the LXX but, rather, a challenge. Understood as a unitary text, the LXX certainly does not exist; there is probably not even a hypothetical *Ur-Septuaginta* text. In fact, we have a plurality of manuscripts and textual traditions. One thinks, for example, of references to the LXX in the *Talmud* which are not found in any known codex, as in the case of Genesis 1. 26 and 11. 7.[19] From the textual point of view, therefore, a future theology of the LXX will always have to be a 'plural' theology.

To this methodological precaution we must add another: behind every (translated) book of the LXX lies a different translator; therefore, to recognize the different nature of each book is a fundamental presupposition for a theology of the LXX.[20] However, that does not prevent us from seeking common aspects, even theological ones, among the different texts of the LXX which, in each case, arose from within a fairly homogeneous cultural and religious environment. Moreover, these observations are also true for the Hebrew Bible. How is it possible, in fact, to seek agreement between the Pentateuch and Qoheleth? Yet, taken overall, there exists a theology of the Hebrew Bible if for no other reason than that it speaks of the same God, and this goes for Qoheleth too. In an interesting article, Roger Le Déaut, described the LXX, taken as a whole, as a document of Alexandrian theology.[21] Moreover, as Martin Rösel observes, it is possible to adopt a comparative approach and highlight the differences but also the common points between the various books of the LXX.[22]

---

16 See also Anna Passoni Dell'Acqua, 'I LXX: punto di arrivo e di partenza per diversi ambiti di ricerca', *Annali di Scienze Religiose*, I (1996), 17–31.

17 Gert J. Steyn, 'Which "LXX" are we Talking about in NT Scholarship? Two Examples from Hebrew', in *Die Septuaginta — Texte, Kontexte, Lebenswelten: Internationale Fachtagung veranstaltet von Septuaginta Deutsch (LXX.D), Wuppertal 20.-23. Juli 2006*, ed. by Martin Karrer and Wolfgang Kraus, WUNT, 219 (Tübingen: Mohr Siebeck, 2008), pp. 697–707.

18 See Douglas, 'Limitations', pp. 116–17.

19 See Hans Ausloos, 'Sept défis posés à une théologie de la Septante', in *Congress Volume: Stellenbosch 2016*, ed. by Louis C. Jonker, Gideon R. Kotzé and Christi M. Maier (Leiden: Brill, 2017), pp. 228–50 (pp. 233–34).

20 See Cook, 'Towards the Formulation', p. 636.

21 Roger Le Déaut, 'La Septante: un Targum?', in *Études sur le judaïsme hellénistique*, ed. by R. Kuntzmann, LeDiv, 119 (Paris: Cerf, 1984), pp. 147–95 (p. 176 n. 142).

22 Rösel, 'Towards a "Theology of the Septuagint"', especially p. 255. Cf. the criticisms of Rösel advanced by Ausloos, 'Sept défis', p. 248 n. 62.

A further methodological precaution is to keep in mind that, with regard to the translated books, the LXX is precisely and primarily a translation.[23] But it must also be remembered that the books composed directly in Greek are very much influenced by the already existing texts of the LXX, even when they are distant in style from the LXX, at least in part, as is the case for the book of Wisdom.[24] The first task towards a future theology of the LXX is, therefore, a constant comparison with the Hebrew text. Authors such as Jan Joosten[25] remind us of the difficulty of this comparison, a difficulty which is well known to all. In fact, the LXX's changes to the Hebrew text do not always arise from theological motives; at times, it is a question of linguistic or cultural reasons, often arising from the fact that the Greek text presupposes a different Hebrew *Vorlage*, as is clear from the discoveries at Qumran and, in various cases, a better text than the MT. In the end, it is not always possible to grasp the translator's intention.[26] Moreover, it is also true, as Emanuel Tov reminds us yet again, that we must also ask whether the translators always really understood their Hebrew text.[27] As still happens today, the translators faced the risk of conjectures, misunderstandings and real errors.

However, we agree with Jonathan Cook when he observes that 'It is exactly in the differences between the source text and the target text that interpretation takes place. This interpretation could be understood as exegesis or theology'.[28] Hans Ausloos cites

---

23 Ausloos, 'Sept défis', pp. 236–37.

24 See Luca Mazzinghi, 'The Style of the Book of Wisdom', in *Handbuch zur Septuaginta/Handbook of the Septuagint*, ed. by Eberhard Bons and Jan Joosten (Gütersloh: Gütersloher Verlagshaus, 2016), III. Die Sprache der Septuaginta/The Language of the Septuagint, pp. 386–92.

25 Jan Joosten, 'Une théologie de la Septante? Réflexions méthodologiques sur l'interprétation de la version grecque', *Révue de Théologie et de Philosophie*, 132 (2000), 31–46.

26 See Ausloos, 'Sept défis', p. 240 n. 38, with further bibliography. Martin Rösel observes that, even in the case where a text of the LXX must be attributed to a different Hebrew *Vorlage*, that does not necessarily exclude theological consequences; Martin Rösel, 'Eine Theologie der Septuaginta. Präzisierungen und Pointierungen', in *Theologie und Textgeschichte: Septuaginta und Masoretischer Text als Äußerungen theologischer Reflexion*, ed. by Frank Ueberschaer, Thomas Wagner and Jonathan Miles Robker (Tübingen: Mohr Siebeck, 2018), pp. 25–43. We would have a theological emphasis which the LXX shares with other witnesses to the text (in this case, Hebrew). However, these are complicated cases: theology proper to the LXX or the different theology of a different Hebrew text? Cf. the problem of the LXX of Jeremiah which many hold to reflect a more original Hebrew text. See also Ausloos, 'Sept défis', pp. 244–47, who discusses the text of the LXX of I Kings 19. 17 and that of Genesis 1. 2. Are these actually different theologies from the MT? See also Dirk Kurt Kranz, 'The "Religious Status" of the Septuaginta: The End of a Paradigm', in *Sophia — Paideia. Sapienza e educazione (Sir 1,27): Miscellanea di studi offerti in onore del prof. Mario Cimosa*, ed. by Gillian Booney and Rafael Vicent (Roma: LAS, 2012), pp. 33–53.

27 Emanuel Tov, 'Did the Septuagint Translators Always Understand Their Hebrew Text?', in Emanuel Tov, *The Greek and the Hebrew Bible: Collected Essays on the Septuagint*, VT.S, 72 (Leiden: Brill, 1999), pp. 203–18.

28 Cook, 'Towards the Formulation', p. 622; Ausloos, 'Sept défies', pp. 238–39; Joosten, 'Une théologie', p. 33.

some possible examples such as Isaiah 6. 10 and 9. 5; one could add Qohelet 11. 9, part of a translation which is overall very literal.[29] But the examples could be multiplied.[30]

It still remains to register a further methodological precaution. Despite the usefulness, and even the attraction of enterprises like that of the French edition of the LXX, it is always necessary to distinguish between the intention of the translator and the way in which the tradition has taken up the texts of the LXX. This is especially true of the interpretations of the LXX offered by the New Testament; one thinks, for example, of Matthew 3. 17 and parallels, a text which refers to LXX-Gen 22. 2; the messianic interpretation belongs to the NT and is not necessarily present in the text of the LXX.[31]

However, the necessary methodological precautions which many authors offer around the construction of a theology of the LXX should not lead us into absolute conclusions like that of Emanuel Tov: 'es gibt keine "Theologie" der ganzen LXX', a conclusion repeated by authors such as Ausloos.[32] However, if by 'theology' we mean what Folkert Siegert writes, 'Theologie ist denkerisches Bemühen um Gottes Wort',[33] then, considered from this point of view, the LXX certainly contains a theology even if mostly an implicit one. In any case, equally certainly, the LXX offers a reflection which is also intellectual on what the translators hold to be the word of God.[34] We should recall the path followed by the German project of the *Septuaginta Deutsch*; the starting point is the Greek text (Old Greek) and, at the same time, the conviction

---

29 In Qohelet 11. 9, the term 'blameless', ἄμωμος, is absent from the edition of Rahlfs but present in the three great codexes A, B, and S; to be added also μή, with B and S, thus καὶ μή ἐν ὁράσει. Here, the Greek translator moralizes on the Hebrew text which actually contains an explicit invitation to enjoy one's youth.

30 See Tov, 'Theologically Motivated Exegesis'.

31 See Ausloos, 'Sept défis', pp. 147–48.

32 Emanuel Tov, 'Die Septuaginta in ihrem theologischen und traditionsgeschichtliche Verhältnis zur hebräischen Bibel', in *Mitte der Schrift? Ein jüdischchristliches Gespräch*, ed. by Martin Klopfenstein and others, Judaica et Christiana, 11 (Bern: Peter Lang, 1987), pp. 237–68 (p. 239). Ausloos, 'Sept défis', p. 250: 'Il ne semble guère possible de parler de "la" théologie de la Septante'. Cook, 'Towards the formulation', p. 637 shows himself less sceptical, even if he thinks the appearance of an overall theology of the LXX premature.

33 Cited in Martin Rösel, 'A Theology of the Septuagint? Clarifications and definitions', in Martin Rösel, *Tradition and Innovation: English and German Studies on the Septuagint*, SBLSCS, 70 (Atlanta: SBL, 2018), pp. 273–90 (p. 279). This goes for the classical perspective formulated by Gerhard von Rad, *Old Testament Theology*, 2 vols (London: SCM Press, 1975), I. The Theology of Israel's Historical Traditions, p. 105: 'The subject-matter which concerns the theologian is, of course, not the spiritual and religious world of Israel and the conditions of her soul in general, nor is it her world of faith, all of which can only be reconstructed by means of conclusions drawn from the documents: instead, it is simply Israel's own explicit assertions about Jahweh'.

34 See Rösel, 'A Theology of the Septuagint?', p. 278. Barr, *The Concept of Biblical Theology*, p. 249 speaks of theology in these terms: 'Theology is a reflective activity in which the content of religious expressions is to some extent abstracted, contemplated, subjected to reflection and discussion, and deliberately reformulated'. See R. Timothy McLay, 'Why Not a Theology of the Septuagint', in *Die Septuaginta — Texte, Theologien, Einflüsse: 2. internationale Fachtagung veranstaltet von Septuaginta Deutsch (LXX.D), Wuppertal 23.-27.7. 2008*, ed. by Wolfgang Kraus and Martin Karrer, WUNT, 252 (Tübingen: Mohr Siebeck 2010), pp. 607–20 (p. 610).

that this text is more than a translation. In fact, the translators are set as mediators between the tradition they have received and the cultural context in which they live.[35]

In my own opinion, the task of discovering a theology of the LXX is not beyond our grasp. In any case, as Timothy McLay writes, a theology of the LXX ought to have the same legitimacy and the same principles as a theology of the Hebrew Bible or of the New Testament.[36] As I have already mentioned, and following the example of what Georg Fischer has written about the theologies of the Old Testament, a future theology of the LXX must undoubtedly be founded on the theologies of the individual books[37] but not be limited to these.[38] Jan Joosten,[39] who confines his discussion to the books present in the Hebrew canon and translated into Greek, observes that if we take account of an overall approach which considers all the factors which could have influenced a particular translation, the variants of the LXX which present their own theological characteristics are actually very few and scattered among the different books (one thinks of monotheistic tendencies, the nature of idols, angels, anthropomorphisms which are toned down by comparison with the MT and so on).

It is necessary, however, to add a thematic approach, that is, how a particular theme or *motif* is treated in the LXX; also to be added is a lexical approach related to the lexical equivalents of the LXX and their possible theological tenor. The results of this type of methodologies, comments Joosten, are not exciting when it comes to the possibility of an overall theology of the LXX. However, an important aspect highlighted by Joosten is the so-called literal nature of the LXX, something studied in the most technical of details by Emanuel Tov.[40] According to Joosten, such literalism, to which we must add the tendency to harmonise the Scriptures, is already in itself the expression of a precise theology: a theology of the word of God contained in the Hebrew text which the translator intends to offer to his readers in Greek. Therefore, from this point of view too, it is possible to speak of a theology of the LXX.

---

35 '[...] the original translators of the LXX wanted to mediate between the tradition and the contemporary situation. This includes a relation to the *Vorlage* as well as the possibility of conscious modifications and attempts to bring things up to date'; Wolfgang Kraus, 'Contemporary Translations of the Septuagint: Problems and Perspectives', in *Septuagint Research: Issues and Challenges in the Study of the Greek Jewish Scriptures*, ed. by Wolfgang Kraus and R. Glenn Wooden, SBLSCS, 53 (Atlanta: SBL, 2006), pp. 63–83 (p. 70).

36 McLay, 'Why Not a Theology of the Septuagint?', pp. 616–20. See also Timothy Michael Law, *When God Spoke Greek: The Septuagint and the Making of Christian Bible* (Oxford: Oxford University Press, 2013), p. 170: 'Regardless of which explanation explains each deviation, one is hard pressed to claim the theological vision of the Septuagint and the Hebrew Bible are identical'.

37 See Cook, 'Towards a Theology', p. 636.

38 See Rösel, 'Towards a "Theology of the Septuagint"', p. 255. In the Italian sphere, Mario Cimosa, 'È possibile scrivere una "teologia" della Bibbia Greca (LXX)?', in *Initium Sapientiae: Scritti in onore di Franco Festorazzi in occasione del suo 70. compleanno*, ed. by Rinaldo Fabris, SuppRivBiblt, 36 (Bologna: EDB, 2000), pp. 51–64.

39 See Joosten, 'Une théologie de la Septante'.

40 See Emanuel Tov, *The Text-Critical Use of the Septuagint in Biblical Research*, JBS, 8, Revised and Enlarged 2nd edn (Jerusalem: Simor, 1999), pp. 50–66.

3. Where and How the Theology of the LXX Overlaps with Biblical Theology

For the most part, the classical treatments of biblical theology ignore the LXX. The celebrated *Theology of the Old Testament* of Gerhard von Rad (first edition, 1957) seems to take for granted that the text of the Old Testament is the Masoretic text.[41] Brevard S. Childs's attempt to provide a biblical theology of both the Testaments[42] does not give any place to the LXX, not even to the non-translated books like Wisdom and Maccabees because they are considered apocryphal (an aspect surely a little paradoxical in that he is proposing a 'canonical' approach). Thus, Rolf Rendtorff's *Theology of the Old Testament*, published in 1999, does not give any consideration to the text of the LXX.[43] Closing his already-mentioned book, *When God spoke Greek*, Timothy M. Law asks how Western theology would have developed if it had taken the LXX into consideration.[44]

In 1936, the German historian, Viktor Eherenberg, in his study, *Ost und West*, wrote that the LXX constitutes 'das Buch ohne das Christentum und abendländische Kultur undenkbar sind'.[45] Martin Rösel offers a similar thought: '[...] Christian Biblical Theology should no longer be performed without taking the LXX into account'.[46] We must also mention the work of Mogens Müller, *The First Bible of the Church: A Plea for the Septuagint*.[47] In any case, through the history of its results, the French translation, *La Bible d'Alexandrie*, has highlighted the importance of the LXX for the New Testament and for patristic theology. In passing, I note that the Roman Church has adopted as its official biblical text a translation from the Hebrew, Jerome's *Vulgata*, but, in its liturgy, has continued to use the version of the Psalms also translated by Jerome but according to the LXX. If all this is the case, the question is: how is it possible to integrate the LXX within biblical theology? There is obviously

---

41 Gerhard von Rad, *Theologie des Alten Testaments*, 2 vols (München: Christian Kaiser, 1957–60).

42 Brevard S. Childs, *Biblical Theology of the Old and the New Testaments* (London: SCM Press, 1992).

43 Rolf Rendtorff, *Theologie des Alten Testament. Ein kanonischer Entwurf*, 2 vols (Neukirchen-Vluyn: Neukirchener, 1999–2001).

44 See Law, *When God Spoke Greek*, pp. 167–72.

45 Victor Eherenberg, *Ost und West: Studien zur geschichtlichen Problematik der Antike* (Praga: Röher, 1935), pp. 24–25.

46 Rösel, 'A Theology of the Septuagint', p. 284–85.

47 We recall here some conclusions of Müller which are important for biblical theology: 'In a biblical theological context where the Bible includes both the Old and the New Testaments, it should be therefore out of question to exclusively recognize *Hebraica veritas a priori* at the cost of *Graeca veritas*'; Mogens Müller, *The First Bible of the Church: A Plea for the Septuagint* (Sheffield: Sheffield Academic Press, 1996), pp. 119–20. This is because the Jewish Bible consists of both the Hebrew and the Greek texts. A little later, he writes: 'In a biblical theological context we must insist that the Septuagint is at least part of canon. For in a Christian theological context, it is historically incorrect to put the Septuagint in brackets when it comes to the question of the Old Testament of the Church. The history of the reception has a significance of its own' (pp. 122–23). See from the same Mogens Müller, 'Biblia semper interpretanda est. The Role of the Septuagint as a Hellenistic Version of the Old Testament', in *Sophia — Paideia. Sapienza e educazione (Sir 1,27): Miscellanea di studi offerti in onore del prof. Mario Cimosa*, ed. by Gillian Booney and Rafael Vicent (Roma: LAS, 2012), pp. 17–31.

a whole path to be pursued but the many contemporary studies of the LXX provide a good starting point.

As a conclusion to these reflections, I would like to suggest some possible paths to pursue concerning the role of the LXX and its theology within a survey of biblical theology.

First of all, we have to tackle the problem of the canon: to introduce the text of the LXX within a survey of biblical theology means to take into consideration textual forms which, in some cases, like Jeremiah (and, obviously, Esther), represent real alternatives to the Masoretic text. Not only that: it is well known that, in the great uncial codexes, the order of the books of the Old Testament is very different from that of the Masoretic Codexes of Leningrad and of Aleppo, and not only because of the presence of the texts that have not been translated. These 'canonical' lists are not even uniform; all that is not without consequences for biblical theology. A single example: in *Codex Sinaiticus*, the final book of the LXX is Job which closes, as is well known, with a verse added by the Greek translator, relating to Job's future resurrection; here, Matthew's Gospel follows on immediately. *Codex Alexandrinus*, on the other hand, concludes with the Psalms of Solomon which, in Psalms of Solomon 17, contain a clear messianic opening, whereas *Codex Vaticanus* closes the LXX with the book of Daniel, an obvious link with Matthew's 'Son of Man'.[48]

This canonical plurality and textual diversity lead us into accepting the conclusions of Wolfgang Kraus: 'Denn Bibel in unserem Sinn gab es noch nicht. Es gab die biblischen Traditionen in verschiedenen Fassungen';[49] thus, continues Kraus, this demolishes the theses of Gese and Stuhlmacher that there exists a continuity between the Hebrew Bible, the LXX and the NT; the plurality of texts does not allow this 'continuum'. It also rules out the possibility that texts like the Vulgate, or, at the opposite pole, Luther's Bible, can be used to establish a biblical theology. However, not even the MT by itself can be considered as 'the' biblical text. On the other hand, neither can the LXX by itself. Moreover, in the NT period, it still did not exist in its complete form. Essentially, we have a

---

48   See Adrian Schenker, 'L'Ecriture Sainte subsiste en plusieurs formes canoniques simultanées (Réponse à l'exposé du prof. Max Seckler)', in *L'interpretazione della Bibbia nella Chiesa: Atti del Simposio promosso dalla Congregazione per la Dottrina della Fede* (Città del Vaticano: Libreria Editrice Vaticana, 2001), pp. 178–86. For the order of the books in the various textual traditions, see Peter Brandt, *Endgestalten des Kanons: Das Arrangement der Schriften in der jüdischen und christlichen Bibel*, BBB, 131 (Berlin: Philo Fine Arts, 2001). A summary of the various positions concerning the relationship between the Hebrew canon and that of the LXX is also found in William Edward Glenny, 'The Septuagint and Biblical Theology', *Themelios*, 41/2 (2016) <http://themelios. thegospelcoalition.org/article/the-septuagint-and-biblical-theology)> [accessed 09 January 2021]; an extensive bibliography and a summary treatment of the problem is now to be found in Konrad Schmid, *Theologie des Alten Testaments* (Tübingen: Mohr Siebeck, 2019), pp. 118–22.

49   Wolfgang Kraus, 'Die hermeneutische Relevanz der Septuaginta für eine Biblische Theologie', in *Die Septuaginta — Text, Wirkung, Rezeption: 4. Internationale Fachtagung veranstaltet von Septuaginta Deutsch (LXX.D), Wuppertal 19.-22. Juli 2012*, ed. by Wolfgang Kraus and Siegfried Kreuzer, WUNT, I 325 (Tübingen: Mohr Siebeck, 2014), pp. 3–25 (p. 20). See Kraus's criticism of Childs on p. 21.

plurality of texts, of canonical forms and of textual traditions which include both the MT and the LXX. For Kraus, this has considerable consequences for a biblical theology. Like the MT and the NT, the LXX can and must be a source for biblical theology. It is true that the LXX is primarily and principally a translation (though not only that if we extend the discussion to the texts originally in Greek); but, even so, it represents both possible alternative readings which in not a few cases are better than the Masoretic text, as well as constituting the oldest comment on and actualisation of it.

Secondly, we have to tackle the great theological themes which emerge from the existing studies on the LXX; themes which refer to the great structures of thought which are shared by both the Hebrew Bible and the LXX as well as the New Testament, not to mention those intertestamental texts which did not make it into any canon, either Jewish or Christian.

First of all, we shall look at the way in which the LXX speaks of God.[50] Eberhard Bons has shown that a careful study of the divine vocabulary in the LXX, especially in the Psalter and in the prophetic *corpus*, produces some statements that are significant and of clear interest for biblical theology. In summary, these are: 1. The LXX mostly gives a faithful rendering of the anthropomorphisms and the divine titles; 2. But it does reject a literal translation of some anthropomorphisms and so emphasises the transcendence of the God of Israel; 3. Although without an unequivocal monotheism, the LXX highlights the unique nature of the God of Israel; 4. The LXX presents the God of Israel with a series of attributes unknown to the Hebrew Bible; 5. The LXX performs minor corrections aimed at putting across particular theological concepts such as, for example, universalism. In this connection, in Psalm 8. 6; 97(96). 7; 138(37). 1 the LXX introduces ἄγγελοι instead of אֱלֹהִים which is used in Hebrew in the sense of 'gods'; these are additions of notable theological richness which are not without importance in aiming at an overall biblical theology.[51] In

---

50 Eberhard Bons, 'Parlare di Dio in greco: traduzione, inculturazione, revisioni teologiche nella versione dei LXX', *RicStoBib*, 21/1–2 (2010), 113–24; 'Die Rede von Gott in den Psalmen[LXX]', in *Im Brennpunkt: Die Septuaginta*, ed. by Dieter Böhler and Heinz-Josef Fabry, BWANT, 174 (Stuttgart: Kohlhammer, 2007), III, pp. 182–202. See also Martin Rösel, 'Theo-logie der griechischen Bibel zur Wiedergabe der Gottesaussagen im LXX-Pentateuch', *VT*, 48 (1998), 49–62; on the Psalter, see, in particular *Der Septuaginta-Psalter: Sprachliche und theologische Aspekte*, ed. by Erich Zenger, HBS, 32, (Freiburg: Herder, 2001); Frank Austermann, *Von der Tora zum Nomos: Untersuchungen zur Übersetzungsweise und Interpretation im Septuaginta-Psalter*, MSU, 27 (Göttingen: Vandenhoeck & Ruprecht, 2003).

51 Of the LXX of the Psalms, it can be affirmed that 'Der Übersetzer sich nicht nur als *interpres*, als Dolmetscher, verstand, sondern auch — und vor allem — als *expositor*, als Schriftgelehrter'; Bons, 'Die Rede von Gott in den Psalmen[Lxx]', p. 48. See Arie van der Kooij, 'Zur Frage der Exegese im Septuaginta-Psalter', in *Der Septuaginta-Psalter und seine Tochterübersetzungen: Symposium in Göttingen 1997*, ed. by Anneli Aejmelaeus and Udo Quast, MSU, 24 (Göttingen: Vandenhoeck & Ruprecht, 2000), pp. 366–79; Eberhard Bons, 'Le Dieu et le dieux dans le Psautier de la Septante', in *Le monothéisme biblique: Evolution, contexte et perspectives*, ed. by Eberhard Bons and Thierry Legrand, LeDiv, 244 (Paris: Cerf, 2011), pp. 129–43. By the same author and with good methodological notes, Eberhard Bons, 'Dieu dans le corpus prophétique de la Septante. Quelques exemples d'exégèse intra-biblique et d'innovation théologique', in *Les recueils*

any case, the translators have left the mark of an exegetical process animated by a believing hermeneutic.

Bons's studies can now be supplemented by various others. I recall, in particular, the congress held at Salonica in 2014, the proceedings of which were published in 2016, edited by Evangelia Dafni with the title *Gottesschau — Gotteserkenntis*.[52] I find especially significant the study by Martin Rösel, 'Wie Gott sich erkennen lässt: Gottesschau und Gotteserkenntis in der Septuaginta'. Rösel concludes his work by recalling that this type of analysis — in this case relating to the knowledge and the vision of God in the LXX — enables the construction of a theology not only of the individual books of the LXX, but also of the whole. Perhaps, Rösel observes, not so much a theology in the modern (I would add 'Christian') sense of the term but nonetheless the LXX introduces important modifications with regard to the image of God offered by the MT.[53]

A study of the biblical theology of the Old Testament, but also of the New, has to include results like those just recorded concerning the figure of God. The same can be said of the other great themes such as Messianism, eschatology,[54] the nature of the other gods and of idols, the relationship between Israel and the peoples (and, in the New Testament between the Church and the world) or more specific themes such as that of prayer, a theme already studied by Mario Cimosa for the whole of the LXX.[55] Cimosa shows how it is possible, through a careful lexical analysis, to arrive at theological conclusions which are valid, not only for the LXX but for the influence which it had on the New Testament.

For many scholars, the LXX, as a whole, has to be considered as the Old Testament which was used in the New,[56] even if this statement is to be taken with the due reservations. In the New Testament period, in fact, the LXX as such did not yet exist,

---

prophétiques de la Bible: Origines, milieux et contexte proche-oriental, ed. by Jean-Daniel Macchi and others (Genève: Labor et Fides, 2012), pp. 465–79. See also Anna Passoni Dell'Acqua, 'La metafora biblica di Dio come roccia e la sua soppressione nelle antiche versioni', *Ephemerides Liturgicae*, 91 (1977), 417–53.

52 Evangelia Dafni (ed.), *Gottesschau – Gotteserkenntnis*, WUNT, 387 (Tübingen: Mohr Siebeck, 2017). See therein, in particular, the essays of Emanuel Tov, 'Textual Problems in the Description of Moses's Ascent to Mt. Sinai in Exodus 19, 24, 32 and 34', pp. 3–18; Jan Joosten, 'Seeing God in the Hebrew Bible and the Septuagint', pp. 19–27; Hans Ausloos, 'Beyond Maximalism and Minimalism: The Theophany in 1Kings 19:11–12 and the Theology of the Septuagint', pp. 29–39. This last essay intends to highlight the reason why it is so difficult to affirm whether the LXX has always translated the MT or a different *Vorlage*, if it has understood the text or if it has actually intended to insert theological variants there. Cf. again Mario Cimosa, 'The Revelation and Knowledge of God in the Septuagint: Exodus, the Wisdom Books and the Psalms', pp. 43–61; Martin Rösel, 'Wie Gott sich erkennen lässt: Gottesschau und Gotteserkenntnis in der Septuaginta', pp. 163–76.

53 Rösel, 'Wie Gott sich erkennen lässt', p. 176.

54 Rösel, 'Towards a Theology', p. 262.

55 Mario Cimosa, *La preghiera nella Bibbia greca: Studi sul vocabolario dei LXX* (Roma: Dehoniane, 1992).

56 See especially Müller, *The First Bible of the Church*, p. 116. Remaining solely on the lexical level, one thinks of the New Testament use of words like ἐλπίς-ἐλπίζω or κτίζω which cannot be explained without the linguistic (but also theological) background provided by the LXX.

or did not exist as a whole (one thinks of Daniel, for example). In any case, a biblical theology of both Testaments must avoid falling into the danger of eliminating the Hebrew Bible in favour of the LXX.

This is a risk run by a famous textual critic such as Dominique Barthélemy who wrote (before changing his opinion and returning to the MT):[57]

> the Masora is nothing other than a sclerotic and archaising form. Its dictatorship, imposed after the coming of Jesus, resulted in the silencing of the development of a text which until then was still in process of its full evolution.

He added, not without polemic:

> If [the Septuagint] was *the final actualisation* of the Mosaic message before the nations *before Pentecost*, it is the canonical and, therefore, the original form of the Old Testament for the people of Pentecost. Moreover, as such, it was received by the Church, until a Jerome, newly endowed with Jewish culture and covered with a rabbinic veneer, achieved, with a measure of success and despite the protests of Augustine, what the African had not managed to obtain from Origen: a replacement of the Church's Old Testament with the Bible of the rabbis.

Although it would not be so for many members of the Orthodox churches, this is an extreme position. The rifts which it would provoke with Judaism are clear (see, in this connection, the recent remarks of Wolfgang Kraus concerning the works of Crüsemann).[58] It is a thesis which, on the historical and literary plane, does not take account of a real textual plurality. The proposal of Natalio Fernández Marcos[59] is more satisfactory: it would involve publishing new biblical translations in two parallel columns (as done in Italy by the new CEI Bible 2008 for the two books of Esther) or, following the great uncials, adding after the Hebrew text that of the LXX which immediately precedes the New Testament.[60] According to Fernández Marcos, from a Christian perspective, the relationship between promise and fulfilment would be much more visible.

---

57   See Dominique Barthélemy, 'L'Ancien Testament a mûri à Alexandrie', in *Études d'histoire du texte de l'Ancien Testament*, OBO, 21 (Göttingen: Vandenhoeck & Ruprecht, 1978), pp. 127–39 (pp. 138–39); 'La place de la Septante dans l'Église', in *Études d'histoire du texte de l'Ancien Testament*, OBO, 21 (Göttingen: Vandenhoeck & Ruprecht, 1978), pp. 111–26. See also similar considerations, even if expressed in more moderate tones, in Hans Hübner, *Teologia biblica del Nuovo Testamento*, 3 vols (Brescia: Paideia, 1997), I. Prolegomeni, pp. 67–73.

58   See Kraus, 'Die hermeneutische Relevanz', pp. 4–9.

59   Natalio Fernández Marcos, 'La Biblia griega en la historia y en la teología: el retorno de la Septuaginta', *EstBib*, 72 (2014), 467–82.

60   The Danish scholar, Knud Jeppesen, 'Biblia hebraica — et Septuaginta: A Response to Mogens Müller', *SJOT*, 10/1–2 (1996), 271–81 (pp. 280–81), responds to Müller's book, *The First Bible of the Church*, claiming that, if in translations of the Bible, the Hebrew Bible still has to be used, 'in biblical theology there is much to say in favour of letting the Septuagint have the same weight as the Hebrew text — therefore in this case *Biblia Hebraica* and *Septuaginta*'.

I shall conclude by recalling a Father of the Church who was certainly not an advocate for the LXX. In his prologue to the books of Solomon, Jerome writes: 'si cui sane Septuaginta interpretum magis editio placet, habet eam a nobis olim emendatam; neque enim si nova condimus ut vetera destruamus'.[61]

Thus, it is not a question of preferring one Bible at the expense of another or of destroying one version in favour of another — and, moreover, it is not being claimed that the MT is to be considered 'older' than the LXX! — but of accepting what is now a clear textual plurality and, consequently, a theological plurality. Such a conclusion will certainly be able to arouse fears in the fundamentalists of every colour and of every religious faith, but we can only benefit from a better understanding of a text which by its very nature is plural, and that is the case with the biblical text. Thus, if we wish to read things from a perspective of faith, this textual and theological plurality can only respond to the multiform way of speaking of the God of the Bible.

---

61   Cf. PL XXVIII, 1308.

Biblical Index